CRIMINAL BEHAVIOR: A PSYCHOSOCIAL APPROACH

FIFTH EDITION

Curt R. Bartol
Castleton State College

PRENTICE HALL, UPPER SADDLE RIVER, NEW JERSEY 07458

Library of Congress Cataloging-in-Publication Data

BARTOL, CURT R.
   Criminal behavior: a psychosocial approach/Curt R. Bartol.—5th ed.
     p. cm.
   Includes bibliographical references and index.
   ISBN 0-13-787649-1
   1. Criminal psychology.   2. Criminal behavior—United States.
  I. Title.
  HV6080.B37 1998
  364.3—dc21   98-41092
                                                   CIP

Editorial director: Charlyce Jones Owen
Editor in chief: Nancy Roberts
Senior acquisitions editor: John Chillingworth
Managing editor: Sharon Chambliss
Marketing manager: Christopher DeJohn
Editorial/production supervision: Kari Callaghan Mazzola
Electronic page makeup: Kari Callaghan Mazzola
Electronic art creation: John P. Mazzola
Interior design: John P. Mazzola
Cover director: Jayne Conte
Cover design: Kiwi Design
Cover art: W. Stepanova, 20th century, "Composition" 1920;
   Tretiakov Gallery, Moscow, Russia/Superstock
Buyer: Mary Ann Gloriande

This book was set in 10/12 Palatino by Big Sky Composition
and was printed and bound by Hamilton Printing Company.
The cover was printed by Phoenix Color Corp.

© 1999, 1995, 1991, 1986, 1980 by Prentice-Hall, Inc.
Upper Saddle River, New Jersey 07458

Printed in the United States of America
10 9 8 7 6 5 4

ISBN 0-13-787649-1

Prentice-Hall International (UK) Limited, *London*
Prentice-Hall of Australia Pty. Limited, *Sydney*
Prentice-Hall Canada Inc., *Toronto*
Prentice-Hall Hispanoamericana, S.A., *Mexico*
Prentice-Hall of India Private Limited, *New Delhi*
Prentice-Hall of Japan, Inc., *Tokyo*
Pearson Education Asia Pte. Ltd., *Singapore*
Editora Prentice-Hall do Brasil, Ltda., *Rio de Janeiro*

To Anne, a colleague in all things that matter

CONTENTS

PREFACE

Criminal Behavior: A Psychosocial Approach is a textbook about criminal behavior from a psychological perspective. More specifically, this text portrays the criminal offender as being embedded in and continually influenced by multiple systems within the psychosocial environment. One focus of the book is that adequate theory, well-executed research, and effective application of knowledge to the "crime problem" require an understanding of the many levels of events that influence a person's life course—from the individual to the family, peers, schools, neighborhoods, community, culture, and society as a whole. The fifth edition views the criminal offender as existing on a continuum, ranging from the serious, repetitive offender who begins his or her criminal career at a very young age to the occasional offender who may offend at any point in the life course.

The study of crime, called criminology, is a multidisciplinary enterprise, with the various disciplines (e.g., sociology, psychiatry, psychology, anthropology, genetics, biopsychology, economics, political science, history) examining the different levels of explanations from different perspectives. The vast majority of current criminological texts focus on sociological theories and research on crime. Unfortunately, while they attempt to cover psychological perspectives on crime, they rarely describe it accurately. Authors continue to regard "psychology" from a classical Freudian or psychoanalytic viewpoint, often combined with a vague biological-genetic "trait" or dispositional focus. Occasionally, "learning" is described but current research in the area is neglected. This state of affairs is troubling because psychology is one of the core disciplines contributing to the understanding of criminal behavior.

This book reviews the contemporary research, theory, and practice concerning the psychology of crime as comprehensively and accurately as possible. Increasingly, research in criminological psychology is focusing on the cognitive characteristics of the criminal offender. Researchers examining the psychology of the offender are delving into offender perceptions, reasoning, beliefs, decision-making, and attitudes. Therefore, the continuing challenge of psychological criminology is the systematic integration and organization of the cognitive, motivational, and affective processes of the offender that interact with the vast array of social environmental factors. The book examines the causes, classification, prediction, prevention, intervention, and treatment of criminal behavior from a social psychological perspective. This challenging spirit will be reflected throughout the pages of the text.

The organization of *Criminal Behavior* runs from broad, theoretical positions on crime to specific criminal offenses. Developmental and biopsychological positions are presented in the early chapters, while social and learning viewpoints come later.

The book views a majority of criminal offending as belonging to two major groups: (1) the adolescent offending group, in which offending is a response to group and social pressures; and (2) the life-course-persistent offending group, in which a lifelong pattern of antisocial behavior is apparent. Current interventions are promising with the first group, but are less likely to be successful with the second group unless started early in the child's life course. Some of the changes in this fifth edition include a completely rewritten chapter on drugs and crime to reflect new and expanding research in the area, and a completely rewritten chapter on juvenile delinquency focusing on prevention, intervention, and treatment. Also, in order to reflect the early developmental aspects of criminal behavior, the delinquency chapter is now the second chapter in the book. The white-collar and occupational crime section has been rewritten and better represents contemporary viewpoints in this rapidly expanding area.

The text also includes expanded coverage of the psychosocial aspects of antisocial behavior, including attention deficit/hyperactivity disorders (ADHD), conduct disorders, and learning disorders. Expanded coverage is also directed at the emerging research on the female psychopath, measurement of psychopathy, and the childhood of the psychopath.

New sections on computer crime (cybercrime), stalking (including cyberstalking), hate crimes, and psychological victimization are now included. I have tried to be more sensitive to the victimization aspects of crime, particularly as it affects groups that are vulnerable to prejudice and discrimination.

The research coverage of crime scene analysis (criminal profiling), bombing, terrorism, burglary, shoplifting, arson, and robbery is updated and more in-depth. The concept of dangerousness, the new strategies in the area of assessment and prediction of dangerous individuals, and the emerging controversies on the assessment and classification schemes of sex offenders are more fully addressed.

This text is designed to be a core text in undergraduate and graduate courses in criminal behavior, criminology, the psychology of crime, crime and delinquency, and forensic psychology. The book is heavily research-based and provides a readable summary of contemporary research in all areas of crime. The major goal is that students of criminal behavior will, as a result of reading this text, avoid oversimplified, prejudicial, dogmatic answers to the complex issues involved in crime. If, after studying the text with an open mind, the reader puts it down seeking additional information, and if the reader has developed an avid interest in discovering better answers, then this text will have served its purpose.

The material contained in this book has been classroom tested for over twenty years. During these years, many students have made very helpful suggestions and incisive comments about the readability of the text and the relevancy of the topics. To them, I owe an immeasurable amount of gratitude. I would also like to thank the many professional reviewers who have provided invaluable recommendations for improving the text material over the years, including this edition's reviewers: William J. Clark of Tidewater Community College, Carol Y. Thompson of Texas Christian University, and Carol Warner of Webster University. My assistant, Corey Belden, carefully reviewed the manuscript and was extremely helpful in the collection of research materials. My other assistant, Sarah Brechnock, critically read the manuscript from a student perspective and was invaluable in the development of the indexes. Anne, my "colleague in all things that matter," continually provided professional advice and support throughout all phases of the book. Kari Callaghan Mazzola of Big Sky Composition has been very skillful, competent, and meticulous in the production of this fifth edition. Very special thanks are due Sharon Chambliss, managing editor at Prentice Hall, who has been there during the writing, editorial, and production phases of several editions of the book. Her professional competence, skillful assistance, and understanding patience has made the writing and ongoing revisions much easier, and has been greatly appreciated.

Curt R. Bartol

INTRODUCTION
TO CRIMINAL BEHAVIOR

rime intrigues people. Sometimes it attracts us, sometimes it repels us, occasionally it does both at once. It can amuse, as when we hear about capers and practical jokes that presumably do not harm anyone. It can frighten, if we believe that what happened to one victim might happen to us. Crime can also anger, as when a beloved community member is brutally killed. Violent crime in particular draws attention; consider the rampant excitement and fear in a neighborhood or small town when news of a local murder hits the street.

While interest in crime has always been high, understanding why it occurs and what to do about it has always been a problem. Public officials, politicians, "experts," and streetcorner philosophers continue to offer simple and incomplete solutions for obliterating crime: more police officers on the streets, closed-circuit TV, street lights, sturdy locks, karate classes, stiff penalties, speedy imprisonment, or capital punishment. Academe invariably offers abstract interpretations and suggestions that often have little practical value. As in most areas of human behavior, there is no shortage of experts but there are few effective solutions.

Our inability to prevent crime is partly due to our problems in understanding criminal behavior, a complex phenomenon. Because crime is complex, explanations of crime require complicated, involved answers. Psychological research indicates that most people have limited tolerance for complexity and ambiguity. People apparently want simple, straightforward answers, no matter how complex the issue. Parents become impatient when psychologists answer questions about child rearing by saying, "It depends"—on the situation, on the parents' reactions to it, on any number of possible variables. This preference for simplicity helps to explain the popularity of do-it-yourself, 100-easy-ways-to-a-better-life books.

This text presents criminal behavior as a vastly complex, poorly understood phenomenon. Readers looking for simple solutions will either have to reorient their thinking, set the text aside, or read it in dismay. There is no all-encompassing psychological explanation for crime, any more than there is a sociological, anthropological, psychiatric, economic, or historic one. In fact, it is unlikely that sociology, psychology or any other discipline can formulate basic "truths" about crime without help from other disciplines and areas of research. Criminology needs all the interdisciplinary help it can get to explain and control criminal behavior. An integration of the data, theory, and general viewpoints of each discipline is crucial.

To review accurately and adequately the plethora of studies and theories from each relevant discipline is far beyond the scope of this text, however. Our focus is the psychological perspective, although other viewpoints will also be described. The psychology of crime is really a subdivision of the general field of **forensic psychology**. Forensic psychology refers broadly to the production and application of psychological knowledge to the civil and criminal justice systems. It includes such areas as police psychology, correctional psychology (including institutional and community corrections), psychology and law, victim services, and the delivery and evaluation of intervention and treatment programs for juvenile and adult offenders. Forensic psychology is a rapidly emerging field of both academic study and professional application.

The primary aim of this text is to review and integrate recent scholarship and research in the psychology of crime, compare it with traditional approaches, and offer a theoretical framework for the study of crime. We cannot begin to do this task without first calling attention to philosophical questions that underlie any study of human behavior.

PERSPECTIVES OF HUMAN NATURE IN THEORIES OF CRIME

All theories of crime have underlying assumptions about human nature. Three major ones can be identified. One perspective views humans as creatures of conformity who want to do the "right" thing. To a large extent, this assumption represents the foundation of the humanistic perspectives in psychology. Human beings are basically "good" people trying to live to their fullest potential. An excellent example of this **conformity perspective** in criminology is the **strain theory** of Robert K. Merton. Merton's strain theory argues that humans are fundamentally conforming beings who are strongly influenced by the values and attitudes of the society in which they live. In short, most members of a given society desire what the other members of the society desire. The "right" thing, therefore, is what a society or a group within a society says is the "right" thing. American society, according to strain theorists, advocates that the accumulation of wealth or status is all-important and represents the symbols that all members should strive for. Strain theorists contend that humans, being fundamentally conformists, readily buy into these notions. However, access and the means for reaching these well-advertised goals are not equally available to everyone. Some have the education, the social network, personal contacts, and family influence to attain these goals. The socially and economically disadvantaged, however, do not have the opportunities, the education, nor the necessary social network for attaining material wealth and economic or political power. Thus, the strain theory predicts that crime and delinquency occur when there is a *perceived* discrepancy between the materialistic values and goals cherished and held in high esteem by a society and the availability of the legitimate means for reaching these goals. Under these conditions, a *strain* between the goals of wealth and power and the means for reaching them develops. Groups and individuals experiencing a high level of this strain are forced to decide whether to violate norms and laws to attain some of this sought-after wealth or power, or give up on the American dream and go through the motions, withdraw, or rebel.

A second perspective assumes that human beings are basically undisciplined creatures who, without the constraints of the rules and regulations of a given society, would flout society's conventions and commit crime indiscriminately. The belief that humans are fundamentally "unruly" forms the **nonconformist perspective**. Good illustrations of this perspective are found in neurobiological theories, to be discussed in Chapters 3 and 4, and Travis Hirschi's **social control theory** to be discussed in several chapters. Social control theory contends that crime and delinquency occur when an individual's ties to the conventional order or normative standards are weak or largely nonexistent. In other words, the socialization that normally holds one's basic human nature in check is incomplete or faulty. This position fundamentally perceives human nature as "bad" or "antisocial," an innate tendency that must be *controlled* by society. In this sense, social control theory subscribes to **Darwinism**.

The third perspective sees human beings as born basically neutral (neither inherently conforming nor unruly); they learn virtually all their behavior, beliefs, and tendencies from the social environment. This third approach is the **learning approach**, exemplified most comprehensively by social learning theory, to be a main topic in Chapter 5, and Edwin H. Sutherland's differential association theory. Differential association theory provides a good illustration of this perspective. Criminal behavior, according to this theory, is learned, as is all social behavior, through *social interactions* with other people. It is *not* the result of emotional disturbance, mental illness, or innate qualities of "goodness" or "badness." Rather, people learn to be criminal as a result of messages they get from others who were also taught to be criminal. Consequently, an excess of "messages" favorable to law violation over unfavorable messages promotes criminal activity. The conventional wisdom that bad company promotes bad behavior, therefore, finds validity in differential association theory.

PERSPECTIVES IN CRIMINOLOGY

Criminology is the multidisciplinary study of crime. Many disciplines are involved in the collection of knowledge about criminal action, including psychology, sociology, psychiatry, anthropology, biology, neurology, political science, and economics. Over the years, the study of crime has been dominated by three disciplines—sociology, psychology, and psychiatry—but other disciplines or subdisciplines are becoming more actively involved. For example, criminal anthropology is rapidly emerging as an active participant (Rafter, 1992).

Although our main concern in this text is with *psychological* principles, concepts, theory, and research relevant to criminal behavior, considerable attention will be placed on the research knowledge of the other disciplines, particularly sociology and psychiatry. Again, criminology needs all the help it can get in its struggle to understand, explain, and prevent criminal behavior.

It is not easy to make sharp demarcations between disciplines, since they overlap considerably in focus. For example, what distinguishes a given theory as sociological, psychological, or psychiatric is sometimes simply the stated professional affiliation of its proponent. The reader should also realize that condensing any major discipline into a few pages hardly does it justice. To obtain a more adequate overview, the interested reader should consult texts and articles within those disciplines.

SOCIOLOGICAL CRIMINOLOGY

Sociological criminology has a rich tradition in examining the relationships of demographic and group variables to crime. Variables such as age, race, gender, socioeconomic status, interpersonal relationships, and ethnic-cultural affiliation have been shown to have significant relationships with certain categories and patterns of crimes. Sociological criminology, for example, has allowed us to conclude that young, African-American males from disadvantaged backgrounds are disproportionately overrepresented as perpetrators and victims of homicide. The many reasons for this overrepresentation are reflected in the various perspectives and research findings that will be covered in the book.

Sociological criminology also probes the situational or environmental factors that are most conducive to criminal action, such as the time, place, kind of weapons used, and the circumstances surrounding crime. In addition, the sociological approach examines the underlying social conditions that may encourage criminal behavior, such as inequities in educational and employment opportunities, or unequal treatment by agents of the criminal justice system.

PSYCHOLOGICAL CRIMINOLOGY

Psychology is the science of behavior and mental processes. **Psychological criminology**, then, is the science of the behavior and mental processes of the criminal. While sociological criminology focuses on groups and society as a whole, psychological criminology focuses on *individual* criminal behavior—how it is acquired, evoked, maintained, and modified. Both social and personality influences on criminal behavior are considered, along with the mental processes that mediate that behavior. Personality refers to all the biological influences, psychological traits, and cognitive features of the human being that psychologists have identified as important in the mediation and control of behavior. Recently, psychological criminology has shifted its focus to the cognitive aspects of offending. Psychological criminology also examines and evaluates prevention, intervention, and treatment strategies that have been tried in reducing criminal behavior.

In the past, psychologists assumed that they could best understand human behavior by searching for stable, consistent personality **dispositions** or traits that exert widely generalized effects on behavior (Mischel, 1973). Many psychologists studying crime, therefore, assumed they should search for the personality traits or variables underlying criminal behavior. They paid little attention to the person's environment or situation. Presumably, once personality variables were identified, it would be possible to determine and predict which individual was most likely to engage in criminal behavior. As you will learn, the search for any single personality type of the murderer, rapist, or psychopathic killer has not been fruitful. Psychologists who provide law enforcement agencies with profiles of the rapist still at large, based solely on personality variables, are at best engaging in unvalidated clinical judgment and unsubstantiated hunches. However, psychologists can offer statistical probability about some demographic and behavioral patterns of certain offenders. For example, they might determine, roughly, that a rapist is probably young, white, unemployed, from the area, and so forth. They might also offer possible motives for the attack, based on research findings and accompanied by the necessary caveats. This "profile" information, however, is based on the collected knowledge from all sectors of criminology, including psychology, sociology, anthropology, psychiatry, political science, history and economics. The mission of this book is to provide this interdisciplinary knowledge.

Criminal profiling refers to the process of identifying personality traits, behavioral tendencies, and demographic variables of an offender based on characteristics of the crime (Bartol & Bartol, 1994). To a very large extent, the profiling process is dictated by a data base collected on previous offenders who have committed similar offenses. Currently, profiling is at least 95 percent an art based on speculation and only 5 percent science. The topic will be covered in more detail in Chapter 9.

In recent years, reconstruction of the personality profile and cognitive features (especially intentions) of *deceased* individuals has gained some popularity. This postmortem psychological analysis is called reconstructive psychological evaluation (RPE) or equivocal death analysis (Poythress, Otto, Darkes, & Starr, 1993). The analysis is also known as a **psychological autopsy** (Brent, 1989; Ebert, 1987; Selkin, 1987), although the "autopsy" analysis is often reserved for suicide cases. The psychological autopsy is frequently done to determine the reasons and precipitating factors for the suicide.

The RPE differs from criminal profiling in two important ways: (1) The profile is constructed on a dead person; and (2) the identity of the person is already known. Like criminal profiling, however, the reliability and validity of the RPE and its variants (psychological autopsies) has yet to be demonstrated and remains open to debate.

PSYCHIATRIC CRIMINOLOGY

The terms *psychology* and *psychiatry* are often confused by the lay person and even by professionals and scholars in other disciplines. Psychiatric concepts and theories are often believed to be accepted tenets in the field of psychology. In reality, the two professions often see things quite differently, even though there are commonalities.

American **psychiatric criminology**, also called **forensic psychiatry**, has traditionally followed the Freudian, psychoanalytic, or psychodynamic tradition. The father of the psychoanalytical theory of human behavior was the physician-neurologist Sigmund Freud (1856–1939), whose followers are called Freudians. Many contemporary psychoanalysts subscribe to a modified version of the orthodox Freudian position and are therefore called neo-Freudians. Still other psychoanalysts follow the tenets of Alfred Adler and Carl Jung, who broke away from Freud and formed schools of their own.

Collectively, all psychoanalytic positions form the psychodynamic school, which explains behavior in terms of motives and drives. This perspective views human nature as *innately* antisocial. That is, humans are biologically driven to get what they want when they want it, unless they are held in check by internal (conscience) and external (society) forces. Without an organized society with rules and laws, humans (especially men because of their biology) would aggress, plunder, steal, and even kill at will.

The psychoanalytic position assumes that we must delve into the abysses of human personality to find unconscious determinants of human behavior, including criminal behavior. Consider the following comments by two forensic psychiatrists. "The criminal rarely knows completely the reasons for his conduct" (Abrahamsen, 1952, p. 21). "Every criminal is such by reason of unconscious forces within him..." (Roche, 1958, p. 25). Psychoanalytic and psychodynamic theories acknowledge that behavior varies across situations. However, they conclude that there are enduring and generalized underlying dynamic or motivational dispositions that account for this diversity. "Surface" behaviors indirectly signal or symbolize dynamic, underlying attributes. Psychological defenses distort and disguise the "true" meaning of external or observed behaviors. The trained clinician, therefore, must interpret the significance of these external behaviors, since the actor is not aware of their purpose.

The Freudian, psychoanalytic, and psychodynamic positions strongly endorse the view that the prime determinant of human behavior lies within the person and that after the first few years of life the environment plays a very minor role. Consequently, criminal behavior is believed to spring from within, primarily dictated by the biological urges of the unconscious. The environment, culture, or society cannot be held responsible for crime rates; biopsychological needs and urges within the individual are the culprits.

It would be unfair, however, to simply classify contemporary psychiatric criminology as heavily Freudian or psychoanalytical. Contemporary psychiatric criminology is much more diverse and is considerably less steeped in the traditional belief that criminals are acting out their uncontrolled animalistic, unconscious, or biological urges. Therefore, *traditional* psychiatric criminology will be distinguished from *contemporary* psychiatric criminology throughout the text. The traditional psychiatric view will represent psychoanalytic, Freudian, and psychodynamic perspectives; whereas the contemporary psychiatric view will represent the diverse and rich knowledge gained through research and clinical experience.

One critical problem with *traditional* psychiatric criminology is its failure to develop a replicable research data base, partly because its concepts are ambiguous (presumably residing in the intangible recesses of the mind) and are not often conducive to empirical or scientific examination. The vagaries of the id, the ego, the superego, unconscious urges and impulses, behavioral symbolism, and psychosexual development as explanations of crime are well-known to most criminologists, and they hold a dominant place in traditional psychiatry. However, they are not accepted by most contemporary psychologists and many contemporary psychiatrists. In fact, most Freudian and Neo-Freudian concepts have never found a secure place in mainstream psychology, especially within the academic and research realms.

DEFINITION OF CRIMINAL BEHAVIOR

In a text of this nature, one initial task must be to define criminal behavior and determine the object of our study. It is not easy to do this, since we are confronted with definitional as well as methodological dilemmas. Not only must we decide how to define crime and the criminal, but we must also struggle with the many statistical problems associated with crime reporting and interpretation.

Crime itself is "an intentional act in violation of the criminal law committed without defense or excuse, and penalized by the state as a felony or misdemeanor" (Tappan, 1947, p. 100). Criminal behavior, therefore, is intentional behavior that violates a criminal code, intentional in that it did not occur accidentally or without justification or excuse. To be held criminally responsible, a person must have known what he or she was doing during the criminal act and must have known that it was wrong. Obviously, this legal definition encompasses a great variety of acts, ranging from homicide to minor traffic violations.

In a text of this type, we are confronted with several dilemmas. Should we restrict ourselves to a legal definition and study only those individuals who have been convicted of crime? Or should we include individuals who indulge in antisocial behaviors but have not been detected by the criminal justice system? Perhaps our study should include persons predisposed to be criminal, if such persons can be identified. As a review of criminology textbooks and literature attests, there is no universal agreement as to what group or groups should be targeted for study.

If we abide strictly by the legal definition of crime and base research and discussion only on those people who have committed crimes, do we consider only those who have been convicted and incarcerated, or do we include those who have probably broken the criminal law but are not convicted? Even by conservative estimates, 36 to 40 million persons—16 to 18 percent of the total U.S. population—have arrest records for nontraffic offenses (U.S. Department of Justice, 1988). Furthermore, how can we include individuals who violate the law but escape detection or those who come to the attention of law enforcement officials but are never arrested?

Trying to study criminal behavior on the basis of incidence presents other problems for social scientists. Incidence of crime is usually measured in one of three ways:

1. Official police reports of arrests, such as those tabulated and forwarded to the FBI for publication in its annual national statistical report on crime, the *Uniform Crime Reports (UCR)*
2. Self-report studies, where members of a sample population are asked what offenses they have committed and how often

3. National or regional victimization studies, which sample a population of households or businesses asking respondents how often they have been victims of specified crimes

UNIFORM CRIME REPORTS

The Federal Bureau of Investigation's *Uniform Crime Reports* (*UCR*), compiled since 1930, is the most cited source of U.S. crime statistics. The UCR is an annual document (released to the public sometime between late July and early September) containing arrest information received on a voluntary basis from local and state law enforcement agencies throughout the United States. Interestingly, federal law enforcement agencies do not report through the traditional UCR program, although a newly revised reporting system has been implemented that requires federal agencies to report. This new system—called the National Incident-Based Reporting System—will be described shortly.

The first UCR was published with fewer than a thousand agencies reporting; the 1996 UCR data collection was based on nearly sixteen thousand city, county, and state law enforcement agencies, representing about 98 percent of the U.S. population (FBI, 1997). The UCR is the only major data source permitting a comparison of national data broken down by age, sex, race, and offense. The more recently developed FBI *Supplementary Homicide Report* contains data on victim and offender demographics, the offender-victim relationship, the weapon used, and the circumstances surrounding the homicide.

The UCR divides crimes a number of ways, including by age, gender, and race of person arrested, and city and region of the country where the crime was committed. Crimes are also categorized according to seriousness. Serious crimes are called **index crimes** (or **Part I crimes**) (see Table 1-1), nonserious crimes are **nonindex crimes** (or **Part II crimes**) However, this distinction can be misleading. For instance, larceny-theft, which includes shoplifting, is categorized as an index crime, whereas fraud and drug offenses are classified as nonindex crimes. Examples of nonindex crimes include vandalism, carrying weapons, and buying, receiving, and possessing stolen property. Table 1-1 contains definitions of both index and nonindex crimes reported in the UCR. These definitions are not necessarily legally accurate but are primarily broad classifications created by the FBI for statistical reporting purposes. Figure 1-1 shows the proportion of the entire index that each of the eight index crimes represents.

In order to be recorded in the UCR, a crime must, at a minimum, meet the following requirements:

- Be perceived by the victim or by someone else
- Be defined as a crime by the victim or the observer
- In some way become known to a law enforcement agency as a crime
- Be defined by that law enforcement agency as a crime
- Be accurately recorded by the law enforcement agency
- Be reported to the FBI compilation center

Table 1-1   Definitions of Index Crimes and Nonindex Crimes in Uniform Crime Reports

	Index Crimes
Murder and Nonnegligent Manslaughter	The willful (nonnegligent) killing of one human being by another.
Forcible Rape	The carnal knowledge of a female forcibly and against her will. Included are assaults and attempts to commit rape by force or threat of force. Statutory rape (without force) and other sex offenses are excluded.
Robbery	The taking or attempting to take anything of value from the care, custody, or control of a person or persons by force or threat of force or violence and/or by putting the victim in fear.
Aggravated Assault	An unlawful attack by one person upon another for the purpose of inflicting severe or aggravated bodily injury. This type of assault is usually accompanied by the use of a weapon or by means likely to produce death or great bodily harm. Attempts to inflict injury are included.
Burglary	The unlawful entry of a structure to commit a felony or theft. There are three classifications: forcible entry, unlawful entry where no force is used, and attempted forcible entry.
Larceny-Theft	The unlawful taking, carrying, leading, or riding away of property from the possession or constructive possession of another. It includes crimes such as shoplifting, pocket-picking, purse-snatching, thefts from motor vehicles, thefts of motor vehicle parts and accessories, and bicycle thefts.
Motor Vehicle Theft	The theft or attempted theft of a motor vehicle, including the stealing of automobiles, trucks, buses, motorcycles, motorscooters, and snowmobiles.
Arson	Any willful or malicious burning or attempt to burn, with or without intent to defraud, a dwelling house, public building, motor vehicle or aircraft, or personal property of another.

	Common Nonindex Crimes
Other Assaults (Simple)	Assaults and attempted assaults where no weapon is used and that do not result in serious or aggravated injury to victim.
Forgery and Counterfeiting	Making, altering, uttering, or possessing, with intent to defraud, anything false in the semblance of that which is true.
Fraud	Fraudulent conversion and obtaining money or property by false pretenses.
Embezzlement	Misappropriation or misapplication of money or property entrusted to one's care, custody, or control.
Stolen Property	Buying, Receiving, Possessing: Buying, receiving, and possessing stolen property, including attempts.
Offenses against the Family and Children	Nonsupport, neglect, desertion, or abuse of family and children.
Drug Abuse Violations	State and/or local offenses relating to the unlawful possession, sale, use, growing, and manufacturing of drugs.
Sex Offenses (Except Forcible Rape, Prostitution, and Commercialized Vice)	Statutory rape and offenses against chastity, common decency, and morals.
Gambling	Promoting, permitting, or engaging in illegal gambling.
Vandalism	Willful or malicious destruction, injury, disfigurement, or defacement of any public or private property, real or personal, without consent of the owner or persons having custody or control.

Source: Adapted from FBI (1997). *Uniform Crime Reports, 1996* (Washington, DC: U.S. Department of Justice).

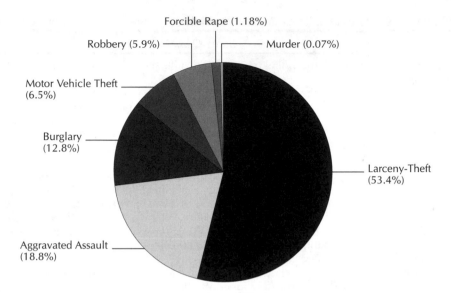

Figure 1-1   Percent Distribution of Index Crimes
(Source: U.S. Department of Justice, *Uniform Crime Reports, 1997.*)

A term that is frequently used in the UCR is **clearance rate**. The clearance rate refers to the proportion of reported crimes that have been "solved." The clearance rate for violent crimes in 1996 was 47 percent, and 18 percent for property crimes (FBI, 1997). The clearance rate was highest for murder (67 percent) and lowest for burglary and motor vehicle theft (14 percent each). (See Figure 1-1.)

UCR data are not without problems. The compilation center relies on the accuracy and compliance of local and state agencies to report crime statistics, and the data do not consider early discretionary decision making by law enforcement officers. In addition, the index category emphasizes street crime to the neglect of the equally serious occupational, corporate, and professional crime, although it is likely that future reports will begin to include these more "professional" occupational crimes.

Official crime statistics, like those of the UCR, are generally believed to underestimate most criminal offenses and are routinely criticized for errors and omissions. The total number of criminal offenses committed, known as the **dark figure**, will probably never be known, but estimates from a victimization survey conducted by the U.S. Census Bureau suggest that out of every one hundred offenses committed, seventy-two are never recorded in the official statistics (Skogan, 1977). However, Skogan also notes that most unreported violations appear to be minor property offenses rather than more serious crimes. Figure 1-2, based on 1987 through 1996 UCR data, shows that arrest rates for serious property crimes peak at around age seventeen or eighteen, just before the age range where many courts begin prosecuting offenders as adults.

With increasing age, and particularly after age twenty, property arrests decline. On the other hand, arrests for violent crime gradually peak and show a gradual decline with age. The UCR also provides data on the number of law enforcement officers killed or assaulted, and some characteristics of homicide victims.

Two additional crime categories now followed by the FBI but not traditionally included in the *Uniform Crime Reports* are hate crimes and terrorism. We now turn our attention to these two very important criminal categories.

HATE CRIMES

In 1989, Congress mandated that the FBI collect data on "hate" or bias crimes. Known as the **Hate Crime Statistics Act** (and signed into law by President Bush in April 1990), it requires data collection of violent attacks, intimidation, arson, or property damage, that are directed at a person or group of persons because of race, religion, sexual orientation, or ethnicity. In September 1994, the *Violent Crime Control and Law Enforcement Act* amended the *Hate Crime Statistics Act* to add disabilities, both physical and mental, to the hate crimes category. The disability bias data collection began in January 1997.

Figure 1-2   Percent Distribution of Index Crimes by Age
(Source: U.S. Department of Justice, *Uniform Crime Reports, 1997.*)

   Documenting hate or bias crimes is difficult because the intentions of the offender are not always that clear-cut. Recent data (FBI, 1997) suggest that a majority of hate crimes are motivated by racial hatred (63 percent), followed by religious bias (14 percent), sexual-orientation bias (12 percent) and ethnic bias (11 percent). Eighty percent of the hate crime victims were individuals, while the remaining victims were businesses, religious organizations, or an assortment of other targets.

   A vivid example of a hate crime occurred in early June, 1998 in Jasper, Texas. James Byrd Jr., a 49-year old African American, was walking home from a family party when he was offered a ride by three white men, all of them known white-supremacists. The men drove Byrd to a remote dirt road where they severely beat him. Then Byrd was chained to their pickup truck by the ankles and dragged along the road, tearing his body to pieces. Police found Byrd's head, neck, right arm, torso, shoes, a wallet, and other personal items scattered along the route. A mile-long blood trail on the road marked the gruesome scene.

TERRORISM

The FBI defines terrorism as, "the unlawful use of force or violence against persons or property to intimidate or coerce a Government, the civilian population, or any segment thereof, in furtherance of political or social objectives" (FBI, 1996). Terrorism may be either domestic or international, depending on the origin, base, and objectives of the terrorist organization.

   The number of victims killed or injured by terrorists differs widely from year to year. For example, on April 9, 1995, a truck bomb destroyed the Federal Building in Oklahoma City, killing 168 citizens and injuring hundreds of others. This attack was the deadliest terrorist incident ever committed on U.S. soil. In another incident that year, terrorists derailed a twelve-car Amtrak train near Hyder, Arizona, killing one and seriously injuring twelve others. Consequently, the number of people killed or injured in terrorist attacks in the United States increased sharply in 1995. In 1994, no American in the United States died in a terrorist attack; whereas six people were killed in the World Trade Center bombing in 1993.

   There are various ways to classify terrorism. The FBI classifies terrorists according to political leanings. For example, right-wing terrorists are extremist groups that generally adhere to an antigovernment or racist ideology, and often engage in a variety of hate crimes and violence. Gun-control legislation, the United Nations involvement in international affairs, and clashes between dissidents and law enforcement are the more recent stimuli that have encouraged right-wing militia groups to become more active. Vivid examples include the Unabomber, who sent mail bombs to individuals involved with technology, killing three and seriously injuring twenty-three over a seventeen-year period. The intention of the Unabomber was to stop the Industrial Revolution and technological progress in American society. Another example of right-wing extremists was the bombing of the Alfred P. Murrah Federal Building in Oklahoma City, referred to previously.

   Special interest extremists, particularly violent antiabortion advocates, continue to be a problem in the United States. International terrorists who view the United States as a primary target are likely to increase substantially in future years.

THE NATIONAL INCIDENT-BASED REPORTING SYSTEM

During the late 1970s, the law enforcement community called for the expanded use of the UCR and more detailed information on crime than the statistics offered in the UCR. In response, the UCR reporting system was evaluated under federal contract by ABT Associates of Cambridge, Massachusetts. Recommendations of the research firm are reported in *A Blueprint for the Future of the Uniform Crime Reporting System*, published in 1985. These recommendations formed the basis of the National Incident-Based Reporting System (NIBRS) under the *Uniform Federal Crime Reporting Act* passed by the U.S. Congress in 1988 (Public Law No. 100–690, 102 Stat. 4181). In this Act, Congress required all federal law enforcement agencies, including those agencies within the Department of Defense, to collect and report data to the FBI on two categories of offenses: Group A, which includes forty-six serious offense categories, such as arson, assault, homicide, fraud, embezzlement, larceny-theft, and sex offenses; and Group B, which includes eleven less serious offenses, such as passing bad checks, driving under the influence of alcohol, engaging in disorderly conduct, drunkenness, nonviolent family offenses, and liquor law violations (see Table 1-2 for a list of Group A offenses).

In the Group A Incident Report information, a crime is viewed along with all its aspects, including information about the victim, weapon, location of the crime, alcohol/drug influence, type of criminal activity, relationship of victim to alleged offender, residence of victims and arrestees, and a description of property and its value. Presumably, this added information will become an indispensable tool for law enforcement agencies and researchers, because it will provide them with detailed data about when and where specific types of crime take place, what forms they take, and the characteristics of their victims and perpetrators. Group B arrest reports contain only information about the arrestee and the circumstances of the arrest.

States were also invited to participate in the project. State and federal agencies participating in the NIBRS use automated systems to report information on Group A and Group B offenses to the FBI on a monthly basis. Ultimately, this new approach is intended to be a paperless (electronic) reporting system. However, the new system is expected to take several years to implement completely. So far, progress has been slow and the new system is unlikely to be fully implemented for several more years. Consequently, much of the crime and arrest data reported in this text will be based on the information provided in the more recent UCR and other government documents.

The anticipated benefits of the NIBRS are primarily through the more precise information it should provide to researchers and investigators about when and where crime takes place, its form, and the characteristics of its victims and offenders. Another primary objective of NIBRS is to get a better handle on the nature and extent of crimes involving illicit drugs.

Table 1-2   The National Incident-Based Reporting System (NIBRS) Group A Offenses

Arson	*Kidnapping/Abduction*
Assault Offenses	*Larceny-Theft Offenses*
Aggravated assault	Pocket picking
Simple assault	Purse snatching
Intimidation	Shoplifting
Bribery	Theft from building
Burglary/Breaking and Entering	Theft from coin-operated machines
Counterfeiting/Forgery	Theft from motor vehicle
Destruction/Damage/Vandalism of Property	Theft of motor vehicle parts/accessories
Drug/Narcotic Offenses	Motor vehicle theft
Drug/narcotic violations	Pornography/obscene materials
Drug/equipment violations	*Prostitution Offenses*
Embezzlement	Prostitution
Extortion/Blackmail	Assisting or promoting prostitution
Fraud Offenses	*Robbery*
False pretenses/swindle/confidence game	*Sex Offenses, Forcible*
Credit card/ATM fraud	Forcible rape
Impersonation	Forcible sodomy
Welfare fraud	Sexual assault with an object
Wire fraud	Forcible fondling
Gambling Offenses	*Sex Offenses, Nonforcible*
Betting/wagering	*Stolen Property Offenses*
Operating/promoting/assisting gambling	*Weapon Law Violations*
Gambling equipment violations	
Sports tampering	
Homicide Offenses	
Murder/nonnegligent manslaughter	
Negligent manslaughter	
Justifiable homicide	

Source: The National Center for the Analysis of Violent Crime, Annual Report, 1992 (Quantico, VA: FBI Academy, 1992), p. 22.

SELF-REPORT STUDIES

Many researchers believe that self-report (SR) studies provide a more accurate estimate of actual offenses than do local police or UCR statistics, even though respondents may inflate or deflate reports of their criminal activity. In a dated but revealing SR survey (Wallerstein & Wyle, 1947), 1,698 persons were asked to indicate on a list of forty-nine criminal offenses which, if any, they had committed. The list included felonies and misdemeanors but excluded traffic violations. Ninety-one percent of the nearly 1,700 respondents admitted they had committed one or more offenses for which they might have received jail or prison sentences. The average number of offenses for each person was eighteen. None of the sample had served an actual prison sentence. This study suggests that most people have broken the criminal law at some point in their lives.

In another study by Short and Nye (1957), three thousand high school students, with a guarantee of anonymity, were administered questionnaires about their unlawful actions. Not only did the results confirm the high incidence of unlawful behavior reported by the Wallerstein and Wyle study, but it also showed that the unlawful conduct was evenly distributed across all socioeconomic classes. Even if the offenses were not serious ones, if these SR studies are representative, violations of the law are common across all levels of society, at least among young people.

Most SR investigations focus on delinquency rather than adult offending. The SR data are gathered either through interviews (personal or telephone) or questionnaires. In most SR measures, subjects are asked to indicate whether they have engaged in any of the listed illegal activities and, if so, how often. Nettler (1984), in his review of the SR research, concludes the following, according to SR data:

- Almost everyone, by his or her own admission, has violated some criminal law.
- The amount of "hidden crime" (the dark figure) is enormous.
- Most of the infractions are minor.

The last point is an important one because it is the basis for much of the criticism directed at SR studies. Most of the offenses included in a majority of SR questionnaires are relatively minor ones—so minor that they are likely to distort one's impressions of criminal offending unless the content of the questions are known. For example, the questionnaire used by Short and Nye was a twenty-three-item delinquency scale that included such questions as whether one has ever defied his or her parents' authority (to their face). Realize, of course, that the researchers were asking high school students (grades nine through twelve) questions about behaviors that were violations of the law for youth at that time (called status offenses). Other items included whether one had ever skipped school without a legitimate excuse, taken little things (worth less than $2), bought or drank beer, wine, or liquor, had sexual relations with persons of the opposite sex or the same sex, or gone hunting or fishing without a license. More "serious" violations listed were running away from home, fist fights, gang fights, taking a car for a drive without the owner's (including parents') knowledge, use of narcotic drugs, theft (over $50), and vandalism.

Recent SR studies, responding to the criticisms of earlier investigations, have directed their questions at more serious criminal activities. Still, we must be careful about drawing far-reaching conclusions based on the information from SR research unless the nature of the questions is known, as well as who was asked, why, and how. At this point, however, SR studies do suggest that minor criminal activity is extensive and widespread, at least among youth. Furthermore, SR studies continually show that the number of individuals involved in serious crimes is relatively small, but those few who do engage in serious criminal activity commit a lot of crimes. Moreover, persistent, repetitive offenders do not specialize in any one crime (such as larceny) but show considerable versatility in criminal involvement,

committing a wide variety of offenses, violent as well as nonviolent. We will discuss this behavioral pattern in more detail in the next chapter.

DRUG ABUSE SELF-REPORT SURVEYS

Two extensive, nationwide self-report surveys dominate the data gathered on
drug abuse in the United States: *The National Household Survey on Drug Abuse* and
The Monitoring the Future Study. The National Household Survey on Drug Abuse
(NHSDA) is an ongoing survey of the noninstitutionalized population of the
United States, twelve years old or older. The survey has been conducted by the
Federal government since 1971, and is the primary source of statistical information on the use of illegal drugs in the United States. It is designed to estimate the
rates of drug use, the number of users, and other aspects related to illicit drugs,
alcohol, cigarettes, and smokeless tobacco.

The survey collects data by administering questionnaires to a representative
sample of the population at their places of residence. The sample includes residents of households, noninstitutional group quarters (e.g., shelters, rooming
houses, dormitories), and civilians living on military bases. The interview takes
about one hour to complete and incorporates procedures designed to maximize
honest reporting of illicit drug use. In 1996, 18,269 persons were interviewed.

The Monitoring the Future Study (MFS) is a nationwide survey of high school-
ers in the United States conducted at the Institute for Social Research at the
University of Michigan and sponsored by research grants from the National
Institute of Drug Abuse. Since 1991, the project has included not only high school
seniors but eighth and tenth grade students as well. The MFS also conducts a follow-up survey of each graduating class for a number of years after their initial
participation. The mission of the MFS is to predict future trends of drug abuse
based on current youth drug use. We will describe these surveys and their informative results in more detail in Chapter 12.

VICTIMIZATION SURVEYS

Additional sources of data on criminal offending are victimization surveys. The
main source of victimization data on crime is the **National Crime Victimization
Survey (NCVS)**, originally called the **National Crime Survey (NCS)**. The Bureau
of the Census interviews, on a staggered schedule, a large national sample of
households (approximately fifty thousand) representing over one hundred thousand persons over the age of twelve. Crimes committed against children below
age twelve are not counted for privacy reasons and because the designers of the
survey believe that younger respondents, compared to adults, are not as likely to
provide accurate information. The households are asked about crimes they experienced during the previous six months.

The original impetus for the NCVS came from the President's Commission on
Law Enforcement and Administration of Justice in 1966. The Commission wanted
to supplement the UCR because of the widespread dissatisfaction with and distrust of the accuracy of this source. After considerable experimentation and a vari-

ety of pilot projects to test methods and their feasibility, the NCVS was fully implemented in July 1973. While the survey has generally been regarded as an effective instrument for measuring crime, the National Academy of Sciences concluded that the survey's methodology and scope could be improved. Consequently, the NCVS has undergone several changes and improvements since it was begun in 1973. The most recent significant changes in the NCVS occurred in 1992 when a redesigned interview method was put into place to improve survey methods and collect previously unreported data. This redesign and other ongoing developments of the NCVS have significantly changed the way in which the survey gathers data and information on victimization. The effects of these methodological changes on data are described in a report published by the Bureau of Justice Statistics entitled *Effects of the Redesign on Victimization Estimates* (BJS Technical Report, April 1997 [NCJ-16438]).

The survey is currently designed to measure the extent to which households and individuals are victims of rape, robbery, aggravated assault, simple assault, household burglary, motor vehicle theft, and theft. It also provides many details about the victims (such as age, race, sex, education, income, and whether the victim and the offender were related to each other) and about the crimes themselves. Specifically, the NCVS interviewer wants to know the following:

- Exactly what happened
- When and where the offense occurred
- Whether any injury or loss was suffered
- Whether the crime was reported to the police
- The victim's perception of the offender's gender, race, and age

According to NCVS data, 35 million victimizations occurred in 1995 (Bureau of Justice Statistics, 1997). About 5.5 million households were burglarized, and another 8.8 million had something stolen (e.g., a bike left on the front lawn). The NCVS also reported that 1.6 million individuals were victims of aggravated assault (assailant inflicted, intended, or threatened to inflict serious bodily harm), and nearly a million individuals said they had been victims of a robbery. Over 13 million individuals had something stolen during the year.

If we examine the *rates* (victimization rate per one thousand persons age twelve or older) we find discernible decreases in 1995 NCVS data compared to previous years. In 1995, rape, robbery, and aggravated assaults, for example, were at or near a twenty-three-year low. The rates of theft and household burglary have steadily declined since the late 1970s. The 1995 burglary rate, for instance, is about half the rate reported in 1973. The motor vehicle rate in 1995 is substantially below the record 1991 high.

Victimization surveys are considered a good source of information about crime incidents, independent of data collected by law enforcement agencies throughout the country. Often, the offending trends reported through NCVS data procedures differ substantially from those found in police data (Ohlin & Tonry, 1989).

Throughout the course of this text we will refer to victimization studies in order to get a better grasp on criminal activity as well as to learn how crime affects victims. In many instances, however, we will use surveys conducted by researchers independent of the NCVS. One excellent and meaningful survey sponsored by the National Institute of Justice (NIJ) in collaboration with the Centers for Disease Control and Prevention (CDC) involved an examination of the extent and nature of stalking in American society. The survey, known as the National Violence against Women Survey, was conducted by the Center for Policy Research (Tjaden, 1997).

STALKING: A CONTEMPORARY EXAMPLE OF VICTIMIZATION DATA

Stalking is defined as "a course of conduct directed at a specific person that involves repeated physical or visual proximity, nonconsensual communication, or verbal, written, or implied threats sufficient to cause fear in a reasonable person" (Tjaden, 1997, p. 2). Systematic information on stalking in the United States is limited, despite the attention it receives from the media and the legislatures (Tjaden, 1997). Most of the previous research has focused on the stalking of famous persons, entertainment personalities, or politicians, known as "celebrity stalking." However, a substantial increase in the stalking of "noncelebrities" over the past decade has generated numerous media accounts of stalking victims and passage of antistalking laws in all 50 states and the District of Columbia (Tjaden & Thoennes, 1998). Legal definitions of stalking vary widely from state to state. While most states define stalking in their statutes as the willful, malicious, and repeated following and harassing of another person, some include such activities as lying-in-wait, surveillance, nonconsensual communication, telephone harassment, and vandalism (Tjaden & Thoennes, 1998). Some states specify that at least two stalking events must occur before the conduct can be considered illegal.

In an attempt to fill in the large gap in our knowledge about stalking, the Center for Policy Research conducted a comprehensive victimization survey of eight thousand women and eight thousand men eighteen years of age or older on issues relating to violence (Tjaden & Thoennes, 1997). The survey revealed that 8 percent of women and 2 percent of men reported they had been stalked at some point in their lives (Tjaden, 1997). Overall, the survey indicated that approximately 1.4 million Americans are victims of stalkers every year, a surprisingly large number. In most cases, the stalking lasted less than one year, but some people were stalked for over five years. It is estimated that one out of every twelve women and one out of every forty-five men in the United States has been stalked during his or her lifetime (Tjaden & Thoennes, 1998).

The survey found that the motives of most stalkers were to control, intimidate, or frighten their victims. This observation was made by both male and female victims. Eighty-seven percent of the time the stalker was male, and 80 percent of the time the victim was female. In most stalking incidents, the victims (particularly women) knew their stalker. About half of the female victims were stalked by current or former marital or cohabiting partners, and a majority of these women (80 percent) had been physically assaulted by that partner either during the relationship, during the stalking episode, or during both. In about one-third of the cases, stalkers vandalized the victim's property, and about 10 percent of the time the stalker killed or threatened to kill the victim's pet. In nearly half the cases, the stalker made overt threats to the victim. The survey dispels the myth that most stalkers are psychotic or delusional. Only 7 percent of the victims perceived their stalkers as "crazy" or abusers of drugs or alcohol.

Half of all victims reported the stalking to the police, and about one-quarter of the female victims obtained a restraining order. Not surprisingly, 70 percent of all restraining orders were violated by the assailant. About one-quarter of victims in cases where a restraining order was violated pursued prosecution. When prosecution was pursued, most cases resulted in conviction of the stalker and well over half received jail time. Although most of the stalking stopped within two years, the emotional and social effects of being stalked continued for many victims long after the incident. About one-third of the stalking victims sought psychological treatment because of the emotional and social trauma that resulted from the stalking episodes.

Meloy (1998) asserts that stalkers rarely cause serious physical injury to their victims, threaten them with weapons, or use weapons. Even so, the psychological trauma is often substantial. In a survey of 145 stalking victims (120 females, 25 males), Doris Hall (1998) reports that the experience of being stalked for months or even years is akin to psychological terrorism. A majority of the victims said their entire lives changed as a result of being stalked. "Many move or quit jobs, some change their names, others have gone underground, leaving friends and family in order to escape the terror" (Hall, 1998, p. 134). Some change their physical appearance or wear disguises. Others become exceedingly suspicious of the motives of others, often leading them to follow lonely and isolated lives. Many victims constantly worry that the stalker will find them, and that the entire experience will start all over again.

What terminates stalking? Some stalkers stop their activity toward the current victim when they find a new love interest. About 18 percent of the victims in the Center for Policy Research Survey indicated the stalking stopped when their assailant got a new spouse, partner, or boyfriend/girlfriend. Informal law enforcement interventions also seem to help. Fifteen percent said the stalking ceased when the assailant received a warning from the police. More formal interventions such as an arrest, conviction, or restraining orders do not appear to be very effective. When it comes to persistent, frightening stalking that creates risks to personal safety, the survey suggests that the most effective method may be to relocate as far away from the offender as possible with no information of whereabouts provided to the offender.

A new form of stalking that has emerged in recent years is **cyberstalking**, the use of the internet for stalking. "Because e-mail is used daily by what some experts say are as many as 35 million people, and it is estimated that there are approximately 200,000 stalkers in the United States, the Internet is a perfect forum with which to terrorize their victims" (Jenson, 1996, p. 1). "Chat rooms" and e-mail have provided far-reaching and unregulated opportunities for cyberstalkers to harass unsuspecting victims, especially women. Unfortunately, victims of cyberstalking cannot be adequately protected due to the lack of enforceable laws to prosecute and deter this behavior (Jenson, 1996). And there are substantial obstacles to using criminal and civil law to thwart the persistent cyberstalker, bringing into question whether it is possible to regulate this type of behavior at all. J. Reid Meloy (1998) points out that the internet provides a means of stalking that lacks the usual social constraints. "Only written words are used, and other avenues of sensory perception are eliminated; one cannot see, hear, touch, smell, or emotionally sense the other person" (Meloy, 1998, p. 11). The lack of face-to-face interaction with their victims and the overall anonymity encourages some individuals who would not ordinarily behave in such a fashion to act out their fantasies. An example of cyberstalking is provided by Jenson (1996), who describes a South Carolina woman who had been stalked by an unknown cyber-stalker for several years via e-mail. Not only had the stalker threatened her life, but he also threatened to rape her daughter. The stalker also posted the woman's home address on e-mail for 25 million people to see.

To date, very little systematic research has been conducted to examine the prevalence and incidence of cyberstalking, the personal characteristics of cyber-stalkers, effective deterrents to cyberstalking, or even the psychological conse-quences of being cyberstalked, but the internet does provide an extremely inviting avenue for cyberstalkers that will have substantial ramifications in the future.

THE FOCUS OF THE BOOK

Some scholars have argued (e.g., Sellin, 1970; Tappan, 1947) that one who engages in undetected criminal activity is not a criminal in the strictest or opera-tional sense, because a criminal is by definition one who has been detected, arrested, and convicted. However, from a psychological point of view, we encounter problems when we limit ourselves to studying persons legally defined as criminals. Legal classifications are determined by that which society, at some point in time, considers socially harmful or, in some cases, morally wrong. Therefore, because each society has a different and changing set of values, what may be judged a criminal act in one may not meet the criteria in another, or even in the same society at a later time. Many states in the United States differ signifi-cantly in their criminal codes and are continually revising them. Chemical (drug) possession, prostitution, and dissemination of obscene material are examples of activities that generate ever-changing statutes, and if not changing statutes, selec-tive enforcement.

Members of every society (and consequently every society's judicial system) perceive and process violators of the criminal code with some discrimination, so that the offender's background, social status, personality, motivation, sex, age, race, and legal counsel, as well as the circumstances surrounding the offense, all may affect the legal process. It is highly likely that individuals who have been arrested, convicted, and punished represent a distinctly different sample from those who participate in illegal activity but avoid detection, conviction, or pun-ishment.

Approximately one-fifth of those arrested go to trial, according to Sarbin (1979), who describes the legal process of becoming a criminal. First, the agents of social control (usually the police) label the individual as a suspect. Next, the agents may decide that the suspect should be arrested. Third, the arrested party may be charged with a crime, at which point he or she becomes a defendant. Fourth, the defendant may be tried and convicted, at which point he or she becomes a felon. Finally, the felon may be incarcerated in a correctional facility and be labeled a convict, inmate, prisoner, or criminal. At each step in the process there is a funneling effect that shows that fewer and fewer individuals reach each subsequent step in the criminal justice process. Hart and Sacks (1958) called this the "great pyramid of legal order," and Galanter (1974) called it the "legal iceberg." Hundreds of thousands of individuals get filtered out, for a variety of reasons.

One reason is the error and subjectivity that cannot realistically be removed from determinations of guilt or innocence. Another is the sentencing process. It has been demonstrated that the characteristics of the victim may influence how much punishment is assigned to the offender. Landy and Aronson (1969) report evidence that if the victim is a respectable citizen (i.e., successful and altruistic), the offender will receive a stiffer sentence than if the case involves an "unrespectable" victim (i.e., despicable and dishonest). Jones and Aronson (1973) found that defendants who raped a married woman or virgin were more likely to receive longer sentences than defendants who raped a divorced woman. It has also been found that the more serious a traffic accident the greater the tendency for jurors to believe that the principals involved were at fault and negligent (Walster, 1966). Such discrepancies in sentencing have led to widespread demands for determinate sentencing, where the punishment is carefully calibrated to the offense and there is less room for discretion on the part of judges or juries.

The aforementioned studies support Lerner's hypothesis (1970, 1980) that people need to believe they live in a just world where the undeserving are appropriately deprived or punished. This just world hypothesis predicts, for example, that some victims of rape, assault, or homicide are assumed by many people to have gotten what they deserved or asked for. The implications of this hypothesis in relation to juries' determinations of guilt, and therefore to the determination of who are criminals, are obvious.

It is generally acknowledged, therefore, that incarcerated individuals are not representative of the "true" criminal population. Yet, with rare exceptions, researchers studying the "criminal mind" use as subjects only those individuals who have reached the final stage of the legal process; inmates in correctional institutions. Consequently, if we discuss only legally determined criminals, we will be neglecting a considerable segment of the population that actually breaks the law. To some extent, we have little choice but to do just that. Because this book is based on research, the kinds and amounts of available empirical data dictate to a great extent what will be covered. On the other hand, we can go beyond this point and study the *behavior* that generally qualifies as criminal. From this perspective, we can include the vast body of psychological research that deals with such areas as aggression, "deviant" sexual behavior, and moral development. However, our focus will be on the *persistent, repetitive offender,* whether detected or undetected by the criminal justice system. In other words, in this text we will concentrate on the individual who has frequently committed serious crimes or antisocial acts over an extended period of time (at least several years).

THE SCOPE OF THE BOOK

This text begins with broad theoretical issues surrounding the origins of criminal behavior and moves to more specific offending in the later chapters. Chapter 2 describes the developmental and family influences on children who become delinquent and examines why some go on to become adult offenders. Some effective treatment and prevention themes are outlined in this early chapter. Chapters 3 and 4 concentrate on possible genetic and psychoneurological factors in the development of criminal behavior. The chapters include contemporary and classic theory and research related to the biological explanations of deviant and criminal behavior. In Chapter 5, greater attention is directed at learning factors and social influences on criminal behavior. In this sense, the early part of the text progresses from internal or dispositional theories through environmental or situational theories of criminal behavior, and toward an interactive combination of both. Ultimately, we place heavy emphasis on the internal cognitive or mediational processes.

Chapter 6 focuses on the mentally disordered offender and considers the extent of his or her involvement in crime. In Chapter 7, the book begins discussing specific offenses, beginning with violent crimes. Chapter 7 presents in broad terms some of the instigators and regulators of violence. Chapter 8 continues this theme with a focus on homicide and aggravated assault and its attempt to offer psychological explanations for these violent offenses. Chapter 9 addresses specific issues concerning homicide, including crime scene analysis, mass, and serial murders.

The review of specific offense categories continues with an extensive examination of the research and theoretical development on sex crimes in Chapter 10. Chapter 11 focuses on a wide variety of economic offending. Chapter 12 assesses the validity of the relationship between drugs and crime. Finally, Chapter 13 focuses on the treatment and prevention of serious and violent criminal behavior in general.

The major goal of this book is to encourage the reader to appreciate the enormous complexity of crime and to avoid oversimplified, prejudicial, dogmatic answers to the challenging questions posed by crime. If, after studying the text with an open mind, the reader seeks further information about offending and develops an avid interest in discovering innovative answers and creative solutions to the "crime problem," then this text will have fulfilled its mission.

2

JUVENILE DELINQUENCY:
DEVELOPMENTAL FACTORS

Juvenile justice was officially ushered into the United States on the last day of the 1899 session of the Illinois legislature, when that body passed the seminal **Juvenile Court Act**. This comprehensive child welfare law defined a delinquent as a child under the age of sixteen who violated a state law or any village or city ordinance. It also established this country's first juvenile court and regulated juvenile institutions within the state. The philosophy underlying the law was that juvenile offenders should not be given the same punitive and retaliatory treatment as adults, but rather be given individual attention for their own protection as well as that of society (Chute, 1949). In addition, the law included provisions for dealing with dependent and neglected children.

Although other states had adopted various procedures and regulations relevant to their wayward and neglected youth, the Illinois Act was the first comprehensive attempt at codification. It rapidly became the model for juvenile justice, and by 1911 twenty-two states had adopted similar measures. By 1925, all but two states had established juvenile courts (Tappan, 1949). Today, they exist in some form in every state, either separately or as part of a family court system.

Most programs directed at preventing or treating juvenile delinquency in the early twentieth century were created and managed by psychiatrists, psychologists, or social workers. Not surprisingly, they called for individual counseling and psychotherapy for youthful offenders, usually by a social caseworker or a clinical practitioner. Illinois was also a pioneer in this area, since the first clinic established to provide psychiatric diagnoses to juvenile courts, the Juvenile Psychopathic Institute, opened its doors in Chicago in 1909. Shortly thereafter, the Judge Harvey H. Baker Child Guidance Clinic was established in Boston (Chute, 1949).

In 1930, however, a monumental project was undertaken—again in Chicago—by sociologists proposing a different approach to the prevention of juvenile offenses. Called the Chicago Area Project, it paved the way for a reassessment of existing treatment and preventive programs for delinquents. It also represented the first systematic challenge by sociologists to the domination of psychologists and psychiatrists in both private and public juvenile programs (Schlossman & Sedlak, 1983).

The Project, which lasted thirty years, has been amply described, lauded, and criticized in the sociological and criminal justice literature. Essentially, it immersed researchers and volunteers into communities with higher than average rates of delinquency. The researchers obtained oral histories and accounts of juvenile activities, organized recreational programs, offered "curbstone counseling," and mediated with police and juvenile justice agencies on behalf of community youth. The Project de-emphasized the individualized casework approach and drew attention to the role of the community as an agent of informal social control to prevent delinquency. Readers interested in more detail about the Project might refer to Schlossman and Sedlak's (1983) instructive history and assessment.

Lloyd Ohlin (1983) traces three major shifts in federal policy regarding youth offending, beginning in the 1960s. He attributes the first shift to the Chicago Project and others like it. In the early 1960s, Ohlin notes, federal policymakers drew on community organization strategies to foster community responsibility for juvenile misbehavior and funded a variety of social programs toward that end. The programs in general were not successful, however, partly due to naiveté and partly due to the massive social changes in society that were occurring during the 1960s. "We are much more aware today that juvenile justice depends on the successful operation of a broad formal and informal network of social relationships that guide youth development" (Ohlin, 1983, p. 464). Ohlin notes that "the growing gap between expectation and achievable results fostered disillusionment, alienation, social unrest, and ultimately, abandonment of the programs themselves" (Ohlin, 1983, p. 464). He also suggests, however, that we can learn valuable lessons from the failure of those early community programs.

The second shift in social policy was spearheaded by a series of presidential commissions studying the broad problems of crime and violence. In 1967 the first of these commissions, the President's Commission on Law Enforcement and Administration of Justice, set the tone. Its primary task was to recommend ways to identify and control delinquents and status offenders. The Commission recommended six major strategies: (1) decriminalization of status offenses (such as running away from home); (2) diversion of youth from court procedures into public and private treatment programs; (3) extension of due process rights to juveniles in the same spirit as they had been extended to adult offenders; (4) deinstitutionalization, whereby delinquents would be cared for in group homes or small treatment centers instead of the traditional large institutions, reform schools, or training schools; (5) diversification of services; and (6) decentralization of control of juvenile proceedings and care. Ohlin notes that, although the Commission's recommendations were well received, implementation of the strategies has been "spotty."

In addition, implementation has been somewhat overshadowed by a third change in social policy, which began in the mid-1970s, with a nationwide shift toward a law-and-order commitment. Apparently in response to a rapidly growing fear of crime and serious juvenile delinquency, the public began to demand quicker punishments and mandatory sentencing procedures, first for adults and eventually for juveniles. Ohlin notes that this new focus reflects in part a strong conservative reaction to the liberal policies advocated by the National Crime Commissions of the 1960s.

A fourth cycle has emerged during the 1990s, a cycle characterized by broad legislative reform. Those policy makers calling for reform of the juvenile justice system have spurred legislation in a variety of states lowering the age at which youths may be tried as adult offenders for serious violent offenses like rape or murder. In 1994, for example, states introduced more than seven hundred bills to move more youthful offenders from specialized facilities to adult prisons (Krisberg, 1995). There is also a greater preoccupation with chronic, violent offenders, who actually comprise a very small proportion of the juvenile offender population.

DEFINITION OF JUVENILE DELINQUENCY

Juvenile delinquency is an imprecise, nebulous, social, clinical, and legal label for a wide variety of law- and norm-violating behavior. At first glance, a simple legal definition seems to suffice: *Delinquency is behavior against the criminal code committed by an individual who has not reached adulthood*. But the term "delinquency" has numerous definitions and meanings beyond this one-sentence definition. In some states the legal definition also includes status offending, which is not behavior against the criminal code but is behavior prohibited only for juveniles. For example, running away, violating curfew laws, and truancy all qualify as **status offenses**.

Social definitions of delinquency consist of a wide variety of youthful behaviors considered inappropriate, such as aggressive behavior, truancy, petty theft, vandalism, or drug abuse. The behavior may or may not have come to the attention of the police. Psychological definitions of delinquency include conduct disorder and antisocial behavior. **Conduct disorder** is a diagnostic term used to represent a group of behaviors characterized by *habitual* misbehavior, such as stealing, setting fires, running away from home, skipping school, destroying property, fighting, being cruel to animals and people, and frequently telling lies. The child may or may not have been arrested for these behaviors. Some of these behaviors are not even against the criminal law. The term "conduct disorder" is more fully described in the American Psychiatric Association's *Diagnostic and Statistical Manual* (1994, 4th edition), commonly referred to as the *DSM-IV*. The DSM-IV divides conduct disorders into two categories, depending on the onset of the misbehaviors. If the misconduct began in childhood (before age ten), it is called conduct disorder: childhood-onset type. If the misconduct began in adolescence, it is called conduct disorder: adolescent-onset type.

The clinical term "antisocial behavior" is usually reserved for more serious habitual misbehavior, especially a behavioral pattern that involves direct and harmful actions against others. It is to be distinguished, however, from the term "antisocial personality disorder," a diagnostic label reserved primarily for adults who displayed conduct disorders as children or adolescents, and continue serious offending well into adulthood. We will discuss antisocial personality disorders in more detail in Chapter 6.

Legally, a juvenile delinquent is one who commits an act defined by law as illegal and who is adjudicated delinquent by an appropriate court. The legal definition is usually restricted to persons under eighteen, but states vary in their age distinctions. At this writing, four states give criminal courts, rather than juvenile courts, automatic jurisdiction over juveniles at age sixteen, and eight states do so at age seventeen. Several other states are considering lowering their age restrictions. All states allow juveniles to be tried as adults in criminal courts under certain conditions and for certain offenses. Some states (e.g., New York) allow children as young as age seven to be tried as adults for certain offenses. Under federal law, juveniles may be prosecuted under the criminal law at age fifteen.

Juvenile courts are part of the civil court system and differ significantly from criminal courts in both terminology and procedure. For example, juvenile courts accept petitions of delinquency rather than criminal complaints; conduct hearings, not trials; adjudicate juveniles delinquent rather than criminal. In general, juvenile court proceedings are not open to the public. However, juveniles are still protected by many due process safeguards associated with criminal trials, such as written notice of charges, legal representation, the right to confront and cross-examine witnesses, and protection against self-incrimination.

The juvenile justice system is fraught with inequities, and scholars have proposed numerous philosophical, structural, and procedural changes to better balance the interests of society, the child, and the parent (e.g., Schultz & Cohen, 1976; American Bar Association, 1979). It is not our purpose here to deal with these problems at any length or to evaluate the recommendations for change. They only serve to provide a backdrop for our main topic, which is the behavior of youths adjudicated delinquent, and how serious criminal behavior in youths is acquired and maintained. Our main focus throughout this chapter will be on the chronic, repetitive offender who moves from adolescence to adulthood in a continuing cycle of offending and reoffending.

THE NATURE AND EXTENT OF JUVENILE OFFENDING

The nature and extent of delinquent behavior—both what is reported and unreported to law enforcement agencies—is essentially an unknown area (Krisberg & Schwartz, 1983; Krisberg, 1995), even more so than adult crime. We simply do not have complete data on the national incidence of juvenile delinquency. We do have some statistics collected by law enforcement agencies, the courts, and facilities for delinquents, but the figures are woefully incomplete and inaccurate. As Barry Krisberg (1992, p. 2) notes, "Put simply, the amount of crime committed by juveniles is unknown and perhaps unknowable."

Usually, unlawful acts committed by delinquents are placed into five major categories:

1. Unlawful acts against persons
2. Unlawful acts against property

3. Drug offenses
4. Offenses against the public order
5. Status offenses

Most referrals to juvenile court are for crimes against property (46 percent), followed by offenses against the public order (21 percent), status offenses (17 percent), crimes against persons (11 percent), and drug offenses (5 percent). The first four categories are comparable in definition to crimes committed by adults. Status offenses, on the other hand, are acts that only juveniles can commit and that can be adjudicated only by a juvenile court. As discussed earlier, typical status offenses range from misbehavior, such as violations of curfew, running away from home, and truancy, to offenses that are interpreted very subjectively, such as unruliness and unmanageability. The judicial system historically has supported differential treatment of male and female status offenders. Adolescent girls, for example, have often been detained for incorrigibility or running away from home, when the same behavior in adolescent boys was ignored or tolerated. Until recently, about three times as many girls were held for status offenses as boys (U.S. Department of Justice, 1988). In recent years, as a result of suits brought on behalf of juveniles, many courts have put authorities on notice that this discriminatory approach is unwarranted, and the practice appears to be diminishing. Moreover, under the federal law, juveniles are no longer overtly punished for status violations. Nevertheless, some research indicates that officials circumvent the rules by reaching for ways to bring adolescents, particularly girls, under the aegis of juvenile courts (Chesney-Lind, 1986).

It has been argued that, because status offenses lend themselves to so much subjectivity, they should be removed from the purview of all state juvenile courts (American Bar Association, 1979). Some states have clearly moved in this direction. On the other hand, many have de-emphasized status offenses or replaced them completely with statutes allowing the detention and/or supervision of youngsters who are presumably in need of protection either from their own rash behavior or the behavior of others, such as "bad" companions. These statutes are usually referred to as PINS or CHINS laws (person or child in need of supervision). Under these laws, runaways or incorrigible youngsters are subject to juvenile court jurisdiction, often at the instigation of their parents, even though they may not have committed an act comparable to a crime.

The trend in recent years has been to remove status offenses from juvenile court jurisdictions, but the jurisdiction does remain in some states. Therefore, even though status offenses are a category that is slowly being phased out, it is important that we are familiar with the term because of its long, controversial history in juvenile justice.

In this chapter, we will cover violent and property offenses broadly because serious or habitual juvenile offenders rarely restrict their behaviors to one type of offense category. Youth crime data are collected from a variety of sources: (1) official records of police arrests, such as the FBI's UCR; (2) self-reports of victimization, such as the *National Crime Survey*; (3) self-reports of delinquent involvement, where national samples of youth are asked to complete questionnaires about their own behavior, such as in the *National Youth Survey* (Elliott, Ageton, & Huizinga, 1980); (4) juvenile court processing, as reported by the *National Center for Juvenile Justice (NCJJ)*; (5) juvenile corrections, as reported in the monograph *Children in Custody (CIC)*; and (6) probation and parole statistics, as reported in various governmental publications. The last three sources of information have the major disadvantage of greatly underestimating the number of actual offenses, since even more than in the criminal system, a very high proportion—perhaps a majority—of cases are either undetected or are dismissed before reaching the courts. In other words, because of parental involvement, negotiations, and compromises, many offenders do not require adjudication. To add to the problem of obtaining statistics on juvenile offenders, juvenile court dockets do not always reflect serious offending. Referrals by parents, schools, probation officers, and other courts, either for status offenses or for supervision, make up much of a court's delinquency workload. Because of this confusion, perhaps the most complete official nationwide compilation of juvenile offenses today remains the UCR, despite its serious shortcomings.

Although all these sources of data are far from perfect, many contemporary researchers interested in the correlates and causes of juvenile delinquency prefer the unofficial data gained from self-report survey research (Hindelang, Hirschi, & Weis, 1981). They prefer these data for several reasons. First, many researchers are highly skeptical about the validity of official government data such as UCR reports. Second, victimization surveys are limited, because victims often do not know the age of the offender. Therefore, while these surveys may provide important information about crime in general, they may not accurately reflect the involvement of juveniles. Third, self-report data seem consistent with modern theories of delinquency and crime, many of which were formulated before self-report measures were even adequately developed. In other words, self-report procedures appear more valid than either official reports or victim accounts. Addressing one criticism of self-report studies, Hindelang and his fellow researchers (1981) noted that adolescents generally did not resist reporting their own unlawful behavior, although there are, of course, exceptions.

In spite of these advantages, self-report surveys are a relatively new development in juvenile crime research and, as such, do not adequately estimate the incidence of juvenile offending. They may be quite accurate as far as they go, but they do not yet reach enough young people to provide a valid assessment. Moreover, as described in Chapter 1, they have traditionally focused on trivial offenses rather than serious law-violating behavior, although designers of the National Youth Survey have made promising strides toward controlling for this problem. Official data, by contrast, offer extensive—often nationwide—information on the type of delinquency that concerns law enforcement officials. Yet they are limited in the sense that, like all official data, they may reflect errors in reporting and discretionary treatment. Therefore, although we will often refer to official data—such as arrest records—in the following pages, it is with the caveat that these data may not be truly representative of delinquent behavior.

Public opinion surveys consistently reveal that many people believe serious youth crime is increasing at a steady and alarming rate (Krisberg, 1992). Since the available nationwide data are sketchy and incomplete, it is difficult to reach firm conclusions about the nature and characteristics of youth crime. Prior to 1989, there was little evidence that youth crime was skyrocketing. Official juvenile statistics between 1960 and 1988, when adjusted for population increases, revealed that the juvenile offending rate was not increasing, but was remaining largely the same from year to year. Victimization data obtained by the National Crime Survey (NCS) showed a similar pattern. Moreover, both revealed that serious juvenile offenses (defined in accordance with the Sellin-Wolfgang scale) remained steady or actually declined (Laub, 1983; Galvin & Polk, 1983). True, the serious offense rates, which peaked during the mid-1970s, were substantial, but they did not increase. In fact, the UCR data indicate that between 1979 and 1988, the number of persons under eighteen arrested for index crimes actually dropped by nearly 18 percent (U.S. Department of Justice, 1989a).

Between 1989 and 1994, however, the arrest rates for juveniles increased significantly—but not alarmingly. The available data suggest that between the 1980s and the early 1990s, juvenile arrests for all crimes increased 20 percent. If we consider violent and property crimes separately, we find a similar pattern, especially for violent crimes. In 1980, juveniles were known to be the offender in 8 percent of all homicides. In 1994, they were known to be the offender in 16 percent of all homicides, a significant increase (Sickmund, Snyder, & Poe-Yamagata, 1997). After more than a decade of increases, homicides by juveniles dropped in 1995 (17 percent). Nearly all of the decline was in homicides by African-American juveniles (Sickmund et al., 1997). In fact, the juvenile arrests rate for violent crime in 1996 dropped 9 percent from 1995 and 12 percent from 1994, marking the second year of decline after steady increases the previous six years. The reasons for these statistical increases and decreases are unknown, although the media and experts are full of conflicting explanations. Unfortunately, scientific answers to the youth crime question must wait for empirical research to analyze the partial data sufficiently and offer more systematic explanations for these trends.

Self-report studies and official data do show, however, that only a small percentage of the juvenile population engages in serious delinquent behavior. It is also important to note that only about 3 to 15 percent of serious offenses ever result in "police contact," again according to some self-report studies (Weis & Sederstrom, 1981). Research utilizing self-report surveys by Elliott, Dunford, and Huizinga (1987) suggest that serious, repetitive juvenile offenders escaped detection 86 percent of the time over a five-year period. These figures further suggest that the incidence of offending may be substantially underestimated by official arrest data. In other words, a small percentage of youth are committing a substantial amount of undetected offenses, or offenses for which they are not adjudicated.

How does violent juvenile crime compare with the incidence and rate of property offenses—burglary, larceny-theft, and motor vehicle theft? According to the 1996 UCR data, the four violent index categories (murder and voluntary manslaughter, forcible rape, robbery, and aggravated assault) represent only 4 percent of all juvenile arrests. If we consider all eight index offenses (adding larceny-theft, motor vehicle theft, burglary, and arson), we find that 88 percent of juvenile arrests were for larceny-theft, motor vehicle theft, and burglary, indicating that a vast majority of juvenile crime is acquisition crime.

National arrest rates, victimization studies, and self-report data generate different estimates of the incidence of delinquency. Furthermore, the available data are extremely inadequate for answering even the most basic questions about youth crime trends or characteristics of juvenile offenders (Krisberg, 1992). Krisberg (1992, p. 2) argues that unless the federal or state governments are willing to make a strong commitment of new research funds to the collection and analysis of nationwide data on youth crime, "the knowledge base supporting delinquency prevention-and-control efforts will remain woefully inadequate."

However, as we noted, a series of longitudinal and self-report studies conducted in recent years do show that most serious property and violent offenses are being committed by a small but significant segment of the youth population, and that this segment tends toward high recidivism (Bartol & Bartol, 1998). In addition, frequent offenders do not specialize in any one particular kind of offending, such as theft or larceny. Instead, they tend to be involved in a wide variety of offenses, ranging from minor property crimes to highly violent ones. Longitudinal research also indicates that repetitive offenders were unusually troublesome in school, earning poor grades, and that they have inadequate or poor social skills. Furthermore, these troublesome behaviors began at an early age, and the more serious the offender, the earlier these childhood patterns appeared. With these observations in mind, we will now turn our attention to a topic directly relevant to the psychosocial nature of this text, namely the social and psychological factors that appear to be correlated with delinquent behavior among young people.

SOCIAL RISK FACTORS

POVERTY, SOCIAL CLASS, AND DELINQUENCY

Social class and general effects of poverty have been a central focus in research studies of crime and delinquency for over a century. Most pre-1960 sociological theories of delinquency considered it as a crucial element in explanations for crime and delinquency. These theories predicted an inverse or negative relationship between **social class** and offending: the lower the social class, the greater the likelihood of involvement in delinquent or criminal behavior. During the mid-1950s and early 1960s, researchers began to wonder if social class or poverty connection to offending was really all that strong. Much of this doubt stemmed from the findings of self-report studies that suggested that juvenile offending was as prevalent among middle-class youth as it was among lower-class youth.

There is little doubt, however, that poverty has a strong connection to persistent, violent offending, as measured by official, victimization, and self-report data. Accumulating research evidence strongly indicates that poverty is one of the most robust predictors of adolescent violence for both males and females (Sampson & Wilson, 1993; Hammond & Yung, 1994; Hill et al., 1994). This strong connection between poverty and violence holds whether we are referring to victims or offenders. Children and youth living under conditions of poverty are more likely to be victims, and they are also more likely to be offenders. Preschool children living in a low-income family characterized by poor housing and unemployment are especially at high risk to become delinquent and/or to become victimized (Dodge, 1993a; Farrington, 1991). Poverty in this context refers to a situation in which the basic resources to maintain an average standard of living within a specific geographical region are lacking. This may include the absence of sufficient income to meet basic necessities of life.

The exact nature of the relationship between poverty and violence is not well understood. For example, poverty is often accompanied not only by inequities in resources, but also by discrimination, racism, family disruption, unsafe living conditions, joblessness, social isolation, and limited social support systems (Hill et al., 1994; Sampson & Lauritsen, 1994). Youth living under poverty conditions are more likely to drop out of school, to be unemployed, to carry a firearm, to be victimized, and to be a witness to a variety of violence. Furthermore, poverty affects people differently. For instance, the values of different ethnic and cultural groups provide a cultural context wherein poverty is perceived differently (Guerra et al., 1995). Some subgroups or minority groups may perceive material deprivation and poverty as more acceptable if everyone else within that cultural context is in the "same boat."

Poverty influences the family in many ways. It influences children through its impact on parents' behavior toward children. For instance, the stress caused by poverty in urban settings is believed to diminish parents' capacity for supportive and consistent parenting (Hammond & Yung, 1994). This situation may lead to coercive and highly aggressive methods of child control. Coercive methods of child control are more direct, immediate, and easy to administer. They require less time and energy to administer, compared to parenting that emphasizes sensitivity, interpersonal skills, and patient understanding. It is much easier to slap a child than it is to explain and utilize more thoughtful parenting strategies. Furthermore, parenting that utilizes aggressive and violent tactics often provides models and a violent context that promote the cycle of violence in the next generation. Living in disadvantaged environments may also lead to the belief that economic survival and **social status** depends greatly on being aggressive and violent to others.

PEER ASSOCIATION

Adolescents live in two separate worlds: one for the family and the other for friends (Berndt, 1979). Adolescents—especially those in the middle class—often seek advice from family in matters of finance, education, and career plans, but in making decisions about their social lives—dress, drinking, dating, drugs, recreational activities—adolescents overwhelmingly want to be attuned to the opinions of their peers (Sebald, 1986).

Consistently, the research literature finds peer association one of the strongest and most consistent single predictors of delinquency (Loeber & Dishion, 1983; Pepler & Slaby, 1994). A national, longitudinal self-report survey conducted by Elliott, Huizinga, and Ageton (1985) also reports that association with delinquent peers is one of the strongest predictors of delinquency. Those adolescents who report having delinquent friends are more likely to report delinquent offending themselves.

The relationship between peers and drug use seems especially strong. For example, Richard Johnson and his associates (Johnson, Marcos, & Bahr, 1987) found that peers have considerable influence on both the frequency and the type of drug used. They conclude, "It is not so much that adolescents use drugs because drug use of the friends makes drug use seem right or safe; rather, they apparently use drugs *simply because their friends do*" (p. 336).

However, peer influence is a complicated process. It is highly unlikely that peer influence by itself provides a complete picture of the development of serious delinquency and crime. Serious delinquency is the end product of many influences, including peers, family, and the social environment in general. Furthermore, there is no evidence in the research literature that association with delinquent peers precedes or even encourages offending (Farrington, 1987). In other words, the adolescent may have been prone to frequent antisocial behavior prior to the association with delinquent friends. Therefore, we cannot assert that delinquent peers *cause* other peers who associate with them to become delinquent, but serious delinquents do tend to hang around with delinquent peers, although their delinquent behavior was often apparent before their peer association. The research is strong that aggressive children are rejected by peers (Pepler & Slaby, 1994). However, research has found that these rejected children seek out and associate with other rejected children who share similar values and goals (Cairns & Cairns, 1991; Cairns et al., 1988).

Farrington (1987) notes that those delinquents who associate with delinquent friends over extended periods of time persist in offending as adults. The research also shows that peer influences may be important when it comes to *property* offending for juveniles, but the link is weak or nonexistent when it pertains to adult *violent* offending (Farrington & Hawkins, 1991; Raine, 1993).

PSYCHOLOGICAL RISK FACTORS

DEVELOPMENTAL FACTORS

There is good evidence that serious, persistent delinquency patterns begin in early childhood. Learning experiences begin early and build on themselves. Researchers have noted differences in impulsiveness, social skills, and feelings for others between children who ultimately became serious delinquents and nondelinquents during their early school years. Even at an early age, aggressive, belligerent children are unpopular and are excluded from peer groups (Hartup, 1983; Patterson, 1982; Olweus, 1978). In fact, Coie, Underwood, and Lochman (1991) contend that aggressiveness is the single most important reason for a child to be rejected by peers.

As a group, highly aggressive, troublesome children demonstrate social and interpersonal skills that are below average for their age. Those children who continue offending into adolescence and young adulthood are troublesome in school, beginning as early as the first grade (Farrington, 1987), and perform below average in most school achievement tasks (Schafer & Polk, 1967; Kelly, 1980). Low achievement, low vocabulary, and poor verbal reasoning have been found to correlate significantly with later delinquency (Farrington, 1979).

Stealing is another early predictor of delinquency. In fact, in a literature review by Loeber and Dishion (1983), habitual stealing—as reported by parents and teachers—emerged as one of the strongest predictors of later delinquency. Furthermore, youngsters who engaged in stealing, even at the elementary school level, also tended to be simultaneously demonstrating other problem behaviors such as lying, truancy, and running away. Frequent dishonesty appears to be another behavioral pattern that predicts quite early a tendency toward repetitive offending (Loeber & Dishion, 1983; Farrington, 1979). Research and theoretical development by Terrie Moffitt and her colleagues (1993a, 1993b) encourage us to view delinquency as proceeding along at least two developmental paths. On one path we see a child developing a lifelong trajectory of delinquency and crime at a very early age, probably around three or even younger. Moffitt (1993a, p. 679) observes: "Across the life course, these individuals exhibit changing manifestations of antisocial behavior: biting and hitting at age four, shoplifting and truancy at age ten, selling drugs and stealing cars at age sixteen, robbery and rape at age twenty-two, and fraud and child abuse at age thirty." These individuals, whom Moffitt calls **life-course-persistent** (**LCP**) offenders, continue their antisocial ways across all kinds of conditions and situations. Moffitt reports that many of these LCP offenders exhibit neurological problems during their childhoods, such as difficult temperaments as infants, attention-deficit disorders or **hyperactivity** as children, and learning problems during their later school years. Judgment and problem-solving deficiencies are often apparent when the children reach adulthood. LCP offenders generally commit a wide assortment of aggressive and violent crimes over their lifetimes.

LCPs as children miss opportunities to acquire and practice prosocial and interpersonal skills at each stage of development, partly because they are rejected and avoided by their childhood peers, and partly because their parents and other caretakers become frustrated and give up on them (Coie, Belding, & Underwood, 1988; Coie, Dodge, & Kupersmith, 1990; Moffitt, 1993a). Moffitt (1993a, p. 684) writes that "… if social and academic skills are not mastered in childhood, it is very difficult to later recover from lost opportunities." Furthermore, as noted previously, disadvantaged homes, inadequate schools, and violent neighborhoods are factors that are very likely to exacerbate the ongoing and developing antisocial behavioral pattern.

The great majority of "delinquents" are those individuals who begin offending during their adolescent years and most often stop offending somewhere around their eighteenth birthday. Moffitt labels these individuals **adolescent-limited** (**AL**). Their developmental histories do not demonstrate the early and persistent antisocial problems that members of the LCP group manifest. However, the frequency—and in some cases, the violence level—of the offending during the teen years may be as high as that of the LCP youth. In effect, the teenage offending patterns of the AL and that of the LCP may be highly similar (Moffitt et al., 1996). "The two types cannot be discriminated on most indicators of antisocial and problem behavior in adolescence; boys on the LCP and AL paths are similar on parent-, self-, and official records of offending, peer delinquency, substance abuse, unsafe sex, and dangerous driving" (Moffitt et al., 1996, p. 400). That is, a professional could not easily identify the group classification (AL or LCP) simply by examining juvenile arrest records, self-reports, or the information provided by parents during the teen years.

According to Terrie Moffitt and her colleagues (Moffitt et al., 1996), the AL delinquent is most likely, during the teen years, to be involved in offenses that symbolize adult privilege and demonstrate autonomy from parental control. Examples include vandalism, drug and alcohol offenses, theft, and "status" offenses such as running away or truancy. In addition, AL delinquents are likely to engage in crimes that are profitable or rewarding, but they also have the ability to abandon these actions when prosocial styles become more rewarding. For example, the onset of young adulthood brings on opportunities not attainable during the teen years, such as leaving high school for college, obtaining a full-time job, and entering a relationship with a prosocial person. AL delinquents are quick to learn that they have something to lose if they continue offending into adulthood. During childhood, in contrast to the LCP child, the AL youngster has learned to get along with others. They normally have a satisfactory repertoire of academic, social, and interpersonal skills that enable them to "get ahead." Therefore, the developmental histories and personal dispositions of the AL youth allow them the option of exploring new life pathways, an opportunity not usually afforded the LCP youth.

Another example of the developmental perspective is found in a study conducted by Daniel Nagin and Kenneth Land (1993). These researchers were able to identify four developmental paths in British boys: the never-convicteds (NCs), the adolescence-limiteds (ALs), the high-level chronics (HLCs), and the low-level chronics (LLCs). The offending paths of the ALs followed the typical contour: Offending began late, reached a peak at age sixteen, and then showed a precipitous decline to zero by age twenty-two (Nagin, Farrington, & Moffitt, 1995). The LLC curve showed a rise through early adolescence, reached a plateau, and remained at the same level well past age eighteen. The HLC group (essentially the same as Moffitt's LCP) showed an early and frequent antisocial and offending pattern that continued through adolescence at a high rate and remained high well into adulthood. A very common feature of the chronic offender is a behavioral pattern characteristic of attention deficit disorder. It should be emphasized, however, that persons who have been diagnosed with attention deficit disorder are not necessarily chronic offenders. On the other hand, chronic juvenile offenders tend to be diagnosed ADHD at some point during their development.

HYPERACTIVITY AND ATTENTION DEFICIT DISORDERS

The term "hyperactive syndrome" (also called minimal brain dysfunction, hyperkinesis, attention deficit disorder, or currently **attention deficit hyperactivity disorder [ADHD]**) includes a heterogeneity of behaviors, but the central three are: (1) inattention (does not seem to listen, or is easily distracted); (2) impulsivity (acts before thinking, shifts quickly from one activity to another); and (3) excessive motor activity (cannot sit still, fidgets, runs about, is talkative and noisy).

ADHD is the leading psychological diagnosis for American children (Cowley, 1993). Educators note that ADHD children have difficulty staying on task, remaining cognitively organized, sustaining academic achievement in the school setting, and maintaining control over their behavior. Satterfield (1987) notes that, while most childhood disorders are temporary and are not predictive of psychopathology in later life, the hyperactive syndrome presents a different story. "The hyperactive child presents a remarkably immutable syndrome that forecasts an ominous picture of the future. The clinical picture often worsens as the child grows older, with resulting adolescent problems of academic failure and serious antisocial behavior" (Satterfield, 1987, p. 146). Although the common belief is that one eventually outgrows hyperactivity, the evidence is that the key symptomatic features of hyperactivity persist into adulthood (af Klinteberg, Magnusson, & Schalling, 1989; Thorley, 1984). It is estimated that over 10 million Americans are affected by the disorder, three-quarters of them males (Cowley, 1993).

ADHD is a puzzling problem, the cause of which is largely unknown. Some scientists contend that ADHD children are born with a biological predisposition toward hyperactivity; others maintain that some children are exposed to environmental factors that damage the nervous system. Rolf Loeber (1990) demonstrates how exposure to toxic substances during the preschool years often retards or negatively influences children's neurological development, often resulting in symptoms of ADHD. For example, children exposed to low levels of lead toxicity (from paint) are more hyperactive and impulsive, and are easily distracted and frustrated. They also show discernible problems in following simple instructions. The causal factors of ADHD are probably multiple and extremely difficult to identify.

Some researchers observe that ADHD children do not possess effective strategies and cognitive organization with which to deal with the daily demands of school work. These children often have particular difficulty in understanding and using abstract concepts. ADHD children also seem to lack cognitively organized ways for dealing with new knowledge.

Although many behaviors have been identified as accompanying ADHD, the overriding theme is that ADHD children are perceived as annoying and aversive to those around them. Although ADHD children are continually seeking and prolonging interpersonal contacts, they eventually manage to irritate and frustrate those people with whom they interact (Henker & Whalen, 1989). They are often rejected by peers, especially if they are perceived as aggressive (Henker & Whalen, 1989). This pattern of peer rejection appears to continue throughout the developmental years (Reid, 1993).

As research on ADHD accumulates, it is becoming increasingly apparent that ADHD is not so much a disorder of activity as it is a *disorder of interpersonal relationships*. Even those ADHD children who are not aggressive and who manage to control some of their "hyperactivity" still have problems with their social interactions. They lack friendship and intimacy (Henker & Whalen, 1989). Terrie Moffitt (Moffitt & Silva, 1988; Moffitt, 1993b) observes that a very large number of

ADHD children report delinquent behaviors by early adolescence. She also found that children between the ages of five and seven who demonstrate the characteristics of both ADHD and delinquent behavior not only have special difficulty with social relationships but also have a high probability of consistent serious antisocial behavior into delinquency and beyond (Moffitt, 1990). Experts argue that the most common problem associated with ADHD is delinquency and substance abuse. The data strongly suggest that youth with symptoms of both ADHD and delinquent behavior are at very high risk for developing lengthy and serious criminal careers (Moffitt, 1990; Satterfield, Swanson, Schell, & Lee, 1994). David Farrington (1991) in his well-cited research also found that violent offenders often have a history of hyperactivity, impulsivity, and attention deficit problems.

The most common method of treatment for ADHD is stimulant medication (methylphenidate or Ritalin). However, this approach is marked by limited success and numerous side effects, some of them severe. Counseling and psychotherapy are often used, often in conjunction, but they too have had very limited success with this puzzling phenomenon, particularly over the long term. ADHD children generally demonstrate multiple problems that can be best treated through treatment strategies that include all the factors impinging on the child at any given time. These treatment approaches are called "multisystemic" and will be dealt with more fully in Chapter 13.

CONDUCT DISORDERS

ADHD frequently co-occurs with a diagnostic category called "conduct disorders" (Offord, Boyle, & Racine, 1991; Reid, 1993). As mentioned previously, conduct disorder (abbreviated CD) is a term often used by mental-health professionals to represent a cluster of behaviors characterized by persistent misbehavior. Examples of this misbehavior include stealing, fire setting, running away from home, skipping school, destroying property, fighting, frequently telling lies, and cruelty to animals and people. According to the *Diagnostic and Statistical Manual-IV* (*DSM-IV*), published by the American Psychiatric Association (1994), the central feature of conduct disorder is the *repetitive* and *persistent* pattern of behavior that violates the basic rights of others.

Behavioral indicators of a conduct disorder can be observed in the context of interactions with parents well before school entry (Reid, 1993). For instance, children who are aggressive, difficult to manage, and noncompliant in the home at age three, often continue to have similar problems when entering school. Furthermore, these behaviors show remarkable continuity through adolescence and into adulthood. CD children frequently have significant problems with school work, a behavioral pattern that often results in the label "learning disability." Similar to ADHD children, aggressive CDs are at high risk for strong rejection by their peers (Reid, 1993). This rejection generally lasts throughout the school years and is very difficult to change (Reid, 1993). As described above, children who are consistently socially rejected by peers miss critical opportunities to develop normal interpersonal and social skills. Lacking effective interpersonal skills, these youth are forced to get their needs met through more aggressive means, including threats and intimidation.

The DSM-IV identifies two subtypes of conduct disorders based on the onset of the repetition and persistence of the misbehavior: the *childhood-onset type* and *adolescent-onset type*. According to the DSM-IV, childhood onset type occurs when the pattern begins prior to age ten. The adolescent-onset type, on the other hand, is characterized by the absence of any pattern before age ten. The DSM-IV also notes that if the CD pattern begins before age ten, the prognosis is not good, compared with a more favorable prognosis for a later onset. The DSM-IV is consistent with LCP (life-course-persistent) and AL (adolescence-limited) antisocial behavioral patterns reported by Moffitt, Reid, and others.

An estimated 6 to 16 percent of the male population is believed to have behavioral features of CD. The prevalence in girls ranges from 4 to 9.2 percent (Cohen, Cohen, & Brook, 1993; Zoccolillo, 1993). A recent study by Anna Bardone and her colleagues (Bardone, Moffitt, & Caspi, in press) found that CD patterns in girls is a strong predictor of a lifetime of problems, including poor interpersonal relations with partners/spouses and peers, criminal activity, early pregnancy without supportive partners, and frequent job loss and firings. Similar to CD boys, CD girls appear destined for a life of interpersonal conflict with the social environment.

Contrary to statements found in many crime and delinquency textbooks, few contemporary psychologists believe that delinquent offenders, as a whole, are emotionally disturbed or psychologically maladjusted youths in need of conventional psychotherapy. Rather, mainstream psychology views delinquency, including frequent offenders, as a learned behavior, acquired and maintained like all other human behavior. Most psychologists consider behavior a function of the environment (social) interacting with individual (psychological) factors.

Over the past three decades, the psychological study of crime has shifted away from accepting personality traits as major determinants of criminal and delinquent behavior toward a more interactive cognitive and developmental focus.

FAMILY BACKGROUND

It is estimated that over 13 million American families with children are maintained by only one parent (Department of Commerce, Bureau of Census, 1996). Studies based on official data have traditionally found that delinquents come from homes where parents are divorced or separated more often than do nondelinquents (Glueck & Glueck, 1950; Monahan, 1957; Eaton & Polk, 1961; Rodman & Grams, 1967; Flynn, 1983). This has led to conclusions that the single-parent home could be blamed for much delinquency. Since the 1970s, with the emergence of self-report data, these conclusions have been questioned.

The relationship between the single-parent home and delinquency carries excessive baggage in that it is confounded with so many other variables and influences. For example, there appears to be an inverse relationship between divorce rates and social economic class or status (Belsky, Lerner, & Spanier, 1984). Couples at the lower end of the socioeconomic status spectrum have the highest divorce rates, while couples in the upper-middle and upper classes have the lowest rates. Thus, it may not be the broken home or single-parent situation per se that is directly contributing to delinquency, but perhaps some combination of poverty level, job opportunities, educational level, or other interacting variables is the causal factor.

Also, the term "broken" or single-parent home is ambiguous. Homes may be broken by a wide variety of circumstances—death, desertion, divorce, or separation. In addition, we cannot assume that all these separations affect families the same way. For example, there is some evidence that children from single-parent homes that are relatively conflict free are less likely to be delinquent than children from conflict-ridden "intact" homes (Gove & Crutchfield, 1982). Furthermore, the composition of the broken homes must be considered. That is, who is living in the broken home—grandparents, stepparent, relatives, or friends?

While the relationship between single-parent homes and delinquency is a commonly reported one, we are far from explaining it. It is clear that, if the single-parent home is a risk factor, it is probably confounded by a complex of other interacting variables. However, as Flynn (1983, p. 13) asserts: "One point is indisputably clear in the literature: A stable, secure, and mutually supportive family is exceedingly important in delinquency prevention."

Gerald Patterson (1982, 1986) concluded years ago that the families of delinquency-prone children support the use of antisocial behavior in their children by inadvertently reinforcing such behaviors and by failing to reinforce prosocial ones. Within these families, continual aversive exchanges were observed between parents and the aggressive children, suggesting that these children may be both the architects and the victims of aggressive interactions (Pepler & Slaby, 1994).

PARENTAL DISCIPLINARY PRACTICES

Other researchers have discovered that the lack of parental supervision appears to be a strong predictor of serious, violent delinquency (Loeber & Stouthamer, 1986; Pepler & Slaby, 1994). Furthermore, factors such as inconsistent parental disciplinary practices (McCord, 1979) and harsh, physical punishment by parents are also strongly correlated with delinquency (Straus, 1991). Inconsistent or physically harsh discipline in the home may result in more delinquency than consistent and reasoning forms of discipline. Delinquents repeatedly complain that their parents were unfair and nonobjective in administering discipline (McCord, McCord, & Zola, 1959; Glueck & Glueck, 1950), a complaint voiced much less frequently by nondelinquents. We should easily see why this type of discipline is a problem. First, it yields inconsistent dispensation of reinforcement. This means that socially desirable behaviors, if engaged in, will not be strengthened in the home environment. If a nine-year-old plays a spirited game of hide-and-seek with her younger sister, she may be ignored by the parent on one occasion, chastised for being too noisy the next. Second, punishment contingent on the whim and mood of a parent rather than on any specific behavior on the part of the child contributes to an extremely unpleasant and unpredictable environment. Physical punishments of slapping, hitting, and punching provide a pattern to be modeled when youngsters are themselves frustrated and disenchanted. Murray Straus (1991) concluded that although harsh physical punishment produces some conformity in children during the short term, over time it tends to increase the probability of violent delinquency and crime. Straus further discovered that parents who believe in physical punishment not only hit the children more often but are more likely to go beyond ordinary physical punishment and actually assault the child. For example, they may resort to punching and kicking, which, of course carry greater risk of injury to the child. Research by Leonard D. Eron and his colleagues (Eron, Huesmann, & Zelli, 1991) reveals that this cycle of violence and aggression remains in aggressive-prone families for at least three generations. In one of the very few studies examining the parenting practices of minority families living within the inner city, Gorman-Smith et al. (1996) found that some aspects of family relationship characteristics and parenting practices are consistently linked to violent delinquency, regardless of ethnic or socioeconomic characteristics. Three of the most influential factors are poor parental monitoring, poor discipline, and a lack of family cohesion.

It is important to remember that the relationship between parental disciplinary tactics and delinquency does not occur in isolation. Straus (1991) reports that in several studies he conducted, 90 percent of the parents surveyed used some kind of physical punishment with their three- and four-year-olds. If there were a simple, direct relationship between parents' use of physical punishment and violence, the violence rates would be far greater than they are now.

A lack of parent-child involvement and parental rejection have also been found to be strong predictors of serious delinquency (Farrington, 1991). Brown (1984) cites evidence that emotional abuse and neglect may play an even more critical role in the development of delinquency than does physical punishment. Emotional abuse includes such behaviors as frequently screaming at the child, calling the child insulting names, excessively criticizing, or generally ignoring the child. Neglect usually refers to a gross lack of proper supervision and physical care.

After reviewing the research literature, Loeber and Dishion (1983) discovered that family factors could increase the power of prediction of delinquency and crime if they were combined. Combining several family factors—such as family size, quality of parental supervision, parental drinking habits, employment history, and criminality—are more impressive than any single factor, particularly in reference to male delinquency. Loeber and Dishion concluded that children from large families that are characterized by employment problems, disorganization and instability, inadequate supervision, conflict and disharmony, and poor parent-child relationships are at much greater risk of becoming delinquent than children from families without these features.

INTELLIGENCE AND DELINQUENCY

For some time, criminologists (and many psychologists) have been eager to label the relationship between intelligence and delinquency invalid and spurious. Even to mention the connection may prompt a derisive reaction reserved only for

Lombroso's classical born-criminal theory. Years ago, Hirschi and Hindelang (1977, p. 572) wrote: "Today, textbooks in crime and delinquency ignore IQ or impatiently explain to the reader that IQ is no longer taken seriously by knowledgeable students simply because no differences worth considering have been revealed by research." As Hirschi and Hindelang noted, these textbooks are wrong, since one of the most consistent findings in the delinquency literature is that delinquents do, as a group, score lower on standard intelligence tests than nondelinquents do. The essential point that Hirschi and Hindelang made was that the inverse relationship between IQ scores and delinquency continues to be documented by the research, for whatever reason. Why this difference exists should be at the heart of the controversy.

In their 1977 article, Hirschi and Hindelang hypothesized that an indirect causal relationship exists between IQ and delinquency. By indirect they meant that a low IQ leads to poor performance and negative attitudes toward school, which in turn leads to delinquency. A high IQ, on the other hand, leads to good performance and positive attitudes toward school, which in turn leads to the internal acceptance of conventional values and conformity (nondelinquency). Therefore, Hirschi and Hindelang saw school performance and attitudes as "intervening variables" that mediate between IQ and delinquency.

However, one fundamental flaw in the Hirschi and Hindelang argument is the common assumption that IQ reflects intelligence. The term IQ is an abbreviation of the intelligence quotient derived from a numerical score on a so-called "intelligence" test. The term "IQ" originated out of what is now called, the **psychometric approach**. The word "psychometric" means "mental measurement." Traditionally, the psychometric approach has searched for individual differences in persons through the use of psychological tests, including intelligence tests, scholastic aptitude tests (e.g., SAT), school achievement tests, personality inventories, and other specific abilities tests. The various tests are used for many purposes, such as selection, diagnosis, and evaluation. The psychometric approach continues to be widely used by practicing psychologists and mental health professionals. Increasingly, the term **psychometric intelligence**, abbreviated **PI**, is preferred to the traditional term "IQ" (Neisser et al., 1996). We will, therefore, use the more accurate term "PI" for the remainder of the book.

Satisfactory performance on a vast majority of intelligence tests depends greatly on language acquisition and verbal development. Usually, a person must have considerable experience using and defining words—particularly English words. The examinee must be able to make conventional connections and see distinctions between verbal concepts. The examinee must also know the facts that the test designer deems important to know within mainstream culture. At the very least, almost all intelligence tests measure some aspect of academic skills that are taught in school or that predict success in school. A vast majority of psychologists today would agree that PI scores are strongly influenced by social, educational, and cultural experiences. In short, all intelligence tests are culturally biased.

More importantly, PI scores and the concept of intelligence should not be confused. The term PI merely refers to a standardized score from a test. Intelligence, on the other hand, is a broad, all-encompassing ability that defies any straightforward or simple definition. It means many things to different people. Intelligence includes ability ranging from musical talent to logical mathematical skills. The term may also include wisdom, intuition, judgment, and even humor. It is, therefore, extremely important to make a distinction between PI and intelligence. While delinquents, as a group, do score lower on intelligence tests, this observation should not be construed as documenting that delinquents are less intelligent than nondelinquents. For example, Brazilian street children are masters at doing the math required for survival in their street business even though they have failed mathematics in school (Carraher, Carraher, & Schliemann, 1985; Neisser et al., 1996).

The relationship between PI test scores and school performance is strong and consistent. "Wherever it has been studied, children with high scores on tests of intelligence tend to learn more of what is taught in school than their lower-scoring peers" (Neisser et al., 1996, p. 82). Schools help develop certain intellectual skills and attitudes. Quality schools generally have positive effects on PI. Preschool programs (e.g., Headstart) show significant positive effects on children during their early school years, and recent research shows that these gains do not fade when the program is over, provided there is periodic intervention during the child's middle school years.

There is also a relationship between PI and years of education, and, to a lesser extent, between social status and income. Interestingly, researchers have found that there has been a steady worldwide rise in PI scores in recent years. In what is know as the "Flynn effect" (after James Flynn who first noticed the increase), youth in technologically advanced countries have shown a gain of about three PI points per decade. In the United States, however, while psychometric intelligence scores have increased, scores on scholastic aptitude tests (such as the SAT) have decreased or remained the same.

Average PI scores do vary between ethnic groups. For example, many studies using different tests and samples typically show African Americans scoring significantly lower than whites (Neisser et al., 1996). Studies show, however, that his psychometric gap has been consistently decreasing since 1980 (Vincent, 1991). Asian Americans and whites, on average, score about the same on PI tests; Native Americans score slightly lower than other groups on verbal skills, but this slight difference may be the result of chronic middle-ear infections common among Native American children (McShane & Plas, 1984a, 1984b). Latinos, who make up the second-largest and fastest-growing minority group in the United States, typically score somewhere between African Americans and whites. It is unclear what these reported differences mean, but there is no evidence to support the view that ethnic differences in psychometric intelligence are due to genetics or biological factors. Although genetics may play a role in *individual* differences in psychometric intelligence, there is no evidence for ethnic *group* differences.

Group differences in PI are most likely due to a combination of factors, dominated by cultural and social influences. According to Boykin (1986, 1994), for instance, the African-American culture is often in conflict with the values and expectations of the American school system. To varying degrees, the black culture "includes an emphasis on such aspects of experience as spirituality, harmony, movement, verve, affect, expressive individualism, communalism, orality, and a socially defined time perspective" (Neisser et al., 1996, p. 95). According to Boykin, black children often find their cultural background in conflict with the culture of the school system, and consequently they become alienated from both the process and products of that educational system.

The influence of poverty—such as poor nutrition, inadequate prenatal care, lack of adequate child-care facilities, and inaccessibility to educational, occupational, and training opportunities—also play critical but largely unknown roles. In the final analysis, we really don't know much about psychometric intelligence, although its relationship to socioeconomic status, educational level, and academic achievement does clearly exist.

PI scores are crude indices of mainstream language skills that are heavily influenced by experience. In general, rich and varied experiences increase PI scores, and limited experience decreases them (Garbarino & Asp, 1981; Neisser et al., 1996). School experiences, if positive, may increase language skills; if negative, they may stagnate, or even decrease, language skills. PI scores are also strongly influenced by the type of test used, its content, the many characteristics of testing situations, and the training and skill of the examiner.

Still, even with these many variations, the inverse relationship between PI scores and the tendency toward delinquency are consistently reported (e.g., Binder, 1988; Quay, 1987; White, Moffitt, & Silva, 1989). As PI scores go down, the probability of misconduct increases, and vice versa. Children with low PI scores are at a higher risk for delinquency behavior, and as Anne Crocker and Sheilagh Hodgins (1997, p. 434) write: "To our knowledge, no study has failed to confirm this relation." The relationship is particularly strong for verbal PI scores (Culberton, Feral, & Gabby, 1989; Kandel et al., 1988). Furthermore, as noted by Crocker and Hodgins (1997), the relationship between low PI scores and delinquency appears to be independent of socioeconomic status, race, and detection by the police (Moffitt, 1990; Lynam, Moffitt, & Stouthamer-Loeber, 1993). Moreover, it should be emphasized that this relationship is not specific to delinquency; the relationship is equally robust for adult offenders. Crocker and Hodgins (1997) examined the criminality of mentally deficient men and women in a Swedish birth cohort composed of over fifteen thousand subjects. The subjects were followed from birth to age thirty. Subjects who were placed in special classes for the mentally retarded (both at the elementary and high school level) were compared with normal subjects. Subjects considered mentally retarded were more likely to have been convicted for criminal offenses, including violent ones, than normal subjects. Crocker and Hodgins also found that, similar to mentally normal subjects, conduct problems in childhood (before age twelve) were predictive of adult antisocial behavior in both mentally deficient male and female groups.

What does the relationship between PI scores and delinquency and crime mean exactly? It probably means that delinquents as a group, particularly serious delinquents, have had limited experiences in mainstream society, faulty parenting, and poor school experiences, but more research is necessary before further explanation is advanced. Related to the PI question is the issue of learning disabilities. There is considerable empirical support that juvenile delinquents have a far greater incidence of learning disabilities than nondelinquents (Brier, 1989; Lombardo & Lombardo, 1991; Scaret & Wilgosh, 1989). However, similar to the PI question, it is very unclear what the relationship means.

GENDER AND JUVENILE OFFENDING

It is a well-known fact that boys far outnumber girls in most types of offending, particularly violent offending. Victimization data, self-report data, and official data all support this gender gap in criminal offending. In addition, the reported ratios of male to females for most crimes have remained basically the same for decades, regardless of cultural or societal changes. Males have been so overrepresented in violent crimes (approximately a nine-to-one ratio) for so long that some theorists have suggested that hormonal and biological factors are the most logical explanation for these gender differences (Wilson & Herrnstein, 1985).

Recent research by developmental psychologists is beginning to shed considerable light on the gender difference in juvenile offending. There is growing recognition that biology is not the primary factor—or even a significant factor—in explaining the differences in gender offending, including violent offending (Adams, 1992; Pepler & Slaby, 1994). Research by Eleanor Maccoby (1986), for example, indicates that girls and boys learn different types of prosocial behavior, with girls being more accommodating than boys. The current work of cognitive psychologists suggests that there may be socialized and cultural differences in the way boys and girls perceive their worlds. Social learning theorists have long held that girls are "socialized" differently from boys, or taught not to be aggressive. Anne Campbell (1993, p. 19) argues that "boys are not simply more aggressive than girls; they are aggressive in a different way." According to Campbell, boys and girls are born with the potential to be equally aggressive, but girls are socialized not to be overtly aggressive, whereas boys are encouraged to be aggressive.

In summary, the evidence strongly indicates that cultural and psychosocial factors play a major role in determining gender differences in offending. Biological and genetic factors appear to play a less significant role than previously believed.

PREVENTION AND TREATMENT OF JUVENILE OFFENDING

The number of intervention, prevention, and treatment programs that have been attempted on children at risk and juvenile offenders runs into the thousands. Very few programs, however, have demonstrated success or significant effectiveness in reducing delinquency or crime. This lack of success is especially clear in programs that try to change serious delinquent offenders or life-course persistent offenders (Borduin et al., 1995; Moffitt, 1993a). Restrictive interventions for serious juvenile offenders, such as residential treatment and incarceration, have been especially ineffective and extremely expensive. At this writing, the average cost of incarcerating a juvenile for just one year is close to $34,000, and some estimates go as high as $64,000 (Coordinating Council, 1996).

The reasons for the many failures in preventing or treating delinquency are multiple. There has been, however, a smattering of success stories with specific prevention and treatment programs. The overriding characteristics of these success stories is that (1) they begin early (either before or during the first grade); (2) they work with or within the many changing environments the child faces each day; and (3) they focus on the family. Let's examine each critical point more closely.

There is clear evidence to indicate that the earlier the signs of antisocial or delinquent behavior, the more serious or violent the antisocial behavior will be later (Tolan & Thomas, 1995). As noted earlier in the chapter, Terrie Moffitt (1993b; Moffitt et al., 1996) finds cogent evidence that the LCP delinquent shows discernible signs of antisocial behavior as early as age three. Furthermore, the LCP offender who enters adolescence fully engaged in delinquent behavior is usually highly resistant to change. Consequently, effective prevention must begin early, preferably before entry into the first grade. Nancy Guerra and her colleagues (Guerra et al., 1995) observe that aggressive and antisocial behavior may begin to develop much earlier in children living in the most economically deprived urban neighborhoods, suggesting that intervention and prevention programs must begin even earlier for some children. Furthermore, this observation appears to hold for both boys and girls (Tolan & Thomas, 1995). Consequently, preschool programs, such as Project Headstart and the Perry Preschool Project, hold enormous potential for the reduction or eradication of crime. Preliminary investigations have demonstrated that these programs can be effective and their long-term effects are encouraging (Mulvey, Arthur, & Reppucci, 1993; Berrueta-Clement et al., 1987).

There is little doubt that living conditions in the poorest inner-city neighborhoods are extremely harsh and the daily onslaught of violence, substance abuse, child abuse, and economic hopelessness are highly disruptive to a child's normal development. For the child exposed to an adverse family life, inadequate living standards, and little opportunity to develop even the rudiments of social and interpersonal skills for dealing effectively with others, the damage may be irreparable. Clearly, the longer a child is exposed to these adverse conditions, the more difficult it will be to modify his or her life course away from serious delinquency and adult crime. Hence, intervention programs must not only begin early in the child's development but must also be skillfully directed at as many causes and negative influences as possible.

Prevention programs that have demonstrated long-term success have used multifaceted approaches focusing on treating children through their broad social environment, and with particular sensitivity to the family's cultural background and heritage. And there is little doubt that intervention programs that neglect gender, ethnicity, socioeconomic status, and other demographic characteristics are destined to fail.

Research has continually shown that the most successful interventions concentrate on the family while recognizing the other powerful influences outside the family. Scott Henggeler and his colleagues (Henggeler & Borduin, 1990;

Henggeler, Melton, & Smith, 1992; Scherer et al., 1994) have designed a treatment approach for serious juvenile offenders that focuses on the family while being responsive to the many other contexts surrounding the family, such as the welfare system, the neighborhood, and the school. Called **multisystemic therapy (MST)**, the approach has shown very promising results. While peer influences are important during development, using peers to change deviant behavior has largely been unsuccessful (Dishion & Andrews, 1995; Chamberlain, 1996). In some instances, the use of peer groups in treatment settings may actually increase deviant and criminal behavior.

Effective intervention targets the known risk factors that occur along the child's developmental path. Before birth, successful intervention begins with ensuring prenatal health care and maternal nutrition, together with the elimination of toxic materials in the environment. Intervention must also include reduction of intrafamilial violence and the elimination of maternal alcohol and drug abuse (including tobacco). For children born into disadvantaged families living in inner cities, serious efforts must be directed at reducing the extreme economic deprivation that exists, especially among ethnic minorities.

Unfortunately, some very large gaps in our knowledge about intervention and prevention still remain. For instance, it is essential that more culturally sensitive and culture-specific interventions are developed. Researchers and practitioners alike need to develop an understanding, appreciation, and integration of the benefits of culturally diverse perspectives in dealing with highly aggressive and violent children and adolescents. It is also critical that researchers closely examine whether or how the developmental course of antisocial behavior varies by gender and ethnicity. Surprisingly, very few studies have focused specifically on low-income urban minority children where living conditions are extremely harsh (Guerra et al., 1995).

PREVENTION STRATEGIES

Future research concentrating on delinquency and crime prevention will likely examine the topic from the public health model. This model divides prevention strategies into three somewhat overlapping categories: (1) primary prevention; (2) secondary prevention; and (3) tertiary or treatment-based prevention. **Primary prevention** is designed to prevent behavior before any signs of the behavioral pattern emerges. Usually, primary prevention programs are established early in the developmental sequence of the child, preferably before the ages of seven or eight. These programs are usually found within the school system where there are large groups of young children. Examples include Project Headstart (Zigler, 1994), the Perry Preschool Project (Berrueta-Clement et al., 1987), and the many school-based prevention programs directed at first and second graders (Tolan & Guerra, 1994).

Secondary prevention programs are designed for children who show some early signs of aggressive, antisocial, conduct disorder, or delinquent behavior but have not yet been formally classified as delinquent. The basic assumption of secondary programs is that early detection and early intervention will prevent the child from engaging in more serious criminal actions later on. A well-known example of this preventive strategy is juvenile diversion. The diversion program offers services to youth arrested for minor offenses in the hope that the services will prevent deeper involvement in crime. The services offered vary widely from jurisdiction to jurisdiction. Diversion programs are operated under different auspices, including private groups, probation departments, social services, and the juvenile courts themselves. In another example, police in Honolulu, Hawaii, established a Saturday morning program whereby juveniles arrested for minor offenses were given the option of being referred to juvenile court or reporting weekly to a community center for classes on decision making, anger management, and conflict resolution. Usually, parents of the juvenile are also expected to attend.

The third or **tertiary prevention** strategy is often described by researchers and practitioners as "treatment" or "counseling" for already involved delinquents. The distinction between secondary and tertiary prevention is often blurred, however. This is because both approaches require the identification of at-risk children for the intervention services, and often provide the same services. For our purposes, we will use the term "tertiary prevention" for those programs designed to reduce serious delinquent or criminal behavior. In most cases, tertiary prevention or treatment strategies for serious delinquents are carried out in residential (institutional) settings.

SUMMARY AND CONCLUSIONS

Scientists can now point with confidence to a large list of risk factors associated with juvenile delinquency and criminal behavior but not one single variable on the list is the overwhelming favorite as the cause of the problem. In this chapter we began to examine some of the risk factors associated with crime and delinquency. Among these factors are poverty and social economic class. It is difficult to disentangle poverty and social class, however, from the many other influences that impinge on the young lives existing within adverse environments. Discrimination, racism, family disruption, unsafe living conditions, joblessness, social isolation, and limited social networks all play roles in the formation of crime and delinquency.

We have examined the potential roles played by conduct disorders, ADHD, intelligence, and gender. We have seen that the backgrounds of persistent offenders are littered with numerous impediments to normal development. Moreover, there is a growing body of evidence that people who experience a series of failures and lack personal efficacy tend to view many aspects of their environments as fraught with danger (Bandura, 1989). Lacking interpersonal skills and personal efficacy, and living in a social environment that fails to provide suitable opportunity to develop competence, many youths resort to a mean, bitter, "I-don't-care" approach to life. These embittered youths begin to contaminate all their social environments with this antisocial approach, and the social environments react similarly in an ongoing, bidirectional interaction. Of course, not all youths react this way to this set of circumstances. Some, because of a certain temperament interacting with a myriad of experiences, acquire interpersonal competencies, academic skills, and effective strategies to avoid a pattern of persistent offending as a way of life.

Social environments and peer groups are important in the development of internal standards, but people do not automatically model actions. They extract and process their own standards from the multiplicity of actions and reactions of individuals around them. From all this divergent information, people develop personal standards against which they measure and evaluate their own conduct. For example, violence is simply triggered by individual characteristics of temperament, biological predispositions, or personality factors. It is more likely to be a function of the way in which an individual "perceives ... events, makes meaning of them, anticipates others' reactions, and chooses to act on these events" (Eron & Slaby, 1994, p. 10). From the preschool years, highly aggressive or violent individuals have been found to show habits of thought that reflect lower levels of social problem-solving skills and higher endorsement of beliefs that support the use of violence. We will learn later in the text that a minority of highly aggressive and violent offenders began their criminal careers during adulthood. That is, there are a few violent individuals who did not display overt aggressive tendencies during childhood, but something happened during adulthood that prompted them to become violent and serious offenders.

The evidence is clear that prevention and intervention must begin early, preferably during the preschool years. Early intervention is especially critical for children growing up in inner-city neighborhoods where risk factors for delinquency are more prevalent. Research strongly indicates that intervention becomes more difficult and encounters more intransigent behavior patterns from teenagers who exhibit antisocial behavior from an early age. The life-course-persistent offender who enters adolescence fully engaged in delinquent or antisocial behavior is usually highly resistant to change. The adolescence-limited offender, on the other hand, is far more likely to be responsive to intervention and treatment strategies during the teen years. Adolescence-limited offenders are also more likely to show spontaneous recovery from their delinquency patterns as they embark on a more responsible, "adult" life course.

Throughout the remainder of this text, it will be obvious that theories emphasizing cognitive processes (i.e., beliefs, values, thoughts) are favored in contemporary psychological explanations of crime and delinquency. Our beliefs, values, images of ourselves, and our philosophies are the primary guides of our behavior. They are reference points for justifying our conduct to ourselves and to others. Most people try to live according to their internal standards and respond to others according to their perspectives of human nature. If our friends, models, and heroes perceive life and the human condition in a certain way, we may well do the same. If cruelty, insensitivity to others, and a selfish orientation is the norm, this may be reflected both in our approach to life and in our perceptions of criminal behavior. Moreover, if we believe that "everyone does it," we have neutralized the stigma attached to the conduct. Youth is a time when we begin to formulate basic philosophies of life. In most instances, delinquency seems to be an expression of the values the juvenile has either adopted or has been exposed to through significant models in the environment.

3

ORIGINS OF CRIMINAL BEHAVIOR: BIOLOGICAL FACTORS

Many—perhaps most—contemporary criminologists would agree with the following statement: "Genetics may play a role in criminality, but it is only an insignificant one. There is little doubt that environment is the principal determinant and cause of criminal behavior." Poverty, high unemployment, poor education, faulty parenting, overpopulation, and group values that deviate from society's norms are often considered the major culprits producing crime. Heredity-based physiological components are scoffed at, and their possible role as causal agents in criminality is often dismissed.

Why so? Perhaps because accepting heredity as a factor in criminal behavior implies that criminal acts are unavoidable, inevitable consequences of the "bad seed," "bad blood," or "mark of Cain." Heredity is destiny. Little can be done to prevent the ill-fated person from becoming a criminal. A classic illustration of this viewpoint is Cesare Lombroso's doctrine (1911) that some criminals are born that way.

Most behavioral scientists—and many social scientists—recognize, however, that behavioral traits result from an **interaction** of hereditary and environmental factors. We no longer ask whether behavior is due to heredity or environment; we agree that both are involved in a complex way. However, researchers usually focus on one or the other for intensive study. In this chapter, we will discuss the work of psychologists who study heredity and biopsychology as factors in the genesis of criminal behavior.

Biopsychologists, as they are called, try to determine which genetic and neurophysiological variables play a part in criminal behavior, how important they are, and what can be done to modify them. Biopsychologists do not believe that genetic or neurophysiological components are the sole causal agents. Most would say that understanding the social environment is as important as understanding the biological one. However, they have chosen to concentrate on the biological elements. We will introduce their work and assess their results after we have taken a brief look at the history of biopsychological research in criminality.

THE BORN CRIMINAL

A pioneer researcher on the relationship between crime, genetics, and personality was Cesare Lombroso (1836–1909), the Italian physician and self-termed criminal anthropologist introduced in Chapter 1. Lombroso's original and basic premise, published in *L'Uomo Delinquente* [*Criminal Man*] in 1876, was that some people are born with strong, innate predispositions to behave antisocially. He was greatly influenced by the views that Charles Darwin expounded in *The Descent of Man*, especially the notion that some people are genetically closer to their primitive ancestry than others (Savitz, 1972). The criminal, Lombroso believed, represented a separate species that had not yet evolved sufficiently toward the more "advanced" *homo sapiens*. This species was genetically somewhere between modern humans and their primitive origins in physical and psychological makeup. He called this evolutionarily retarded species *homo delinquens* and considered those individuals mutations or natural accidents living among civilized humans.

Lombroso collected extensive data on the physical measurements of Italian prisoners and Italian military personnel (noncriminals). He concluded that the criminal was distinguished by certain physical anomalies: an asymmetrical skull, flattened nose, large ears, fat lips, enormous jaws, high cheekbones, and Mongolian eye characteristics (1972). Moreover, *homo delinquens*, also derisively called the "born criminal," had an affinity for tattoos, "cruel games," and orgies, and had a peculiar primitive slang, all believed to be behavioral throwbacks to savage, undeveloped human or subhuman species. Lombroso maintained that the born criminal's artworks were often faithful reproductions of the first crude artistic attempts of primitive people. The implications were that this primitive creature, who instinctively demonstrated behaviors useful in the wild in the millennia past, could not adjust socially and morally to the demands of modern times.

L'Uomo Delinquente went through several revisions, and by 1897 it had grown to three volumes comprising 1,903 pages. With each edition Lombroso modified his theory from the dogmatic one of 1876 to a more flexible but still basically genetic version. For example, early Lombrosian theory asserted that all criminals met the physical dimensions and psychological characteristics outlined. Later, possibly responding to criticism, Lombroso concluded that the born criminal actually accounted for only about one-third of the criminal population (Lombroso-Ferrero, 1972). The other two-thirds comprised a wide assortment of criminal types. Lombroso also suggested at this point that environmental factors were significant in the development of certain types of crime (Wolfgang, 1972). In 1911, Gina Lombroso summarized her father's last work and translated it into English. Still another rendition, *Crime: Its Causes and Remedies*, was published a year later.

According to Cesare Lombroso, offenders who were not born criminals fell into one of six categories. *Habitual* or *professional criminals* violated the law systematically and engaged in crime as a trade or occupation. The degrading influence of prisons (which Lombroso called "criminal universities"), including daily contact with other hard-core prisoners, played a significant role in the development of this offender. A second type was the *juridical criminal*, who violated the law not because of any "natural depravity" but simply from lack of prudence, care, or forethought—the impulsive type. *Criminals of passion* violated the law because of their "intense love, honor, noble ambition, or patriotism." They may have murdered to defend their honor, their loved ones, or their country. *Criminaloids* had "weak natures" and were highly susceptible to good and bad example. They had innate characteristics very similar to those of born criminals, but the environment was an important determinant of their criminal action. *Born criminals*, by contrast, were dictated by strong biological predispositions to crime. Lombroso also recognized the *morally insane* and *hysteric criminal* types.

Born criminals, the biologically predisposed, exhibited a lack of guilt or remorse for any wrongdoing (although they often alleged repentance) and a peculiar inability to learn the distinction between good and evil. Lombroso reported that they did not develop close friendships and were likely to betray companions and accomplices. They displayed "exaggerated notions of their own importance," were impulsive, cruel, and had a high tolerance for pain.

Lombroso at first considered the female offender to be very similar to the male offender, both psychologically and in physical appearance (Wolfgang, 1972). Singling out prostitution as representative of female crime, he saw it as an **atavism** (a throwback to primitive times) and suggested that most prostitutes were born criminals who lacked a "mother sense." He later modified this view. On second thought, the born criminal woman did not clearly exhibit the same physical anomalies as the male born criminal. Psychologically, however, she was more terrible and cruel than any man, almost monster-like (Wolfgang, 1972). Lombroso based this on his belief that women in general have many traits in common with children, such as revenge, jealousy, and an inclination toward "vengeances of a refined cruelty."

Lombroso had a devoted following, which, as we noted in Chapter 1, became known as the *Italian school of criminology*. His outrageous pronouncements often embarrassed other criminologists, however, and they sought ways to refute him. In 1913, Charles Goring (1913/1972) published an influential monograph reporting the results of a study comparing the physical measurements of three thousand English convicts to those of an equal number of nonconvicts. He did not find the significant physical differences reported by Lombroso. Goring's research, however, was plagued by numerous methodological flaws, as were Lombroso's own investigations. Nevertheless, it proved devastating to the Lombrosian position. Armed with Goring's findings and eager to put the genetics and crime issue to rest, many criminologists quickly wrote the born criminal's obituary.

Although opinion varies about the value of Lombroso's contributions, there is little doubt that he had considerable impact on research directed at the relationship between genetics and the criminal personality. The late Stephen Shafer (1976, pp. 41–42), for example, suggested that Cesare Lombroso could easily be called the father of modern criminology because his theories have stimulated research and empirical investigations on the criminal's personality as well as the social environment. Abrahamsen (1960, pp. 6–7) comments that Lombroso will be remembered "for disproving the assumption that a criminal committed a criminal act because his will was free and so was unquestionably responsible for his act." Abrahamsen agrees that Lombroso paved the way for examining the criminal personality. Wolfgang (1972, p. 287) states: "The clinical, psychological, and psychiatric analyses of today that report data on personality traits ... are similar to, but much more refined and sophisticated than many of the findings reported by Lombroso."

PHYSIQUE AND CRIME

Theorists have linked physical characteristics with personality ever since Hippocrates outlined a typology of physiques and tried to relate them to personality. He also introduced the concept of humors, or body fluids, which presumably influenced personality (Hall & Lindzey, 1970). The modern path in constitutional psychology was set by the German psychiatrist Emil Kretschmer (1925), who distinguished four types of body structures and tried to connect them to specific mental disorders. He called one physique the *pyknic* and noted that it was characterized by a short, fat stature. A second type, exhibiting height and very thin features, was the *leptosomatic* or *aesthenic*. The muscular, vigorous physique was called the athletic type. The fourth, the *dysplastic*, represented an incongruous mixture of different physiques in different parts of the body, making it appear "rare, surprising and ugly" (Hall & Lindzey, 1970).

More pertinent to our discussion of crime is the theory of William H. Sheldon (Sheldon & Stevens, 1942; Sheldon, Hartl, & McDermott, 1949), who developed a similar but superior classification of body type in the United States and related physique to delinquency. Sheldon's method is called **somatotyping**. After extensively collecting and documenting physical measurements, Sheldon found he could delineate three basic body builds: the **endomorphic** (fat and soft), **ectomorphic** (thin and fragile), and **mesomorphic** (muscular and hard) (see Figure 3-1). The reader with some background in embryology will recognize that the terms refer to layers of the embryo. The endodermal embryonic layer develops primarily into the digestive viscera, and thus individuals who are plump (endomorphs) are tied to the digestive system. The mesodermal layer of the embryo develops into muscle; therefore, the tough, muscular body, well-equipped for strenuous activity, is labeled the mesomorph. The ectodermal layer is developmentally responsible for the nervous system. The ectomorph has a large brain and central nervous system compared to the rest of his or her body, which is usually tall and thin.

We should emphasize that Sheldon avoided making sharp distinctions between body types or somatotypes. People were scored on the basis of three 7-point scales corresponding to the three somatotypes, with a 7 indicating that they were exclusively that body type. This was a rare occurrence, however. For example, a "pure" mesomorph would have a somatotype of 1-7-1, with the 1s denoting that he or she was devoid of that particular body build. A 3-2-5 person would be primarily ectomorphic (5), but have some features of endomorphs (3) and mesomorphs (2). The average body build would be assigned a 4-4-4 index, indicating constitutional balance (see Figure 3-1).

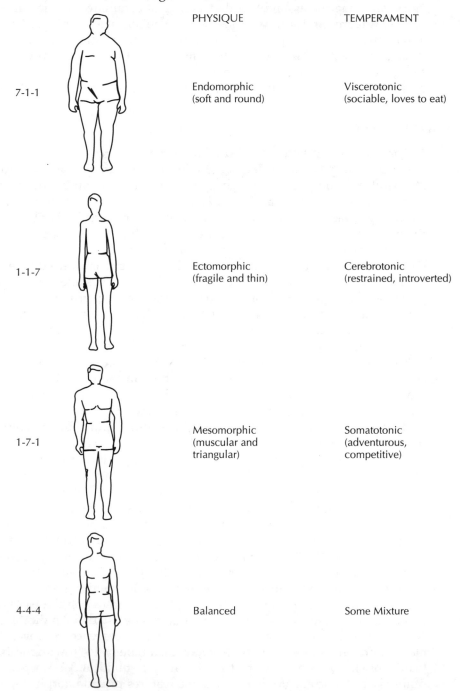

	PHYSIQUE	TEMPERAMENT
7-1-1	Endomorphic (soft and round)	Viscerotonic (sociable, loves to eat)
1-1-7	Ectomorphic (fragile and thin)	Cerebrotonic (restrained, introverted)
1-7-1	Mesomorphic (muscular and triangular)	Somatotonic (adventurous, competitive)
4-4-4	Balanced	Some Mixture

Figure 3-1   Sheldon's Somatotypes in Relation to Physique and Temperament

Sheldon found a strong **correlation** between personality (or temperament) and somatotype—in other words, he linked certain personality types with certain body types. One personality loves comfort, food, affection, and people. This type is usually even-tempered and easy to get along with. Sheldon labeled this disposition *viscerotonia* and, as you might have guessed, he connected it closely to the basic endomorph. A second personality type ordinarily needs vigorous physical activity, risk taking, and adventure. A person with this temperament, according to Sheldon, is more likely to be indifferent to pain and aggressive, callous, even ruthless in relationships with others. This cluster of personality traits was called *somatotonia* and was linked with the mesomorph. *Cerebrotonia* labels the person who is inhibited, reserved, self-conscious, and afraid of people; it correlates highly with the ectomorphic body build.

Sheldon began to test his theory in 1939 by exploring the relationship between delinquency and physique. His first study involved nearly four hundred boys in a residential rehabilitation home. Biographical sketches—family background, medical history, mental and educational performance, and delinquent behavior—were collected for each boy, and they were all assigned somatotype ratings. Sheldon studied his delinquents for eight years, comparing them to a group of male college students. He found that the college men generally clustered around the "average" somatotype of 4-4-4. Delinquents, on the other hand, tended to be heavily mesomorphic, but there were also signs of endomorphy. Ectomorphs were rare in the delinquent group. On the basis of his study, Sheldon concluded that there were definite somatotypic and temperamental differences between delinquent and nondelinquent males.

Subsequent investigations (primarily on males) provided additional, although not very strong, support for Sheldon's findings. Glueck and Glueck (1950, 1956) found that mesomorphs were proportionately overrepresented in the delinquent population (60 percent, with 30 percent endomorphs). In general, their findings established that delinquent boys were larger and stronger than nondelinquent boys. In another study, Cortes and Gatti (1972) reported that delinquent subjects (one hundred boys adjudicated delinquent by the courts) were much more mesomorphic than nondelinquents (one hundred male high school seniors). Fifty-seven percent of their delinquent group could be easily classified as mesomorphic compared to 19 percent of the nondelinquents. These percentages roughly correspond to those cited by Glueck and Glueck (1950) in their study of five hundred youths. Hartl, Monnelly and Elderkin (1982) claim that, in their thirty-year follow-up of Sheldon's original group, the relationship between mesomorphs and antisocial behavior still holds.

Later, more sophisticated research reached different results. McCandless, Persons, and Roberts (1972) found physique unrelated to either self-reported delinquency or the seriousness of the criminal offenses. Wadsworth (1979), using data from the British National Survey, reported that delinquents, especially those who committed serious offenses, were generally smaller in stature and appeared to reach puberty later than their nondelinquent peers. While no somatotyping was done, the results suggest that the delinquents were not mesomorphs, since mesomorphs reportedly reach puberty before the other body types (Rutter & Giller, 1984). Finally, in their longitudinal study of working class boys in London, West and Farrington (1973) reported little association between delinquency and either height-weight ratios or physical strength.

Wilson and Herrnstein (1985, p. 90) in their influential but controversial book, *Crime and Human Nature,* concluded that the evidence on the relationship between physique and crime "leaves no doubt that constitutional traits correlate with criminal behavior." Some of the evidence does suggest a relationship between body build and crime, but there is also a significant amount of evidence that indicates that there may be no relationship. Thus, the research is equivocal and far from conclusive. While it may make logical sense to argue that the mesomorph's physique, because it is so muscular and strong, is well suited for involvement in aggressive or antisocial acts, much more sophisticated and well-executed research needs to be conducted before we can get a better understanding of the physique-crime connection. In a recent study, Sampson and Laub (1997) found evidence that mesomorphy is a poor predictor of adult arrests for any crime, including violence. Thus, while mesomorphy seems related to official delinquency, it does not seem related to criminal offending during adulthood.

ATTRACTIVENESS

Some researchers have studied physical features, such as facial characteristics, and related them to body build, criminal activity, or treatment by the criminal justice system. Staffieri (1967) found that body build significantly influenced whether one was judged attractive, with mesomorphs generally receiving the highest ratings. Cavior and Howard (1973), concentrating on facial features, found that both African-American and white delinquents were rated significantly less attractive than nondelinquents. Moreover, correctional personnel often comment that inmates, as a group, have "uglier" faces than the general population. Thompson (1990) estimates that, in any given year, there are 250,000 moderately disfigured offenders in prison. Perhaps facial unattractiveness plays a role in the development of crime and/or increases the probability of being adjudicated delinquent by the courts. Research has found that attractive children are favored by adults and other children. In fact, attractive children are less negatively evaluated than less attractive children, even when they have committed identical antisocial acts (Dion, 1972; Dion, Berscheid, & Walster, 1972). In one study using a simulated jury, good-looking defendants were treated more gently and were considered less dangerous than a comparable group of unattractive defendants (Sigall & Ostrove, 1978).

The thesis that physical unattractiveness might have something to do with criminal behavior has been applied to rehabilitation. In the mid-1970s, corrective surgery was offered to inmates with facial deformities at Rikers Island, as part of a pilot project testing the value of plastic surgery as a rehabilitative measure (Kurtzberg, Mandell, Lewin, Lipton, & Shuster, 1978). The surgery was to be performed just prior to prison release. After extensive medical and psychological screening, 425 inmates were divided into four groups. Depending on his group, the inmate would receive either surgery, counseling, both, or neither (the control group).

The results, though complex, showed some support for the benefits of a new image. The offenders who seemed to benefit most from the intervention were non-addicts who received surgery; they were substantially less likely to engage in crime during a one-year follow-up period than a comparable group of offenders who received no surgery. Interestingly, the group that received counseling alone committed more detected crime during the follow-up period than even the group that had neither counseling nor surgery. Although the study's results are not clearcut, they do suggest that physical improvements also improve prisoner self-image and the likelihood of acceptance by others. Possibly, the individual with the improved appearance has less need to defend or prove his or her worth through crime or to react aggressively to slights or challenges. And, possibly, the slights and challenges are fewer in number.

Based on a nationwide survey, Thompson (1990) estimates that five to six thousand inmates in the United States undergo some type of cosmetic or reconstructive surgery each year. Moreover, Thompson, in his review of the research literature, found that six of the nine studies examining recidivism rates after cosmetic or reconstructive surgery concluded that reoffending was significantly reduced following the surgical treatment. However, since there are a number of methodological problems in all these studies, other interpretations and conclusions of the data are possible. It is also unclear whether corrective surgery reduces recidivism over the long haul or merely delays a return to prison.

MINOR PHYSICAL ANOMALIES (MPAS)

In recent years, there has been renewed interest in the relationship between physical attributes and temperament. Specifically, some researchers have focused on minor physical anomalies—such as asymmetrical ears, soft and pliable ears, curved fifth fingers, ocular hypertelorism (widely spaced eyes), multiple hair whorls, webbed toes, furrowed tongue—and learning disabilities, hyperactivity, schizophrenia, aggressiveness, and clumsiness. These minor physical anomalies, or MPAs, seem to correlate (albeit weakly) with some temperamental and behavioral attributes in children. For example, high numbers of MPAs are found in active, aggressive, and impulsive preschool boys (Paulhus & Martin, 1986) and in boys demonstrating conduct disorders (Halverson & Victor, 1976). MPAs are generally not noticed either by people who have them or by others. They are discernible only to trained observers and do not significantly interfere with attractiveness. The occurrence of MPAs is hypothesized to be associated with teratogenic factors (factors that produce physical defects in the developing embryo) operating within the first trimester of pregnancy.

The assumption is that the same teratogenic factors that produce minor physical abnormalities also affect the central nervous system in a way that contributes to behavioral problems and developmental deviations. Presumably, hyperactivity, impulsiveness, restlessness, and inattentiveness are all potential reflections of central nervous system defects that go hand-in-hand with MPAs. While the hypothesis connecting MPAs with a propensity toward delinquent or criminal behavior is intriguing, very little research has attempted to test the hypothesis directly. In a study by Mednick and Kandel (1988), an experienced pediatrician assessed MPAs in 129 twelve-year-old boys, and then the researchers followed the boys' development until they were twenty-one years old. The researchers discovered that MPAs were related to violent offending, but only if the boys were from unstable, nonintact homes. Boys from stable homes did not show the relationship. Furthermore, Mednick and Kandel did not find an MPA relationship for property crimes, only violent crimes. In another study, Brennan, Mednick, and Kandel (1993) found that subjects who had delivery complications at birth and a high number of MPAs were more likely to be adult violent offenders than individuals who had only one of those conditions, or neither of them. These results suggest that disruptions in the normal development of the nervous system may render the individual at some risk to engage in violent behavior. Clearly, much more research is needed before further conclusions can be advanced.

TWIN STUDIES

One way to determine the role of genetics in criminality is to compare the incidence and type of criminal convictions among identical and fraternal twins. Fraternal twins (also called dizygotic twins) develop from two different fertilized eggs and are no more genetically alike than ordinary siblings. Identical twins (monozygotic twins) develop from a single egg; they are always the same sex and share all the same genes. Theoretically, the twin method of research assumes that similar environments exert similar influences on each member of a twin set. Therefore, differences are presumably due to genetic factors.

Some investigators suggest that identical twins are so physically alike that they probably elicit similar social responses from their environment, more so than fraternal twins. In this sense, they are more likely to develop similar personalities. There may be merit to this viewpoint, but research does not yet support it. Rather, some research has found that identical twins reared apart are more alike in some personality attributes than are identicals reared in the same home environment (Shields, 1962; Canter, 1973). When reared together, identicals may make a conscious effort to accentuate their individual identities, whereas when reared apart they may have less need to be different.

Concordance, a key concept in twin study research, is the genetics term for the degree to which related pairs of subjects both show a particular behavior or condition. It is usually expressed in percentages. Assume that we want to determine the concordance of intelligence among twenty pairs of identical twins and twenty pairs of fraternals. If we find that ten pairs of the identical twins have approximately the same IQ score, but only five pairs of the fraternals obtain the same score, our concordance is 50 percent for identicals, 25 percent for fraternals. The concordance for identicals would be twice that of fraternals, suggesting that hereditary factors play an important role in intelligence. If, however, the two concordances were about the same, we would conclude that genetics is irrelevant, at least as represented in our sample and measured by our methods.

Numerous twin studies using this concordance method have strongly indicated that heredity is a powerful determinant of intelligence, schizophrenia, depressions, neurotic disorders, alcoholism, and criminal behavior (Claridge, 1973; Rosenthal, 1970, 1971; McClearn & DeFries, 1973; Hetherington & Parke, 1975). The first such study relative to criminality was reported by the Munich physician Johannes Lange (1929) in his book *Crime as Destiny* (Rosenthal, 1971; Christiansen, 1977). The title reflects Lange's Lombrosian conviction that criminal conduct is a predetermined fate dictated by heredity. He found a criminality concordance of 77 percent for thirteen pairs of adult identical twins and only 12 percent for seventeen pairs of adult fraternal twins. Auguste Marcel Legras (1932) then found a 100 percent criminal concordance for five pairs of identicals. Note that both of these studies used small samples. Subsequent studies, using more sophisticated designs and methods of twin identification and sampling, continued to find a substantially higher criminal concordance for identical twins when compared to fraternals. The levels were not as high as those reported by either Lange or Legras, however. Table 3-1 summarizes relevant investigations of criminal concordance. Although these tabulated investigations differed in method and definitions of criminality, the combined concordance levels demonstrate that, where criminal behavior is concerned, identical twins seem better matched than fraternal twins.

Hans Eysenck reviewed other twin studies, found similar concordances, and concluded: "Thus concordance is found over four times as frequently in identicals as in fraternals, a finding which seems to put beyond any doubt that heredity plays an extremely important part in the genesis of criminal behaviour" (Eysenck, 1973, p. 167). Rosenthal, however, injects a word of caution, stressing the many pitfalls of the concordance twin method and the ramifications of using different legal defini-

Table 3-1   Summary of Twin-Criminality Studies Showing Pairs and Concordance Rates

Researcher	Identical Twins			Fraternal Twins		
	No. of Pairs	Pairs Concordant	Percent	No. of Pairs	Pairs Concordant	Percent
Lange (1929)	13	10	77	17	2	12
Legras (1932)	4	4	100	5	0	0
Rosanoff (1934)	37	25	68	60	6	10
Kranz (1936)	31	20	65	43	20	53
Stumpfl (1936)	18	11	61	19	7	37
Borgstrom (1939)	4	3	75	5	2	40
Rosanoff et al. (1941)	45	35	78	27	6	18
Yoshimasu (1961)	28	17	61	18	2	11
Yoshimasu (1965)	28	14	50	26	0	0
Hayashi (1967)	15	11	73	5	3	60
Dalgaard & Kringlen (1976)	31	8	26	54	8	15
Christiansen (1977b)						
Males	71	25	35	120	15	13
Females	14	2	21	27	2	8
Totals	**339**	**185**	**55**	**426**	**73**	**17**

tions of criminality. Nevertheless, he allows, "… it is clearly not possible to rule out the potential fact that genetic factors may indeed be the primary source of the higher concordance rate in MZ (identical) as compared to DZ (fraternal) twins" (Rosenthal, 1975, p. 10).

Eysenck further complicates the issue by suggesting that twin studies may actually have deflated the true concordance rate, since it is likely that identical twins were often confused with fraternal twins, especially in the earlier studies. If the twins are of the same sex, it is difficult to distinguish identicals from fraternals from appearance alone. Today, blood type, fingerprints (which are highly similar but not identical), and various genetically determined serum proteins allow differentiation. Since these methods were not available to earlier investigators, Eysenck contends that mix-ups may have confounded the results. However, the concordance rates may just as easily have been inflated as deflated.

As Table 3-1 shows, twin studies have not invariably found high criminal concordance rates in favor of identical twins. One study by Dalgaard and Kringlen (1976) found no significant difference between identicals and fraternals. The Dalgaard-Kringlen sample included all the registered male twins born in Norway between 1921 and 1930. However, 32 percent of the sample was deleted from the analysis for various reasons, which might have affected the results. Also, the label "criminal" was applied to traffic violations, military offenses, and treason during World War II, as well as to all actions against the penal code. This was a broader definition than was used in most twin studies. The late Karl O. Christiansen, who devoted much of his research work to twin studies, could not explain the lack of significant differences reported by Dalgaard and Kringlen. He advocated an additional study to determine whether "some special conditions exist in Norway that would dampen the expression of genetic factors…" (Christiansen, 1977a, p. 82).

Overall, despite procedural and definitional problems and except for the Dalgaard-Kringlen data, the studies examining concordance rates among twins have consistently indicated higher concordance for identicals. More recent research, however, indicates that these higher concordance rates may hold only for adult offending and not for juvenile offending (Blackburn, 1993). In a careful review of the literature, Adrian Raine (1993, p. 79) concludes: "Summary statistics from 13 twin analyses show that 51.5 percent of MZ twins are concordant for crime compared to 20.6 percent for DZ twins, indicating substantial evidence for genetic influences on crime."

The twin data clearly suggest that it might be wise to consider heredity a significant component in criminality. This is not to say, however, that it is the sole or even the most important causal factor of criminality. Genetic studies also reveal that environmental factors are extremely important.

ADOPTION STUDIES

Another method used to identify crucial variables in the interaction between heredity and environment is the adoption study, which helps identify environments most conducive to criminality. There have been exceedingly few such investigations, however, and those few have been fraught with methodological problems.

One of the first adoption studies was carried out in Denmark by Schulsinger (1972), who explored the incidence of psychopathy in the biological relatives of adopted adults. Schulsinger compared fifty-seven adopted adults whom he diagnosed psychopathic to a control group of fifty-seven nonpsychopathic adopted adults. The two groups were matched for sex, age, social class, and age of transfer to the adopting family. The study's direct implications for criminal behavior are questionable, because Schulsinger defined psychopathy by his own loose criteria. Individuals who were impulse-ridden and who exhibited acting-out behavior qualified. As we will see in Chapter 4, these descriptions do not necessarily connote either psychopathy or criminality.

Schulsinger found that 3.9 percent of the biological relatives of psychopathic adoptees could also be classified as psychopathic, whereas only 1.4 percent of the control group's biological relatives could. The results just failed to reach statistical significance, indicating that we should be very cautious about accepting their implications. It is interesting, though, that psychopathy—even given its loose definition—was about two and a half times greater in the family backgrounds of acting-out adoptees.

Crowe (1974) conducted a better-designed study, a follow-up of fifty-two persons relinquished for early adoption by female offenders. Ninety percent of the biological mothers were felons at the time of the adoptive placement, the most common offenses being forgery and passing bad checks. Twenty-five of the adoptees were female, and all were white. Another fifty-two adoptees with no evidence of criminal family background were selected as a control group and matched for sex, race, and age at the time of adoption.

For the follow-up phase of the study, Crowe selected thirty-seven index and thirty-seven control subjects who had by then reached age eighteen. (*Index* subjects in research are those subjects who are of major concern.) Seven of the index adoptees had arrest records: As adults, all seven had at least one conviction, four had multiple arrests, two had multiple convictions, and three were felons. Of the thirty-seven matching controls, two had adult arrest records and only one of these had been convicted. Each subject's personality was diagnosed by three clinicians based on test results and data gathered in an interview; no family background was included. The clinicians made their diagnoses independently of one another and without knowing the subject's group. Six of the adoptees born of female offenders were labeled "antisocial personality"; one control group subject was labeled "probable antisocial personality."

Crowe found a positive correlation between the tendency of the index group to be antisocial and two other variables: the child's age at the time of adoptive placement, and the length of time the child had spent in temporary care (orphanages and foster homes) prior to that placement. The older the child of an offender upon adoptive placement and the longer the temporary placement, the more likely would the child grow up antisocial. The control group members were not affected by these conditions. This suggests either that the two adoptee groups responded differently to similar environmental conditions or that the adoption agency placed the offspring of female offenders in less desirable homes—and there was no indication that this selective placement had occurred.

Hutchings and Mednick (1975) also conducted a study examining the effects of genetics and environment. They reasoned that if there is a genetic basis for criminality, then there should be a significant relationship between the criminal tendencies of biological parents and those of their children who were adopted by someone else. In 1971, using Copenhagen adoption files, Hutchings and Mednick identified 1,145 male adoptees, who were by then thirty to forty-four years old. They were matched with an equal number of nonadoptee controls on sex, age, occupational status of fathers, and residence. The researchers learned that 185 adoptees (16.2 percent) had criminal records, compared to 105 nonadoptees (8.9 percent). A check on the biological fathers of the adoptees revealed that they were nearly three times more likely to be involved in criminal activity than were either the adoptees' adoptive fathers or the fathers of the nonadopted controls. Furthermore, there was a significant relationship between the criminality of the sons and that of the fathers. Where the biological father had a criminal record and the adoptive father had none, a significant number of adoptees still became criminal (22 percent); but where the biological father had no record and the adoptive father had a criminal record, the number of adoptees who pursued criminal activities was lower (11.5 percent). If both the biological and adoptive fathers were criminal, the chances were much greater that the adoptee would also be criminal than if only one man was criminal. Hutchings and Mednick concluded that genetic factors continue to exert strong influences in the tendency toward criminality, even though environmental factors also play important roles.

One serious limitation to the Hutchings-Mednick data, as well as to any adoption study, is that agencies often try to match the adopted child with the adoptive family on the basis of the child's biological and socioeconomic background. The Crowe study involving the children of offenders found no evidence of this, but the Danish agency used in the Hutchings-Mednick investigation confirmed that this was done. To their credit, the researchers not only recognized this problem, but also admonished that extrapolations to American society should be made cautiously, since Danish society is more homogeneous in cultural values and race.

The most comprehensive adoption study to date was conducted by Mednick, Gabrielli, and Hutchings (1984, 1987). These researchers compared the court convictions of 14,427 adoptees (adopted between the years 1927 and 1947) in a small European country with conviction records of their biological and adoptive parents. The study showed a significant relationship between the conviction history of the adoptees (for both males and females) and their biological parents. Specifically, if either biological parent had been convicted of a crime, the risk of criminality in the adoptee (the biological child) increased significantly. This relationship was especially strong for male adoptees who were chronic or persistent offenders. As we might expect, chronic offenders accounted for a disproportionate share of the total offending for the entire cohort. Interestingly, there was no evidence that the type of crime committed by the biological parent had any relation to the type of crime committed by the biological child. Both the biological parent and biological child tended to engage in crime but selected different kinds of crime. There was also no indication that the adopted children knew about the criminality of their biological parents. The researchers concluded that some factor transmitted by criminal parents increased the probability that their children would engage in criminal behavior. Elsewhere, Gabrielli and Mednick (1983, p. 63) commented, "It is reasonable ... to conclude that some people inherit biological characteristics which permit them to be antisocial more readily than others."

In summary, twin and adoption studies suggest that genetic components may contribute significantly to a tendency to become criminal, but they have also found that environment is highly important (Ellis, 1982; Blackburn, 1993; Raine, 1993). The available data so far indicate that some people may be born with a biological predisposition to behavior that runs counter to social values and norms, and that environmental factors may either inhibit or stimulate it. To help pinpoint this possible predisposition, we turn now to the theory and research of the British psychologist Hans J. Eysenck.

EYSENCK'S THEORY OF PERSONALITY AND CRIME

The late Hans J. Eysenck (Eysenck & Gudjonsson, 1989) was convinced that sociological theory has little to offer toward the understanding and treatment of crime. "In many ways we disagree with various sociological theories that have become so popular since World War II but which, we believe, are fundamentally erroneous and counter to fact" (Eysenck & Gudjonsson, 1989, p. 1). Instead, Eysenck argues that psychological knowledge provides the key answers and strategies for the prevention of criminal behavior. "We believe that psychology is a fundamental discipline which underlies any advances we may make in the prevention of crime, and the treatment of criminals" (Eysenck & Gudjonsson, 1989, p. ix). Not only will psychology lead the way toward the solution of crime, Eysenck told us, but the neurological underpinnings of personality are one of the prime determinants of antisocial and criminal behavior.

Eysenck (1977) proposed that criminal behavior is the result of an *interaction* between certain environmental conditions and *inherited* features of the nervous system. He believed that a comprehensive theory of criminality must allow for an examination of the neurophysiological makeup and the unique socialization history of each individual. Statements that crime is caused by social conditions such as poverty, poor education, or unemployment are as inaccurate as hereditary and biological explanations. "Crime cannot be understood in terms of heredity alone, but it can also not be understood in terms of environment alone" (Eysenck, 1973, p. 171). Eysenck also suggested that different combinations of environmental, neurobiological, and personality factors give rise to different types of crime (Eysenck & Eysenck, 1970). This position implies that different personalities are more susceptible to certain crimes than others, an issue we will return to shortly.

Unlike most contemporary theories of crime, Eysenck's theory places heavy emphasis on genetic predispositions toward antisocial and criminal conduct.

Eysenck (1996, p. 146) asserted "genetic causes play an important part in antisocial and criminal behaviour. This simple fact is no longer in doubt." It is important to note at the outset that he was not suggesting that individuals are born criminal, but rather that some people are born with nervous system characteristics that are significantly different from the general population and that affect their ability to conform to social expectancies and rules. "It is not crime itself or criminality that is innate; it is certain peculiarities of the central and autonomic nervous system that react with the environment, with upbringing, and many other environment factors to increase the probability that a given person would act in a certain antisocial manner" (Eysenck & Gudjonsson, 1989, p. 7). Eysenck isolated features of the central and autonomic nervous systems to account for a substantial portion of the differences found in personality in general. The way each individual's nervous system functions may be as unique as his or her personality characteristics. Carrying this a step further, we could posit that some nervous systems are more likely to engage in criminal activity because of their reactivity, sensitivity, and excitability.

Based on a series of empirical studies and statistical analyses, Eysenck argued that there are four higher order factors of personality—one higher order factor for ability called "g" (general intelligence), and three higher order factors for temperament, called **extraversion**, **neuroticism**, and **psychoticism**. Eysenck believed that the ability factor is an important factor in the cause of criminality, but is less important than the temperament factors. He wrote, "we may conclude that intelligence is a factor in the causation of criminality but that its contribution is probably smaller than one might have thought at first" (Eysenck & Gudjonsson, 1989, p. 50).

Most of the research on crime and personality has focused on extraversion and neuroticism, which are essentially the core concepts of Eysenckian theory. Eysenck did not identify psychoticism until he found a need to account for behaviors not fully explained by extraversion or neuroticism.

Eysenck visualized each of the three temperament or personality factors on a continuum, with the neuroticism and extraversion lines at right angles and intersecting. Psychoticism is on a separate continuum. Most people fall in the intermediate or midpoint area of each, and people rarely are at either extreme (see Figure 3-2; most people fall within the square). The extraversion dimension runs from the extreme pole extraversion to the extreme pole introversion, with the middle range called ambiversion. Thus, depending on where a person falls on this dimension, that person may be an extravert, introvert, or ambivert. The neuroticism continuum runs from the polar ends of neuroticism to stability, with no middle label. Psychoticism runs from tough-mindedness (high psychoticism) to tender-mindedness (low psychoticism), also with no label for the middle majority. The extraversion dimension is believed to reflect basic functions of the central nervous system (CNS), which consists of the brain and spinal cord, while neuroticism represents functions of the peripheral nervous system (nerve pathways outside the central nervous system). As yet, neither Eysenck nor other researchers have postulated a nervous system mechanism for psychoticism.

Eysenck developed several self-report questionnaires to measure these personality variables, the best known being the British Maudsley Personality Inventory

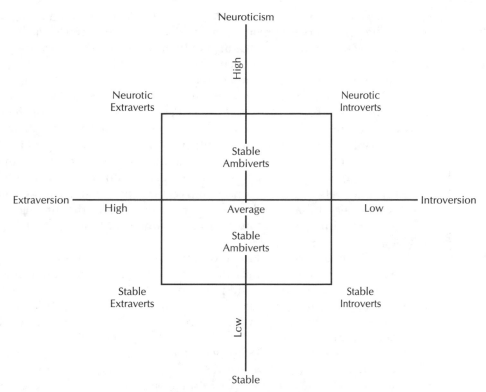

**Figure 3-2   Illustration of Eysenck's Personality Dimensions
for Neuroticism and Extraversion**

(MPI) and its American editions, the Eysenck Personality Inventory (EPI) and the Eysenck Personality Questionnaire (EPQ). The questionnaires have stimulated extensive research to explore both their validity and Eysenck's concept of personality. Overall, worldwide research has supported the general theory, but when it is applied to criminality, the support begins to crumble. We will review some of this research later in this chapter, after examining more closely the basic concepts behind each dimension.

EXTRAVERSION

Behavioral Characteristics and Incidence   Usually, two out of every three people will score in the "average" range on the extraversion dimension, thus making them clinically uninteresting ambiverts. Roughly 16 percent of the population are extraverts, and another 16 percent introverts.

According to Eysenck, the typical extravert is sociable, impulsive, optimistic, and has high needs for excitement and for a varied, changing environment. Extraverts tend to lose their temper quickly, become aggressive easily, and be unreliable. They like to have people around, they enjoy parties, and they are usually very talkative. The typical introvert, on the other hand, is reserved, quiet, and cautious. He or she keeps feelings under close control and generally tries to avoid excitement, change, and most social activities. Introverts tend to be reliable and unaggressive and to place great value on ethical standards (Eysenck & Rachman, 1965). Ambiverts exhibit some features of both extraversion and introversion, but not to the same degree or consistency as extraverts and introverts.

Think of the extraversion dimension as a continuum representing a progressive need for stimulation, which can be defined as the impact stimuli have on areas of the brain. The impact is analogous to the taste of food. Some people have a relatively consistent tendency to prefer spicy, hot foods that have more impact on their taste centers (Szechuan cuisine), while others more often choose bland foods (macaroni and cheese), because they do not desire the high taste impact. Some people prefer and actively seek out more stimulation or stimulus impact from other areas of their lives as well—they like rousing music, perpetual bustle, psychedelic drugs. Eysenck maintained that people at the extraversion end of the dimension require high levels of stimulation from their environment because of their biological makeup.

If you conceptualize the dimension this way, you may find that the popular term "extrovert" (note the spelling) takes on added meaning. Extroverts are sociable creatures who like to be around people and to be immersed in activity because of the stimulation this provides them. It is important to note, though, that our everyday usage of the nouns *extrovert* and *introvert* are not identical to Eysenck's polar classifications.

Because extraverts have higher needs for excitement and stimulation to break the daily boredom, they are also most likely to run counter to the law. They tend to be impulsive, fun-loving, thrill-seeking people who are willing to take chances and stick their necks out. They enjoy pranks and practical jokes, and find challenge in opportunities to do the unconventional or even the antisocial thing. In addition, some features of the extraverted nervous system not only encourage stimulation seeking but also inhibit the acquisition and internalization of society's rules, as we will see shortly.

Physiological Bases of Extraversion-Introversion   Eysenck (1967) hypothesized that people differ along the extraversion-introversion axis because of genetic differences in certain mechanisms in their central nervous system, particularly the tiny but complex network of neurons located in the central part of the brain stem called the reticular activating system (RAS) (see Figure 3-3). The RAS, which we will discuss in detail in Chapter 4, is believed to act as a sentinel that awakens and keeps alert the portion of the brain called the cerebral cortex. All higher level functions, like thinking, memory, and decision making, occur in the cerebral cortex (French, 1957). The RAS arouses the cerebral cortex and keeps it alert to incoming stimuli. Nerve pathways communicating information to the cerebral cortex branch off into collateral pathways traveling to the RAS. In effect, these collaterals "tell" the RAS to alert the brain to incoming information.

Eysenck postulated that both extraverts and introverts inherit a RAS that handles cortical arousal in a unique way, differently from the RAS of the general population. The extravert's RAS does not seem to generate cortical excitation or

Cerebral Cortex

Amygdala

Thalamus

Cerebellum

Reticular Activating System

Spinal Cord

Figure 3-3   Location of the Reticular Activating System (RAS) Relative to Other Brain Structures

arousal effectively. In fact, it appears to reduce the impact of stimulation and the arousal properties of stimuli before they can reach the cortex. The introvert, on the other hand, apparently has inherited a RAS that amplifies stimulation input, keeping cortical arousal at relatively high levels. So we have the extravert, who is cortically underaroused, seeking additional stimulation to achieve an optimally aroused cortex, and the introvert, who is cortically overaroused, trying to avoid stimulation. The ambivert, who obtains an intermediate level of arousal, is generally content with moderate amounts of stimulation.

In Chapter 4 we will also discuss the concept of optimal level of stimulation or cortical arousal. One motivation behind human behavior is the desire to achieve a just-right level of stimulation and cortical arousal. Too much stimulation becomes aversive and even painful, while too little results in boredom and eventual sleep. It is assumed that the extravert, because of the dampening effect of the RAS, needs higher levels of stimulation to maintain that just-right or optimal level of cortical arousal. The introvert, because of the amplifying effect of the RAS, desires relatively lower levels of stimulation. This explains the typical extravert's attraction to spicy foods, loud music, and vividly colored objects, and the introvert's preference for bland foods, soft music, and cool or dark-colored objects.

The extravert's stimulation needs are well documented (see Eysenck, 1967, 1981). As mentioned previously, the greater tendency of extraverts to seek sensation is presumably more likely to put them in conflict with the law. Eysenck suggested that most people involved in criminal activity are cortically underaroused and have a strong drive to obtain stimulation or sensation from their environment. They are thus drawn to risk taking, joy riding, and illegal activities that have high stimulation value. Put quite simply, most criminals are extraverts.

Before leaving the section on extraversion, let's digress for a moment on the effects of alcohol on cortical arousal. Alcohol is a general central nervous system depressant. It lowers cortical arousal to the point that one may pass out or fall asleep. The extravert without alcohol is already "half in the bag," and with alcohol he or she is even less alert. For introverts, however, alcohol has the effect of lowering a normally high cortical arousal to a point where they become more extraverted, behaviorally and physiologically. Thus, the usually quiet, reserved person may become boisterous or perform a soft shoe routine on the coffee table after a few drinks. The drunk introvert now has an extraverted arousal level and seeks more stimulation.

Eysenck supposed that the active, aroused cortex is a better inhibitor of activity than the poorly aroused one. Therefore, high cortical arousal leads to inhibition, while low cortical arousal allows subcortical regions of the central nervous system to function without restraint. Alcohol lowers the alertness of the cortex, which presumably lessens its censorship over the primitive, subcortical regions of the nervous system. This facilitates inappropriate, antisocial behaviors usually held in check by the cortex. Thus, according to the Eysenckian perspective, under the influence of alcohol, introverts will do things they normally would not do. On the other hand, even relatively small quantities of alcohol influence the extravert, who already functions at a low level of cortical arousal, toward even more uninhibited behavior. The correlation between alcohol and crime is a strong one and will be discussed in greater detail in Chapter 12.

By now, you should have a basic understanding of one of Eysenck's personality dimensions. We will now move on to consider the second dimension, which is equally important.

NEUROTICISM

Like extraversion, neuroticism is a significant variable in the relationship between personality and crime. Sometimes called *emotionality*, this dimension reflects an innate biological predisposition to react bodily to stressful events. Basically, neuroticism deals with the intensity of emotional reactions. It is believed to occur in the general population in the same frequencies as extraversion, with 16 percent of the population falling above and below one standard deviation from the mean.

A person high on the neuroticism scale reacts intensely and lastingly to stress. In fact, even under low-stress conditions, the person is likely to be moody, touchy, sensitive to slights, anxious, and to complain of various physical ailments like headaches, backaches, and digestive problems. He or she tends to overreact to stress and have difficulty returning to a normal, calm state. People high in emotionality also have a strong propensity to develop neurotic features such as phobias and obsessions. Their opposites, persons at the other end of the continuum, display emotionally stable, calm, and even-tempered behavior. They tend to keep their wits about them under stress and intense excitement and to select appropriate reactions to emergencies. Researchers testing Eysenckian theory refer to high emotionality individuals as *neurotics* and their counteropposites as *stables*.

Neurophysiological Bases of Neuroticism-Stability

Whereas the extraversion-introversion dimension is linked to the central nervous system, the neuroticism-stability continuum relates to the autonomic nervous system, which can be divided into the sympathetic and parasympathetic nervous systems (see Figure 3-4). The *sympathetic system* activates the body for emergencies by increasing heart rate, respiration flow, blood flow, pupil dilation, and perspiration. The *parasympathetic system* counterbalances the sympathetic; it brings the body back to its normal arousal state. According to Eysenck, differences in emotionality are due to variances in the sensitivity of these subdivisions, which are both under the control of the so-called visceral brain or *limbic system*. In addition to a complicated array of neuronal circuitry, the limbic system includes the neurological structures known as the hippocampus, amygdala, cingulum, and hypothalamus. The hypothalamus appears to exert the greatest amount of control over the autonomic nervous system and thus represents the central mechanism in emotionality.

Neurotics are believed to have unusually sensitive limbic systems, so they achieve emotionality quickly, and it lasts longer (The term *neurotic* as used here should not be confused with the neurotic classification of mental disorders, which will be discussed in Chapter 6). Theoretically, it may be that their sympathetic system is activated quickly while their parasympathetic system is slow in counterbalancing this. Stables, low in emotionality, may possess an underactive sympathetic system and an overactive parasympathetic system.

Although autonomic activation appears to produce a generalized arousal state in everyone, there is good reason to believe that each person reacts to the stress in unique ways. Some of us tense the muscles in our neck, forehead, or back; others breathe more heavily; for others, the heart pumps faster. This tendency for response specificity may account for the various forms of neurotic behaviors displayed by humans reacting to stress. Some complain of headaches, others of digestive problems or backaches. (Obviously, we are not suggesting that all backache sufferers are neurotics.)

Eysenck assumed that the person high on emotionality is more likely to engage in criminal activity than the person low on that dimension. He based this assumption on the consistent research finding that emotionality can serve as a drive, pushing an individual to resort to habitual ways of behaving. Under high emotionality (high drive) a person is more vulnerable to his or her habits—good or bad. Thus, if the individual has acquired antisocial habits, he or she will be more driven to commit them under high drive than low drive conditions. Neuroticism, therefore, encourages whatever mindless or habitual behaviors the person has acquired. Furthermore, because habits are usually not as well ingrained in the young as they are in the old, we would expect neuroticism to be an important factor with respect to adult criminals, less so with adolescents, and least so with young children (Eysenck, 1983).

The two dimensions we have looked at thus far are usually combined in classi-

SYMPATHETIC

PARASYMPATHETIC

Thalamus

Hypothalamus

Constricts
Pupil

Dilates Pupils

Stimulates
Salivation

Inhibits Salivation

Relaxes Bronchi

Constricts
Bronchi

Accelerates Heart

Decelerates
Heart

Inhibits Activity

Stimulates
Activity

Small
Intestine

Small
Intestine

Secretion of
Adrenaline and
Noradrenaline

Contracts
Bladder

Relaxes
Bladder

Chain
Ganglia

**Figure 3-4   Illustration of the Sympathetic and Parasympathetic Subdivisions
of the Autonomic Nervous System**

fying an individual's personality. That is, based on Eysenck's personality inventories, a person will be a neurotic introvert, a stable extravert, a neurotic ambivert,
and so forth. If we accept Eysenck's views up to this point, we should agree that
the neurotic extravert is the most likely of the possible personality types to be
involved in criminal behavior.

PSYCHOTICISM

No neurophysiological mechanism has been established to explain the characteristics of psychoticism, Eysenck's most recently formulated dimension. Eysenck (1996) does suggest, however, high levels of the male hormone testosterone combined with low levels of the enzyme monoamine oxidase and the neurotransmitter serotonin may play a significant role in the formation of psychoticism.

Psychoticism seems to be highly similar to primary psychopathy, which we will discuss in Chapter 4. Behaviorally, psychoticism is characterized by cold cruelty, social insensitivity, unemotionality, disregard for danger, troublesome behavior, dislike of others, and an attraction to the unusual. "Psychotics" are hostile toward others and enjoy duping or ridiculing them. It is important that we distinguish between Eysenck's psychotics and persons who are psychotic in the clinical sense of being out of touch with reality. Although this latter label is losing favor among clinicians, it appears frequently enough in literature to warrant making the distinction. Psychosis as a classification of mental disorder and abnormality will be dealt with in Chapter 6.

Eysenck's psychoticism dimension has not received the research attention that extraversion and neuroticism have. However, he hypothesizes that, like extraversion and neuroticism, psychoticism will prove to be a striking characteristic of the criminal population. He suggests that psychoticism will be especially prominent in hardcore, habitual offenders convicted of crimes of violence (Eysenck, 1983). Furthermore, unlike neuroticism, it apparently is important at all stages of development, from childhood through adolescence to adulthood.

Thus far we have only defined Eysenck's dimensions and, in the case of neuroticism and extraversion, we have isolated the physiological mechanisms that control them. None of this explains, however, why neurotics, extraverts, and psychotics are more likely to be criminal. The reason has to do with some very basic psychological principles to which we now turn our attention.

CRIME AND CONDITIONABILITY

A basic premise of this text is that criminal behavior is learned. Traditionally, psychologists have delineated three major types of learning: **classical** or **Pavlovian conditioning**, **instrumental** or **operant learning**, and **social learning**. It is important now to examine these processes more carefully if we are to approach an understanding of why some people engage in crime.

The student with a background in introductory psychology will recall Ivan Pavlov's famous experiments with dogs who learned to salivate at the sound of a bell. Pavlov discovered that pairing a neutral stimulus (in this case a bell) with a significant stimulus (for example, food) would result in the dogs' eventually learning to associate the sound of the bell with that of food. How do we know the dogs learned to make that association? Because they salivated at the mere sound of the bell, a response they usually reserved for food. The process of learning to respond to a formerly neutral stimulus (bell) that has been paired with another stimulus that already elicits a response (salivation) is basically *classical* or *Pavlovian conditioning*. In classical conditioning, animals (or persons) have no control over the situation, even over what happens to themselves. The animal is "forced" to take the consequences. The bell will ring and food will appear shortly afterward, regardless of what the animal does. In anticipation, and without any effort on its part, the animal salivates. This learning occurs not because of any reward or gain, but merely because of the *association* between the bell and the food.

In *instrumental learning*, the process is quite different. The learner must do something to the environment in order to obtain a reward or, in some cases, to avoid punishment. Instrumental learning is based on learning the consequences of behaving a certain way: If you do something, there is some probability that a certain rewarding event (or at least an avoidance of punishment) will occur. A child may learn, for example, that one parent will give her a piece of candy to quell a temper tantrum; the other parent will not yield. The child will eventually learn to use temper tantrums when Dad's around, but not to use them in front of Mom (or vice versa).

One important aspect of instrumental learning should be stressed: There must be a goal driving the animal or person to operate on the environment. That is, the individual must have a purpose or expectation for his or her behavior, must expect a reward for the response. A reward or reinforcement is the event that increases the likelihood of a response. Classical conditioning, by contrast, results from an association between stimuli and takes place without reward.

Social learning is more complex than either classical conditioning or instrumental learning, because it involves learning from watching others and organizing social experiences in the brain. Since Eysenck did not deal directly with social learning principles, we will reserve this topic for Chapter 4.

Eysenck (1977) turns the question of criminal behavior around from the usual, "Why do people become criminal?" to "Why don't more people engage in criminal behavior?" To answer this with the adage, "Crime doesn't pay" is nonsense, since there is evidence that for much of the criminal population, crime does pay. After all, one of the chief motivators of behavior may be the desire to gain reward and pleasure (referred to as *hedonism*). "It would seem ... that a person may, with a fair degree of safety, indulge in a career of crime without having to fear the consequences very much" (Eysenck, 1964, p. 102). According to Eysenck, those detected, convicted, and incarcerated often represent that portion of the criminal population who are of lower intelligence, poorly taught, unable to afford an influential attorney, or simply unlucky. So, if instrumental learning is a major factor, there should be substantially more crime, because people would be more often than not rewarded for operating criminally on their environment. Moreover, when punishment does occur, it is so long in coming that it cannot reasonably be considered a deterrent. Eysenck suggests, in fact, that delayed and sometimes arbitrary punishment may actually encourage criminal activity.

To explain why more people do not become criminal, Eysenck contends that classical conditioning has a stronger effect on most people than instrumental learning. That is, most people behave themselves because they have been classically conditioned during childhood about the rules of society. That guiding light, superego, conscience, or whatever it is that makes us feel uncomfortable before, during, and after a socially and morally disapproved act is, according to Eysenck, a *conditioned reflex*. In a traditional family environment, children may be verbally reprimanded or physically punished for behavior that is against the social mores. Immediately after engaging in a socially or morally frowned-upon act, say, punching a friend, a child finds that punishment quickly follows.

Let's return to Pavlov's dog experiments for a moment and substitute the food with painful shock. Immediately following the sound of the bell, the dog receives a severe electrical shock (punishment) through the grids in the floor of the cage. After a number of trials (bell followed by shock) the dog, rather than salivating at the bell, begins to shake in fear. The animal has been classically conditioned to fear the sound of the bell, even when shock no longer follows it. The dog now associates shock with the bell rather than food.

Eysenck asserts that basically the same sequence occurs in childhood— inappropriate behavior followed by reprimand. For example, child punches another child, mother reprimands. Following a few repetitions of this sequence, the thought of punching stimulates fear of the consequences. In essence, "by punishing antisocial behavior numerous times, parents, teachers, and others concerned with the upbringing of the child, including his or her peers, perform the role of the Pavlovian experimenter" (Eysenck, 1983, p. 60). The child associates punching with punishment, and this bonding between the behavior and the aversive consequences should deter him or her from performing the act. Moreover, the closer the individual comes to performing the act, the stronger the association (fear) becomes.

Most people, Eysenck believes, do not participate in criminal activity (he prefers the term antisocial behavior) because after a series of trials they have made strong connections between deviant behavior and aversive consequences. On the other hand, those persons who have not made adequate connections, either because of poor conditionability (e.g., extraverts) or because the opportunity to do so was not presented (socialization), are more likely to display deviant or criminal behavior. According to Eysenck, these people do not anticipate aversive events strongly enough to be deterred; the association has not been sufficiently developed.

Pavlov observed that dogs differ widely in their conditionability to the sound of a bell and theorized that these differences come from properties of their nervous systems. Eysenck also made this observation, commenting that "German Shepherds are very law abiding: They are easily conditioned and are well known to animal fanciers and shepherds for this property. Basenjis, however, are natural psychopaths, difficult or almost impossible to condition, disobedient and antisocial" (Eysenck, 1983, p. 61). Eysenck advanced the same observation concerning humans: Extraverts condition less readily than introverts due to biological differences in their nervous systems. Introverts condition better and therefore are less likely to engage in behavior contrary to society's laws and mores.

The principles of conditioning have been firmly established in the field of psychology as a valid explanation for many forms of behavior. The conditioning process appears to be a powerful force in the socialization of children, particularly in the suppressing of undesirable behaviors. There is every reason to believe that it may be a critical process in determining who becomes involved in deviant or criminal behavior. However, there is also evidence that conditioning can serve as an *instigator* of such behavior. As we will see in later chapters, the association between *pleasurable* events and specific behavior is also an extremely powerful motivator of criminal activity.

According to Eysenck, the conditioned conscience has two effects on behavior: It may prevent us from indulging in forbidden activities, or it may make us feel guilty after we commit them. The conditioned conscience inhibits us from engaging in antisocial activities by its association with prior adverse consequences. In addition, once we have committed the act we tend to feel uncomfortable about our transgressions. Eysenck (1983) supposed the difference rests in the timing of the aversive consequences. Reprimanding a child before or during an act would produce different effects than reprimanding a child after the act. The former situation would result in feelings of discomfort before the act (or while committing it); whereas the latter would produce discomfort (guilt) after the act.

What part does neuroticism or emotionality play? As noted earlier, Eysenck predicted that neuroticism functions as a drive strongly encouraging the performance of behavior previously acquired during childhood. That is, neuroticism amplifies existing habits in a person's repertoire of responses. If a neurotic extravert has not been properly conditioned to avoid stealing and has engaged in frequent, successful stealing in the past, neuroticism will function as a strong force or drive toward the old habit—stealing. In other words, behavior (inappropriate or appropriate) = prior conditioning or learned habits x (intensified by) emotionality.

According to Eysenck (1983, p. 65), "The general growth in permissiveness in homes, schools, and courts has led to a significant reduction in the number of conditioning contingencies to which children are exposed. It would follow as a direct consequence that they would grow up with a much weaker conscience, and consequently that many more children would be led to engage in criminal and antisocial activities." In essence, Eysenck is asserting that increases in crime may be traced directly to conditions within the home or schools that are not conducive to the development of a conditioned conscience toward avoiding antisocial conduct.

THE EVIDENCE FOR EYSENCK'S THEORY

Now that we have scrutinized Eysenck's theory of criminality, the relevant question becomes, "Can we find research to support it?" Eysenck's theory of criminality predicts that criminals, as a group, will demonstrate lower levels of cortical arousal (extraversion), higher levels of autonomic (sympathetic) arousal (neuroticism), and be more tough-minded (psychoticism). In short, he postulates that criminals will score high on the E, N, and P scales of the Eysenck Personality Questionnaire (EPQ), and that these dimensions are more than merely correlated with crime; they are *causally* related to it.

In some cases the research supports Eysenck's hypothesis, but many studies also refute the hypothesis. Although some research seems to damage the theory, these results do not necessarily mean that Eysenck is wrong. Research findings that fail to support parts of a theory suggest that the theory might be modified to account for the new data, provided the experiments were carefully conducted. The theory as a whole may still be promising and useful.

Passingham (1972) reviewed all literature on Eysenck's theory prior to 1972 and found flaws in the basic experimental design of most of the experiments. He noted that few of the studies used adequate controls to compare criminal and non-criminal populations. A control group, of course, should be matched as closely as possible to the experimental group, with all relevant variables (e.g., socioeconomic class, economic and cultural background, and intelligence) the same. Without an adequate control group, meaningful comparisons and valid conclusions are impossible. For example, suppose we designed a study to determine whether the personalities of criminals are significantly different from those of noncriminals, and suppose we used college students as a control group. If we found a significant difference, we could only conclude that the criminals differ from college students. But a college sample very probably differs from a criminal sample on a number of significant variables, such as socioeconomic class. Since college students are generally middle class or higher, and since criminals studied in the research usually are not, the results might reflect a difference between social classes, not necessarily between criminal and noncriminal personalities. The college group, therefore, is not an adequate control group.

Passingham also found that most researchers explaining Eysenck's theory did not delineate subgroups of offenders. They merely selected a heterogeneous sample of prisoners, administered questionnaires, and made comparisons and conclusions based on responses from a control group, often poorly selected. Prisoners are prisoners for a constellation of reasons and offenses. Eysenck recognized this when he commented (1971, p. 289) that "not all crimes are likely to be equally highly correlated with extraversion, and some types of criminals, such as the recidivist 'old lag,' lacking entirely in the social skills needed to make a success of living outside an institution, may in fact show introverted tendencies." In fact, many murderers and sex offenders do show strong introverted patterns. It is imperative, therefore, that researchers study categories of offenders to determine whether certain personalities are linked to certain offenses. A recent review by Farrington, Biron, and LeBlanc (1982) indicates that some of the aforementioned problems have been corrected, but many still remain.

In general, Eysenck's prediction that the criminal and antisocial populations should score significantly higher on the extraversion scale has not been consistently supported (Passingham, 1972; Allsopp, 1976; Feldman, 1977; Farrington, Biron, & LeBlanc, 1982). The results are especially inconsistent for adult male offenders and for delinquents of both sexes. While some studies (e.g., Price, 1968; Buikhuisen & Hemmel, 1972) report high extraversion scores for these two groups, other investigations cite evidence that they score lower than the general population (e.g., Hoghughi & Forrest, 1970; Cochrane, 1974). Some researchers found no difference between prisoners and delinquents compared to control groups (e.g., Little, 1963; Burgess, 1972). Other studies found significantly higher E scores (extraversion) for *violent* offenders compared to other types of offenders (Gossop & Kristjansson, 1977). Studies separating the extraversion characteristics that reflect impulsiveness from those that reflect sociability found that adult male prisoners score higher on impulsiveness than do male noncriminals, but score lower than noncriminals on sociability (S. B. G. Eysenck & H. J. Eysenck, 1970, 1971). This may reflect the irrelevance of the sociability questions for incarcerated prisoners, since sociability tendencies may be dampened in a correctional institution.

Berman and Paisey (1984) examined the relationship between antisocial behavior and personality in convicted American juvenile males. Subjects were divided into two groups: Thirty juvenile males convicted of assault or confrontation with a victim—called the assaultive group—and thirty juvenile males convicted of offenses involving property without confrontation with a victim—called the nonassaultive group. These male juveniles were being held in the Dade County Juvenile Detention Center (Miami, Florida) awaiting sentencing. All were English-speaking whites. The assaultive group, compared to the nonassaultive group, scored significantly higher on all three of the Eysenckian personality dimensions, P, E, and N, particularly on P.

In Spain, Silva, Martorell, and Clemente (1986) compared the Junior EPQ scores of 42 delinquent males confined in a reformatory to 102 nondelinquent males. They found that P and N scores were significantly higher in the delinquent group. However, contrary to what Eysenck predicted, E scores were significantly higher in the nondelinquent group. In London, Lane (1987) compared "60 pupils with convictions" with "60 pupils without convictions." The criminal group scored substantially higher on the P scale, whereas the noncriminal group scored higher on the N scale. There were no differences between the groups on the E scale. Lane asserted somewhat discouragingly, "Extraversion … for so long the central feature of the theory on conduct disorder and criminality, fails to hold up consistently" (p. 805). Moreover, neuroticism scores were consistently in the opposite direction than that which Eysenck predicted, with the noncriminal group scoring higher than the criminal group. Psychoticism scores were not significant, neither higher nor lower for either group. Lane concludes, "A way of resolving these variations may be to take the argument outside the narrower conditioning model and place it within a broader multifactorial and interactive concept which links individual differences with behavioural and sociological analyses" (p. 806).

The aforementioned studies used official data, comparing EPQ scores of convicted delinquents with nondelinquents, or the scores of one group of convicted delinquents with another group. Some studies have not used officially recognized offenders, but have tapped the incidence of offending in the general population through self-report (SR) questionnaires. The most popular SR scale in Great Britain is the Antisocial Behavior Scale (ABS), originally developed by Gibson (1967), and later revised by Allsopp and Feldman (1976). However, research using the ABS has not been supportive of Eysenck's theory of criminality either. Jamison (1980), using 1,282 secondary school children (ages thirteen to sixteen) in and around London, found a robust correlation between self-reported antisocial conduct and the P scale, but a negligible or weak relationship with N and E respectively. Powell and Stewart (1983), also using British subjects from the secondary and junior schools, found that self-reported antisocial behavior was strongly related to scores on the P scale, weakly to the E scale, and negligibly to the N scale. Similar results have been reported by Rushton and Chrisjohn (1981) on Canadian college students.

The research results examining the relationship between neuroticism and criminal or antisocial conduct are clear: It is not supported. Moreover, the relationship between extraversion and antisocial conduct is only weakly supported, but the relationship between psychoticism and crime appears to be moderately supported. The failure of E scale findings to support Eysenck's hypothesis strongly may reflect a weakness in his argument that most criminals are poor conditioners. While many may have "faulty consciences," the poor conditioning perspective seems too limited. It might be more accurate to suggest that some criminals have offended because of poor conditionability, others because they perceived antisocial behavior as one of the few avenues available to them for gaining something, and still others for a combination of both reasons or other reasons. Most inmates are not in prison because of a failure to associate social transgressions with feelings of guilt and anxiety. Rather, they are incarcerated for a variety of offenses, prompted by a variety of motives, and associated with a variety of social situations. Because the E scale, which reflects conditionability, is not sensitive enough to account for this, more prisoner subgroup research is needed.

Bartol and Holanchock (1979) administered the Eysenck Personality Questionnaire to 398 inmates at a maximum security prison in New York state. Sixty-two percent were African American, 30 percent Hispanic, and about 7 percent white. The sample was divided into six offender groups according to conviction history: homicide, aggravated assault and attempted murder, rape and sexual assault, robbery, burglary, and drug offenses. When the inmate had committed offenses in more than one category, he was classified according to the most serious. A control group comprised persons who were in waiting rooms at various state employment agencies in predominantly African-American and Hispanic areas of New York City. We found 187 males who agreed to fill out the EPQ; from all indications, this control group matched the criminal group in age, race, socioeconomic class, and employment history.

All six criminal groups scored lower than the control group on the E scale, but there were significant differences among the criminal subgroups. Sex offenders were the most introverted, followed by burglars. Robbery offenders were the most extraverted.

While demonstrating the ability of the EPQ to distinguish among offenders in this particular sample, the aforementioned study does not support Eysenck's position on extraversion. Although there appeared to be many reasons for this lack of support, a dominant one was cultural. Prisoners in our study were generally from the African-American or Hispanic regions of New York City and had been convicted of violent crimes. Eysenck studied predominantly European white prisoners convicted of property crimes. This observation stresses the importance of considering cultural factors when studying heterogeneous criminal populations.

Farrington, Biron, and LeBlanc (1982) found little support for the Eysenckian theory of criminality in their review of the literature, which included their own recent investigation of antisocial individuals in London and Montreal. "Our conclusion is that, at the present time, it seems unlikely that the Eysenck theory, the Eysenck scales, or the Eysenck items are of much use in the explanation of delinquency" (p. 196).

We should not discard the Eysenckian theory this blithely, however. Enough studies find some support for it to warrant speculation and research on why the results are equivocal. Are they due to cultural differences, sampling differences in either offender or control populations, or the wording of questions on the personality inventory? Also, the P scale has been somewhat supported by recent research using both convicted delinquents and SR offenders. This finding suggests that people who engage in antisocial or criminal conduct tend to be insensitive, aggressive, impulsive, tough-minded individuals who are highly self-centered. Obviously, more research should be directed at this personality dimension.

Although Eysenck's theory is in a state of flux, we have given it a considerable amount of attention here for three reasons. First, the theory is one of the few comprehensive statements about the role of genetics in antisocial behavior. We still have much to learn from this attempt, and perhaps some modifications will strengthen its explanatory potential. Second, Eysenck's theory recognizes the interaction of the environment—specifically via classical conditioning—with characteristics of the nervous system. Of particular importance is the attention Eysenck gives to individual differences in the nervous system as a biological basis for personality in general (Nebylitsyn & Gray, 1972). Criminology cannot afford to discount the existence of biological factors in antisocial behavior, even if these factors account for the behavior of only a small percentage of the population. At this point, however, it appears that Eysenck's emphasis on classical conditioning as a primary explanation of criminality and his tendency to ignore other forms of learning and mediational (cognitive) processes may be the theory's most damaging weaknesses. In addition, Gordon Trasler (1987) notes that even the concept of conditionability is fraught with difficulties and encourages much debate among contemporary psychologists. There is even considerable debate about what the term means, and the empirical evidence examining the concept remains elusive and conflicting. Finally, Eysenck's theory is unique because it represents one of the few attempts by a psychologist to formulate a general, universal theory of criminal behavior.

SUMMARY AND CONCLUSIONS

Realizing that crime, like all human behavior, results from an interaction between heredity, neurophysiology, and environment, we have in this chapter looked at the research on the genetic and biological makeup of persons who become criminal. A pioneer in genetic-biological criminology, Cesare Lombroso, asserted that there is a "born criminal," physically distinct from the general population and *predisposed* to act antisocially. Lombroso's theory was periodically revised, but the final version retained the notion of innate criminal tendencies, at least in some offenders. Lombrosian theory was soon put to rest, but it prompted other theorists to posit that there might be more to crime causation than social and environmental factors alone.

Later theorists studied the relationship of body build (Kretschmer) or body type (Sheldon) to crime. Theirs and later studies supported a *correlation* with crime, but questionable methodology often made it impossible to determine whether a *causal* relationship existed. To what extent genetically determined physical characteristics may influence criminal behavior remains unknown.

The genetic factor has also been explored in twin and adoption studies. Generally, empirical studies have found a high concordance rate between identical twins engaged in crime, lending some credence to genetic predisposition. Even when separated at birth, identicals tend to be similar in their pursuit of criminal careers. There have been few adoption studies, primarily because of the inaccessibility of records. Researchers in this area who say their research supports the genetic viewpoint admonish that the environment can either stimulate or inhibit any inborn tendency toward criminality.

Eysenck proposed an interaction theory of crime, seeing it as the result of environmental conditions (primarily classical conditioning) working on inherited features of the nervous system. The essence of Eysenckian theory is that individuals with certain types of nervous systems (introverts) condition better, or learn the mores of society much more readily than individuals with other types (extraverts and ambiverts). In other words, introverts link transgressions with disapproval much sooner than others do. Some people would say introverts have a stronger conscience and experience more fear prior to their transgressions and more guilt after committing them. However, as we will note in Chapter 10, this quick associative or conditioning ability also means that introverts are more likely to acquire sexually deviant behavior.

Eysenck hypothesized that neuroticism or emotionality intensifies existing habits, which in some cases may be antisocial ones. Individuals with high emotionality may be more driven toward antisocial habits than individuals with low emotionality. Psychoticism, a dimension that has received less research attention, appears to correlate with features of the psychopath and frequent offenders.

It is obvious that the Eysenckian position needs considerable revision and refinement. As it now stands, the theory has flaws that could be fatal. One glaring weakness is its reliance on classical conditioning to the exclusion of mediational (cognitive) factors and social learning. Despite these problems, Eysenck's work represents a broad, testable theory of criminality that continues to stimulate international research.

One thing needs to be emphasized in the conclusion of this chapter. Assigning a major role in the causation of criminal behavior to diverse neurological deficits and nervous system functioning is overly simplistic. While biopsychology and neurophysiological factors may play some role in the formation of criminal behavior, it is far more likely that crime—especially violent behavior—develops as a result of a series of complicated interactions with significant others in the social environment.

THE PSYCHOPATH: A FOCUS ON BIOPSYCHOLOGICAL FACTORS

Throughout its history, the term **psychopath** has been controversial and used to describe a wide variety of attitudinal, emotional, and behavioral features. In the early nineteenth century, the French psychiatrist Philip Pinel felt a need to distinguish the person who habitually exhibited asocial and antisocial actions (not necessarily criminal), but did not exhibit signs of mental illness as it was then understood. He coined the term *manie sans delire* (mania without frenzy) to describe this behavior disorder, which included such features as cruelty, irresponsibility, and immorality (Rotenberg & Diamond, 1971). In 1837 the British psychiatrist J. C. Pritchard renamed the clinically strange group of disorders "moral insanity," presuming that they manifested a "derangement" and a failure to abide by society's expectations of religious, ethical, and cultural conduct. To Pritchard, this was evidence of a mental disease. His term was accepted and used by both the public and the medical profession for over a half century. In 1888, however, the German psychiatrist J. Koch decided that moral insanity had unwarranted negative connotations, and he proposed another designation, "psychopathic inferiority." Our modern conception of the psychopath is derived directly from Koch's label.

Psychopathic inferiority, as conceived by Koch, encompassed numerous behaviors, some of which are still linked with the psychopathic personality as we recognize it today, but many of which are associated instead with neurotic or personality disorders. The early psychiatrists believed that this disorder was constitutional, likely inbred by a genetic strain that produced a basic flaw in one's personality. There were implications, which in some respects continue today, that psychopaths were evil, human vessels of the devil, bent on destroying the moral fabric of society—"the devil made them do it."

Emil Krapelin, who had an affinity for classification schemes, delineated seven categories of psychopath in his *Textbook of Psychiatry* in 1913. The seven subtypes were the excitable, the unstable, the impulsive, the eccentric, the liars and swindlers, the antisocial, and the quarrelsome. All represented constitutional predispositions. Not to be outdone, Kahn (1931) suggested sixteen trait-syndromes for the psychopath. In 1930, G. E. Partridge considered psychopathy an exclusively social, rather than mental, maladjustment and proposed the term **sociopath** to replace psychopath (Pennington, 1966).

To stem the proliferation of symptoms and labels and to check the resulting ambiguity, the American Psychiatric Association in 1952 dropped *psychopath* and officially adopted *sociopath*, or, more specifically, "sociopathic personality disturbance, antisocial reaction." Contemporary researchers and clinicians use the terms interchangeably. The purist, however, considers the sociopath a *habitual* criminal offender who fails to learn from experience. The psychopath may or may not be criminal, and presumably manifests specific empirically verifiable behaviors and biological predispositions that differ from those of the general population.

In 1968, the American Psychiatric Association again changed its label, this time to "personality disorder, antisocial." The DSM III (1980), DSM III-R (1987), and the DSM-IV (1994) continued to use the term, and it refers specifically to an individual who exhibits "a pervasive pattern of disregard for, and violation of, the rights of others that begins in childhood or early adolescence and continues into adulthood" (DSM IV, p. 645). In other words, the antisocial personality disorder is closely allied with *persistent* criminality. For example, approximately 80 percent of the incarcerated male offenders in Canadian federal prisons met the DSM-III-R criteria for antisocial personality disorder (Correctional Service of Canada, 1990; Hare, Forth, & Stachan, 1992).

Robert Hare (1970) proposed a useful scheme to outline three categories of psychopaths, the primary, the secondary or neurotic, and the dyssocial. Only the **primary psychopath** is a "true" psychopath. The other two categories meld a heterogeneous group of antisocial individuals who comprise a large segment of the criminal population. **Secondary psychopaths** commit antisocial or violent acts because of severe emotional problems or inner conflicts. They are sometimes called acting-out neurotics, neurotic delinquents, symptomatic psychopaths, or simply neurotic characters. The third group, **dyssocial psychopaths**, display aggressive, antisocial behavior they have learned from their subculture, like their gangs or families. In both cases, the label "psychopath" is misleading, because the behaviors and backgrounds have little if any similarity to those of primary psychopaths. Yet both secondary and dyssocial psychopaths are often incorrectly called psychopaths because of their high recidivism rates. In recent years, the term "sociopath" is often used by criminologists and sociologists to refer to the repetitive offender who does not respond appropriately to treatment, rehabilitation, or incarceration. The term "antisocial personality disorder" (ASP) is used by psychiatrists and many psychologists to refer to those offenders who demonstrate a "failure to conform to social norms with respect to lawful behaviors as indicated by repeatedly performing acts that are grounds for arrest" (American Psychiatric Association [APA], 1993, p. T-4). However, ASP is more narrow than primary psychopathy because it restricts its definition to behavioral indicators. Hare's definition of primary psychopathy includes emotional elements and in the future is likely to include cognitive aspects. However, with each new publication of the DSM, the characteristics used to describe the ASP are increasingly similar to Hare's primary psychopathy.

This text adopts Hare's scheme, considering primary psychopath an experimentally and clinically useful designation. It is distinguished from secondary or neurotic psychopaths in its behavioral, cognitive, and neurophysiological features. From this point on, when we refer to the psychopath, we mean the primary psychopath. He or she is unique: neither neurotic, psychotic, nor emotionally disturbed, as commonly believed. Primary psychopaths are usually not volcanically explosive, violent, or extremely destructive. They are more apt to be outgoing, charming, and verbally proficient. They may be criminals—in fact, in general they run in perpetual opposition to the law—but many are not. The term **criminal psychopath** will be used to identify those primary psychopaths who engage in repetitive antisocial or criminal behavior.

The late Ferdinand Waldo Demara Jr., the "Great Impostor," who forged documents and tried dozens of occupations without stopping to obtain a high school education, is a good example of a primary psychopath. A brief description of some of his exploits may help put the primary psychopath in perspective. (See Critchton, 1959, for a more complete version.)

Demara frequently came into contact with the law, primarily because he persisted in adopting fake identities. He once obtained the credentials of a Dr. French, who held a Harvard Ph.D. in psychology. Demara was in the U.S. Navy at the time, awaiting a commission on the basis of other forged documents, but when he realized he was in danger of exposure via a routine security check, he decided he would prefer the Dr. French identity. He dramatized a successful suicide by leaving his clothing on the end of a pier with a note stating that "this is the only way out." Navy officials accepted his "death," and Demara became Dr. French. With his impressive credentials in hand, he obtained a Dean of Philosophy position in a Canadian college, successfully taught a variety of psychology courses, and assumed administrative responsibilities.

He developed a friendship with a physician, Joseph Cyr, and learned the basics of medicine from their long conversations. He eventually borrowed and duplicated Cyr's vital documents—birth, baptism, and confirmation certificates, school records, medical license—and obtained a commission in the Royal Canadian Navy as Dr. Cyr. He read extensively to nurture his growing knowledge of medicine.

During the Korean War, Demara/Cyr was assigned to a destroyer headed for the combat zone. The ship met a small Korean junk carrying many seriously wounded men, who were brought on board for emergency medical care. Three men were in such critical condition that only emergency surgery could save their lives. Although Demara had never seen an operation performed, he hurriedly reviewed his textbooks. With unskilled hands, he operated through the night. By dawn, he had not only saved the lives of the three men, but also had successfully treated sixteen others.

Demara/Cyr's deeds were broadcast over the ship's radio and disseminated, along with his photo, by the press. The real Dr. Cyr, shocked to see Demara's visage over his own respected name, immediately exposed him. Demara was discharged from the Canadian Navy which, to save itself from additional embarrassment, allowed him to leave without prosecution.

The exploits of this great impostor are far more typical of the primary psychopath than are violence and bizarre perversions. To the public, the term *psychopathic killer* conjures images of a maniac gone berserk with a lust for wanton murder. Psychopathic rapists supposedly torture and murder their victims because they hated their mothers or want to get back at women for some other reason. In fact, most crimes of primary psychopaths are petty and without apparent rationale. Their criminal actions are often inappropriate and astonishingly immature pranks performed without regard for the embarrassment of others or for personal risks. Joy rides, drunken brawls, and spontaneous break-ins are more likely to be part of the psychopath's pattern than are serious offenses.

This is not to say that psychopaths never commit heinous and brutal crimes. They sometimes do. Neville Heath—charming, handsome, and intelligent—murdered two young English women in two of the most brutal and sadistic sexual murders ever uncovered (Critchley, 1951; Hill, 1960). Like Demara, Heath had an extraordinary career, much of it in the armed forces. Unlike Demara, his brushes with the law were serious and occasionally ended in imprisonment. He was commissioned and dishonorably discharged on three separate occasions, once each in the British Royal Air Force, the Royal Armed Service Corps, and the South African Air Force. He flew in a fighter squadron in the RAF until he was court-martialed for car theft at age nineteen. He then committed a series of thefts and burglaries and was sentenced to Borstal Prison. Pardoned in 1939, he joined the Royal Armed Service Corps but was dismissed for forgery. On his way home to England, he jumped ship and eventually managed to obtain a commission in the South African Air Force until his past caught up with him. When not in trouble, Heath was regarded as a daring, confident, and highly charming officer—and a rake. After the third court-martial, he developed a taste for sadistic murder.

You may be able to identify other examples of primary psychopaths at their worst. The notorious Charles Manson, who in the 1960s exhibited an uncanny ability to attract a devout cluster of unresisting followers, is one probable example. Another is Henri Landau, "Bluebeard," born in Paris in 1869 and hanged fifty-one years later. Bluebeard was said to have "loved" 283 women and murdered at least 10 of them. He forged, swindled, seduced, and murdered, and he assumed multiple occupations, including toy salesperson, physician, lawyer, and engineer. His modus operandi was to seduce women and charmingly persuade them to hand over their money and property for safekeeping.

Throughout the remainder of this chapter we will examine in more detail the behavior, physiology, and background of the primary psychopath, who will hereafter be called simply the psychopath.

BEHAVIORAL DESCRIPTION

One respected authority on the behavioral characteristics of the psychopath is Hervey Cleckley (1976). His often-quoted text, *The Mask of Sanity*, describes in clear and empirically useful terms the major behaviors demonstrated by the full-fledged psychopath, as distinct from the other psychopathic types referred to previously.

Superficial charm and average to above-average intelligence are two of the psychopath's main features, according to Cleckley, and they are both especially apparent during initial contacts. Psychopaths usually impress others as friendly, outgoing, likable, and alert. They often appear well-educated and knowledgeable, and they display many interests. They are verbally skillful and can talk themselves out of trouble. In fact, their vocabulary is often so extensive that they can talk at length about anything (Hare, 1991). However, systematic study of their conversation reveals that they often jump "from one topic to another and that much of their speech is empty of real substance, tending to be filled with stock phrases, repetitions of the same ideas, word approximations, abstract terms and jargon used in a superficial or inappropriate fashion, logically inconsistent statements and phrases, and half-formed sentences" (Hare, 1991, p. 57). As Hare (1996, p. 46) notes: "In some respects, it is as if psychopaths lack a central organizer to plan and keep track of what they think and say." However, since psychopaths are so charming and manipulative, these language shortcomings are not readily apparent.

Psychometric studies indicate that psychopaths usually score higher on intelligence tests than the general population (Hare, 1970), particularly on individually administered tests. In fact, Hare wryly comments, the psychopaths who were the sample for his studies were probably the least intelligent of their ilk, since they were not quite bright enough to avoid being convicted for their offenses. (Hare has conducted much of his research on imprisoned psychopaths.)

Psychopaths also do not seem to be plagued with mental disorders, either mild or severe. They lack any symptoms of excessive worry and anxiety, irrational thinking, delusions, severe depressions, or hallucinations. Even under high pressure conditions they remain cool and calm, as did Ian Fleming's fictitious James Bond, probably a prime example. Feasibly, the doomed psychopath might enjoy a steak dinner (au poivre) with gusto just before being executed. The infamous multiple murderer Herman W. Mudget, alias H. H. Holmes, retired at his normal hour the evening before his execution, easily fell asleep, slept soundly, and woke up completely refreshed. "I never slept better in my life," he told his cell guard. He ordered and ate a substantial breakfast an hour before he was scheduled to be hanged. Until the moment of death, he remained remarkably calm and amiable, displaying no signs of depression or fear (Franke, 1975).

Not everyone agrees with the view that psychopaths do not suffer from some mental disorder. Some clinicians argue that psychopathy and schizophrenia are part of the same spectrum of disorders (Hare, 1996). Some forensic clinicians maintain that they occasionally see a mentally disordered offender who qualifies as both a psychopath and a schizophrenic (Hare, 1996). There is some evidence to suggest that it is not uncommon to find psychopaths who seem mentally disordered in maximum security psychiatric units for highly violent or dangerous patients.

Other principal traits of the psychopath are selfishness and an inability to love or give affection to others. According to Cleckley, egocentricity is always present in the psychopath and is essentially unmodifiable. The psychopath's inability to feel genuine, meaningful affection for another is absolute. Psychopaths may be likable, but they are seldom able to keep close friends, and they have great difficulty understanding love in others. They may be highly skillful at pretending deep affection, and they may effectively mimic appropriate emotions, but true loyalty, warmth, and compassion are foreign to them. Psychopaths are distinguished by flat emotional reaction and affect. And since psychopaths have so little need to receive or give love, psychopaths, as a group, have relatively little contact with their families, and many change their residences frequently (Hare, 1991). In addition, they do not usually respond to acts of kindness. They show capacity only for superficial appreciation. Paradoxically, they may do small favors and appear considerate. One prototype mowed the lawn for his elderly neighbor and slipped her some schnapps when she was ill—the next morning he stole her car.

Psychopaths have a remarkable disregard for truth and are often called "pathological liars." They seem to have no internalized moral or ethical sense and cannot understand the purpose of being honest, especially if dishonesty will bring some personal gain. They have a cunning ability to appear straightforward, honest, and sincere, but their claims to sincerity are without substance.

Psychopaths are unreliable, irresponsible, and unpredictable, regardless of the importance of the occasion or the consequences of their impulsive actions. Impulsivity appears to be a central or cardinal feature of psychopathy (Hart & Dempster, 1997). This pattern of impulsive actions is cyclical, however. Psychopaths may, for months on end, be responsible citizens, faithful spouses, and reliable employees. They may experience great successes, be promoted, and gain honors, as did Demara and Heath. Skillfully as they have attained these socially desirable goals, they have an uncanny knack of suddenly unravelling their lives. They become irresponsible, and may pass bad checks, sabotage the company computer, go on a drunken spree, or steal the boss's car. They also tend to have a "bad temper" that flares quickly into an argument and attack. Psychopaths may later say they are sorry and plead for another chance—and most will probably get it. Invariably, if the psychopath is a young adult, the irresponsible behavior will return.

Even small amounts of alcohol prompt most psychopaths to become vulgar, domineering, loud, and boisterous and to engage in practical jokes and pranks. Cleckley notes that they choose pranks that have no appeal for most individuals, and that seem bizarre, inappropriate, and cruel. They lack genuine humor and, not surprisingly, the ability to laugh at themselves.

Cleckley describes a potentially promising, brilliant physician in his early forties who was loved by his patients and had managed to develop a thriving practice during his "upswing" periods. His negative, psychopath behaviors, however, were colossal blunders:

> This man's history shows a great succession of purposeless follies dating from early manhood. He lost several valuable hospital appointments by lying out sodden or by bursting in on serious occasions with nonsensical uproar. He was once forced to relinquish a promising private practice because of the scandal and indig-

nation which followed an escapade in a brothel where he had often lain out disconsolately for days at a time.

Accompanied by a friend who was also feeling some influence of drink he swaggered into his favorite retreat and bellowed confidently for women. Congenially disposed in one room, the party of four called for highballs. For an hour or more only the crash of glasses, scattered oaths, and occasional thuds were heard. Then suddenly an earnest, piercing scream brought the proprietress and her servants racing into the chamber. One of the prostitutes lay prostrate, clasping a towel to her breast, yelling in agony. Through her wails and sobs she accused the subject of this report of having, in his injudicious blunderings, bitten off her nipple. An examination by those present showed that this unhappy dismemberment had, in fact, taken place. Although both men had at the moment been in bed with her, the entertainer had no doubt as to which one had done her the injury.

Feeling ran strong for a while, but, by paying a large sum as recompense for the professional disability and personal damage he had inflicted, the doctor avoided open prosecution. Before a settlement had been made, the guilty man attempted to persuade his companion to assume responsibility for the deed. It would be less serious for the other man, he argued, since his own prominence and professional standing made him a more vulnerable target for damaging courtroom dramatics and for slander. His companion, however, declined this opportunity for self-sacrifice with great firmness. (Cleckley, 1976, pp. 206–207)

Although above average in intelligence, psychopaths appear incapable of learning to avoid failure and situations that are potentially damaging to themselves. Some theorists suggest that the self-destructive, self-defeating deeds and attitudes reflect a need to be punished to mitigate the guilt they subconsciously experience, or more simply, that they are driven by a masochistic purpose. Evidence refuting these explanations will be offered later in this chapter.

When a psychopath drifts into criminal activity, impulsivity will usually prevent him or her from performing like a professional criminal. Psychopaths are more likely to participate in capers and hastily planned frolics, or in spontaneous, serious crimes for immediate satisfaction. The professional criminal has purpose and a plan of action; the psychopath is impulsive and lacks long-range goals.

A cardinal fault of psychopaths is their absolute lack of remorse or guilt for anything they do, regardless of the severity or immorality of their actions and irrespective of their traumatic effects on others. Since they do not anticipate personal consequences, psychopaths may engage in destructive or antisocial behavior—such as forgery, theft, rape, brawls, and fraud—by taking absurd risks and for insignificant personal gain. When caught, they express no genuine remorse. They may readily admit culpability and take considerable pleasure in the shock these admissions produce in others. Whether they have bashed in someone's head, ruined a car, or tortured a child, psychopaths may well remark they did it "for the hell of it."

Psychopaths have little capacity to see themselves as others perceive them. Instead of accepting the facts that would normally lead to insight, they project and externalize blame onto the community and family for their misfortunes. Interestingly, educated psychopaths have been known to speak fluently about the psychopathic personality, quoting the literature extensively and discussing research findings, but they cannot look into their own troublesome antics or mount a reasonable attack on their actions. They articulate their regrets for having done something, but the words are devoid of emotional meaning, a characteristic Cleckley calls **semantic aphasia**. Johns and Quay (1962) remarked that psychopaths "know the words but not the music." Similarly, Grant (1977) notes that the psychopath knows only the book meaning of words, not the living meaning. Hare (1996, p. 45) concludes: "In short, psychopaths appear to be semantically and affectively shallow individuals."

Finally, an important behavioral distinction underlying much of Cleckley's description is what Quay (1965) refers to as the psychopath's profound and pathological stimulation seeking. According to Quay, the actions of the psychopath are motivated by an excessive *neuropsychological* need for thrills and excitement. It is not unusual to see psychopaths drawn to such interests as race car driving, skydiving, and motorcycle stunts. We will examine this alleged need for stimulation in the pages to follow.

THE CRIMINAL PSYCHOPATH

Although some psychopaths have little contact with the criminal justice system, many have continual contact with the system because of persistent offending. In some cases, this persistent offending is extremely violent in nature. Hare (1996, p. 38) posits: "The case with which psychopaths engage in ... dispassionate violence has very real significance for society in general and for law enforcement personnel in particular." Hare refers to a report by the Federal Bureau of Investigation (1992) that found that nearly half of the law enforcement officers who died in the line of duty were killed by individuals who closely matched the personality profile of the psychopath.

Currently, the best measuring instrument of criminal psychopathy is the twenty-two-item **Psychopathy Checklist (PCL)** (Hare, 1980) and its twenty-item revision (**PCL-R**) (Hare, 1991). More recently, a twelve-item version has been developed, called the *Psychopathy Checklist: Screening Version (PCL:SV)* (Hart, Cox, & Hare, 1995; Hart, Hare, & Forth, 1993). All three checklists are conceptually and empirically similar. The instruments are largely based on the Cleckley conception of psychopathy, but are designed primarily to identify psychopaths in male prison, forensic, or psychiatric populations. All three assess the affective, interpersonal, behavioral, and social deviance facets of criminal psychopathy (Hare, Hart, & Harpur, 1991; Hare, 1996). Typically, trained examiners, after a semistructured interview with the inmate and a review of his institutional file, score the inmate 0, 1, or 2, depending on the extent he has the disposition described by each item on the checklist. A score of 30 or above qualifies the inmate as a primary psychopath. Inmates with scores between 21 and 29 are classified as "middle" subjects who show many of the features of psychopathy but do not fit all the criteria. Scores below 21 are considered "nonpsychopaths." So far, the research has strongly supported the reliability and validity of the PCL, PCL-R, and the PCL:SV for distinguishing criminal psychopaths from criminal nonpsychopaths (Hare, Forth, & Stachan, 1992; Hare, 1996). Howard (1990) argues, however, that the PCL may have some problems in distinguishing between psychopaths and those individuals with severe mental disorders, primarily because both groups have a serious deficiency in emotionality.

Current data suggest that about 1 percent of the general population and 15 to 25 percent of incarcerated offenders meet the PCL-R criteria for psychopathy (Hare et al., 1992; Hare, 1996). Moreover, those offenders who meet the PCL-R criteria manifest violent and aggressive behaviors—including verbal abuse, threats, and intimidation—at a much higher rate than other inmate populations (Hare et al., 1991). They are "responsible for a markedly disproportionate amount of the serious crime, violence, and social distress in every society" (Hare, 1996, p. 26). Psychopathy appears to be especially high among convicted rapists, with reports as high as 35 to 43 percent among serial rapists or rapists who killed their victims (Hare, 1996).

Many of the murders and serious assaults committed by nonpsychopaths occurred during domestic disputes or extreme emotional arousal. On the other hand, this pattern of violence is rarely observed for criminal psychopaths (Hare et al., 1991; Williamson, Hare, & Wong, 1987). Criminal psychopaths frequently engage in violence as a form of revenge or retribution, or during a bout of drinking. Many of the attacks of nonpsychopaths are toward women they know well, whereas many of the attacks of criminal psychopaths are directed toward men who are strangers. Hare et al. (1991, p. 395) observe that the violence committed by criminal psychopaths was callous and cold-blooded "without the affective coloring that accompanied the violence of nonpsychopaths." Research also indicates that rapists who have psychopathic characteristics are more likely to have "nonsexual" motivations for their crimes, such as anger, vindictiveness, sadism, and opportunism (Hart & Dempster, 1997).

Research studies report that the recidivism rate of psychopaths is very high. In one study (Serin, Peters, & Barbaree, 1990), the number of failures of male offenders released on unescorted temporary absence program was examined. The failure rate for psychopaths was 37.5 percent, while none of the nonpsychopaths failed. The failure rate during parole was also examined. While 7 percent of nonpsychopaths violated parole requirements, 33 percent of the psychopaths violated their requirements. In another study (Serin & Amos, 1995), 299 males offenders were followed for up to eight years after their release from a federal prison. Sixty-five percent of the psychopaths were convicted of another crime within three years, compared to a reconviction rate of 25 percent for nonpsychopaths. Quinsey, Rice, and Harris (1995) found that within six years of release from prison, more than 80 percent of the psychopaths convicted as sex offenders had violently recidivated, compared to a 20 percent recidivism rate for nonpsychopathic sex offenders. A persistent offending history in conjunction with high scores on the PCL-R are probably one of the most powerful predictors of violent recidivism available anywhere.

What kind of treatment is available for those adult offenders who qualify as psychopaths? Hare (1996, p. 41) asserts: "There is no known treatment for psychopathy." Based on the research examining the effectiveness of various treatment programs, he is right. Hare (1996, p. 41) writes: "This does not necessarily mean that the egocentric and callous attitudes and behaviors of psychopaths are immutable, only that there are no methodologically sound treatments or 'resocialization' programs that have been shown to work with psychopaths. Unfortunately, both the criminal justice system and the public routinely are fooled into believing otherwise." Psychopaths, of course, volunteer for various prison treatment programs and show "remarkable improvement" and present themselves as model prisoners. They are skillful at convincing therapists, counselors, and parole boards that they have changed for the better. Upon release, however, there is a high probability that they will reoffend. In fact, there is some evidence to suggest that psychopaths who participate in therapy are more likely to engage in violent crime following the treatment than those psychopaths who did not receive treatment. Rice, Harris, and Cormier (1992) investigated the effectiveness of an intensive therapeutic community program offered in a maximum security facility. The study was retrospective in that the researchers examined records and files ten years after the program was completed. The results showed that psychopaths who participated in the therapeutic community exhibited higher rates of violent recidivism than did the psychopaths who did not. The results were the reverse for nonpsychopaths: Nonpsychopaths who received treatment were less likely to reoffend than nonpsychopaths who did not receive treatment. The researchers admonish that the psychopaths used in the study were an especially serious group of offenders. Eighty-five percent had a history of violent crimes. Whether less serious psychopathic offenders will show similar results is unknown. The researchers conclude: "(T)he combined results suggest that a therapeutic community is not the treatment of choice for psychopaths, particularly those with extensive criminal histories" (Rice, Harris, & Cormier, 1992, p. 408). Hare (1996) suggests that group therapy and insight-oriented treatment programs may help the psychopath develop better ways of manipulating and deceiving others.

THE FEMALE PSYCHOPATH

There are few statistics on the ratio of male to female psychopaths, but it is generally believed that the males far outnumber their female counterparts. Robins (1966) reports that only 15 percent of the psychopaths in her study were female. Salekin, Rogers, and Sewell (1997) reported that the prevalence rate of psychopathy for female offenders in a jail setting was 15.5 percent, compared to the usual 25 to 30 percent prevalence rate reported for men. Because the known psychopathic population is dominated by men, little research has been directed at the women, although both Hare and Cleckley included female psychopaths in some of their work. However, Hare's PCL and PCL-R have been developed almost exclusively on male criminal psychopaths. Some preliminary studies using the PCL-R suggest that female criminal psychopaths may demonstrate different behavioral patterns than male criminal psychopaths (Hare, 1991).

There is some evidence that female psychopaths are less aggressive and violent than male psychopaths (Mulder, Wells, Joyce, & Bushnell, 1994). Female psychopaths may also recidivate less often than male psychopaths (Salekin, Rogers,

Ustad, & Sewell, 1998). In fact, the evidence suggests that psychopathic female inmates may have recidivism rates that are no different than the recidivism rates reported for nonpsychopathic female inmates (Salekin et al., 1998).

A classic study on female psychopaths was a longitudinal fifteen-year study on women in prison conducted by Guze (1976). Psychopathy, Guze notes, is the most frequent personality diagnosis of women felons. It is often accompanied by diagnoses of alcoholism and "hysteria," an outdated personality disorder attributed to adolescent girls and young women. Guze notes that drug dependence is also significantly more frequent among arrested female psychopaths, appearing in 58 percent of the psychopath population compared to 8 percent of convicted female nonpsychopaths.

Guze found that antisocial symptoms in female psychopaths typically began around age eleven. Forty-two percent of the adult psychopaths had a history of juvenile arrests and runaway status offenses. In a finding reflective of moral biases and discriminatory treatment of women, Guze noted that 65 percent had arrest records for sexual misconduct, such as prostitution. Furthermore, many had a history that included incest and illegitimate pregnancies. It is difficult to separate the status offenses and so-called victimless crimes from the property or violent crimes in Guze's survey. He notes, for example, that recidivism was greatest among psychopaths under age thirty, but it is unclear whether this figure refers to status offenses, adult sexual offenses, or serious crime. Interestingly, 72 percent of the female psychopaths who had ever married had been married at least once to a psychopath or an alcoholic.

Robins (1966) found that female psychopaths followed the same behavioral patterns as male psychopaths, except that they were more frequently involved in sexual misconduct. In her sample, 79 percent of the females displayed abnormally high sexual activity and "excessive" interest in sexual matters. This finding is common in other female psychopath research. In the absence of other behavioral descriptors, it suggests that the psychopath label may have been attached indiscriminately to women who were believed to engage inappropriately in sexual activity.

Cleckley (1976) describes one female psychopath whose nonsexual behavioral characteristics were clearly in evidence before sexual characteristics appeared. "Roberta," a twenty-year-old patient, began to steal small items from stores and from relatives at age ten. As an adolescent, she obtained dresses, cosmetics, candy, perfume, and other articles by charging them to her father without his knowledge. Her schoolwork was mediocre, but her intelligence was clearly superior. She demonstrated overt kindness to animals, but when her own dog was killed by a car, she did not seem to mind. During her teens, she became truant and began to stay out all night. When her parents expressed alarm, she admitted her errors but continued her erratic behavior. Her parents complained that they could not understand her. "It's not that she seems bad or exactly that she means to do wrong," said her father. "She can lie with the straightest face, and after she's found in the most outlandish lies she still seems perfectly easy in her own mind."

When Roberta was expelled from the local high school for excessive truancy, her desperate parents sent her to a series of boarding schools, from which she was either expelled or ran away. Once back home, she added more antisocial habits to her repertoire. Her father employed her as a bookkeeper in his business, but she managed to embezzle considerable sums of money. Attempts to reason with her did nothing to change her behavior; she seemed totally untroubled.

Up to this time, Roberta had displayed little interest in sex and had experienced only mild kissing and "necking," which she found "vaguely" pleasurable. She eventually ran away from home with no purpose except to wander. At this point, she discovered that prostitution was an effective way to obtain money and lodging. When police officers returned her to her home, she ran to her parents, threw herself into their arms, and expressed her affection. She said she was sorry for the distress she had caused them, but the penitence was devoid of feeling. She was unaffected by the inevitable gossip that surrounded her return to her small town (adapted from Cleckley, 1976, pp. 46–55).

In general, research on possible gender differences in psychopathy is complicated by a tendency to equate sexual activity in women with abnormal stimulation-seeking behavior. When "excessive" or "aberrant" sexual activity is separated from other behaviors, female psychopaths may have characteristics largely similar to their male counterparts. Salekin et al. (1997) have found evidence for at least two broad categories of female psychopaths. One category appears to be characterized by a lack of empathy or guilt, interpersonal deception, sensation seeking, and proneness to boredom. The other group appears to be characterized by early behavioral problems, promiscuous sexual behavior, and adult antisocial (not violent) behavior. In recent years we have seen a renewed interest in studying the female psychopath.

RACIAL/ETHNIC DIFFERENCES

Kosson, Smith, and Newman (1990) noticed that most measures of psychopathy have been developed using white inmates as subjects. In their research, they found that psychopathy, as measured by Hare's PCL, does exist in African-American male inmates in a pattern that resembles white male inmates. However, Kosson et al. found one important difference. The African-American criminal psychopaths tended to be less impulsive than white criminal psychopaths. This finding raises some questions as to whether the PCL is entirely appropriate to use with African-American inmates. The racial/ethnic area has been neglected and needs much more research attention.

BASIC NEUROPHYSIOLOGICAL CONCEPTS AND TERMINOLOGY

Contemporary research favors the view that psychopathic behavior results from a complex interaction between neurophysiological and learning or socialization factors. It is important, therefore, to become familiar with additional neuropsychological vocabulary and basic structures of the nervous system, some of which appeared in Chapter 3. The concepts presented here will also lay the foundation for topics in later chapters (e.g., Chapter 7 on aggression and violence, Chapter 10 on sexual offenses, and Chapter 12 on drugs) as well.

The human nervous system can be divided into two major parts, either on the basis of structure or function. The structural division—the way it is arranged physically—is perhaps the clearest distinction.

The central nervous system (CNS) and the peripheral nervous system (PNS) are the two principal parts. The CNS comprises the brain and spinal cord, and the PNS comprises all nerve cells (called neurons) and nerve pathways located outside the CNS (see Table 4-1). In other words, those nerves that leave the spinal cord and brainstem and travel to specific sites in the body belong to the peripheral (outside) nervous system. This includes all the nerves connecting the muscles, skin, heart, glands, and senses to the CNS.

The basic function of the PNS is to bring all the outside information to the CNS, where it is processed. Once the CNS has processed information, it relays the interpretation back to the PNS if action is necessary. When you place your finger on a hot object, the PNS relays this raw datum (it is not yet pain) to the CNS, which interprets the datum as the sensation of pain, and in return, relays a command to the PNS to withdraw the finger. The PNS cannot interpret; it only transmits information to the CNS and carries communications back. In the following pages, we will consider the significance of each of these systems to the diagnosis of psychopathy.

CENTRAL NERVOUS SYSTEM (CNS)

Structurally, the CNS consists of the brain and spinal cord. Interpretation, thoughts, memories, and images all occur in the cerebral cortex (the highest center of the brain). It is the processing center for stimulation and sensations received from the outside world and the body via the PNS. The cerebral cortex, which is the outer surface of the human brain, contains about 10 to 13 billion nerve cells, or neurons. Each neuron has a complicated communication link to numerous other neurons, creating an extremely complex and poorly understood communications network. Although the physical structures of the brain do not directly concern us, the electrical and arousal properties of the cortex are relevant in understanding the electroencephalograms (brainwave patterns) and psychological characteristics of the psychopath.

Table 4-1   Divisions of the Human Nervous System

I. Central Nervous System
   A. Brain
   B. Spinal Cord
II. Peripheral Nervous System
   A. Skeletal Nervous System (communicates with voluntary muscles)
   B. Autonomic Nervous System
      1. Parasympathetic (relaxes and deactivates after emergencies)
      2. Sympathetic (activates for emergencies)

Electrical activity in the CNS became the subject of serious study in the late 1920s, when the German psychiatrist Hans Berger developed sophisticated equipment enabling him to record oscillatory electrical potentials on the scalps of human subjects. The electrical oscillations recorded from the cortex are electroencephalograms (EEGs); the device that records them is the electroencephalograph. Because of the oscillatory characteristics of the EEGs, they are referred to as brainwaves. Berger's technique allowed the study of electrical properties of the brain without discomfort to the subject. His work was not immediately recognized, and it was not until the early 1940s that his discovery accelerated investigations of the brain.

Berger (1929) discovered that when EEG recordings were made of the relaxed adult, usually with eyes closed, the electrical activity generally oscillated between eight and twelve cycles per second (CPS). He called this brainwave pattern, which appeared with some consistency under relaxed conditions, *alpha rhythms*. Nevertheless, he did not know what brain function he was recording. To this day, investigators remain uncertain of the exact meaning of brain rhythms, despite rapid technological advances in recording hardware. Many believe that brainwaves represent the synchronous, almost symphonic firing of billions of neurons, the purpose of which remains unknown. We do know, as did Berger, that the EEG is an ever-changing reflection of the cortex's arousal levels and is sensitive to various changes in both the external and the internal (mood and thought) environments. By studying alpha rhythms, researchers have learned the characteristics of the cortex during sleep, drug ingestion, development, and malfunction, such as epileptic seizures. EEG patterns have also provided us with partial hints about the way the psychopath's cortex functions. Some of the cortical functions of the psychopath appear to be significantly different from the nonpsychopath.

Subsequent to Berger's findings, researchers delineated several other cortical rhythms. The *delta rhythm* spans one-half to three CPS, has high voltage, and indicates that the cortex is at its lowest stage of activity and arousal. The *theta rhythm* has four to seven CPS, less voltage than delta, and represents a stage slightly higher in cortical arousal. Together, delta and theta are often referred to as slow wave activity, because of their relatively low frequency or oscillation rates. Alpha rhythms, which have eight to twelve CPS, represent a higher level of cortical arousal than slow wave activity and are "normal" rhythm for the relaxed adult. *Beta rhythms* have thirteen to thirty CPS, low voltage, and reflect active cognitive processes, thinking, or general arousal states. Beta rhythms are sometimes referred to as desynchronic of alpha, since they occur under conditions that block the occurrence of alpha. For example, if an EEG recording is being made while a person is relaxed with eyes closed and someone suddenly calls out the person's name, there will be an immediate blocking of alpha with resultant beta rhythms. For our purpose, it is important to remember that beta reflects high states of cortical activity and arousal.

EEGs seem to change with age. The delta and theta rhythms that predominate in childhood give way to alpha and beta in normal adulthood, except during sleep, when the delta and theta patterns return. Throughout infancy, childhood, and adolescence, the brain rhythms also become progressively more regular, and the cortex increases its potential for higher states of arousal. At birth, brain rhythms are irregular and often nonexistent. During the first year, delta begins to occur with some regularity on both sides of the brain (Fois, 1961). After the first year, the theta rhythm dominates the EEG pattern, eventually giving way to alpha rhythms, which begin to dominate at about age ten. The alpha gradually becomes regular and usually "matures" at around age fourteen. Beta rhythms develop at around age sixteen. The rhythms in the developing human are particularly susceptible to psychological stress and other factors in the environment. Highly irregular theta rhythms, for example, accompany older children having temper tantrums. They become more regular if the child lies down and calms down. The stages of sleep are also delineated on the basis of brain rhythms, the lighter stages characterized by theta patterns and the deeper stage by deltas. Other things being equal, the more aroused and alert the cortex, the higher the frequency and the lower the voltage of the brainwaves.

Adrian Raine (1993) points out that there have been hundreds of studies examining the EEGs of criminals, delinquents, psychopaths, and violent offenders. Further, Raine notes that a large number of studies (e.g., Volavka, 1987; Milstein, 1988) find a variety of EEG abnormalities in certain criminal populations, especially those populations who engage in *repetitive violent offending*. On the other hand, most of the research has major methodological flaws that make any firm conclusions unwarranted. We now turn our attention to some of the EEG research on psychopathy.

EEG RESEARCH ON PSYCHOPATHS

When researchers discovered that brainwaves could be monitored, they began to hypothesize individual differences in those patterns and to devise experiments to test those hypotheses. In a pioneer study during World War II, Hill and Watterson (1942) investigated the EEG patterns of 151 male British military personnel who were not adjusting to military service and were believed to be psychopathic. The investigators divided the men into three classifications: aggressive, mixed, and inadequate psychopaths. The groups actually represented heterogeneous clusters of personality disorders and obviously failed in many respects to meet Cleckley's or Hare's criteria as we have presented them. One group, however, the aggressive psychopaths, closely resembled Hare's criminal psychopath. Men in this group had a history of "violence to others regardless of the consequences, repeated destruction of property, or a combination of such kinds of aggressive impulsive behavior" (Hill & Watterson, 1942, p. 47). The results indicated that 65 percent of the aggressive psychopaths demonstrated abnormal EEGs, compared to 15 percent of a group of "normals" used as controls. Most abnormal EEGs were of a slow-wave variety—delta and theta; the control group exhibited the usual adult alpha and beta patterns.

This study prompted many other EEG studies using individuals with various kinds of behavior disorders, including psychopathy. Subsequent studies of psychopaths have consistently revealed significantly higher incidences of EEG abnormality of a *slow-wave* variety (e.g., Craft, 1966; Hare, 1970). In a series of studies conducted by Knott and his colleagues (1953), between 49 and 58 percent of seven hundred psychopaths had EEG abnormalities, mostly of a slow-wave variety. It should be noted that between 10 and 15 percent of the general population show abnormal EEGs, with "abnormal" being defined in a number of ways. Additional studies by Ehrlich and Keogh (1956) and Arthur and Cahoon (1964) also found that well over half of the psychopaths measured had abnormal EEGs, with most reflecting slow-wave patterns. It should be noted, however, that many of the EEG studies failed to employ a strict criteria of psychopathy (Raine, 1993), and therefore, some of the research findings may be based on a hodgepodge of criminal populations.

Assuming that many of the EEG studies did use primary psychopaths, it is unclear why many psychopaths display slow-wave activity (immature brainwave patterns). As noted, it is not even clear what cortical functions the EEG represents. Do EEG abnormalities generate psychopathic behavior, or does psychopathic behavior cause EEG abnormality? The answer is not known. It could be that neither causes the other.

Hare (1970) suggests that slow-wave activity represents delayed brain maturation. Since some evidence indicates that EEG patterns of many psychopaths resemble those of children, it is arguable that the brain and cortical functioning of the psychopath is immature and childlike. Hare refers to this as the **maturation retardation hypothesis**, also known as the "maturation lag hypothesis." It is appealing because the behavioral patterns of the psychopath—self-centeredness, impulsivity, inability to delay gratification, and inordinate stimulation seeking—resemble the behaviors of children.

There is also evidence that, with increasing age, the immature EEG patterns of some psychopaths develop into mature ones, and that there is a corresponding change toward more socially approved behavior (Gibbens, Pond, & Stafford-Clark, 1955). Robins (1966) found support for this observation, discovering that the change was most likely to occur between the ages of thirty and forty. It may be that the psychopath's cortex matures later in life than those of the normal adult. It should be emphasized, however, that the EEG evidence to date is sketchy and fragmented, and considerably more data are necessary before a maturation retardation hypothesis deserves widespread support.

In several cross-sectional and longitudinal studies of the criminal histories of male psychopaths and nonpsychopaths, Hare and his colleagues (Hare, McPherson, & Forth, 1988; Hare & Jutai, 1983; Hare, 1986; Harpur & Hare, 1994) did find that the criminal activities of the criminal psychopath decrease at around age forty. The decrease is more dramatic for nonviolent crimes than for violent ones, however (Hare et al., 1992). Hare, McPherson, and Forth (1988) further observe that the psychopath's dramatic decline in prison time and conviction rate after age forty is often preceded by an equally dramatic increase in these variables between the ages of twenty-five and thirty. The reasons for these discernible shifts remain unknown and are largely left to speculation. One popular hypothesis is "burnout." That is, the frequent wear-and-tear of convictions and prison time eventually takes its toll on the antisocial activities of the criminal psychopath. Hare, however, finds the burnout hypothesis highly unlikely because the psychopath is relatively free of stress, tensions, anxieties, and conflicts that typically lead to emotional burnout. Of course, another favorite hypothesis is maturational lag, described earlier. Other hypotheses include learned strategies for remaining out of prison, or the cognitive realization that the future is bleak without changes in lifestyle. After all, even the criminal psychopath may eventually learn after a series of aversive consequences for antisocial behavior. In sum, the available evidence does suggest a reduction in offending (although not necessarily a complete termination of offending) at around age forty for most male criminal psychopaths, but the reasons for this career shift remain unknown. Hare (Hare et al., 1992) cautions, however, that although some psychopaths become less criminal with age, they often remain disagreeable people right into old age. They continue to demonstrate the same egocentric, manipulative, and callous traits characteristic of the psychopath well past forty (Hare, 1996). Moreover, not all psychopaths show a dramatic decrease in gross criminal behavior at middle age but many remain criminally active well beyond age forty.

Positive Spikes   In the late 1950s and early 1960s, some researchers (e.g., Niedermeyer, 1963; Kurland, Yeager, & Arthur, 1963) noticed that a brain rhythm of a different variety occurred during sleep in many psychopaths and highly aggressive individuals. Against a background of the usual slow-wave activity found in sleep, spontaneous bursts of brainwaves with frequencies of six to fourteen CPS appeared in certain locations of the cortex (especially in the temporal lobe) in 66 percent of the aggressive subjects. These individuals had a history of uncontrollable and violent episodes of destructive urges usually triggered by small, trivial slights. The aggressive explosions often resulted in extensive damage to property and injury or death to others. The brain-wave bursts are called positive spikes, and they have also been found to occur in the brainwaves of psychopaths during awakened states. Researchers observe that, following the aggressive episodes, the individual expresses no guilt, but is fully aware of the aggressive or even violent behavior (Hare, 1970).

In sum, contemporary research focusing on central nervous system characteristics reveals definite indications of inordinate amounts of abnormal brainwave patterns, mostly of a childlike nature, in the EEGs of psychopaths. The data suggest that the psychopathic central nervous system is immature and perhaps does not develop fully until around age forty to forty-five. There are also data to suggest that highly aggressive criminal psychopaths may demonstrate other abnormal brainwave patterns, such as positive spikes. We should be cautious, however, in making firm conclusions about the complex relationships between brainwave activity and primary psychopathy. Research conducted two or more decades ago may have used a less precise definition of psychopathy in assigning categories.

HEMISPHERE ASYMMETRY

The human brain can be divided anatomically into two cerebral hemispheres—a right and a left. These two cerebral hemispheres seem to coexist in some sort of reciprocally balancing relationship in cortical functioning and information processing. For most individuals, the right hemisphere specializes in nonverbal functions, whereas the left specializes in verbal or language functions. Furthermore, the left hemisphere processes information in an analytical, sequential fashion. Language, for example, requires sequential cognition and the left seems to be the best equipped for this operation. The right hemisphere, on the other hand, seems to process information holistically and more globally. For example, the right is involved in the recognition of faces, a complicated process requiring the processing of information all at once or simultaneously. Thus, the right and left hemispheres are two functionally differentiated information processing systems.

In addition to information processing, research is now finding that these two cerebral hemispheres also make different contributions to human emotions. The right hemisphere appears to be particularly important in the understanding and communication of emotion. The left seems to be closely tied to self-inhibiting processes, in contrast to the right which appears to be more spontaneous and impulsive (Tucker, 1981). Furthermore, the two hemispheres must have a balance of contribution from each for normal judgment and appropriate self-control (Tucker, 1981).

Hare (Hare & Connolly, 1987; Hare & McPherson, 1984) hypothesizes that criminal psychopaths manifest an abnormal or unusual balance between the two hemispheres, both in language processing and in emotional or arousal states. Hare notes that criminal psychopaths are often strikingly inconsistent with their verbalized thoughts, feelings, and intentions. Criminal psychopaths seem to be highly peculiar in the organization of certain perceptual and cognitive processes. It seems as though their left hemisphere is, in some ways, deficient in linguistic processing because they do not rely on the verbal sequential operations to the extent that a majority of individuals do. Since language plays a very important role in the self-regulation of behavior, one of the contributing factors in the extremely impulsive, episodic behavior of psychopaths may reside in some deficiency in their use of internal language. This characteristic was pointed out some time ago by Flor-Henry (Flor-Henry, 1973; Flor-Henry & Yeudall, 1973), who was convinced that psychopathy is closely linked to left-hemispheric language dysfunction.

Nachshon (Nachshon, 1983; Nachshon & Denno, 1987) points out that many studies have found that a disproportionate percentage of violent, repetitive offenders have left hemispheric dysfunction. Moreover, several researchers have argued that left-handedness may be an indicator of left hemispheric dysfunction and have predicted that left-handedness will be overrepresented in the criminal or psychopathic population. Fitzhugh (1973) reported that about one-third of a group of juvenile delinquents were left-handed, while Andrew (1978) found that about one out of five adult male offenders preferred their left hand. However, in a later study, Andrew (1980) reported that the left handers seemed to be less violent than right-handed offenders. On the other hand, Nachshon and Denno (1987), in their investigation of 1,066 black male children—whose mothers participated in the Philadelphia Collaborative Perinatal Project—found that nonoffenders (based on official statistics) showed a significantly higher incidence of left-handedness than offenders. Thus, the research results are far from conclusive. Researchers have used different samples, have not been very definitive about their sample composition, and have used a variety of procedures and methods in obtaining and analyzing the data. Much more needs to be done before we can entertain any conclusions about left versus right preferences or left versus right hemispheric functioning in criminal or psychopathic populations.

FRONTAL NEUROPSYCHOLOGICAL STUDIES

Some studies suggest that psychopaths may suffer from frontal lobe problems or dysfunctions. The frontal lobe refers to that section of the cerebral cortex we commonly call the forehead. It is believed to be responsible for foresight, planning, and regulation of impulses. Gorenstein (1982) and Newman, Patterson, and Kossen (1987) report findings that indicate psychopaths may have some defects in frontal lobe processing. On the other hand, research by Hare (1984), Hoffman, Hall, and Bartsch (1987), and Sutker and Allain (1983) failed to support the frontal lobe hypothesis.

At this point, the evidence for the frontal lobe hypothesis is, at best, weak and confusing. Furthermore, frontal lobe dysfunction may not be simply limited to psychopaths, but may be a feature characteristic of many other types of offenders (Raine, 1993).

STIMULATION SEEKING

Quay (1965) suggests that the psychopath's behavior represents an extreme form of stimulation seeking. Physiologically, psychopaths do not receive the full impact of sensations from the environment. Therefore, in order to get the optimal amount of stimulation necessary to keep the cerebral cortex satisfied, they must engage more frequently in exciting forms of behavior.

Several studies have supported Quay's hypothesis. For example, Wiesen (1965) found that psychopaths worked harder for visual (colored lights) and auditory (music on a radio) stimulation than did a group of nonpsychopaths. In a second experiment that provided continued bombardment of lights and music, Wiesen also demonstrated that nonpsychopaths worked harder than psychopaths to obtain three seconds of silence and relative darkness.

Skrzpek (1969) delineated psychopaths and "neurotic delinquents" on the basis of a behavior rating list for psychopathy and neuroticism developed by Quay (1964). He found that conditions that increased "cortical arousal" (e.g., where the subject was required to make difficult auditory discriminations) decreased preference for visual complexity in both the psychopathic and neurotic groups, but was most pronounced in the latter. On the other hand, a brief period of stimulus deprivation (presumably low cortical arousal) increased preference for complexity in both groups, but a significantly greater increase was shown by the psychopaths.

In an attempt to test Quay's hypothesis that deficient responsivity of the nervous system might account for pathological stimulation seeking, Whitehill, DeMyer-Gapin, and Scott (1976) conducted an experiment using 103 boring slides of "concrete facades of a modern college campus building." As subjects, the researchers used fifty-five institutionalized "disturbed" preadolescent boys. The professional staff at the institution rated eight boys psychopathic (antisocial) and eight neurotic. A group of seven "normal" noninstitutionalized adolescent boys, matched with the index subjects for age, were used as controls. The average age was 11.5. Results showed that the psychopathic and normal boys looked at the slides significantly less than the neurotic group. More importantly, the psychopathic preadolescents showed a significant decrease in viewing time earlier than the other groups, suggesting that they became bored more quickly than the other groups. Whitehall concluded that the data support the pathological stimulation-seeking hypothesis and favored a physiological ingredient in the formulation of psychopathy. In another project, Orris (1969) found that, compared to nonpsychopaths, psychopathic boys performed more poorly on a boring task requiring continuous attention and that they engaged more in boredom-relieving activities like singing or talking to themselves.

OPTIMAL AROUSAL OF THE CEREBRAL CORTEX

A number of theorists have postulated (e.g., Berlyne, 1960; Hebb, 1955; Fiske & Maddi, 1961) that organisms seek to maintain preferred or optimal levels of stimulation, with stimulation referring to the amount of sensation and/or information processed by the cortex. In effect, their theories argue for an inverted U-shaped function, with intermediate levels of stimulation most preferred and the extremes least preferred (see Figure 4-1). Insufficient amounts of stimulation lead to boredom, which can be reduced by an increase in stimulation-seeking behavior. On

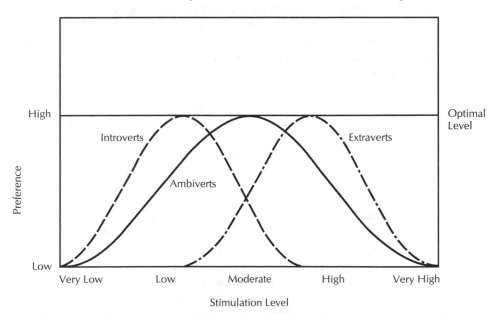

Figure 4-1 Optimal Levels of Stimulation for Ambiverts, Introverts, and Extraverts
(Note that introverts reach their optimal level sooner than ambiverts or extraverts do.)

the other hand, exceptionally high levels of stimulation are also aversive and may promote behavior designed to avoid stimulation in an effort to bring the stimulus input to a more pleasurable level.

Cortical arousal appears to have a direct relationship with the amount of stimulation received by the cortex. Low stimulation produces a relatively low level of cortical arousal, whereas high levels of stimulation initiate high cortical arousal. To fall asleep, we must lower the cortex's arousal level by minimizing external and internal stimulation (noises, lights, thoughts). If we do not wish to fall asleep, but our cortical arousal is low (e.g., during a boring lecture), we seek excitement to increase the arousal level. On the other hand, if stimulation becomes excessive, such as via a blaring radio or the pandemonium of rush hour traffic, we are distressed if unable to control the stimulus input. Some psychologists argue that much behavior can be explained as an attempt by the person to maintain optimal or just-right levels of stimulation—levels that are the most comfortable and pleasurable to the individual.

It is generally agreed that there are individual differences in the quality and quantity of stimulation necessary for each person to reach the hypothetic optimum. Some of this individual difference may be attributed to certain physiological structures, particularly those found in the brainstem. Eysenck (1967), you will recall, hypothesized that personality differences are largely due to differential needs for stimulation, which are dictated by functional properties of the reticular formation.

The reticular formation can be conveniently divided into several anatomical areas. Chief among these is the reticular activating system (RAS), a tiny but complex nerve network located in the central portion of the brainstem. The RAS underlies our attentiveness to the world and acts as a sentinel that activates the cortex and keeps it alert. Sensory signals or inputs from all parts of the body must travel through the brainstem on their way to the processing center, the cortex. Inside the brainstem, they branch into two major pathways (see Figure 3-3). One major pathway goes through a relay station known as the thalamus; the other travels through the RAS which, in turn, alerts the cortex to incoming information being routed through the thalamic pathway. The RAS-generated arousal is nonspecific in that it energizes the entire cortex and not any specific area. Therefore, any particular stimulation or sensation, from the outside world or from inside the body, has both a coded message (which travels through the thalamus) and a nonspecific arousing effect (which travels through the RAS).

The RAS can also decrease cortical arousal. If certain incoming stimuli are no longer significant or relevant, the cortex "tells" the RAS to filter out that particular group of stimuli. That process is called adaptation or **habituation**. Therefore, repetitive and insignificant stimuli are prevented by the RAS from unnecessarily bombarding the cortex with meaningless detail.

Contemporary research and theory suggests that the psychopath has a pathological need for excitement and thrills because of some deficiency in or excessive habituation property of the RAS. We emphasize the word "suggest" because, while the research seems consistent in demonstrating that psychopaths appear to have a strong need for stimulation, research has not clearly identified what neurophysiological mechanisms are involved. However, mainstream theory concerning the neurophysiological processes are as follows. The RAS either does not activate the cortex sufficiently to receive the full impact of the incoming information, or else it adapts too quickly, thereby shutting down the cortex's activation before it receives complete information. Either way, the psychopath is unable to reach optimal arousal levels with the same amount of stimulation that normals find adequately arousing. So, the psychopath engages in behaviors that society refers to as thrill-seeking, chancy, antisocial, or inappropriate in order to reach satisfying optimal cortical arousal.

The general concept of arousal has been used interchangeably with cortical arousal throughout this chapter. In discussing psychopathy, many investigators refer to other forms of arousal, like autonomic (anxiety) or behavior arousal. Basically, these terms mean the same thing. Many states of activation or arousal involve overlapping systems (Korman, 1974). Thus, although there may be slightly different processes and mechanisms involved in different states of arousal, all must involve the heightened arousal levels of the cortex.

In an interesting experiment, Chesno and Kilmann (1975) tested the arousal hypothesis of psychopathy by manipulating stimulation variables (aversive white noise and shock) and personality variables (psychopaths, neurotics, and normals). Ninety male offenders incarcerated in a maximum security penitentiary were selected for the experiment by various criteria. Psychopaths were classified according to Cleckley's criteria. The procedure involved an avoidance learning task, with electric shock being administered for certain incorrect choices by the subject. During the avoidance learning task, each subject received either 35, 65, or 95 decibels of white noise through earphones. (White noise is an auditory stimulus that sounds like a hissing radiator.)

If the arousal hypothesis is correct, the underaroused psychopath under low levels of stimulation should require some form of increased stimulation. Since errors in avoidance learning led to electric shock, psychopaths would be most likely to commit errors and benefit by the stimulation provided by the electric shock. Accordingly, as external stimulation increases (higher levels of white noise), the psychopath should have a decreased need for stimulation and, therefore, should learn to avoid the shock more effectively. The results of the study supported the hypothesis. Psychopaths made significantly more avoidance errors than the other groups as the stimulation decreased, which suggests that they prefer punishment to boredom. The finding may explain the well-known inability of psychopaths to benefit from punishment in situations low in stimulation, like prisons or even classrooms. It might even be that imprisoned psychopaths would "learn better" if the conditions under which they were incarcerated were more stimulating.

Therefore, psychopaths apparently do not learn to avoid aversive circumstances because of underarousal. However, if their arousal is increased, their avoidance learning should correspondingly increase. Furthermore, there is evidence that if incentives (e.g., money or other rewards) are used, avoidance learning in psychopaths also increases. In summarizing the research on this topic, Newman and his colleagues (Newman, Patterson, Howland, & Nichols, 1990; Newman & Kosson, 1986; Newman, 1987) have been very active in studying how rewards or incentives change the avoidance learning patterns of psychopaths. With adequate incentives, psychopaths become highly motivated to learn certain tasks and requirements. In fact, psychopaths under incentive conditions may learn better than nonpsychopaths. Raine (1993, p. 228) writes: "Psychopaths do indeed learn poorly when the reinforcer is physical or social punishment, but they do appear to learn well when (1) their arousal is increased, or (2) they are sufficiently motivated by financial incentives."

PERIPHERAL NERVOUS SYSTEM

The PNS is subdivided into a *skeletal division*, comprising the motor nerves that innervate the skeletal muscles involved in body movement, and an *autonomic division*, which controls heart rate, gland secretion, and smooth muscle activity. Smooth muscles are those muscles found in the blood vessels and gastrointestinal system; they look smooth under a microscope in comparison to the skeletal muscles, which look striped or textured.

The autonomic segment of the PNS is extremely relevant to our discussion of the psychopath, because here, too, research has consistently uncovered a significant difference between the psychopath's and the general population's reactivity or responsiveness to stimuli. The autonomic division is especially important, because it activates emotional behavior and responsivity to stress and tension. It can be subdivided into the *sympathetic* and *parasympathetic systems* (see Figure 3-4).

The sympathetic system is responsible for activating or arousing the individual for fight or flight before (or during) fearful or emergency situations. As you will recall, the psychopath displays a James Bond-like coolness, even in stressful situations. We might explain this in one of two ways. Either the sympathetic nervous system does not react sufficiently to stressful stimuli, or the parasympathetic system springs into action in the psychopath more rapidly than in nonpsychopaths. There is research support for both of these positions.

Before discussing in more detail the psychopath's autonomic nervous system, we should note the principles and techniques of measuring autonomic activity. Emotional arousal, which is largely under the control of the autonomic nervous system, can be measured by monitoring the system's activity, such as heart rate, blood pressure or volume, and respiration rate. The most commonly used physiological indicator of emotional arousal, however, is skin conductance response (SCR), also known as the galvanic skin response (GSR). Since skin conductance response is the label most advocated by contemporary researchers (Lykken & Venables, 1971), it will be used throughout this chapter.

SCR is simply a measure of the resistance of the skin to conducting electrical current. Although a number of factors in the skin influence its resistance, perspiration seems to play a major role. Perspiration corresponds very closely to changes in emotional states and has, therefore, been found to be a highly sensitive indicator of even slight changes in the autonomic nervous system. Other things being equal, as emotional arousal increases, perspiration rate increases proportionately. Small changes in perspiration can be picked up and amplified by recording devices, known as polygraphs or physiographs. An increase in perspiration lowers skin resistance to electrical conductance. In other words, skin conductance increases as emotional arousal (anxiety, fear, and so on) increases.

We noted earlier that psychopaths lack the capacity to respond emotionally to stressful or fearful situations. Essentially, they give the impression of being anxiety-free, carefree, and cool, and they display a devil-may-care attitude. We would expect, therefore, that compared to the normal population, the psychopath has a comparatively underactive, underaroused autonomic nervous system. What has the research literature revealed?

AUTONOMIC NERVOUS SYSTEM RESEARCH

In a pioneering study, Lykken (1957) hypothesized that since anxiety reduction is an essential ingredient in learning to avoid painful or stressful situations, and since the psychopath is presumed to be anxiety-free, then the psychopath should have special difficulty learning to avoid unpleasant things. Recall that two characteristic features of psychopaths are their inability to learn from unpleasant experiences and their very high recidivism. Lykken carefully delineated his research groups according to Cleckley's criteria. His psychopaths (both males and females) were drawn from several penal institutions in Minnesota and were classified as either primary or neurotic psychopaths. College students comprised a third group of normals.

Lykken designed an electronic maze that subjects were expected to learn as well as possible in twenty trials. There were twenty choice points in the maze, each with four alternatives, with only one being the correct choice. Although three alternatives were incorrect, only one of these would give the subject a rather painful electric shock. Lykken was primarily interested in discovering how quickly subjects learned to avoid the shock, a process called **avoidance learning**. He reasoned that avoidance learning would be rewarded by the reduction of anxiety on encountering the correct choice point, but since psychopaths are presumably deficient in anxiety, their performance should be significantly worse than that of normals. The hypothesis was supported.

Prior to the maze portion of the experiment, Lykken measured the skin conductance changes of each subject while he or she tried to sit quietly for thirty to forty minutes. During this time, the subjects would periodically hear a buzzer and occasionally receive a slight, brief electric shock several seconds after the buzzer. Eventually, the buzzer became associated with the shock. In normal individuals, the sound of the buzzer itself produced an anxiety response in anticipation of the electric shock (classical conditioning) and was reflected by a substantial increase in SCR. Psychopaths, however, were considerably less responsive to this stress. Furthermore, psychopaths were incapable of learning to avoid the painful electric shocks, while the normals learned significantly better.

Lykken's data indicate that psychopaths do in fact have an underresponsive autonomic nervous system and, as a result, do not learn to avoid aversive situations as well as most other people. More recent research continues to support these findings (Ogloff & Wong, 1990). Does this provide at least a partial explanation for why psychopaths continue to get into trouble with the law, despite the threat of imprisonment?

Schachter and Latane (1964) followed up on Lykken's work by using similar apparatus and basic procedures, with the exception of one major revision. Each subject was run through the maze twice, once with an injection of a harmless saline solution, once with an injection of adrenaline, a hormone that stimulates physiological arousal. Subjects were prisoners selected on the basis of two criteria: how closely they approximated Cleckley's primary psychopath and how incorrigible they were, as measured by the number of offenses and time in prison. Prisoners high on both criteria were primary psychopaths; prisoners relatively low were normals.

Injections of adrenaline dramatically improved the performance of the psychopath in the avoidance learning task. In fact, with adrenaline injections, the psychopaths learned to avoid shocks more quickly than did normal prisoners with similar injections. On the other hand, when psychopaths had saline injections, they were as deficient in avoidance learning as Lykken's psychopaths.

Since anxiety is presumed to be a major deterrent to antisocial impulses, the manipulation of arousal or anxiety states by drugs may suggest policy implications for the effective treatment of convicted psychopaths. Specific drugs apparently have the potential to increase the emotional level of psychopaths to a point equivalent to the level of the general population.

Subsequent research by Hare (1965a, 1965b) found that primary psychopaths have significantly lower skin conductance while resting than do nonpsychopaths. In a major study, Hare (1968) divided fifty-one inmates at the British Columbia Penitentiary into three groups—primary psychopaths, secondary psychopaths, and nonpsychopaths—and studied them under various conditions, while constantly monitoring their autonomic functioning. The experimental conditions also permitted the observation of a complex physiological response known as the orienting response (OR).

The OR is a nonspecific, highly complicated cortical and sensory response to strange, unexpected changes in the environment. The response may take the form of a turning of the head, a dilation of the eye, or a decrease in heart rate. It is made in an effort to determine what the change is. Pavlov referred to the OR as the "what-is-it" reflex. It is an automatic, reflexive accompaniment to any perceptible change, and it can be measured by various physiological indices. The OR produces, among other things, an increase in the analytical powers of the senses and the cortex.

Hare found that not only did psychopaths exhibit very little autonomic activity (skin conductance and heart rate), but also that they gave smaller ORs than did nonpsychopaths. His data suggest that psychopaths are less sensitive and alert to their environment, particularly to new and unusual events.

Hare later reported intriguing data relating to the heart or cardiac activity of the psychopath. The aforementioned conclusions were based on skin conductance data. When cardiovascular variables are considered, however, some apparent anomalies appear. While skin conductance is consistently low, cardiac activity (heart rate) in the psychopath is often as high as that found in the nonpsychopathic population (Hare & Quinn, 1971). Hare comments, "The psychopaths appeared to be poor electrodermal [skin conductance] conditioners but good cardiovascular ones" (Hare, 1976, p. 135). That is, although psychopaths do not learn to react to stimuli as measured by skin variables, it appears that they learn to react autonomically as well as nonpsychopaths when the heart rate is measured. Hare suggests that the psychopath might be more adaptive to stress when "psychophysiological defense mechanisms" are brought into play, thereby reducing the impact of stressful stimuli.

Hare and his colleagues designed experiments in which the heart rate could be monitored throughout the experimental session. In one experiment, a tone preceded an electric shock by about ten seconds (Hare & Craigen, 1974). In anticipation of the shock, psychopaths exhibited a rapid acceleration of heartbeat, followed by a rapid deceleration of heart rate immediately before the onset of the noxious stimulus (a "normal" reaction is a gradual but steady increase in heart rate until the shock). However, their skin conductance remained significantly lower than that of nonpsychopaths. Therefore, psychopaths appear to be superior conditioners when cardiac activity is measured, indicating that they do indeed either learn or inherit autonomic adaptability to noxious stimuli. Hare suggests that this accelerative heart response is adaptive and helps the psychopath tune out or modulate the emotional impact of noxious stimuli. This, he speculates, may be the reason that skin conductance responses are relatively low in the psychopath.

Lykken (1955) also conducted experiments testing the performance of psychopaths on polygraph equipment. If psychopaths are generally underaroused, we would expect that lie detectors would be unable to differentiate their deceptive from their truthful responses, since polygraphs rely on physiological reactivity to questions. Also, psychopaths should have no trouble being deceptive, since they are typically adept at manipulating and deceiving others. Lykken's research confirmed these expectancies. Psychopaths emitted similar skin conductance responses, regardless of whether they were lying or telling the truth. Nonpsychopaths displayed significant differences in reactivity; their lie ratios, reflected by skin conductance, were larger than those of psychopaths. Because of the artificial atmosphere of the laboratory compared to real-life situations, particularly stressful ones, Lykken admonished against uncritical acceptance of his findings until further testing.

Few studies have since directly examined the relationship between psychopathy and lie detection. However, Raskin and Hare (1978) did re-examine the Lykken study, using more sophisticated equipment and better standardization for lie detection. Using twenty-four psychopathic prisoners and twenty-four nonpsychopathic prisoners, they found that both groups were equally easily detected at lying about a situation involving a $20 mock theft. This contradictory finding underscores the fact that fine tuning is still needed if we are to understand the neurophysiological characteristics of the psychopath.

There is evidence, for example, that sufficiently aroused or motivated psychopaths will give physiological responses to interesting events that equal the responses of nonpsychopaths (Hare, 1968). On the other hand, when it comes to highly stressful, serious occasions, psychopaths appear to have incomparable skill at attenuating guilt or aversive reactions (Lykken, 1978). The simulated crime scene in the Raskin-Hare experiment was not only relatively unstressful; it may also have been regarded by the psychopath as an interesting "game." The acid test for the lie detection hypothesis will rest with carefully designed experiments under real-life, highly stressful situations. The present data do not justify firm conclusions. Christopher Patrick and his colleagues (Patrick, Bradley, & Lang, 1993) conducted a study designed to test in what ways the startled reflex action in psychopaths differs from the normal population. These researchers note that psychophysiological research on the psychopath has relied almost exclusively on skin conductance and cardiovascular measures. The researchers found that criminal psychopaths (measured by Hare's PCL-R) exhibited much lower startled responses under aversive conditions than nonpsychopaths. Their findings confirm previous research showing that criminal psychopaths give smaller autonomic responses under aversive conditions than do other nonpsychopathic offenders. Hare (1993, 1996) postulates that psychopaths suffer from a general "hypoemotionality." That is, it appears that psychopaths fail to experience the full impact of any kind of emotion—positive or negative. The psychopath may be born with this hypoemotionality and that may account for their lack of remorse throughout their lifetimes.

In summary, the research reviewed thus far allows us to make four tentative conclusions about the autonomic functioning of the psychopath. First, psychopaths appear to be both autonomically and cortically underaroused, both under rest conditions and under some specific stress conditions. They are much more physiologically "drowsy" than nonpsychopaths. Second, because they lack the necessary emotional equipment, psychopaths appear to be deficient in avoidance learning, which might account partially for their very high recidivism rates. Third, some data suggest that if emotional arousal can be induced, such as by adrenaline, psychopaths can learn from past experiences and avoid normally painful or aversive situations, such as prison, embarrassment, or social censure. And fourth, with adequate incentives, such as monetary rewards, psychopaths can learn from past experiences and avoid aversive consequences as well as anyone.

Adrian Raine (1993), in his excellent review of the relevant research, finds that many of these psychophysiological indicators discussed for psychopaths may be characteristic of repetitive, violent offenders in general. In fact, in reference to *resting heart rate* levels in *noninstitutionalized offenders*, he concludes: "This is probably the best replicated and most robust biological finding on antisocial behavior reported to date" (p. 190).

We noted earlier that psychopaths are profoundly affected by alcohol, even in small amounts. Alcohol is a general CNS depressant, decreasing arousal levels in the nervous system. Research indicates that underaroused psychopaths are already half asleep and "half in the bag"; alcohol has the general effect of "bagging" them completely. Therefore, we would expect not only that the psychopath would get intoxicated more rapidly than the nonpsychopath of comparable weight, but also would probably pass out sooner. We would also expect the psychopath to have few sleep difficulties. Steven Smith and Joseph Newman (1990) found that a higher percentage of criminal psychopaths have been polydrug users when compared to criminal nonpsychopaths. In addition, criminal psychopaths were particularly heavy alcohol abusers, and alcohol may have played a very significant role in prompting their extensive antisocial behavior.

CHILDHOOD OF THE PSYCHOPATH

We have discussed the behavioral descriptions and biopsychological components of psychopaths. Now, how did they get that way? Criminal behavior and other behavior problems are often assumed to be rooted in the home, usually in homes with conflict, inadequate discipline, or poor models. From our discussion of the biopsychological components of psychopaths, however, it is obvious that the answer is not that simple. Psychopathy seems to be a result of a highly complex interaction of biopsychological, situational, and learning factors.

Cleckley (1976) is not convinced that any common precursors exist in the family backgrounds of psychopaths, even though relatively homogeneous classifications of psychopathy do exist. However, even if we accept that neurophysiological factors may be causal factors in the development of psychopathy, this does not mean they are hereditary. In fact, there is little evidence to support a strong genetic influence on psychopathy. It is possible, though, that psychopaths are born with a biological predisposition to develop the disorder, independent of any genetic factors. In line with the Eysenckian view, it could be that psychopaths have a nervous system that interferes with rapid conditioning and association between transgression and punishment. Because of this defect, the psychopath fails to anticipate punishment and, hence, feels no guilt (no conscience). As an alternative to the defect argument, it is possible that certain aspects of the psychopath's nervous system simply have not matured. Another possibility is that a lack of oxygen at birth or early in development adversely affected the RAS.

It appears that psychopathy can be identified early. In a poll of Canadian psychiatrists, 12.7 percent were convinced that the psychopath could be diagnosed prior to age eight, and another 66 percent believed that the disorder could be identified before age eighteen (Gray & Hutchison, 1964). The DSM-IV specifies that in order to qualify as having an antisocial personality disorder, certain behavioral patterns must be evident before age fifteen. In a longitudinal study conducted by Robins (1966), clinical records verified that 95 percent of adult psychopaths investigated had demonstrated psychopathic behaviors thirty years previously, as children. After an extensive review of the literature, Quay (1972) notes that psychopathic behaviors in adults are probably labeled "conduct disorders" or "excessive aggressiveness" in children. Childhood behaviors that elicit those labels include extreme disobedience, disruptiveness, fighting, temper tantrums, irresponsibility, and attention seeking.

ADHD AND PSYCHOPATHY

Considerable research has linked the psychopath's inordinate stimulation needs with the behavior of the ADHD (attention deficit/hyperactive disorder) child. If the psychopath's physiological underarousal is based on a dysfunction of the nervous system, we would expect to find the same lack of responsivity during his or her childhood. Some hyperactive children, then, may be candidates for adult psychopathy.

In a thirty-year follow-up of children seen in a child guidance clinic, Robins (1966) found that approximately one-third of those children showing hyperactivity symptoms were diagnosed psychopathic. Similar to neurophysiological features of the psychopath, ADHD appears to be closely linked to low levels of cortical arousal (Satterfield, 1978, 1987).

In an ongoing longitudinal study begun in the mid-1970s and conducted by the Long Island Jewish Medical Center in combination with the New York State Psychiatric Institute, 16 percent of the individuals diagnosed ADHD were abusing drugs, compared to 3 percent of the controls (Cowley, 1993). Twenty-seven percent (versus 8 percent of the controls) had been diagnosed as having antisocial personalities. "By their early 20s, the kids from the hyperactive group were twice as likely to have arrest records, five times as likely to have felony convictions and nine times as likely to have served time in prison" (Cowley, 1993, p. 48). Still, we will need to distinguish between ASPs and criminal psychopathy before tentative conclusions can be advanced.

Stimulant drugs (particularly Ritalin) are often prescribed to relieve the excessive hyperactivity. You might expect that stimulants would increase rather than decrease motor activity. However, they appear to have a specific influence on the RAS and other brainstem structures, improving their efficiency and allowing more arousal and/or information to reach the cortex (e.g., Bartol, 1975). Thus, the use of stimulant drugs to control hyperactive children has a paradoxical effect.

If hyperactive children have low cortical arousal, they will require greater amounts of stimulation to reach their optimal level of arousal. Cantwell (1975) notes that hyperactive children do not display greater amounts of motor activity on the playground, but rather in such places as the classroom, where they are required to control stimulus input. In these situations, it is likely that the arousal level drops below their normal requirement. Thus, the underaroused child will seek increased amounts of stimulation and excitement. One way of getting this is to "cut up" in the classroom and upset others, behavior which is very similar to that of the adult psychopath, who "cuts up" in society.

If children receive adequate stimulus input, such as would be provided by stimulant drugs affecting the activity of the RAS, they no longer need the surplus activity, stimulation, or personal attention. This explanation may account for the fact that behavior modification techniques have been largely ineffective for treating classroom ADHD.

After an extensive review of the literature on hyperactive children, Cantwell (1975) found a common thread in adult psychopathy and childhood ADHD. Note in the following quote, however, that he uses sociopath as a synonym for psychopath, which we have warned against doing earlier in this chapter:

> Recent research on waking autonomic functions and EEG patterns in sociopathic adults and in hyperactive children suggest that both groups may have the same underlying neurophysical abnormality: lower levels of basal resting physiological activation than age-matched normals.... It would also suggest that ... there may be a genetically transmitted neurophysiological abnormality that leads to hyperactivity in childhood and sociopathy in adulthood. (Cantwell, 1975, p. 199)

The problem with the Cantwell review, of course, is the equation of psychopathy and sociopathy. It is impossible to tell whether the literature he cites was based on true psychopaths or antisocial individuals with a long history of criminal behavior (sociopaths).

Mendelson, Johnson, and Steward (1971) interviewed the mothers of eighty-three children, ages twelve to sixteen, who had been diagnosed hyperactive several years earlier. Seventy-five percent of the children were still exhibiting hyperactive behavior at follow-up. Mothers complained that the children had a "rebellious attitude" and were generally incorrigible. According to Mendelson, 22 percent of the children continued to demonstrate excessive antisocial behavior and seemed destined to become psychopaths. About 60 percent had had contact with the police, 17 percent on at least three occasions. Twenty-five percent of this group had been referred to juvenile court. More than a third of the 83 children had threatened to kill their parents, 7 percent carried weapons, and 15 percent had set fires.

Similar findings were reported by Weiss, Minde, Werry, Douglas, and Nemeth (1971) in a five-year follow-up study of adolescents who had earlier been diagnosed hyperactive. A great majority of mothers (70 percent) complained that "emotional immaturity" was their child's biggest problem. Thirty percent of the children had no steady friends at follow-up. Twenty-five percent continued to exhibit antisocial behavior regularly. Sixteen percent had been referred to court, and 3 percent were in a reform school at the time of the follow-up study.

Satterfield (1987) examined the relationship between official arrests and ADHD. The study was an eight-year longitudinal analysis of 150 hyperactive and 88 normal children. The data revealed that hyperactives were far more likely to have been arrested for serious crimes than normal children. Moreover, hyperactives were twenty-five times more likely to have been institutionalized for antisocial behavior than normals.

Research on neurophysiological factors in hyperactive children also supports a link between psychopathy and ADHD. Several studies have found that 40 to 50 percent of hyperactive children have abnormal EEGs (Satterfield, 1973; Capute, Niedermeyer, & Richardson, 1968; Hughes, Crawford, Barker, Schumann, & Jaffe,

1971), especially reflected in abnormal slow-wave activity. You may recall that this cortical feature is common in adult psychopathy. In another series of studies, Satterfield and colleagues (Satterfield & Dawson, 1971; Satterfield, Atoian, Brashears, Burleigh, & Dawson, 1974) found that many hyperactive children consistently demonstrated low skin conductance levels. The lower their skin conductance level, the greater their restlessness, hyperactivity, and impulsiveness as reported by their teachers. The children showing the lowest arousal (lowest skin conductance and cortical arousal as measured by EEGs) were most responsive to stimulants (specifically, methylphenidate). Following the drug treatment, the children showed a significant increase in arousal as measured by skin conductance and EEGs and a decrease in motor activity.

Recent research has focused on developing a more refined classification system of the hyperactive syndrome (Satterfield, 1987; af Klinteberg et al., 1989). Much of the study has been directed at distinguishing between "pure" hyperactivity, characterized by a high degree of impulsivity, and "aggressive" hyperactivity, characterized by hostility and aggressiveness. In fact, af Klinteberg et al., (1989) suggest that impulsivity may be a better predictor of adult criminal behavior than aggressiveness.

Other recent research also continues to support the relationship between ADHD and criminal psychopathy (Loeber & Stouthamer-Loeber, 1998). Rolf Loeber and Magda Stouthamer-Loeber (1998, p. 246) point out that ADHD appears to do three things in development of repetitive aggressive and violent behavior: (1) It is associated with poor cognitive and academic functioning; (2) it is implicated in the maintenance of oppositional (antisocial) behavior; and (3) it activates an early, accelerated development of aggressive behaviors, conduct problems, and substance abuse.

From the aforementioned research, it appears likely that some childhood ADHD is a precursor of some adult psychopathy, a finding that underscores the neurophysiological factors in psychopathy. In general, however, with the exception of the work on ADHD, few studies have been directed at the neurophysiological components of potential psychopaths during early childhood.

A more fruitful avenue for exploring the childhood of the psychopath—especially the criminal psychopath—would be close examination of the life-course-persistent (LCP) offender described by developmental theorists, particularly Terrie Moffitt and her colleagues. The reader will recall that this theory was explored in Chapter 2 in some detail. Developmental theory postulates that LCP offenders manifest antisocial behavior across all kinds of conditions and situations in their childhoods. Neurologically, LCPs demonstrate a variety of minor neuropsychological disorders, such as difficult temperaments as infants, attention deficit disorders or hyperactivity as children, and learning and language problems as adolescents. Socially, LCPs are rejected by their peers during their preteen years and are annoying to adults. Emotionally, they exhibit virtually no empathy or concern for others, show very little bonding to family, and often are sadistic and manipulative. They are highly impulsive and lack insight. As they develop, LCPs commit a wide assortment of aggressive and violent crimes across life spans. A careful reading of LCPs developmental histories often shows a striking resemblance to the symptomology of criminal psychopaths.

PARENTAL LOSS

Research literature often suggests that psychopathy results primarily from a faulty family environment, with researchers offering various interpretations of precisely what the "fault" was. In a background study on outpatients at a psychiatric clinic in Perth, Western Australia, Greer (1964) identified parental loss as a major factor. Parental loss was defined as the complete loss or continuous absence of one or both natural parents for at least twelve months before the child had reached age fifteen. Greer found that 60 percent of seventy-nine patients identified as psychopaths had suffered parental loss. That figure compared to 28 percent of the 387 neurotic subjects and 27 percent of 691 normals.

Greer's results should be viewed cautiously, since the psychopaths were classified according to the American Psychiatric Association 1952 guidelines. The sample, therefore, probably included a rather heterogeneous group of psychopaths. Nevertheless, three findings are particularly intriguing. First, significantly more female than male psychopaths had experienced parental loss. Second, a large proportion of the psychopaths had lost a parent before they reached the age of five. Third, psychopaths as a group were much more likely to have lost both parents.

It has also been reported that parental loss in psychopaths is more likely to be paternal than maternal (Oltman & Friedman, 1967), and that the more severe the psychopathic behavior, the more likely there is to be parental loss in the individual's background (Craft, Stephenson, & Granger, 1964). Parental rejection or loss have been found in many other studies, but criteria for defining psychopathy have been too varied to draw meaningful conclusions. Hare (1970) also notes that most of the studies have relied on biased and retrospective data, obtaining background information either from the psychopath (who is a far from reliable source), or from parents, relatives, and friends. The information thus gathered is after the fact and likely to be distorted so facts will fit the behavior.

Buss (1966) described two types of parental behavior he felt are conducive to psychopathic patterns. In the first type, parents are cold and distant to the child, allowing no close relationship to develop. In the second type, discipline, rewards, and punishment are inconsistent and capricious. Instead of learning right from wrong, the child learns to avoid blame and punishment by lying or by other manipulative means.

After an extensive overview of the research on the causes of psychopathy, McCord and McCord (1964) concluded, "Extreme emotional deprivation or moderate rejection coupled with other environmental conditions or with neural damage to inhibitive centers, best account for the development of psychopathy" (McCord & McCord, 1964, p. 87). According to this view, extreme emotional deprivation by itself can account for some psychopathy, but the McCords noted that a substantial number of deprived psychopaths also have some undefined malfunction in the nervous system. In addition, all psychopaths have experienced parental rejection to some degree.

Cleckley (1976) rebels at this approach, asserting that the theory of parental loss and rejection has been oversold. He is skeptical about any consistent family background pattern emerging from the research, noting that a large percentage of psychopaths in his studies had family backgrounds that seemed happy and conducive to excellent adjustment. According to Cleckley, if there is a negative element in the family background, it must be extremely subtle and abstruse, out of the parents' awareness, and therefore something they should not be blamed for. As a possibility, he suggests an incapacity on the part of the parents for simple warmth, for the "true intimacy that seems to be essential for biologic soundness (substantiality) in some basic relationships" (Cleckley, 1976, p. 411). Parents may be fair, kind, and genial, and demonstrate other superior qualities, but they may lack that one subtle but essential ingredient necessary to develop basic warmth and feeling in the child. Moreover, that one special quality may be nearly impossible to isolate for purposes of experimental study.

Hare and his colleagues (Hare et al., 1992) find no support for the hypothesis that psychopaths come from a "poor" or "inadequate" family life. Hare does not dispute the research that finds that a "poor," abusive family life is associated with the early emergence of criminal behavior in *nonpsychopaths*, but when it comes to psychopaths, the inadequate or dysfunctional family link is weak or nonexistent.

Phares (1972) believes that one plausible family background explanation of psychopathy is parental pampering and overindulgence. Some children are allowed to escape punishment for antisocial and aggressive behavior by apologizing or by promising not to do it again. They learn to be exceptionally skillful at manipulating others with suitable verbalizations and by being "cute." Phares contends that parents actually reinforce antisocial behavior by allowing children to receive rewards and escape punishment (also highly rewarding) for psychopathic behaviors. In addition, such children rarely have to endure frustration or delayed gratification, since parents cater to their every whim. The children will likely carry these useful behaviors into adulthood.

In the Robins (1966) longitudinal study, most psychopaths were found to have fathers who were either themselves psychopathic or were alcoholic. Robins notes that three of the consequences of having an antisocial, ineffectual father are the inconsistent discipline he provides, marital discord in the family, and a faulty model for the child. Robins did not find a significant relationship between parental rejection and loss and psychopathic behavior, however.

The research on family background, although equivocal, suggests that parental responses to a physiologically based need for stimulation may be crucial. The fact that a child has inordinate stimulation needs does not destine him or her to psychopathy. If parents are effective models, consistent in discipline, and use consistent reinforcement techniques rather than avoidance learning, the child's chances of developing into a moral, sensitive adult are increased. On the other hand, if parents are absent from the home, ineffectual, or inconsistent in discipline, the child will probably not learn appropriate social and moral behavior.

However, it appears likely that certain temperamental dispositions of activity, reactivity, emotionality, and sociability that exist at an early age render a child a high risk to engage in behaviors that run counter to society's rules. Highly active children move into (and often against) their environments at a higher pace and more impulsively than less active children. Moreover, children with highly irritable, nasty temperaments are apt to elicit decidedly different responses from parents and the social environment than children who are temperamentally more relaxed and pleasant. Parents able to tolerate ADHD and deal with it effectively provide a better emotional fit than those unable to tolerate a child moving at a high pace toward his or her environment. Parents unable or unwilling to deal with the fast-paced, irritable child may provide an inadequate home environment for "normal" development.

A typical developmental pattern would be ADHD in early childhood, perhaps accompanied by a learning disability, a behavioral problem in the middle school years, juvenile delinquency as an adolescent, and a psychopathic or antisocial personality disorder in adulthood. While this pattern is emerging, the psychopathic personality learns, by reward, how to manipulate others verbally. The words "I'm sorry" or "I won't do it again" take on strong reinforcing properties, despite their insincerity.

SUMMARY AND CONCLUSIONS

The primary psychopath should be distinguished from people who may be classified as psychotic, neurotic, or emotionally disturbed. The primary psychopath should also be distinguished from the sociopath, who is similar in many ways. However, sociopath usually refers to a person who *habitually* violates the law and who does not learn from past experience. The psychopath as discussed here may or may not run afoul of the law. In addition, psychopaths demonstrate a variety of behavioral and neurophysiological characteristics that differentiate them from other groups of individuals. Hare has proposed the term *criminal psychopath* to describe those persistent and repetitive offenders of the law. In this sense, the criminal psychopath and sociopath are similar in their offending patterns.

Psychopaths most often function in society as charming, daring, witty, intelligent individuals, high on charisma but low on emotional reaction and affect. They appear to lack moral standards or to manifest genuine sensitivity toward others. If criminals, they become the despair of law enforcement officials because their crimes appear to be without discernible or rational motives. Even worse, they show no remorse or ability to be rehabilitated. Furthermore, the diagnostic category "antisocial personality disorder" as defined in the DSM-III and the DSM-IV is becoming increasingly similar to Robert Hare's definition for criminal psychopath.

We reviewed much of the neurophysiological research suggesting that the psychopath is different from the rest of the population on a number of physiological measures. The psychopath seems to be underaroused, both autonomically and cortically, a finding that may account for his or her difficulty in learning the rules of society. There is some evidence, however, to suggest that with adequate incentives, psychopaths may learn societal expectations very well. Recalling our discussion of Eysenck's theory in Chapter 3, it is clear that the psychopath would be a stable extravert with high psychoticism. The psychopath, like the extravert, apparently is not aroused enough to profit as easily from the classical conditioning that perhaps sets most of us on the straight and narrow path in childhood. If, in addition to this physiological lack, the psychopath's family situation leaves him or her without appropriate models, then he or she is doubly cursed.

Many psychopaths also apparently have abnormal brain-wave patterns, mostly of a slow-wave childlike variety, which suggests that their nervous system is immature, at least until middle age. There are indications of more than the usual amounts of positive spikes, which are brain-wave bursts that correlate with aggressive episodes and impulsivity. Research has failed to discover, however, whether these abnormalities engender psychopathic behavior or vice versa. There is also little evidence to support a strong hereditary influence, although we should not overlook the possibility that psychopaths may be born with a biological predisposition to the disorder.

Studies on the childhood of psychopaths strongly suggest that they may have been ADHD as children, causing chaos for parents and teachers. It would be folly to maintain, though, that the ADHD child of today is the psychopath of tomorrow. Perhaps because they are physiologically underaroused, psychopaths do not respond as well to admonishments, threats, or actual punishment as do their nonpsychopathic peers. They do not learn society's expectations and the rules of right and wrong, possibly because anxiety-inducing disciplinary procedures are not that anxiety-producing for them. In many respects, the criminal psychopath follows a developmental path highly similar to the life-course-persistent offender described by developmental theory, outlined in Chapter 2.

There are still numerous gaps in our knowledge of the psychopath, one being in the area of gender differences. Research on female psychopaths is scant. Some research suggests that behavioral characteristics for females are generally similar to those of male psychopaths, with slightly more emphasis among females on sexual acting-out behavior. This probably reflects a cultural bias, however, since women have been traditionally chastised more than men for behavior deemed inappropriate according to sexual mores. However, research on female criminal psychopaths that have used Hare's PCL-R implies that their behavioral patterns may be somewhat different than male criminal psychopaths.

One feature of psychopaths is abundantly clear, however. They do not seem to think like mainstream society. They appear to perceive situations and approach life differently than most people. This variation in cognitive style is characteristic of many so-called "deviant" individuals, whether or not they are criminal. We will discuss this phenomenon again in the chapters on homicide and violence and sexual offenses.

ORIGINS OF CRIMINAL BEHAVIOR: LEARNING FACTORS

People do not come into situations empty headed. They have an infinite store of living experiences and an extensive repertoire of strategies for reacting to events. Up to this point, we have not acknowledged these strategies, concentrating instead on heredity and neurophysiology and the significant roles they may play in the development of criminal behavior. These biological factors appear to account in part for individual differences in susceptibility to classical conditioning. Since the capacity to be conditioned strongly affects fear of reprisal, it determines the degree of inhibition of socially undesirable criminal behavior. However, classical conditioning presumes that the human being is an automaton. Pair a neutral stimulus with a closely following painful event and the alert, intact robot will eventually, and automatically, connect the stimulus with the pain. This sequence is probably a very powerful factor in many behaviors, but certainly not in all. Conditioning is only one of several factors involved in the acquisition of criminal behavior.

To understand criminal behavior, it is crucial that we regard all individuals—whether or not they violate the rules of society—as active problem solvers who perceive, interpret, and respond to their environments uniquely. For the moment, consider unlawful behavior as subjectively adaptable rather than deviant. In this sense, unlawful conduct is a response pattern that a person has found to be effective, or thinks will be effective, in certain circumstances.

Violent crimes like aggravated assault and homicide are sometimes called "irrational," "uncontrollable," "explosive," or "motiveless," and therefore are believed to resist or defy analysis (e.g., President's Commission on Law Enforcement and Administration of Justice, 1967). Later in this text, we will find, however, that different types of violence can be placed into different theoretical frameworks. The decision to act violently may be a quick one, but the violent behavior is usually not irrational or uncontrollable, although in a very small percentage of cases it may be. Even behavior that may arise out of a severe mental disorder, however, may be adaptive, even when it is not legally culpable.

Engaging in criminal behavior might be one person's way of adapting or surviving under physically, socially, or psychologically dire conditions. Another person might decide that violence is necessary to defend honor, protect self, or reach a personal goal. In either case, the person is choosing what he or she believes is the best alternative for that particular situation. It is not, of course, necessarily the alternative that others would choose, nor what society condones. What, besides susceptibility to classical conditioning, accounts for the difference? In a very general sense, learning—both operant (or instrumental) and social learning—is an extremely important component in the equation. In the following pages we will expand the concept of conditioning to include these two distinct forms of learning, which play a major role in the acquisition and maintenance of criminal behavior. Later, we will introduce situational factors that appear to affect the learning process. Since each of these topics springs from the school of psychological thought called behaviorism, we will begin our discussion there.

BEHAVIORISM

Behaviorism "officially" began in 1913 with the publication of a landmark paper by John B. Watson (1878–1958), "Psychology as the Behaviorist Views It." The paper, which appeared in *Psychological Review*, is considered the first definitive statement on behaviorism, and Watson is thus acknowledged as the school's founder. However, Watson was by no means the first to discuss the basic elements of behaviorism. Its roots can be traced back at least to Aristotle (Diserens, 1925), and ingredients are also found in the positivism of both Auguste Comte (1838) and Antoine Cournot (1858) (Titchener, 1914). The point is that Watson's behaviorism represents a recurring phase in the cyclical history of psychology. A psychology of consciousness or mind is followed by a psychology of action and behavior (behaviorism), from which a psychology of mind and consciousness re-emerges. Today, psychology is moving once again toward a psychology of mind, especially cognitive processes. But that's another story, one we will cite periodically throughout this text. For the moment, let's return to Watsonian behaviorism, which has heavily influenced psychological interpretations of criminal behavior.

Watson frequently declared that psychology was the science of behavior. He believed that psychologists should eliminate the mind and all of its related "vague" concepts from scientific consideration because they could not be observed or measured. He was convinced that the fundamental goal of psychology was to understand, predict, and control human behavior, and that only a rigidly scientific approach could accomplish this.

Greatly influenced by Pavlov's research on classical conditioning, Watson thought that psychology should focus exclusively on the interplay between stimulus and response. A stimulus is an object or event that elicits behavior. A response is the elicited behavior. Watson was convinced that all behavior—both animal and human—was controlled by the external environment in a way similar to that described by Pavlov in his initial study—stimulus produces response (sometimes called S-R psychology). Therefore, for Watson, classical (or Pavlovian) conditioning was the key to understanding, predicting, and controlling behavior, and its practical applicability was unlimited.

The chief spokesperson for behaviorism for several decades was B. F. Skinner (1904–1990), who has been the most influential psychologist in the United States during the twentieth century. The Skinnerian perspective especially dominated the application of behavior modification or behavior therapy in the correctional system and in many institutions for the mentally handicapped or disturbed. Some contemporary theories about criminal behavior (e.g., Akers, 1977, 1985) try to integrate Skinnerian behaviorism with sociological perspectives. It is worthwhile, therefore, to spend some time sketching the Skinnerian approach to human behavior in general before assessing its impact on criminology.

Like Watson, Skinner believed that the primary goal of psychology is the prediction and control of behavior. And like Watson, he believed that environmental or external stimuli are the primary—if not the sole—determinants of all behavior, both human and animal. The environmental stimuli become **independent variables** and the behaviors they elicit the **dependent variables**. In the behavioral sciences, a variable is any entity that can be measured. A behavior (or response) is called "dependent" because it is under the control of (or dependent on) one or more independent variables. The consistent relationships between independent and dependent variables (stimulus and response) are scientific laws. Thus, according to Skinner, the aim of behavioristic psychology is to uncover these laws, making possible the prediction and control of human behavior.

Unlike Watson, Skinner did not deny the existence and sometimes usefulness of private mental events or internal stimuli. He emphasized, however, that these stimuli are not needed by a science of behavior, since the products of mental activity can be explained in ways that do not require allusion to unobserved mental states. Specifically, mental activity can be explained by observing what a person does, and it is what a person does that counts. Watson, remember, insisted that consciousness and mind simply do not exist. Thought, to Watson, was little more than tiny movements of the speech apparatus.

At this point, we must emphasize the need to distinguish between behaviorism as a *perspective on human nature* and a *method of science*. As a method of science, behaviorism posits that knowledge about human behavior can be best advanced if scientists use referents that have a *physical* basis and can be *publicly* observed by others. Since private events that happen inside our heads cannot be seen by others, they cannot be subjected to the rules of science. According to Skinner, behavioral science data must be comparable to be verified or disconfirmed. Otherwise, psychology would remain a philosophical exercise steeped in armchair speculation and untestable opinions. Self-proclaimed experts could continue to assert that shoplifting is an addiction, just like alcoholism, without being taken to task about the validity of their statements. Only a well-executed, systematic study where the terms shoplifting and addiction are clearly spelled out and rigorously tested will advance our knowledge about the accuracy of the shoplifting-addiction connection. Therefore, every psychological experiment, every sentence written into a psychological report, should be anchored to something that we can all observe, or that is testable by another professional. Rather than merely saying that someone is anxious or angry, we must identify the precise behaviors that prompt us to make these interpretations. This offers a basis for others, including the person being observed, to agree or disagree with us. "You're twitching in your chair. You must be apprehensive." "No, I'm not! It's that damned woolen underwear my aunt sent from Vermont."

Concerning behaviorism as a perspective of human nature, Skinner—and a majority of psychologists with a strong behavioristic leaning—embraced the view that humans differ only in degree from their animal ancestry. The behavior of humans follows the same basic natural laws as that of all animals. Like Darwin, Skinner saw no radical differences between humans and animals. Even human language and conceptual thinking are nondistinctive. Verbal behavior "is a very special kind of behavior, but there is nothing by way of processes involved that would distinguish it from non-verbal behavior and hence [verbal behavior] would not distinguish man from the [other] animals" (Skinner, 1964, p. 156). To Skinner, therefore, research on subhumans like monkeys, rats, and pigeons has great value; if carefully done it will reveal lawful relationships between all organisms and their environments.

Skinner was also clearly a strong **situationist**. All behavior is at the mercy of stimuli in the environment, and individuals have virtually no control or self-determination. Independent thinking and free will are myths. Animals and humans alike *react*, like complicated robots, to their environments. The environmental stimuli and the range of reactions are complex and infinite, but with careful research, this complexity is not unmanageable. Complex human behavior can be broken down into more simple behavior, a procedure sometimes referred to as **reductionism**. In other words, complicated behavior can be best understood by examining the simplest stimulus-response chains of behavior. This point brings us to the issue of **operant conditioning**.

Skinner accepted the basic tenets of classical conditioning, but asserts that we need an additional type of conditioning to account more fully for all forms of behavior. Recall Ivan Pavlov's experiments with the hungry dogs. The dogs did not operate on their environments to receive rewards; the event (food) occurred regardless of what they did. Skinner called this "responding conditioning" and contrasted it to a situation in which a subject does something that affects the situation. In other words, subjects behave in such a way that reinforcement is forthcoming. To uncover this operant conditioning principle, Skinner established an association between *behavior* and its *consequences*. He trained pigeons (apparently less troublesome and less expensive than dogs) to peck at keys or push levers for food. The pecking or pushing are operations on the environment. The operation should not be construed to imply self-determination, however. It is simply a *reaction* to stimuli in order to receive a certain consequence or reward. In this sense, the behavior that emerges from operant conditioning—although not automatic— is no more indicative of free will than is the behavior that emerges from classical conditioning.

The learning that comes about through operant conditioning was described before Skinner's time, but he is credited with drawing contemporary attention to it. In the early nineteenth century, for example, the philosopher Jeremy Bentham observed that human conduct was controlled by the seeking of pleasure and the avoidance of pain. In essence, this is what is meant by operant learning. It assumes that people do things solely to receive rewards and avoid punishment. The rewards may be physical (e.g., material goods, money), psychological (e.g., feelings of importance or control over one's fate), or social (e.g., improved status, acceptance).

Skinner called rewards **reinforcement**, defining that term as anything that increases the probability of future responding. Furthermore, reinforcement may be either positive or negative. In **positive reinforcement**, we gain something we desire as a consequence of certain behavior. In **negative reinforcement**, we avoid an unpleasant event or stimulus as a consequence of certain behavior. For example, if as a child you were able to avoid the unpleasantness of certain school days by feigning illness, your malingering was negatively reinforced. Therefore, you were more likely to engage in it again at a future date, under similar circumstances— high school dress-up day, class discussion day in a difficult college course, or the day the district supervisor was scheduled to visit the office. Thus, both positive and negative reinforcement can increase the likelihood of future behavior.

Negative reinforcement is to be distinguished from punishment and extinction. In punishment, an organism receives noxious or painful stimuli as consequences of behavior. In **extinction**, a person or animal receives neither reinforcement nor punishment. Skinner argued that punishment is an ineffective way to eliminate behavior, because it merely suppresses it temporarily. At a later time, under the right conditions, the response is very likely to reoccur. Extinction is far more effective, because once the organism learns that a behavior brings no reinforcement, the behavior will be dropped from the repertoire of possible responses for that set of circumstances.

According to Nietzel (1979), C. R. Jeffery (1965) was one of the first behaviorists to suggest that criminal behavior was learned according to principles of Skinnerian operant conditioning. Shortly afterwards, Burgess and Akers (1966) agreed with this, and further hypothesized that criminal behavior was both *acquired* and *maintained* through operant conditioning. But, as Nietzel points out, most of the direct evidence for this claim comes from experiments with animals. Evidence that the same occurs in humans is scarce and replete with possible alternate interpretations.

The premise that operant conditioning is the basis for the origin of criminal behavior is deceptively simple: Criminal behavior is learned and strengthened because of the reinforcements it brings. According to Skinner, human beings are born neutral—neither good nor bad. Culture, society, and the environment shape behavior. Therefore, behavior will be labeled good, bad, or indifferent, as society chooses. What is judged "good" behavior in one society or culture may be labeled "bad" in another. Members of one group in a society may believe that it is "bad" for a child to pretend that a block of wood is a toy truck and "good" to hit the child with a rod to stop that behavior. To others, the behavior of the adults who hit the child is "bad." Depending on the severity of the punishment, it may also be aggravated assault.

Skinner was convinced that searches for individual dispositions or personalities that lead to criminal conduct are fruitless, because people are ultimately determined by the environment in which they live. He does not completely discount the role of genetics in the formation of behavior, but he sees it as a very minor one; the dominant player is operant conditioning. According to Skinner and his followers, if we wish to eliminate crime, we must change society through behavioral engineering based on a "scientific conception of man." Having agreed on rules and regulations (having defined what behaviors constitute antisocial or criminal offenses), we must design a society in which members learn very early that reinforcement will not occur if they transgress against these rules and regulations, but will occur if they abide by them.

This is a tall order, since the reinforcements for behavior are not always obvious and may actually be highly complex. Property crimes like shoplifting and burglary, or violent crimes like robbery, appear to be motivated in many cases by a desire for physical rewards. However, they may also be prompted by a desire for social and psychological reinforcements, such as increased status among peers, self-esteem, feelings of competence, or simply for the thrill of it. It is a safe bet that much criminal behavior is undertaken for reinforcement purposes, positive or negative. The problem then becomes, how do we identify those reinforcements and how do we prevent them from happening, or at least minimize their value?

Contemporary psychology still embraces a behavioristic orientation toward the *scientific study* of behavior, but has grown cool toward the Skinnerian perspective of human nature. All behaviorists are not Skinnerians. Many find Skinner's brand of behaviorism too limiting (e.g., Bandura, 1983, 1986). While they agree that a stimulus can elicit a reflexive response (classical conditioning) and that a behavior produces consequences that influence subsequent responding (operant conditioning), they are also convinced that additional factors must be introduced to explain human behavior.

This brings us to the topic of mental states and brain-mediational processes, which Skinner urged us to shun. In recent years, many psychologists have been examining the roles played by self-reinforcement, anticipatory reinforcement, vicarious reinforcement, and all the symbolic processes that occur within the human brain. To avoid confusion, we must now begin to distinguish Skinnerian behaviorism from other forms, including social behaviorism (social learning) and differential association-reinforcement.

SOCIAL LEARNING

Early learning theorists worked in the laboratory, using animals as their primary subjects. Pavlov's, Watson's, and Skinner's theories, for example, were based on careful, painstaking observations and experiments with animals. The learning principles gleaned from their work were generalized to a wide variety of human behaviors. In many cases, this was a valid process. Few psychologists would dispute the contention that the concept of reinforcement is one of the most soundly established principles in psychology today.

However, behaviorists also suggested that, since all human behavior is learned, it can also be changed using the same principles by which it was acquired. This generated a plethora of behavior therapies or behavior modification techniques. Use learning principles to establish conditions that change or maintain targeted behaviors and *voilà*! therapeutic success! The apparent simplicity of the procedures and methods was especially appealing to many clinicians and other professionals working in the criminal justice system, and behavior modification packages sometimes guaranteed to modify criminal behavior were rushed to correctional institutions.

But oversimplification is dangerous when we deal with human complexity. Human beings do respond to reinforcement and punishment, and behavior therapy based on learning principles can change certain elements of behavior. Moreover, humans can be classically conditioned, although there are individual differences in their susceptibility. When we lose sight of the person and overemphasize the environmental or external determinants of behavior, however, we may be overlooking a critical level of explanation. Remember that human beings are, in large part, active problem solvers who perceive, encode, interpret, and make decisions on the basis of what the environment has to offer. Thus, internal factors, as well as external ones, may play significant roles in behavior. This is the essence of **social learning theory**, which suggests that to understand criminal behavior we must examine perceptions, thoughts, expectancies, competencies, and values. Each person has his or her own version of the world and lives by that version.

To explain human behavior, social learning theorists place great emphasis on cognitive variables, which are the internal processes we commonly call thinking and remembering. Classical and operant conditioning ignore what transpires between the time the organism perceives a stimulus and the time it responds or reacts. Skinnerian behaviorists claim, "If we can account for the facts by using observable behavior, why worry about the labyrinths of internal processes?" Social behaviorists, however, counter that this perspective offers an incomplete picture of human behavior.

The term *social learning* reflects the theory's strong assumption that we learn primarily by observing and listening to people around us—the social environment. In fact, social learning theorists believe that the social environment is the most important factor in the *acquisition* of most human behavior. They do accept the necessity of reinforcement for the *maintenance* of behavior, however. Criminal behavior, for example, may be initially acquired through association and through observation, but whether or not it is maintained will depend primarily upon reinforcement (operant conditioning). For example, if a boy sees someone he admires (i.e., a role model) successfully pilfering from the local sporting goods store, the boy may try some pilfering of his own. Whether he continues that behavior, however, will depend on the personal reinforcement or value it assumes. If no reinforcement is forthcoming (he fails to pocket a baseball because someone else walked into the store, or he finds that the gym shorts he stole do not fit), then the behavior will probably drop out of his response repertoire (extinction). If the behavior brings aversive results (punishment), this will inhibit or suppress future similar behavior.

Several clusters of psychologists are enrolled in the social learning school of thought. We will focus first on the work of two prominent representatives, Julian Rotter and Albert Bandura, since they seem to have the most to offer to the study of criminal behavior from the social learning perspective.

EXPECTANCY THEORY

Julian Rotter is best known for drawing attention to the importance of expectations (cognitions) about the consequences (outcomes) of behavior, including the reinforcement that will be gained from it. In other words, before doing anything, we ask, "What has happened to me before in this situation, and what will I gain this time?" According to Rotter, whether a specific pattern of behavior occurs will depend on our expectancies and how much we value the outcomes. To predict whether someone will behave a certain way, we must estimate that person's expectancies and the importance he or she places on the rewards gained by the behavior. Often, the person will develop "generalized expectancies" that are stable and consistent across relatively similar situations (Mischel, 1976).

The hypothesis that people enter situations with generalized expectancies about the outcomes of their behavior is an important one for students of crime. Applying Rotter's theory to criminal behavior, we would say that when people engage in unlawful conduct, they expect to gain something in the form of status, power, security, affection, material goods, or living conditions. The violent person, for example, may elect to behave that way in the belief that something will be gained. The serial murderer might believe that God has sent him on a mission to eliminate all "loose" women; the woman who poisons an abusive husband looks for an improvement in her life situation. Simply to label a violent person impulsive, crazy, or lacking in ego control fails to include other essential ingredients in the act. Although self-regulation and moral development are involved—concepts we will discuss in later chapters—people who act unlawfully perceive and interpret the situation and select what they consider to be the most effective behavior under the circumstances. Usually, when people act violently, they do so because that approach has been used successfully in the past (at least they believe it has been successful). Less frequently, they have simply observed someone else gain by employing a violent approach, and they try it for themselves. This brings us to Bandura's imitational model of social learning.

IMITATIONAL ASPECTS OF SOCIAL LEARNING

An individual may acquire ways of doing something simply by watching others do it; direct reinforcement is not necessary. Bandura (1973b) introduced this idea, which he called **observational learning** or **modeling**, to the social learning process. Bandura contends that much of our behavior is initially acquired by watching others, who are called *models*. For example, a child may learn how to shoot a gun by imitating TV characters. He or she then rehearses and fine tunes this behavioral pattern by practicing with toy guns. The behavior is likely to be maintained if peers also play with guns and reinforce one another for doing so. Even if the children have not pulled the triggers on real guns, they have acquired a close approximation of shooting someone by observing others do it. It is likely that just about every adult and older child in the United States knows how to shoot a gun, even if they have never actually done so: "You aim and pull the trigger." Of course, shooting safely and accurately is much more complicated, but the rudimentary know-how has been acquired through **imitational learning** (also called modeling or observational learning). The behavioral pattern exists in our repertoires, even if we have never received direct reinforcement for acquiring it.

According to Bandura, the more significant and respected the models, the greater their impact on our behavior. Relevant models include parents, teachers, siblings, friends, and peers, as well as symbolic models like literary characters or TV or movie personages. Rock stars and athletes are modeled by many young people, which is one reason we are exposed to so many public figures touting everything from cosmetics to a drug-free life to beer. Interestingly, the commercial and public service advertisements often miss the point. In observational learning, it is not so much what the model says as what the model does that is effective. If football stars actually avoided the use of drugs in their daily lives, their messages to youth might be more effective.

The observed behavior of the model is also more likely to be imitated if the observer sees the model receive a reward. Conversely, it is less likely to be imitated if the model is punished. Bandura believes—much like Rotter—that once a person decides to use a newly acquired behavior, whether he or she performs or maintains it will depend on the situation and the expectancies for potential gain. This potential gain may come from outside (the praise of others, financial gain) or it may come from within (self-reinforcement for a job the individual perceives as well done).

Much of Bandura's research was directed at the learning of aggressive and violent behavior. We will be returning to his theory, therefore, in Chapter 7. At this point, however, be aware that a substantial body of experimental findings gives impressive support to his views. For example, preschool children who watched a film of an adult assaulting an inflated plastic rubber doll were significantly more likely to imitate that behavior than were a comparable group who viewed more passive behavior (Bandura & Huston, 1961; Bandura, Ross, & Ross, 1963). Many studies employing variations of this basic procedure report similar results, strengthening the hypothesis that observing aggression leads to hostility in both children and adults (Walters & Grusec, 1977). Apparently, people who observe aggressive acts not only imitate the observed behavior but also become generally more hostile.

To some extent, social learning as it is discussed by Rotter and Bandura humanizes the Skinnerian viewpoint, since it provides clues about what transpires inside the human brain (or mind). It draws our attention to the cognitive, mediational aspects of behavior, while classical and operant conditioning focus exclusively on the environment. Social learning theorists use *environment* in the social sense, which includes the internal as well as the external environment. Skinnerians prefer to limit relevant stimuli to external surroundings.

DIFFERENTIAL ASSOCIATION-REINFORCEMENT THEORY

Ronald Akers (1977, 1985; Burgess & Akers, 1966) proposes a social learning theory of deviance that tries to integrate the core ingredients of Skinnerian behaviorism, the social learning theory as outlined by Bandura, and the differential association theory of criminologist Edwin H. Sutherland. Akers calls his theory **differential association-reinforcement (DAR)**. Briefly, the theory states that people learn to commit deviant acts through interpersonal interactions with their social environment.

To understand DAR theory, we must grasp Sutherland's **differential association theory**, which dominated the field of sociological criminology for over four decades. It was first set forth in the third edition (1939) of Sutherland's *Principles of Criminology* and restated in 1947. Although Sutherland died in 1950, the theory was left intact in Donald R. Cressey's subsequent revisions of the original text.

Sutherland believed that criminal or deviant behavior is learned the same way that all behavior is learned. The crucial factors are with whom a person associates, for how long, how frequently, how personally meaningful the associations, and how early they occur in the person's development. According to Sutherland, in our intimate personal groups we all learn definitions, or normative meanings (messages), favorable or unfavorable to law violation. A person becomes delinquent or criminal "because of an excess of definitions favorable to violation of law over definitions unfavorable to violation of law. This is the principle of differential association" (Sutherland & Cressey, 1974, pp. 80–81).

Note that criminal behavior does not invariably develop out of association or contacts with "bad companions" or a criminal element. The messages, not the contacts themselves, are crucial. Furthermore, deviant messages must outweigh conventional ones. Therefore, Sutherland also believed that criminal behavior may develop even if association with criminal groups is minimal. For example, law-abiding groups—such as parents—may communicate subtly or bluntly that it is all right to cheat, or that everyone is basically dishonest. This is an extremely important point that will be reiterated when we discuss moral development.

Sutherland's theory is probably popular among social scientists because, as one writer put it, "it attempts a logical, systematic formulation of the chain of interrelations that makes crime reasonable and understandable as normal, learned behavior without having to resort to assumptions of biological or psychological deviance" (Vold, 1958, p. 192). However, the theory is also ambiguous; because of this feature it has not drawn much empirical research (see Gibbons, 1977, pp. 221–228). How are a person's contacts to be measured and weighed? Also, as Cressey (Sutherland & Cressey, 1974) admits, the theory does not specify what kinds of learning are important (e.g., operant, classical, modeling). Neither does it adequately consider individual differences in the learning process.

Akers (1985) tries to correct some of the problems with differential association theory by reformulating it to dovetail with Skinnerian and social learning principles. He proposes that most deviant behavior is learned according to principles outlined in Skinner's operant conditioning, with classical conditioning playing a secondary role. Furthermore, the strength of deviant behavior is a direct function of the amount, frequency, and probability of reinforcement the individual has experienced by performing that behavior in the past. The reinforcement may be positive or negative, in the Skinnerian meanings of the terms.

Crucial to the Akers position is the role played by *social* and *nonsocial reinforcement*, the former being the more important. "Most of the learning relevant to deviant behavior is the result of social interactions or exchanges in which the words, responses, presence, and behavior of other persons make reinforcers available, and provide the setting for reinforcement" (Akers, 1985, p. 45). It is also important to note that most of these social reinforcements are symbolic and verbal rewards for participating or for agreeing with group norms and expectations. For example, doing something in accordance with group or subcultural norms is rewarded with "Way to go," "Great job," "Good going," a pat on the back, or a friendly grin. Nonsocial reinforcement refers primarily to physiological factors or material acquisition that may be relevant for some crimes, such as drug-related offenses or burglary.

Deviant behavior, then, is most likely to develop as a result of social reinforcements given by significant others, usually within one's peer group. The group first adopts its own *normative definitions* about what conduct is good or bad, right or wrong, justified or unjustified. These normative definitions become internal, cognitive guides to what is appropriate and will most likely be reinforced by the group. In this sense, normative definitions operate as *discriminative stimuli*—social signals transmitted by subcultural or peer groups to indicate whether certain kinds of behavior will be rewarded or punished within a particular social context.

According to Akers, two classes of discriminative stimuli operate in promoting deviant behavior. First, *positive discriminative stimuli* are the signals (verbal or nonverbal) that communicate that certain behaviors are encouraged by the subgroup. Not surprisingly, they follow the principle of positive reinforcement: The individual engaging in them gains social rewards from the group. The second type of social cue, *neutralizing* or *justifying discriminative stimuli*, neutralize the warnings communicated by society at large that certain behaviors are inappropriate or unlawful. According to Akers, they "make the behavior, which others condemn and which the person himself may initially define as bad, seem all right, justified, excusable, necessary, the lesser of two evils, or not 'really' deviant after all" (Akers, 1977, p. 521). Statements like "Everyone has a price," "I can't help myself," "Everyone else does it," or "She deserved it" reflect the influence of neutralizing stimuli.

The more people define their behavior as positive or at least justified, the more likely they are to engage in it. If deviant activity (as defined by society at large) has been reinforced more than conforming behavior (also defined by society), and if it has been justified, it is likely that deviant behavior will be maintained. In essence, our behavior is guided by the norms we have internalized and for which we expect to be continually socially reinforced by significant others.

Akers accepts the validity of Bandura's modeling as a necessary factor in the initial acquisition of deviant behavior. But its continuation will depend greatly on the frequency and personal significance of *social reinforcement*, which comes from association with others.

Akers's social learning theory has received its share of criticism. Some scholars consider it tautological or circular: Behavior occurs because it is reinforced, but it is reinforced because it occurs. Kornhauser (1978) points out that there is no empirical support for the theory. Still, the theory remains a very popular one within sociological criminology.

FRUSTRATION-INDUCED CRIMINALITY

Several learning investigators (e.g., Amsel, 1958; Brown & Farber, 1951) have noted that when organisms—including humans—are prevented from responding in a way that had previously produced rewards, their behavior often becomes more energetic and vigorous. Animals bite, scratch, snarl, and become irritable; humans may snarl and become irritable and rambunctious (and may also bite and scratch). Researchers assume that these aroused responses result from an aversive internal state of arousal which they call *frustration*.

Thus, when behavior directed at a specific goal is blocked, arousal increases and the individual experiences a drive to reduce it. Behavior is energized, but more significantly, the responses that lead to a reduction in the arousal may be strengthened or reinforced. This suggests that people who employ violence to reduce frustration will, under extreme frustration, become more vigorous than usual, possibly even resorting to homicide. It also suggests that violent behavior directed at reducing frustration will be reinforced, since it reduces unpleasant arousal by altering the precipitating event or stimuli.

Leonard Berkowitz (1962) conducted numerous studies relating frustration to criminality. He divided criminal personalities into two main classifications: the **socialized** and the **individual offender**. You have already met socialized offenders. We have discussed them throughout this chapter as products of learning, conditioning, and modeling. They offend because they have learned to, or are expected to, as a result of their interactions with the social environment. The individual offender, by contrast, is the product of a long, possibly intense series of frustrations resulting from unmet needs. According to Berkowitz, both modeling and frustration are involved in the development of criminal behavior, but one set of life experiences favors a particular criminal style. "Most lawbreakers may have been exposed to some combination of frustrations and aggressively antisocial models, with the thwartings being particularly important in the development of 'individual' offenders and the antisocial models being more influential in the formulation of the 'socialized' criminals" (Berkowitz, 1962, p. 303).

Berkowitz adds an important dimension to frustration, suggesting that it is particularly intense if an individual has high expectancy of reaching a goal (Berkowitz, 1969). People who anticipate reaching a goal, and who feel they have some personal control over their lives, are more likely to react strongly to interference than those who feel hopeless. In the first case, delay or blockage may generate intense anger and even a violent response, if the frustrated individual believes that type of response will eliminate the interference. The power of frustration may well have been what Maslow (1954) was referring to when he stated that crime and delinquency represent a legitimate revolt against exploitation, injustice, and unfairness. The frustration hypothesis also fits neatly into theories offered by radical or conflict criminologists. Individuals who feel suppressed by the power elite and feel they have a right to reap society's benefits may well experience intense frustration at continuing domination.

The frustration-induced theory helps to explain the behavior of looters during unexpected events like floods, fires, urban riots, or electrical blackouts. For example, between April 30 and May 3, 1993, businesses in Los Angeles were burned and looted largely by African Americans who were frustrated by a jury's acquittal of four white L.A. police officers in the March 1991 beating of African-American motorist Rodney G. King. Fifty-eight people were killed in the four days of rioting, and damage was estimated to be at least one billion dollars. People of all ages and race or ethnic backgrounds were stealing everything from food and alcohol to firearms and stereos. The rioting triggered smaller uprisings in several other cities, including San Francisco, Atlanta, Seattle, Las Vegas, and Miami. Authorities concluded that the riots were brought on by frustrations with economic, social, and political inequalities found in many sectors of American society, including the court system. The Los Angeles riot was similar to the August 1965 uprising of the Watts section of L.A., when thirty-four were killed and one thousand were injured. The riot was prompted by deeply felt frustrations with the same perceived inequalities in American society. Since 1965, there have been at least eight violent riots in major cities brought on by frustrations with the expanding inequalities found in America.

The frustration-induced theory would suggest that individuals who commit larceny under these situations have materialistic goals (e.g., their fair share of middle-class goods) that they have not yet attained. Society blocked the goals, and the individuals became impatient and frustrated. When the opportunity to loot arises, they are there to take it. Demographic profiles of the 2,706 adults arrested and charged with looting during the New York City blackout of 1977 support this theory. The defendants had "stronger community ties" and higher incomes than the average defendant in the criminal justice system (*New York Times*, August 14, 1977). Only about 10 percent were on welfare; approximately half were gainfully employed. Sixty-five percent of those arrested were African American and 30 percent were Hispanic. These data indicate that these defendants were, in general, eager to eliminate further delays in meeting their expectancy for a better life.

On the other hand, a good argument could be made for a modeling or social learning explanation. The data may represent nothing more than the naive response of a group of lower-middle-class violators who modeled seemingly rewarding behavior but lacked the streetwise knowledge to escape detection. The more sophisticated groups, perhaps more representative of larceny suspects as a group, may have looted early and fled. The others, imitating the early groups, were still looting when the police arrived.

Berkowitz hypothesizes that the more intense and frequent the thwartings or frustrations in a person's life, the more susceptible and sensitive the person is to subsequent frustration. Thus, the individual who frequently strikes out at society in unlawful or deviant ways may have encountered numerous severe frustrations, especially during early development, but has not given up hope. In support of this argument, Berkowitz cites the research findings on delinquency (e.g., Glueck & Glueck, 1950; Bandura & Walters, 1959; McCord, McCord, & Zola, 1959), revealing that delinquent children, compared to nondelinquents, have been considerably more deprived and frustrated during their lifetime. Berkowitz also suggests that parental neglect or failure to meet the child's needs for dependency and affection are internal, frustrating circumstances that germinate distrust of all others within the social environment. This generalized distrust is carried into the streets and school, and the youngster may exhibit a "chip on the shoulder." The frustration of not having dependency needs met prevents the child from establishing emotional attachments to other people. The individual may thus become resentful, angry, and hostile toward other people in general.

SITUATIONAL INSTIGATORS AND REGULATORS OF CRIMINAL BEHAVIOR

Most contemporary theories and research support the view that human behavior results from a mutual interaction between personality and situational variables. However, several behavioral and social scientists (e.g., Goldstein, 1975; Gibbons, 1977; Petersen, 1977) complain that much crime research and theory neglects situational variables in favor of dispositional factors. They contend that criminality in many cases may simply reflect being in the wrong place at the wrong time with the wrong people. For example, Gibbons comments: "In many cases, criminality may be a response to nothing more temporal than the provocations and attractions bound up in the immediate circumstances out of which deviant acts arise" (Gibbons, 1977, p. 229). Skinner, of course, exemplifies the position that behavior is controlled by environmental contingencies and events.

Haney (1983) discusses **fundamental attribution error**, which refers to a common human tendency to discount the influence of the situation and explain behavior by referring to the personality of the actor instead. Fundamental attribution error is a concept that applies to making attributions about others, not ourselves. For example, when correctional counselors were asked why inmates had committed the crimes that put them in prison, the counselors attributed the causes almost exclusively to dispositional or personality factors (such as "laziness," or meanness) rather than to environmental factors, such as upbringing, poverty, or social factors (Saulnier & Perlman, 1981). The inmates, on the other hand, said that factors they believed landed them in prison were largely external in nature, such as poverty, poor employment opportunities, and physical and sexual abuse. When it comes to ourselves, we engage in **self-serving biases**, where we tend to attribute good things about ourselves to dispositional factors, and bad things to events and forces outside ourselves. For example, when we do well on an exam, we tend to attribute the cause to our intelligence and study habits. On the other hand, when we do poorly, we tend to attribute the cause to a poorly designed or unfair exam.

Haney believes that personality or internal states account very little for how we act. He contends that the important determining influence is the situation in which we find ourselves. In essence, Haney is arguing that, given the appropriate circumstances, anyone might engage in culpable criminal behavior, that we all have our price.

Situations are rarely static. Our behavior influences them to some extent, and they in turn influence our behavior. This reciprocal interaction between person and environment is one reason why students of crime are beginning to pay more attention to victimology—victims often influence the course of criminal actions, particularly violent ones. At this point we will turn our attention to two situational factors that seem to play a particularly important role in antisocial behavior, authority and deindividuation.

AUTHORITY AS AN INSTIGATOR OF CRIMINAL BEHAVIOR

Sometimes people behave a certain way because someone with power told them they must, even though the actions do not "set right" with their own principles. Kelman and Hamilton (1989) refer to this phenomenon as "crimes of obedience." "A crime of obedience is an act performed in response to orders from authority that is considered illegal or immoral by the larger community" (Kelman & Hamilton, 1989, p. 46). The classic example of the influence of authority is the military order to kill indiscriminately or to commit some other atrocity, such as Lieutenant William Calley's carrying out the massacre of villagers at My Lai in Vietnam. Other examples abound. An example of crimes of obedience in a political/bureaucratic context is the Watergate scandal, where on June 17, 1972, a group of men under the auspices of the White House broke in and tried to bug the Democratic National Headquarters in the Watergate apartment complex. The Iran-Contra scandal provides another example. Crimes of obedience appear to be widespread in the corporate world, an issue we will deal with in more detail in Chapter 11.

In an attempt to delineate some of the variables involved in obedience to authority, Stanley Milgram (1977) designed a series of experiments, using as subjects persons who volunteered (for money) in response to a newspaper ad. The experiments, which eventually received intensive public scrutiny and are now cited in nearly every introductory psychology textbook, studied the amount of electrical shock people were willing to administer to others when ordered to do so by an apparent authority figure.

The subjects were adult males, ages twenty to fifty, who represented a cross section of the socioeconomic classes. They were told that the researchers were studying the effects of punishment on memory. The experiment required a "teacher" and a "victim." Unknown to the volunteers, the victim was part of the experiment, a confederate who had been trained to act in a certain manner as part of the experimental design. In a rigged coin toss, the naive subject (the volunteer) always became the teacher and the confederate the victim. The victim-learner was taken to an adjacent room and strapped into an "electric chair" in the presence of the "naive" teacher.

Next, the teacher was led back to a room where he saw a simulated shock generator—a frightening apparatus with thirty toggle switches presumably capable of delivering thirty levels of electric shock to the learner in the adjacent room. Each level was marked in volts ranging from 15 to 450 and accompanied by a switch. In addition, labels indicated "slight shock," "danger: severe shock," and beyond, to an "XXX" level. Each time the learner gave an incorrect answer to a learning task, the teacher was instructed to administer a stronger level of shock. The victim, who did not of course receive any shock at all, purposefully gave incorrect answers; he had also been trained to scream in agony, plead with the subject to stop, and pound on the wall when the higher levels of shock were administered.

Milgram wanted to discover how far people would go under the orders of an apparent authority figure (the experimenter). He may have found more than he bargained for. Almost two-thirds of the subjects obeyed the experimenter and administered the maximum shock levels. In subsequent experiments, using similar experimental conditions but different subjects (including both males and females), Milgram continued to find similar results.

Many of Milgram's subjects, while obeying the experimenter's instructions, demonstrated considerable tension and discomfort. Some stuttered, bit their lips, twisted their hands, laughed nervously, sweated profusely, or dug their fingernails into their flesh, especially after the victim began pounding the wall in protest (Milgram, 1963). After the experiment, some reported that they wanted to stop punishing the victim but continued to do so because the experimenter would not let them stop. Milgram (1977, p. 118) concluded: "The individual, upon entering the laboratory, becomes integrated into a situation that carries its own momentum."

In subsequent studies, Milgram modified the procedure to determine more precisely what conditions inhibited or promoted this extreme obedience. For example, he varied the psychological and physical distance between the subject and the victim. To increase the psychological distance between the two, Milgram eliminated the cries of the victim that had been programmed into the original experiment. In another experiment, to minimize the physical and psychological distance between them, the subject sat next to the victim.

In general, Milgram found that the subjects obeyed the experimenter less as physical, visual, and auditory contact with the victim increased. However, the nearer the *experimenter* got to the "teacher," the more likely the teacher was to obey. Milgram found no evidence of significant personality or sex differences in the studies where shocking behavior was concerned, but he did find that female teachers were more distressed about their task than their male counterparts.

The psychological and physical distance variable suggests some interesting implications. If we were to analogize between Milgram's studies and violent actions, we would expect that the more impersonal the weapon or situation (psychological and physical distance) the greater the *likelihood* for destruction and serious violence. Certainly, killing someone with a firearm at a distance versus killing someone point blank are two different tasks. And both methods differ from choking someone to death with one's bare hands. It would appear that the firearm offers a more impersonal and possibly easier way to eliminate someone, and thus is more likely to lead to violent behavior. Admittedly, this suggestion makes some quantum jumps from a psychological experiment in an artificial setting, but it is a point worth considering when we discuss the relationship between weapons and violence in Chapter 8.

In assessing the profound influence of commands from an authority figure, we should also pay close attention to the reactions of the subjects in Milgram's study. Individual differences were noted in the way the subjects reacted to the situation, but not in their actual willingness to shock. Although some subjects refused to continue with the experiment when they believed that they were hurting the victim, most (about 65 percent) administered the full range of shock levels. Most also displayed anxiety and conflict.

Milgram noted a curious dissociation between word and action. Many subjects said they could not go on, but nevertheless they did. Some justified their action by concluding that the experimenter would not permit any harm to come to the victim. "He must know what he is doing." Other subjects expressed different interpretations and expectancies, such as the belief that the scientific knowledge gained in the experiment justified the method. It is interesting to note that people who have not undergone the ordeal are quite convinced that they would be members of the defiant group who refused to deliver the extreme levels of shock. Later studies conducted both in the United States and abroad confirmed Milgram's findings, however (Penrod, 1983).

Milgram suggests that our culture may not provide adequate models for disobedience to authority. He admonishes (1977, p. 120) that his studies raise the possibility that human nature or, more specifically, the kind of character produced in American democratic society, cannot be counted on to insulate its citizens from brutality and inhuman treatment at the direction of malevolent authority. A substantial proportion of people do what they are told to do, irrespective of the context of the act and without limitations of conscience, so long as they perceive that the command comes from a legitimate authority.

Milgram's theory may account to some extent for irrational acts committed under the influence of authority. Milgram would probably explain the refusal of the U.S. attorney general to fire the Watergate prosecutor as a refusal to perceive the president as a legitimate authority figure. Alternately, there may have been a psychological affinity to the prosecutor. In either case, Milgram would probably find personality factors irrelevant. Other theorists would argue that it is precisely such factors that account for resistance to authority.

DEINDIVIDUATION

Philip Zimbardo designed a number of studies testing the influence of **deindividuation**, the process of losing one's identity and becoming part of a group, as a situational variable. Deindividuation apparently follows a complex chain of events. First, the presence of many other persons encourages feelings of anonymity. Then, the individual feels he or she loses identity and becomes part of the group. Under these conditions, he or she can no longer be singled out and held responsible for behavior. Apparently, this feeling then generates a "loss of self-awareness, reduced concern over evaluations from others, and a narrowed focus of attention" (Baron & Byrne, 1977, pp. 581–582). When combined, these processes lower restraints against antisocial criminal behavior and appear to be basic ingredients in mass violence.

In one experiment, Zimbardo (1970) purchased two used cars, left one abandoned on a street in Manhattan, New York, and the other on a street in Palo Alto, California (about 55,000 population in the late 1960s). Zimbardo's deindividuation hypothesis predicted that, due to the large population of New York, people would more likely lose their identity and feel less responsible for their actions. Consequently, New Yorkers would be more likely to loot the abandoned vehicle. This is exactly what happened. Within twenty-six hours, the New York car was stripped of battery, radiator, air cleaner, radio antenna, windshield wipers, side chrome, all four hubcaps, a set of jumper cables, a can of car wax, a gas can, and the only tire worth taking. Interestingly, the looting was not done by delinquents or members of a criminal subculture; all the looters were well-dressed, middle-class whites. On several occasions the looting was done by entire families: children and parents together in a family enterprise.

On the other hand, the car in Palo Alto was untouched during the seven days it was left abandoned. At one point during a rainstorm, a passerby actually lowered the hood to prevent the motor from getting wet. Why such a dramatic difference?

Zimbardo suggests that the anonymity of the New York residents worked in combination with situational cues implying that they could get by without repercussions. Zimbardo's hypothesis contends that in high population areas, who cares what you are doing as long as you are not bothering others or damaging a concerned party's property? Passersby in New York even stopped and chatted with the looters. In Palo Alto, people could be more easily identified. Moreover, a person engaging in this kind of behavior would expect to be the target of social disapproval or gossip.

Deindividuation is not necessarily associated with crowds or massive populations, however. The effect may be achieved by a disguise, a mask, or a uniform also worn by others, or it may be achieved by darkness (Zimbardo, 1970). Research data indicate that people tend to be more abusive, aggressive, and violent when their identity is hidden. This phenomenon might explain why, throughout history, war paints, masks, and costumes have been donned by warriors preparing for battle (Watson, 1973). Even contemporary soldiers, guerrillas, and military advisers are deindividuated by their uniforms. Deindividuation also helps explain the apparent ease with which members of groups such as the Ku Klux Klan regress from being apparently respectable citizens by day to violent, hooded terrorizers by night. Again, however, it is too simplistic to assume that no dispositional or other factors are at work.

The disguise aspect of deindividuation was vividly illustrated in another sobering Zimbardo experiment (1973) known as the Stanford Prison Experiment.

Zimbardo and his colleagues simulated a prison environment in the basement of the psychology building at Stanford University, with all the physical and psychological trappings of an actual prison: bars, prison uniforms, identification numbers, uniformed guards, and other features that encouraged identity slippage. Student volunteers were screened through clinical interviews and psychological tests to ensure that they were emotionally stable and mature. According to Zimbardo, the subjects finally selected were "normal," intelligent college students from middle-class homes throughout the United States and Canada. They were paid $15 a day for participating.

The experiment required two roles, guard and prisoner, which were assigned by random coin toss. The randomization assured that there were no significant differences between the two groups. The "prisoners" were unexpectedly "arrested" and brought to the simulated prison in a police car. There they were handcuffed, searched, fingerprinted, booked, stripped, "deloused," given a number, and issued a prison uniform. Each prisoner was then placed in a six by nine foot cell with two other inmates.

The guards wore standard uniforms and mirrored sunglasses to encourage deindividuation. In addition, they carried symbols of power: a night stick, keys to the cells, whistles, and handcuffs. Before the prisoners could do even routine things (e.g., write a letter, smoke a cigarette), they had to obtain permission. Guards drew up their own formal rules for maintaining law and order in the prison (sixteen rules in all) and were free to improvise new ones.

Within six days, both guards and prisoners had completely absorbed their roles:

> Three prisoners had to be released during the first four days because of hysterical crying, confusion in thinking, and severe depression. Many others begged to be paroled, willing to forfeit the money they had earned for participating in the experiment.
>
> About a third of the guards abused their power and were brutal and demeaning. Other subjects did their jobs as tough but fair correctional guards, but none of these supported the prisoners by urging the brutal guards to ease off. The realism of the prison was apparently striking. "The consultant for our prison ... an ex-convict with sixteen years of imprisonment in California's jails, would get so depressed and furious each time he visited our prison, because of its psychological similarity to his experiences, that he would have to leave" (Zimbardo, 1973, p. 164).

The situation became such that Zimbardo decided to terminate the experiment during the sixth day, instead of proceeding through the planned two weeks.

The experiment prompted him to conclude: "Many people, perhaps the majority, can be made to do almost anything when put into psychologically compelling situations—regardless of their morals, ethics, values, attitudes, beliefs, or personal convictions" (1973, p. 164). Much the same conclusion had been reached by Milgram with respect to the influence of authority figures.

Although the Stanford Prison Experiment underscores the crucial importance of situational variables in determining behavior, there were still significant individual differences in the way the subjects responded to the conditions. For example, only one-third of the guards became brutally enthralled with their power. Rather than making far-reaching conclusions on the basis of how a total of twenty-one subjects (both guards and prisoners) responded, it would be much more fruitful to give some attention to individual variables. For example, it would have been helpful to examine the values, expectancies, competencies, and moral development of the participants, in combination with the situational factors. What developmental factors most likely predisposed individuals to act the way they did, and exactly how did they perceive the situation? What did they expect to gain by their behavior? We will return to the deindividuation issue when we discuss mass violence in Chapter 8 and offer other perspectives of what happens to people caught up in the excitement of the crowd.

SUMMARY AND CONCLUSIONS

We have reviewed Skinnerian behaviorism, the social learning theories of Rotter and Bandura, the semisocial learning theories of Akers and Hogan, and the Berkowitz frustration theory in this chapter. Each emphasizes to varying degrees the importance of learning in the development and maintenance of criminal behavior.

Our perspective of human nature influences what factors we consider paramount in the acquisition of criminal behavior, such as learning factors or the biological determinants discussed in Chapters 3 and 4. Until now, we have focused on the possible *origins* of criminal behavior: biological factors, classical conditioning, operant conditioning, and observational learning. We have also introduced some of the *external reinforcements* involved in the maintenance and regulation of criminal behavior. They include tangible rewards as well as social and psychological ones. Collectively, external reinforcements that bring us material, social, or psychological gain are called *positive reinforcements*. Behaviors that enable us to avoid unpleasant circumstances are negatively reinforced.

Also included in the regulation of behavior is *vicarious reinforcement*, which consists of both observed reward and observed punishment. When we observe others (models) receiving rewards or punishments for certain behavior, we tend to alter our behavior correspondingly. Models are extremely important in the acquisition and regulation of criminal behavior. They are reference points for what we should and can do in a particular set of circumstances. Therefore, models may act as inhibitors or facilitators of behavior. People internalize the actions and philosophies of significant models, thereby making them part of their own behavioral repertoire and cognitive structure. In the next chapter we will elaborate further on the influences of models.

Lastly, we discussed some situational *instigators of crime*, such as authority figures and the environmental factors involved in the process of deindividuation. In some instances, people engage in illegal or violent conduct because they are told or ordered to do so. In other instances, the personal sense of identity appears to be lost in the excitement of the crowd. Under these deindividualized conditions, people may do things they normally would not do. We will return to these topics in Chapters 7 and 8.

THE MENTALLY
DISORDERED OFFENDER

Scientific investigations of abnormal behavior and criminal behavior have much in common. When we differentiate either one from "normal" behavior, we encounter vague definitions, classifications that invite numerous exceptions, and unwieldy and complex variables. In addition, both abnormal and criminal behavior are deviant in the sense that they stray from what is considered normal, expected, and approved conduct in society. In this sense, the criteria for determining what behaviors constitute normality may fluctuate according to the dominant economic, social, and political philosophies concurrently operating within any given society. With regard to criminal behavior, this point is easily illustrated by both past and present laws governing the use and sale of alcoholic beverages and other drugs. With abnormal behavior, it is easily illustrated by the fact that homosexuality was considered both abnormal and a mental disorder until 1973. In our discussion of deviant behavior, therefore, we are necessarily constricted by the boundaries established in society at this point in time.

Despite complexities in definition and criteria, psychologists have made some progress toward understanding the deviant human mind. Researchers have learned, for example, that most deviant behavior (both abnormal and criminal) is probably acquired through the same fundamental processes as nondeviant behavior. Deviant behavior seems to represent learned response patterns for coping with perceived threats, fears, and stress, and generally, for surviving in one's world (real or imagined). Problems arise when we try to classify and simplify these response patterns, since so many factors go into each individual's discovery of what works best for him or her. As many clinicians are too well aware, human behavior rarely follows a set, predictable pattern to correspond neatly to textbook descriptions or guidelines in a diagnostic manual. Toch and Adams (1989) note that classifications of people are often byproducts of resource allocation. That is, classification systems are often implemented for funding purposes and for the convenience of staff needs.

In the psychological study of both criminal and abnormal behavior, labels are of limited use. With respect to criminal behavior, they inform us about conduct but not about motivations. We know that a person who has committed petty larceny stole an item or items of relatively nominal value, but we have no idea what led to that conduct. In abnormal behavior, labels are even more of a problem, since they are based on response patterns that may not be manifested in outward behavior. When we say a person is schizophrenic, for example, we may be referring to hallucinations that may not be clearly obvious to an observer. In behavior that is both criminal and abnormal, the problem is, of course, greater.

Diagnostic labels are shorthand summaries of a cluster of behaviors. They are not explanations for why people do things. Since labels explain nothing, the psychological study of the criminal behavior that is presumably abnormal must go beyond them and try to explain its principal causes. In this chapter, therefore, we focus on the mental disorders and their alleged relationship with crime. In doing so, we will find that this relationship is not as strong as is often assumed. We will begin with a brief presentation of the concepts traditionally used by the psychiatric, psychological, and legal professions to describe and predict abnormal behavior. Next, we will examine criminal responsibility, competence to stand trial, and the issues of **determinism** and free will, which are all viewed by the legal and psychiatric professions from very different perspectives. Finally, we will examine the concept of dangerousness as it applies to clinical prediction.

MENTAL DISORDERS AND CRIME

It is a popular misconception that the brutal, violent, and apparently senseless crime is usually committed by someone who is mentally ill or "sick." A man who sexually assaults, tortures, and kills a four-year-old child has to be sick. How else could he do this? An alternate explanation focuses on the subhuman perspective: If not sick, the person is an animal. Although this second approach is gaining ground, perhaps reflecting public impatience with perceived insanity loopholes in the criminal justice system, there is still wide public subscription, mirrored in popular literature, to a presumption of mental illness, particularly when outrageous, inexplicable crimes are at issue. The media have been instrumental in developing the mental disorder and violence connection. John Monahan (1992) cites a survey (Gerbner, Gross, Morgan, & Signorielli, 1981) that showed that on prime-time American television, 73 percent of all individuals characterized as mentally disordered were also depicted as violent. In another analysis (Shain & Phillips, 1991), 86 percent of all print stories dealing with former mental patients focused on the violence of the patients, especially if the topics dealt with serial or mass murder (Monahan, 1992).

The media's tendency to make the mentally ill-violent connection is not new. Throughout the history of civilization, there has been a strong tendency to forge this link between mental illness and violent behavior (Monahan, 1981). Most societies and their legal systems have been confused about and often frightened by mental disorder. In fact, the first mental hospital in the American colonies was established after Benjamin Franklin argued forcefully that the mentally ill were prone to violence and should be confined, involuntarily if need be, to protect society (Monahan & Geis, 1976). It should be emphasized, however, that not all people believe that mental disorders inevitably or frequently lead to violence. Surveys, for example, suggest that only about one-quarter of the U.S. adult population strongly subscribe to such a view (Monahan, 1992).

The acceptance of this link centers on the assumption that mentally ill people do not play by the rules of society, are unpredictable, and cannot control their own actions. Since they are apt to do anything at any given time, these "crazy people" are potentially dangerous. On the other hand, we also assume that people who commit senseless or incomprehensible violent acts are obviously crazy and sick. Thus, mentally ill people are dangerous, and people who commit bizarre crimes are mentally ill.

Before we can examine the validity of these beliefs, we must define our terms. **Mental illness** is a disorder of the mind that is judged by experts to interfere substantially with a person's ability to cope with life on a daily basis. It presumably deprives the person of freedom of choice, but it is important to note that there are degrees to this deprivation. Mental illness is manifested in behavior that deviates notably from normal conduct. Use of the term *illness* encourages us to look for etiology, symptoms, and cures and to rely heavily on the medical profession both to diagnose and treat. More important, it encourages us to excuse the behavior of persons plagued with the "sickness." If we use the term **mental disorder**, however, we are not so conceptually limited. Mental disorder need not imply that a person is sick and to be pitied or less responsible for his or her actions. Therefore, although *mental illness* is still used in the psychological, psychiatric, and legal literature, and is the term favored in both civil and criminal law, we prefer the less restrictive *mental disorder*.

Mental disorders are manifested in a variety of behaviors, ranging in severity from what Morse (1978) calls "crazy behavior" to conduct that is essentially innocuous. Crazy behavior is that which is obviously strange and unusual and cannot be logically explained. A nineteen-year-old male skipping along the sidewalk with a pie plate on his head and reciting "Wee Willie Winkle" is exhibiting strange behavior. If it is fraternity initiation week on the local campus, there may be a logical explanation. In the absence of such an explanation, the behavior becomes "crazy." In this instance, clinicians might call the behavior *psychotic*, symptomatic of a severe mental disorder. It is not necessarily dangerous, however—a crucial distinction.

The concept of mental disorder, therefore, may connote bizarre, dramatic, harmful, or mildly unusual behaviors whose classifications are published in the **Diagnostic and Statistical Manual of Mental Disorders (DSM)**. Compiled by committees appointed by the American Psychiatric Association, the DSM is the guidebook for clinicians who seek to define and diagnose specific mental disorders. It is reviewed and revised periodically to conform to the contemporary, mainstream thinking of psychiatrists and other mental health professionals. Thus, until 1973, as we noted earlier, homosexuality was considered a mental disorder; today it is no longer so. In a sense, then, mental disorders are whatever the psychiatric profession wishes them to be.

The DSM-III—the manual published in 1980—differs substantially in content from the DSM-II, which appeared in 1968. The DSM-III-R, published in 1987, has made some changes but does not significantly affect the disorders described in this chapter. Today, the DSM-IV is used by virtually every mental health professional in the United States to guide diagnosis and to justify third-party reimbursement for treatment. The DSM-IV (the fourth edition), published in 1994, was developed in an effort to maximize empirical input and to minimize subjectivity and bias. It is now the standard of mental disorders used by mental health professionals for diagnosis, research guidance, and reimbursement criteria.

For our purposes, three major changes between the DSM-II, DSM-III, and DSM-IV are important: (1) a shift in focus from the *causes* of mental disorders to their behavioral indicators; (2) a reclassification of what were formerly called **neuroses**, and (3) an expansion of the subcategories of **psychosis**. The previous DSM was steeped in psychoanalytic, psychodynamic traditions and etiology. Its categories were based on assumed psychodynamic causes. The DSM-III and DSM-III-R try to eliminate theory and etiology and concentrate on description and classification, although it is debatable to what extent this has been accomplished (Charney, 1980; Schacht, 1985; Wakefield, 1992). If there is substantial research or clinical agreement on the causes of a disorder, this information is included; otherwise, there is generally no speculation. Instead, clinicians are offered more detailed, concrete bases for making diagnoses. Each category is described extensively, and its observable behaviors are carefully outlined.

The second major difference is reflected in the committee's decision to drop the label neurosis, because there was little agreement about its meaning. Neurosis has been replaced by three separate major categories: (1) **anxiety disorders**, which include phobias, generalized anxiety disorders, and obsessive compulsive disorders; (2) **somatoform disorders**, which include somatization and conversion disorders; and (3) **dissociative disorders**, including amnesias, fugues, and multiple personality. Since neurosis has been traditionally used to encompass all these categories, the Committee recommended that they could be subsumed under the term **neurotic disorders**. It is preferable, however, to use the distinct categories.

When we refer to "crazy behavior," we are not usually talking about neurotic disorders. Generally, these disorders do not result in major problems or discomfort to others in society; only the person affected usually feels the discomfort. In essence, a neurotic disorder is an emotional reaction that distresses the individual (and perhaps indirectly those closest to him or her) and that the individual finds unacceptable. However, the person maintains contact with reality, and the behavior does not typically violate social norms. For example, although agoraphobia (an abnormal fear of open spaces) is a mental disorder from a professional point of view, it is not the type of "crazy behavior" that concerns the public. The neurotic disorders may be relatively enduring and recurrent, but they are generally regarded as mild. Furthermore, since these disorders are rarely associated with violent, frightening actions, they do not play a role in discussions of responsibility for criminal behavior.

A third change in the new edition of the DSM revolves around the subcategories of psychosis. In DSM-II, psychosis was a major section comprising schizophrenia, paranoid states, and major affective disorders (severe depression).

Psychosis as a separate category does not appear in DSM-III. Instead, schizo-phrenic disorders, paranoid disorders, affective disorders, and "psychotic disor-ders not elsewhere classified" appear as separate major categories. For our pur-poses, since a large segment of the research we will be discussing was conducted before this change, we will retain the labels "psychosis" and "psychotic behavior," which should be viewed as generic terms covering each of the four just cited.

Although many other changes characterize the DSM-III, the aforementioned are of greatest concern to us here. Changes in other categories, such as in psycho-sexual disorders, will be alluded to as they pertain to the topics being discussed later in this text. For the present, the three categories of mental disorders most rele-vant are (1) schizophrenic disorders, (2) paranoid disorders; and (3) the personality disorder called "antisocial personality disorder." Note that the first two fall into the "psychotic" category; the third is a separate category under the general label "per-sonality disorders." They are relevant because they are most likely to be associated with violent or antisocial behavior and are most often cited to support an insanity defense to criminal charges. We will review each of these disorders and then assess their relevance to criminal behavior.

Before describing each of the disorders, the term mental disorder should be more carefully defined. According to the DSM-IV (p. xxi), a mental disorder

is conceptualized as a clinically significant behavioral or psychological syndrome or pattern that occurs in an individual and that is associated with present distress (e.g., a painful symptom) or disability (i.e., impairment in one or more important areas of functioning) or with a significantly increased risk of suffering death, pain, disability, or an important loss of freedom. In addition, this syndrome or pattern must not be merely an expectable and culturally sanctioned response to a particu-lar event, for example, the death of a loved one. Whatever its original cause, it must currently be considered a manifestation of a behavioral, psychological, or bio-logical dysfunction in the individual.

While the newer DSM-IV recognizes that no definition adequately identifies precise boundaries for the concept "mental disorder," nor is the concept able to cover all situations, the DSM-IV continues to utilize the definitions of DSM-III and DSM-III-R, as serviceable as any other available definition.

As noted by Wakefield (1992), there are two basic principles that guide the DSM-IV definition for mental disorder. First, the mental condition must have nega-tive consequences for the person. That is, the person must be experiencing some pain, distress, discomfort, or disability. The second principle rests on the assump-tion that a mental disorder is a dysfunction of some internal process within the person that for some reason has gone haywire. This principle differentiates the dis-order from the normal or expected internal processes that result from some trauma or tragedy of daily living, such as the loss of a loved one. We now turn to the spe-cific disorders.

SCHIZOPHRENIC DISORDERS

Schizophrenia is the mental disorder that people most often associate with "crazy behavior," since it frequently manifests itself in highly bizarre actions. It is a mental disorder that continues to be extremely complex and poorly understood

(Andreasen & Carpenter, 1993). The disorder generally begins early in life, often leads to social and economic impairment, and leaves traces on its victims for the rest of their lives (Andreasen & Carpenter, 1993). Behavioral manifestations of schizophrenia are varied, but there are some common characteristics.

Severe breakdowns in thought patterns, emotions, and perceptions are common. Spells of extreme social withdrawal from others are also typical. The thoughts and cognitive functioning of the schizophrenic person become disorganized and fail to correspond to reality, and his or her speech will reflect this. The most common example is a loosening of associations, in which ideas shift between totally unrelated or only obliquely related subjects. Thought becomes fragmented and bizarre, and delusions—false beliefs about the world—are common. For example, persons with schizophrenia may believe that everyone is plotting to destroy them, or that God has sent them on a mission to kill all red-haired prostitutes.

Typical features of the person with schizophrenia also reflect inappropriateness of emotions or affect (e.g., indiscriminate giggling or crying), or emotional flatness, where very little—if any—emotional reaction is exhibited. The voice is monotonous, the face immobile and expressionless. The major disturbances in perception are various forms of hallucinations, which involve sensing or perceiving things or events that others do not sense or perceive. The most common hallucinations are auditory, with the individual hearing voices or sounds that no one else in the vicinity hears.

The DSM-IV outlines five characteristic symptoms of schizophrenia, at least two of which must be manifested before a diagnosis can be entertained: (1) delusions; (2) hallucinations; (3) disorganized speech; (4) grossly disorganized behavior; and (5) inappropriate affect. Furthermore, the social, self-care, and/or the occupational life of the individual must show signs of being markedly below the level achieved prior to the onset. In addition, there must be continuous signs of the disturbance for at least six months.

The DSM-IV recognizes five subtypes of schizophrenia: (1) disorganized; (2) catatonic; (3) paranoid; (4) undifferentiated; and (5) residual. Following is a brief summary of the essential features of each subtype:

1. Disorganized type: Inappropriate affect (flat, incongruous, or silly emotional responses) and marked incoherence and disorganization in thought patterns. Associated features include grimaces, strange mannerisms, complaints of nonexistent physical ailments, extreme social withdrawal, and other oddities of behavior.

2. Catatonic type: Severe disturbances in muscular and voluntary movement. Extended periods of mutism are common. Parrotlike and senseless repetition of a word or phrase just spoken by another person is also common. Prominent grimacing is another frequent characteristic. The catatonic may assume a bizarre posture for long periods of time (usually several hours) and then fly into an overactive, agitated state of screaming and throwing things.

3. Paranoid type: Characterized by delusions and hallucinations (usually auditory hallucinations). Paranoid schizophrenics may be convinced that the FBI is following them with the intent of capturing them and leading them to their death. Or, the paranoid schizophrenic may believe that the world is inhabited by extraterrestrials who are plotting to take over the world. Of all the schizo-

phrenic types, the paranoid is the most frequently represented in criminal behavior.

4. Undifferentiated type: This type shows psychotic symptoms that cannot be classified into any of the foregoing categories.

5. Residual type: These individuals have had at least one episode of schizophrenia, and there is evidence that some of the symptoms are continuing. For example, the person may still display blunted emotions or illogical thinking, but no other symptoms.

The DSM-IV identifies a sixth category, *schizophreniform disorder*, a behavioral pattern that shows at least two indicators of delusions, hallucinations, disorganized speech, grossly disorganized behavior, and emotional inappropriateness. It is a temporary disorder and underscores the difficulty in classifying schizophrenic disorders in general. In order to qualify for schizophreniform disorder, the symptoms must persist for at least one month but less than six months. If the symptoms continue more than six months, the clinician is encouraged to classify the disorder into one of the five longer-lasting types.

DELUSIONAL DISORDERS

The **delusional disorders** (also called **paranoid disorders**) is the presence of one or more *nonbizarre* delusions that persist for at least one month. The judgment of whether the delusions systems are bizarre or nonbizarre is considered especially important in deciding between a delusional disorder and schizophrenia. In addition, delusional disorders do not have clear boundaries, since they often accompany other disorders like schizophrenia, organic mental disorder, paranoid personality disorder, and depressions. The essential feature of all delusional disorders is the delusional system, which most often includes persecutory beliefs about being spied on, cheated, conspired against, followed, drugged, maliciously maligned, harassed, or obstructed. An important manifestation of the disorder is that the delusions are not necessarily bizarre or grossly disorganized. That is, they are reasonably believable and not completely far-fetched. Generally, these false, persecutory beliefs are accompanied by anger, resentment, and sometimes violence. Suspiciousness, either generalized or directed at one or more persons, is common. The DSM-IV (1994) recognizes seven different types of delusional disorders, but the persecutory type is the one most closely associated with criminal conduct, especially violent criminal conduct.

ANTISOCIAL PERSONALITY DISORDER

The DSM-III and the DSM-III-R criteria for the antisocial personality disorder have been among the most frequently criticized because of their vagueness and lack of empirical anchoring (Widiger, Frances, Pincus, Davis, & First, 1991). The DSM-IV, however, has tried to address these problems by incorporating into its criteria more empirically based attributes. As mentioned in Chapter 4, many of the new criteria closely follow the Robert Hare definition of the criminal psychopath.

The essential feature of an **antisocial personality disorder** (ASP) is a history of continuous behavior in which the rights of others are violated. The individual must be at least eighteen years of age and must have a history of some symptoms of conduct disorder before age fifteen. The pervasive pattern of disregard for and the violation of the rights of others, must also be indicated by at least three of the following behavioral patterns:

1. Failure to conform to social norms or the criminal law, as reflected by frequently performing acts that are grounds for arrests.
2. Irritability and unusual aggressiveness, as indicated by repeated physical fights or assaults.
3. Consistent irresponsibility, as reflected in a poor work history or failure to honor financial obligations.
4. Impulsivity or a failure to plan ahead is characteristic at all ages.
5. Deceitfulness, as reflected in frequent lying, use of aliases, or conning others for personal profit or pleasure.
6. Reckless disregard for the safety of others or self is standard.
7. Lack of remorse or guilt for wrongdoings, as indicated by being indifferent to or rationalizing having hurt, mistreated, or stolen from another.

Additional symptoms, as outlined in the DSM-IV, include stealing, fighting, truancy, and resisting authority that are typical childhood symptoms. ASPs lack empathy and tend to be callous, cynical, and contemptuous of the feelings, rights, and sufferings of others. Furthermore, ASPs frequently exhibit precocious and aggressive sexual behavior, excessive drinking, and the use of illicit drugs. There is a marked impaired capacity to maintain lasting, close, warm, and responsible relationships with family, friends, or sexual partners.

On average, ASPs fail to become independent, self-supporting adults. They spend most of their lives in institutions (usually correctional facilities) or remain highly dependent on their families. Other accompanying features include restlessness, an inability to tolerate boredom, and a belief that the world is hostile. ASPs often complain of tension and depression. They are often impulsive and unable to plan ahead.

Antisocial personality disorder occurs more frequently in males than females. It is estimated that about 3 percent of the American male population and about 1 percent of the American female population fall into this category (DSM-IV). Furthermore, the disorder is more common in lower-socioeconomic populations, partly because it is connected with impaired earning capacity, and partly because of the greater likelihood of being raised in an one-parent family with inadequate models and resources. Lastly, the DSM-IV concludes that the disorder runs in families, possibly due to a genetic link that predisposes the child.

The validity of the antisocial personality disorder as a meaningful concept has been debated. Blackburn (1988) contends that there is no single type of abnormal personality that is prone to chronic rule violation. Furthermore, the diagnostic label "antisocial personality disorder" remains "a mythical entity" that fails to be meaningful for theory development, research, clinical communication, or prediction. "Such a concept is little more than a moral judgment masquerading as a clinical diagnosis. Given the lack of demonstrable scientific evidence of clinical utility of the concept, it should be discarded" (Blackburn, 1988, p. 511). Other clinicians find ASP a very useful diagnostic category, and with increasing research the concept is gaining increasing support.

MENTAL DISORDERS AND VIOLENCE

Long-term inpatient care or hospitalization of the mentally disordered is a practice that has largely disappeared. Consequently, the mentally disordered have become a more visible presence within the community. When problems arise, often it is the responsibility of law enforcement officials to handle the situation. "As a result, the jails and prisons may have become the long-term repository for mentally ill individuals who, in a previous era, would have been institutionalized within a psychiatric facility" (Teplin, 1984, p. 795).

Previous research literature consistently supported the position that severely mentally disordered individuals are no more likely to commit serious crimes against others than the general population (Brodsky, 1973, 1977; Henn, Herjanic, & Vanderpearl, 1976a; Rabkin, 1979; Monahan, 1981). However, more recent research (Klassen & O'Connor, 1988, 1990; Monahan, 1992) finds that male mentally disordered patients, who have a history of at least one violent incident, have a high probability of being violent within a year after release from the hospital. Furthermore, schizophrenia seems to be the disorder most closely connected to violence (Blackburn, 1993).

Other research (Swanson & Holzer, 1991; Swanson, Holzer, Ganju, & Jono, 1990) suggests that currently mentally disordered patients are involved in violent behavior far more often than the nondisordered members of the general population. Furthermore, this difference persists even when demographic and social factors are taken into account (Monahan, 1992). John Monahan (1992) stresses two things about the research showing a connection between mental disorders and violence. First, the relationship refers only to people currently experiencing a serious mental disorder. People who have experienced a serious mental disorder in the past and are not showing symptoms currently are not prone to engage in violent behavior. Second, a great majority (over 90 percent) of the currently mentally disordered are not violent. Media portrayals of common psychotic killers driven berserk by blood thirsty delusions are sensational, frightening, and perhaps entertaining, but in reality the phenomenon is rare. Two additional things about the recent research should be emphasized. First, the mental disorder/violence link holds for the seriously mentally disordered (psychotic individuals). And second, the relationship is stronger for those seriously mentally disordered individuals who currently have a history of violent behavior.

Bonta, Law, and Hanson (1998) argue that psychopathology or mental disorder—past or current—as a major predictor of criminal conduct and violence in *offenders* is very much open to question. Based on an extensive review of the recent research literature, Bonta and his colleagues concluded that offenders with mental disorders were no more criminally prone or violent than offenders without mental disorders. In fact, offenders with mental disorders were less likely to recidivate than nondisordered offenders. Note again that key word in the Bonta et al. review is "offender." Whether the same holds true for nonoffenders remains a debatable issue.

Rabkin's (1979) review of the criminal behavior of discharged mental patients sheds further light on the relationship between crime and mental disorders. A significant number of studies in her literature review found that the arrest rate for discharged mental patients was higher than the rate for the general population, especially for assaultive behavior. Rabkin suggested two explanations for the disproportionate arrest rates. First, a small subset of patients who had criminal records prior to hospital admission continued their antisocial ways soon after discharge from the mental institution. These habitual offenders significantly inflated the arrest rates for all mental patients. Patients without prior criminal records were substantially below the arrest rates for the general population. Rabkin suggests that the upward trend in arrest rates is partly due to policy and procedural changes in many mental institutions that allowed patients to return to the community much sooner than in the past, and partly due to the increasing tendency of courts to refer habitual offenders for psychiatric diagnosis. In other words, courts—at least during the period under review—were likely to refer for psychiatric diagnoses people who were criminally prone and who, in a less psychiatrically conscious era, would have been standardly processed through the criminal justice system. And as we might suspect, diagnosticians probably cooperated by tagging on a label that would facilitate, although not guarantee, a commitment to a mental institution.

The second factor accounting for the disproportionate arrest rates is diagnostic. Rabkin found that most criminal offenses after discharge were committed by individuals who had been diagnosed with alcoholism, substance addiction, or personality disorder. The first two diagnostic categories appear consistently in the research. It has also been suggested that so-called personality disorders are often classified as such only because the clinician could find no other way to label a person acting antisocially. Alcoholism and substance addiction are in the fringe areas of traditional diagnoses because they do not represent what are considered serious or typical mental disorders. When these three categories were omitted, Rabkin found that the arrest rates among the discharged patients, without a criminal history, were comparable to those reported in the general population. "When patients with arrest histories, primary diagnoses of substance abuse, and personality disorders are considered separately, the remainder of the patient group appears to be considerably less dangerous than are those members of the general public who are not mentally ill" (Rabkin, 1979, p. 26).

In another landmark research project, Henn and his colleagues conducted an extensive series of investigations on all defendants referred by a St. Louis, Missouri, court for psychiatric assessment over a ten-year period (Henn, Herjanic, & Vanderpearl, 1976a). Focusing on a sample of 1,195 defendants accused of a variety of crimes and referred for psychiatric assessment, Henn learned that the most frequent diagnosis was personality disorder, accounting for nearly 40 percent of all the diagnoses. Two-thirds of those classified as personality disorders were specifically designated antisocial personality. The second most frequent diagnosis was schizophrenia (which also included those labeled probable schizophrenia), comprising 17 percent of the total. The other diagnostic labels (based on DSMs I and II) were evenly distributed and of low frequency.

It is interesting to note that 93 percent of the defendants were diagnosed *something*, which may reflect, in part, a perceived obligation on the part of the evaluation team to tag on a diagnosis of some sort. Of course, this could also reflect sophistication on the part of the referring judges, who were able to detect a likely mental disorder.

Henn also found frequent references to alcoholism, primarily as a secondary diagnosis, in the diagnostic reports. Alcoholism cut across all diagnostic categories, with the notable exception of schizophrenia, where only a few cases were reported. The combination of alcoholism and drug addiction as a secondary diagnosis was common in persons labeled antisocial personality. These findings support those reported by Guze (1976), who found the diagnosis of alcoholism prevalent among offenders with a diagnosis of antisocial personality disorders.

Teplin (1984) conducted a well-executed study on the tendency of police officers to arrest mentally disordered individuals. Trained graduate students in psychology observed 1,382 police-citizen encounters (involving 2,555 citizens) and evaluated the mental status of the citizens according to specific criteria (a symptom checklist that listed the major characteristics of severe mental disorders). The police determined that 506 citizens qualified as suspects, and they arrested 148. The graduate students classified 30 of the 506 suspects and 14 of the 148 suspects arrested as exhibiting definite symptoms of mental disorders. Therefore, the police arrested 20 percent more individuals with symptoms than without symptoms. However, considering that many disordered individuals tend to have annoying symptoms, such as verbal abuse, belligerence, and disrespect, the slightly higher probability of arrest is hardly surprising. In addition, the police officers failed to recognize the behavior as representing a mental disorder in a large number of cases, believing the individuals were simply being disrespectful and asking for trouble.

In summary, the research literature fails to support the belief that the severely mentally disturbed, as a group, tend to be killers or unpredictable violent offenders. However, there is some research that strongly indicates that individuals who are currently seriously mentally disordered, and who have a history of violence, are dangerous and prone to engage in violent behavior. Furthermore, it is possible, as some clinicians believe, that the more bizarre violent offenses are committed by the mentally disordered, particularly those categorized as schizophrenic or paranoid. Moreover, the more extreme violence of schizophrenics is typically directed to family members or acquaintances, and bizarre self-mutilation is more likely than mutilatory murders (Blackburn, 1993). However, Ronald Blackburn (1993, p. 274) admonishes: "Although there appears to be an increased risk in schizophrenia, particularly in paranoid schizophrenia, it must be reiterated that only a small minority of patients in this category are violent, and that the disorder itself is rarely sufficient to account for violent acts in instances where they occur."

Individuals experiencing affective (mood) psychoses are less likely to be violent, but when affective psychoses are associated with violence, they are usually manifest in females within the context of **extended suicide**, where the offender kills self as well as others in the environment (Blackburn, 1993).

Research does indicate that alcoholism, substance abuse, and antisocial personality disorders are overrepresented in criminal offenses. In the case of alcoholism and substance abuse, the evidence may be clearcut. In the case of personality disorders, it may reflect clinician subjectivity. An evaluating agency may assume at the outset that the individual referred for evaluation is antisocial, because he or she has already had contact with the criminal justice system. Add this to the belief that the court is expecting a label of some sort, and the final result may well be a contaminated diagnosis.

Mental disorders in those incarcerated in prison are sometimes cited as evidence of a link between crime and abnormal behavior. The incidence and nature of disorders among the convicted are difficult to determine, however. Recent research reveals, for example, that the rates of serious mental disorders among prison inmates vary widely, ranging from 5 percent to 16 percent psychotic (Teplin, 1990). In the New York correctional system, it is estimated that about 8 percent of the inmates have "severe" mental disabilities and another 16 percent have "significant" mental disabilities (Steadman, Fabisiak, Dvoskin, & Holobean, 1987). However, it is unclear whether the mental disorders were present prior to incarceration, or developed as a result of being incarcerated. It is possible that prison conditions have some deleterious effects on mental states. Therefore, an individual may become mentally disordered after being institutionalized, and that fact may not be reflected in the research. We will assess more fully the potential deleterious effects of imprisonment in Chapter 13.

THE MENTALLY DISORDERED OFFENDER AND CRIMINAL RESPONSIBILITY

The term *mentally disordered offender*, for purposes of our discussion, refers to the person believed both to be mentally disordered and to have committed a serious criminal act. In some cases, mentally disordered offenders have only been charged with, not convicted, of a crime. In that sense, offender is used loosely. Four categories of individuals are included: (1) those found Incompetent to Stand Trial (IST); (2) those found Not Guilty of a Crime by Reason of Insanity (NGRI); (3) Mentally Disordered Sex Offenders (MDSO); and (4) those administratively transferred from a prison to a mental hospital ("transfers"). The first three categories have been adjudicated by the courts. Most mentally disordered offenders have been committed involuntarily to a security section of a mental hospital (or hospital prison), presumably for psychotherapeutic reasons. Occasionally, mentally disordered offenders, specifically ISTs, are allowed to remain in the community, but are subjected to a regimen of outpatient therapeutic services.

Steadman and his colleagues (Steadman, Monahan, Hartstone, Davis, & Robbins, 1982), in a national survey that will be cited extensively throughout this section, found that 20,143 persons were admitted to state and federal institutions in the United States during 1978 as mentally disordered offenders. Transfers from prisons to mental institutions accounted for 54 percent of the total. ISTs represented about 32 percent, NGRIs about 8 percent, and MDSOs another 6 percent. The Steadman figures indicate that the national admission rates for mentally disordered offenders have remained about the same at least since 1967, despite some changes in state and federal statutes during the period.

THE INSANITY DEFENSE

The best known of the mentally disordered offender categories, due to the wide publicity it attracts, is the judicial determination of **Not Guilty by Reason of Insanity (NGRI)**. **Insanity** is a legal term, not a psychiatric or psychological one; it should be used only in the context of a criminal offense. Insanity refers to a person's *state of mind at the time an offense was committed*. A finding of insanity means that the person was mentally disordered at the time of his or her offense, and thus cannot be held criminally responsible for his or her actions. The law assumes that mental disorder can rob an individual of free will or the ability to make appropriate choices. If this is the case, the individual is not responsible for crimes committed while suffering from the mental disorder. Note that insanity should not be equated with mental illness or serious mental disorder. That is, the evidence that a person was mentally ill at the time of the crime will not necessarily result in a determination of insanity.

Insanity defenses, especially if they are successful, receive extensive media coverage and commentary. When John Hinckley, charged with an attempt on the life of President Reagan, was found NGRI by a federal jury, there was widespread public indignation accompanied by numerous demands for repeal of the insanity defense in both federal and state law. Since the Hinckley acquittal by reason of insanity in June 1982, at least thirty-four states have made some kind of alteration to their insanity statutes (Steadman, McGreevy, Morrissey, Callahan, Robbins, & Cirincione, 1993). Moreover, in response to the public outcry against the Hinckley acquittal, the U.S. Congress passed the Insanity Defense Act of 1984. The public and some professionals (attorneys, judges, mental health workers, criminal justice personnel) believed the federal law should be changed.

It is important to note that the number of insanity defenses is small in the United States compared to the total number of criminal cases. Unfortunately, there are no *systematic, nationwide* data on how often the insanity defense is actually used (McGinley & Paswark, 1989). County, state, and federal levels of government rarely share information about these issues (Steadman et al., 1993). Steadman and his colleagues write: "County level information on insanity pleas, for example, is rarely, if ever, aggregated to the state level, meaning almost nothing is known about the earliest stages of the insanity defense process" (Steadman et al., 1993, p. 3). However, there are some very good estimates based on studies conducted by independent and governmental researchers. These researchers estimate that insanity defenses are used in only one percent of all U.S. felony criminal cases (Callahan, Steadman, McGreevy, & Robbins, 1991; Simon & Aaronson, 1988; Steadman et al., 1993). We have far more knowledge about the number of *acquittals* by reason of insanity than we do about the number of actual defenses

(Steadman et al., 1993). The number of acquittals by NGRI occur in only 22 to 25 percent of all cases invoking the defense (Callahan et al., 1991; Steadman & Braff, 1983; Burton & Steadman, 1978).

In the United States, acquittals are far more difficult to obtain from juries (jury trials) than from judges (bench trials), a pattern that underscores the pervasive negative attitude the American public has toward the insanity defense. For instance, Callahan et al. (1991) found, in an eight-state study involving nine thousand defendants who pleaded NGRI, that only 7 percent of the acquittals were handed down by juries. The remaining 18 percent were decided by judges. In another study, Boehnert (1989) found that 96 percent of defendants found insane had gone before a judge. Thus, it seems wise for defendants who plan to use the insanity defense to have a bench trial (where the judge decides) rather than a jury trial.

Callahan et al. (1991) found that successful NGRI defendants, compared to unsuccessful defendants, tended to be older, female, better educated, and single. They also had a history of prior hospitalization and were considered extremely disturbed. Furthermore, 15 percent of the acquitted defendants had not themselves raised the insanity defense, indicating that they were so disordered that an insanity verdict was essentially imposed on them.

Defense attorneys have generally not recommended that their clients plead insanity unless they were charged with a serious offense and the evidence against them was overwhelming. When the possible penalty is capital punishment or life imprisonment without parole, an insanity defense becomes more palatable to the defense. In many jurisdictions, however, insanity acquittees are automatically confined to mental institutions, even without a finding of present mental illness. They might be confined for as long as necessary to produce substantial improvement in their condition. In fact, research shows that persons found NGRI on average spend at least as much time in a mental institution or treatment facilities as they would have spent in prison if convicted (Golding & Roesch, 1987). Furthermore, in the past, authorities administering treatment of NGRI individuals were at liberty to use a wide range of therapeutic devices to remedy the deviant condition.

Over the past two decades, there have been several changes in the way NGRIs and other adjudicated mental conditions (e.g., ISTs) can be treated. In general, the U.S. Supreme Court has restricted what the mental health system can do to NGRIs. For example, in 1992, the Court, in *Foucha v. Louisiana*, ruled that insanity aquatics may not be held in psychiatric facilities once they are no longer mentally disordered. Once they are evaluated as no longer mentally disordered, they must be released from the facility immediately and given back their liberties.

INSANITY STANDARDS

The insanity defense has been recognized in English courts for over seven hundred years (Simon, 1983). Since the American legal system is derived from British law, American courts have generally recognized it as well. Standards or tests to determine insanity vary widely among the states, but they usually center around one of three broad models of criminal responsibility: the M'Naghten Rule, the Brawner Rule, or the Durham Rule. Moreover, all the insanity standards are fundamentally based on two criteria: **irrationality** and **compulsion** (Morse, 1986). If it can be established that a person was not in control of his or her mental processes (was thinking irrationally) and/or was not in control of his or her behavior (was driven by compulsion) at the time of the offense, then there are grounds for absolving that person of some or all responsibility for the offense. Jurisdictions, however, differ in the extent they accept both these criteria. That is, some jurisdictions prefer one criteria over the other.

THE M'NAGHTEN RULE: THE RIGHT AND WRONG TEST

The **M'Naghten Rule** has been around in some form since at least the eighteenth century. The current rule was formulated in 1843 when Daniel M'Naghten, a Scottish woodcutter, was accused of killing a man he believed to be the prime minister. M'Naghten thought he was being persecuted by the Tories and their leader, Prime Minister Sir Robert Peel. He fired a shot into a carriage transporting Peel's secretary, Edward Drumond, thinking Peel himself was in the carriage. There was no question that M'Naghten had committed the act, but the court believed he was so mentally deranged that it would be inhuman to convict him, since it was clear he was not in control of his faculties. He was found Not Guilty by Reason of Insanity and was committed to the Broadmoor Mental Institution, where he remained until his death twenty-two years later.

In 1851, the M'Naghten Rule was adopted in the federal and most state courts in the United States. It is deceptively simple, and therein lies its popularity. It states that a person is not responsible for a criminal act if, "at the time of committing the act, the party accused was labouring under such a defect of reason, from disease of the mind, as not to know the nature and quality of the act he was doing; or if he did know it ... he did not know he was doing what was wrong" (M'Naghten, 1843, p. 718). Essentially, the rule states that if a person, because of some mental disease, did not know right from wrong at the time of an unlawful act, or did not know that what he or she was doing was wrong, that person cannot be held responsible for his or her actions.

Thus, the M'Naghten Rule, sometimes referred to as the **right and wrong test**, emphasizes the *cognitive elements* of (1) being aware and knowing what one was doing at the time of the illegal act; or (2) knowing or realizing right from wrong in the moral sense. The rule recognizes no degree of incapacity. You are either responsible for the action or you are not. There are no in-betweens.

Some states supplement M'Naghten with an irresistible impulse test. This test recognizes or assumes that people may realize the wrongfulness of their conduct, be aware of what is right or wrong in a particular set of circumstances, but still be powerless to do right in the face of overwhelming pressures from uncontrollable impulses. In other words, there are conditions under which people presumably cannot help themselves. The M'Naghten Rule alone would not cover those circumstances, since it requires that the person did not know right from wrong.

THE BRAWNER AND ALI RULE

The **Brawner Rule**, which is largely based on an insanity rule suggested by the Model Penal Code (MPC), is another rule for determining insanity. The Model Penal Code was proposed in 1962 by a group of legal scholars called the American Law Institute (ALI). The Code was drafted to serve as a model for legislatures seeking to modernize and rationalize their criminal statutes. According to the Brawner Rule, "A person is not responsible for criminal conduct if at the time of such conduct as a result of mental disease or *defect* (italics added), he lacks substantial capacity either to appreciate the criminality [wrongfulness] of his conduct or to conform his conduct to the requirements of the law" (*U.S. v. Brawner*, 1972, p. 973). It must be demonstrated that the disease or mental defect *substantially* and directly (1) influenced the defendant's mental or emotional processes, or (2) impaired his or her ability to control behavior. The Brawner Rule, unlike M'Naghten, recognizes *partial* responsibility for criminal conduct as well as the possibility of an irresistible impulse beyond one's control. It also excludes from the definition of mental disease or defect any repeated criminal or otherwise antisocial conduct. This provision (called the **caveat paragraph**) was intended to disallow the insanity defense for criminal psychopaths who persistently violate social mores and often the law. Thus, psychopathic or antisocial personality disorders cannot claim that their abnormal condition is a mental disorder, disease, or defect.

THE DURHAM RULE: THE PRODUCT TEST

The **Durham Rule** was created in 1954 in *Durham v. U.S.* by the same court that later rejected it in favor of the Brawner Rule. Monte Durham, a twenty-six-year-old resident of the District of Columbia, had a long history of mental disorder and petty theft. His crime of the moment was burglary, but he was acquitted, because his unlawful act was considered to be "the product of a mental disease or mental defect" (*Durham v. U.S.*, 1954, p. 874). While the M'Naghten Rule focuses on knowing right from wrong (the mental element in a crime), Durham assumes that one cannot be held responsible if an unlawful action is the product of mental disease or defect.

There is nothing in the Durham Rule that relates directly to the person's mental judgment. If the person has a disease or defect, lack of culpability is easily assumed. The rule was later clarified in *Carter v. U.S.* (1957), which held that mental illness must not merely have entered into the production of the act, it must have played a necessary role.

Many states were attracted to the apparent simplicity of the Durham Rule, since it seemed more straightforward and comprehensible to juries. However, it soon became apparent that definitions of "mental illness" are vague and subjective, a situation that fostered the widespread discretionary power of psychiatry and considerable misuse of mental health experts during trial. Moreover, virtually any defendant could be excused, once mental disease or defect had been established, and the Durham Rule quickly lost its popularity.

The well-publicized NGRI acquittal of John Hinckley Jr., for his assassination attempt of President Ronald Reagan in March 1981, sparked a public outcry for the elimination of the insanity defense, and prompted legislative bodies and many professional organizations to reexamine it. The American Bar Association and the American Psychiatric Association, for example, proposed new, more restrictive standards (Steadman et al., 1993). Nearly one hundred different reforms in thirty-four jurisdictions occurred soon after Hinckley's acquittal, the most active insanity reform period in American history. In most instances, these reforms reflected a return to the M'Naghten Rule in a modified, more restrictive form (Steadman et al., 1993). Three states—Montana, Idaho, and Utah—have abolished the insanity defense altogether, an action upheld by the U.S. Supreme Court in *Cowan v. Montana*. In the Cowan case, Joe Junior Cowan, believed to be suffering from paranoid schizophrenia, broke into a Forest Service residence quarters in a remote section of Montana (see Biskupic, 1994). He beat forestry worker Maggie Doherty until she was unconscious. Cowan's lawyer argued that at the time of the attack Cowan was in a state of psychotic delusion which caused him to run "crazily" around Doherty's house, looking into the windows and yelling, "It's my house" and "Who are you?" The trial judge still found Cowan guilty of attempted murder and aggravated burglary and sentenced him to 60 years in prison (Biskupic, 1994). The Montana Supreme Court upheld the conviction, concluding that neither the constitutional guarantee of due process nor the constitutional prohibition against cruel or unusual punishment gives a defendant the right to an insanity defense. The U.S. Supreme, without comment from the Justices, let stand the Montana ruling, opening the door for other states to eliminate the insanity defense. We will now examine two of the more popular variants of the insanity defense that have been tried in recent years by various legislative bodies.

THE INSANITY DEFENSE REFORM ACT

Amid public clamors to abolish the insanity defense completely, Congress passed the **Insanity Defense Reform Act of 1984**, which kept the defense in the federal law but modified it in important ways. Rita Simon and David Aaronson (1988, p. 47) assert: "The *Hinckley* verdict was unquestionably the decisive influence on congressional modifications to the insanity defense." Essentially, Congress made it more difficult for persons using the insanity defense in federal courts to be acquitted. The Insanity Reform Act changed the Brawner/ALI Rule—the rule that has been most consistently adhered to in all federal circuits (except the Fifth Circuit) since its adoption during the early 1970s—to one patterned along the lines of the M'Naghten Rule. Specifically, a defendant cannot be held responsible if "… at the time of the commission of the acts constituting the offense, the defendant, as a result of a severe mental disease or defect, was unable to appreciate the nature and quality or the wrongfulness of his acts. Mental disease or defect does not otherwise constitute a defense" (18 U.S.C., sec 20[a] [1984]).

In addition, the new federal standard changed the Brawner/ALI Rule in three principal ways (Simon & Aaronson, 1988). First, the Act abolished the irresistible impulse test (commonly called the **volitional prong**) of the Brawner/ALI Rule. The inability to control one's actions because of mental defect was no longer acceptable as an excusing condition. Second, the Act modified the "cognitive" requirement by replacing the phrase "lacks substantial capacity … to appreciate" with "unable to appreciate." The intention was to tighten the requirement to a total lack of ability to appreciate that what they did was wrong (Simon & Aaronson, 1988). Third, under the new law, the mental disease or defect must be severe, to emphasize that certain behavioral disorders (especially personality disorders) do not qualify as a defense. It is still too early to tell what long-term effects the Act will have on insanity verdicts in the federal courts.

GUILTY BUT MENTALLY ILL (GBMI)

Also in response to disenchantment with the insanity defense, some states have introduced a new verdict alternative, **Guilty but Mentally Ill** (**GBMI**). Michigan was the first to adopt this alternative in 1975, and by 1992 eleven other states had followed Michigan's lead. In fact, the GBMI verdict became one of the most popular insanity reforms after John Hinckley's acquittal. The GBMI option is intended as an alternative to, not a substitute for, the NGRI verdict. Although states differ in the standards and procedures associated with the GBMI verdict, the major intention of the option was to reduce the number of insanity acquittals, hold the defendant blameworthy, but still recognize the presence of a mental disorder. Thus, it allows the court to render a "middle-ground" verdict in the case of allegedly mentally disordered defendants. The verdict allows juries, for example, to reconcile their belief that a defendant who commits a crime should be held responsible with the belief that he or she also needs help.

Research on the GBMI laws indicate that they may not have accomplished their intended purposes. In Michigan, for example, insanity acquittals have remained stable while guilty verdicts have generally declined (Smith & Hall, 1982). The same findings have been reported in other states that have adopted the GBMI (McGinley & Paswark, 1989). Furthermore, defendants who have elected to use the GBMI have received longer sentences and had longer confinements than "sane" defendants found guilty of similar charges (Callahan, McGreevy, Cirincione, & Steadman, 1992; Steadman et al., 1993). In addition, research indicates that those individuals found GBMI are no more likely to receive psychotherapy or rehabilitative services than other mentally disordered defendants in the prison system (Morse, 1985; Slobogin, 1985). Therefore, mentally disordered defendants are unlikely to pursue the GBMI alternative in the future unless significant changes are made in the law. Instead, they are more likely to take their chances with the traditional insanity defense.

Currently, there is considerable evidence that defendants charged with a serious violent crime often elect the GBMI alternative after plea bargaining, suggesting that defense attorneys have been more willing to accept a GBMI verdict rather than go to trial and risk their client's life (Steadman et al., 1993).

INCOMPETENCY TO STAND TRIAL

Some persons charged with a crime are considered so intellectually and/or psychologically impaired that they are unable to understand the charges or the judicial process, or unable to cooperate rationally with their attorneys in their own defense.

Specifically, the U.S. Supreme Court has held that defendants are competent to stand trial if they have "sufficient present ability to consult with their lawyer with a reasonable degree of rational understanding ... and a rational as well as factual understanding of the proceedings..." (*Dusky v. U.S.*, 1960, p. 402). If determined to be **Incompetent to Stand Trial (IST)**, they are so adjudicated and remitted to a mental institution, or less frequently, to an outpatient therapeutic program, until rendered competent. Generally, the trial is held in abeyance until the defendant is found competent, or, alternately, the case is dismissed.

Evaluations for competency to stand trial represent the most common referral for criminally-related forensic assessments (Cruise & Rogers, 1998). Recent data indicate that approximately twenty-five thousand criminal defendants nationwide, or about one in fifteen, are evaluated for their competency to stand trial each year by state and federal courts (Nicholson & Kugler, 1991; Cruise & Rogers, 1998). Moreover, about four out of every five defendants evaluated for competency to stand trial are found competent (Grisso, 1986; Nicholson & Kugler, 1991). Incompetency to stand trial has no direct relevance to insanity, and the two determinations must be viewed distinctly. Criminal responsibility, which is at the core of the insanity defense, and competency to stand trial refer to a defendant's mental state/capacity at *two different points in time*. In an insanity claim, the law asks, "What was the defendant's state of mind at the time the offense was committed?" In competency considerations, the question becomes, "What is the defendant's state of mind at the present time, or at the time of the trial?" An individual who was seriously mentally disordered at the time of an offense may have enough mental stability by the time of the trial to be competent to stand trial. On the other hand, a person may be of sound mind during the unlawful act, but may later become disordered or disoriented and be determined IST. Furthermore, the competency issue can be raised at any time during the actual proceedings.

Persons found IST, therefore, have not been convicted of any crime, but they may nevertheless be institutionalized for treatment. In recent years, however, ISTs have asserted constitutional rights in connection with their status, including the right to the "least restrictive or drastic alternative" in treatment (Winick, 1983). They have been successful to some extent in lower courts, but the U.S. Supreme Court has not ruled on this matter.

Research on persons found IST indicates that they are highly similar in background characteristics. Most have limited social and occupational skills and a history of prior criminal charges and psychiatric hospitalizations (Williams & Miller, 1981). Compared to the general population, ISTs are disproportionately unmarried, African American, and poorly educated (less than ninth grade education) (Steadman, 1979). More recent research has continued to support Steadman's earlier findings (Nicholson & Kugler, 1991). In fact, a review by Nicholson and Kugler (1991) finds that all individuals referred for competency evaluations (not just those found IST) are largely single, unemployed, and poorly educated.

Individuals adjudicated IST are much more likely than criminal defendants to be charged with violent offenses (Nicholson & Kugler, 1991). Furthermore, the seriousness of the criminal charges against them seem to play a greater role in determining the length of their confinement than the severity of the mental disorder. IST defendants are often diagnosed psychotic or with other serious mental disorders. Nicholson and Kugler (1991, p. 364) conclude: "… defendants who manifested disorientation and impaired memory, poor judgment, thought and communication disturbances, hallucinations, delusions, and bizarre, unmanageable behavior were considered unfit to proceed to trial more often than defendants who did not exhibit such symptoms."

In addition, the IST recidivism rate appears significantly higher than the recidivism rate of comparable offenders not adjudicated mentally disordered (Steadman & Hartstone, 1983). The overall picture indicates that ISTs are marginal individuals with low educational attainment, poor job skills, and a propensity for running afoul of the law. They appear to shuttle back and forth between mental hospitals, and they have few employment or family ties (Steadman, 1979). The IST route, which is often used by criminal defense attorneys as a delaying tactic until community outrage over a heinous crime dissipates, may also represent a tendency to shunt off defendants with little social influence.

In an extensive study of mentally disordered offenders housed in New York state institutions in the mid-1960s, Steadman and Cocozza (1974) found that approximately 40 percent were IST defendants. Another survey by Steadman and his colleagues (1982) a few years later indicated that the IST figure declined to about 32 percent, although these data are incomplete, since only a portion of the institutions surveyed kept records of the actual number of ISTs confined. Thus, about one-third of those involuntarily confined to secure mental hospitals for an *indefinite* period (until somehow rendered "competent") were only *charged with*, not convicted of, a crime. Steadman and Cocozza also discovered (as have other investigators) that a shockingly large number of IST defendants had been confined against their will, sometimes for periods far exceeding the maximum sentence for their alleged offense. More significantly, the Steadman-Cocozza data showed that ISTs had not received any treatment that would enable them to achieve competency; in fact, there were often no guidelines or criteria for determining such competency.

Until the 1970s, the typical procedure for determining incompetency required that defendants be confined within a maximum security institution for a lengthy psychiatric-psychological evaluation (usually sixty to ninety days). Following evaluation, the defendant was granted a hearing on the matter of competency. If the court found the defendant unable to understand the charges or the judicial proceedings, or to help counsel in his or her defense, then the defendant would be automatically committed to a secure hospital for an indefinite period of time—until competent. Theoretically, this indefinite time period could extend—and sometimes did—into a lifetime of involuntary commitment. Effective treatment was either not provided or could not be offered, and it was anyone's guess what actually constituted competency.

Mentally disordered offenders, as a group, receive very little psychotherapy, and when it is provided, its effectiveness is highly debatable. In fact, no consistently effective therapy has yet been developed for many serious mental disorders.

The traditional form of "talk" psychotherapy is effective primarily for intelligent and articulate individuals plagued with neurotic disorders and motivated to change. Almost all presently existing forms of psychotherapy are ineffective for people demonstrating bizarre or antisocial behavior, especially if they have limited intelligence or education. Psychoactive drugs do not seem to change a patient's mental state permanently, only render them more manageable temporarily. Many psychotherapists are willing to admit that if they cannot produce marked improvements within the first six months of treatment, they will not do so thereafter, however long they try (Walker, 1978).

Courts are beginning to ameliorate the many injustices perpetuated against mentally disordered offenders, injustices often promoted by the numerous disparities between criminal law and mental health law (Wexler, 1977, 1981). The U.S. Supreme Court restricted both the length of time for IST evaluation and the limits of legal confinement (*Jackson v. Indiana*, 1972), and has protected prisoners being transferred to mental institutions without benefit of a hearing on the issue of their mental condition (*Vitek v. Jones*, 1980). Today, individuals found IST, with little likelihood of being restored to competency, often have their cases *dismissed without prejudice*. However, in many jurisdictions, the prosecutor still retains the option of reinstituting charges if the person does regain competency at some later time.

DRUGS AND INCOMPETENT DEFENDANTS

In some cases, the judicial system may feel there is strong interest in bringing an IST defendant to trial, particularly if psychoactive drugs can stabilize the mental condition and render the defendant competent. Psychoactive drugs are "those drugs that exert their primary effect on the brain, thus altering mood or behavior, or that are used in the treatment of mental disorders" (Julien, 1992, p. xii).

In *U.S. v. Charters* (1988), the Supreme Court ruled that an IST defendant could be forced to take psychoactive drugs against his will at the discretion of medical personnel. In *Tran Van Khiem v. U.S.* (1992), the Supreme Court again held that a murder defendant found IST could be treated with psychoactive drugs against his will. The Court ruled against the defendant in the case, because the government's interest in bringing him to trial was greater than the defendant's interest in avoiding the effects of the drugs (Bartol & Bartol, 1994). However, in *Riggins v. Nevada* (1992), the Court affirmed the right of a defendant claiming *insanity* to be free of psychoactive drugs during his trial. Thus, the issue of whether an IST defendant should be forced to take measures that render him or her competent for trial remains unsolved at this point, but is likely to be addressed frequently in the near future.

TRANSFERS

A third way a person may attain mentally disordered offender status (besides NGRI and IST) is by exhibiting severely disturbed behavior while incarcerated in a prison or correctional facility. The Steadman-Cocozza 1974 analysis revealed that 40 percent of the mentally disordered population were "mentally ill" inmates who had been transferred out of prison and into secure mental hospitals. The most recent Steadman survey (1982) found that number had increased to over 54 percent of the mentally disordered population. About 96 percent of transfers from a prison to a mental hospital were male. Roth (1980) estimates that between 15 and 20 percent of prison inmates exhibit sufficient psychological "pathology" to warrant psychiatric attention, although this does not mean they warrant transfer. According to Roth, about 5 percent of the disorders would qualify as psychosis.

Because states differ greatly in the transfer options they provide for mentally disordered prisoners, it is difficult to distinguish a general pattern in either the disorders or the circumstances surrounding the transfers. However, in 1980, the U.S. Supreme Court began to address the transfer practice, in *Vitek v. Jones*. The Court ruled that the transfer of an inmate to a mental health hospital requires, at a minimum, an administrative hearing to determine whether such transfer is appropriate. The Supreme Court recognized the special nature of confinement in a mental health facility and the stigma that often accompanies a commitment (Churgin, 1983). Furthermore, transfer to a mental institution not only entails forced treatment of almost any variety, but also may substantially reduce chances for parole, since parole boards may be reluctant to release into the community a prisoner who was recently in a mental hospital setting.

THE MENTALLY DISORDERED SEX OFFENDER

A fourth way of being adjudicated a mentally disordered offender is through **Mentally Disordered Sex Offender** (MDSO) statutes. Although the number of states that use MDSO statutes is steadily decreasing, this legal status still warrants some brief comment concerning how it is used.

The legal literature often refers to these laws as "sexual psychopath statutes," but the term psychopath is not really appropriate for a vast majority of these offenders. Other than the label, the statutes have little in common. In most cases, the legislative intention was to provide special dispositional procedures for persons who exhibit a tendency to commit sex offenses, but each state has developed its own set of procedures and definitions. Either explicitly or implicitly, the statutes depict the sexual psychopath as a mentally disordered individual who is particularly *dangerous* to children, women, or both.

In 1937, Michigan became the first state to enact a sexual psychopath statute. It was joined by California in 1939. At one time nearly thirty states had sexual psychopath statutes. In 1963, the change in terminology to "mentally disordered sex offender" took place (Dix, 1983). The earlier statutes sought to "intercept" the "sexual psychopath" even before he was convicted of a crime (Morris, 1982). Today, statutes generally require a conviction, usually of a sex crime, which may range from indecent exposure to forcible rape. Morris (1982, p. 136) notes that the early statutes represented "immediate legislative reactions to sensational sexual crimes," and that they illustrated "a legislative capacity to conceal excessive punitiveness behind a veil of psychiatric treatment.… At base lies the false assumption of a connection between sexual offenses and mental illness.…" The statutes were also based on the equally false premise that sexual offenders start with minor sexual offenses (e.g., indecent exposure, voyeurism) and move on to more serious ones (e.g., forcible rape).

In recent years there has been a strong move to repeal and abolish MDSO statutes (Dix, 1983). This shift in policy is likely due in part to the many constitutional challenges to discriminatory procedures, inadequate treatment, indeterminate sentencing, and the frequently vague terminology of the statutes. This state of flux with regard to MDSO statutes creates problems for the researcher. There is too little consistency and such a lack of uniformity that it is almost impossible to reach valid conclusions about who gets legally labeled MDSO.

Some studies have made the effort, however. The Steadman project, for example (Steadman et al., 1982), found that virtually all MDSOs are male. In 1978, state and federal courts filed approximately 3,600 requests for clinical evaluations for possible MDSO status. The major determining factor as to whether an offender received this status appeared to be past criminal record. Those with prior sex-related criminal records (other than the current offenses) were far more likely to be evaluated MDSO than those with no prior sex-related criminal record or with a non-sex-related record (Konecni, Mulcahy, & Ebbesen, 1980). Dix (1976) found that 85 to 90 percent of the MDSOs committed to California's Atascadero State Hospital had a prior history of sex offenses. The available evidence suggests that courts rely heavily on the offender's social history and prior criminal record to make their determinations, rather than on facts surrounding the current charge.

Sturgeon and Taylor (1980) compared 260 MDSOs to 122 offenders convicted of sex crimes but not adjudicated MDSO. White sex offenders were more likely to be found MDSO and referred for treatment in a mental health facility, while African-American and Hispanic sex offenders were nearly twice as likely to be sent to prison. Similar results were reported by Pacht and Cowden (1974), who also found that MDSOs tend to be older and have more prior sexual offenses on their records than other persons convicted of a sexual offense. MDSOs are usually committed to a mental institution for an indeterminate length of time. If the 1978 Steadman survey (Steadman et al., 1982) is representative, MDSOs are also committed for a longer period of time than other mentally disordered offenders.

The procedures used by the law to assign MDSO status, as well as the treatment of offenders once they have been so assigned, raise ethical, philosophical, and legal issues that are beyond the scope of this text. To some extent, these same issues relate to adjudication and treatment of mentally disordered offenders in general. Cohen (1980) offers a comprehensive legal assessment of the areas in civil and criminal law that represent questionable deprivations of individual liberty in the name of the individual's or society's best interest.

For our purposes, however, we should reiterate that the mentally disordered offender classifications are usually based on the assumption that these individuals are dangerous to the community, often more so than persons convicted of crimes but not mentally disordered. This presumably justifies more extensive—and in some cases indefinite—confinement. MDSOs are considered especially dangerous to women and children. NGRIs and ISTs are presumed dangerous because they have already committed a criminal act, regardless of its nature, although they have not been convicted. Transfers are dangerous to the prison community and must be confined elsewhere. Dangerousness has a variety of implicit meanings, however, and is seldom defined adequately in the statutes. Furthermore, researchers and clinicians have a very difficult time not only defining it but, more important, evaluating and predicting it. This is not to suggest that mentally disordered offenders are never a threat to society. Those who are should be identified and confined, and a bona fide effort made to provide them with treatment. On the other hand, as we will discover in the next section, dangerous behavior is almost always overpredicted.

MENTAL DISORDERS AS UNIQUE DEFENSES

During the past decade, defendants have used a variety of special mental disorders in an effort to absolve themselves completely of criminal responsibility or to support a claim of diminished capacity or diminished responsibility. These **unique defenses** include multiple personality disorder, post-traumatic stress disorder, amnesia, pathological gambler's syndrome, battered woman syndrome, and sexual addiction. We will cover the first four unique defenses in this section, while the latter two will be discussed later in the book.

POST-TRAUMATIC STRESS DISORDER (PTSD)

According to the DSM-IV, **post-traumatic stress disorder (PTSD)** is "the development of characteristic symptoms following exposure to extreme traumatic stress or involving direct personal experience of an event that involves actual or threatened death or serious injury, or other threat to one's physical integrity; or witnessing an event that involves death, injury, or threat to the physical integrity of another person; or learning abut unexpected or violent death, serious harm, or threat of death or injury experienced by a family member or other close associate" (p. 424). The precipitating event would be substantially distressing to almost anyone, and is "usually experienced with intense fear, terror, and helplessness" (p. 424).

PTSD was formally recognized as a distinct disorder in the 1980 edition of the DSM-III following efforts by veterans' groups to have mental health professionals recognize a "post-Vietnam syndrome" that led to a variety of disabling symptoms (Appelbaum, Jick, Grisso, Givelbar, Silver, & Steadman, 1993). Since being formally recognized, PTSD has been a syndrome that has been broadly applied to war veterans, survivors of the Holocaust, survivors of major disasters, and victims of rape, child abuse, spousal abuse, and sexual harassment.

Surveys estimate that between 1 and 2 percent of all Americans suffer from PTSD (Sutker, Uddo-Crane, & Allain, 1991). One study estimated that PTSD affected 31 percent of all male and 27 percent of all female Vietnam veterans (Kulka, Schlenger, Fairbank, Jordan, Hough, Marmar, & Weiss, 1991).

The symptoms of PTSD include "flashbacks," recurrent dreams or nightmares, or painful, intrusive memories of the traumatic event. A diminished responsiveness, a don't-care attitude, or psychological "numbing" to the external world are common, particularly during the weeks following the event. Feelings of alienation or detachment from the social environment are also characteristic, a pattern that leads to difficulty in developing close, meaningful relationships with others. Other symptoms include sleep problems, being easily startled, considerable difficulty concentrating or remembering, and extreme avoidance of anything that reminds them of the event. Even anniversaries of the trauma are often enough to precipitate symptoms. These individuals tend to be moody, depressed, and difficult to be around or work with. They often move from job to job, relationship to relationship.

PTSD has been used to support a defense of NGRI, in both violent and nonviolent cases (Monahan & Walker, 1990, 1994). For example, PTSD has been used as an excusing condition for drug trafficking (e.g., *U.S. v. Krutschewski*, 1981). Evidence to date, however, shows that using PTSD in the courts as an *insanity defense* is no more successful than other mental disorders (Appelbaum et al., 1993). Moreover, PTSD defendants, as a rule, do not follow the stereotypic images portrayed by the media as "tortured but essentially upstanding veterans, who at some point, become overwhelmed by their symptoms, 'snap,' and commit a violent crime" (Appelbaum et al., 1993, p. 233). Specifically, the research evidence reveals that defendants who use PTSD as an insanity defense have been in as much trouble and involvement with the criminal justice system as other defendants who use the insanity defense (Appelbaum et al., 1993).

When the PTSD defense has been successful, it usually results in a finding of *diminished responsibility*, rather than the complete absolution of responsibility (NGRI) for the defendant. PTSD has also been cited in plea bargaining and in presentence reports (Monahan & Walker, 1990). Appelbaum and colleagues (1993) find that, in cases involving veterans, PTSD is frequently used as evidence for diminished responsibility in deciding cases for pretrial diversion, plea bargaining, and sentencing.

The primary legal argument used by the defense is that the defendant was in a PTSD dissociative state when he committed the act. This has been especially the approach used by PTSD Vietnam veterans. For example, in *State v. Felde* (1982), the defendant who shot a police officer "claimed that he was in a dissociative state and that he believed that he had been captured by the North Vietnamese at the time he shot the officer" (McCord, 1987, p. 65). In *U.S. v. Crosby* (1983), the defendant, charged with kidnapping and assault with a deadly weapon, claimed he was in a dissociative state caused by PTSD at the time of the incident. In *Miller v. State*, the defendant, charged with a prison escape, argued that he thought he was still in Vietnam and his only intention was to get back to the United States.

In addition to its role as the underlying mental condition for the insanity defense, PTSD has also been used to excuse or mitigate criminal responsibility in cases involving battered women (Appelbaum et al., 1993). Generally, the battered woman claims that the abuse had been so extensive and brutal that she suffered PTSD, and in that dissociative mental state, killed the abuser (usually her husband). Also, evidence that an alleged rape victim shows the symptoms of PTSD has been accepted in some courts as proof that the victim has indeed been raped (Appelbaum et al., 1993).

Methods for objective assessment of PTSD generally lack solid validity and the diagnosis depends almost exclusively on self-report. Therefore, there is considerable opportunity for faking the disorder, especially if the individual rehearses and practices the symptoms. Appelbaum et al. (1993, p. 230) conclude that the problem of PTSD in the courts as an excusing condition is "particularly acute with something as new, as 'unverifiable,' as potentially useful, and as politically charged as PTSD."

PATHOLOGICAL GAMBLERS' SYNDROME

The syndrome of **compulsive gambling** began with psychoanalytic case studies during the early part of the twentieth century (Cunnien, 1985). Compulsive gamblers, the early case studies concluded, are neurotics with an insatiable, unconscious desire to lose what was gained (Cunnien, 1985). The DSM-IV describes pathological gambling as the inability to resist impulses to gamble, despite the dire consequences to family, interpersonal relationships, and daily living. "The essential feature of Pathological Gambling is persistent and recurrent maladaptive gambling behavior that disrupts personal, family, or vocational pursuits" (DSM-IV, p. 615). It is a progressive and eventually overwhelming urge to engage in gambling behavior. The disorder may afflict as many as 1 to 3 percent of the adult population, and is more common among males than females (DSM-IV). In a survey of 1,200 residents of Ontario, Insight Canada Research (1998) found that about 8 percent of Ontarians could be classified as "problem gamblers," while 0.9 percent are probable pathological gamblers. Pathological gambling usually begins during adolescence in males, and later in life in females (DSM-IV). Pathological gamblers are often overconfident, very energetic, and easily bored, but sometimes exhibit stress, anxiety, and depression during their losing streaks.

The distinguishing characteristic of pathological gambling from "normal" or social gambling is its "addictive" nature. Addicted gamblers are believed to be unable to walk away from a gamble and are tense and restless if gambling is denied them.

Pathological gambling became fully recognized in the DSM-III in 1980 as a serious mental disorder, and since that time the disorder has been used by defendants as an excuse for a variety of illegal activities. The crimes with which defendants have been charged are not gambling offenses, but rather crimes committed for monetary gain. The defendants contended that money was necessary in order to support their pathological gambling habit (McCord, 1987). For example, in *U.S. v. Gillis* (1985), the defendant, who was charged with interstate transportation of stolen vehicles and forged securities, argued that he engaged in these illegal activities to support his gambling habit. The following are additional examples where similar defenses were used: *U.S. v. Davis* (1984), where the defendant was charged with forging and converting government checks payable to deceased relatives; *U.S. v. Gould* (1984), where the defendant was charged with bank robbery; and *U.S. v. Lewellyn* (1985), where the defendant was charged with embezzlement, making a false statement and mail fraud.

In general, defendants using this defense have been unsuccessful, because they have been unable to demonstrate a connection between "the syndrome and the inability of the defendant to resist the impulse to commit crimes in order to support the gambling urge" (McCord, 1987, p. 67). However, it should be noted that the pathological gambling defense has been occasionally successful, as seen in *State v. Lafferty* (1984) in a case involving embezzlement, and in *State v. Campanaro* (1980) in a case involving forgery.

Cunnien (1985, p. 89) writes: "There are ... no available data to suggest whether pathological gambling and attendant criminal behavior are uncontrollable or merely uncontrolled." He further concludes, "It remains unproven that impulses to gamble are uncontrollable" (Cunnien, 1985, p. 98).

MULTIPLE PERSONALITY DISORDER

The essential feature of **multiple personality disorder** (MPD) (now called **dissociative identity disorder**) is "the existence within the person of two or more distinct personalities or personality states that recurrently take control of behavior" (DSM-IV, p. 484). Furthermore, "each personality state may be experienced as if it has a distinct personal history, self-image, and identity, including a separate name" (DSM-IV, p. 484). Periodically, at least two personalities take full control of the individual's behavior. The change or transition from one personality is often very sudden (seconds to minutes), and is generally triggered by stress or some relevant environmental stimuli. Often, hypnosis can also bring about this shift into another personality.

According to the DSM-IV, each of the personalities may be aware of some or all the other personalities in varying degrees. There may be as many as a hundred different identities. The disorder occurs about three to nine times more frequently in females than in males. Persons who experience MPD are highly suggestible and impressionable, and can be readily hypnotized either by themselves or others. Reported cases of MPD have historically been extremely rare. However, between 1980 and 1989 the number of cases diagnosed in the United States rose dramatically, from two hundred to at least six thousand (Slovenko, 1989). Part of this increase is due to the American Psychiatric Association officially recognizing the disorder in the DSM-III.

On occasion, MPD has been used successfully as an excusing condition for criminal responsibility. In *State v. Rodrigues* (1984), a defendant accused of three counts of sodomy and one count of rape on young girls was acquitted on the basis of MPD. In *State v. Milligan* (1978), Billy Milligan claimed he had twenty-four separate personalities and was found Not Guilty by Reason of Insanity in criminal charges of raping three women. In general, however, MPD has not been a successful defense (Slovenko, 1989). One of the more well-known cases in which the MPD defense was tried involved serial killer Kenneth Bianchi, known as the Hillside Strangler. The Hillside Strangler was given wide publicity because of the brutality and sadistic quality of his murders. The victims were young, attractive women who were raped and strangled, and whose nude bodies were conspicuously displayed on the hillsides in the Los Angeles area. The Hillside Strangler was responsible for at least a dozen murders during a one-year period (1977–1978).

Much of the following material was acquired from an article written by Martin T. Orne, David F. Dinges, and Emily Carota Orne (1984), and the interested reader is encouraged to study that paper. Throughout his adult life, Bianchi's most consistent career aspiration was to become a police officer, and he even attended a junior college program in police science. Although he repeatedly applied for positions at various police departments, he was not successful at landing a job. However, he did obtain employment as a security guard.

Overall, Bianchi was unable to sustain a successful career pattern, holding at least twelve different jobs during the nine-year period following high school. His background was a series of deceit, lies, scams, and illegal activities, ranging from the use of stolen credit cards to the pimping of juvenile prostitutes. During his last year in Los Angeles, Bianchi masqueraded as a psychologist, complete with an office and answering service. He obtained false diplomas and credentials by placing a classified ad in the *Los Angeles Times*, offering a position to a recently graduated psychologist. He requested that the applicants send not only résumés, but also their official university transcripts as well. From the hundreds of applications he received, he obtained enough information to forge a transcript and diploma with his name on them.

At age nineteen, Bianchi married a high school girlfriend, but the marriage lasted less than eight months. At age twenty-six, he began to live with a woman in a common-law relationship; she bore him a son. After the birth of his son, his common-law wife moved to Bellingham, Washington, where Bianchi joined her three months later. In Bellingham, he obtained a job as a supervisor for a private security agency. Bianchi, however, was arrested on January 11, 1979, for the murders of two women in Washington—murders that followed a pattern similar to the Hillside Strangler in California.

Despite considerable evidence against him, Bianchi insisted that he was innocent. Eventually, he maintained under hypnosis that his alter personality "Steve" had done the killings. Since Steve did the killings, Ken Bianchi argued he should not be held responsible and pleaded NGRI under the State of Washington's M'Naghten Rule. The court appointed a team of experts to determine if Bianchi really was suffering MPD. The court (*State v. Bianchi*, 1979) posited that if the experts could agree, the insanity defense might prevail. The team of experts, however, after careful examination of his past and present behavior, found no basis for Bianchi's claim of MPD. Although Bianchi knew the "textbook version" of MPD (probably knowledge gained during the time he impersonated a psychologist), he was less than convincing on the more subtle aspects of the disorder recognized by the experts. The team concluded that Bianchi was a psychopath. Bianchi then quickly changed his plea to guilty in order to avoid the death penalty.

It became clear during the intensive evaluation of his background that Bianchi killed for sexual gratification, and it probably was no accident that the Hillside murders began during his common-law wife's pregnancy and ceased with the birth of his son (Orne et al., 1984). The murders in Bellingham, Washington, occurred during the time Bianchi's common-law wife was nursing the child, a time when Bianchi found her sexually unappealing.

There is considerable debate among practitioners and scholars as to whether the syndrome MPD actually exists, and it is sometimes referred to as the "UFO of psychiatry" (Ondrovik & Hamilton, 1991). In most instances, MPD may possibly be iatrogenic—that is, unintentionally caused by clinicians or practitioners themselves (Comer, 1992). This means that practitioners who firmly believe in and are perceptually sensitive to MPD look for and interpret a variety of behaviors as symptoms of MPD. In effect, the practitioner may develop the syndrome in the patient, and the patient, in turn, learns to believe that he or she is afflicted with MPD. It has also been argued that implicit and explicit suggestions during hypnosis can shape segments of self into the appearance of MPD (Orne et al., 1984). Regardless of whether the syndrome is developed by others, or if there is such a thing as several personalities actually "possessing" a physical body, the important point is that the syndrome is *often subjectively* real to the patient. And the person who experiences MPD often plays each of the roles well and convincingly. Martin Orne and his colleagues (Orne et al., 1984, p. 120) observe: "So striking are the behavioral differences between personalities that the assertion is often made that one would need to have the dramatic skills of Sarah Bernhardt or Sir Laurence Olivier, along with a detailed knowledge of psychiatry, to effectively simulate such radically different persons."

Everyone to some degree hosts a number of subpersonalities (Slovenko, 1989). One aspect of our subpersonalities is our moods: One day we may be cool and withdrawn, and the next day, warm and sociable. The situation also makes a big difference. For example, each person is different at home with parents as compared to spending time with friends. At home, parents might treat you like the immature sixteen-year-old they remember, and you find yourself assuming that role quickly and easily. The old conflicts and squabbles with your parents return, just like years ago.

In summary, the validity of MPD as a viable entity is very much open to debate by both the mental health and legal professions. At present, there is very little solid evidence that the syndrome, as a bona fide mental disorder in which one personality completely controls the other(s), actually exists.

AMNESIA

Amnesia refers to complete or partial memory loss of an event, series of events, or some segment of life's experiences, either due to physical trauma, neurophysiological disturbance, or psychological factors. According to the DSM-IV, "Individuals with an amnestic disorder are impaired in their ability to learn new information or are unable to recall previously learned information or past events" (p. 156). Amnesia is not simply forgetting a name, a date, an incident, but is reserved for severely impaired ability to remember past material (retrograde amnesia) or to acquire and retain new material (anterograde amnesia).

Some researchers have identified a classification of amnesia called **limited amnesia**, which is "a pathological inability to remember a specific episode, or small number of episodes, from the recent past" (Schacter, 1986b, p. 48). Limited amnesia may be caused by emotional shock, alcohol or drug intoxication, or a blow to the head. Therefore, limited amnesia is not ongoing, nor does it involve extensive memory loss. Rather, the loss is temporary and restricted to a specific event or incident.

In general, the courts have not been receptive to amnesia as a valid condition in either the insanity defense, or as a condition that promotes incompetence to stand trial (Rubinsky & Brandt, 1986). Paull (1993) notes that there have been cases in at least twenty states and five federal circuit courts where the court has held that amnesia per se does not render a defendant incompetent. One reason for this judicial "hard line" approach to amnesia is the suspicion that the defendant may be faking the memory loss. It is easy for people to simply say they cannot remember committing the crime, and it is difficult for psychologists to determine whether a person can or cannot remember. Alcoholic intoxication presents a favorite alibi for reprehensible behavior, and is the most commonly invoked excusing condition in criminal cases. "When I drink I go blank about some things" is the usual line. It is intriguing to note that 30 to 65 percent of persons convicted of homicide claim they cannot remember the crime, usually because of alcoholic intoxication at the time of the offense (Schachter, 1986b). A similar pattern exists for other violent crimes (e.g., rape) as well.

However, the courts have not been very sympathetic to defendants who rely on excuses based on alcohol or drug intoxication. This is because the courts hold the person blameworthy since he or she should have known, at the outset, the risks involved in drinking alcohol or taking drugs. Thus, attempts to use amnesia as the foundation of an insanity defense have met with strong judicial resistance. For example, one court held that "insanity is the incapacity to discriminate between right and wrong while amnesia is simply the inability to remember" (Rubinsky & Brandt, 1986, p. 30). Therefore, amnesia per se fails to qualify as a mental disorder that robs a person of the ability to distinguish between right and wrong.

DANGEROUSNESS

In August 1966, Charles Whitman, a University of Texas student majoring in architectural engineering, murdered his wife and his mother. Shortly thereafter, he carried his personal arsenal in a footlocker to the observation deck of the 307-foot-tall University Tower. He proceeded to load a number of high-powered, scope-equipped rifles and began randomly shooting at people near the observation deck and on the ground far below. Whitman managed to shoot forty-four victims, killing fourteen, before a police officer and a citizen climbed to the tower and ended the tragedy by shooting Whitman himself.

An investigation revealed that the twenty-five-year-old Whitman had consulted a psychiatrist five months before the incident, and, during a two-hour interview, had described "overwhelming violent impulses" and great fear of his inability to control them. He had also revealed a compelling need to "go up on the tower with a deer rifle and start shooting people." Whitman did not return for further consultation after the initial two-hour session. Nevertheless, when the news of his contact with a psychiatrist was disseminated, there was public outcry and many questions about why he was not treated, confined, or referred to the proper author-ities. Similar questions were raised when the public learned that James Huberty, who killed twenty-two fast-food restaurant patrons in the summer of 1984, had also had contact with a mental health clinic. In Huberty's case, social workers had apparently tried without success to return his telephone calls.

Are clinicians obligated to notify others of the dangerousness of their clients? This issue was raised in a California suit charging that a University psychologist failed to do just that (*Tarasoff v. Regents of the University of California*, 1974). Prosenjit Poddar was a voluntary outpatient at a University of California-Berkeley clinic. During his therapy sessions with a clinical psychologist, Poddar articulated fan-tasies of harming, or perhaps even killing, Tatiana Tarasoff, whom he had met at a dance. The psychologist, who learned from one of Poddar's friends that he planned to purchase a gun, became increasingly concerned. When the patient discontinued therapy, clinic officials wrote to the police requesting their help in getting Poddar committed to a mental institution. Police investigated the case, interviewed Poddar, warned him to stay away from Tatiana, but did not pursue the commitment, appar-ently because California's new civil commitment law was difficult to interpret. Two months later, Poddar killed Tatiana Tarasoff by stabbing her, though he was carry-ing his newly purchased gun. He was charged with first-degree murder. Tarasoff's family sued the University clinic, claiming the psychologist had been negligent in not warning the young woman or the family of the danger.

The Tarasoff case, undoubtedly familiar to all clinicians, addressed very directly the question of what duty therapists owe to third parties in warning them of possible harmful behavior from their clients. The California Supreme Court ruled that a psychotherapist has an obligation to use reasonable care to protect intended victims. We will set aside the many implications of the decision with regard to patient-therapist confidentiality, as well as the numerous questions it poses about precisely what type of warning is sufficient. Implicit in the duty found by the California court is the capacity to predict dangerousness.

The court apparently believed that mental health professionals can predict with considerable accuracy who is or will be dangerous and who will not. The law has been relying on predictions of dangerousness for a long time, dating at least as far back as the sixteenth century (Morris & Miller, 1985). Yet researchers and clini-cians have long struggled both to define dangerousness and to predict its occur-rence. After the Tarasoff case, dangerousness generated more controversy than even the insanity defense (Simon & Cockerham, 1977). The concept is a crucial one, because both criminal and civil statutes provide for the incarceration or involun-tary confinement of those believed to be dangerous. In criminal law, persons con-victed of serious crimes are confined in part to protect society from further harm. Furthermore, both adults and juveniles are subject to detention even before being convicted of a crime or adjudicated a delinquent if they are believed dangerous. Decisions regarding whether to parole prisoners are largely based on whether they are dangerous. In involuntary civil commitment, persons believed to be dangerous to themselves or to others because of a mental disorder may be confined until that disorder is corrected.

There is no question that a person is dangerous who has been violent in the past and indicates by word or deed that he or she plans to do serious harm to others. Someone who has committed a series of murders, mutilations, or rapes, and who attests to planning to do more of the same, is certainly—by anyone's definition—a dangerous individual. If a person has no history of violence and threatens harm, however, the situation becomes more problematic. In this context, clinicians have difficulty reaching a consensus on who is dangerous and who is not. For example, if you are asked to list whatever you consider dangerous behavior, your list will very probably differ in both length and content from your next door neighbor's. Some lists will include behavior that promotes psychological harm, such as terrorizing or threatening others, while others will include behavior that produces damage to property, like defacing a valuable stamp collection. As Nigel Walker (1978) points out, some people have very long lists, others quite short ones.

DEFINITION OF DANGEROUSNESS

The problem of defining dangerous behavior is shared by legislatures and courts as well as by clinicians. All states and all courts recognize that behavior that is likely to result in *physical harm* is dangerous. They begin to differ when behaviors that lead to property damage or psychological injury are involved. One example of psychological injury is the effect on a young woman produced by a person who continually shadows her, observes her public movements, perhaps even photographs her.

Some courts have ruled that this type of behavior can cause irreparable emotional damage. They conclude that a threat of "psychological trauma is ... as much a menace to the health or safety of others as is possible physical injury" (Developments in the Law, 1974, p. 1237; henceforth called Developments). This form of psychological damage has prompted many state legislatures to pass "stalking laws" that state that persons who continually follow and otherwise harass other individuals can be charged with a criminal offense.

Some state statutes and courts also permit damage to property to qualify as dangerous behavior. The extensive legal protection afforded property ownership in our society supports the reasonableness of this conclusion (Developments, 1974). In the *Jones v. U.S.* (1983) case, which supported the automatic and indefinite confinement of a NGRI individual whose offense was petty larceny, the Supreme Court reflected this view. It noted that "crimes of theft frequently may result in violence from the efforts of the criminal to escape or the victim to protect property or the police to apprehend the fleeing criminal" (*Jones v. U.S.*, 1983, p. 3050, footnote 14). In this and other cases, the Court has apparently accepted the argument that dangerousness to property is a proper standard to use in evaluating the need for confinement.

Psychologists and psychiatrists are not generally involved in dangerousness predictions unless some type of mental disorder is at issue. That is, in most criminal law, individuals like judges, juries, and parole board members make decisions about dangerousness without any help from clinicians. In civil commitments and in situations involving the insanity defense, competency to stand trial, or mentally disordered sex offenders, psychologists and psychiatrists are more likely consulted. Many clinicians believe that when the possible outcome is confinement, only behavior that leads to, or is likely to lead to, bodily injury should be considered dangerous. Possible damage to property should not qualify, and psychological damage is far too elusive to form the basis for legal judgments, clinical evaluation, or empirical conclusions. Currently, most jurisdictions agree that a *substantial probability of risk of serious bodily harm* to self or to others constitutes dangerousness, and that risks to property and emotions do not.

Even if we accept this limitation, one hurdle remains: the need to define clearly both seriousness and substantial risk or probability of bodily harm. Neither problem has been resolved to the satisfaction of most scholars of the legal system. Some incidents of bodily harm are clearly serious—murder, mutilation, rape, and bodily injury requiring lengthy hospitalization. What about a broken arm, a black eye, a cut requiring several stitches? Is the mentally disordered person who periodically engages in fist fights a dangerous individual? Currently, the legal definitions of dangerousness are largely restricted to physical or tangible harm of a serious nature, but this standard may change as the legal system sorts out the balance between a person's liberty and the public's safety (Monahan & Shah, 1989).

PREDICTION OF DANGEROUSNESS

The prediction of dangerousness and violence is perhaps the most complicated and controversial issue in the entire field of forensic psychology (Borum, 1996). Today, many researchers and scholars (e.g., Steadman et al., 1993) consider the prediction of dangerousness (also known as risk assessment) to be one of the most important issues in both criminal and civil matters worldwide.

However, the psychological research literature consistently concludes that clinicians are unable to specify the type or severity of harm an individual may cause, or to predict with great accuracy the probability of harm even occurring. Years ago, Alan Stone (1975, p. 33) wrote:

> It can be stated flatly on the basis of my own review of the published material on the prediction of dangerous acts that neither objective actuarial tables nor psychiatric intuition, diagnosis, and psychological testing can claim predictive success when dealing with the traditional population of mental hospitals. The predictive success appropriate to a legal decision can be described in three levels of increasing certainty: Preponderance of the evidence, 51 percent successful; clear and convincing proof, 75 percent successful; beyond a reasonable doubt, at least 90 percent successful.

Stone asserted that mental health professionals have failed to predict dangerous behavior by even the lowest criterion, a *preponderance of the evidence*. The U.S. Supreme Court, however, has ruled that preponderance is too low a standard to use in committing presumably dangerous mentally disordered individuals and has upgraded the evidence for dangerousness standard to clear and convincing proof. We will return to this decision (*Addington v. Texas*, 1979) shortly. In line with Stone's conclusion, Cocozza and Steadman (1976) assert that "any attempt to commit an individual solely on the basis of dangerousness would be futile if psychiatric testimony were subjected to any of these three standards of proof" (p. 1101). They add that the psychological research has demonstrated "clear and convincing evidence of the inability of psychiatrists or anyone else to predict dangerousness accurately" (p. 1099).

Wexler (1981) is not so pessimistic, however. He believes that clinicians are asked only to testify to the potential likelihood of dangerousness, and that is perfectly possible on the basis of characteristics of the individual such as age, gender, clinical diagnosis, history of violence, use of drugs, or verbal threats. He comments, "It may well be possible in a given case to prove *even beyond a reasonable doubt* the existence of given characteristics and their probabilistic association with violent behavior" (1981, p. 61).

Although Wexler's point seems well taken, we must still be concerned about the tendency of clinicians to *overpredict* dangerousness, which may occur even with a clear and compelling standard. In other words, even a variety of factors that might convince a court that the evidence is clear and compelling lend themselves to overprediction. As John Monahan (1981, 1984) notes, studies of clinical predictions of dangerousness show a strong tendency to *overpredict*, a pattern that holds for criminal offenders as well as mentally disordered patients. At a minimum, the most sophisticated predictive methods yield 60 to 70 percent false positives (people who were predicted to be dangerous but did not engage in harmful behavior) (Rubin, 1972; Kozol, Boucher, & Garofalo, 1972; Wenk, Robison, & Smith, 1972). In a ten-year follow-up investigation of 592 convicted male offenders, mostly sex offenders (Kozol, Boucher, & Garofalo, 1972), two of every three persons predicted dangerous were false positives, even after extensive background data and results of independent clinical exams by psychiatrists had been made available to those doing the predicting. Moreover, because of some flaws in the design of the study, the odds for accurate prediction were very much in the researchers' favor (Monahan, 1976; Steadman, 1976; Dix, 1980). A continuing body of research in the area of dangerousness prediction with respect to the mentally disordered continues to find that false positives outnumber true positives by a margin of two to one (Wettstein, 1984; Monahan, 1988).

The ratio of false to true positives deserves some attention. False positive is a descriptor we use for persons who are labeled dangerous (positive), but who do not engage in harmful behavior during a specific period of time after release from custody (false). True positives are persons predicted to be dangerous (positive) who do engage in subsequent harmful behavior (true). (See Table 6-1.) For example, assume a team of mental health professionals concludes that ten persons are dangerous. If, during a two-year period following release, six do engage in harmful behavior, we have a 60 percent rate of true positives and a 40 percent rate of false positives. On the other hand, the team may predict that ten people will not engage in violent behavior (negatives). If some of them do, they are called false negatives. True negatives are those predicted not to engage in harmful behavior within a certain period of time and who do not. Thus, if the team predicts that seven out of ten people will not engage in harmful behavior, and five of the ten do

Table 6-1   Four Possible Outcomes of Prediction

		Criterion Behavior	
		Did	*Did Not*
	Will	True positive	False positive
Prediction			
	Will Not	False negative	True negative

not, the team was wrong in two cases. We therefore have a ratio of 20 percent false negatives to 50 percent true negatives.

In many ways it is clearly advantageous for mental health professionals to predict more positives than negatives, especially if there is some question about whether a person is dangerous. The *Tarasoff* decision also encourages this trend. Clinicians who fail to warn and protect the community by not detecting persons who eventually commit violent or harmful acts will likely pay a higher social and professional price than clinicians who overpredict dangerousness.

A 1966 U.S. Supreme Court decision, *Baxstrom v. Herold*, facilitated extensive social science research on the accuracy of dangerousness prediction. Johnnie Baxstrom had been convicted of second-degree assault and sentenced to a two-and-one-half- to three-year term in a New York State prison. After two years, prison psychiatrists found him dangerous and mentally disturbed, and he was transferred to Dannemora State Hospital for the criminally insane. Despite his requests to be transferred to a civil mental health institution, based on the fact that his prison term was near its expiration date, the Department of Mental Hygiene determined that Baxstrom could not be cared for in a civil hospital because he was potentially dangerous. He remained institutionalized at Dannemora long after his maximum prison term had expired (by three years). The Supreme Court, with Chief Justice Warren writing the opinion, ruled that Baxstrom had been denied equal protection of the law by being confined in an institution for the criminally insane beyond the expiration of his maximum criminal sentence and without the benefit of a hearing to evaluate his "potentially dangerous" classification. The Court therefore ordered that "in order to accord the petitioner the equal protection of the laws, he was and is entitled to a review of the determination as to his sanity [and dangerous propensities] in conformity with proceedings granted all others civilly committed..." (p. 109).

The Court's ruling directly influenced the confinement of at least 967 other patients held under similar circumstances in secure institutions for the mentally disordered throughout New York State. These "Baxstrom patients," who on the average had spent eight years in involuntary confinement beyond the expiration of their criminal sentences, were quickly provided hearings. Against the advice of corrections psychiatrists and physicians, many were released. The Baxstrom patients were predominantly nonwhite, lower socioeconomic class, middle-aged males. Although a vast majority had arrest records and many had previous con-

CHAPTER 6

victions, only 58 percent had been convicted of violent crimes (Steadman, 1976). On the average, the patients had been institutionalized continuously for fourteen years.

The Baxstrom patients were considered some of New York's most dangerous mental patients, but follow-up reports found that predicted dangerousness had been grossly overstated (false positives) (Monahan, 1976). Steadman and Cocozza (1974) followed up eighty-five Baxstrom patients and discovered that 20 percent were rearrested, but only 7 percent were convicted, usually for minor violations such as vagrancy and public intoxication. An examination of both in-hospital and community behaviors revealed that only 20 percent of the "extremely dangerous" patients were assaultive toward others during the four-year follow-up period (Steadman, 1976). A prominent variable predicting whether Baxstrom patients demonstrated assaultive behavior was age: The younger the patient, the more likely he or she was to engage in assaultive behavior. Even using the Legal Dangerousness Scale (Cocozza & Steadman, 1976), a measure of four criminal background characteristics, there were two false positives for every three patients predicted to be violent, again underscoring the inaccuracy of clinical prediction.

The Baxstrom decision also affected a similar group of mentally disordered offenders in Pennsylvania (*Dixon v. Attorney of the Commonwealth of Pennsylvania*, 1971). Dixon patients were transferred to civil mental hospitals for reevaluation and treatment or release, after a court ruled unconstitutional a state statute that permitted the indefinite confinement of civilly and criminally committed patients without periodic hearings.

The Dixon patients had notable past histories of mental problems and criminal offenses. Forty-three percent had been hospitalized in the past, and 90 percent were diagnosed psychotic on current admission. Over 80 percent had prior arrest records, 64 percent had previously served jail and prison sentences, and 39 percent had committed five or more offenses in the past. The patients were institutionalized indefinitely at Fairview on the basis of presumed dangerousness. The Dixon patients were followed over a number of years by Thornberry and Jacoby (1979). After their court-ordered transfer to civil and less secure mental hospitals, only 19 percent were involved in some kind of violence within the hospital setting. Two-thirds of the Dixon patients were discharged from the civil hospitals within nine months of the transfer. During a four-year follow-up, about 24 percent were arrested, and only one-quarter of these arrests were for violent offenses. Overall, the incidence of false positives—where clinicians had predicted harmful or violent behavior that did not occur—was 67 percent, or two out of every three predictions.

Criminal justice personnel have tried a variety of measures to predict dangerousness. In 1965, in an effort to predict violent recidivism among parolees, researchers in the California Department of Corrections developed a violence-prediction scale based on background information like age, prior offenses, drug usage, and length of imprisonment. Each offender released on parole was evaluated according to this scale (Wenk, Robison, & Smith, 1972). Researchers isolated about 3 percent of the parolees as most violent, but only 14 percent of this most violent group actually violated parole by engaging in violent or harmful acts.

Five percent of the entire parolee sample violated parole with violent actions. Although the most violent group were nearly three times more likely to be violent, it should be stressed that a majority (86 percent) of the "dangerous" parolees did not display violent behavior while on parole, nor did 95 percent of the entire parolee population.

In another procedure developed by the California Department of Corrections, all parolees released into supervision were classified into one of six categories, based on aggressive behavior and psychiatric evaluation of violence potential (Wenk, Robison, & Smith, 1972). The categories ranged from serious aggressive (those who had committed one or more acts of major violence) to low level aggressive (no recorded history of aggression). Results of the study, involving 7,712 parolees, revealed that those regarded as most potentially aggressive (two highest aggressive groups) were no more likely to be violent than the less potentially violent groups (two lowest aggressive groups). The rate of conviction and imprisonment for crimes involving violence for the potentially aggressive groups was 3.1 per thousand parolees, compared to 2.8 per thousand parolees for the potentially least aggressive groups, an insignificant difference. Furthermore, for every correct identification of a potentially aggressive individual, there were 326 incorrect ones.

In a third project, Wenk and his colleagues (1972) studied 4,146 youthful offenders admitted to the Reception Guidance Center at Deuel Vocational Institute, California, during a two-year period. The researchers wanted to determine which background data were most useful in predicting violence during a fifteen-month parole period after the offenders' release from the institution. During the fifteen-month period, 104 or 2.5 percent of the youths violated parole by displaying violent (assaultive) behavior.

To isolate predictive variables of violent behavior, the researchers combined and divided the background data in a number of ways. One procedure revealed that general recidivism (any violation of parole) and violent recidivism (violation of parole by violence) were highest for multiple offenders, youths who had been admitted to the institution on several occasions. In another procedure, youthful offenders with a history of actual violent behavior (which may or may not have resulted in institutionalization) were found to be three times more likely to be involved in violent recidivism during the fifteen-month parole period. It is tempting to jump to the conclusion that multiple offenders and youths with histories of violence are dangerous. Yet Wenk and his colleagues admonish that if they were to make predictions based on the same background data, they would still be accurate only once in twenty predictions. Only a small proportion of youths with violent backgrounds engaged in violence during parole. We should emphasize that the violent behavior was defined as a conviction for a violent crime. In fact, other studies have shown that when arrest records for violent crimes are used, the accuracy of prediction gets better (Monahan, 1981). However, even with this increase in accuracy, the false positive rate continues to hover around 60 percent.

It is quite clear that clinicians tend to overpredict dangerous behavior, under the premise that it is better to be safe than sorry. It is also quite clear that predictions of dangerousness, in general, are inaccurate. What accounts for this inaccuracy?

First, the behavior being predicted, violence, occurs relatively infrequently in the daily lives of even the most frequent offender. Therefore, the prediction of an infrequent behavior is akin to finding a needle in a haystack of behaviors. Violent behavior happens (or is reported) so infrequently that if you say it will happen, the odds are already against you. Secondly, while human behavior is generally consistent across time (temporal consistency), it is often inconsistent across situations (trans-situational consistency). More specifically, people tend to act the same way during their lifetimes, if the situations eliciting this behavior are basically the same. However, if the situations are different, as is so characteristic of life, people are unlikely to act the same way. As noted earlier, for example, most of us act differently with our parents than we do with our friends, or we act one way with members of the same sex, but another way with members of the opposite sex. Thus, mental health professionals would be substantially more accurate, if they could be certain that the social environment remained the same. In reality, the social environment is always changing, rendering the predictions based on one situation inapposite for another.

Overall, the best predictor of future behavior is past behavior. Past violence will suggest a probability of future violence. Furthermore, the more the behavior has occurred in a variety of situations, the more accurate will be the predictions. A person who manifests violence frequently and across many different situations will be far more easy to predict than a person who is only occasionally violent in some situations. If clinicians were able to modify Wexler's (1981) suggested approach and base the likelihood of dangerousness strictly on those characteristics associated with age and past behavior, their predictions might be more accurate. Recent research strongly indicates that the best predictors of criminal conduct and violence are age, criminal history, antisocial peers, and substance abuse (Andrews & Bonta, 1994; Bonta, Law, & Hanson, 1998; Gendreau, Little, & Goggin, 1996).

CURRENT DANGEROUSNESS MEASURES

In recent years, a number of dangerousness measures (generally called risk assessment instruments) have been developed, mostly by Canadian psychologists. These risk assessment instruments generally require a clinician or assessor to evaluate an individual based on information in certain areas of background and behavioral patterns. The first of these instruments was the Dangerous Behavior Rating Scheme (DBRS) developed by Christopher Webster and Robert Menzies (1993). The scale underwent considerable research development but became a disappointment when it failed to predict dangerousness and violence to a satisfactory level. A second, more promising attempt is the Violence Risk Assessment Guide (VRAG) developed by Grant Harris, Marnie Rice, and colleagues (Webster, Harris, Rice, & Quinsey, 1993). The VRAG is based on data from 618 men with prior histories of significant violence who were initially confined at the Oak Ridge Division of the Penetanguishene Mental Health Center in Ontario, Canada. Oak Ridge is a maximum security facility providing assessment and treatment for persons referred from the courts, correctional services, and other provincial psychiatric hospitals (Webster, Harris, Rice, & Quinsey, 1993). Twelve variables believed to predict future violence make up the VRAG. The variables include separation of parents by age sixteen or younger, schizophrenia, elementary school maladjustment, alcohol abuse history, and symptoms of psychopathy. The 618 violent men in the project were followed for ten years. Overall, 31 percent of the subjects committed another violent offense, usually within seven years after release (Rice, 1997). The best predictor of violent recidivism was the score of the psychopathy scale (i.e., PCL-R). "It alone predicted better than any combination of other criminal history variables…" (Rice, 1997, p. 415). On the other hand, the presence of a mental disorder did not predict violence. Based on preliminary research, Rice concludes: "[O]ur work and that of others on the prediction of violence has shown that long-term criminal violence can be predicted with a considerable degree of accuracy among men who have already been apprehended for a violent criminal offense" (p. 418).

Another promising instrument for evaluating risk is the Historical/ Clinical/Risk Management (HCR-20) scale developed by Christopher Webster and his colleagues (Webster, Douglas, Eaves, & Hart, 1997). The HCR bases its predictive power on three major areas: Past or historical factors, clinical or current factors, and risk management factors. The HCR contains ten historical items, five clinical items, and five risk management items, for a total of twenty items. The historical items include "previous violence," which, as we have learned, is one of the strongest predictors of future violence. Another historical or "H" item is "young age at first violent incident" (Webster et al., 1997, p. 267). In other words, the younger the person at the time of the first violent incident, the greater the likelihood that a violent pattern will persist into the future. "Early maladjustment" at home, at school, or in the community is another predictive H item. Other H items in the HCR-20 are relationship instability, employment problems, substance use problems, and major mental illness (particularly psychotic or mood-disorders). Clinical or "C" items include lack of insight, negative attitudes (antisocial, hostile, anger), and "active symptoms of major mental illness" (Webster et al., 1997, p. 263). Active symptoms of serious mental illness that include delusional systems characterized by sadistic fantasies, and homicidal and suicidal ideation are especially related to violence prediction. Risk management or "R" variables are related to the future circumstances of the individuals they are evaluating. That is, is the person being evaluated likely to have adequate housing, meals, daily activities, and finances. Research suggests that individuals without these basics are at higher risk for violence than those who have these needs managed and taken care of. Examples of R items are lack of personal support, noncompliance with remediation attempts, feasibility of future plans, and stress. The researchers of the HCR-20 find that the historical (H) items are the strongest for predicting future violent behavior (Webster et al., 1997), and C items are second strongest (Borum, 1996). The HCR-20 is still in its infancy and will need ongoing research before it receives widespread acceptance as a valid risk assessment instrument.

Henry Steadman, John Monahan, and their colleagues (1994) are currently directing an extensive study examining violence toward others by the mentally disordered. The project is sponsored by the Research Network on Mental Health and Law of the John D. and Catherine T. MacArthur Foundation, and is called the

MacArthur Risk Assessment Study. The project involves one thousand patients discharged from mental institutions in three locations: Pittsburgh, PA, Worcester, MA, and Kansas City, MO. The ultimate goals of the project are threefold: (1) to improve the validity of clinical risk assessment, (2) to improve the effectiveness of clinical risk management, and (3) to provide useful information for reforming mental health and policy. With the data from this recently published study, researchers and practitioners should get a good idea of what particular variables are most helpful in improving predictions of dangerousness in the mentally disordered.

SUMMARY AND CONCLUSIONS

In this chapter, we focused on the relationship between mentally disordered individuals and crime. In order to begin to understand this relationship, we must go beyond labels, which do not explain why someone behaves in a certain way. Furthermore, labels are assigned by the mental health profession, and, along with definitions, may change with each edition of the DSM, the standard diagnostic manual used by most clinicians.

With the exception of persons with an antisocial personality disorder, individuals with mental disorders—as a whole—are no more likely than the general population to commit crimes, including violent crimes. There is, however, one notable exception. Currently mentally disordered patients who have a history of violence are involved in violent behavior far more often than the nondisordered members in the general population. This relationship appears to be especially significant if the current mental disorder is accompanied by three symptoms: (1) feeling that others wish to do one harm; (2) feeling that one's mind is dominated by forces beyond one's control; and (3) feeling that others' thoughts are being put into one's head (Monahan, 1996).

Bonta et al. (1998) raise some serious questions as to whether mentally disordered offenders are more likely to recidivate than nondisordered offenders. Preliminary data from recent research suggest that mentally disordered offenders are less likely to commit another crime than normal offenders. As Bonta and his colleagues point out, the ongoing MacArthur study (Steadman et al., 1994) may eventually provide the definitive answer on the role of mental disorders in violent behavior, at least for civil patients.

We also reviewed the various categories of mentally disordered offenders, including those found Not Guilty by Reason of Insanity, those found Incompetent to Stand Trial, Mentally Disordered Sex Offenders, and transfers. Legal determinations of these categories vary from jurisdiction to jurisdiction. Furthermore, in recent years many court decisions have affected the way mentally disordered offenders are adjudicated, confined, and treated.

Recent research reveals that fewer than 1 percent of all criminal cases involve the insanity defense, and when the defense is raised, it rarely succeeds. And when it does succeed, it is rarely a bargain. The amount of time spent in a mental institution or treatment facility is generally at least as long as the amount of time the offender would have served in prison had he or she been found guilty.

Incompetence to stand trial is another key legal determination of the mentally disordered defendant. ISTs tend to be marginal members of society with few family ties, no job, prior hospitalization, and who are slightly older than most criminal defendants.

In the past twenty years, we have seen the emergence of many special or unique defenses based on psychological states. Although these defenses have received considerable attention from the media, the courts have been very reluctant to accept them as excusing or mitigating conditions for criminal actions. Defendants have claimed lack of responsibility, or diminished responsibility, by using post-traumatic stress disorder, multiple personality disorder, compulsive gambling disorder, and amnesia.

Lastly, we reviewed the complex literature on the dangerous offender. Traditionally, clinicians have overestimated the potential violence of mentally disordered populations, engendering debate about the proper criteria for assessing dangerousness. How many persons are forcefully confined, on the basis of dangerousness, without justification? Accurate predictions of dangerousness are extremely elusive. Overall, the best predictor available is past behavior. Those who were violent in the past, compared to those without such a history, are more likely to offend in the future. Several new risk assessment instruments have been developed in recent years that show considerable promise in accurately predicting dangerousness in certain individuals.

Monahan and Shah (1989) find that the history of dangerousness in both civil commitment and criminal confinement in the United States can be characterized by three changes over the past twenty-five years. First, the type of mental disorder that triggers a dangerousness assessment has changed from some vague, open-ended concept of mental illness to a more definitive, serious mental disorder that could be labeled "psychotic." Second, the definition of dangerous behavior has changed from an ambiguous notion of undesirable activity to a specific concern with tangible violence or physical harm. And third, while psychologists and psychiatrists can provide technical advice to the court about mental disorders and their risks, the ultimate decisions about who should be incarcerated or released involve the courts, who must balance the social and moral issues between a person's liberty and the public's safety.

HUMAN AGGRESSION
AND VIOLENCE

There is ample evidence of the long history of human involvement in aggression and violence. The 5,600 years of recorded human history, for example, include 14,600 wars, a rate of more than 2.6 per year (Baron, 1983; Montagu, 1976). Some writers argue that aggression has been instrumental in helping people survive. Through centuries of experience, humans learned that aggressive behavior enables them to obtain material goods, land, and treasures; to protect property and family; and to gain prestige, status, and power. In fact, we might wonder whether the human species could have survived had it not used aggression.

Aggression warrants an entire chapter because it is the basic ingredient in violent crime. Furthermore, by studying aggression, psychologists have made substantial contributions to society's effort to understand violence and crime. Is human aggression instinctive, biological, learned, or some combination of these characteristics? If it results from an innate, biological mechanism, the methods designed to control, reduce, or eliminate aggressive behavior will differ significantly from methods used if aggression is learned.

Perspectives of human nature emerge very clearly from the scholarly and research literature on aggression. Some writers and researchers believe that aggressive behavior is basically physiological and genetic in origin, a strong residue of our evolutionary past. This physiological, genetic contention is accompanied by compelling evidence that explanations of human aggressive behavior may be found in the animal kingdom from which it originated. On the other hand, researchers who subscribe to the learning viewpoint believe that, while some species of animals may be genetically programmed to behave aggressively, human beings learn to be aggressive from the social environment. The learning position also offers cogent evidence to support its theory. Other researchers remain on a theoretical fence, accepting and rejecting some aspects of each argument.

If aggression and violence represent a built-in, genetically programmed aspect of human nature, we may be forced, as Baron (1983) suggests, toward a pessimistic conclusion. At best, we can only hope to hold our natural, aggressive urges and drives temporarily in check. Furthermore, we should design the environment and society in such a way as to discourage violence, including administering immediate and aversive consequences (punishment) when it is displayed. Even better—and setting aside ethical or legal considerations for the moment—we might consider psychosurgery, electrode implants, and drug control—all effective methods for the reduction, if not the elimination, of violence.

If, on the other hand, we believe that aggression is learned and is influenced by a wide range of situational, social, and environmental variables, we can be more optimistic. Aggression is not an inevitable aspect of human life. Once we understand what factors play major roles in its acquisition and maintenance, we will be able to change human behavior by manipulating these factors.

By most accounts, animal aggression reflects the biological programming carried in the genes to ensure the survival of the species. Humans, with their enormously complex and sophisticated cerebral cortex, rely heavily on thought, associations, beliefs, and learning; these become primary determinants of behavior. Theorists differ over the degree to which genetic programming contributes to human behavior. Are people aggressive and violent because their animal instincts continue to promote this particular behavior? And, if the evolutionary aggressive drives still reside within the subcortical structures of the brain (below the cortex in the "old" brain), as some writers tell us they do, are they modifiable? If not, how can we best prevent people from attacking and killing one another? On the other hand, a difference-in-kind perspective suggests that genetic predispositions, or biological precursors of aggression, have a minimal influence on human behavior, if they have any influence at all. After defining aggression, we will return to these different points of view.

DEFINING AGGRESSION

The task of defining human aggression is surprisingly difficult, as many social psychologists have discovered. Forcibly jabbing someone in the midsection is certainly defining it by example—or is it? Now what about jabbing someone more softly, in jest? Would everyone consider football and boxing aggressive behaviors? If someone pointedly ignores a question, is that an example of aggression? What if someone spreads malicious gossip? If a burglar breaks into your home and you reach for your trusty but rusty rifle, aim it at the intruder, and pull the trigger, is yours an act of aggression? Is it any less so if the rifle does not fire? If someone sits passively on a doorstep and blocks your entry, is this aggression?

Some social psychologists define aggression as the intent and attempt to harm another individual, physically or socially, or in some cases, to destroy an object. This definition seems adequate for many situations, but it has several limitations. Refusing to speak does not fit well, since it is not an active attempt to harm someone. The person blocking entry also is not trying to injure anyone. Most psychologists place these two behaviors in a special category of aggressive responses and call them passive-aggressive behaviors, since they are generally interpreted as aggressive in intent, although the behavior is passive and indirect.

As fascinating as passive-aggressive behavior may be, it is generally irrelevant when we discuss crime, since the aggression we are concerned about is the type that manifests itself directly in violent or antisocial behavior. We might stretch the point by suggesting that the doorstep sitter is trespassing, in which case he or she might be charged with a criminal offense. In general, however, the aggressive behavior we wish to focus on in this chapter will not be of the passive-aggressive kind.

In an effort to conceptualize the many varieties of human aggression, Buss (1971) tried to classify them based on the apparent motivation of the aggressor (see Table 7-1). You may easily find exceptions and overlapping categories in the Buss scheme, but that emphasizes how difficult it is to compartmentalize human aggressive behavior. It also epitomizes the many definitional dilemmas that hamper social psychologists studying aggression.

Before trying to settle on a satisfactory definition of aggression, it may be useful to recognize two types, **hostile** (or **expressive**) and **instrumental aggression**, a distinction first made by Feshbach (1964). They are distinguished by their goals, or the rewards they offer the perpetrator. Hostile (or expressive) aggression, which we are most concerned with in this chapter, occurs in response to anger-inducing conditions, such as insults, physical attacks, or personal failures. The aggressor's goal is to make a victim suffer. Most homicides, rapes, and other violent crimes directed at harming the victim are precipitated by hostile aggression. The behavior is characterized by the intense and disorganizing emotion of anger, with anger defined as an arousal state elicited by certain stimuli, particularly those evoking attack or frustration. Angry at the economic system that deprived him of a job, a sniper may take potshots at passing motorists and feel satisfaction at having lashed out "successfully" at society.

Instrumental aggression begins with competition or the desire for some object or status possessed by another person—jewelry, money, territory. The perpetrator tries to obtain the desired object regardless of the cost. Instrumental aggression is usually a factor in robbery, burglary, larceny, and various white collar crimes. The thief's obvious goal in a robbery is to obtain cash-value items. Usually, there is no intent to harm anyone. However, if someone interferes with the thief's objective, he or she may feel forced to harm that person or risk losing the desired goal. Instrumental aggression is usually also a feature of calculated murder committed by a hired, impersonal killer.

Table 7-1   Varieties of Human Aggression

	Active Direct	Indirect	Passive Direct	Indirect
Physical	Punching the victim	Practical joke, booby trap	Obstructing passage, sit-in	Refusing to perform a necessary task
Verbal	Insulting the victim	Malicious gossip	Refusing to speak	Refusing consent, vocal or written

Source: A. H. Buss, "Aggression Pays," in J. L. Singer (ed.), *The Control of Aggression and Violence.* New York: Academic Press, 1971, p. 8.

Bandura (1973a) notes that most definitions of aggression imply that it is solely concerned with behaviors and intentions residing within the perpetrator (or performer). Going a step further, he suggests that the adequate definition of aggression must consider both the "injurious behavior" of the perpetrator and the "social judgment" of the victim. Thus, a soft poke in the belly may qualify as aggression if it is done derisively and if the recipient interprets it that way. A textbook on criminal behavior, however, must focus on aggression as manifested in conduct, not as it is perceived by a victim. For our purposes, therefore, we define aggression as *behavior perpetrated or attempted with the intention of harming another individual physically or psychologically* (as opposed to socially) *or to destroy an object*. This definition encompasses all the behaviors described in Buss's typology. Aggressive behavior, of course, will not always qualify as criminal. Furthermore, we will define violence as *destructive physical aggression intentionally directed at harming other persons or things*. Violence may be methodical or random, sustained or fleeting, intensive or uncontrolled. It always harms or destroys the recipient or is intended to do so (Daniels & Gilula, 1970).

THEORETICAL PERSPECTIVES ON AGGRESSION

Behavioral and social scientists have debated for over a half century whether humans are born aggressive and naturally violent, or born relatively free of aggressive tendencies. This debate, part of a wider controversy about the respective merits of nature and nurture, touches every school of thought in human behavior. According to the first perspective, humans are programmed aggressive to defend themselves, family, and territory from intruders. According to the second, humans become violent by acquiring aggressive models and actions from society.

PSYCHOANALYTIC VIEWPOINTS

Sigmund Freud, the father of psychoanalysis and a physician by training, was convinced that human beings are susceptible from birth to a build-up of aggressive energy, which must be dissipated or drained off before it reaches dangerous levels. This is known as the **psychodynamic** or **hydraulic model** since it bears a close resemblance to pressure build-up in a container. If excessive pressure accumulates in the container—the human psyche—an explosion is likely to occur, as demonstrated by tirades that may involve violence. According to the traditional Freudian perspective, people who have tirades are blowing off the excess steam of aggressive energy.

Freud suggested that violence in all of its forms is a manifestation of this aggressive energy discharge. Internal energy accumulates to dangerous levels when people have not discharged it appropriately through a process called catharsis, one of the most important concepts in psychoanalytic psychotherapy. Catharsis may be accomplished by actual behavior (playing football, for example) or may occur vicariously (watching football). The Freudian-psychodynamic position predicts that children who participate in or avidly watch school sports will ultimately be less aggressive than children who do not. Freudian psychodynamic followers also maintain that people who engage in violent crime (hostile aggression) have not had sufficient opportunity to "blow off steam" and keep their aggressive energies at manageable levels.

Psychodynamic theorists assume that humans, by their very nature, will always be prone to aggressive impulses. Therefore, if violent crime is to be controlled, the human animal must be provided with multiple but appropriate channels for catharsis (e.g., adequate recreational facilities). In this way, children and adults presumably learn to dissipate aggression in socially approved, appropriate ways. Psychotherapy is one such channel, encouraging catharsis under the guidance of a therapist.

ETHOLOGICAL VIEWPOINTS

Ethology is the study of animal behavior in relation to the animal's natural habitat and compares that behavior to human behavior. In the mid-1960s, a number of ethologists published books and articles about aggression that interested and appealed to the general public. Three especially popular books were Konrad Lorenz's *On Aggression* (1966), Robert Ardrey's *The Territorial Imperative* (1966), and Desmond Morris's *The Naked Ape* (1967). Lorenz has been the chief spokesperson for a theoretical formulation of ethology as it relates to aggression.

A Nobel laureate in biology, Lorenz believed that aggression is an inherited instinct of both humans and animals. One of its main purposes is to enable the animal—and the human being—to defend "staked out" territory, a territory that ensures sufficient food, water, and space to roam and reproduce. If this space is violated, Lorenz argued, the instinctive or genetically programmed response is to attack, or at least to increase aggressive behavior toward the intruder, thus preventing further territory violation. The tendency to attack space violators is referred to as **territoriality**. Lorenz believed it is an innate propensity developed through the lengthy, complex process of evolution. This innate aggressive behavior among members of the same animal species (intraspecific aggression) prevents overcrowding and ensures the best and most powerful mates for the young.

The more deadly the animals' evolutionarily developed weaponry (e.g., fangs, claws, size, and strength), the more intense the innate inhibitions against engaging in physical combat with members of its own species. This innately programmed inhibition is a form of insurance for species survival, Lorenz believed, since constant intraspecific physical combat would eventually extinguish the species. Intraspecies aggression is accomplished, therefore, not by actual combat but by complicated displays of force and superiority, such as a show of teeth, size, or color array. These displays are referred to as ritualized aggression. Through an intricate communication system not yet understood by scientists, the animals transmit signals, after which the more powerful, dominant animal generally wins out. The losing animal demonstrates defeat by various appeasement behaviors, such as rolling over on its back (characteristic of puppies), lowering its tail or head, and emitting cries of defeat. The weaker animal then leaves the territory of the dominant one.

What does all of this have to do with human aggression? Lorenz and other ethologists believe that it is important to understand animal aggression before we can understand human aggression, since humans are part of the animal world and probably follow many of its basic principles. In other words, ethologists subscribe to the difference-in-degree Darwinian perspective. Efran and Cheyne (1974), for example, observed after studying invasion of personal space among humans that "human society may operate through mechanisms which are less uniquely human than is currently fashionable to suggest" (p. 225).

Lorenz raises another issue that, if valid, is more significant to criminal behavior, however. He maintained that human beings have outdistanced the evolutionary process of inhibiting aggression. Instead of developing natural weapons and the species-preserving function of ritualized aggression, humans have developed technological weaponry. Thus, he and many other ethologists believe they can provide at least a partial answer to why human beings wantonly maim and kill members of their own species: They have not developed the ability to engage in the species-preserving behavior of ritualized aggression. Instead, through superior learning ability, they have developed the capacity to annihilate.

The ethological position is intriguing, but it has not been supported by human aggression research (Bandura, 1983; Zillmann, 1983; Montagu, 1973). Zoologists, biologists, and psychologists have tried with little success to apply the Lorenzian tenets to humans. One problem is that the ethological position relies on a strong analogy between animals and humans. Lorenz argued, for example, that the Greylag goose is remarkably similar to the human species (Berkowitz, 1973). However, the human brain makes us remarkably unlike the Greylag goose and considerably less likely to rely on instinct for determining behavior. Research has yet to delineate any instinctive or *invariant* genetically programmed behavior determinant in humans. Furthermore, "the capacity to exercise control over one's own thought processes, motivation, and action is a distinctively human characteristic" (Bandura, 1989, p. 1175).

Ethologists also fail to acknowledge and interpret the vast body of existing scientific research that has tested their position and found it wanting. This curious response—or nonresponse—undermines the validity of their whole presentation. Some critics have referred to ethological theorizing as "scientific-sounding misinformation" (Leach, 1973). To date, therefore, there is little evidence to justify portraying humans as innately dangerous and brutal or as controlled by instinct.

FRUSTRATION-AGGRESSION HYPOTHESIS

Around the time of Freud's death in 1939, a group of psychologists at Yale University proposed that aggression is a direct result of frustration (Dollard, Doob, Miller, Mowrer, & Sears, 1939). According to John Dollard and his colleagues, people who are frustrated, thwarted, annoyed, or threatened will behave aggressively, since aggression is a natural, almost automatic response to frustrating circumstances. Moreover, people who exhibit aggressive behavior are frustrated, thwarted, annoyed, or threatened. "Aggression is always a consequence of frustration" (Dollard et al., 1939, p. 1).

Because of its simplicity and important implications, the **frustration-aggression hypothesis** drew much research, along with much criticism. Psychologists found it difficult not only to decide what frustration was, but also to determine how it could be measured accurately. Researchers also learned that aggression was a much more complex phenomenon than Dollard and his associates had postulated. Frustration does not always lead to aggression, and aggressive behavior does not always signify "frustration." Experiments indicated that people respond to frustration and anger differently. Some do indeed respond with aggression, but others display a wide variety of responses.

Led by Leonard Berkowitz (1962, 1969, 1973), whose general views on some of the causes of criminality were presented in Chapter 4, researchers began to propose a revised, contemporary version of the frustration-aggression hypothesis. According to Berkowitz, frustration increases the probability that an individual will become angry and soon act aggressively (aggression being defined as a behavior in which the goal is to inflict damage or injury on some object or person). In short, frustration facilitates the performance of aggressive behavior. The behavior may be overt (physical or verbal) or implicit (wishing someone dead). Anger, however, is not the only potentially aggressive emotion. Aversive conditions, such as pain, or pleasant states, such as sexual arousal, may also lead to aggressive behavior (Berkowitz, 1973). We will return to this subject shortly.

An important component of the revised frustration-aggression hypothesis is the concept of anticipated goals or expectations. When a behavior directed at a specific goal is thwarted, frustration is likely to result. Thus, the person must have been expecting or anticipating the attainment of a goal or achievement. Mere deprivation of goods will not necessarily lead to frustration. People who are living under deprived conditions may not be frustrated unless they actually expect something better. "Poverty-stricken groups who have never dreamed of having automobiles, washing machines, or new homes are not frustrated because they have been deprived of these things; they are frustrated only after they have begun to hope" (Berkowitz, 1969, p. 15).

Aggression, Berkowitz says, is only one possible response to frustration. The individual may learn others, like withdrawal, doing nothing, or trying to alter the situation by compromise. With this approach, Berkowitz not only emphasizes the importance of learning but also stresses the role of individual differences in response to frustrating circumstances.

The revised frustration-aggression hypothesis, therefore, suggests the following steps: (1) The person is blocked from obtaining an expected goal; (2) frustration results, generating anger; and (3) anger *predisposes* or readies the person to behave aggressively. Whether the person actually engages in aggressive actions will depend in part on his or her learning history, interpretation of the event, and individual way of responding to frustration. It will also depend, however, on the presence of aggression-eliciting stimuli in the environment.

Berkowitz notes that the presence of aggressive stimuli in the external environment (or internal environment represented by thoughts) increases the probability of aggressive responses. A weapon is a good example of such a stimulus. Most people in our society associate firearms with aggression. Berkowitz (1983) likens the firearm to a conditioned stimulus in that the weapon conjures aggressive associations, facilitating overt aggression. A gun, even when not used, is more likely to generate aggressive action than is a neutral object. "The mere sight of the weapon might elicit ideas, images, and expressive reactions that had been linked with aggression in the past…" (Berkowitz, 1983, p. 124).

In one experiment designed to test this hypothesis (Berkowitz & LePage, 1967), angry male subjects were more likely to engage in aggressive action in the presence of a gun than a comparable group of angry subjects in the presence of a badminton racket. This suggests that a visible weapon (such as a law enforcement officer might carry) may actually facilitate, rather than inhibit, a violent response in some people.

The Berkowitz-LePage finding generated much controversy as to whether weapons actually do provoke aggressive behavior. A number of studies tried to replicate the finding, but failed to find evidence of a *weapons effect* (Penrod, 1983). Some researchers believed that many of the subjects used in some of the studies "saw through" the purpose of the study, a research flaw called *demand characteristics*. However, a comprehensive review of the research literature found strong evidence that the weapons effect does—in fact—exist (Carlson, Marcus-Newhall, & Miller, 1990). Carlson et al. concluded: "Aggression-related cues present in experimental settings act to increase aggressive responding. This cue effect occurs more strongly when subjects have been negatively aroused before their exposure to aggression-facilitating cues" (p. 632). The weapons effect has also been found in other countries, including Belgium, Croatia, Italy, and Sweden (Berkowitz, 1994).

It should be mentioned that the aggression-eliciting stimuli need not be aggressive or violent in appearance (i.e., a gun, knife, or bomb) but can be seemingly neutral stimuli. That is, the stimuli need only be associated with aversive events or have a decidedly unpleasant meaning to an individual to intensify aggressive reactions. Even some types of music may facilitate or encourage aggressive behavior (Rogers & Ketcher, 1979).

More recently, Berkowitz (1989) emphasized two important components to the frustration-aggression equation. Aggressive behavior will be generated (1) to the extent that a person perceives the mistreatment as intentional; and (2) to the degree that the frustration experienced is aversive. According to Berkowitz, people become angry and aggressive at being kept from reaching a desired goal, if they think someone had intentionally blocked them from achieving that goal or deliberately and wrongly tried to hurt them. "They are much more likely to become openly aggressive at someone's blocking their goal attainment if they believe their frustrater had deliberately and unjustifiably attempted to keep them from reaching their goal than if they think the thwarting had not been intentional or had not been directed at them personally" (Berkowitz, 1989, p. 68). Thus, self-restraint comes into play when people think they have not been deliberately mistreated or that the blocking of the goal was legitimate. On the other hand, people become angry and aggressive when they perceive they have been treated unfairly or were personally attacked.

Berkowitz also postulates that thwartings or frustrations generate a negative affect, which refers to an emotional state people typically seek to lessen or eliminate. Furthermore, an unexpected interference is more apt to provoke an aggressive reaction than is an anticipated barrier to goal attainment, because the former is usually much more unpleasant. That is, it has more negative affect.

In his more recent reformulation of the frustration-aggression hypothesis, Berkowitz has emphasized the importance of cognitive factors. Currently, it is called the **cognitive-neoassociation model**. It operates in the following manner. During the earlier stages, an aversive event produces a negative affect. This negative affect may be due to physical pain or psychological discomfort. Physical pain as an aversive circumstance is clear, but psychological discomfort needs further elaboration. Being verbally insulted is a good example. While there is no physical pain, personal insults or demeaning comments engender anger, depression, or sadness in just about everyone—all negative affects. Unpleasant feelings or negative affects presumably then give rise, almost automatically, to a variety of feelings, thoughts, and memories that are associated with flight (fear) and fight (anger) tendencies. During this early stage, mediating cognitive processes have little influence beyond the immediate appraisal that the situation is aversive. Some people may act quickly on the basis of these initial emotions without further deliberation or forethought, sometimes engaging in violence. During the later stages, however, cognitive appraisal may go into operation and substantially influence the subsequent emotional reactions and experiences after the initial, automatic responses. These cognitions mediate and evaluate a proper course of action. Aroused people make causal attributions about the unpleasant experience, think about the nature of their feelings, and perhaps try to control their feelings and actions.

Berkowitz emphasizes that any unpleasant feeling or arousal can evoke aggressive, even violent responses. A depressed person can murder his or her family, or a thwarted teenager may violently lash out at authority.

EXCITATION TRANSFER THEORY

Zillmann (1988) has proposed a theory to explain how physiological arousal can generalize from one situation to another. Called **excitation transfer theory**, it is based on the assumption that physiological arousal, however produced, dissipates slowly over time. For example, a mother who receives some anger-producing criticism at work, is likely to still have some residual arousal from that criticism when she arrives home later that evening. When she encounters some annoying event at home, she is apt to "fly off the handle" and overreact to the minor home incident. Consequently, the combination of preexisting arousal, plus anger generated by the irritation at home, may increase the likelihood of aggression. The transfer of arousal from one situation to another is most likely to occur if the person is unaware that he or she is still carrying some arousal from a previous situation to a new, unrelated one.

SOCIAL LEARNING

Why do some people behave aggressively when intensely frustrated, while others change their tactics, withdraw, or seem not to be affected? One major factor may be past learning experiences. The human being, as we noted in Chapter 5, is very adept at learning and maintaining behavior patterns that have worked in the past, even if they only worked occasionally. This learning process begins in early childhood. Children develop many behaviors merely by watching their parents and significant others in their environment, a process we have called modeling or observational learning. A child's behavior pattern, therefore, is often acquired through the modeling or imitation of other people, real and imagined, in the child's environment (Bandura, 1973a). In fact, available research reveals that the conditions most conducive to the learning of aggression are those in which the child (1) has many opportunities to observe aggression, (2) is reinforced for his or her own aggression, or (3) is often the object of aggression (Huesmann, 1988).

Suppose Harris's father returns home harried after a hot and humid day during which he accomplished nothing (frustration). He finds an official-looking letter from the IRS in the mailbox. He opens it, perhaps muttering mild obscenities under his breath, and finds that the IRS apparently suspects he has shortchanged the U.S. government by several hundred dollars, although he knows he has not (more frustration). He is invited for an audit (even more frustration). In response, he slams his fist on the table, exclaims "Damn it!" or some colorful variation, and kicks the nearest chair (just enough not to damage his toe, since he has learned the painful consequences from past similar episodes). Unknown to father, Harris has observed this whole scenario. Several hours later, when his block tower crumbles, little Harris pounds his fist, kicks the living room chair, and curses, "Damn it!"

When a child's imitative behavior is reinforced or rewarded by praise and encouragement from significant models, the probability that the behavior will occur in the future is increased. There is evidence that American parents (consciously or inadvertently) encourage or reinforce aggressive behavior in their children, particularly in their sons. For example, Harris's behavior might have been reinforced if Dad or Mom drew attention to it—"Isn't that cute?"—or if they laughed. In a future episode, the kicking behavior might be directed at the family cat. Many Harrises in our society are expected or encouraged to be hard-hitting linebackers and to hold their own against neighborhood bullies, providing they are approximately the same size. They learn that the child who aggresses successfully against others is often rewarded by status, prestige, and the most attractive toys or material goods.

Bandura (1983) identifies three major types of models: family members, members of one's subculture, and symbolic models provided by the mass media. As we noted in Chapter 2, family members, particularly parents, can be very powerful models up until early adolescence. Beginning in early adolescence, peer models are likely to dominate. Not surprisingly, the highest incidence of aggression is found in communities and groups in which aggressive models abound and fighting prowess is regarded as a valued attribute (Bandura, 1983; Short, 1968; Wolfgang & Ferracuti, 1967).

The mass media, including television, movies, magazines, newspapers, and books, provide abundant symbolic models. Television pervades the life of the growing child, even the very young one, and offers hundreds of potentially powerful aggressive and violent models in a variety of formats, ranging from Saturday morning cartoon film festivals to triple-X-rated cable movies. The effects these models have on children is a highly debated issue and one we will cover later in this chapter.

Since parents are powerful models, we would expect aggressive or antisocial parents to have aggressive or antisocial children. In an old but classic study, Sears, Maccoby, and Levin (1957) interviewed four hundred mothers of kindergarten children about their disciplinary techniques, their attitudes about children's aggressiveness, and the children's expressions of aggression toward peers, siblings, and parents. One of the major findings was that physical punishment by parents was related to aggressiveness in the children. This was especially true when physical discipline was supplemented by high permissiveness toward aggression. In support of this finding, some researchers found that preschoolers played more aggressively when they were watched by a permissive adult than when no adult was visible (Siegel & Kohn, 1959).

Bandura (1973a) argues persuasively that aggressive behavior can be most productively understood and modified if we give attention to the learning principles like those alluded to earlier. As psychologists learn more about human behavior, many are beginning to agree with him.

Social learning theory hypothesizes that the rudiments of aggressive behavior are initially acquired through observing aggressive models or on the basis of direct experience. Then, aggression is gradually refined and maintained by reinforcement. Therefore, people may have an aggressive behavioral pattern, but may rarely express it if it has no functional value or is not condoned by significant others in their social environment. The social learning system acknowledges that biological structures can set limits on the types of aggressive responses that can be learned, and that genetic endowment influences the rate at which learning progresses (Bandura, 1973a). Biology does not program the individual to specific aggressive behavior, however. These behaviors are learned by observation, either deliberately or inadvertently; they become refined through reinforced practice.

In addition, mere exposure to aggressive models does not guarantee that the observer will try to engage in similar aggressive action at a later date. First, a variety of conditions may prevent observational learning from even taking place. Individuals differ widely in their ability to learn from observation. Some people may fail to notice the essential features of the model's behavior or may have a poor symbolic or visual memory. Alternately, they may not wish to imitate the model. Bandura suggests also that one important component of observational learning may be the motivation to rehearse what has been observed. He notes that a mass murderer, for example, may get an idea from descriptive accounts of another mass killing. The incident remains prominent in his mind long after it has been forgotten by others. He continues to think about the crime and to rehearse the brutal scenario mentally until, under appropriate conditions, it serves as a script for his own murderous actions.

Another restriction on observational learning is what happens to the observed model. If the model is reprimanded or punished either during or immediately after an aggressive episode, this will probably inhibit the observer's behavior. The "bad guy" should not get away with violence, if we are to discourage antisocial behavior via the entertainment media.

If aggressive behavior is to be maintained, it needs periodic reinforcement. According to social learning theory, aggression is maintained by instrumental learning. In the *initial* stage of learning, observation is important, but in the later stages, reinforcement is essential. The reinforcement may be positive, as when the individual gains material or social rewards, or it may be negative, if it allows the individual to alter or avoid aversive conditions. If aggressive behavior brings rewards in either of these ways, the person is likely to continue it. A youngster subjected to unmerciful harassment because of his unusual name may be able to stop the teasing with his fists. The reinforcement he gets from his newly found aggressive behavior is negative, but it is still rewarding. Aggression can also allow the individual to feel in control of a situation if things are not going his or her way. The psychological reinforcement offered by feeling in control is an extremely powerful component in any human behavior.

COGNITIVE MODELS OF AGGRESSION

Recent cognitive models for learning aggression have hypothesized that, while observational learning is important in the process, the individual's cognitive capacities and information processing strategies are equally important. Two major cognitive models have emerged in recent years. One has been proposed by Rowell Huesmann and his colleagues (1997), a hypothesis called the **cognitive scripts model**. The other model has been developed by Kenneth Dodge and his colleagues (Dodge, 1986; Dodge & Coie, 1987), and is called the **hostile attribution model**. According to Rowell Huesmann (1988), social behavior in general, and aggressive behavior in particular, are controlled largely by **cognitive scripts** learned and memorized through daily experiences. "A script suggests what events are to happen in the environment, how the person should behave in response to these events, and what the likely outcome of those behaviors would be" (Huesmann, 1988, p. 15). Each script is different and unique to each person, but once established they become resistant to change and may persist into adulthood. For a script to become established, it must be rehearsed from time to time. With practice, the script will not only become encoded and maintained in memory, but it will be more easily retrieved and utilized when the individual faces a problem. Furthermore, the individual's "evaluation of the 'appropriateness' of a script plays an important role in determining which scripts are stored in memory, in determining which scripts are retrieved and utilized, and which scripts continue to be utilized" (Huesmann, 1988, p. 19). The evaluation process includes the confidence that one has in predicting outcomes of the script, the extent to which an individual judges himself or herself capable of executing the script, and the extent to which the script is seen as congruent with the person's self-regulating internal standards. Scripts that are inconsistent or violate one's internalized standards are unlikely to be stored or utilized. An individual with poorly integrated internal standards against aggression, or who is convinced that aggressive behavior is a way of life, is more likely to incorporate

aggressive scripts for behavior. The aggressive child, for example, is apt to insti-
gate aggressive reactions from others, confirming his or her beliefs about the
aggressiveness of human nature in a circular, perpetuating fashion.

Kenneth Dodge and his colleagues discovered that highly aggressive children
often have a **hostile attributional bias**. That is, children prone to violence are
more likely to interpret ambiguous actions as hostile and threatening than are
their less aggressive counterparts (Dodge, 1993). They are apt to see aggression
and violence where there is none. Research consistently indicates that violent
youth "typically define social problems in hostile ways, adopt hostile goals, and
seek few additional facts, generate few alternative solutions, anticipate few consequences for aggression, and give higher priority to their aggressive solutions"
(Eron & Slaby, 1994, p. 10).

Ronald Blackman (1998) also reports research evidence that suggests that persistent lawbreaking by adults represents attempts to master a social environment
perceived as hostile and threatening. Blackburn hypothesizes that highly criminal
offenders approach the world with a well-developed hostile-dominance interpersonal style. That is, rather than simply a reflection of deficits in conscience (as proposed by Eysenck) or self-control (as proposed by Hirschi), frequent criminal
behavior may represent an ongoing attempt to control and dominate others in the
social environment. According to Blackman, chronic criminality can be understood
as "an attempt to maintain status or mastery of a social environment from which
they feel alienated" (1998, p. 174). The well-rehearsed cognitive script of persistent,
life-long offenders, therefore, is to dominate—often in a hostile manner—social
environments they perceive as hostile.

Aggression is a simple, direct way of solving immediate conflicts. If something
is not going your way, approaching the social environment in a threatening, hostile
manner is the most direct way (not necessarily the most effective in the long run)
of confronting your tormentors. On the other hand, prosocial solutions and alternative nonaggressive scripts are less direct and more complex than aggressive
solutions. In essence, they are more difficult to apply. Theoretically, the more cognitively "simple" individual would be more inclined to pursue simplistic and
direct solutions to problems. In addition, because prosocial solutions are more
complicated and more difficult to apply, they also require effective social skills.
However, the development of effective social skills takes time, and those skills will
have a spotty reinforcement history until perfected. Aggressive behavior, on the
other hand, often receives immediate reinforcement for the aggressor, and therefore is more likely to be retained in one's arsenal of strategies for immediate solutions of conflictual situations. After a twenty-two-year longitudinal study, Eron
and Huesmann (1984) concluded that diminished intellectual competence and
poor social skills have an early effect in increasing the likelihood that a child will
adopt characteristically more aggressive styles of behavior to conflict resolution.
Further, the evidence indicates that this aggressive style will persist across situations and time and become a preferred style throughout adulthood. But the relationship is simply not one-way, with limited intellectual competence and inadequate skills causing aggressive behavior. Rather, it appears to be interactive.

Aggressive behavior may interfere with positive social interactions with teachers and peers for intellectual and social advancement, perpetuating a chain of mutually influencing events: aggressive behavior influencing the social environment, and the social environment, in turn, influencing aggressive behavior.

Dolf Zillmann (1988) proposes a similar idea to the cognitive script theory, but, like Berkowitz, emphasizes the importance of physiological arousal and its interaction with cognitions. Zillmann agrees with Hebb (1955, p. 249) that arousal "is an energizer, but not a guide, an engine but not a steering gear." Cognition provides the steering and direction to the energizing effects of anger, fear, or frustration. A long-standing observation in the study of animal and human aggression is that when the organism recognizes or perceives a threat to its welfare and well-being, it can either fight or flee. Following this "recognition of endangerment," physiological arousal quickly sets in, preparing the organism for fight or flight. The "recognition of endangerment," Zillmann reminds us, can be immediate, and the response can be reflex-like. What happens then is also highly dependent on cognition, especially in humans. Very likely, this is when cognitive scripts come in. If the arousal is moderate, the individual with skills and well-integrated standards of prosocial values will probably pursue nonaggressive scripts, although the person may have been angry or threatened at first. However, very high levels of arousal interfere with the complex cognitive processes that mediate our consideration of our internal codes of conduct, as well as our ability to assess the intentions of others and the mitigating circumstances around the incident (Zillmann, 1988). Think of a very stressful or frightening situation that has happened to you, and how difficult it was to think clearly. Or think of a time when you became extremely angry and said or did things you wish you hadn't. At high levels of arousal, our cognitions seem to become narrower and more restricted, almost incapacitated at times. Generally, under these high states of arousal, we resort to strongly established habits to guide and dominate our behavior. In essence, we become "impulsive" and largely unthinking, and cognitions that mediate the diminution of hostile or even violent actions are substantially reduced. However, if we have practiced or rehearsed nonviolent or nonaggressive behaviors as solutions, they are likely to be the habits we resort to under high stress, fear, and high arousal.

OVERT AND COVERT ACTS OF AGGRESSION

Rolf Loeber and Magda Stouthamer-Loeber (1998) recommend that researchers on aggression and violence be mindful of two types of aggressive actions: *overt* and *covert*. According to Loeber and Stouthamer-Loeber, the two forms of aggression are different in: (1) behavior patterns; (2) emotions; (3) cognitions; and (4) development. *Behaviorally*, overt aggression usually involves direct confrontation with victims and the administration of physical harm or threats of physical harm. Covert aggression, on the other hand, does not involve direct confrontation but relies on concealment, dishonesty, or sneaky behavior. In many instances, overt aggression decreases with age, while covert aggression increases with age (Loeber, Lahey, & Thomas, 1991; Stanger, Achenbach, & Verhurst, 1997). However, children who exhibit serious forms of overt aggression (violence) tend to increase their violence as they get older, and often commit both violent and property crimes as adults (Loeber & Stouthamer-Loeber, 1998).

Emotionally, anger is usually an important ingredient in most overt acts of aggression, while more neutral emotions are characteristic of covert actions. Violent actions are usually accompanied by high levels of arousal brought on by anger. Covert actions, on the other hand, tend to be less emotional acts, such as fraud, theft, embezzlement, and a variety of occupational crimes. *Cognitions* are also different between the covert and overt aggression. As we explained in this chapter, aggressive and violent persons tend to have cognitive deficiencies that make it difficult for them to come up with nonaggressive solutions to interpersonal conflicts and disputes. Covert aggressors also have hostile attributional biases that contribute to violence-prone cognitive processing. People who use covert aggression as a preferred strategy do not demonstrate the degree of cognitive deficiencies in solving their interpersonal problems, nor do they manifest a hostile attributional bias. "Instead, it is postulated that most covert acts are facilitated by specific cognitive capabilities, such as planfulness (i.e., casing situations prior to theft), preoccupations with consumables and property, and lying to escape detection" (Loeber & Stouthamer-Loeber, 1998, p. 250). Occupational crimes, for instance, such as theft of company property, the misuse of information, or software piracy, are often committed with planning and forethought. Crime committed through the use of computers, called cybercrime, is also a good example of covert actions of aggression.

Developmentally, overt aggression generally begins early, especially in boys, as seen, for example, in the case of life-course-persistent offenders. However, Loeber and Stouthamer-Loeber suggest that development of overt aggressive behavior does not necessarily parallel the development of covert actions. Instead, "some children have never been socialized by their parents to be honest and to respect the property of others. This is common among neglectful parents or parents who hold an indistinct or a weak moral stance in these respects" (Loeber & Stouthamer-Loeber, 1998, p. 251). The formation of honesty and respect for the property of others is instilled by parents' teaching and the prosocial models they offer their children. Some covert actions, especially lying, can also evolve as a well-learned strategy that serves to minimize the chances of detection and punishment by adults.

It should be emphasized that not all overt aggressors who engage in violence start early. As Loeber and Stouthamer-Loeber note, "it is necessary to account for the emergence of violence in individuals during adulthood who do not have a history of aggression earlier in their lives" (p. 246). These *late-onset types* represent a minority of adulthood violent offenders, but the hypothesis does suggest that not all highly aggressive and violent individuals manifest aggression in childhood.

In conclusion, violent crimes are overt aggressive behaviors, whereas many property and economic crimes are covert aggressive behaviors.

GENDER DIFFERENCES IN AGGRESSION

While boys engage in more overt aggression and direct confrontation as they grow up, it is not clear if boys are generally more aggressive than girls. The current work of cognitive psychologists suggests that there may be socialized differences in the way girls and boys construct their worlds. Social learning theorists have long held that girls are "socialized" differently than boys, or taught not to be overtly aggressive. Anne Campbell (1993, p. 19) argues that "boys are not simply more aggressive than girls; they are aggressive in a different way." According to Campbell, boys and girls are born with the potential to be equally aggressive, but girls are socialized not to be overtly aggressive, whereas boys are encouraged to be overtly aggressive "to defend" themselves. Loeber and Stouthamer-Loeber (1998, p. 253) conclude from their review of the research that: "In general, gender differences in aggression, as expressed by frustration and rage, are not documented in infancy." They note that only in the preschool period (three to five years of age) do observable gender differences emerge, with boys displaying more overt aggression than girls. Overt aggression in boys becomes especially prominent in boys from elementary school age onward. However, researchers (e.g., Björkqvist, Lagerspetz, & Kaukianinen, 1992; Cairns et al., 1989) also find that girls and women tend to use more covert, indirect, and verbal forms of aggression, such as character defamation and ostracism. Other researchers find that females employ relational aggression, such as exclusion of peers, malicious gossip, and collusion directed at the relational bonds between friendships (Crick, 1995; Crick & Grotpeter, 1995; Loeber & Stouthamer-Loeber, 1998).

In conclusion, there is growing recognition that gender differences in aggression are not simply due to biology, but are primarily due to cultural and socialization processes that promote different kinds of aggression. Environmental cues are also important in cognitive scripts and aggressive strategies individuals employ for various situations. Which script or strategy an individual employs is dependent on which environmental cues are present.

ENVIRONMENTAL FACTORS

POPULATION DENSITY

Closely related to the ethological point of view is one that sees aggression as a result of population density or overcrowded conditions. In areas of high population concentration, personal space is constantly violated. In urban areas, crowded mass transit systems and apartment complexes teeming with people infringe on personal space and territory. Might this overcrowding be a principal factor in crimes of violence and perhaps in personal property offenses?

John B. Calhoun (1961, 1962) conducted a series of provocative studies using domestic rats, and suggested analogies between the rats and humans. He first allowed groups of rats to propagate freely in a limited physical space with adequate quantities of rat chow and water. Eventually, the rat colonies became overpopulated to such an extent that the rodents demonstrated abnormal behaviors.

Normally, male rats find one or more mates, build a nest, and, together with their mates, produce and raise offspring. Although they roam freely, they rarely show interest in another nest. In Calhoun's crowded conditions, however, the males either no longer cared about building a nest or could not defend it from bands of marauding male rats. The marauders entered the nests, attacked the females, and tore up the surroundings. Females were so harassed by these marauders that they lost interest in caring for the young. The marauding rats were those who could not build nests of their own because of lack of space. They developed a lifestyle that revolved around attacking other males and females, physically and sexually.

Calhoun also discovered a group of "juvenile delinquents"—male and female rats without nests who were usually too weak to defend or find a mate. These young rats would gather in large clusters and spend their days milling around the floor of the cage, sometimes fighting, sometimes sleeping, sometimes harassing other rats in the vicinity. Rather quickly, the rat society deteriorated and the population declined. Calhoun's studies have been replicated by other researchers using other animals, with generally similar results.

Can we analogize from rats to humans? The research concerning the effects of crowding on human behavior is far from clearcut. At present, there is no evidence of a relationship between overcrowding and *crime* among humans, but some work suggests a link between overcrowding and *aggression*.

Some investigators have exposed people to crowded conditions combined with various room temperatures (Griffith & Veitch, 1971). In general, as population density and temperature increased, so did subjects' negative feelings toward one another. Other investigations (Freedman, Levy, Buchanan, & Price, 1972) found gender differences in response to overcrowding. Males in same-gender, overcrowded groups were more aggressive and hostile than males in same gender, uncrowded groups. The reverse was true for females. In mixed groups, the gender differences did not occur. This evidence could suggest that men are uncomfortable and hostile in crowded same-gender conditions, while women tend to become more affable and friendly. However, the data also lend themselves to other interpretations. Mueller (1983), for instance, finds that the Freedman data indicate that men in the low-density condition were actually less competitive and aggressive, and only slightly more punitive than women. The issue of gender differences in aggressive behavior as a function of crowding or density is far from resolved.

Freedman (1975) conducted a number of correlational studies in various geographical areas throughout the United States and found no relationship between population density and crimes of violence like murder, rape, and aggravated assault. When populations were matched for socioeconomic class and other relevant variables, crimes of violence actually decreased in proportion to the population as density increased. Freedman attributed this finding to the large number of potential witnesses in high-density areas.

Population density studies, therefore, do not clearly support a relationship between overcrowding and aggression (Mueller, 1983; Harries, 1980; Kirmeyer, 1978). While density may play a significant role in engendering aggressive behavior in animals, in the human population the situation is far more complicated. Overall, the available evidence at this point does not support the view that a city's or a neighborhood's density has a significant influence on crime. However, there is some tentative evidence that density within the home may play a role in aggression and crime (Mueller, 1983; Gove, Hughes, & Galle, 1977; Roncek, 1975).

AGGRESSION AND AMBIENT TEMPERATURE

As temperature increases, violence increases. Or does it? This heat-of-the-night assumption was proposed as a partial explanation for riots and civil disturbances during the late 1960s and early 1970s (Baron, 1977). Later, research spearheaded by Robert Baron (Baron & Ransberger, 1978; Baron & Bell, 1975; Baron & Lawton, 1972; Bell & Baron, 1977) found support for a relationship between ambient temperature and aggression. The relationship seems complex, however. According to Robert Baron, extremely low and high temperatures tend to inhibit aggression, while intermediate levels tend to be associated with it. Baron suggests that when the temperature becomes very unpleasant (too hot or too cold), the person's major concern is to do something self-protective, such as getting a cold drink or donning thermal clothing. In other words, the individual is attempting, as Berkowitz (1989) suggests, to escape aversive circumstances (negative reinforcement). Slightly lower levels of discomfort tend to enhance the likelihood of aggression in some people, however. Picture yourself on an uncomfortably hot, but not excessively humid, summer day. Baron would maintain that your discomfort, compounded by unpleasant odors and other environmental variables, may induce irritability; in potential aggressors, it may produce hostility.

Baron's proposal suggests that collective or individual violence may be prominent at uncomfortable intermediate temperatures, rather than at extremely hot or bitterly cold ones. He hypothesized a similar curvilinear or inverted U-shaped relationship between noise levels and aggression (Baron, 1977). As Penrod (1983) notes, however, these studies do not consider adequately the possible influence of other environmental or situational factors that might be associated with hot weather, such as seasonal unemployment. Recent research by Anderson and Anderson (1984) failed to yield the predicted curvilinear relationship. They found that the number of daily violent crimes increased directly as a function of temperature in two different cities. As temperature increased, violent crime increased in a *linear* fashion. In another study, Anderson (1987) discovered that overall violent crime in the United States was more prevalent in the hotter summer months as well as in the hotter years. The study also revealed that hotter cities have higher violent crime rates than the cooler cities. These relationships also exhibited a linear function rather than a curvilinear one. (See Figure 7-1.)

Other investigators have found that a combination of high temperature and air pollution is highly related to family disturbance and violent behavior (Rotton & Frey, 1985). Kenrick and MacFarland (1986) also found a strong linear relationship between horn honking and ambient temperature, at least up to 106 degrees Fahrenheit. The researchers designed a field study where a car (a 1980 Datsun 200SX) was purposely stalled during a green light at an intersection in the Phoenix metropolitan area. Phoenix, of course, is a city where daily temperatures in excess of 90 degrees are quite common. Results indicated that horn honking was directly linked to the temperature-humidity index. That is, the frequency of horn honking

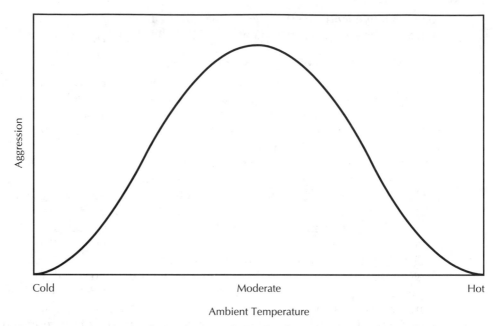

Ambient Temperature

Figure 7-1   Hypothesized Curvilinear Relationship between Aggression and Temperature

increased as temperature increased. The relationship was particularly strong for those honkers who had their windows down (presumably they did not have an air conditioner on or did not have one). In addition to frequency of horn honking, the amount of time spent leaning on the horn also increased as a function of the temperature-humidity index, often accompanied by verbal and nonverbal signals of hostility. The researchers also observed that the highest levels of horn honking were from young male drivers.

Available data also indicate that hotter regions of the world yield more violence, such as murder, rape, assaults, riots, and spouse abuse. In reviewing the research literature on the relationship between violence and temperature in various contexts, Anderson (1989) concludes that there is little doubt of a strong connection between hot temperature and violent crime. Simon Field (1992, p. 340) writes:

> Apart from the criminological universals of age and gender, it would be difficult to find any other factor which is so consistently correlated with violent crime. Under the circumstances the issue receives little attention in the mainstream criminological literature. This is perhaps because the idea that high temperatures induce criminal behaviour is redolent of an outdated environmental determinism, and therefore sits very uneasily with modern sociological theory. Whatever the reasons, the evidence is so compelling that the issue must be addressed.

However, though the relationship seems to be a strong one, it is also likely to be a very complex one. For example, people may be more inclined to drink alcoholic beverages during high temperatures. Therefore, alcohol may be playing a very critical role in the incidence of violence rather than strictly the ambient temperature itself. Field (1992) suggests that the violence-temperature connection may be due to the increased availability of victims who try to beat the heat by getting outside their homes and doing things besides their usual daily activities—such as going to amusement parks.

Field (1992) extended the hypothesis of the violence-temperature relationship by examining the *crime*-temperature relationship, including property crime (burglary, theft, robbery, and criminal damage). In his study, Field looked at temperature and crime statistics in England and Wales over a forty-year period, with particular emphasis on the very complete monthly data between 1977 and 1987. In addition to temperature, he included rainfall and sunshine in his analysis, since rain is often believed to be the police officer's friend by keeping potential victims and offenders off the street. The results showed a consistent and strong statistical relationship between temperature and crime of most types, but no relationship between crime and rainfall or sunshine. Specifically, high temperatures corresponded to high crime rates. Field (1992, p. 347) concludes, "... these findings represent compelling evidence that prevailing temperatures affect the level of most types of crimes in England and Wales." Furthermore, Field contends, "... the findings cannot generally be explained by the hypothesis that temperature causes aggression, for this would not explain the findings concerning property crime" (p. 348). Therefore, the linear hypothesis propounded by Anderson and others is inadequate to explain the findings, suggesting a far more complex relationship than originally supposed. Perhaps temperature affects violence directly, and affects other types of crime indirectly by influencing social behavior. That is, temperature affects property crime by influencing routine activities. In hot weather, for example, the family may be more inclined to go to the beach, leaving their home more susceptible to burglary and themselves more vulnerable to robbery and theft.

OTHER ENVIRONMENTAL FACTORS

The relationships between aggression and other environmental factors, such as noise, air pollution, and even erotica, are relatively new areas of inquiry. With reference to air pollution, for example, some studies indicate that individuals exposed to cigarette smoke are more aggressive than individuals in clean-air conditions (Jones & Bogat, 1978). Some people are even more aggressive when someone is simply smoking (inappropriately) around them (Zillmann, Baron, & Tamborini, 1981), even if the air is not heavily infiltrated with smoke. Other investigators (e.g., Rotton, 1983) report that malodorous pollution also encourages hostile aggressive behavior. There is also some evidence to suggest that loud, unpredictable, or complex noises may influence aggressive tendencies. For example, Konecni (1975) found that angry subjects exposed to loud or complex noise became more aggressive than angry subjects exposed to soft and simple noise. Apparently, the additional arousal instigated by the noise adds to the arousal effects of anger already felt by the subject. This increase in arousal level presumably facilitates aggressive behavior.

The effects of erotica on aggression and violence, and particularly on sex crimes, is an important topic that has received much research attention in recent years. However, because erotica may be conceptually linked with sexual offenses, we will postpone that topic until Chapter 10.

EFFECTS OF MASS MEDIA

Ninety-eight percent of American homes have at least one television set (American Psychological Association, 1993). By the age of sixteen, the average child has spent more time watching television than sitting in a classroom and has probably witnessed more than thirteen thousand killings (Walters & Malamud, 1975).

There are four scenes of violence portrayed on network television to every one scene expressing affection. A three-year study (1994–1997) by four universities on violence on American television revealed that 90 percent of movies shown on television include violence (National Cable Television Association, 1998). Violence was found most frequently on subscription television (85 percent on premium cable, and 59 percent on basic cable), while the lowest incidence of violence was found on PBS at 18 percent. Across three years of the study, nearly 40 percent of the violent incidents on television were initiated by "good" characters who are likely perceived as attractive role models. Sixty-seven percent of the programs portrayed violence within a humorous context. In general, the study found that most media violence is glamorized and that the long-term negative consequences of violent behavior are rarely depicted. Nearly three-quarters of violent scenes contain no remorse, criticism, punishment, or emotional reactions from the perpetrators. Overall, the survey found that the percentage of programs on television that contain some violence remained unchanged over the three-year period of study. One estimate suggests that the average American child sees more than one hundred thousand violent episodes and some twenty thousand murders on television before reaching adolescence (Myers, 1996).

Other surveys found that news coverage of violence against women and children was not used to educate the public but rather to fascinate and entertain (National Media Archive, 1990). In reference to video game preferences, the most popular game category is fantasy violence and other human violence games (Funk & Buchman, 1996). In that same study, the number of girls who listed violent games was equal to the number of boys who listed violent games. Girls favorite games were more likely to fall into the fantasy violent category, whereas boys preferred the human violent games.

It is not surprising that many people are disturbed by media violence and that social science researchers are intrigued by its possible relationship with the violence in our society. Whether exposure to violent media increases violence has been the focus of several public commissions and reports designed to influence social policy (Wood, Wong, & Chachere, 1991). In general, the bulk of the experimental studies reveal that television violence in particular has a significant effect on the frequency and type of aggressive behavior expressed by some adults and some children, especially children of an impressionable age. The relationship between violent television and aggression appears to be particularly strong for young boys who closely identify with the violent characters they see on television, and for children who have difficulty in their interpersonal relationships with their peers (Eron & Huesmann, 1986). In addition, there appears to be a correlation between violence portrayed in the print media, including pornographic literature, and the occurrence of violent crime. However, researchers to date have not established a *causal* link. Freedman (1988, p. 158), for example, warns that "the available empirical evidence does not support the idea that viewing television violence causes aggression." Let us look at some of this research in more detail.

In a classic study by Bandura (1965), sixty-six nursery school children were divided into three groups and shown one of three five-minute films. All three films depicted an adult verbally and physically assaulting a "BoBo," a large inflatable doll with a sand base. One group saw the adult model being rewarded with candy and a soft drink after displaying aggressive behavior. A second group observed the model being spanked and reprimanded verbally. A third group witnessed a situation in which the model received neither punishment nor reward.

After the children saw the film, they were permitted to free play for ten minutes in a playroom of toys, including a BoBo doll. The group that had witnessed the adult model being rewarded for the aggressive behavior exhibited more aggression than the other two groups. In addition, boys were more aggressive than girls. The group that saw the adult model being punished exhibited the lowest amount of aggression in the playroom.

Bandura's research, which included variations on the aforementioned basic design, consistently demonstrated this modeling effect. Furthermore, numerous follow-up studies not only replicated his findings, but also suggested that media violence may have a strong influence on real-life violence in many situations (Baron, 1977). There has also been some suggestion that even news reports of violence may have a **contagion effect** or **copycat effect**, a tendency in some people to model or copy an activity portrayed in the entertainment or news media. Contagion effect is said to occur when action depicted in the media is assessed by certain individuals as a good idea and then mimicked. For example, an ingenious bank robbery, dramatized on television, might be imitated.

A tragic illustration of the copycat effect can be found in a series of school shootings that began in 1997. In October of that year, a sixteen-year-old, having just stabbed his mother to death, arrived at the high school in Pearl, Mississippi, and began randomly shooting his classmates, killing two and wounding seven. Less than two months later, a fourteen-year old male opened fire on a group of fellow high school students participating in a prayer circle in West Paducah, Kentucky. He killed two schoolmates and wounded five others. The West Paducah incident received world-wide media coverage for several weeks, accompanied by extensive stories about the shooter. A few months later, on March 24, 1988, two boys, ages thirteen and eleven, armed with seven handguns and three rifles, opened fire on their classmates as they gathered on the school playground in Jonesboro, Arkansas, killing four very young girls and their teacher and wounding ten others. Of the fifteen killed or wounded, only one was male, indicating that the young shooters were aiming specifically at girls.

After Jonesboro and exactly one month later, came Edinboro, Pennsylvania, where a fourteen-year-old male student began shooting during a school dance, killing a teacher. This incident was followed by another shooting less than a month later in Fayetteville, Tennessee, resulting in the death of a student. A week later, a fifteen-year-old male in Springfield, Oregon, walked into the high school cafeteria and began randomly shooting at fellow students, firing fifty rounds from a .22-caliber semiautomatic rifle in less than a minute. As he stopped to reload the young shooter was tackled and disarmed by a varsity wrestler. During that one minute, however, he managed to kill two classmates and wounded twenty-two others. He had also shot both his parents prior to leaving for school. Less than two weeks later, on June 15, 1998, a fourteen-year-old student, armed with a .32-caliber semiautomatic handgun, opened fire in the hallway of a high school as students took final exams, wounding a basketball coach and a volunteer aide. All of these young shooters had an inordinate interest in guns, had troubled backgrounds, knew the details of the previous school shootings, and had a strong fascination with violence presented through the media.

Exposure to media-portrayed violence does not, of course, automatically promote aggression. Some individuals are affected more than others. Children from low-income families are apparently more influenced by media violence than middle-class children (Eisenhower, 1969); it is not clear whether this reflects exposure to the violence itself or other factors as well. Researchers have found evidence that positive parental models are likely to override violent models on television (Chaffee & McLeod, 1971; Goldstein, 1975). Moreover, television violence seems to have substantially less effect on families where the parents do not rely on aggressive behavior for solving problems (Chaffee & McLeod, 1971).

Researchers have found that aggressive children watch more media violence, identify more with violent characters, and believe more that the violence they observe reflects real life than nonaggressive children (Lefkowitz, Eron, Walder, & Huesmann, 1977; Huesmann, 1988; Huesmann & Eron, 1986). Does this mean that they learned their aggressive styles from the media? The answer is not that clear. Berkowitz (1970) suggests that people who rely heavily on aggression for meeting their needs are more influenced by media violence than are people who do not usually seek violent solutions. Studies have also shown that extremely aggressive adolescents are most strongly attracted to violence portrayed in media entertainment (Berkowitz, 1970; Eron, 1963; Halloran, Brown, & Chaney, 1969).

Repeated exposure to violence on television may habituate heavy viewers to violence. It may also distort one's perception of the world. Heavy television viewers respond to violence with less physiological arousal than do light viewers, suggesting that repeated exposure has desensitized them to violent events (Cline, Croft, & Courrier, 1973; Thomas, 1982). Furthermore, television is heavily populated with villainous and unscrupulous people, portrayals that may give frequent viewers a jaded view of the world. There is some evidence that heavy viewers, compared to light viewers, are less trustful of others and overestimate their chances of being criminally victimized (Gerbner & Gross, 1976).

Black and Bevan (1992) report evidence that movies may have a greater impact on aggressive behavior than television. They argue that television programs are interrupted by commercials, that television viewers talk, leave the room, read, and generally have their attention divided with friends and family. However, in a movie theater, the presentation takes place in the dark, in the presence of many strangers, and the film is viewed without interruption and with focused attention. Therefore, the depiction of violence in the movie theater should be more realistic, salient, and memorable than most presentations seen on television. Black and Bevan found that adults (both men and women) who viewed a violent movie (*Missing in Action*) were more aggressive than those who saw a nonviolent film (*Passage to India*), although the aggression probably dissipated rapidly after leaving the theater.

In an extensive review of the research literature, Wood and colleagues (1991, p. 380) conclude the following:

> Our results demonstrate that media violence enhances children's and adolescents' aggression in interactions with strangers, classmates, and friends. Our findings cannot be dismissed as representing artificial experimental constructions because the studies included in our review evaluated media exposure on aggression as it naturally emerged in unconstrained social interaction.

However, Wood and colleagues admonish that the studies they reviewed focused on short-term media effects since the researchers measured aggressive behavior almost immediately after the film presentation. Long-term effects of media violence remain largely unknown. However, after over three thousand studies on the effects of violent media and aggression, the overwhelming conclusion is that violent television and movies do increase aggressive tendencies in both children and adults.

VICTIM-PRECIPITATED AGGRESSION

So far we have maintained that aggression is principally a learned behavior. Although it may be influenced by a number of variables—temperature, frustration, and situational cues, for example—it occurs because an individual has learned that aggression works. Social learning theory postulates that most aggressive behavior is acquired through modeling and maintained through various forms of reinforcement, especially social reinforcement. However, we have not yet given attention to another parameter, the victim of the aggression. Often, a specific aggressive act is either provoked or facilitated by the behavior of the person who eventually becomes the victim. Specifically, what begins as a heated argument develops into a physical, violent brawl—a process called **escalation**.

Research reviewed by Baron (1977) indicates that most people respond to provocation in kind (e.g., Taylor, 1967; Epstein & Taylor, 1967; Hendrick & Taylor, 1971; O'Leary & Dengerink, 1973). Furthermore, the reciprocated response approximates in intensity the provocation received. The first person then reacts by increasing the provocation. In this way, verbal attacks often lead to physical retaliation and violence. The implication is that in some crimes, the behavior of the victim plays a role in escalating the offender's actions.

The concept of escalation is consistent with social learning theory. That is, we influence our social environment and the social environment influences us in turn.

There is mutual interaction in any interpersonal encounter. Many violent incidents occur between family members, or between persons who know one another well. An investigation often reveals escalating anger and arousal between the participants, often ending in serious injury or even death. We will return to this topic in Chapter 8.

THE PHYSIOLOGY OF AGGRESSION

Although most aggressive behavior reflects a learned way of responding to situations, some theorists and students of aggression argue that physiological factors play a significant role. In recent years, the relationship between physiology and aggression has been broached during discussions of an alleged premenstrual syndrome, drug treatment for sex offenders, and presumed relationships between certain mental or physical defects (schizophrenia, epilepsy) and crimes of violence. While evidence of a strong relationship between aggression and physiological variables does appear to exist for some species of animals, for humans the evidence is far less compelling.

There is experimental evidence that the nervous and endocrine systems of *animals* contribute significantly to their aggressive behavior. The endocrine system secretes hormones into the blood or lymph. Differential roles played by male and female hormones have been connected with differential tendencies toward aggressive behavior. Thus, the male hormone testosterone is believed to facilitate aggression in both the male and female (Moyer, 1971; Goldman, 1977). In animals, the female hormone progesterone, when administered to correct hormonal imbalances, may alleviate symptoms of irritability and tension. There is some dated evidence that women taking birth control pills containing progesterone demonstrate less irritability and hostility than do women not on any pill (Hamburg, Moos, & Yalom, 1968).

Some researchers believe that the differential hormonal effects may partly explain why human males overwhelmingly commit more violent crimes than do human females. In addition, the relationship between the secretion rate of testosterone and the level of overt hostility correlates well in young men, but not older men (Goldman, 1977). The relationship is especially notable in male adolescents with a history of assault or attempted murder. Testosterone may be released in greater quantities when males are younger than when they are older. We underscore, however, that learning and social expectations and cognitions play an extremely powerful role in any statistics that indicate gender differences in criminal behavior.

PREMENSTRUAL SYNDROME (PMS)

At this point, it is relevant to discuss **premenstrual syndrome (PMS)**, which refers to the cyclic physiological and psychological changes that occur prior to the onset of menstruation, usually four to seven days before. Although there is considerable debate about whether premenstrual symptoms are validated and present in enough women to merit diagnosis as a syndrome (Sommer, 1983), the fact that some physiological changes do occur is rarely questioned. These changes may include swelling of the extremities and breasts, fatigue, and headaches. On the other hand, some researchers have also reported positive symptoms associated with PMS, such as increased creativity and physical energy.

The symptoms are believed to be due to changes in the hormonal balance between estrogen and progesterone (Moyer, 1976; Tasto & Insel, 1977). During the preovulation phase (menstrual onset to day fourteen) progesterone dominates over estrogen, a dominance that peaks at approximately day fourteen (ovulation) when the estrogen level begins to increase and eventually dominate. Decreases in progesterone have been associated with high risks of suicide, especially violent suicide (Wetzel, McClure, & Reich, 1971), hospital admissions related to depression and schizophrenia (Tasto & Insel, 1977), and female crime (Dalton, 1964; Moyer, 1971). Because the physiological changes can presumably have a strong influence on behavior, PMS has been used successfully as a criminal defense in British courts. In the United States, a New York case that might have put the syndrome to the test was plea-bargained before it reached the trial stage (Carney & Williams, 1983).

Resistance to a connection between PMS and female criminal behavior is understandable. First, there is too little agreement about whether or not such a syndrome actually exists. Second, if society were to accept PMS as an excusing condition for even a portion of the crime committed by women, the social implications would be shattering. What standards would be used to determine which women were susceptible to PMS, and could any woman be trusted during the premenstrual period? Although these questions may seem overly dramatic, they are not irrelevant if one assumes that, during a significant part of their lives, some women are at the mercy of their biology.

The relationship between the premenstrual syndrome and *violent* crime has yet to be convincingly documented. The first heavily quoted study on the subject was that of Morton and colleagues (Morton, Addison, Addison, Hunt, & Sullivan, 1953). The study was designed to evaluate the effectiveness of various treatments for the relief of premenstrual tension in inmates. Morton, almost as an afterthought, mentioned that 62 percent of his sample of 249 female prisoners had committed violent crimes (murder, manslaughter, and assault) during their premenstrual week. Another 17 percent of the sample had committed violent offenses during menstruation. However, the study had many methodological flaws that make it very suspect. The percentages of crimes were indicated for four-cycle phases (premenstrual week, midcycle, menstruation, and the end of the period), but the lengths of these phases were not provided (Horney, 1978). Furthermore, no statistical analyses were reported, nor were there any explanations of how the data were gathered (Horney, 1978). Moreover, no one has ever been able to replicate the Morton findings.

In another study, Dalton (1961) interviewed 156 newly convicted women in British prisons on their first weekend after sentencing. She reported that 22 percent had committed crimes during their premenstrual period, and another 26 percent during menstruation. Her method for determining these percentages relied exclusively on retrospective memory of the women themselves about their menstrual cycle. Further, Dalton divided the menstrual cycle into seven four-day periods, with menstruation representing days one through four, while the premenstrual period was indicated by days twenty-five through twenty-eight.

There are, however, a number of serious problems in the study. First, crime in the Dalton study did not refer to violence, but rather to *economic* crimes (viz., shoplifting, burglary, embezzlement, forgery, and prostitution). Second, relying on a one-time estimation of self-reported menstrual cycles is fraught with potential for error, particularly since women normally cannot accurately remember their menstrual cycles (McFarland, Ross, & DeCourville, 1989). Third, not all women experience regular twenty-eight day cycles. Therefore, dividing the cycles neatly into seven four-day periods is a very questionable procedure.

Recent research also shows that negative emotions (irritability, loneliness, depression, and so on) do not necessarily increase during premenstrual and menstrual phases for most women. For example, McFarland, Ross, and DeCourville (1989) examined the relationship between women's theories of menstrual distress and their recollections of the physical discomforts and the emotional characteristics that accompany the cycle. Subjects completed daily questionnaires in which they evaluated themselves on emotions and physical symptoms throughout the cycle. Later, the subjects were asked to recall what they had said on the questionnaire during menstruation. The recollections of the women were not only inaccurate, but also consistent with their theories of menstrual distress. "(T)he more a woman believed in the phenomenon of menstrual distress, the more she exaggerated, in recall, the negativity of her symptoms during her last period" (p. 522). Similar observations have been made by Pamela Kato and Diane Ruble (1992), indicating that the intensity of negative emotions experienced during the menstrual state—such as tension, irritability, depression, emotional liability, and anxiety—is open to debate.

In summary, there is no evidence to date that the emotions and moods that presumably accompany PMS facilitate or encourage criminal behavior. In fact, it is highly questionable whether pronounced or intense negative moods even occur during the premenstrual or menstrual state for a majority of women, despite what the "current wisdom" assumes. In their careful review of the literature, Harry and Balcer (1987, p. 318) maintain: "Despite what seems to be substantial interest in the topic, we conclude there is not scientific support for an association between any phases of the menstrual cycle and criminal behavior."

Still, the criminal justice and judicial systems continue to debate whether hormonal balances or imbalances should excuse violent behavior or at least mitigate responsibility (Carney & Williams, 1983), or should have no relevance whatsoever. Although some researchers would have society accept PMS as a substantive defense in crimes of violence (that is, an excusing condition absolving the individual of moral culpability), others believe that such an approach would undermine gains in women's struggle for economic, social, and political equality.

PHYSIOLOGICAL CONTROL THROUGH SURGERY AND DRUGS

Another controversial issue relating to the physiology of aggression is the treatment of violent offenders. Although treatment in the broad sense can mean psychotherapy or psychoanalysis, in the narrow sense it takes on a medical connotation. Those who are violent are administered drugs to dull their senses or overcome the effects of presumably overactive aggression hormones. More drastically, they may be submitted to psychosurgery or castration. The former procedure modifies aggressive centers in the brain; the latter excises the testicles, which contain testosterone, or demolishes their functioning.

It is fairly well documented that castration lessens the tendency for animals to be aggressive. In rare instances, castration of prisoners convicted of sex crimes may have significantly reduced their aggressive episodes (Le Maire, 1956; Hawke, 1950). It may surprise you to learn that compulsory castration was legal in the United States until as late as the 1960s. For example, over 370 "voluntary" bilateral orchidectomies (excision of both testes) were performed on mentally disordered sex offenders in San Diego as a "judicial mandate" (Reiss, 1977).

Treatment with drugs that mimic the chemical composition and action of sexual hormones is more common. For example, medroxyprogesterone (Depo-Provera), which is chemically similar to the female hormone progesterone, is apparently highly effective in lowering testosterone levels (Moyer, 1976). Lowered levels of the aggression-inducing male hormone testosterone presumably lessen the male drive to engage in sexual activity. Depo-Provera, the reasoning goes, will inhibit the excessive and impulsive sexual and aggressive behaviors of sex offenders. There is some evidence to support this assumption. Blumer and Migeon (1973), for example, found that ingestion of high levels of Depo-Provera successfully reduced sexual arousal and the need to engage in sexual "deviations." However, much research needs to be done before researchers recommend widespread usage. Moreover, the use of drugs—like psychosurgery—raises numerous legal questions, many of which have not yet been addressed by the courts.

Recent work in the neuropsychological sciences has provided additional information about aggressive behavior. Advances in technology and instrument sophistication have allowed neuropsychologists to study the potential influence of molecular components, especially substances known as *neurotransmitters*, in facilitating and inhibiting aggression. Neurotransmitters are biochemicals directly involved in the transmission of neural impulses. Without them, communication within the mammalian nervous system would be impossible. Researchers have learned that some of these neurotransmitters—namely norepinephrine, acetylcholine, and serotonin—may significantly influence the cortical and subcortical mechanisms responsible for aggression and violence. No single neurotransmitter solely excites or inhibits aggression, however. Recent research suggests that the neurotransmitter serotonin may play a significant role in aggression and violence (Coscina, 1997; Loeber & Stouthamer-Loeber, 1998; Moffitt et al., in press). Specifically, many individuals who act aggressively toward others or commit violent suicide appear to have abnormally low levels of serotonin.

If certain neurotransmitters are implicated in aggressive behavior, it is not too far-fetched to consider drug regimens for control. Neurotransmitters are strongly affected by drugs. However, since neurotransmitters are the basic chemicals for all behavior, any modification of their levels in the nervous system is likely to affect a large range of behavior and emotions, not only the behavior that researchers are seeking to control. Therefore, although the considerable potential of drugs in controlling and reducing aggression cannot be overlooked, their peripheral effects must be considered.

Some neurophysiologists concentrate their research on trying to identify aggression centers in the brain. Presumably, if the part of the brain that controls or facilitates aggressive or violent behavior could be located, it might be manipulated. The research to date indicates that if an aggression center exists, it is most likely in the general area of the brain stem known as the limbic system, which consists of a diverse group of complicated brain structures and circuitry. Specifically, a small, almond-shaped group of nerve cells in the stem called the amygdala, another structure called the hypothalamus, and a portion of the brain itself called the temporal lobe have been the focus of scientific research. To date, however, we know too little about how our brain works, and we do not know where behavioral centers are located (Chorover, 1980).

When researchers examine the relationship between aggression and brain centers, they usually use the *stereotaxic* procedure, which many researchers believe has great potential for the control of hostile aggression. By drilling a small hole in the skull, researchers are able to penetrate the brain with small insulated wire electrodes for electrical stimulation. They may also insert minute glass hollow tubes (cannulae) to allow them to chemically stimulate specific sites in the brain and stem. The needle electrode, once properly implanted, may be permanently attached to the skull with screw fittings, allowing a small segment of the electrode to protrude from the skull for the attachment of wires or to receive radio transmission from a distance. This procedure of wireless communication is known as *telemetry*. The external part of the electrode is small enough so that it can be covered with hair and thus not be noticeable. The individual feels no pain from the procedure.

Small electric currents are passed through the electrodes to the brain site, stimulating the brain structure (or destroying it, if necessary, with direct current or high-frequency alternating current). In this way, aggressive and violent behavior may be stimulated or inhibited, depending on whether the site has an excitatory (facilitating) or inhibitory effect on aggressive behavior. If the researcher applies low frequency alternating current to an area with a facilitating function, the individual will probably behave aggressively; conversely, when current is applied to an inhibitory area, the person will be mild-mannered.

As a result of the aforementioned research, it is now possible for scientists to implant electrodes into a specific region of the human brain and monitor brainwave patterns by computer, even when the individual is some distance away from the laboratory. When a brainwave configuration known to be associated with violent behavior in that particular individual occurs, the computer activates an electrical stimulation to the brain site.

Violence may also be controlled by producing permanent alterations of brain tissue (lesions) by surgical, electrical (direct current), or chemical means (collectively called *psychosurgery*). Lesions in the temporal lobe of the brain were performed on several prisoners in California (Valenstein, 1973). The Japanese neurosurgeon Hirataro Narabayashi claims success with amygdala operations on a diversity of patients plagued by aggressive, uncontrollable, destructive, and violent behavior. He reports that about 68 percent of his patients showed a significant decline in aggressive, violent behavior (Valenstein, 1973).

What are the social implications of such scientific practices? To what extent are they justified? Some investigators assert that we should control the antisocial elements in our society by any perfected biochemical, electrical, or surgical means necessary. In the early 1970s, the then-President of the American Psychological Association, Kenneth B. Clark, urged his colleagues to make full use of these breakthroughs in biological research, which he referred to as **psychotechnology**. Assuming that no individual would choose to be a criminal if he or she were "not impelled by some forms of internal, biochemical, or external, social forces—or some combination of both" (1971, p. 1056), Clark commented:

> The implications of an effective psychotechnology for the control of criminal behavior and the amelioration of the moral insensitivities which produce reactive criminality in others are clear. It would seem, therefore, that there would be moral and rational justification for the use of compulsive criminals as pretest subjects in seeking precise forms of intervention and moral control of human behavior.

Clark also suggested that world leaders be required to submit themselves to perfected forms of psychotechnological and biochemical intervention so that their potentially aggressive, hostile impulses could be controlled. This would be justified, since it would prevent the mass destruction of civilization.

Since Clark's widely quoted address, few psychologists have called for similar drastic interventions, although biochemical intervention and surgical techniques on the human brain (psychosurgery) are increasingly sophisticated. The medical, legal, moral, and ethical ramifications if Clark's proposals were to be carried out on a large scale would be overwhelming, and the questions posed would be unanswerable. Who would decide which technique should be used on whom? Which individuals would be required to submit to psychosurgery, and which would be encouraged to? What are the constitutional rights of the subjects? Although some courts have already begun to answer some of these questions with respect to institutionalized individuals, there remain numerous unsettled issues that are not within the scope of this text.

Furthermore, biological alleviation of aggressive behavior would undoubtedly affect socially desirable behaviors as well. There is evidence to suggest that aspects of a person's emotional, cognitive, and intellectual functioning may be significantly affected by biological manipulation of the brain. Neuronal networks in the central nervous system do not function in physiological isolation. It is estimated that the brain contains between 10 and 13 billion brain cells (neurons) whose interconnecting pathways form the most complex intercommunication network in the known universe. Each nerve cell or neuron may play some role in behavior. Scientists talk about areas or structures in the brain that may account for some type of behavior, but they know that each of these areas contains numerous neurons and supportive cells that contribute to a variety of functions. Thus, surgical, electrical, or chemical intervention to affect aggression may also incidentally affect other behaviors that need not and should not be changed.

BRAIN PATHOLOGY AND AGGRESSION

Routine postmortem examinations on chronically antisocial, violent persons generally find no noticeable lesion or malformation in the limbic system or other areas of the central nervous system (Goldman, 1977). This does not necessarily mean there was no physiological abnormality. The instruments used in the postmortem analysis may not have been sophisticated enough to detect them. Alternately, the individual's violent behavior might have reflected biochemical or neurotransmitter substances rather than malformation or damage to neural structures. In some instances, however, individuals were found to have symptoms of serious brain diseases. Richard Speck, who murdered eight student nurses in Chicago, reportedly displayed such symptoms (Valenstein, 1973). Charles Whitman, who killed passersby from the top of a university tower, was found in an autopsy to have a large tumor in the area of the amygdala (Mark & Ervin, 1970). Even so, it is not clear that these abnormalities directly affected Speck's and Whitman's violent behavior.

Furthermore, it is extremely unlikely that a majority of criminals in our society suffer from brain pathology or significant dysfunction. A small proportion of violent crime may be committed by people with brain diseases, but disease does not account for an appreciable portion of the aggression in our society.

Abnormal brainwave patterns, introduced in Chapter 4, are more common, however. A significant number of prisoners who have committed violent crimes apparently display these patterns (Valenstein, 1973; Mark & Ervin, 1970). You may recall that one category of abnormal brainwave patterns, slow-wave activity, is especially apparent in the temporal lobe region of the brain. Hare (1970) estimates that 2 percent of the general population exhibits this phenomenon, compared to 8.2 percent of the convicted murderer population and 14 percent of aggressive psychopaths. A second type of abnormal brainwave activity, positive spike activity, occurs in less than 2 percent of the general population. However, it has been estimated that anywhere between 20 and 40 percent of individuals with a history of impulsive, aggressive, and destructive behavior display positive spikes (Hare, 1970). The destructive and violent responses are often precipitated by relatively mild provocations, but they can result in severe damage to property and injury or death to others. Do abnormal brainwaves cause violent behavior? Or does violent behavior cause abnormal brainwaves? It is impossible to tell. At present, the research on brainwave patterns has uncovered only correlations, which do not signify cause and effect. The evidence to date indicates only that some forms of brain pathology or dysfunctions are found in a very small percentage of those who are violent—nothing more.

HEREDITY AND THE XYY CHROMOSOME

Some early investigators believed that criminal behavior and predispositions to be violent were a result of heredity. The most prominent proponent of this view was Lombroso, who was convinced that a criminal "type" could be identified by specific physical characteristics, such as an unsymmetrical head and jaw, a low forehead, protruding ears, and bushy, connected eyebrows.

More contemporary inquiries on the relationship between genetics and criminality have focused on the so-called XYY chromosomal syndrome. The impetus for this research was a study by Jacobs and his associates (Jacobs, Brunton, Melville, Brittain, & McClermont, 1965), who reported that the presence of an extra Y chromosome in the male is significantly associated with the triad of tall stature, mental retardation, and an unusually high level of aggressive behavior. After the Jacobs study was released, some investigators hypothesized that the XYY chromosomal anomaly was closely related to violent criminal activity in males.

Chromosomes are chains of genetic material known as DNA that contain hereditary instructions for the growth and production of every living cell in the organism. Chromosomes control physical traits such as eye and hair color and height, and they may have substantial influence on many psychological predispositions and temperaments. For example, chromosomes may account for a predisposition to depression. Each cell in the human body normally possesses forty-six chromosomes, or twenty-three pairs. One pair in each cell is responsible for sex determination and sex characteristics. One member of the pair is always an X, but the other member may be either an X or a Y, depending on the sex of the individual. They are named after their appearance under a microscope. Each cell of the normal woman has two X chromosomes, while each cell of the normal man has an X and a Y. In rare instances, however, a genetic anomaly occurs in males in that two Y chromosomes pair with a single X—hence the phenomenon XYY. Rather than the usual forty-six chromosomes, the individual has forty-seven.

The principal characteristics associated with the presence of an extra Y chromosome include unusual height, episodes of violent aggression, and borderline intelligence—although there are many exceptions. Severe acne or scars from acne are also a characteristic.

A number of infamous murderers apparently had the XYY abnormality. One was Robert Peter Tait, who was convicted of beating to death a seventy-seven-year-old woman in Australia (Fox, 1971). The XYY characteristic was discovered after his trial but did not delay his execution. The XYY genotype was first used as a basis for criminal defense in 1968, at the trial of Daniel Hugon in Paris. Hugon was charged with the brutal murder of an elderly prostitute. Although convicted, he received only seven years imprisonment. It is not certain that the court considered the XYY abnormality a mitigating factor in determining his sentence, however (Fox, 1971). In the United States, criminal defendants have not used the defense successfully. "Big Bad John" (Sean) Farley, a 6 foot 8 inch 240-pound giant who murdered and mutilated a Queens, New York woman in 1969, was convicted in spite of his plea of insanity due to chromosomal imbalance. Finally, Richard Speck, who murdered eight student nurses, possessed some of the physical features associated with the XYY chromosome. After his conviction, researchers examined his chromosomal structure. Although there was considerable confusion at the time the results were released, it has been concluded that Speck's genetic structure does not include the abnormality.

Although XYY has not been used as a criminal defense, there is some empirical support for its relationship with crime. So far, however, there is little evidence that violence and XYY go hand in hand. After an extensive review of the world literature, Jarvik, Klodin, and Matsuyama (1973) concluded that the presence of the XYY configuration in the general population averages between 0.11 and 0.14 percent; among mental patients it is significantly higher, averaging between 0.13 and 0.20 percent. However, in criminal populations, Jarvik found that XYY occurred in 1.9 percent of the cases. Jarvik's research combined information from twenty-six studies, including 5,066 criminal subjects. The 1.9 percent figure for the presence of the XYY chromosome, however, constitutes a very small percentage of the total prison population and seems to represent very little of the violence in our society. In another study, XYY prisoners were found to have fewer assault incidents than comparable groups of "normal" XY prisoners (Price & Whatmore, 1967). A great majority of the XYY crimes were against property.

EPILEPSY AND VIOLENCE

Between 1889 and 1970, there were only fifteen court cases in the United States in which epilepsy had been used as a defense against charges of murder, homicide, manslaughter, or disorderly conduct (Delgado-Escueta, Mattson, & King, 1981). However, during the 1970s medical researchers implied that there was a causal relationship between temporal lobe epilepsy and violence (Goldstein, 1974; Pincus, 1980). This implied relationship resulted in a rash of diminished responsibility or insanity defenses for violent acts beginning in 1977. Presumably, the person plagued with this disorder is prone to uncontrollable periods of violence and destruction. Available research fails to support any relationship between violence and epilepsy in general or violence and psychomotor epilepsy, however (Valenstein, 1973; Blumer, 1976).

Although angry, irritable behavior between seizures is commonly reported in chronic temporal lobe epileptics, they rarely inflict physical harm (Blumer, 1976). In rare cases, some violence may occur in the confusional state that takes place immediately after an epileptic seizure, if the individual is provoked. During this brief rage attack, the person appears to lose control and may even destroy some furniture or strike a family member. Rarely is there actual physical injury, and rarely are criminal charges brought. Furthermore, it is not clear whether aggression occurs because of the seizure itself, associated brain damage that often accompanies psychomotor seizure activity, or is independent of the seizure itself (Herzberg & Fenwick, 1988). Available evidence indicates that if violence does occur during the seizure episode, the violent behavior is probably due to a long-standing response pattern of the individual and is not directly related to the seizure itself.

SUMMARY AND CONCLUSIONS

In this chapter we reviewed the major psychological perspectives on aggression and violence. Answers to what can be done about aggression and violent crime rest ultimately on one's perspective of human nature. If one believes that aggression is innate and part of our evolutionary heritage, a position held by mainstream psychoanalytic and ethological thought, then the conclusion must be that aggression is part of life, and that little can be done to alter this basic ingredient of human nature. Clues for reducing aggression are found in the behavior demonstrated throughout the animal kingdom. If, on the other hand, one believes that human aggression is acquired, then the key becomes principles of human learning and thought, and hope that one can change this acquired behavior for the betterment of humankind. The distinction between the innate and learning viewpoints has been somewhat oversimplified, but most contemporary theories on aggression fall within one or the other camp. At this point, the learning perspective has garnered considerably more empirical support than the innate perspective. Cognitive factors are especially important in explanations of human aggression.

However, as more research data are published, the learning perspective becomes increasingly complex, and additional factors must be considered. For one thing, physiological arousal certainly plays a major role in aggressive and violent behavior, as suggested by Berkowitz (1989). High levels of arousal seem to facilitate (not cause) aggressive behavior in certain situations. Extremely high arousal seems to interfere with our sense of self-awareness and internal control, rendering us more susceptible to environmental cues and to mindless or habitual behaviors. In this sense, under very high arousal, we may not stop to consider the consequences of our violent behavior. This point raises serious questions about the value of capital punishment or life sentences as general deterrents to common violent crime.

The different types of aggressive behavior were also emphasized in this chapter. Overt and covert forms of aggression must be considered in any discussion of crime. Overt aggressors are more likely to be involved in both violent and serious property-economic crimes, whereas covert aggressors are more prone to be involved in property offenses, particularly occupational crime. And although the conventional wisdom has been that boys are more likely to commit highly aggressive crimes, the evidence suggests that girls may be equally involved in aggressive behavior of a different kind.

Situational and neurophysiological factors also contribute significantly to aggressive behavior. Aggressive stimuli, crowds, pollution, temperature, smells, and central nervous system pathology all must be entertained as possible contributors. Social learning theorists also note that the media and the models they provide substantially affect our attitudes, values, and overall impressions about violence. Attitudes, beliefs, and thoughts refer to the cognitive processes that are beginning to emerge as contenders for a leading role in the psychological explanation of criminal behavior. Operant and classical conditioning remain important, but they do not adequately address the many intricacies of criminal behavior.

We end the chapter with a concise summary statement by Rowell Huesmann who, after reviewing the research literature, concludes: "No one causal factor by itself explains more than a small portion of individual differences in aggressiveness" (1997, p. 70). He hastens to add, however, that "early learning and socialization play a key role in the development of habitual aggression" (1997, p. 70).

CRIMINAL HOMICIDE
AND ASSAULT

I f the news and entertainment media are reasonably decent barometers of human interest, homicidal violence must be one of Western civilization's most fascinating subjects and, along with sex, the most marketable. Usually, the more bizarre, senseless, or heinous the murder, the more extensive press coverage it receives, followed shortly thereafter by books, television specials, and movies. Unusual mass murders, serial murderers, and so-called motiveless killings are especially popular. Yet on a national level, homicides consistently account for only about 1 or 2 percent of all violent crimes reported in the FBI's UCR and other official statistics, numbering around twenty thousand in 1996 (FBI, 1997; see Figure 8-1). If we consider its percentage distribution among all index crimes, murder represents only 0.2 percent of the total. Furthermore, a vast majority of these criminal homicides offer very little mystery or intrigue. In most cases, criminal homicides involve angry friends, spouses, or acquaintances killing friends, spouses, or acquaintances.

The disproportionate amount of attention paid to criminal homicides may be explained in a variety of ways. One way might be to draw a parallel to the popularity of the occult, the mysterious, and the macabre. We crave our science fiction, our tales of terror, even our haunted houses. Perhaps we need a certain amount of excitement and arousal to prevent our lives from becoming too mundane and boring. Psychologists have long known that novelty produces arousal and excitement and breaks monotony (Berlyne, 1960). This human need for stimulation—which, as we learned in Chapter 3, is greater in some people (extraverts) than others (introverts)—may partly explain the appeal of roller coasters, sky jumping, race car driving, and gambling. These same people may enjoy films featuring vampires, werewolves, psycho-murderers, or torture chambers. Or, these vicarious pleasures might be enjoyed by individuals not wishing to seek out excitement directly. In either case, they add zest to life.

The marketability of murder might also be explained by curiosity or exploratory behavior, which is very closely related to excitement and arousal. One purpose of curiosity is to allow organisms to adjust to their environments (Butler, 1954). An individual or an organism explores a new situation to satisfy

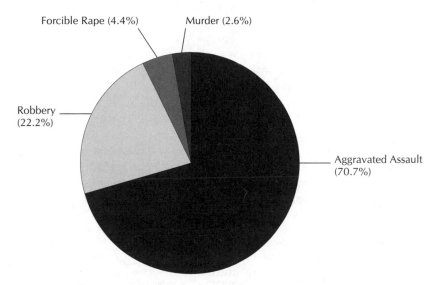

Figure 8-1   Violent Crime Distribution in the United States
(Source: U.S. Department of Justice, *Uniform Crime Reports, 1997.*)

this curiosity—which is theorized to be a physiological drive state—and in the process of discovering information, adapts to the new situation. Curiosity about murder might help us prepare for the possibility that a similar event might happen to us. Reading about bizarre, seemingly irrational homicides might help us to identify danger signals. Information about the incident gives clues about who murders, who gets murdered, and under what circumstances.

Extensive exposure to violence may immunize us from its horror, however. Many social commentators have advanced cogent arguments that Western civilization has become conditioned or jaded to cruelty and inhumane behavior. In addition, the attention that the news media give to violence makes it seem more widespread and frequent to people than it really is. This phenomenon is called by social psychologists the **availability heuristic**. Heuristics refer to cognitive shortcuts that people use to make quick inferences about their world. When the news media show graphic and frightening accounts of violence, people are likely to incorporate these vivid details into cognitive shorthand and have them readily available for future reference. When they think of violence at a later time, they remember the most vivid and horrific accounts, increasing their fear of violent crime and augmenting its incidence in their minds.

To speculate about why we are attracted to accounts of murder and violence, or to wonder about the effects of repeated exposure, may not seem to address the main focus of this chapter, which is the violent offender. Speculation becomes relevant, however, when we shift the focus to the individual who is part of a society that seems to have an inordinate need to seek out stimulation or to know details of crimes. When that individual is insensitive to suffering and begins to create his or her own excitement by torturing and murdering, we have a social problem.

Psychology, as we will see in this chapter, can offer some suggestions for understanding and solving this problem.

After defining our terms, we will examine situational and dispositional factors that occur consistently in homicide and aggravated assault, beginning with data gathered by sociological researchers. We should emphasize that the statistics are offered only to provide a broad perspective of the incidence, prevalence, and sociological correlates of violent crime. We will then consider family violence in some detail.

Thus far in this text, theoretical issues have been introduced with minimum application to specific offenses. Beginning here and throughout the remainder of this text, we will interweave the theories and concepts previously outlined with specific categories of criminal behavior.

DEFINITIONS

Criminal homicide is causing the death of another person without legal justification or excuse. Legally, the term **murder** is reserved for the "felonious killing of one human being by another with malice aforethought" (Nettler, 1982, p. 3). The UCR, however, includes both murder and nonnegligent manslaughter under the rubric criminal homicide for reporting purposes (see Figure 8-2). The essential difference between murder and manslaughter is that malice aforethought must be present for murder, whereas it must be absent for manslaughter. In this sense, manslaughter is not as serious as murder. Therefore, nonnegligent manslaughter is killing another human being without premeditation. In other words, the offender's original intent was not to kill the victim; however, he or she became so agitated and emotionally

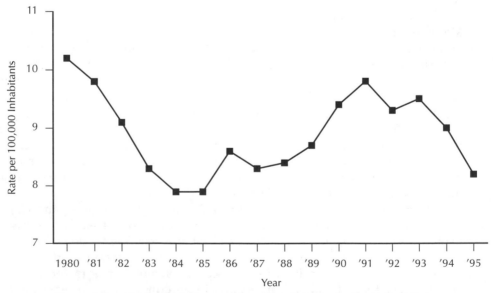

Figure 8-2   Murder and Nonnegligent Manslaughter in the United States
(Source: U.S. Bureau of Justice Statistics, 1996.)

upset in a particular situation that he or she lost partial control of his or her self-regulatory system. Since we are concerned with both murder and nonnegligent manslaughter, we will use the general term **homicide**. We are not concerned with suicides, accidental deaths, negligent manslaughter, or justifiable homicide (the killing of a person by a law enforcement officer in the line of duty or, in some cases, the killing of a person in the act of committing a felony by a private citizen).

Assault is the intentional inflicting of bodily injury on another person, or the attempt to inflict such injury. It becomes **aggravated assault** when the intention is to inflict serious bodily injury. Aggravated assault is often accompanied by the use of a deadly or dangerous weapon. **Simple assault** is the unlawful, intentional inflicting of less than serious bodily injury without a deadly or dangerous weapon, or the attempt to inflict such bodily injury, again without a deadly or dangerous weapon.

Criminologists generally study aggravated assault and homicide together, primarily because they view many aggravated assaults as failed homicide attempts (Doerner & Speir, 1986; Doerner, 1988). Dunn (1976) challenges this practice. He notes that the aggravated assault rate is at least twenty times that of homicide. "Given this disparity in rates, it is difficult to imagine that even one-quarter of all aggravated assaults were attempted homicides or would have been homicides except for the intervention of medical care" (Dunn, 1976, p. 10). Therefore, it may be unwarranted to consider aggravated assault as being in the same league as homicide; the two may differ in important variables, including the motives of the perpetrator. A purist, therefore, would try to maintain an aggravated assault-homicide distinction.

For our purposes, it is neither realistic nor desirable to do so. Not realistic, since much of the relevant research on offender characteristics collapses the categories into one, under the rationale that people who kill usually have a history of assaultive behavior. It is not desirable, since, from a psychological point of view, the two types of behavior are very comparable. Often, the type of weapon used determines the final outcome. The high-powered bullet, as an obvious example, is in most cases far more lethal than the knife (Gillin & Ochberg, 1970; Block, 1977). A stabbing or even a beating may represent behavior similar to that displayed in homicide with a Saturday night special. In law, the distinctions between murder and aggravated assault are crucial; in psychology, they are less so.

Block (1977) contends that death is a highly plausible outcome of any violent crime, including robbery and rape. Criminal homicide, then, is violent behavior carried too far. In general agreement with Block, we will designate criminal homicide and aggravated assault as one form of violent behavior, although the statistics section will separate them briefly. In later chapters, we will discuss other forms of violent behavior, including rape, armed robbery, and arson.

SOCIOLOGICAL CORRELATES OF HOMICIDE

RACE/ETHNIC ORIGIN

One the most consistent findings reported in the sociological criminology literature is that African Americans in the United States are involved in criminal homicide at a rate that far exceeds their numbers in the general population. Wolfgang (1958,

1961) studied 588 homicides reported in Philadelphia from 1948 to 1952 and found that about 73 percent of the offenders and 75 percent of the victims were African American. Furthermore, in 94 percent of all the reported cases, African Americans killed African Americans or whites killed whites, indicating that most homicide is intraracial. More recent data from 1996 continue to show this trend: 93 percent of the African-American victims were slain by African-American offenders, whereas 85 percent of the white murder victims were killed by white assailants (FBI, 1997).

Numerous studies in the past three decades have consistently reported the preponderance of African-American offenders and the intraracial nature of homicide (Pokorny, 1965; Voss & Hepburn, 1968; Munford, Kazer, Feldman, & Stivers, 1976; Zimring, Mukhergee, & Van Winkle, 1983; Humphrey & Palmer, 1987; Hewitt, 1988). Most of the studies have focused on various geographical areas, especially urban areas. In a nationwide study, Riedel, Zahn, and Mock (1985) report that African Americans are still more likely to be offenders in at least 50 percent of all homicides, and that generally homicides tend to be intraracial.

In a ten-year study of criminal violence in Chicago between 1965 and 1974, Richard Block (1977) found that the incidence of homicide more than doubled, but the proportion of involvement by race changed very little. In 1965, 78 percent of all offenders and 72 percent of all homicide victims were African American; in 1974, the figures were 78 percent and 70 percent, respectively. In 1965, 90 percent of the homicide victims and offenders were members of the same race; this compared to an 88 percent intraracial incidence rate reported in 1974.

African Americans constitute about 12 percent of the U.S. population, but they account for over 50 percent of all arrests for violent crimes. About 52 percent of those arrested for murder and about 39 percent arrested for aggravated assault are African American (FBI, 1997). In general, African Americans comprise on the average about 40 percent of the prisoners in local jails and nearly 50 percent of prisoners in state and federal facilities. Hispanics constitute about 6 percent of the U.S. population and account for about 12 percent of the arrests for violent crimes. However, only about 1 percent of those arrested for homicide are Hispanic. In addition, Hispanics make up only about 7 percent of the state and federal prison population.

Today, homicide is the leading cause of death for both male and female African Americans, aged fifteen to thirty-four (Hammond & Yung, 1993; Humphrey & Palmer, 1987). African Americans from inner cities and low socioeconomic status are the most at risk. Nationwide, African-American males have a 1 in 30 chance of becoming a homicide victim during their lifetime. White males, on the

Table 8-1   Leading Cause of Death, Age 15–24

White Males	African-American Males
1. Accidents	1. Homicide
2. Suicide	2. Accidents
3. Homicide	3. Suicide

other hand, have a 1 in 179 chance (see Table 8-1). African-American females have a 1 in 132 chance of becoming a homicide victim, while white females have a 1 in 495 chance.

Obviously, these figures may reflect a variety of societal inequalities, including lack of opportunities, racial oppression in its many forms, and possible discriminatory treatment by the criminal justice system. For example, a similar pattern exists for Native Canadians and Native Americans. While Canadian Indians constitute only 3 to 3.5 percent of the total population of Canada, they represent 9 percent of the penitentiary population in the country (Hartnagel, 1987). In the prairies and northern sections where the populations of Native Canadians are higher, they make up over 40 percent of the jail and penitentiary population. The American Indian (persons of Indian, Eskimo, or Aleut descent) has a homicide rate that is more than double that of whites, but not quite as high as African Americans (Bachman, 1992). The sociological literature abounds with explanations for the racial disparity in crime rates. Interestingly, Ronet Bachman (1992), in her research, found that the American Indian has one of the highest suicide rates of all Americans, while African Americans have the lowest. Bachman suggests that American Indians live in a subculture that "tolerates" both external (homicide) and internal (suicide) forms of violence.

GENDER DIFFERENCES

The relationship between homicide and gender is also very robust, although not quite as strong as that between homicide and race. Wolfgang reported that 82 percent of the murderers and 76 percent of the victims in his Philadelphia sample were male. Specifically, the homicide offender rate per 100,000 was 41.7 for African-American males, 9.3 for African-American females, 3.4 for white males, and only 0.4 for white females. Notice how the race factor emerges strongly in combination with the gender factor. That is, the group displaying by far the highest incidence of homicide is the African-American males.

UCR data consistently reveal that the annual arrest rates for murder run about 90 percent male, 10 percent female (FBI, 1997). Studies in Houston (Pokorny, 1965), Chicago (Voss & Hepburn, 1968; Block, 1977), Atlanta (Munford et al., 1976), North Carolina (Humphrey & Palmer, 1987), Muncie, Indiana (Hewitt, 1988), England (Gibson & Klein, 1961), Israel (Landau, Drapkin, & Arad, 1974), nine different U.S. cites (Zahn & Rickle, 1986), and across the United States in general (FBI, 1997) have also confirmed the very high ratio of males to females when homicide is at issue. Furthermore, there are substantial situational and victim differences between murders committed by males and by females, a topic that will reappear in Chapter 9.

Interesting cultural differences also emerge when we examine victim statistics. The English study, for example, found that 60 percent of the victims were females; U.S. studies hover around a 25 percent figure for female victims. In the Israeli study, 51 percent of the victims of Jewish homicide offenders were female, compared to only 34 percent of the victims of non-Jewish offenders. These data illustrate the importance of considering possible cultural determinants and the nature of interpersonal relationships when homicide rates are examined.

AGE

With monotonous regularity, national statistics from all sources continue to underscore the fact that about half of all those arrested for violent crime are between the ages of twenty and twenty-nine. The young are also the victims. For example, homicide deaths among youths (age fifteen to twenty-four) have increased 300 percent during the past three decades to become the number two cause of death (after accidents) for this age group (Lore & Schultz, 1993).

In the United States, the median age of homicide offenders is twenty-nine (Riedel, Zahn, & Mock, 1985). By far the highest rate of offending occurs among young, African-American males, aged eighteen to twenty-two (FBI, 1997). There is some evidence of a small increase in violent crime committed by the elderly, a phenomenon just beginning to attract research attention (Newman, Newman, & Gewirtz, 1984). According to the UCR, arrests for the elderly for serious crimes more than doubled between 1977 and 1996. Still, in 1996, persons aged sixty-five and older accounted for less than 1 percent of all arrests and .007 percent of all arrests for violent crimes (FBI, 1997).

As we learned in Chapter 2, most offending histories tend to be short, usually dropping off dramatically somewhere between late adolescence and early adulthood. However, some have long, protracted careers, involving a series of petty and serious crimes well past young adulthood, although even a majority of these "career criminals" seem to burn out soon after age forty.

SOCIOECONOMIC CLASS

Criminologists have long assumed that crime, including violent crime, is found primarily among the lower socioeconomic class. Recent research (e.g., Williams, 1984; Smith & Bennett, 1985; Bailey, 1984; Blau & Blau, 1982; Hawkins, 1985) continues to support the observation that violence appears to be associated with the lower class or with economic and social discrimination.

Research and commentary by Tittle (Tittle & Villemez, 1977; Tittle, 1983) challenges both the theory and empirical research based on class distinctions in criminal activity, however. Tittle argues that criminologists have established their theories and conducted their research on the basis of unfounded assumptions about the lower class. After reviewing thirty-five self-report studies, Tittle and Villemez (1977) asserted that the supposed link between social class and crime was a myth.

Other criminologists believe that a rejection of the relationship is premature. Brathwaite (1981) reviewed over a hundred studies and disagreed with Tittle's conclusions, finding considerable support for the view that individuals in the lower class commit more crime than those in other classes. Elliott, Ageton, and Huizinga (1980), after analyzing data from their self-report youth survey, emphasized the importance of distinguishing between serious crime against persons and property and nonserious offenses. They noted that lower-class youth are proportionately more involved in serious crimes than other youth.

Thornberry and Farnworth (1982) propose a reorientation toward social status rather than social class. A person's own social status, they argue, is more relevant to criminal activity than the social class of his or her family. Using data from a birth cohort study, they found few class differences in the delinquent activity of youth. However, the same individuals as adults were significantly more likely to be involved in criminal activity if they had low social status.

For the moment, there is little doubt of a relationship between socioeconomic position in society and adult violent behavior (excluding white collar or occupational crime), but what this relationship means remains unclear. In Chapter 2, we also learned that the relationship between crime and poverty is complex, involving a myriad of factors.

VICTIM–OFFENDER RELATIONSHIP

Until about a decade ago, research consistently indicated that in at least two-thirds of all homicides the offender and the victim knew one another well (Wolfgang, 1958; Bullock, 1955; Svalastoga, 1956; Driver, 1961; Hepburn & Voss, 1970; Wong & Singer, 1973). In the Wolfgang data, the victim and offender were strangers in only about 14 percent of the cases. In a Chicago investigation, Hepburn and Voss (1970) reported a slightly higher victim-offender unfamiliarity figure, 19 percent.

Recent UCR data (FBI, 1997) show that over half the murder victims in 1996 were either related to the offender (12 percent) or acquainted with the offender (35 percent). Among all female murder victims in 1996, about 30 percent were slain by husbands or boyfriends, while only 4 percent of the male victims were killed by wives or girlfriends.

Men are victimized by violent strangers at an annual rate more than double that of women (FBI, 1997). The chance of becoming the victim of a violent crime perpetrated by a stranger increases with age for women, but remains about the same across all ages for men (U.S. Department of Justice, 1989b).

While the homicide offender and his or her victims frequently have similar demographic characteristics, this observation holds primarily for family and acquaintance homicide. When it comes to stranger homicide, there is a clear tendency for the offender to be younger and of a different race than the victim (Riedel, Zahn, & Mock, 1985).

WEAPONS

Guns and knives are the two preferred instruments for inflicting death, but this preference is somewhat influenced by gender, race, geography, and other parameters. For example, in Philadelphia during the early 1950s, stabbing was the most common lethal method (Wolfgang, 1958), whereas in Chicago during the 1960s and early 1970s, shooting was preferred (Hepburn & Voss, 1970; Block, 1977). Later, firearm-related homicides in Chicago increased almost threefold (Block, 1977). However, death inflicted by other weapons increased only slightly.

Nationwide data now indicate that firearms are used in over two-thirds of all homicides, while knives are used in less than 14 percent (FBI, 1997). Specifically, of the 15,848 murders reported in 1996 in the United States, 10,744 (68 percent) were caused by firearms (see Table 8-2). Half of these firearm homicides are committed with handguns. Furthermore, about three-quarters of the law enforcement officers killed each year in the line of duty are killed by persons wielding handguns.

In 1994, 44 million Americans owned 192 million firearms, 65 million of which were handguns (Cook & Ludwig, 1997). Although there are enough firearms to provide every American adult with one, only 25 percent of the adults actually own guns. Seventy-four percent of gun owners possess two or more. Gun ownership is highest among middle-aged, college-educated people of rural small-town America (Cook & Ludwig, 1997). About 14 million adults (approximately one-third of gun owners) carry firearms for protection. Two-thirds who carried guns kept them in their vehicles, while the others sometimes carry them on their person.

About every fourteen minutes someone in America dies from a gunshot wound. About half of those deaths are suicides, about 44 percent are homicides, and 4 percent are unintentional shootings (Washington Post, October 12, 1993). Moreover, a study in the *New England Journal of Medicine* (Washington Post, October 12, 1993) contradicts the common view that having a gun protects people from violence. The study discovered that households with guns are three times more likely to result in the death of a household member than gunless households.

Table 8-2   Murder Victims, Types of Weapons Used, 1992–1996

Weapons	1992	1993	1994	1995	1996
Total	22,716	23,180	22,084	20,232	15,848
Total Firearms	15,489	16,136	15,463	13,790	10,744
Handguns	12,580	13,212	12,775	11,282	8,594
Rifles	706	757	724	654	546
Shotguns	1,111	1,057	953	929	673
Other guns	42	37	19	29	20
Firearms, not stated	1,050	1,073	992	896	911
Knives or cutting instruments	3,296	2,967	2,802	2,557	2,142
Blunt objects (clubs, hammers, etc.)	1,040	1,022	912	918	733
Personal weapons (hands, fists, feet, etc.)[1]	1,131	1,151	1,165	1,201	939
Poison	13	9	10	14	8
Explosives	19	23	10	192	14
Fire	203	217	196	166	151
Narcotics	24	22	22	22	32
Drowning	29	23	25	30	24
Strangulation	314	331	287	237	243
Asphyxiation	115	111	113	137	92
Other weapons or weapons not stated	1,043	1,168	1,079	968	726

[1]Pushed is included in personal weapons.

Source: U.S. Department of Justice, *Uniform Crime Reports, 1997.*

OTHER FACTORS

Several other factors associated with violent crime are reported consistently in the research:

Temporal Factors Homicides tend to increase during the summer months, although some recent research (e.g., Cheatwood, 1988) suggests that the month of December has the highest incidence of homicide in the United States. Weekends, especially the hours between 8 P.M. Saturday and 2 A.M. Sunday, are clearly when homicides most often occur (Wolfgang, 1958; Hepburn & Voss, 1970; Block, 1977).

Prior Arrests According to the Wolfgang data, two-thirds of all homicide offenders had previous arrest records. More important, when offenders had prior records, they were likely to involve offenses against persons rather than against property, and they were usually violent offenses. Recall that the past track record of the offender is perhaps the single most useful factor for predicting future offenses. The Wolfgang study suggested that many homicidal offenders had patterns of engaging in violent behavior to resolve conflicts.

Victim Precipitation Wolfgang also found that about 26 percent of the cases were victim-precipitated: The victim contributed in some significant way to his or her own demise. Hepburn and Voss (1970) found that about 38 percent of Chicago homicides seemed provoked by the victim. Studies do suggest that offender motives for killing are often based on minor altercations and domestic quarrels in which both parties were actively aggressive. Recall the phenomenon of escalation presented in the previous chapter, where we noted that some people tend to retaliate in kind to insults or blows. Moreover, verbal quarrels very often escalate to physical altercations. Separated from the context in which they took place, the precipitating factors of violent behavior are often pitifully trivial. Victim precipitation figures may change as more homicides are committed with strangers as victims, however.

Alcohol This continually emerges as a factor associated with homicide. Wolfgang reported that in nearly two-thirds of the cases, either the victim, the offender, or both had been drinking immediately prior to the slaying. The noteworthy relationship between alcohol and violence will be discussed in detail in Chapter 12.

SOCIOLOGICAL CORRELATES OF ASSAULT

Assault has not drawn nearly the amount of research, publication, or popular interest that homicide has. And yet, aggravated assault is the most common type of violent crime, accounting for nearly 60 percent of all violent crimes reported to police (FBI, 1997; see Figures 8-1 and 8-3). On the average, approximately one million incidents of aggravated assault and over 600,000 of simple assault are reported

Figure 8-3   Aggravated Assaults in the United States
(Source: U.S. Bureau of Justice Statistics, 1996.)

annually. In 1996, there were 388 reported victims of aggravated assault for every 100,000 people in the United States, the lowest rate in 8 years (FBI, 1997). About 7 out of every 1,000 are victims of simple assault. Moreover, there are about 240,000 nonfatal gunshot injuries annually, and about 4 to 6 nonfatal injuries occur for every fatal shooting (Washington Post, 1993).

African Americans make up about 40 percent of those arrested for assault, aggravated or simple. Like homicides, assaults are overwhelmingly intraracial (Dunn, 1976; Block, 1977; FBI, 1997).

The victim and offender know one another or are relatives in at least 50 percent of the reported assault cases (U.S. Department of Justice, 1988, 1989b, 1993; FBI, 1997). As might be expected, the lethal firearm is significantly less often employed in assault than in homicide. In his Chicago study, Block (1977) found that the weapons most commonly used in assault incidents were hands, fists, or feet. Dunn (1976) found similar results in a project undertaken in New York's Westchester County. In 1996, 34 percent of the aggravated assaults were committed with blunt objects or dangerous weapons (FBI, 1997). Personal weapons (e.g., hands, fist, or feet) were used in 26 percent of the assaults, firearms in 22 percent, and knives or cutting instruments in 18 percent of the incidents.

About half of those arrested for assault are young. A vast majority are below the age of twenty-five. In addition, males outnumber females seven to one in total arrests for assault.

The remainder of the chapter will focus on family violence and its many variants. And in Chapter 10, we shall concentrate on specific types of criminal homicide and the psychological explanations for violence in general.

FAMILY VIOLENCE

About one of every five murders and nonnegligent manslaughters in the United States involves a family member killing another family member, with a majority (about 50 percent) involving spouse killing spouse. Similar statistics have also been reported in Canada (Silverman & Mukherjee, 1987). Homicide within the family accounts for 45 percent of all murders in England and Wales (Home Office, 1986; d'Orban & O'Connor, 1989). A neglected area of research in family violence is homicide followed by suicide, where a family members kills other family members and then kills himself or herself. One reason for the neglect is that homicide-suicides are relatively rare, accounting for less than 2 percent of all homicides. Research has consistently shown, however, that a high proportion of homicide-suicides (usually well over 50 percent) involves spouses, especially ex-spouses (Stack, 1997).

Research on the incidence of family violence among African Americans has been largely inadequate (Plass, 1993). Based on what is known, however, violence within the African-American family is similar to that found for white families, except at higher rates. "As is the case for all types of homicide, African Americans are victimized by lethal violence at the hands of family members at rates that are many times higher than those for other racial groups in the United States" (Mercy & Salzman, 1989). Approximately 7 percent of all arrests made for simple or aggravated assaults involved family members (U.S. Department of Justice, 1989a). However, self-report victimization studies suggest that at least 20 percent of simple or aggravated assaults involve family members (U.S. Department of Justice, 1989b). Although these official statistics are woefully incomplete, they still underscore the considerable magnitude of family violence.

Some variant of family violence has probably existed since the primordial beginnings of family life. However, with the notable exception of intrafamilial homicide, family violence has not been traditionally regarded as serious crime or worthy of criminal prosecution in this country. State governments and the courts have long claimed that family relationships require or deserve special immunity, including the views that parents have a right to discipline children physically; that a husband possesses the divine right to have sexual access to his wife; or that nagging women or disobedient children often provoke and deserve the beatings they receive (Pleck, 1989). This view has been energetically challenged in recent years by various interest groups attempting not only to acquaint the public about the problem but to activate lawmakers and the criminal justice system toward more stringent legal and social sanctions.

The modern era of family violence interest and research began in 1962 when a Denver pediatrician (C. Henry Kempe) and four of his medical colleagues published a paper in the *Journal of the American Medical Association* entitled "The Battered Child Syndrome" (Kempe, Silverman, Steele, Droegemueller, & Silver, 1962). The paper documented evidence of repeated multiple bone fractures of children suspected of being abused, and the article *gradually* became instrumental in the "rediscovery" of serious child abuse. The article was certainly not the sole precipitating factor in prompting the reexamination of child abuse. During the 1960s, a very large and influential child welfare movement, bent on drawing public and professional attention to the plight of abused and neglected children, was also taking hold.

In the early 1970s, the women's movement was highly influential in the rediscovery of wife beating, and shortly thereafter drew attention to marital rape. What began as a women's right issue soon picked up support as a law-and-order issue (Pleck, 1989). The women's movement spawned legislation to increase or establish penalties for wife beating, to strengthen civil remedies, and to make it easier for women victims to file criminal charges against their assailants (Pleck, 1989). During the 1980s, several other types of family violence, from sibling violence to filial abuse of the elderly, have been acknowledged and empirically investigated. Thus, family violence includes spouse abuse, child abuse, sibling violence, abuse of the elderly, and child-to-parent violence. Currently, child abuse research is the most advanced, sophisticated, and extensive in the field of family violence (Finkelhor & Lewis, 1988). The problem of child abuse has also been the most widely publicized. Nationwide polls in 1976 revealed that only 10 percent of the general population considered child abuse a serious problem. In 1983, however, over 90 percent of the population considered it a serious problem (Wolfe, 1985).

However, despite the current interest and public concern about family violence, we still know very little about it. Systematic study of family violence is new and often poorly designed. Even definitions, terms, and concepts in the field are excessively broad, ambiguous, and applied inconsistently, jeopardizing the comparability, generalizability, and reliability of the research findings (Weis, 1989). For example, it is unclear what behaviors should be included under the rubric family violence. Should verbal threats, shouting, slapping, aggressive gestures, intimidation, or spanking be included as examples of violence? Or only the more serious, physical forms of violence such as punching, stabbing, striking, shooting, and burning? Surveys conducted during the 1960s and 1970s, for example, indicated that between 84 to 97 percent of all parents used physical punishment at some time to discipline their children (Gelles, 1982). Surely we cannot conclude that 90 percent of the American parents were abusive during that era. Rather, this high incidence of corporal punishment was due to the widespread and firmly held tradition that a spanking now and then did the child some good. Although that tradition is currently shifting toward less or no corporal punishment, there still remains considerable controversy as to whether parental spankings and slaps constitute abuse.

It is also unclear how the term violence differs from abuse, maltreatment, neglect, and emotional and social deprivation. As noted by Gelles (1982), the **battered child syndrome** quickly gave way to the terms child abuse, child abuse and neglect, and child maltreatment. Child abuse, once restricted to physical violence by Kempe and his associates, has become increasingly broad, encompassing an extensive range of behaviors and misbehaviors by parents and caretakers. Furthermore, it also remains unclear what relatives or intimates should be included in family violence. Should lovers, intimate friends, common-law spouses, distant relatives, ex-spouses, or separated spouses also be included? Therefore, a troubling aspect of family violence research is that terms are defined differently and often unclearly, and an assortment of family members are included in the sample, making reliable comparisons between studies difficult and valid conclusions nearly impossible to come by. In addition, each study collects data from a variety of sources and often uses substantially different procedures and methodology to tabulate and analyze the data.

For our purposes, research on family violence will be divided into four major questions: (1) How much family violence is there; (2) what are the common characteristics (or correlates) of the offenders and victims; (3) is family violence fundamentally different from other kinds of violence (such as street violence); and (4) what are the causes of family violence? We will explore the research in these four areas, keeping in mind the critical problems in definition, sampling, and methodology just described. It should be pointed out that intrafamilial sexual abuse, although mentioned in the following sections, will be discussed in greater detail in Chapter 9.

INCIDENCE AND PREVALENCE

Estimates on the prevalence and incidence of family violence differ widely. The term **incidence** in this section will refer to the total number of cases (frequency) per year. **Prevalence** will refer to the proportion or ratio of the population involved, such as the number of children experiencing abuse per 1,000 children in the general population.

In 1967, Gil (1970) found only 6,000 confirmed annual cases of child abuse in the United States. However, Light (1973) reanalyzed Gil's data and concluded that between 200,000 and 500,000 children are physically abused in the United States every year. Light further estimated that between 465,000 and 1,175,000 children are severely neglected or sexually abused annually. Nagi (1975), based on nearly 2,000 interviews with all relevant public and private agencies throughout the state of Florida, surmised that about 167,000 cases of physical child abuse are reported each year nationwide. He further speculated that another 91,000 cases remain unreported. The National Incidence Study (NIS), sponsored by the National Center on Child Abuse and Neglect, estimated that 625,000 American children were neglected or abused during 1980 (U.S. Department of Health and Human Services, 1982). Approximately 208,000 of this total were physically assaulted children, and serious injury occurred in another 137,000 cases. An estimated 1,200 to 1,500 children are killed each year by a parent or parent figure (Emery & Laumann-Billings, 1998). Eighty-five percent of these children are under the age of five years (Lung & Daro, 1996).

In 1986, a second National Incidence Study (NIS-2) was conducted. As in 1980, information was gathered from state or local child protective service agencies as well as from the public schools, children's hospitals, police and sheriff's departments, mental health agencies, probation departments, and county health departments. However, the definitions for abuse and neglect were broader and more inclusive in the NIS-2, as we will see. The NIS-2 found that between 1980 and 1986 the number of child abuse and neglect cases increased dramatically, even when the original NIS-1 definitions were used. In 1986, 1,025,900 children were abused or neglected, an increase of over 400,800. When the revised definitions were applied, the number of those maltreated swelled to 1,584,700 children. Of this total, 675,000 were found to be abused children, including 358,300 physically abused children, 155,900 sexually abused children, and 211,100 emotionally abused children. Emotional abuse is comprised of three kinds of maltreatment: (1) close confinement; (2) verbal or emotional assault; or (3) other. Close confinement refers to incidents where the child was tied or bound, or confined in a closet or very small enclosure for long periods of time. Verbal or emotional assault refers to cases where the child was *habitually* belittled, denigrated, scapegoated, or threatened with sexual or physical abuse. "Other" refers to cases where the basic necessities of food, water, shelter, or sleep were withheld for extended periods, or where an attempted physical or sexual assault took place.

The NIS-2 also delineated physical abuse cases according to the severity of the injury. Approximately 1,100 cases of physical injury resulted in the death of the child, although more recent data suggest that as many as 5,000 children die annually as a result of maltreatment (Reiss & Roth, 1993). Another 160,000 cases (2.5/1,000 children) were classified as serious because the injuries were evaluated as life-threatening, such as loss of consciousness, breathing cessation, broken bones, third-degree burns, or extensive second-degree burns over the child's body. Another 952,600 children (15.1/1,000 children) received moderate injury from physical abuse. Moderate referred to injury or pain which persisted for at least forty-eight hours, including bruises, burns, depression, and observable emotional distress. Female children were subjected to more abuse of all three kinds (physical, sexual, and emotional) than male children. In addition, female preschool children are more frequently homicide victims of their mothers than are male preschool children (Mann, 1993).

The NIS-2 admonishes, however, that the dramatic increase in the incidence and prevalence of child abuse and neglect between 1980 and 1986 may be more a reflection of better recording procedures and more awareness of child maltreatment by public and private social agencies (and the general public) than any explosion of maltreatment. "The NIS-2 study indicates that the increase of incidence of child abuse and neglect between 1980 and 1986 is probably due more to an increase in the recognition of child maltreatment by community professionals than it is due to an increase in the actual occurrence of maltreatment" (U.S. Department of Health and Human Services, 1988, p. xv).

A third National Incidence Study (NIS-3) conducted during 1993 and 1994 showed a sharp increase in the number of serious cases of child abuse and neglect. NIS-3 data reveal an estimated 1,553,800 children in the United States were abused or neglected, reflecting a 67-percent increase since the NIS-2 estimate and a 149-percent increase since the NIS-1 estimate (Sedlak & Broadhurst, 1996). The substantial increase reported by the NIS-3 probably stems from improved recognition of more subtle cues of abuse—"those that indicate abusive and neglect behaviors that have not yet resulted in harm or injury" (Sedlak & Broadhurst, 1996, p. 10).

The American Humane Association, or AHA (1987), collects data on the abuse and neglect of children from child protective service agencies in all fifty states, the District of Columbia, Puerto Rico, the U.S. Virgin Islands, Guam, and the

Marianas. The Association defines abuse as a report of intentional, nonaccidental injury, harm, or sexual assault inflicted on a child. Neglect is defined as any care-taker not providing essential care to a child, such as food, clothing, shelter, medical attention, education, or supervision. In 1986, a total of 2,086,112 children were abused or neglected in the United States and its territories, a statistic substantially higher than the one reported by NIS-2 for the same year. Three percent of these children receive serious or major physical injury, and another 18 percent receive "minor" physical injury annually. Thus, according to the AHA data, the preva-lence of child abuse and neglect is approximately 32 out of every 1,000 American children compared to the NIS-2 rate of 24 per 1,000.

The discrepancy between the NIS-2 and the AHA figures is probably due to a number of things. As noted earlier, each agency defines things differently, collects data from different sources, and varies significantly in procedures and methodol-ogy. The AHA data, for instance, include cases that have been substantiated on fur-ther investigation as well as cases that were determined to be unfounded. NIS-2 data were based on more substantiated or documented cases.

Some of the best designed research has come out of the Family Research Laboratory at the University of New Hampshire. In a 1975 survey, based on inter-views with 2,143 married (or cohabiting) couples, Straus, Gelles, and Steinmetz (1980) concluded that 36 out of every 1,000 American children (ages three through seventeen) experienced a "serious assault" during the year. Nationwide, this amounts to about 1.7 million seriously abused children annually. Moreover, the New Hampshire group discovered that most children (94 percent of those abused) were not assaulted just once but repeatedly over the course of a year, with an aver-age of over ten serious assaults per year. In 1985 the New Hampshire group (Straus & Gelles, 1986) conducted a similar study, although rather than relying on face-to-face interviews as in the earlier study, they interviewed 6,002 couples via telephone. Surprisingly, they discovered that the incidence of child abuse, although still distressingly high, had actually decreased 47 percent between 1975 and 1985. They attributed this decrease to enhanced public awareness, increased social and legal sanctions, better resources, and more extensive and knowledgeable social services during the ten-year period.

PREVALENCE AND INCIDENCE OF SPOUSE ABUSE

Studies estimating the prevalence and incidence of spousal violence also differ dra-matically in their figures. Steinmetz (1977) estimated that out of a population of 47 million couples, 3.3 million wives and over a quarter of a million husbands are subjected to severe beatings by their spouses. In a national survey conducted in 1975 by the New Hampshire group (Straus, Gelles, & Steinmetz, 1980), 28 percent of the married persons interviewed said they had experienced marital violence at some point in the marriage. In 1996, 30 percent of female murder victims were slain by their husbands, ex-husbands, or boyfriends, compared to 3 percent of the male murder victims who were killed by their wives, ex-wives, or girlfriends (FBI, 1997). Sixteen percent reported some kind of *physical violence* between spouses dur-ing the year of the survey. Interestingly, in the 1975 national survey and in a later one (1985) (Straus & Gelles, 1986), no significant differences were found between men and women in overall self-reported rates of aggressing against their spouses. In fact, in more recent surveys, women were reported as engaging in all forms of aggression against their spouses at rates equal to or greater than those for men (O'Leary, 1988; O'Leary, Barling, Arias, Rosenbaum, Malone, & Tyree, 1989). Furthermore, some of this aggression apparently is not reciprocated by husbands but is initiated and continued by the wife alone. However, a strong caveat must be inserted here. Adult women respondents tend to overreport—both perpetration and victimization—in surveys of this type, while men generally underreport (Weis, 1989). Furthermore, severely battered women, especially those who have been victimized over a long period, tend to *underestimate* both the frequency and severity of the abuse they experience (Frieze & Browne, 1989). Therefore, conclusions about the extent of partner abuse must remain very tentative. The most common forms of aggression for both men and women appear to be pushing, grabbing, or shoving. However, the impact of men's physical aggression on women is usually more deleterious than women's physical aggression toward men (O'Leary, 1988).

The 1985 New Hampshire survey also suggests that wife physical abuse decreased by 27 percent between 1975 and 1985. Thus, contrary to reports of an epidemic of wife beating during the 1970s and 1980s, the UNH data refute this claim. The available evidence also suggests that much spousal abuse does not begin during the marriage. Some research indicates, for example, that over one-third of women about to be married have been victims of physical violence from their fiances (O'Leary & Curley, 1986).

PREVALENCE AND INCIDENCE OF ELDERLY ABUSE

Estimates of the proportion of elderly persons (persons sixty-five or older) who are abused range from 4 to 10 percent, but it is difficult to make confident estimates because of a lack of reliable statistics (Pagelow, 1989; Pillemer & Suitor, 1988). Best incidence estimates suggest that between 500,000 and 2.5 million elderly persons are abused by their caretakers each year (Pagelow, 1989). Pillemer and Finkelhor (1988) focused on the Boston metropolitan area and found that 3 percent of the elderly suffered from one of three kinds of abuse: physical abuse, chronic verbal abuse, or neglect. The researchers extrapolated that about 1 million elderly persons are similarly abused throughout the United States.

SIBLING AND CHILD-TO-PARENT ABUSE

Violence between siblings is believed to be the most common form of intrafamilial violence, but surprisingly little is known about it (Gelles, 1982; Ohlin & Tonry, 1989). While professionals may recognize intrafamilial violence of parent-to-child, spouse-to-spouse, they still may find it difficult to recognize sibling violence and abuse. Steinmetz (1981) reported that two-thirds of the adolescent siblings in the family sample she studied used physical violence to resolve conflict. Families having only sons consistently experience more sibling violence than do families that have only daughters (Straus, Gelles, & Steinmetz, 1980). It is estimated that three children in a thousand annually used a gun or knife on a sibling in the United

States (Gelles, 1982). The victims of the more extreme forms of sibling violence tend to be younger siblings. For example, Fehrenbach and colleagues (Fehrenbach, Smith, Monastersky, & Deisher, 1986) reported that over 40 percent of the victims of adolescent rape were younger siblings, usually less than twelve years of age.

Child-to-parent abuse has also become an important topic. Three teenagers (ages fifteen to seventeen) in a hundred (3.5 percent) were reported as kicking, biting, punching, hitting with an object, beating up, threatening, or using a gun or knife against a parent (Gelles, 1982). The killing of parents (parricide) is usually committed by sons (Lubenow, 1983; Pagelow, 1989), but is the rarest form of intrafamily homicide. Mothers are killed (matricide) far more often than fathers (patricide) by both adolescents and adult sons and daughters. Female parricide is exceptionally rare in all countries of the world (d'Orban & O'Connor, 1989). When daughters are involved in parricide, they often secure the help of a male friend or sibling to commit the violence. In Britain, boys most often kill a parent (or parents) with explosive violence in response to prolonged provocation and parental brutality and abuse (d'Orban & O'Connor, 1989).

MULTIASSAULTIVE FAMILIES

According to recent statistics, at least 7 percent of all intact families are multiassaultive (Hotaling & Straus, 1989). That is, some families are characterized by continual cycles of intrafamily physical aggression and violence. Siblings hit each other, spouses hit each other, parents hit the children, and the older children hit the parents. Findings support the notion that assault is a generalized pattern in interpersonal relations that crosses settings and is used across targets (Hotaling & Straus, 1989). Men in families in which children and wives are assaulted are five times more likely to have also assaulted a nonfamily person than are men in nonassaultive families. A similar pattern holds for women from multiassaultive families, although the relationship is not as strong. Sibling violence is particularly high in families in which child assault and spouse assault are present, with boys displaying significantly more assaultive behavior (Hotaling & Straus, 1989). Moreover, children from multiassaultive families have an inordinately high rate of assault against nonfamily members (Hotaling & Straus, 1989). These children are also more likely to be involved in property crime, to have adjustment difficulties in school, and to be involved with police (Hotaling & Straus, 1989). Since a vast majority of the studies have been correlational in design, it is not possible to determine causal directions. It is simply extremely difficult to tell what is causing what in this complicated web of interrelated variables. However, it is quite clear that multiassaultive family members are violent and antisocial across a variety of settings, including toward both family members and society in general, and may demonstrate this behavioral pattern throughout most of their lifetimes.

ETIOLOGY

For some time, the scholarly and popular literature have concluded that both abusive parents and abusive spouses have themselves been the victims of family violence during their childhoods (Megargee, 1982). Some research suggests that highly violent offenders may have been subjected to more severe and frequent physical and psychological abuse during their childhoods than other offenders (Hämäläinen & Haapasalo, 1996). Individuals grow up to be abusive because they were abused themselves, a belief referred to as the cycle-of-violence hypothesis. However, the consequences of physical assault of children are neither so simple nor so absolute as many public pronouncements would have us believe (Garbarino, 1989). Publications supporting the cycle-of-violence hypothesis rarely present empirical data to support their claims (Gelles, 1982; Pagelow, 1989). When data are presented, they are based on small case studies and correlations are marginal or, at best, modest. Much of the literature, however, suffers from the "woozle effect." The **woozle effect**, a term first used in a Winnie-the-Pooh story, and later adopted by Houghton (1979), refers to the tendency of one study to cite another study's data or conclusions, but without mentioning the methodological limitations and problems inherent in the first study (Gelles, 1982). For example, one study might conduct a self-report survey of a nonrepresentative sample of battering husbands (who were forced by the courts to attend a battering husband workshop in Apples, Wisconsin). Many of these battering men, perhaps mindful of the social sanctions and legal consequences facing them, and hoping to reduce culpability, assert they were victims of severe physical abuse as children. Since no control group was used (nonbattering husbands) and the sample was nonrepresentative (husbands convicted and assigned by the court within a single geographic and cultural area of the country), the researchers make modest or tentative conclusions, stressing the limited external validity of their findings. The woozle effect occurs when other writers or researchers cite this flawed and highly tentative study, without mentioning its acknowledged limitations, as *conclusive* evidence for the cycle of violence hypothesis.

In short, the cycle of violence and the overall consequences of abuse and neglect are not well documented, and the resilience of human beings rules out any simple cause and effect relationship between maltreatment and future behavior (Garbarino, 1989). In many cases, rather than finding that abusive parenting is the logical consequence of being victimized as children, the opposite sequence is likely to take place. Realizing and sensitive to the enormous psychological and social costs of family violence, many victims of child abuse may be less likely than their nonabused peers to commit aggressive acts as adults within their families. Garbarino (1989, p. 222), for example, writes, "Many victims of child abuse, probably most, survive it and avoid repeating the pattern in their own child rearing."

Another traditional belief is that battered women allow themselves to be battered (Frieze & Browne, 1989). Others have argued that victims of spouse abuse are masochistic, consciously and unconsciously precipitating the violence to which they are subjected (Megargee, 1982). Still others have depicted battered wives as lacking self-esteem, being highly passive and dependent on their husbands, and willing to place greater value on maintaining the marriage above their safety (Megargee, 1982).

Abusive husbands have been depicted as extremely possessive and unreasonably jealous men who treat their wives like property coveted by other men. This depiction led to other assumptions about the inadequacy, incompetence, and low self-esteem of these abusive husbands who saw threat to their masculinity everywhere. Alcohol abuse is also often seen as part of the clinical picture. Similarly, men who abuse their children were seen as incompetent, immature individuals, overwhelmed and frustrated by the responsibilities of parenting. The violence of both the abusive husband and the abusive father was seen as irrational and expressive, precipitated by frustration and extreme anger. Some professionals have suggested that street violence is generally rational and instrumental, whereas family violence is predominately irrational and expressive (see Megargee, 1982; Hotaling & Straus, 1989).

The empirical evidence for these depictions is meager, equivocal, and confusing. Some studies find some support for these correlates, others provide no support. Despite several attempts at psychological typologies for wife and child abusers (Megargee, 1982), there does not seem to be any evidence for "typical" psychological profiles for either wife batterers or child abusers. However, recent research results look promising for a typology that might help in the prevention, intervention, and treatment of abusers. In an extensive review of the research literature, Holtzworth-Munroe and Stuart (1994) identified three primary types of male spouse batterers: Type 1 batterers who abuse family members only; Type 2 batterers who abuse family members because of emotional problems; and Type 3 batterers who are generally violent toward both family members and persons outside the family. Type 1 abusers are the more common, tend to be less aggressive than the other two, and also tend to be more remorseful for their actions. They are generally inadequate, passive men who are dependent on others. Type 2 batterers tend to be depressed, inadequate individuals who are emotionally volatile and who display indicators of personality disorders and psychopathology. The Type 3 batterer is an individual who is antisocial, criminally prone, and violent across situations. They are more likely to abuse alcohol and are generally more belligerent toward almost everyone. They are also most likely to be involved in serious violence toward a spouse.

The search for demographic variables has been equally mixed and inconclusive (Weis, 1989; Hotaling & Straus, 1989). Wife and child abuse appears to cut across socioeconomic, religious, and ethnic lines. Even current research on gender does not reveal clear trends for women or men as assaulters of spouse, child, or parent.

Alcohol and drug abuse seems to play a role as an exacerbater, but not as a cause, of the family violence. Abusive men with severe alcohol or drug problems are apt to abuse their partners both when drunk and when sober. However, abusive husbands who drink heavily are violent more frequently, and inflict more serious injuries on their partners than do abusive men who do not have a history of alcohol or drug problems (Frieze & Browne, 1989). A similar pattern also holds for men who abuse their children. Many use alcohol as an excusing agent that allows them to escape some culpability for their antisocial or violent actions, as well as to avoid the full impact of legal sanctions. Babcock, Waltz, Jacobson, and Gottman (1993), in some very promising research, examined the interactions of marital power, interpersonal strategies, and communication skills as predictors of marital violence. They reasoned that husbands who are unable to effect their intentions through negotiation or general communication skills are more likely to resort to physical aggression—pushing, slapping, beating—to achieve their intentions. This is especially the case if the wives are more verbally competent, more educated, or have better jobs than their husbands. For example, previous research suggests that women with jobs that are higher in status than their husband's jobs experience more life-threatening violence than wives who were occupationally similar to their husbands (Hornung, McCullough, & Sugimoto, 1981). Frustrated with some combination of power discrepancy between him and his wife, the husband's only effective expressive retort may be physical aggression. The study by Babcock et al. (1993, p. 47) showed "… that poor husband communication, as well as discrepancies in education and decision-making power favoring the wife, were … associated with husband-to-wife aggression." Moreover, husbands who battered their wives were more likely to be in relationships where their demands were met with their wives' withdrawal (e.g., defensiveness, passive inaction, "stonewalling," or the "silent treatment"). The researchers interpreted the withdrawal pattern as one of power (the individual has resources the other partner wants); whereas the demanding role represented a weak position (the individual wants something the other partner has). This research emphasizes the importance of studying the reciprocal interaction of a relationship if we are to understand family violence more fully.

Once violence has occurred in a relationship, it tends to be repeated (Frieze & Browne, 1989). Over time, violence, if not adequately sanctioned, may also become more severe and more frequent. Furthermore, being violently victimized by an intimate over an extended period of time may result in emotional reactions and psychological scars decidedly different than those incurred by victims of violent crime by strangers. We need more research on the patterns of abuse over the life course of a family before we can offer conclusions.

The elderly appear to be maltreated in much the same way that children are maltreated—with one notable exception: financial exploitation (Pagelow, 1989). The likeliest candidates for elder abuse appear to be white women between the ages of seventy-five and eighty-five, middle to lower class, Protestant, and suffering from some form of physical or mental impairment (Pagelow, 1989). Only 5 percent of the elderly are placed in institutions or rest homes, although 85 percent of them have at least one chronic illness (Hudson, 1986). Most are living at home. Abusive caretakers tend to lack resources, feel trapped, and may be abusing drugs or alcohol. Two-thirds of abusive caretakers are forty years old or older, and most are sons and daughters of the victims. Spouses constitute the second largest abuser category. Male caretakers are more likely to abuse the elderly physically, while women caretakers are prone to abuse them psychologically or neglect them. However, both men and women are equally likely to exploit them financially. The most common abuse is a combination of psychological abuse and neglect (Pagelow, 1989). Elder abuse victims do not ask for help and may refuse assistance.

IS FAMILY VIOLENCE DIFFERENT FROM GENERAL VIOLENCE?

As noted earlier, some clinicians and writers have suggested that family violence is fundamentally different from general (or street) violence and thus should be examined separately (Megargee, 1982). Physical violence against children and spouses are "special" cases of violence that require family-based theories to explain them. Wife abusers are psychologically distressed, and their violence is irrational. As also mentioned earlier, child abusers are depicted as incompetent and immature, unable to cope with the responsibilities of parenting, and holding unrealistic expectations of children. Similarly, child abusers are extremely emotional and irrational in their assaults. Street offenders, on the other hand, presumably use violence in a deliberate, rational way to gain things, such as material goods, status, or other social reinforcements. General violent offenders utilize violence for a purpose, whereas family violent offenders are lashing out in anger and without discernible purpose.

Empirical evidence for differences between criminal violence in the streets and family violence is weak and equivocal, with most of the studies being unsystematic or seriously flawed methodologically (Hotaling & Straus, 1989). The evidence we have so far, however, strongly suggests that the etiology of violent behavior may be very similar, whether it is used against a family member or a nonfamily member. Violent people tend to be violent generally, both within and outside the family context. They are aggressive and assaultive toward a large variety of targets and across a wide array of settings.

BATTERED WOMAN SYNDROME

The term **battered woman syndrome** was coined and developed by Lenore Walker (1979), a psychologist who specializes in domestic abuse. Walker has identified a cluster of behavioral and emotional features that, she believes, are often shared by women who have been physically and psychologically abused over a period of time by the dominant male figure in their lives. Feelings of low self-esteem, depression, and helplessness are among the important components that frequently accompany the syndrome.

Research on domestic violence finds that a great majority of battered women either remain in lifelong abusive relationships, leave the relationship, or are killed by their abusers. Very rarely do battering relationships get better. A small minority of abused women kill their abusers. Although evidence for the battered woman syndrome is being admitted into the trials of women who do kill their abusers (Schuller & Vidmar, 1992), it is rarely successful in bringing about an acquittal (Browne, 1987; Ewing, 1990).

Currently, there is considerable debate concerning the reliability, validity, and usefulness of the diagnosis "battered woman syndrome" (Bartol & Bartol, 1994). One of the major problems with the concept is the tendency for mental health and law professionals to regard it as a single entity representing some kind of mental or behavioral disorder. However, battered women demonstrate a wide range of behavioral patterns that often reflect survival skills and adaptation to a serious, life-threatening situation.

INFANTICIDE, NEONATICIDE, AND FILICIDE

The United States has the second highest child homicide rate in the world (Northern Ireland is first) (Baron, 1993; Christoffel & Liu, 1983). Child homicide is not randomly distributed, but occurs with greater frequency across the globe in areas characterized by poverty, racial minorities, and urbanization (Baron, 1993). A majority of child homicides are the result of parents killing their own child.

Although the term **infanticide** literally means the killing of an infant, it has become synonymous with the killing of a child by a parent. Several years ago, Resnick (1970) recommended that the killing of one's children be divided into two separate categories, **neonaticide**, which refers to the killing of the newborn within the first twenty-four hours after birth, and **filicide**, which refers to the killing of a child older than twenty-four hours. Infants and small children are more likely to be killed by their mothers than their fathers (Reiss & Roth, 1993). Moreover, newborns, infants, and children ages one to four are more vulnerable to homicide than are children ages five to nine (Reiss & Roth, 1993).

Traditionally, women who kill their children have been viewed by the legal system and the psychiatric profession as suffering from severe emotional problems, rendering them either insane (the legal system) or psychotic (the psychiatric profession). If the woman wasn't "crazy," then the woman was obviously morally flawed, calloused, or non-caringly cold. Ania Wilczynski (1991, 1997) observes that in England and Wales, these women are still viewed as either "mad" or "bad." Mothers, after all, are supposed to act in a loving, warm, selfless and protective fashion—at all costs—toward their children (Wilczynski, 1991). Any deviation from this stereotype promotes a conclusion that the women are either mentally ill and need to be treated with sympathy; or, alternatively, fundamentally wicked or callous, and therefore need to be punished harshly. However, the overwhelming perception of the criminal justice system in England (and perhaps throughout North America) is that women who kill their children are "mad" and "abnormal," whereas men who kill their children are perceived as "bad" and "normal" (Wilczynski, 1997). Interestingly, in 1938 England passed the *Infanticide Act*, based primarily on the assumption that a mother who kills her infant is probably mentally disturbed and psychotic. Today, the courts of England continue to convict on the grounds of "infanticide"—that is, the mother killed her child while mentally ill. Rarely is there conviction of murder or manslaughter.

Wilczynski (1991) studied twenty-two prosecuted cases of maternal infant-killings (where a mother killed her child under the age of twelve months) in England and Wales between 1971 and 1989. In fourteen of the cases, the women were seen as emotionally disturbed. They were seen as "… essentially good women and mothers, for whom something had gone tragically wrong" (Wilczynski, 1991, p. 74).

Following the psychiatric tradition, Resnick (1969, 1970) concluded that two-thirds of the mothers who commit filicide are psychotic, compared to only 17 percent of the women in the neonaticide group. He also found that a vast majority of the filicide group suffered from serious depression, while very few women in the neonaticide group exhibited this feature. Furthermore, suicide attempts accompany one-third of the filicides, but rarely accompany neonaticide.

Coramae Richey Mann (1993) investigated the patterns and characteristics of maternal filicide in six major U.S. cities (Chicago, Houston, Atlanta, Los Angeles, New York, and Baltimore) between 1979 and 1983. Although the data set for the study consisted of 296 cleared homicide cases in which the offender was female, Mann restricted her research sample to twenty-five maternal filicides of preschool children (ages birth to five years). Because of the small sample size, any far-reaching conclusions must be viewed cautiously.

Mann found that 40 percent of the women who killed their preschool children had arrest records. One offender had fifteen misdemeanor arrests, while another had six felony arrests. Twenty-five percent had arrest records for violent crime. Moreover, twelve of the twenty-five filicide offenders had recorded child abuse histories where court or social service intervention took place. Most of the victims were killed in the bathroom (30 percent), or the bedroom (26 percent), usually on Sunday morning. Manual methods were used in 80 percent of the cases—hands or feet (52 percent), suffocation or strangulation (16 percent), or drowning (12 percent). The killing of older children (ages four or five) tended to be more brutal.

Although the most frequent victim was a African-American female infant under the age of two years, Mann admonishes that her sample was too small to advance any firm conclusions about racial patterns. Mann also emphasizes that location is a critical variable when examining the racial/ethnic factor in filicide. Large metropolitan cities, for example, are far more likely to have a minority population than more affluent, suburban areas. While a majority of the offenders were initially charged with murder, only 19 percent were convicted of that charge. Forty percent of the women who killed their preschool children were sent to prison, most often on a conviction of manslaughter, and another 36 percent received a probation sentence. The remaining six cases were either not processed, dismissed, or received special treatment from the court and their dispositions were sealed. A determination of a mental disorder of the offenders was apparently rare.

THEORETICAL EXPLANATIONS OF FAMILY VIOLENCE

The development of theory requires well-designed and executed research. Without theoretical testing through sound research, speculations and free-floating explanations abound without empirical anchoring. This describes what is happening in the field of family violence. Gelles and Straus (1979), for example, were able to identify fifteen different theories attempting to explain family violence. Weis (1989, p. 123) observes that "the field is, with few exceptions, characterized by descriptive work, with little hypothesis testing, causal modeling, or attempts to construct and test integrated theories of the different types of family violence."

The systematic study of family violence, however, is a new undertaking. Thus, it suffers from a constellation of uncoordinated research and a matrix of poorly integrated theory, as all new sciences do. Furthermore, the family is a difficult social situation to study. It is a complex social system consisting of many roles, and it is a private social group where interactions and behaviors are invisible to outsiders. Social interactions are more intense, emotional, and consequential than other interactions (Weis, 1989). In addition, family influences do not flow in one direction; they are apt to be multidirectional, a process called **reciprocal influence** (Bartol & Bartol, 1998). For example, while the parents affect the development of the child, the child also affects the development and psychological growth of the parents, including their marital relationship, relationships with friends, and even the level of job satisfaction. Reciprocal influence implies that the social environment influences the individual, and the individual, in turn, has an impact on the social environment. Therefore, theories that are sensitive to the reciprocal interactionism of family dynamics are the best candidates to advance our knowledge about family violence.

CESSATION OF FAMILY VIOLENCE

Although theories of family violence are underdeveloped, the effectiveness of various procedures or strategies to reduce family violence can still be tested. Unfortunately, there have been very few systematic evaluations of the effectiveness of particular strategies in combating family violence (Elliott, 1989).

One of the more influential investigations examining the effectiveness of police responses to spouse abuse was the Minnesota Domestic Violence Experiment (Sherman & Berk, 1984). The police officers participating in this project handled marital conflict one of three ways: arrest, separating the parties, or advising (or mediating) the parties. Follow-up of the effectiveness of these approaches over a six-month period indicated that arrest was the most effective police response for reducing misdemeanor family assaults. However, the study has serious design problems that undermine both its external validity and internal validity. Moreover, there is some evidence that the impact of an arrest wears off over a relatively short period of time (eight to twelve months), and the assaults return to their original level (Elliott, 1989).

The effectiveness of the legal sanctions of prosecution, conviction, and sentencing in deterring subsequent family violence is also questionable. There are also many unanswered questions about the effectiveness of community services and care for family violence victims (Saunders & Azar, 1989).

Much of the contemporary work and commentary has been directed at reducing wife abuse. Fagan (1989) hypothesizes that a large segment of the rewards and support men receive for abusing their wives derives from a long-standing cultural stereotype that men must be dominant and show women who is boss. One very "masculine" way of achieving and maintaining this expected dominance is through physical aggression and, if necessary, some violence. Some of the reinforcement comes from the satisfaction of maintaining this physical dominance and the positive social status that accompanies domination over wives advocated by one's peer group and subculture. Accordingly, men subscribing to this subculture socialize together, drink together, and participate in male-oriented recreation activities, generally excluding their wives from these activities. This male subculture provides a social milieu that supports and encourages traditional male dominance in male-female relationships, even if it requires violence now and then. Frequent contacts with this exclusive male sub-culture by the husband, combined with increasing social isolation of the wife, are particularly associated with the more severe forms of wife abuse (Bowker, 1983; Fagan, 1989). Presumably, the more deeply immersed into this subculture a man is, the more likely he is to batter his wife.

To what extent some women also support this male-dominating tradition is largely unknown, but knowledge about the degree to which women explicitly or implicitly favor this belief system may be extremely important in a deeper under-standing of the dynamics of the relationship. This is not to imply that a subculture that supports male domination in a marriage necessarily advocates violence in car-rying out this dominance, but research does suggest that many wife batterers man-age to isolate their families socially while receiving considerable encouragement and support for physical aggression from their social network of friends. It is not unusual in rural areas, for example, for abusive husbands to see to it that their wives and children are physically isolated, while they continually go hunting, fish-ing, and drinking with their friends.

An effective way of breaking the wife-abuse cycle, therefore, is to change the abuser's attitudinal system and social network of friends that support or at least condone physical male domination of family relationships. Obviously, this strategy will not be easy to apply in many abusive behavioral patterns. Abusers have had a lifelong learning experience in developing belief systems, and probably have had considerable reinforcement history for their aggressive actions toward women from their subculture. "Leaving the subculture is not unlike leaving the world of the addict or the alcoholic" (Fagan, 1989, p. 408).

To initiate a motivation to change a behavioral pattern of wife abuse often requires establishing a series of situations where the psychological costs for the abuse outweigh its psychological benefits. Legal sanctions may be one way, but many batterers realize that these sanctions are normally weak and without teeth. However, serious attempts by the criminal justice system to put some bite into these legal sanctions (such as arrests, criminal charges, and conviction) may begin to prove effective over the long haul. It is important to note that it is unlikely that any one arrest or single event will promote a wish to change. It is more likely that a series of aversive and costly events, such as strong legal sanctions, combined with social sanctions from the community (public disclosure, visits by social agencies) and emotional sanctions from the victim (reporting the abuse to authorities, leav-ing the home, separating, threatening divorce) will wear the abuser down to a point where he makes a decision to change his behavioral patterns.

However, the more severe and protracted the violence is, the more difficult it may be to stop, despite formal external interventions—legal or otherwise (Fagan, 1989). Legal and social sanctions for spouse abuse may work for less chronic and severe situations. However, legal sanctions, regardless of the nature and strength of the sanction, may not only be ineffective for the more serious cases, but could possibly lead to escalation in violence. Therefore, social, legal, and emotional sanc-tions may be more effective with individuals who do not have an extensive history of repetitive and serious violence.

As we shall see in Chapter 10, it is one thing to get a person to decide to stop acting a certain way. It is quite another for an individual to continue to avoid that behavior. Research clearly demonstrates that the maintenance of positive behavior is far more difficult to achieve than stopping the negative behavior.

SUMMARY AND CONCLUSIONS

In this chapter, we began to narrow our focus to consider specific offenses. Previous chapters were broader, in that they dealt with general theoretical orientations to crime. Here, we reviewed the major sociological data on violence, and summarized empirical and clinical research on family violence.

Sociological and official data indicate that homicides are rare compared to the total incidence of violent crime. In the United States, violent crime is often committed by young males living in environments that implicitly or explicitly advocate violence for the resolution of conflict. Guns (especially handguns) are commonly used in the crime. Certain minority groups—African Americans and Hispanics in the United States and Indians in Canada—are overrepresented in violent crime statistics. Most often, the victim and the offender are family members, friends, or acquaintances. While assaults are far more common than homicide, the same sociological features appear, particularly for aggravated assault.

About one of every five criminal homicides in the United States and Canada involves a family member killing another family member. The ratio appears even higher in England and Wales. The chapter reviewed the national data on family violence in general, spouse abuse, child abuse, elderly abuse, sibling abuse, and child-to-parent abuse. The research on battered child syndrome and the battered woman syndrome were summarized. The research data on infanticide, neonaticide, and filicide were examined. There is a discernible tendency in many cultures to assume a woman who kills her children is mentally disordered. However, whether a similar cultural proclivity exists when a man kills his own children is unknown. Some recent research indicates that many women who kill their own children have a history of violence and child abuse prior to the homicide.

The chapter focused on the ordinary—perhaps more mundane—aspects of criminal homicide and assault. In the next chapter, we will focus on some of the more frightening types of criminal homicide where victims are killed by strangers, randomly, or simply when the opportunity arises.

CRIMINAL HOMICIDE:
A CLOSER LOOK

This chapter will take a more detailed look at **criminal homicide**, including several investigative methods commonly used to identify offenders. We will look at various kinds of criminal homicide, including serial murder, sexual sadistic murder, mass murder, product-tampering homicide, and murder at the workplace. We will also examine the validity of numerous reports that certain so-called satanic cults regularly engage in human sacrifice and torture. Although homicides covered in this chapter are relatively rare, the social and emotional impact they have on a community—and a society as a whole—is considerable. The fear and terror they engender can alter the lifestyles of thousands. Moreover, they draw extensive media coverage; some of it is accurate, but much of it lacks a solid understanding of the psychosocial aspects involved in the crime. Therefore, it is important that we give some attention to what we know—and do not know—about these well-publicized offenses. Finally, we will end the chapter by discussing some of the current psychological theories and research that try to explain contemporary violence.

INVESTIGATIVE METHODS

According to John Douglas and Corinne Munn (1992a), there are three important features of offender behavior that may be evident at the scene of a crime: (1) the modus operandi; (2) the personation or signature; and (3) staging. **Modus operandi** (the **MO**) refers to the actions and procedures an offender engages in to commit a crime successfully. It is a behavioral pattern that the offender learns as he or she gains experience in committing the offense. Since the offender generally changes the MO until he or she learns which method is most effective, investigators may make a serious error if they place too much significance on the MO when linking crimes, however (Douglas & Munn, 1992c).

Anything that goes beyond what is necessary to commit the crime is called the **personation**, or the **signature**. For example, a serial offender may demonstrate a repetitive, almost ritualistic behavior from crime to crime, an unusual pattern that is not necessary to commit the offense. The signature may involve certain items that are left or removed from the scene, or other symbolic patterns, such as writings on the wall. If the victim is murdered, the signature may include unusual body positions or mutilations. In very rare instances, the signature may involve a "DNA torch," where the offender pours gasoline over the genital areas of the victim and sets the victim and the structure or motor vehicle on fire in an effort to destroy any evidence of sexual assault. A signature may also involve the repetitive acts of domination, manipulation, and control used by a serial rapist (Douglas & Munn, 1992b). The signature is often thought to be related to the unique cognitive processes of the offender, and, in this sense, may be more important to an investigator than the MO.

Staging refers to the intentional alteration of a crime scene prior to the arrival of the police. As Douglas and Munn (1992a) note, staging is usually done for one of two reasons: either to redirect the investigation away from the most logical suspect, or to protect the victim or the victim's family. Staging is frequently done by someone who has an association or relationship with the victim. For example, staging done by the family with the intent to protect the victim may be seen in autoerotic fatalities. **Autoeroticism**, a term coined by Havelock Ellis, refers to self-arousal and self-gratification of sexual desire. In some instances, the method of autoeroticism may result in the death of the victim, such as self-strangulation or hanging. Douglas and Munn (1992a) assert that in about one-third of autoerotic fatalities the victim is nude, and in about another one-third the victim is clothed in a costume, such as female clothing. Under these conditions, friends or family members may alter the scene to make the victim more "presentable" to the authorities. In some instances, they may even stage a criminal homicide.

In some instances, an offender may engage in **undoing**, a behavioral pattern found at the scene where the offender tries to psychologically "undo" the murder. For example, the offender may wash and dress the victim, or place the body on a bed, gently placing the head on a pillow and covering the body with blankets. This pattern typically occurs in offenders who become especially distraught about the death of the victim. Very often, the offender has a close association with the victim. In other cases, an offender may try to dehumanize the victim by engaging in actions that obscure the identity of the victim, such as excessive facial battery. Other offenders may employ more subtle acts of dehumanization, such as covering the victim's face with some material or object, or placing the victim face down.

Crime scenes are also classified as organized, disorganized, or mixed (see Tables 9-1 and 9-2). An **organized crime scene** indicates planning and premeditation on the part of the offender. The crime scene shows signs that the offender maintained control of himself and the victim. Often, the victim is moved from the abduction area to another secluded area, and perhaps the body is moved to still another area. Furthermore, the offender in an organized crime usually selects his victims according to some personal criteria. The infamous serial killer Ted Bundy, for example, selected young, attractive women who were similar in appearance. He was also successful in the abduction of these young women from highly visible areas, such as beaches, campuses, and ski lodges, indicating considerable planning and premeditation (Douglas, Ressler, Burgess, & Hartman, 1986).

Table 9-1   Profile Characteristics of Organized and Disorganized Murders as Classified by the FBI

Organized	Disorganized
Average to above-average intelligence	Below average intelligence
Socially competent	Socially inadequate
Skilled work preferred	Unskilled work
Sexually competent	Sexually incompetent
High birth order status	Low birth order status
Father's work stable	Father's work unstable
Inconsistent childhood discipline	Harsh discipline as a child
Controlled mood during crime	Anxious mood during crime
Use of alcohol with crime	Minimal use of alcohol
Precipitating situational stress	Minimal situational stress
Living with partner	Living alone
Mobility (car in good condition)	Lives/works near crime scene
Follows crime in news media	Minimal interest in news media
May change job or leave town	Significant behavior change

Source: *FBI Law Enforcement Bulletin*, 1985, p. 19.

A **disorganized crime scene** demonstrates the offender committed the crime without premeditation or planning. The crime scene indicators suggest the individual acted on impulse or in rage, or under extreme excitement. The disorganized offender obtains his victim by chance, often without specific criteria in mind. For example, Herbert Mullin of Santa Cruz, California, killed fourteen people of varying types (e.g., an elderly man, a young girl, and a priest) over a four-month period (Douglas et al., 1986). Generally, the victim's body is found at the scene of the crime. The **mixed crime scene** has ingredients of both organized and disorganized crime aspects. For example, a crime may have begun as a carefully planned one, but deteriorated into a disorganized one when things did not go as planned.

CRIMINAL INVESTIGATIVE ANALYSIS (PROFILING)

Criminal investigative analysis (CIA) (also called **crime scene analysis**) is an attempt to derive hypotheses about an offender based on the analysis of a crime scene, victim information, and current knowledge of offenders from previous research (Knight, Warren, Reboussin, & Soley, 1998). Essentially, it is a form of retroclassification, or classification that works backwards (Douglas, Burgess, Burgess, & Ressler, 1992). Different names and labels have been used for CIA, including profiling, psychological profiling, criminal behavior profiling, investigative profiling, crime scene profiling, and crime scene analysis. Homant and Kennedy (1998) recommend that crime scene profiling be divided into four somewhat overlapping categories: (1) psychological profiling; (2) offender profiling; (3) geographical profiling; and (4) equivocal death analysis. Homant and Kennedy suggest that psychological profiling be reserved for the strategy of

Table 9-2   Crime Scene Differences between Organized and Disorganized Murderers as Classified
             by the FBI

Organized	Disorganized
Planned offense	Spontaneous offense
Victim a targeted stranger	Victim/location known
Personalizes victim	Depersonalizes victim
Controlled conversation	Minimal conversation
Crime scene reflects control	Crime scene random and sloppy
Demands submissive victim	Sudden violence to victim
Restraints used	Minimal use of restraints
Aggressive acts prior to death	Sexual acts after death
Body hidden	Body left in view
Weapon/evidence absent	Weapon/evidence often present
Transports victim or body	Body left at death scene

Source: *FBI Law Enforcement Bulletin*, 1985, p. 19.

interviewing and testing of individuals to determine whether their characteristics match the research-based characteristics of a class of offenders. For example, a suspect might be interviewed and evaluated in an effort to determine if he fits into an empirically established typology of offenders. Offender profiling, according to Homant and Kennedy, is a method of classification that is strictly empirical in approach. It requires gathering of a large amount of empirical data that are systematically analyzed for behavioral and personality characteristics. From these data, a "profile" is often developed that characterizes a certain offender type. "Investigative profiling is best viewed as a strategy enabling law enforcement to narrow the field of options and generate educated guesses about the perpetrator" (Douglas et al., 1992, p. 21). Other researchers write: "A psychological profile focuses attention on individuals with personality traits that parallel traits of others who have committed similar offenses" (Pinizzotto & Finkel, 1990, p. 215). In short, criminal profiling is an attempt to identify demographic variables and behavioral patterns of an offender based on characteristics of previous offenders who have committed similar offenses.

Psychological profiling was used by the Office of Strategic Services (OSS) during World War II, primarily to profile enemy leaders and their proclivities (Ault & Reese, 1980). After the war, profiling was largely shelved until the FBI started using it again during the early seventies. The FBI's National Center for the Analysis of Violent Crimes and the Behavioral Science Unit receive numerous requests for profiles from various law enforcement agencies, primarily for cases involving homicide (65 percent), rape (35 percent), or kidnapping (8 percent) (Pinizzotto, 1984). The FBI, before rendering information on a case, often requests (1) color photos of the crime scene; (2) the nature of the neighborhood (economic and social data); (3) the medical examiner's report; (4) a map of the victim's travels prior to the death; (5) a complete investigative report of the incident; and (6) complete background of the victim, including habits and lifestyle. Forensic psychologists and psychiatrists, working independently or for a government agency, are also often asked to provide information on various criminal behaviors.

Ideally, a profile tries to identify "what," "why," and "who." However, Anthony Pinizzotto and Norman Finkel (1990) conclude from their research that criminal profiling is much more complex than this, involving a "multilevel series of attributions, correlations, and predictions" (p. 230). Much profiling is guesswork based on hunches and anecdotal information accumulated through years of experience, and it is full of error and misinterpretation. Currently, profiling is probably at least 90 percent an art and speculation and only 10 percent science. However, the FBI Behavioral Science Unit (BSU) together with the Child Abduction & Serial Killer Unit (CASKU) and the Profiling and Behavioral Assessment Unit (PBAU) are developing research programs to bring more science and scholarship into profiling and crime scene investigation. Furthermore, very rarely does profiling provide the specific identity of the offender, nor is it intended to. Criminal profiling basically tries to narrow the field of investigation (Douglas, Ressler, Burgess, & Hartman, 1986). Broadly, criminal profiling suggests the kind of person who might have committed the crime under investigation, but exact identity is extremely remote.

A profile report normally includes the gender, age, marital status, education level, and some broad identification of the occupation of the offender. There is also some prediction or estimation as to whether the offender will strike again, whether he or she has a police record, and what types of victims are at risk. In some instances, the profiler will try to identify possible motivational factors for the crime as well as the offender's personality traits.

Experienced profilers assert that profiling of *serial* offenders is most successful when the offender demonstrates some form of psychopathology at the crime scene, such as sadistic torture, evisceration, post mortem slashings and cuttings, and other mutilations (Pinizzotto, 1984). The reasoning behind this conclusion is that when a person is mentally disordered, he or she shows greater consistency in behavior from situation to situation. Whether mentally disordered persons are more consistent in their behavioral patterns than normals remains an open question, however. It is likely that some are, and some are not.

Profiling appears to be particularly useful in serial sexual offenses, such as serial rape and serial sexual homicides (Pinizzotto & Finkel, 1990). This is because we have a more extensive research base on sexual offending than we do on homicide. Furthermore, profiling is largely ineffective at this time in the identification of offenders involved in fraud, burglary, robbery, political crimes, theft, and drug-induced crime because of the limited research base.

Computer-based models of offender profiles developed from extensive statistical data collected on similar offenses hold considerable promise. To date, however, there is very little research on the utility, reliability, and validity of criminal profiling in general. And the FBI agrees with this assessment. "At present, there have been no systematic efforts to validate these profile-derived classifications" (Douglas et al., 1992, p. 22).

Pinizzotto and Finkel (1990) did try to assess the accuracy of profiling in a study involving four trained FBI experts, six trained police detectives, six experienced detectives without training, six clinical psychologists naive about criminal profiling, and six untrained undergraduate students. The results, in general, were not strongly supportive of profile accuracy. Trained experts were somewhat more accurate in profiling the sexual offender, but were not much better than the untrained groups in profiling the homicide offender. The researchers also tried to identify any qualitative differences in the way experts and nonexperts processed the information provided. Overall, the results showed that experts did not process the material any differently than the nonexperts. This finding suggests that the cognitive methods and strategies used by expert profilers are not discernibly different from the way nonexperts process the available information about the crime. The artificiality of the experiment and the quality of information given the groups may have been influential factors in this observation, however. What the researchers did find is that some trained profilers were more interested and skillful in certain areas than other profilers. Some profilers, for example, were good at gaining information from the medical reports, whereas others were better at gaining clues from the crime scene photos. This finding indicates that group profiling by a team of trained experts may be more effective than utilizing one single profiler.

In recent years, reconstruction of the personality profile and cognitive features (especially intentions) of deceased individuals has gained some popularity. This postmortem psychological analysis is called **Reconstructive Psychological Evaluation (RPE)** or **equivocal death analysis** (Poythress, Otto, Darkes, & Starr, 1993). The analysis is also known as a psychological autopsy (Brent, 1989; Ebert, 1987; Selkin, 1987), although the "autopsy" analysis is often reserved for suicide cases. The psychological autopsy is frequently done to determine the reasons and precipitating factors for the suicide.

The RPE differs from criminal profiling in two important ways: (1) The profile is constructed on a dead person; and (2) the identity of the person is already known. Like criminal profiling, however, the reliability and validity of the RPE and its variants (psychological autopsies) have yet to be demonstrated and remain open to debate.

In summary, much serious research needs to be done on profiling accuracy, usefulness, and processing before any tentative conclusions can be advanced in the area. Raymond Knight and his colleagues (Knight et al., 1998) have made a solid step in that direction.

MULTIPLE MURDERERS

One of the most frightening and perhaps incomprehensible types of homicide is the random killing of groups of people, either in one episode or individually over a period of time. Although multiple murders are still rare occurrences, when they do happen they cannot escape attention, and they remain etched in the public consciousness. Who today cannot recall the slaughter of twenty-one patrons at a

McDonald's in San Ysidro, California, in July 1984, by James Oliver Huberty, or the mass murder of twenty-two patrons at Luby's Cafeteria in Killeen, Texas, on October 16, 1991. Most people still recall the planned, separate murders of thirty-three young men and boys in the cellar of the suburban Chicago home of John Wayne Gacy during the late 1970s. During the early 1990s Jeffrey Dahmer lured at least seventeen boys and young men into his home in Milwaukee, where he drugged, killed, and dismembered them. The public was shocked to learn the details of how Dahmer ate the victims' flesh and had sex with the corpses. The crimes of David Berkowitz, known as the infamous Son of Sam, and those of the Hillside Strangler, the Boston Strangler, and Theodore Bundy are all classic multiple murders in the United States that have received extensive media coverage.

In England, we have had Jack-the-Ripper in earlier times, and more recently, Peter Sutcliffe, the Yorkshire Ripper who killed thirteen women in the red-light districts of Northern England. Dennis Nilsen became England's first serial killer to prey on the homosexual subculture, committing at least fifteen known murders (Jenkins, 1988).

More recently in the United States, there has been a rash of multiple murders where an individual goes into a school building or business establishment and begins shooting randomly with a semiautomatic firearm. A typical scenario reads like the following: On Friday night, August 8, 1993, a Fort Bragg soldier, heavily armed and shouting about President Clinton and homosexuals in the military, went into a restaurant in Fayetteville, North Carolina, and began shooting people at random. Before he was shot down, he managed to kill four and wound six others in a restaurant that he had never visited prior to his onslaught.

Serial murder is usually reserved for incidents where an individual (or individuals) kills a number of individuals (usually a minimum of three) over time. The time interval—sometimes referred to as the cooling-off period—may be days or weeks, but more likely months or years. The cooling-off period is the main difference between serial murders and other multiple murders (Douglas, Ressler, Burgess, & Hartman, 1986). The murders are premeditated and planned, and the offender usually selects specific victims. **Spree murder** normally refers to the killing of three or more individuals without any cooling-off period, usually at two or more locations. A bank robber who kills some individuals within the bank, flees with hostages, and kills a number of people while in flight during a statewide chase would be an example of a spree murderer. **Mass murder** involves killing three or more persons at a single location with no cooling-off period between murders. The FBI identifies two types of mass murder: classic and family (Douglas et al., 1986). An example of a **classic mass murder** is when an individual barricades himself or herself inside a public building, such as a fast food restaurant, randomly killing the patrons and any other individual he or she has contact with. An example is James Huberty at MacDonald's, or the Fort Bragg soldier in North Carolina described previously. Another example is Sylvia Seegrist (nicknamed Ms. Rambo because of her military-style clothing), who began shooting people at a Pennsylvania mall in October, 1985, killing three and wounding seven (Douglas et al., 1986). She was sentenced to life imprisonment.

A **family mass murder** is where at least three family members are killed (usually by another family member). Very often, the perpetrator kills himself or herself, an incident that is classified as a mass murder/suicide.

SERIAL MURDERERS

Serial murders seem to be on the increase in the United States and England. In the United States during the 1950s and 1960s, there were only two cases of an individual killing ten or more victims over a period of time. Since 1970, however, there have been at least forty known individuals who qualify as serial murderers (Jenkins, 1988). The U.S. Department of Justice concluded that there were about thirty-five serial murderers active at any given point in the United States during the 1970s and 1980s (Jenkins, 1988). However, it remains debatable whether serial murders are on the increase, or whether the dramatic improvement in communication and computer networks among law enforcement agencies and the news media may account—at least in part—for the statistical increments in the crime. Prior to 1970, information exchange between agencies was difficult and primitive by today's standards, and therefore, serial murderers who moved from one geographic location to another (which they commonly do) probably went undetected.

Mass murderers also seem to be on the increase in the United States, although the phenomenon remains rare in England. Available estimates indicate that as many as 3,500 to 5,000 victims are slain by serial or mass murderers in the United States each year (Holmes & Deburger, 1988). This estimate may be much too high, however, since it accounts roughly for 14 to 20 percent of all criminal homicides committed each year across the entire country.

Several years ago, Jenkins (1988) noted that victims of serial murderers tend to be young women, especially active prostitutes. Today, the primary victims of serial killers tend to be children of both sexes (ages eight to sixteen). In response to the increase in child victims, FBI Director Louis Freeh created a specialized unit to focus on investigation of child abduction and murder. The unit is called the "Child Abduction and Serial Killer Unit." In addition, the Missing and Exploited Children's Task Force (MECTF) was created by Congress in the 1994 Crime Bill to assist in investigating the most difficult cases of missing and exploited children. Both the Child Abduction and Serial Killer Unit and the MECTF work closely with the National Center for Missing and Exploited Children. In 1987, the Office of Juvenile Justice and Delinquency Prevention (OJJDP) conducted six studies in an effort to determine the incidence of abducted children by nonfamily members. Two definitions of abductions were developed: a legal abduction and a stereotypical abduction (FBI, 1997). The legal abduction definition included an incident involving the coerced and unauthorized taking of a child by a nonfamily member more than twenty feet or longer than one hour, or the luring of a child for the purpose of committing another crime. The stereotypical abduction definition included—in addition to meeting the legal definition criteria—abduction by a stranger whereby the child is gone overnight, or is killed, or is transported a distance of fifty miles or more, or the child is ransomed, or kept permanently. The studies estimated that there were between 3,200 to 4,600 legal definition abductions, 200 to 300 stereotypical definition abductions, and that at least 100 were murder victims (FBI, 1997).

Unlike the typical violent individual who demonstrates a propensity for violence at an early age, serial murderers generally begin their careers of repetitive homicide at a relatively late age. Jenkins (1988) concludes that most start their careers between the ages of twenty-four and forty. Interestingly, the median age of arrested serial murderers is thirty-six. Arrests typically occur about four years after they begin killing. While serial murderers have extensive police records, the records reflect a series of petty theft, embezzlement, and forgery, rather than a history of violence (Jenkins, 1988). Surprisingly, they also do not have extensive juvenile records. Jenkins concludes that the English cases do not provide any early indicators or predictors of eventual murderous behavior. When British serial murderers committed their first murder, about half were married, had a stable family life, and had usually lived in the same house for many years. A majority had stable jobs, and, disconcertingly, a good number had been former police officers or security guards.

Serial murderers kill about four people per year, an average that seems to be characteristic of both British and American offenders. However, the evidence does not support any notion that they kill on the basis of some compulsion or irresistible urge. Rather, the murder appears to be more a result of opportunity and the random availability of a suitable victim.

Holmes and Deburger (1988) have recently analyzed the characteristics of serial killers in the United States. In general, the patterns and characteristics of the British sample correspond closely to the American. However, while the British serial murderers generally stay in the same neighborhood, many of their American counterparts prefer to move around the country, committing murders in a number of states and jurisdictions. Holmes and Deburger also note that serial murder is predominately white males killing white females. There are exceptions, of course. Jeffrey Dahmer, a thirty-one-year-old white male, killed at least nine African-American males in 1991, and apparently killed many more over a ten-year period. Victims, both in the British and American samples, tend to be strangers or individuals whom the killer met only briefly before, a pattern that makes it particularly difficult for law enforcement agencies to identify the assailant. Moreover, the motive for the killing is usually aberrant and extremely difficult for those who seek the murderer's arrest to understand.

Although relatively rare, there have been at least three dozen female serial murderers in U.S. history. Hickey (1991) identified thirty-four documented female serial murderers, with 82 percent of them acting after 1900. Moreover, there are some discernible differences between female and male serials. For example, only about one-third of female serials killed strangers, in contrast to males who almost exclusively prefer strangers (Holmes, Hickey, & Holmes, 1991). Most victims of female serials are husbands, former husbands, or suitors. For example, Belle Gunness murdered an estimated fourteen to forty-nine husbands or suitors in LaPorte, Indiana (Holmes et al., 1991). Nannie Doss killed eleven husbands and family members in Tulsa, Oklahoma.

Female serials murder primarily for material or monetary gain, such as insurance benefits, will allocations, trusts, and estates. Furthermore, the method of killing is usually through poisons (usually cyanide) or overdoses of pills. Approximately half of the female serial killers had a male accomplice. Some women murdered because of involvements in cults or with a male serial murderer. A good example of cult involvement is the female following of the Charles Manson family. An example of involvement with a male serial murderer is Charlene Gallego, the common-law wife of serial killer, Gerald Gallego (Holmes et al., 1991). Charlene helped Gerald select, abduct, and murder at least ten individuals.

Jenkins (1993) contends that the current popular image of the serial murderer—a white male who kills for sexual motives—may be an inaccurate one. He argues that a lack of a **victimological perspective** encourages confusion and distorted information. He suggests that our current knowledge about serial murderers is strongly influenced by two factors: availability of the victims and the attitudes of law enforcement agencies toward those victims. Rather than strictly focusing on individual and personality attributes of the offender, he believes we should also examine the *social opportunity* to kill. In other words, what we know about serial murder may be strongly influenced by the nature and type of the potential victims.

To illustrate, Jenkins provides the case of Calvin Jackson, who was arrested in 1974 for murder committed in a New York apartment building. Actually, Jenkins was a serial murderer, but none of his victims caused the police to suspect a serial killer. Jackson's killings took place in a single-occupancy hotel where the guests were poor, socially isolated and largely forgotten, and mostly elderly. Time after time, the police were called to the hotel to deal with cases of death or injury due to alcohol, drugs, or old age. When foul play was suspected, the police never considered it the work of a serial murderer, because the nature of the victims did not fit the stereotypic profile. Since there was no evidence of grotesque sexual abuse of the victim (the victim stereotype), there was little reason for the police to entertain the possibility of a serial murderer. Other serial murderers may set up situations where murders resemble drug-related homicides. Therefore, our current knowledge of serial murderers may be restricted to a certain category of offender.

An examination of the victim selection of *known* serial murderers will reveal that killers prefer the group of people offering easy access, transience, and a tendency to disappear without causing much alarm or concern. Victims are often prostitutes, especially streetwalkers, street runaways, young male drifters, and itinerant farm workers. Young women in or near a university or college campus, or the elderly and solitary poor appear to be the groups next preferred. The strongest determining factor in victim selection for both groups seems to be easy availability of potential victims. Rarely do known serial murderers break in and kill middle-class strangers in their homes, for example—although the entertainment media often use this portrayal of serial murder to instill fear into the audience. It should be pointed out, however, that although serial killers begin their murderous careers by selecting highly vulnerable victims, they may, as their killings continue, gain substantially more confidence in their ability to abduct more "challenging" victims. Fortunately, very few serial killers become this successful before they are arrested.

Jenkins further suggests that dramatic increases in serial murder are directly related to dramatic increases in potential victims, such as severe downturns in the economy or deinstitutionalization of mental patients that result in putting more vulnerable people on the streets.

Interestingly, thirty-one of the fifty-two known cases of serial murderers in the United States since 1971 have occurred in the western states, especially California (Jenkins, 1993). Only four have occurred in the northeastern states. The reasons for this geographical distribution remains largely a mystery, although the answer probably lies in some combination of lifestyles, economic conditions, and the availability of potential victims.

Perhaps an effective method for reducing serial murder is to identify and protect specific high-risk groups and regions, and to take whatever social measures are needed to reduce their vulnerability. Focusing on the offender through criminal profiling and other investigative measures is usually of limited usefulness, because most serial killers are apprehended by a mixture of fortuitous events and carelessness by the offender. In the meantime, community leaders and authorities should concentrate on reducing the availability of potential victims.

While African Americans are overrepresented in "normal" homicide cases, only one-fifth of known American serial murderers are African American. One answer to this discrepancy may lie in how serial murder is identified and investigated. For example, law enforcement agencies may be less prone to investigate African-American victims as casualties of serial murderers if they are found in a rundown apartment complex located in a poverty-stricken, crime-infested neighborhood. Under these circumstances, law enforcement officials are more likely to conclude that the victim is simply another fatality in the long stream of never-ending violence found in certain segments of American society.

TYPES OF SERIAL MURDERERS

Holmes and Deburger (1988) make a gallant attempt to classify serial murderers into a typology based on motive. They identify four major types: (1) visionary; (2) mission-oriented; (3) hedonistic; and (4) power/control oriented. The *visionary type* is driven by voices or visions that demand that a particular group of people be destroyed, such as prostitutes, homosexuals, or derelicts. The visionary killer often operates on the basis of a "directive from God." In many instances, this type qualifies as psychotic or crazy. The *mission-oriented type* determines that there is a particular group of people that must be destroyed or eliminated. He sees no visions, hears no voices, and functions on a day-to-day basis without demonstrating crazy or psychologically aberrant behavior. The *hedonistic type* strives for pleasure and thrill seeking, and feels that people are objects to use for one's own enjoyment. Reportedly, the hedonistic killer gains considerable pleasure from the murder event itself. The *power/control type* strives to get satisfaction by having complete life-or-death control over the victim. Sexual components may or may not be present, but the primary motive is the extreme power over the helpless victim.

At least two more types could be added to the Holmes-Deburger list: the *recognition seeker* and the *material-gain seeker*. Some serial murderers may kill primarily for the challenge of it and the recognition they receive from the media. For example, serial killer Donald Evans claims he murdered at least seventy victims in twenty-one states during a fourteen-year period. Apparently, the victims consisted of the most vulnerable members of society, running from prostitutes to elderly, helpless women. After he was arrested, he proudly proclaimed himself as the most prolific serial killer in U.S. history, and asked for the death penalty. The material-gain seeker kills serially for money and material rewards, such as we find in many women serial murderers discussed previously, who kill husbands and suitors for insurance, will distribution, and other material acquisition.

Despite the extensive media coverage and several interesting books on the subject in recent years, there have been very few well-designed, empirically based studies on serial murderers during the past ten to fifteen years. Much of the available information has been gathered through anecdotal, interviews or case study methods, which, while informative and interesting, fail to provide a systematic and functionally useful data base for predicting and identifying these offenders.

A PSYCHIATRIC PERSPECTIVE

Based on clinical observations and experience, Lunde (1976) summarizes the characteristics of both serial and mass murderers, which he considers, from a psychiatric perspective, the same. Thus, he uses the term "mass murderer" as a collective term to include both types. According to Lunde, mass murderers are almost always psychotic and kill either for no apparent reason or for an apparent but perverse (often sexual) reason. He compares mass and single murderers on a number of factors. As mentioned previously, mass murders in the United States are almost always performed by white males, while single murders are most often committed by African Americans. The mass murderer is rarely intoxicated during the episode, while single murders are often associated with alcohol consumption by the offender, victim, or both. Lunde also notes that mass murderers rarely know their victims well. The choice of victims is usually not random or coincidental, however. The offender usually selects victims possessing specific attributes; there is a significant physical, social, or psychological feature about the victim that attracts the offender. Even mass murderers who randomly shoot into a group of people are making some deliberate choice of victims, as we shall see in the next section. Other mass killers have preyed on young African-American boys, college women, or prostitutes.

Lunde believes that most mass murderers fall into two psychiatric classifications: paranoid schizophrenia or sexual sadism. We have already discussed the salient features of paranoid schizophrenia in Chapter 6, and we will not review that particular syndrome here. We might suggest, however, that Lunde would probably place Huberty in this category, along with Jim Jones, who orchestrated the deaths of some nine hundred members of his "Church of God" in Jonestown, Guyana.

It is a mistake, however, to assume along with Lunde that almost all mass (serial) murderers are seriously mentally disordered in the clinical sense of that term. While their thought patterns may be considered to be extremely aberrant when it comes to sensitivity and concern for other human beings, a vast majority of serial killers fail to qualify as psychotic or crazy in the traditional scheme of mental disorders. Serial killers have developed versions of the world characterized by values, beliefs, perceptions, and general cognitive processes that facilitate repetitive murder, often in a brutal, demeaning, and cold-blooded manner. They commit the type of murders that draw interest, send spine-chilling fear into the community, and appear incomprehensible. They draw considerable expenditure from law enforcement agencies in both time and money in their detection and arrest. Motives are difficult to determine and seem to be based on psychological rewards rather than material gain. But the labels "sick," "crazy," or "psychotic" explain little and offer little hope in the quest for understanding the processes involved in the development of this behavior.

SEXUAL SADISTIC MURDERER

Sexual sadism, in its extreme form, is "a deviation characterized by torture and/or killing and mutilation of other persons in order to achieve sexual gratification" (Lunde, 1976, p. 48). The sexual sadistic offender engages in multiple means of torture, using psychological torment that is often combined with physical methods of torture to heighten his sexual arousal. The sight of suffering and the helplessness of the victims increasingly excites him.

The sexual acts of this offender are paired with domination, degradation, and violence. Anal and/or oral sexual penetration are often used by this offender because he perceives this behavior as more degrading to the victim than vaginal penetration (Dietz, Hazelwood, & Warren, 1990). Object penetration is also common. Victims, who are apparently viewed only as objects to be used as sources of pleasure, are almost always women, but homosexual sadistic murders have also occurred (e.g., Gacy and Dahmer). The victims are often bound, blindfolded, and/or gagged.

Sexual bondage is common in sadistic murders. **Sexual bondage** refers to the restriction of movement in a way that enhances the sexual arousal of the offender (Dietz et al., 1990). For example, the victim may be bound in a variety of suggestive positions, often being photographed. The offender will use elaborate and excessive binding material that may be tied in a neat and symmetrical manner.

Dietz, Hazelwood, and Warren (1990) examined the characteristics of thirty sexual sadistic offenders (most were known serial murderers) referred to the National Center for the Analysis of Violent Crime. Although their crimes were described as grotesque, bizarre, and horrible, no one who knew them well before their offenses considered them odd or crazy acting. Nor had any of them received psychiatric or psychological attention for sexual sadism before they committed their crimes. During the crime, they are often emotionally detached and distant. After a macabre murder, the sexual sadist may return home calmly and display little if any distress or guilt.

Their crimes are almost always carefully planned. Some offenders even constructed soundproof torture chambers equipped with video equipment and other paraphernalia, such as restraints, torture racks, whips, blindfolds, weapons, and gags. The site of their planned torture is usually isolated to prevent detection. Although they generally do not know their victims, they frequently "capture" their intended victim with considerable forethought and planning. Victims are usually chosen through systematic stalking and surveillance (Douglas et al., 1992). The victim is approached under a pretext, such as requesting or offering assistance, asking directions, or impersonating a police officer (Douglas et al., 1992). Some offenders, however, prefer the "blitz" method, which is an ambush style of attack in which the victim is surprised and quickly overpowered. Strangers are probably sought because they reduce the odds of their being linked to the offender. Sixty percent of the offenders investigated by Dietz and colleagues kept one or more victims captive for periods ranging from twenty-four hours to six weeks before killing or releasing them.

Sadistic murderers usually kill by strangulation, apparently because of the total control over the victim this method offers them. Shooting is too quick and anticlimactic. Following death, victim mutilation is common. The offender usually keeps personal items belonging to the victims (undergarments, shoes, jewelry, driver's license). Many sexual sadists keep records of their crimes in the form of writings, drawings, or photographs (Dietz et al., 1990). Audio or videotapes of the torment of the victim are also kept by many offenders, so that they can relive the crime between kills.

Brittain (1970), a British psychiatrist, posits that sadistic murderers are typically shy, withdrawn, quiet, and mild-mannered. They rarely show anger. They have very few friends and prefer solitary pursuits, like reading and listening to music. According to Brittain, they are usually fascinated by the occult, black magic, werewolves, vampires, and portrayals of horror in both print and electronic media. Douglas and colleagues (1992) report that these offenders often have items in their residence associated with sexual or violent themes, such as pornographic literature, videos, bondage paraphernalia, and detective magazines. Douglas and his colleagues also suggest that gun collections, police uniforms, badges, and materials dealing with law enforcement procedures may be present. They often demonstrate strong attraction for objects that have sexual meaning for them—women's shoes, handbags, stockings, and lingerie. As we will see in Chapter 10, however, it would be incorrect to assume that this tendency leads to sadistic murder.

Characteristically, sadistic murderers are males under age thirty-five. Sadistic murderers often have prior criminal records, although not necessarily for sexual offenses (Douglas et al., 1992). According to clinical data, of all types of murderers, sexual sadists are the most likely to murder again (Lunde, 1976; Brittain, 1970). Furthermore, each time they murder, the next one comes easier. They are drawn to semiskilled employment and generally have a poor work history. About half are married at the time of their offenses, and many have children (Dietz et al., 1990; Douglas et al., 1992). These individuals become dangerous when they have suffered a loss of self-esteem, such as being laughed at by a woman, mocked by acquaintances, or demoted or discharged from employment.

When sadistic murderers are arrested, Brittain (1970) notes, they continue to display little tension or guilt. They may even enjoy describing the incident in detail. They appear to bask in all the attention they receive; it is not uncommon to see them smiling into television and still cameras. They have turned a once-mundane existence into excitement, and they may even feel they have made their mark on history.

Jenkins (1988) makes some important points about what happens to serial murderers once taken in custody. Almost inevitably they attempt a defense of insanity or diminished responsibility, but very rarely succeed. As we discovered in Chapter 6, the public—in Britain, Canada, and the United States—is consistently very reluctant to attribute insanity to extremely violent offenders, particularly in the case of serial or mass murderers.

In summary, most of the knowledge we have on serial murderers is based on clinical observations, investigative reports, and anecdotal data. Some of the material is sensational and overly dramatic, such as that found in popular paperbacks. On the other hand, much of the clinical and investigative material is in agreement and relatively consistent, and it adds greatly to our understanding of the serial offender. Our knowledge of the serial murderer, however, could be greatly expanded with more quantitative data, such as we would find in extensive, systematic data collection and analysis. However, because serial murder is extremely rare compared to other violent offenses, the numbers for a more complete analysis are simply unavailable at this time.

MASS MURDERERS

Surprisingly little research has been directed at mass murderers, especially in comparison to the attention directed at serial murderers. Perhaps this is because mass murder, while frightening, is not as intriguing or mysterious as serial murder. Furthermore, mass murder happens quickly and unpredictably without warning. Then the killing is usually over. And it is often clear who the offender is, and his or her life is usually ended on the spot.

We will not cover, in this section, ideological or political mass murder, such as we find in terrorist attacks, because the motives and features of these world-wide offenses are overwhelmingly diverse. Instead, we will focus our attention on what the FBI calls classic mass murder. Unfortunately, the research on family mass murder is scanty and not detailed or systematic enough to be covered to any great extent.

CLASSIC MASS MURDER

Mass murderers tend to be frustrated, angry people who feel helpless about their lives. They are usually between the ages of thirty-five and forty-five, and they are convinced there is little chance that things will get better for them. Their personal lives have been a failure by their standards and they have often suffered some tragic or serious loss, such as a loss of meaningful employment. George Hennard, for example, the thirty-five-year-old who drove his Ford Ranger pickup into the plate glass window of Luby's Cafeteria in Killeen, Texas, and proceeded to shoot to death twenty-two patrons, had lost his cherished job as a merchant marine.

In addition, mass murders are usually carefully planned, sometimes over very long periods. For example, on November 2, 1991, Gang Lu, a former graduate student at the University of Iowa, sought six specific professors he felt were behind his not getting a $1,000 award for his doctoral dissertation. He managed to kill five of the six within ten minutes before taking his own life. Lu had written five separate letters to people detailing his plans prior to the murder. Likewise, Hennard had apparently planned his onslaught for many months, even studying video documentaries of previous mass murders.

Moreover, the targets selected by mass murderers are either symbolic of their discontent (such as their workplace), or are likely to contain individuals they hate or blame for their misfortunes. George Hennard, for example, had a lifelong hatred for women, and he knew that Luby's Cafeteria during lunch would be filled with them. Hennard moved from victim to victim, frequently selecting women, and methodically shooting each victim in the head at close range as he shouted "bitch." Fourteen of the twenty-two deaths that day were women. Marc Lepine walked calmly through the University of Montreal engineering school (Ecole Polytechnique) with a semiautomatic rifle in search of women to kill. In one classroom, he shouted "I want to kill women!" and as he proceeded to shoot them, he shouted "You're all a bunch of feminists!" He managed to kill fourteen women that day and wounded thirteen more people (four of them men) before he took his own life. In his pocket was a three-page suicide note in which he complained that feminists had always ruined his life. James Oliver Huberty, the McDonald's killer, selected a fast-food restaurant in a Hispanic community (San Ysidro), because he apparently disliked Hispanics and children.

Mass murderers often take a very active interest in guns, especially semiautomatics that maximize the number of deaths in a short period of time. In large measure, the availability of high-powered semiautomatic or automatic weaponry accounts for the increasingly large death toll in recent mass murders. Moreover, mass murderers usually plan to die at the scene, either by committing suicide or by being shot down by law enforcement.

Also, mass murderers are often socially isolated and withdrawn people who are without a strong social network of friends or supports. Their isolation is probably due to some combination of an active dislike of people interacting with their inadequate interpersonal and social skills. The mass murder is their chance to get even, to dominate others, to take control, to call the shots, and to gain recognition.

The remainder of this section will address some specific offenses that have been or possess the strong possibility of becoming mass murder, and that seem increasingly popular in recent years.

PRODUCT-TAMPERING HOMICIDE

Product-tampering homicide refers to death caused by a commercial product that has been sabotaged by someone; it also has the potential to result in multiple deaths. Between 1982 and 1986, there were twelve confirmed deaths directly due to product tampering (Lance, 1988). This form of homicide is rare, and is usually committed for financial gain. The offender usually expects financial gain either through litigation on behalf of the victim (wrongful death), through extortion, or through business operations (Douglas et al., 1992). The business operation strategy refers to attempts to damage a competing business by tampering with its products.

The method most commonly employed in product-tampering homicide is to place cyanide within the product, either before (if the offense involves extortion or business operations), or after purchase in cases claiming wrongful death. Cyanide is often the poison of choice because of its potency (an ounce can kill 250 people) and its availability (Douglas et al., 1992).

Fortunately, although there are numerous threats to tamper, very few are actually carried out. Nearly two-thirds of the threats are directed at retail stores, and the products threatened are usually well-known national brands (Lance, 1988). News of product tampering sometimes prompts a contagion effect (also known as copycat effect), where many people either copy or falsely report the offense. For example, when a baby food company was accused by an individual of having glass in its baby food, more than six hundred complaints of glass particles were immediately received across the country. A vast majority of the complaints were false claims by consumers seeking monetary reward by claiming that glass in the products had caused them some injury. One individual was arrested for deliberately feeding shards of glass to his retarded son in an attempt to obtain money from the baby food company.

AUTHORITY AND WORKPLACE HOMICIDE

An authority or workplace homicide is one wherein an individual murders people that the offender associates with a source of authority that he (or she) perceives did them wrong. According to the FBI (Southerland, Collins, & Scarborough, 1997), the workplace violent offender is usually a disgruntled employee who believes the job is his life, is a loner, has few friends, and lacks a support system. The target of the attack may be a person or persons (usually innocent), working within a building or structure, or for an organization that symbolizes the authority (Douglas et al., 1992).

Data collected by the National Institute for Occupational Safety and Health (NIOSH, 1993) between 1980 and 1989 indicate that approximately 750 people per year are murdered at work, making it the third leading cause of occupational death in the United States (Solomon & King, 1993). In fact, homicide was the leading cause of workplace death for women during those ten years, accounting for 41 percent of all female worker fatalities (Kelleher, 1997). A vast majority of these victims were killed (often randomly) by disgruntled employees who were fired or felt mistreated by the company or agency. Another 30,000 workers and managers are injured each year because of violent attacks by unhappy employees. The organization that has drawn the most authority homicides in recent years has been the U.S. Postal Service. Between 1986 and mid-1993, thirty-eight postal employees were murdered at the workplace by disgruntled present or former employees (Solomon & King, 1993).

It seems that a particular autocratic work environment can be a problem, such as found in large, impersonal bureaucratic organizations. As we discussed previously, when an employee feels frustrated and angry, he or she may be more likely to strike out.

Similar to mass murderers in general, offenders who commit authority homicide tend to be white males who have few social supports, are socially isolated, and who blame others (externalize) for their problems and misfortune, as mentioned earlier. Often, they are seriously depressed. Very often, the offender expects to die at the scene, either killed by the police or by suicide. Authority offenders also tend to be preoccupied with weapons, accumulating a number of them over a period of time with eventual revenge or "occupational martyrdom" in mind. The weapons are often of maximum lethality, such as automatic assault weapons (e.g., AK-47) (Douglas et al., 1992). In most instances, the offender is middle-aged (over thirty and under sixty) (Kelleher, 1997). There is also evidence that workplace offenders tend to have a history of violent behavior, alcohol or drug abuse, and will vocalize, or otherwise act out, violent intentions sometime prior to the authority homicide (Kelleher, 1997). Current data suggest that authority homicides are on the increase (Kelleher, 1997).

A distinction should be made between those incidents where employees are killed or injured by other employees or former employees, and *occupational homicide*, where an employee is killed by a person or persons not connected to the organization. For example, a retail employee murdered by a perpetrator during the commission of an armed robbery represents a very different scenario than authority-workplace homicide. In California, the majority (60 percent) of workplace homicides involve a person entering a small, night-retail establishment, such as a liquor store, gas station, or convenience food store, to commit a robbery (Southerland et al., 1997).

We now turn our attention to another potential offender of multiple homicide: cults. During the past two decades, there have been numerous complaints and allegations that certain satanic cults are murdering humans by the hundreds, or even the thousands. Are these allegations true, or merely a collection of frightening myths?

SATANIC CULTS AND HOMICIDE

Since the Middle Ages, demonology has been closely associated with crime by many Western Christian cultures. This dangerous connection lurked in the midnight landscape of clandestine ceremonies and nocturnal rituals. Secret societies met to worship evil spirits, sacrifice life to those spirits, and practice various forms of black magic.

In the United States, during the 1980s and early 1990s, this deeply entrenched belief in demons resurfaced in full bloom in the form of satanic cults. A **satanic cult** refers to a group of people who "worship" the devil and aspire to possess some of his powers. In Christian theology, Satan is the devil, and represents the greatest enemy of anything good and moral in humankind. It should be emphasized that a satanic cult is more than a group of people who occasionally dabble in devil worship. It refers to an organized belief system of religious worship, consistent devotion, and frequent ritual and ceremony, such as the Church of Satan and the Temple of Set.

Belief in the devil has moved in ebbs and flows in American history. Since the 1960s, there has been an increasing number of Americans who believe in the existence of the devil. For example, one nationwide survey conducted in 1964 found that 37 percent of Americans were certain about the existence of the devil. By 1973, however, this percentage rose to 50 percent (Nunn, 1974; Victor, 1993). A more recent Gallup poll conducted in 1990 found that about 60 percent of Americans were convinced there is a devil (Victor, 1993). Interestingly, the current belief in the devil, or Satan, is more common in America than it is among all other major industrial societies throughout the world (Gallup & Castelli, 1987; Victor, 1993).

The research literature normally identifies three or four levels of participation in a satanic "cult" (Bromley, 1991). At the lowest level are the *dabblers*, who are usually young people experimenting with satanic materials found in heavy metal rock music or in fantasy games such as "Dungeons and Dragons" and computer software games. They are not really serious in their devil worship, although some may wear satanic jewelry or carry "devilish" trinkets. Some juvenile gangs may carry a satanic name (Satan's Chosen), and may vandalize buildings with satanic symbols. But the symbols are largely intended to scare and frighten, and they do not represent actual spiritual commitment to Satan—although a frightened community may think otherwise.

The second level of participation is also not a "cult," but a utilization of symbols and themes as an excuse for antisocial behavior. Serial murderers and other violent offenders, for example, sometimes resort to creating a satanic theme as a rationale for their violent behavior, although there is little evidence they belonged to any cult prior to their violence. People in this group are often referred to as *self-styled satanists*.

The third level of participation involves the "true" satanic cults and churches that practice their religion in an organized and systematic fashion. They are spiritually and intellectually committed to this form of worship. These individuals are called *organized satanists*.

The fourth group, referred to as *traditional satanists*, are those cults commonly believed to be secret, highly organized networks of individuals involved in a host of deviant, evil, and immoral activities. Traditional cults "... subject human victims, preferably children, to obscene torments, then slash them to death, dismember them, and drink their blood and eat their flesh and vital organs" (Stevens, 1991, p. 21). Traditional cults actively promote such deviant activities as violence and murder, child abuse, sexual abuse, drug use, pornography, snuff films, and teen suicides (Best, 1991). Some experts and antisatanist groups claim that many serial murderers are cult members or are in some way influenced by Satan himself. Because of their alleged affiliation with crime and violence, it is this fourth group that we will concentrate on in this section.

Evangelist Bob Larson (1989) claims that up to 70 percent of all crimes committed by adolescents are motivated by the occult. Some mental health experts and law enforcement officials estimate that between 50,000 and 60,000 victims are sacrificed annually by satanic cults, even though the entire national homicide figure rarely exceeds 25,000 (Best, 1991; Bromley, 1991; Stevens, 1991; Victor, 1993; Wright, 1993a). These alarming figures have prompted the organization of groups called the Antisatanist Movement (ASM) and the Anticult Movement (ACM), both led by family-based organizations and conservative religious interests (Bromley, 1991).

Sacrificed victims, the antisatanism groups maintain, come from "throwaway" members of society (derelicts), kidnappings, and abductions. Some police officials claim that 95 percent of all children who disappear each year are victims of occult-related abductions (Best, 1991; Larson, 1989). Many antisatanists believe that the blond virgin child is the most sought-after victim (Victor, 1993). The blond child, as legend has it, is the symbol of innocence, purity, and beauty. Attacks on the blond child represent attacks upon the most cherished traditional values. For example, Jeffrey Victor's research of satanic belief and rumor in western New York state found the most fear-provoking rumor was that "... the Satanic cult was planning to kidnap and sacrifice a blond, blue-eyed virgin" (Victor, 1993, p. 65). Victor further found that when stories were told concerning kidnapping and human sacrifice, 40 percent of the stories specifically mentioned blond, blue-eyed children or virgins.

Antisatanists believe that some of the sacrificial victims are "altar babies." Altar babies are newborns bred specifically for sacrifice by young, unsuspecting women who are impregnated by cult members. One of the best known "breeders" is Lauren Stratford (a pseudonym), who wrote a biographical book, *Satan's Underground: The Extraordinary Story of One Woman's Escape* (1988), describing her unbelievable experiences with the cult. Stratford claimed, for example, to have had three of her own babies taken away for altar sacrifices during her psychological captivity by a satanic cult. The book was widely read by many fundamentalist Christian congregations and confirmed a world view of satanic cults they already strongly held (Wright, 1993a). However, an investigative story by the Christian magazine, *Cornerstone*, found Stratford's story full of contradiction, falsehoods, and unsubstantiated fantasy (Passantino & Passantino, 1989). By early 1990, Stratford's book had been withdrawn by the publisher.

Not all victims are sacrificed, of course. Some are indoctrinated into the cult for future use, such as for breeding vehicles for altar babies. Antisatanist groups claim that initial indoctrination into a traditional satanic cult usually occurs between ages four and six (Bromley, 1991). Antisatanists contend that the satanists operate childcare centers, orphanages, and foster homes as a way to exploit children in their care (Bromley, 1991). These nonsacrificed victims are subjected to a variety of physical and psychological abuse (often sexual in nature), initiation rites, and a long series of indoctrinations. After each indoctrination rite, these future satanists are often returned to their biological parents with their memories repressed or buried deep within their unconscious. Presumably, the terror and frequent brainwashing bestowed on these victims prevent them from remembering the horrible things done to them. Sometimes, usually many years later, these cult victims undergo intensive psychotherapy or hypnosis, and remember some of the things done to them.

The classic example of this phenomenon is the once very popular book, *Michelle Remembers* (published in 1980), written by Michelle Smith and her psychiatrist, Lawrence Pazder. Michelle, being treated for a multiple personality disorder by Pazder, began to remember how she was sexually abused and tortured as a five-year-old child in British Columbia. The abusers, she claimed, were a group of satanists to which her parents belonged. She also recalled seeing babies and adults being ritually butchered. She further maintained that she was frequently fed ashes from the burned remains of the victims. The book is important because it outlines virtually all the major charges that became popular during the 1980s (Jenkins & Maier-Katkin, 1991). Shortly after the peak of this book's popularity, the FBI began receiving similar stories from women across the country (Nathan, 1991). Then, in early 1984, the media began publicizing a sex abuse scandal that allegedly took place at the McMartin Preschool in suburban Los Angeles. The trial was one of the longest (it took six and one-half years) and most expensive criminal court cases in American history. Virginia McMartin, her daughter, Peggy McMartin Buckey, and her grandson, Raymond Cukey—along with five other childcare workers—were accused of sexually abusing hundreds of children for over a twenty-year period. Many of the children reported that they had been subjected to animal sacrifices, had witnessed sex acts performed during secret rites in churches, and were exposed to decomposed corpses in graveyards (Nathan, 1991). Charges were dismissed against all defendants when no convincing evidence was found. Although McMartin was absolved of criminal activity, she lost her school and her life savings, and received little compensation in civil suits.

This widely publicized story prompted the surfacing of similar reports across the country, ranging from preschools and daycare centers, to small-town neighborhoods. These reports were so strikingly similar that by 1985 child abuse experts began using the terms "**satanic ritual abuse**" or "**ritual abuse**" to describe the pattern (Nathan, 1991). By 1987, child protection agencies and police departments were receiving hundreds of disclosures of ritual abuse from distraught parents. Rumors of satanic plots to abduct children led many parents to temporarily withdraw their children from school (Bromley, 1991).

Other events during the 1980s encouraged further concerns about satanic cults. In 1987, John Schlesinger's film, *The Believers*, portrayed devil worship in a powerful and convincing fashion. In addition, the controversial Geraldo Rivera presented a television documentary called *Devil Worship* (Rivera, 1988) that had an enormous impact on the beliefs of the impressionable American public. The Rivera documentary has been widely used as evidence for the horrors of satanic cults at various professional and religious workshops, seminars, and education programs.

In 1989, a year after the Rivera documentary, thirteen mutilated bodies were found in the Mexican border town of Matamoros (Woodbury, 1989). The bodies, all males, had been tortured with razor blades or had their hearts ripped out. "Nearly all had been severely mutilated: ears, nipples, and testicles removed, the eyes gouged from one victim, the head missing from another" (Woodbury, 1989, p. 30). The conclusion by authorities was that it was the work of devil worshippers called the El Padrino Cult. The reporter (Woodbury, 1989, p. 30) concludes the article by stating "... whispers of other demonic bands and hideous deeds swept the Rio Grande valley. As preposterous as the rumors were, they would have sounded far more bizarre a week ago, before the tale of El Padrino and his followers became known."

Further evidence for the current cult epidemic is the sighting of "satanic" graffiti, cemetery vandalism, animal mutations, and some type of violent, local crime, such as horrible murder or unexplained suicide, all symbols that evoke satanic or demonological legends in people's collective imagination (Victor, 1993).

The fear and interests in satanic cults continued unabated into the 1990s. A survey being conducted by the American Bar Association's Center on Children and the Law reports that preliminary data (early 1993) show that 27 percent of county prosecutors have handled cases involving ritualistic or satanic cult abuse (Victor, 1993). Ogloff and Pfeifer (1992) conducted a survey of students at American and Canadian colleges and universities to assess the attitudes of people regarding cults and satanic cults, and to identify those activities in which students believe cults engage. While it is not surprising that 97 percent of the respondents believed that satanic cults exist, it is shocking that 23 percent of the respondents were convinced that these cults routinely participate in human sacrifice.

Some experts claim that the United States, now and in the near future, faces a serious crimewave associated with the occult or satanism that will be unprecedented (Jenkins & Maier-Katkin, 1991).

THE EVIDENCE

What is the evidence for these widespread allegations of crimes by satanic cults? Bromley (1991) notes that not a single defector has managed to leave with any kind of organizational records or hard evidence to support claims of sacrifice or abuse. Mulhern (1991) finds that despite intensive criminal investigations of alleged satanic cult crimes, all have failed to substantiate the allegations. Kenneth Lanning (1989, p. 82), a supervisory special agent of the FBI Behavioral Science and Research Unit in charge of sexual abuse cases, writes: "... a satanic murder can be defined as one committed by two or more individuals who rationally plan the crime and whose primary motivation is to fulfill a prescribed satanic ritual calling for the murder. By this definition, the author has been unable to identify even one documented satanic murder in the United States." Debbie Nathan (1991, p. 76) reports: "Despite continuing concern about ritual abuse, investigations have uniformly failed to turn up the adult witnesses or physical evidence that would be associated logically with ongoing group rites, extreme violence, and pornography production alleged in these cases." Jeffrey Victor (1993, p. 107) asserts: "There is simply no corroborating evidence for the existence of an organized network of Satanic cults whose members sexually molest children in order to brainwash them into a Satanic ideology." And after a carefully conducted sociological research project in western New York on claims and allegations about satanic cult crime, Victor (1993, p. 4) concludes: "… these claims assert that there exists a secret organization, or network, of criminals who worship Satan and who are engaged in the pornography business, forced prostitution, and drug dealing. These criminals also engage in the sexual abuse and torture of children in an effort to brainwash children into becoming life-long Devil worshippers…. My research suggests that they are baseless and misleading. Moreover, these claims exploit the widespread fears, particularly anxieties parents have about their children."

The references cited as evidence for satanic cults as vicious and cruel organizations that destroy human life and morality come almost exclusively from popular print, pop psychology or occult books, newspapers (such as the *National Enquirer*), and television media, and very rarely from scientific research in books or professional journals (MacHovec, 1992).

Antisatanist and fundamental religious groups retort that researchers and scholars fail to understand that these satanic cults are masters at hiding the evidence and brainwashing their members. These groups contend that these satanic cults are much more widely spread than commonly believed by the public, that they are powerful, insidious, secretive, and virtually impossible to detect (Best, 1991). Moreover, the sacrificed bodies go undetected because they are burned in portable high temperature ovens, or are placed in double decker graves under legitimately buried bodies, or the cult eats the bodies (Best, 1991). According to antisatanist groups, cult members become masters at hiding bodies and destroying evidence. In addition, the horrors and torture administered by the cult are intended to be unbelievable, so that few authorities will accept the stories of the few survivors who manage to tell their stories. These groups point out that the striking similarities in survivor stories, however, lend credibility to the atrocities of satanic cults. Moreover, the stories told by children are solid evidence for satanic cults, since children rarely lie. Antisatanist groups argue that children are innocent and pure victims, and have little to gain by lying to adults. However, the research literature indicates that children do make false claims about actions and events that happen to them (Ceci & Bruck, 1993). Children, even very young children, do lie when there is the pressure or motivation to do so. Moreover, people interviewing child witnesses can substantially influence their testimony (Bartol & Bartol, 1994; Ceci & Bruck, 1993).

Other evidence for satanic cults comes from the testimony of adults who were subjected to ritual abuse as children. These "victims" or "survivors" tend to be women in their thirties or forties who generally tell of confronting their satanic past, usually during psychotherapy (Jenkins & Maier-Katkin, 1991). Very often, these survivors are diagnosed as having a multiple personality disorder, which is assumed to be brought on by the trauma suffered at the hands of cult members. Larry Kahaner (1988), a clinician who works with cult survivors, claims that virtually every adult survivor he has known has a multiple personality. Jenny, in the book *Suffer the Child* (Spencer, 1989), claimed to have had several hundred distinct personalities. According to Jenkins and Maier-Katkin

(1991), many of these alleged adult survivors of ritual abuse are seriously emotionally disturbed individuals who have a lengthy record of various psychological disorders and substance abuse. Many come from strict, often puritanical, fanatically religious family backgrounds where severe corporal punishment was commonplace (Mulhern, 1991).

There is some question as to whether clinicians who report a series of satanic cult survivors in their practice may be overly sensitive and biased in their search for satanic cults (Mulhern, 1991). That is, the clinician must believe in the cult before beginning to listen to patients. Impressionable, emotionally disturbed patients may be led to believe in the satanic cult and are inadvertently led by the clinician toward a rich tapestry of stories about the horrors they "experienced" at the hands of the cult. The astute reader will recognize this phenomenon as **iatrogenic**, a concept discussed in an earlier chapter.

If there is no evidence to support the satanic cult-crime connection, why does the myth persist? Many people like the fear and arousal that accompanies stories about strange human-like creatures: devils, vampires, werewolves, bigfoot, Sasquatch, yeti, UFOs, and extraterrestrial aliens. They believe in them because it adds excitement to an otherwise mundane reality. Walk into any new or used book store that carries paperbacks and you will find shelves and shelves of books about satanic cults and the occult, some claiming to be nonfiction.

Historical and anthropological studies have also shown that beliefs in demonology and other mystical evil forces emerge during times of prolonged social anxiety and fears about the breakdown of society (Stevens, 1991). Concern that one's society is "going-to-the-dogs" or that the youth are misguided and overly influenced by evil elements provides a rich environment for blame, persecution, and oppression of certain groups and activities that are targeted by various moral crusades as the culprits in what has gone wrong. Heavy metal music, Dungeons and Dragons, aimless daydreaming, computer games, movies, and the entertainment media in general have all been targeted as agents that poison the mind of the youth in evil ways.

Jeffrey Victor (1993) predicts that the satanic cult scare, and the moral crusade that promotes it, will last—and even intensify—at least until the year 2000. This is especially the case concerning witch hunts for satanists who supposedly engage in the ritual sexual abuse of children. This is because the moral crusade of the Christian right has been joined by many national organizations concerned with child abuse and by highly reputable psychotherapists. Many of these psychotherapists specialize in treating multiple personality disorder patients. In a 1991 survey of members of the APA, 30 percent of the respondents indicated that they had treated at least one client who said he or she had suffered satanic ritual abuse, and (in a second survey) 93 percent of those who treated such a patient believed the story to be true (Wright, 1993a). Self-professed police experts (many of them strong religious fundamentalists themselves) specializing in satanic cults, who give workshops and professional seminars on the topic, also continue to add fuel to the fire.

Victor notes that small towns and rural areas are particularly susceptible to satanic cult scares because they are most deeply affected by lingering economic problems in society, and many fundamentalist Christians reside in them. Some impressionable young adults, mostly women, "remember" when going through psychotherapy that they were victims of satanic ritual abuse, often blaming their parents directly for the abuse. These claims are often encouraged by their psychotherapists, who are often themselves swept along with the overreactions of their patients. Unfortunately, these "... allegations can easily lead to false arrests and ruined community reputations, as they have in many past cases" (Victor, 1993, p. 299).

The phenomenon of an individual remembering ritual abuse many years after it allegedly occurred is known as recovered memory. This **recovered memory syndrome** is based on the assumption that emotionally painful or traumatic events can be unconsciously pushed into the deep recesses of the mind and reside there until brought out by skillful, systematic digging by a therapist or hypnotist. However, there is considerable debate about whether the mind actually works this way. The credibility of the theory is really stretched when considering long-term, frequent, habitual abuse. The evidence so far indicates that people can remember these events, if they want to. Some of the detail may be forgotten, but not all of it. Thus, a majority of people who suddenly remember, in adulthood, a series of traumas that occurred in childhood are believed, by many experts, to be suffering from a **false memory syndrome**. This incident never happened, but some people are susceptible to being convinced that it did.

In reaction to expanding charges of ritual abuse, a number of accused parents in 1992 formed the False Memory Syndrome Foundation, located in Philadelphia. Membership by early 1993 totaled about 3,700, and it is growing rapidly (Wright, 1993b). Martin Gardner (1993) writes that the false memory syndrome is the mental-health crisis of the 1990s. "That traumas experienced as a child can be totally forgotten for decades is the great mental health myth of our time—a myth that is not only devastating innocent families but doing enormous damage to psychiatry" (Gardner, 1993, p. 371).

The remainder of the chapter will highlight some psychological explanations for violent crime in general. In the last chapter and the first part of this one, we became increasingly focused on criminal homicide and we examined specific types of homicide. Now it is time to back up a little and look more broadly at human violence from a theoretical perspective.

PSYCHOLOGICAL FACTORS IN VIOLENT CRIME

IMPULSIVE VIOLENCE

Violent crime is often seen as resulting from the impulsive, spur-of-the-moment, and unpredictable acts of enraged individuals. The person who savagely assaults and sometimes kills is operating on impulse, slashing out at a victim without much forethought or planned strategy. This point of view, of course, partly supports the argument for gun control. If the gun were not available, the perpetrator would not have wounded or killed the victim—at least not as easily. We have also seen that with the significant increase in the technology and availability of rapid fire and automatic weapons, the number of innocent people killed by mass murderers has increased dramatically in the last ten years. The technology and availability of weapons, however, is only part of the story.

Some theorists believe that certain personalities or dispositions are more likely to react violently under certain circumstances than others. In *Violent Men*, Hans Toch (1969) theorizes that most violent episodes can be traced to well-learned, systematic strategies of violence that some people have found effective in dealing with conflictual, interpersonal relationships. Thus, violence is not simply the act of a person acting on impulse; it is the act of one who has habitual response patterns of reacting violently in particular situations. It is Toch's impression that, if we examine the history of violent persons, we will discover surprising consistency in their approaches to interpersonal relationships. They learned, probably in childhood, that violence works for them. They used violent responses effectively to obtain positive and negative reinforcement. They got what they wanted or avoided unpleasant situations by being violent.

Toch posits that humiliating affronts and threats to reputation and status are major contributing factors to violence. A blow to the self-esteem of the person who has few skills for resolving disputes and conflicts (such as verbal skills) may precipitate violence. This is especially true if the person's subculture advocates that disputes be settled through physical aggression.

In a similar vein, Berkowitz hypothesizes that people sometimes react violently, not because they anticipate pleasure or displeasure from their actions, but because "situational stimuli have evoked the response (they) are predisposed or set to make in that setting" (Berkowitz, 1970, p. 140). That is, individuals have been conditioned—specifically, classically conditioned—to react violently by prior experiences in similar situations. In some instances, according to Berkowitz, powerful environmental stimuli essentially produce impulsive behavior. Under these conditions, one's "thinking" becomes highly simplified, responding "mindlessly" to stimuli in a well-learned manner. Thus, some people "fall into" a rage, impulsively striking out automatically in response to unpleasant feelings brought on by aversive or noxious stimuli. Aversive or obnoxious stimuli can be anything from a face one "doesn't like" to physical abuse by another. Nevertheless, the individual is not likely to strike out unless he or she has been in a rage in past situations.

A similar view is expressed by Zillman (1979, 1983), who believes that cognitive or thinking processes are greatly impaired at extreme levels of emotional arousal. Under high excitement, such as anger, behavior normally controlled by thought becomes controlled by mindless habits. Therefore, at very high levels of emotional upset, hostile or aggressive behaviors are likely to become "impulsive," a term Zillman associates with habit strength. The behaviors have been so well learned that they appear quickly and without thought on the part of the individual. In other words, they seem to be "mindless" actions. Impulsive behavior, then, is not unusual, out-of-character behavior; it reflects habitual responses that might be rejected by the individual under low arousal or normal conditions.

Toch, Berkowitz, and Zillman all suggest that when experiencing powerful emotional reactions, many people become incapable of considering the consequences of their violent acts. High arousal inhibits cognitive processing to the point that they may not think before acting. The environment and the relevant external stimuli take control over the internal mediation processes that have been weakened by extremely high levels of arousal. Of course, while these "arousal" perspectives explain the most frequent and common violent incidences found in a majority of societies, many serial and mass murderers, as we learned in this chapter, are more thoughtful and calculating in their killings. These multicide offenders tend to fantasize, dream, and cognitively rehearse their violence before actually participating in it.

OVERCONTROLLED AND UNDERCONTROLLED OFFENDERS

One of the most heuristic explanations of violence was advanced by Edwin Megargee (1966), who identified two distinct personalities in the highly assaultive population: the undercontrolled and the chronically overcontrolled aggressive types. The **undercontrolled personality** has few inhibitions against aggressive behavior and frequently engages in violence when frustrated or provoked. Aggression is a behavioral pattern that becomes the habitual response when the person is upset or angry.

By contrast, the chronically **overcontrolled personality** has well-established inhibitions against aggressive behavior and rigidly adheres to them, even in the face of provocation. This person has learned (or been conditioned) about the consequences (real, imagined, or implied) of engaging in violence. The overcontrolled individual is the socialized, or perhaps oversocialized, person who readily associates violations of social mores and regulations dictated by others with potentially punishing consequences. Even more than others, he or she will often say, "If I violate the rules, I will be punished." Recalling Eysenck's dichotomy, we might posit that the introvert is much like the overcontrolled personality, while the extravert exhibits many features of the undercontrolled.

According to Megargee, however, there may come a time when frustration and provocation overwhelm the overcontrolled person. If this happens, he or she may strike out violently, perhaps even exceeding the violence exhibited by the undercontrolled person. The undercontrolled-overcontrolled typology, therefore, suggests that the more brutal and unexpected slayings are often performed by usually inhibited, restricted individuals. It also seems that numerous family mass murders are committed by overcontrolled family members. Thus, neighbors, friends, and relatives are shocked by a homicide committed by a "nice, quiet, well-mannered boy":

> A 16-year-old choir boy described as a "hell of a nice kid" was arraigned here Thursday as funeral services were held for three girls he is accused of stabbing to death.
>
> The girls' bodies were found Monday, face down in a stream in deep woods about a quarter of a mile from their homes.
>
> The state medical examiner said two of the girls were stabbed 40 times each and the third eight times. The death weapon was believed to be a hunting knife. (Tom Stuckey, Associated Press release, October 14, 1977)

In an empirical test of Megargee's hypothesis, Blackburn (1968) divided a group of violent offenders into extreme assaultives and moderate assaultives. *Extreme assaultives* were defined as those convicted of murder, manslaughter, or attempted murder. *Moderate assaultives* included persons who had wounded with intent to cause serious bodily harm, or who had maliciously wounded or assaulted. On the basis of personality measures, extreme assaultives were significantly more introverted, conforming, and overcontrolled and less hostile than moderate assaultives. Moreover, their extreme aggressive behaviors had occurred only after prolonged or repeated provocation (real or imagined).

In another study (Tupin, Mahar, & Smith, 1973), convicted murderers with a history of violent offenses were found to have a much higher incidence of hyperactivity, fighting, temper tantrums, and other extraverted features during childhood than a comparable group of murderers without previous criminal records of violence. These "sudden murderers"—those without a previous record—were also found in other clinical studies to be introverted and plagued by feelings of inadequacy, loneliness, and frustration (e.g., Weiss, Lamberti, & Blackburn, 1960; Blackburn, Weiss, & Lamberti, 1960). These are all features of the overcontrolled personality type.

Lee, Zimbardo, and Bertholf (1977) reported a limited but pertinent study using a small group of nineteen murderers. Ten were classified as "sudden murderers" because their background reflected no other criminal offenses, while nine were regarded as habitual offenders with prior arrests for violent acts. The Stanford Shyness Survey and Minnesota Multiphasic Personality Inventory (MMPI) were administered to both groups. Eight of the ten sudden murderers indicated they were "shy" on the Stanford Scale, compared to only one of the nine habitual offenders. According to MMPI results, the sudden murderer group tended to be significantly more overcontrolled and passive than the habitual offender group, who tended to be more undercontrolled and assertive. These results combined with other observations suggested to the researchers that people who are overcontrolled are capable of more extreme violence when "inner restraints" break down than are individuals who hold their behavior under looser controls.

At present, there is some evidence to suggest that violent offenders may differ along a continuum of undercontrolled-overcontrolled, with most at the polar ends of the continuum. Moreover, we could further hypothesize that undercontrolled violent offenders will be the habitual criminals. Overcontrolled offenders, who usually do not have criminal records, are more likely to engage in one quick, highly violent or murderous episode.

More recent evidence, however, indicates that undercontrols and overcontrols are found in the nonviolent populations about as often as found in violent populations (Henderson, 1983). This finding implies that the Megargee schema may not offer as much in explaining the various types of violence as originally expected. Furthermore, the over- and undercontrolled dimension does not fully account for the role of situational parameters. For example, persons who are passive and unassertive are more likely to experience intense frustrations and to find themselves in many situations where they feel threatened, insecure, and powerless. The Lee-Zimbardo-Bertholf group (1977) tried to relate this lack of social and verbal skills to the sudden murderer, who is typically a shy individual without the necessary interpersonal skills to assert himself in social situations. Obviously, however, most shy people do not become sudden murderers.

When people lack the skills and strategies to modify at least some of their social situations, feelings of helplessness usually result. These feelings are in turn likely to provoke one of two response patterns: approach (attack) or avoidance (withdrawal). The withdrawal response, as theorized by Martin Seligman (1975), is often called reactive depression or **learned helplessness**. The person feels there is nothing that can be done about his or her predicament, so why bother? This response pattern is vividly illustrated by powerless people living under dire poverty conditions, who perceive that they have little opportunity for change—a life without hope.

On the other hand, an alternative response is to attack, to lash out in desperation, especially if a person believes this response pattern will be effective in improving his or her circumstances. The sudden murderers, who have been passive and pushed around all their lives, may be resorting to one final attempt to change what is happening to them. Their homicidal violence may be a desperate response to gain immediate control over their lives, without consideration for the future consequences of their act. An interesting question might be posed at this point: Which is more adaptive under seemingly hopeless conditions, remaining depressed and hopeless, committing suicide, or doing something violent in a desperate attempt to change things?

COGNITIVE SELF-REGULATION AND VIOLENCE

The subject of impulsive behavior brings us to what some social learning and cognitive theorists call **self-regulatory mechanisms**. Psychological research is finding that this may be an extremely important factor in violent behavior. According to social learning theory (e.g., Bandura, 1983) and social cognition theory (Bandura, 1986, 1989), we are able to exercise considerable cognitive control over our behavior. Cognitive capacity enables us to transcend the present and think about the future as well as the past, even in the absence of immediate environmental cues. This conceptual thinking ability lets us guide our own behavior by thinking about its possible outcomes. However, circumstances sometimes weaken cognitive control and facilitate impulsive actions. Under certain conditions, therefore, our actions are directed more by external stimuli than by cognitive self-regulatory mechanisms.

The self-regulatory process presumes the development and refinement of cognitive structures and concepts, which is learning. As we stated earlier, the world as we know it is based on our cognitive structures, which are nonspecific but organized representations of prior experiences. Some people possess more structures than others, and some deviate from what the social mainstream regards as "accurate" structures of the world and human nature. People with many sophisticated structures can evaluate behavior in more complex ways than can people with few, crude structures. For example, someone with a large storehouse of sophisticated concepts would be less inclined to label a murderer simply as "sick" or "an animal," but see the individual as a complex of different beliefs and motives.

Under normal circumstances, we perceive, interpret, compare, and act on the basis of these structures, which we will refer to as personal standards. If we do not like what we are doing, we can change our behavior, justify it, or try to stop thinking about it. We can also reward and punish ourselves for our conduct. Self-punishment is expressed as guilt or remorse following actions we consider foreign to our standards. In most instances, however, we prefer self-reinforcement to punishment; therefore, we behave in ways that correspond to our cognitive structures. We anticipate the feelings of guilt we will experience for alien actions, and thus we restrain ourselves. "Anticipatory self-condemning reactions for violating personal standards ordinarily serve as self-deterrents against reprehensible acts" (Bandura, 1983, p. 30). Therefore, each of us develops personal standards or codes of conduct that are maintained by self-reinforcement or self-punishment, as well as by external reinforcement and punishment.

Our standards may be built around simplistic beliefs that "There is a sucker in every crowd," or "People are basically mean and brutal," or "The surest route to success is to take care of number one." People who have adopted the "me first" approach and are convinced that rigorous competition and aggression are the best strategies for achieving success may find that aggression—even violent behavior—is a source of self-reinforcement and pride (Toch, 1977). In the extreme, "number one" individuals lack self-reprimands for aggression and harmful conduct. Their personal standards about human nature are a built-in justification for their cruel acts.

Standards are not confined to individuals, but may be characteristic of entire cultures and societies. Some cultures, subcultures, or groups try to develop ethical and moral standards of conduct in their members. We might ask at this point to what extent American society cultivates nonviolent behavior.

Relating all of this specifically to aggression and violence, we can see that personal and group standards dictate much of our behavior. If one's philosophy is that "life is cheap," and if insensitive conduct is the norm, violence can become a way of life. Some people, therefore, are cruel and violent not necessarily to receive reward from the external environment, but because violence reflects their internal standard and implicit theory of human nature. Others, perhaps the majority, have adopted standards and have built cognitive structures that do not condone hurtful or reprehensible conduct.

To some extent, we have oversimplified self-regulatory mechanisms theory in an effort to introduce some of its concepts. Self-regulation does not invariably operate across all situations. Otherwise, how do we explain destructive and reprehensible conduct perpetrated by apparently decent, moral people over the centuries in the name of religious principles and righteous ideologies? What, if anything, justifies deliberate, planned large-scale violence such as bombing or war?

What about terrorism in the name of some higher principle? How do we explain mob violence, where seemingly good people appear to be swept along by their emotions or by the crowd? Why don't self-regulatory mechanisms operate then, when they are so needed?

Social learning theory explains some of this by hypothesizing that under certain circumstances self-regulatory processes become *disengaged* from conduct. "In the social learning analysis, moral people perform culpable acts through processes that disengage evaluative self-reactions for such conduct..." (Bandura, 1983, p. 31). This disengagement may be what takes place in impulsive violence. As described by Berkowitz (1983) and Zillman (1983), high levels of emotional arousal take our attention away from our internal mechanisms of control. When we become extremely angry, for example, we often say and do things we later regret. We feel upset, remorseful, and guilty, and we wish we could take back our words and actions. If we had carefully considered and evaluated the consequences of our behavior, we would probably have acted differently. But under the heat of emotion, our self-regulatory system, with all its standards and values, was held in abeyance. As we get older, however, we generally learn from experience to pay closer attention to our internal control mechanisms, and we engage in fewer impulsive outbursts. This "mellowing" feature may partly account for the lower rates of impulsive violence as age increases.

Regardless of our personal standards against violence or doing harm to others, therefore, we all may occasionally engage in harmful or even violent conduct. When this happens, we use several approaches to convince ourselves of the "rightness" of our actions. We may feel, for example, that under certain conditions some people need to be taught a lesson. An errant child may be hit; an experimental subject may be shocked; a murderer may be executed in the service of justice. The problematic logic of these explanations becomes evident when they are turned about. From a political terrorist's perspective, acts of violence are justified if they accomplish a greater good, like freeing society from a tyrant. Ideally, then, we should very narrowly define conditions under which physical aggression and violence might be justified (e.g., to save another human life).

We may also neutralize our internal standards to some extent by concluding, "Others are doing it, many of them much more than I am." "Most people cheat on their income tax returns. It's part of the game." Certainly, this perspective is relevant to participants engaged in corporate or white-collar crime, a topic we will return to in Chapter 11. In addition, as we saw in the chapter on juvenile delinquency, some groups neutralize their criminal conduct by removing from it the onus of "badness." In fact, engaging in the "bad" conduct may increase one's status within the group.

Another way in which we may downplay our internal standards, especially those against violence, is by convincing ourselves that some individuals are less than human, more animal-like than most. This approach works nicely if we accept the difference-in-degree position on human nature. In other words, we may **dehumanize** people who commit terribly cruel and heinous murders, in effect seeing them as closer to animals than most other people. Some people justify capital punishment on the basis that some criminals are subhuman. Dehumanization helps explain the numerous lynchings of African Americans in U.S. history and the treatment of the Jews in Nazi Germany. In war, we dehumanize the enemy by using derogatory epithets. Like justifying the "rightness" of violence, however, dehumanization also works from both perspectives. Thus, the mass or serial murderer and the individual who continually engages in assaultive behavior, as we have seen, views victims as objects divested of humanity. The offender feels little remorse for any suffering inflicted and does not worry about anticipatory self-punishment. Research has shown, however, that it becomes more difficult to behave cruelly toward others as they become personalized and humanized (Bandura, Underwood, & Fromson, 1975). In other words, if an assailant becomes acquainted with a potential victim, there is less likelihood that he or she will be cruel. This would seem especially true of crimes where killing the victim is not the primary goal.

Finally, we may also disengage our personal standards from our conduct when we are told to do something reprehensible by a legitimate authority. When someone who possesses legitimate power commands us to do something, we are, in a sense, relieved of personal responsibility for the conduct, even if the conduct is alien to our personal standards. The Milgram obedience study discussed in Chapter 4 is a good illustration of this.

In sum, the self-regulatory system we develop is not invariant or automatic, but dynamic and subject to certain experiences and circumstances. Moreover, many events are ambiguous and do not fit readily into our existing cognitive templates. Under these conditions, we are more likely to seek clues from outside sources. Nevertheless, the value of the self-regulatory system is its tendency to guide our behavior toward what we believe is the right thing to do in a particular situation. The more we believe in our internal standards, the less prone we will be to rely on outside sources, even under stress or pressure situations. This suggests that the best internal standards are those we have developed ourselves, rather than those imposed or advocated by an external group, which we embrace only for convenience or for appearances.

Interestingly, women are more likely to see aggression as a breakdown of self-regulatory mechanisms than are men (Campbell, Muncer, & Coyle, 1992). To women, aggressive behavior "... represents a personal failure to adhere to standards of behaviour which they (and others) set for themselves, and consequently they view it negatively" (Campbell et al., 1992, p. 98). Conversely, men are more likely to see aggression as a means of imposing control and dominance over others, and, therefore, regard aggressive behavior as more positive.

Fortunately, most people have developed an internal standard that to wantonly harm another person is wrong. Therefore, the reason that a vast majority of people do not engage in violent behavior is not simply because of a classically conditioned reflex. Rather, it is most likely because they have adopted a belief system that subscribes to the view that it is wrong to harm another human being, at least without just cause. Of course, the human tendency to justify one's behavior—the just-cause argument—is often inseparable from the most heinous violence in human history. We justify large-scale organized violence (wars), claiming we must protect ourselves, family, and way of life from the brutal (less than human) enemy.

The next section focuses on mob behavior and what happens to the self-regulatory mechanisms of normally gentle people caught up in a madding crowd. The crowd, it seems, often robs the individual of his or her identity, and consequently, his or her usual reliance on personal standards of conduct. Some of the most violent behavior is exhibited, not by single individuals, but by excited groups, especially large ones. Physical assaults that occur in the midst of riots or demonstrations, vigilante-instigated lynchings or beatings, gang rapes, and public stonings all illustrate this mob violence.

DEINDIVIDUATION AND CROWD VIOLENCE

The powerful effects of crowds on individual behavior has interested social scientists since the early 1900s. Crowd influence is usually studied under the rubric *collective behavior*, which includes riots, gang rapes, panics, lynchings, demonstrations, and revolutions. For our purposes, we are concerned with collective behavior only as it affects the instigation and maintenance of violence.

One of the first theorists of collective behavior was Gustave LeBon, whose 1896 book *The Crowd* is regarded as the classic study of groups. Because his views were colored by the French Revolution, LeBon did not take kindly to individual behavior swayed by the crowd. Humans in a crowd are like a herd of animals, he said, easily swayed or spooked. LeBon believed that those who normally are non-violent and law-abiding are capable of the kind of violence, intolerance, and general cruelty found in the most primitive savages. The person enmeshed in the mob loses sensibility and the ability to reason, and forfeits his or her own mind to the crowd. The collective mind is dangerously brutal and destructive to people and property. According to LeBon, even educated people become simple-minded and irrational under its influence. Essentially, LeBon claimed, each person comes under the control of the reflexive "spinal cord" rather than the cerebral cortex.

Most of us have seen dramatizations of a "berserk" mob clamoring for the destruction of some political, social, or physical institution or for swift "justice" for an individual or group. Descriptions of mob actions often liken them to brush fires that grow in intensity and are quickly out of control. However, since true mob actions are naturally occurring and spontaneous events, it is difficult to place them under the scrutiny of scientific, systematic investigation. The processes involved in mob action are still not well understood, therefore. Some social psychologists (e.g., Zimbardo, 1970; Diener, 1980) have attempted laboratory studies of mob or group violence, generally by approximating conditions that might bring out aggression and positing that, if allowed to continue, the aggression would likely result in violence. Obviously, they must stop far short of actual violence, so whether it would have occurred remains speculative. The procedure of trying to mimic an event under laboratory conditions is called a **simulation**.

Zimbardo (1970) believes that deindividuation accounts for much of the tendency of otherwise "tame" individuals to engage in antisocial, violent behavior. Recall from Chapter 4 that deindividuation includes a reduction in feelings of personal distinctiveness, identifiability, and personal responsibility. Furthermore, in a crowd the threshold of normally restrained behavior is lowered. In other words, people feel anonymous, less responsible for their behavior, and less inhibited. According to Zimbardo, these conditions encourage the antisocial behavior associated with selfishness, greed, hostility, lust, cruelty, and destruction.

In one widely cited experiment, Zimbardo manipulated two variables, feelings of anonymity and features about the victim. He randomly assigned female college students to deindividuation and "identifiable" groups. Subjects in the deindividuation group wore shapeless white lab coats and hoods over their heads and worked in dimly lit conditions. The experimenters avoided using their names. By contrast, participants in the identifiable groups felt anything but anonymous. They wore large name tags, were greeted by name, worked under fully illuminated conditions, and wore their own clothes with no added lab coats or hoods.

Subjects were told the project was set up to study empathy. The real purpose, of course, was to study the relationship between deindividuation and aggression. Each subject listened to a five-minute recorded interview between her future "victim" and the experimenter. Some victims were portrayed as warm, sincere, honest persons, while others were obnoxious, self-centered, conceited, and critical. After each interview, the subjects were allowed to administer shock to the interviewees they had heard on tape. They were allowed to observe the reactions of their victims by way of a one-way mirror. Aggressive behavior of the subjects was measured by the length of time a painful electrical shock was administered. "Victims"—who actually received no shock—were trained to writhe, twist, and grimace.

Recall now that Zimbardo was manipulating two variables, anonymity (loss of personal identity) and features of the victim (environmental stimuli). Thus, some *subjects* were hooded, others were well identified. Some *victims* were pleasant and likable, others were obnoxious. Zimbardo reasoned that members of the deindividuation group would administer shocks of longer duration because of the diffusion of responsibility and loss of personal identity. He also hypothesized that victim features would be irrelevant, because the heightened arousal experienced under deindividuation would interfere with ability to discriminate between the victims. Put another way, the excitement and resulting arousal engendered by shocking someone without the threat of any repercussions would prevent discernment of the target (the person receiving the shock).

One additional hypothesis was tested. Zimbardo predicted that subjects in the deindividuation group would administer longer shocks as the experiment progressed. He believed the act of administering shock without responsibility would be exciting and reinforcing for its own sake (what he called "affective proprioceptive feedback"). Zimbardo predicted that members of the deindividuation group would increase the duration of shock administered to the victim as the experiment progressed. In brief, the person finds that doing the antisocial behavior feels "so good" each time she does it that the behavior builds on itself in intensity (vigor) and frequency.

Results of the experiment supported all three hypotheses. The deindividuation group shocked victims twice as long as the identifiable group. The deindividuation group also administered the same levels of shock, regardless of the victim's personality features. And finally, this group shocked for longer periods as the experiment progressed. "Under conditions specified as deindividuating, these sweet, normally mild-mannered college girls shocked another girl almost every time they had an opportunity to do so, sometimes for as long as they were allowed, and it did not matter whether or not that fellow student was a nice girl who didn't deserve to be hurt," Zimbardo concluded (1970, p. 170).

Essentially, Zimbardo argues that deindividuated aggression is not controlled by the social environment; it is unresponsive to both the situation and the state or characteristics of the victim. That is, the high arousal generated by the excitement of a crowd reduces both (1) a person's private self-awareness, and (2) his or her ability to discriminate among external stimuli, such as victim characteristics. The participant is no longer guided by self-regulatory mechanisms and is "blind" to such stimuli as the victim's distress or discomfort. The aggressor loses individuality to the collective mind of the crowd; he or she neither feels compassion nor considers the circumstances. The victim may plead, beg, cry, or scream, but these stimuli will have little effect on the crowd behavior. Even a prestigious and powerful authority figure may be unable to stop the violence once self-identity is obliterated by the furor of the crowd.

Zimbardo's research design, like that of Milgram, has been criticized extensively for its questionable use of subject deception and shock (albeit simulated) and its focus on the negative aspects of human behavior. In a sense, these types of experiments constitute a form of psychological entrapment; would people really act this way if not prompted by an experimenter? In the wake of such experiments, the National Institute of Mental Health, the American Psychological Association, and other organizations have adopted ethical guidelines that are applied to the funding and approval of research. Experiments like Zimbardo's, therefore, are unlikely to be replicated. Nevertheless, their possible implications cannot be ignored.

Diener (1980) disagrees with the tenets of Zimbardo's deindividuation theory, postulating that deindividuated behavior is responsive to situational or victim characteristics. He believes that a person's normal self-regulatory behavior is reduced by the unusual and exciting activity of the crowd, and that this reduced private self-awareness creates an *internal* state of deindividuation. Since the individual has trouble retrieving his or her standards of appropriate conduct, he or she becomes more responsive to environmental cues (Prentice-Dunn & Rogers, 1982, 1983). In crowds, people do report a strong loss of individual identity, an overwhelming tendency to concentrate on the moment rather than the future, and substantially altered thinking and emotion (Prentice-Dunn & Rogers, 1983). They become less aware of thoughts, moods, bodily states, and other internal processes. Think of the athlete caught up in the excitement of the game, who continues to play while seriously injured. After the game, the athlete might exclaim about a fractured arm, "It didn't feel that serious!"

According to Diener, because deindividuated individuals do not pay attention to their internal processes, including their self-regulatory capabilities, they depend more on environmental cues for behavioral direction. Thus, when aggressive and violent cues are present, they are far more likely than usual to engage in violence. It is Diener's contention that if the victim of a mob action could, in some way, be "humanized," the crowd might stop its brutality. In other words, perpetrators' attention should be directed toward the victim rather than the violence being displayed by other actors. Diener also believes that participants in a mob action can be made to pay closer attention to their internal regulation norms. His hypothesis deserves to be tested by further research. Of course, whether the cries and pleas of the victim during an attack actually could alter the crowd behavior is a question unlikely to be answered by laboratory research. Furthermore, because the theories of Zimbardo and Diener are based on laboratory studies, we cannot conclude that they generalize to actual situations. They do, however, suggest possible explanations for violent mob behavior.

SUMMARY AND CONCLUSIONS

This chapter took a closer look at specific types of criminal homicide. We also examined the investigative methods and criminal profiling used to identify offenders, particularly serial offenders. Multiple murder was the focus in the early parts of the chapter. Although these offenses are rare, the social and emotional impact they have on a community (and society in general) are substantial. We reviewed the empirical data and professional observations on serial, spree, and mass murder.

We also carefully reviewed the phenomenon of satanic cults and the surprisingly common belief in our society that these cults are involved in a significant amount of ritual abuse and murder through human sacrifice. Investigations and empirical research have revealed no support for claims by certain groups that these cults are involved systematically in widespread ritual abuse or human sacrifice.

The latter part of the chapter focused on psychological explanations of violence in general. That is, when we survey the vast majority of violent crime, we find very little mystery or intriguing characteristics. Serial and mass murder are clearly out of the ordinary of everyday violence. The psychological perspective suggests that three central issues surround *common* violence: (1) self-control, as dictated by self-regulatory mechanisms; (2) emotional arousal; and (3) individual reference points for behavioral guidance, which may be either internal or external. Violence is most often committed while the participants are under very high levels of emotional arousal, particularly anger. High arousal seems to reduce the ability to attend to internal standards of conduct and general self-awareness. Furthermore, high arousal seems to make people feel less responsible for their actions; they often claim, "I don't know what came over me," or "I couldn't help it." In short, high arousal renders people more susceptible to "mindless" behaviors and places them under the influence of external stimuli or events.

Self-regulatory mechanisms develop through socialization and personal beliefs about what is right or appropriate, wrong or inappropriate. Under normal conditions, self-regulatory mechanisms control behavior by providing cognitive templates for what is proper behavior for a specific situation. The effect of arousal on these self-regulatory mechanisms appears especially important in explaining street or domestic violence, where the violence is spontaneous, highly charged, and often used as a way of settling personal conflicts.

Individual construct systems are highly similar to the self-regulation process, but refer in this context to the human ability to justify or neutralize conduct, no matter how reprehensible. Self-regulation refers to behavioral control; the construct system enables a person to perform an act and deal with it later. Human beings, with their intricate cognitive equipment, have an uncanny knack for neutralizing, disregarding, minimizing, rationalizing, and misjudging their deeds. We have an enormous capacity for disengaging our beliefs and our internal standards from our actions. Bandura (1983) lists six common disengagement practices we use for dealing with our own reprehensible, antisocial conduct. It is instructive to examine each of these strategies here.

First, people do not ordinarily engage in antisocial conduct until they have justified to themselves the rightness or morality of their actions. Reprehensible acts can be made honorable through cognitive restructuring. Thus, a distressed father, convinced that he must save his family from the evil of the world, kills his children, his wife, and then himself. In essence, he reconstructed his construct system to fit what he believed was the right thing to do under the circumstances. Another example is that of a moral young man who believes killing is wrong and who voluntarily goes to war to protect his country. At first, these two actions may seem to have nothing in common. However, they both represent cognitive restructuring.

A second disengagement practice—related to the first—is that of people convincing themselves that their violent acts are really trivial and not all that bad compared to what others have done. In war we convince ourselves that the atrocities committed by the enemy are far worse than anything we do. A rapist might convince himself that rape is not really that serious, since no "real" physical harm comes to the victim.

A third strategy involves the power of language. One of the costs of human intellectual ability is the considerable power of words; they allow us to justify our actions with relative ease. We use euphemisms to neutralize reprehensible behavior. For example, intelligence manuals use words like neutralize and terminate instead of assassinate and kill. The euphemisms carry less onus and cause less disruption to moral beliefs. In the chapter on juvenile delinquency, we noted that youth subcultures employ various euphemisms to neutralize their antisocial acts.

A fourth strategy—one most commonly found in group violence—is the diffusion of responsibility. Statements that best typify this practice include: "I was just following orders," "I was just following the crowd," and "The executive board decided that it was in the best interest of the economy (and the company) to continue production, despite some risk to the health of others." These assertions have the effect of displacing responsibility for one's actions to others, or to forces outside oneself.

A fifth strategy is to not even think about the consequences of one's actions. Here, people convince themselves that the consequences are not important. Alternately, they manage to detach themselves from the aftermath of violent actions. For example, the bombardier or the person who pushes the button that will release lethal chemicals onto a civilian population is not only following orders (diffusion of responsibility) but also is probably not allowing himself to think about the tragedy that will result.

Finally, the sixth practice is to dehumanize the victim. "She was loose and got what she deserved." "He was scum." The enemy are labeled "gooks" or something akin to vicious animals. Dehumanization removes all the human, dignifying qualities from the victim or intended victim. As Bandura (1983, p. 32) points out: "Many conditions of contemporary life are conducive to dehumanization. Bureaucratization, automation, urbanization, and high social mobility lead people to relate to each other in anonymous, impersonal ways." These impersonal, dehumanizing aspects of life facilitate violence and make living with it possible.

10

SEXUAL OFFENSES

Sexual behavior in many societies is a subject fraught with moral codes, taboos, norm expectations, religious injunctions, myths, and unscientific conclusions. In the United States, the daring venture of Albert Kinsey and his colleagues in publishing the scientific evidence they had gathered at the Institute for Sexual Research dispelled numerous myths and corrected fallacies about sex. Many still linger, however, especially with reference to the sex offender, for whom society has little tolerance. Moreover, society often does not distinguish between types of sex offenses. "Degenerates" who expose themselves to passersby or watch unsuspecting women undressing are as likely to be feared or to attract disgust and anger as are rapists and child molesters. Often, the community clamors for the strict and speedy prosecution of the offender, who is considered a deranged or evil person (or animal) driven by some inner sinister force, and from whom citizens must be protected.

Sexual offenders are frequently viewed as a homogeneous class of individuals. Research shows, however, that they vary widely in the frequency and type of sexual activity they engage in, and they differ in personal attributes like age, background, personality, race, religion, beliefs, attitudes, and interpersonal skills (Knight, Rosenberg, & Schneider, 1985). There is no single profile that encompasses a majority of sex offenders. The features of their crimes also differ markedly among offenders, including time and place, the gender and age of the victim, the degree of planning the offense, and the amount of violence used or intended (Knight, Rosenberg, & Schneider, 1985).

The causes of sexual offending are neither simple nor straightforward. As the knowledge from systematic study accumulates, it is clear that this behavior is influenced by multiple, interactive factors. Past learning experiences, cognitive expectations and beliefs, conditioning, environmental stimuli, and reinforcement contingencies (both rewards and punishments) are all involved. In this chapter we will review the major research findings on potential causal factors involved in the crimes of rape, child molestation, and exhibitionism. We will also discuss the phenomenon of fetishes, which sometimes leads to minor criminal activity.

Some studies (e.g., Revitch & Schlesinger, 1988) reveal that many sex offenders are not prone to violence or physical cruelty, but rather are timid, shy, and socially inhibited. While this may be correct for a large segment of pedophiles, it is not for rapists, whose attacks often have strong aggressive features. In fact, their sexual aggression can be divided into at least two major categories: instrumental and expressive. **Instrumental sexual aggression** is when the sexual offender uses just enough coercion to gain compliance from his victim. In **expressive sexual aggression**, the offender's *primary aim* is to harm the victim physically as well as psychologically. In some cases the expressive aggression is "eroticized" in that the offender becomes sexually aroused in the presence of physical or psychological brutality.

Regardless of the sex offender's characteristics, motivations, and method of attack or coercion, the social and psychological costs to victims and their families are immeasurable and often devastating. A survey of 3,132 households in the Los Angeles Epidemiologic Catchment Area (ECA) study illustrates this very well. Researchers found that over 13 percent of the individuals interviewed had been victims of sexual assault at least once in their lifetimes (Burnam, Stein, Golding, Siegel, Sorenson, Forsythe, & Telles, 1988; Sorenson, Stein, Siegel, Golding, & Burnam, 1987; Siegel, Sorenson, Golding, Burnam, & Stein, 1987). Two-thirds of the sexually assaulted subjects reported two or more assaults. Moreover, lifetime sexual assault was more frequently reported by women (16.7 percent) than men (9.4 percent). Thirteen percent of the victims were first assaulted between the ages of six and ten, 19 percent between eleven and fifteen, 34 percent between sixteen and twenty, and 15 percent between twenty-one and twenty-five. The experience of being sexually assaulted was associated with substantially higher risks for later onset of serious, self-destructive depression, substance abuse, numerous fears and inhibiting anxieties, and a variety of major interpersonal problems. Overall, the ECA project found that both male and female victims of sexual assault are two to four times more likely to develop serious psychological problems than nonvictims. In this chapter we will focus on the two sexual offenses that are most troubling to society and most tragic to victims—rape and child molestation (pedophilia)—and we will briefly discuss other sexual deviations that may lead to criminal activity.

RAPE

Definitions of rape vary widely from state to state; in many states the term *sexual assault* has replaced rape in the criminal statutes. According to the U.S. Department of Justice, rape is "unlawful sexual intercourse with a female, by force or without legal or factual consent" (U.S. Department of Justice, 1988, p. 2). The UCR defines rape somewhat differently, distinguishing forcible from statutory rape or rape by fraud. **Forcible rape** is "the carnal knowledge of a female, forcibly and against her will" (FBI, 1997, p. 395). It includes assaults and attempts to commit rape by force or threat of force. **Statutory rape** without force is excluded. Statutory rape is the carnal knowledge of a girl, with or without her consent. The critical factor is the age of the victim, an arbitrary legal cutoff point below which a girl is believed not to have the maturity to consent to intercourse or understand the consequences. Age limits vary from state to state, but most set the limit at sixteen or eighteen. Thus, if an adult male engages in sexual relations with a minor female, he may be convicted of statutory rape. **Rape by fraud** is having sexual relations with a consenting adult female under fraudulent conditions. Among the most frequently cited examples is that of the psychotherapist who has sexual intercourse with a patient under the guise of offering treatment.

Many in the general population (including the victims themselves) do not define sexual attacks as rape unless the assailant is a stranger. Thus, if the victim is sexually assaulted by a husband or a boyfriend, she may not report the incident. Criminal justice officials, as well as the general public, often feel marital or date rapes are unimportant because they are believed to happen so rarely, compared to stranger rape, or to be less psychologically traumatic to the victim. Criminal prosecutors, for example, admit they are reluctant to prosecute marital or date rape cases because of concerns that juries will not believe that a woman could be raped by a husband or male friend (Kilpatrick, Best, Saunders, & Veronen, 1988). However, in a survey of the general population conducted by Kilpatrick and colleagues (1988), subjects who had been raped identified their husbands as assailants in 24 percent of the cases and male friends in 17 percent of the cases. These data suggest that over 40 percent of the rapes were committed by husbands or dates, a significant and frequently overlooked statistic in the tabulation of rape.

The classification and study of rape offenses is also hampered by the fact that jurisdictions vary widely in their definitions of rape, often disagreeing with the Department of Justice or UCR guidelines. In the mid-1970s, the National Institute of Law Enforcement and Criminal Justice funded extensive surveys of law enforcement agencies that illustrate these differences (Chappell, 1977a, 1977b). Most agencies reported that vaginal penetration was the criterion for a *minimum* alleged offense to qualify as rape. Over half of the law enforcement agencies surveyed also required evidence of both penetration and force, while another third required evidence of penetration, force, a weapon, and/or resistance by the victim. As might be expected, the average number of rapes reported by the latter agencies was significantly lower than the average number reported by other law enforcement agencies accepting less demanding criteria.

Prosecutors require more stringent evidence than law enforcement agencies before accepting an incident as a probable rape. Most of the 150 prosecutors polled in the Chappell survey set four threshold criteria for filing a complaint of forcible rape: (1) evidence of penetration; (2) lack of victim consent; (3) threat of force; and (4) female gender of the victim. It is intriguing to note, however, that 92 percent of the prosecutors sampled did not have formal guidelines for filing a charge of forcible rape. Therefore, their survey responses were more likely to reflect their own judgments about the minimum threshold requirements for initiating action against an alleged offender.

Although some agencies follow the UCR guidelines for classifying rape, many adopt different classification systems. About one-third have more stringent requirements, one-fifth less stringent. Some jurisdictions distinguish between attempted rape and forcible rape. Many, especially the larger ones, include different degrees of forcible rape (e.g., first- and second-degree). In addition, the term sexual assault may be used rather than rape. In cases involving multiple offenses (e.g., rape plus burglary, homicide, or robbery), the offense considered the more "serious" takes precedence and is more likely to be tabulated in the offense statistics, while the "lesser" crime committed at the same time is not reported. For instance, since homicide is considered to be a more serious crime than forcible rape, homicide-rapes traditionally are tabulated under homicide and not under rape. Therefore, because of these wide variations, we must view statistical comparisons and information pertaining to the "average" rape very cautiously.

INCIDENCE AND PREVALENCE

From all indications, the United States has the highest incidence of rape in the world. During the past decade and according to the UCR, "official" incidence of reported rape in the United States has ranged between 65 and 84 for every 100,000 women (U.S. Department of Justice, 1993). This rate represents 5 to 8 percent of the total violent crime rate. Of course, we must recognize that the actual rape rate is greatly underestimated, partly because of some of the problems listed in the previous section, and partly because of the ordeal women must go through just to report the incident. Victimization studies offer a revealing contrast to the official rates. Russell (1983) selected at random and interviewed 930 women living in the San Francisco area. She learned that 175 of them (19 percent) reported at least one completed extramarital rape and 284 (13 percent) reported at least one attempted extramarital rape. Fifty percent of those reporting these incidents said they had been raped or attacked more than once, and only 8 percent said they had reported any rape incident to law enforcement authorities. A study by Hindelang and his associates (Hindelang, Dunn, Sutton, & Aumick, 1976), designed to gather victimization rates on randomly selected households, found that only about one out of every four forcible or attempted rapes were reported to law enforcement agencies. A study of hitchhike rape estimates that over two-thirds go unreported (Nelson & Amir, 1975). Based on a national sample of college students from thirty-two U.S. colleges and universities, Koss and her colleagues (Koss, Gidycz, & Wisniewski, 1987) discovered that about 28 percent of the college women had been victims of rape or attempted rape (as defined by the UCR). More startling, however, was the finding that virtually none of the incidents were reported to the police and thus were not recorded in official crime statistics. Based on their data, Koss estimates that the victimization rate for women is 3,800 per 100,000, a rate drastically different from the official rates of 65 to 75 per 100,000.

Additional victimization data indicate that there is approximately a one in five chance that a woman will be raped at some time during her lifetime (Furby, Weinrott, & Blackshaw, 1989). If we include *attempted* rape, the odds may be three to one (Russell & Howell, 1983). As mentioned previously, a surprising number of women are sexually victimized while on a date. Approximately 22 percent of college women surveyed indicated they had been subjected to a forced sexual encounter (e.g., fondling, oral sex, or intercourse) by a date at some point in their lives (Yegidis, 1986; Dull & Giacopassi, 1987). Rapaport and Burkhart (1984) found that 15 percent of a sample of college men acknowledged that they had obtained sexual intercourse against their dates' will. Koss, Gidycz, & Wisniewski (1987) report that about 8 percent of their sample of nearly three thousand college men admitted raping or attempting to rape their dates.

For several years, data suggested that rape reporting by victims was on the increase. Chappell (1977a) found that rates of reported rape more than doubled over a ten-year period, and others noted that the numbers continued to increase steadily until 1993 (see Figure 10-1). However, between 1994 and 1996, the reporting of forcible rape in the United States has decreased slightly. For example, the rate per hundred thousand inhabitants decreased 2.7 percent, decreasing from a rate of 37.1 per hundred thousand in 1995 to 36.1 per hundred thousand in 1996 (FBI, 1997). It is too early to tell why the rate has been decreasing in recent years, and probably it is a combination of things rather than any single factor.

The increase in reporting until 1994 probably reflected a higher level of community awareness about rape, the influence of the women's movement, increased training and sensitivity of law enforcement officers, and the gradual revision of statutes and procedures that make the gathering of legal evidence less stressful for the victim. In Chappell's national survey of 150 prosecutors' offices (Chappell, 1977b), 61 percent of the respondents believed that the increased reporting rape rate reflected a change in public attitude toward crime. Another third of the prosecutors felt that the increase was a result of the heightened sensitivity of the criminal justice system. It is interesting to note, however, that a vast majority of the prosecutors felt that the increased rape rate also reflected to some extent a "general pattern of increased violence" in America.

The psychological effects on the rape victim, both during and after the assault,

Figure 10-1   Forcible Rape in the United States
(Source: U.S. Bureau of Justice Statistics, 1996.)

are often severe and incalculable. She is frequently victimized twice—by the assailant and by the criminal justice process. Upon reporting the assault, she is expected to recall and describe personally stressful and humiliating events in vivid detail for law enforcement personnel who are often men. She is also required to undergo a medical examination to establish physical evidence of penetration and use of physical force.

If the victim is able to withstand these stressful conditions, which are sometimes exacerbated by negative reactions from parents, husband, friends, and even by threats from the assailant, she then must prepare for the courtroom, where her privacy is invaded and her credibility may be attacked. Rape trials are usually covered extensively by the press, although most news organizations do not reveal the victim's name or photograph her. Her reputation, however, is especially vulnerable. Ninety-two percent of the prosecutors surveyed by Chappell asserted that victim credibility was one of the most important elements in convincing juries to convict for forcible rape. Therefore, the defense often has concentrated on the victim's prior sexual history to destroy her credibility and to portray her as a demirep. The strategy of disparaging the victim in this way has come under attack in recent years, and many states have revised their evidentiary rules in an attempt to limit the use of a victim's sexual history. Approximately forty states have enacted "rape shield" laws that restrict, to varying degrees, the admissibility of the victim's sexual history into the courtroom (Borgida, 1980). In addition, victim assistants, whose function it is to offer support, give direct services, and advocate for victims, have been instrumental in easing her burden.

Although criminal justice agencies are beginning to be more sensitive to the painful ordeal a victim must go through, the costs are still high. If the woman reports the sexual assault to the police, it means she must devote many hours to the process of the investigation and the subsequent court proceedings (Burt & Katz, 1985). She must bear the costs of missed days of work, childcare, medical expenses for the physical and psychological trauma, and transportation. She may feel a need to change lifestyles, move, and install expensive security systems and locks. Sleeplessness, anxiety, and depression must also be factored into the cost equation. We will discuss these issues in more detail shortly.

SITUATIONAL AND VICTIMIZATION CHARACTERISTICS

The Chappell surveys (1977a, 1977b) found that rapes in large cities are most likely to occur in the victim's residence or, less frequently, outdoors. In cities under a hundred thousand population, and especially in rural areas, they are most likely to occur in motor vehicles, a fact that may reflect the higher frequency of hitchhiking in smaller communities. In fact, hitchhiking (by the victim) accompanied 20 percent of all rapes reported in small cities, compared to 10 percent in large metropolitan areas.

The use of alcohol and other disinhibiting substances is common in rapists. The substance abuse is apparent both in the personal history of the rapist and at the time of the offense. Anywhere between 42 and 90 percent of convicted rapists admit they were under the influence of a disinhibiting substance at the time of the sexual assault, and between 58 and 90 percent exhibit a history of substance abuse (Marques & Nelson, 1989; Pithers, Beal, Armstrong, & Petty, 1989).

Women's fears about being physically harmed in rape are not unfounded. While weapons, especially firearms and knives, are used in only about 25 percent of the reported assaults (U.S. Department of Justice, 1988), about one-fourth of all rape victims sustain injury serious enough to warrant medical attention or hospitalization. *Severe physical injury*, however, is relatively rare, with about 5 percent receiving serious, lasting injury (Williams & Holmes, 1981). Another 39 percent receive minor injury, and 23 percent receive a variety of cuts and bruises (Williams & Holmes, 1981). Further study suggests that women receive more physical and psychological trauma from sexual assault by husbands than by strangers (Kilpatrick et al., 1988). Furthermore, the psychological damage is apparently longer lasting and more damaging, resulting in serious depression, extensive fears, and problems of sexual adjustment.

Victim surveys also indicate that the most commonly used methods of force during date rapes are verbal persuasion, alcohol, or drugs. While weapons are rarely used, physical overpowering (similar to a wrestling match) is commonly reported (Kanin, 1984). Furthermore, data suggest that date rapes occur most frequently in the male's apartment or room, with the next likely location being the female's apartment or room. Very few occur in a car or outside.

Rapists often expect more than vaginal intercourse. In approximately 25 percent of the rapes Chappell studied, the assailant also demanded oral sexual acts; in about 10 percent he demanded both oral and anal sexual acts; in about 6 percent, anal sexual acts only; and in 4 percent other sexual actions. Amir (1971) reported similar patterns.

OFFENDER CHARACTERISTICS

What kind of a person rapes? How did he get that way? Why does he do it? Can the "rapist personality" be easily identified? Are rapists mentally disordered? In this section, we should keep in mind that many studies addressing these questions are based on information obtained from convicted offenders located in prisons, forensic evaluation clinics, or secure psychiatric facilities, a very biased sample, since less than 3 percent of reported rapes in the United States result in a conviction (Battelle Law and Justice Study Committee, 1977).

The most consistent demographic finding is that rapists tend to be young. According to UCR data, over half of those arrested are under age twenty-five, and 80 percent are under age thirty. Henn and his colleagues (Henn, Herjanic, & Vanderpearl, 1976a) reported that 75 percent of those accused of rape and referred to a mental health evaluation team in St. Louis between the years 1952 and 1973 were under age thirty. The Queen's Bench Foundation (1978) found that 70 percent of its sample of seventy-three convicted rapists were under age twenty-five. The National Crime Survey estimates that nearly one-quarter of the rapes or attempted rapes in any given year are committed by offenders between the ages of twelve and twenty. Davis and Leitenberg (1987) found that when both arrest statistics and victim surveys are considered, about 20 percent of all rapes, and about 30 to 50 percent of all cases of child sexual abuse can be attributed to adolescent offenders. In fact, 50 percent of all adult sex offenders report that their first sexual offense occurred during adolescence (Abel, Mittelman, & Becker, 1985).

Another consistent finding is that men accused of and convicted of rape have been in perpetual conflict with society, long before the current rape offense. About one-fourth of those arrested for forcible rape have raped previously, and about one-third have a prior arrest history for violent offenses other than rape (Chappell, 1977a). In a sample of 114 convicted rapists studied by Scully and Marolla (1984), 12 percent had a previous conviction for rape or attempted rape, 39 percent had previous convictions for burglary and robbery, 29 percent for abduction, 25 percent for sodomy, and 11 percent for first- or second-degree murder. Overall, 82 percent had a prior criminal record, but only 23 percent had been convicted of sexual offenses. Gebhard and colleagues (Gebhard, Gagnon, Pomeroy, & Christenson, 1965) reported that 87 percent of their sample of sexual offenders (mostly rapists) had been convicted of some other crime besides their sexual offense prior to age twenty-six.

Occupationally, people arrested for rape tend to come from the so-called blue-collar working class (about 50 percent) and from the ranks of the unemployed (approximately 30 percent). In the Scully and Marolla (1984) study, only 20 percent of all convicted rapists had a high school education or better, and 85 percent came from working-class backgrounds. Very few individuals from the professional or white-collar occupational fields are arrested for rape. A study conducted in England (Wright, 1980) reports that 75 percent of those arrested for rape were in the unskilled working class, and only 2 percent were classified as professional or managerial. Interestingly, when professional people are accused in the United States, their numbers drop precipitously when the rape charge gets to the prosecutor's office, while the other occupational groups remain about the same. At face value, these data suggest that the more affluent or privileged offender is more likely to be filtered out early in the judicial process than the less privileged, less powerful offender.

According to prosecutors, about one-fourth of those accused of rape admitted that the incident was planned and premeditated (Chappell, 1977b). The problem with this statistic, of course, is that most suspects are unwilling to admit premeditation, since it makes the case against them that much stronger. Therefore, it is highly probable that the number of premeditated rapes is substantially higher than those reported by prosecutors. On the basis of an analysis of reported rapes in Philadelphia, Amir (1971) claims that 71 percent were planned. In the Queen's Bench Foundation study (1978), over two-thirds of the convicted rapists interviewed admitted that they had clearly set out to commit a rape.

Traditionally, the rapist has been considered by many clinicians the victim of "uncontrollable urges" (Edwards, 1983), or the recipient of a "disordered personality" (Scully & Marolla, 1984). Psychiatric criminology has, for a long time, dominated the popular literature on the sexual offender and continues to have substantial impact on the thinking of Western civilization. As Scully and Marolla (1985) observe, the psychiatric literature, as well as the general public, have traditionally attributed four fundamental causes for rape behavior. They are: (1) uncontrollable impulses or urges; (2) mental illness or disease; (3) momentary loss of control precipitated by unusual circumstances; and (4) victim instigation. Further, Scully and Marolla assert that each of these statements attribute the cause of the rape behavior to parameters outside of the rapist himself, often to the victim. In other words, the traditional psychiatric literature has consistently attributed the causal factors of sexual deviations to circumstances beyond the offender's direct or immediate control. Empirical research has not supported these assumptions, however. After discussing each in brief, we will outline what researchers have been finding.

Uncontrollable or **irresistible impulse** attribution refers to a psychological state where the normal restraints of self-control are substantially reduced or virtually eliminated by an overwhelming sex drive. The major argument from this perspective maintains that high levels of sexual deprivation may cause a bubbling over of an innate, natural sex drive of such intensity that the individual loses control of his behavior and consequently can no longer help himself. Driven by this powerful, biological force his only release is immediate sexual gratification. Symons (1979), for example, writes that men's sexual impulses are part of human nature and that men innately seek "no-cost, impersonal copulations."

Mental illness or *disease attribution* contends that rape—and most other sexual deviations—is symptomatic of some deep-seated sickness or mental aberration. All sexual offenders are basically "sick" and in need of help. Inherent in this perspective is the conviction that sexually deviant behaviors are similar in causation and represent a single type of psychopathology, usually some form of character disorder (Lanyon, 1986). According to Lanyon (1986, p. 176), this belief "tends to be the view held by the judicial system, by social service agencies, and by the general public." And as Scully and Marolla (1985) point out, "belief that rapists are or must be sick is amazingly persistent" (p. 298). Also related to this perspective is the contention that many rapists are actually latent homosexuals who sexually assault a female to prove their masculinity to themselves and others.

An interesting development within the disease model perspective is the contention that sexual offending represents an addiction (e.g., Carnes, 1983). This sexual-addiction approach is persuasive and appealing because sex offending has some obvious and compelling similarities to other forms of addiction, such as alcoholism, overeating, gambling, shoplifting, and drug abuse. Interestingly, the approach relies heavily on the same treatment strategies advocated by Alcoholics Anonymous (AA) and emphasizes the "twelve steps to recovery." Consequently, various self-help groups have appeared, such as Sex and Love Addicts Anonymous, Sexaholics Anonymous, Sexual Addicts Anonymous, and Sexual Abuse Anonymous. The basic text for Sex and Love Addicts Anonymous (Augustine Fellowship, 1986), for example, states that one's need for a close relationship with another "could be debased by addiction into a compulsive search for sex and romance, or obsessional entrapment in relationships characterized by personal neediness and hyperdependency—in patterns that could forever prevent really meeting the underlying need for authentic experience of self and other" (p. viii). These groups and approaches should not be confused with Relapse

Prevention (RP), a treatment regimen that shows considerable promise in the reduction of sexual offending. We will be discussing this form of treatment near the end of this chapter.

A third popular belief, *drug attribution*, argues that one can momentarily lose control of one's urges in certain circumstances, such as through the use of drugs or alcohol. Alcohol, for example, is believed to remove social and moral constraints, leaving some men at the mercy of their sexual appetites. This desire simply becomes overwhelming, causing some men to attack the most convenient victim. In one study, two-thirds of the men who raped their dates attributed their assaults to excessive drinking (Kanin, 1984). They claimed the date rape was caused by their own inebriation together with a loss of judgment due to high levels of sexual excitement. One-fifth were convinced that there was no way the attack would have occurred had they been sober.

The fourth perspective, *victim attribution*, contends that the victim has, in some way, led the perpetrator into temptation. Rape, according to this view, is a sexual act that is promoted unconsciously by the female. "Nice girls don't get raped," or at least they don't "let it get out of hand." Hitchhike rape, for example, is, according to this view, probably victim-precipitated rape. Because of their unconscious desires, women unwittingly cooperate with the rapist by making themselves available to him in various ways. In the Kanin (1984, p. 96) date rape study, two-thirds of the men said "that although it was probably rape in the legal sense, the fault for the incident resided with the female because of her sexual conduct. According to these males, the sexual demeanor of their victims literally absolved them of guilt so that we are now confronted with something akin to justifiable rape, an analogue to justifiable homicide." Several major surveys conducted on a wide section of the American population strongly suggest that many people continue to believe a victim is at least partially responsible for her rape and that only certain girls get raped (Lottes, 1988).

As noted earlier, empirical study has not supported the validity of these four fundamental assumptions; it does, however, support their persistence. In other words, people continue to believe that rape is caused by drugs, precipitated by the victim, or is the product of mental illness or the offender's uncontrollable urges or addiction. These misconceptions are held by offenders as well as others. Scully and Marolla (1984) interviewed 114 convicted rapists to obtain information about their perceptions, motivations, and afterthoughts and found that most could be divided into two major groups, "admitters" and "deniers." Admitters essentially corroborated the story told by police and victims. Deniers' versions differed significantly from those of police and victims. The researchers identified forty-seven admitters and thirty-two deniers. Apparently, the remainder could not be classified into either category.

Deniers justified their rape behavior primarily by making the victim blameworthy. Five themes ran through these justifications: (1) Women are seductresses; (2) women mean yes when they say no; (3) most women eventually relax and really enjoy it; (4) nice girls don't get raped; and (5) the act was a minor wrongdoing, since the victims were not physically hurt. Thirty-one percent of the deniers said the victim was the aggressor: a seductress who lured them, unsuspecting, into sexual action. About 22 percent said the victim had not resisted enough or that her no had really meant yes. As one offender put it, despite some struggle, "deep down inside I think she felt it was a fantasy come true." Sixty-nine percent of the deniers justified their behavior by claiming not only that the victim was willing, but also that she enjoyed herself, in some cases to an immense degree. Most of the deniers (69 percent) were convinced that "nice girls don't get raped." Their victims, they said, had dressed seductively, were hitchhiking, or were generally known to be "loose."

The belief that bad things happen to bad people and good things happen to good people is called by psychologists the **just world hypothesis** (Lerner, 1980), mentioned in Chapter 1. It is the simplistic belief that one gets what one deserves and deserves what one gets. Just-worlders—people who are most apt to adopt this hypothesis—believe that victims of misfortune or crime deserve their fate. Deniers noted that their victims should not have been in the bar alone, should not have been hitchhiking, or should have worn a bra. The deniers, in this sense, were just-worlders.

A majority of the deniers said that their actions were not reprehensible since they believed they had not physically harmed the victim. Many felt that, although their behavior was not completely proper, it should not have been considered a serious criminal offense, despite the fact that they had threatened their victims with lethal weapons.

Admitters, in contrast to deniers, regarded their behavior as morally wrong and as a serious, harmful attack on their victims. However, most of them tried to diminish their own culpability by asserting that they could not help themselves or were compelled by forces outside their control. Three themes ran through the admitters' justifications: (1) the use of alcohol and drugs; (2) emotional problems; and (3) a "nice guy" self-image. Over three-fourths said they had been under the influence of alcohol or drugs at the time of the attack, and that the substance had influenced their judgment and behavior. They were convinced that the ingested substance had, in effect, reduced their awareness as well as their self-control. Normally, they said, they would not have engaged in such a disgusting act.

Forty percent of the admitters said they believed emotional problems were at the root of their rape behavior, and 33 percent specifically cited an unhappy, unstable childhood, or a marital-domestic situation. Furthermore, 80 percent of the admitters described an upsetting problem or anger-inducing event that occurred prior to the attack. Consistently, Scully and Marolla (1984) found that these men described themselves as being in a rage because of an incident involving a woman with whom they believed they were in love. By contrast, only about 20 percent of the deniers described such problems.

Most of the admitters described themselves as "nice guys," who under normal circumstances would never dream of doing such a violent thing to a woman. In other words, their actions during that violent episode did not represent their true selves. Many expressed regret and sorrow for their victim and apologized to the researchers. We will return to these justifications and excuses later in this chapter.

CLASSIFICATION OF RAPE PATTERNS

Since such a wide variety of sexual offenders are involved in rape, some interesting attempts have been made to categorize rapists according to their behavioral patterns. Researchers at the Massachusetts (Bridgewater) Treatment Center (Cohen, Seghorn, & Calmas, 1969; Cohen, Garafalo, Boucher, & Seghorn, 1971; Knight & Prentky, 1987; Prentky & Knight, 1986) recognized that rape involves both sexual and aggressive features and tried to formulate a behavioral classification system that takes these elements into consideration.

Before we proceed, however, it is important to realize that classification systems are permeated with numerous problems and drawbacks. One obvious problem is that individuals do not fit neatly into a category. Furthermore, there may not be many who do. As astutely noted by Gibbons (1988), classification systems or typologies generally consist "of criminological foundations that assume that real life persons can be found in significant numbers who resemble the descriptions of offenders in the various typologies that have been put forth … researchers have often failed to uncover many point-for-point real-life cases of these hypothesized types of offenders" (p. 9). However, typologies or classification systems are valuable in organizing an otherwise confusing array of behaviors. They are also useful in correctional facilities for risk management, such as deciding where to place an inmate, or in treatment programming, such as deciding what particular treatment modality might be most beneficial for an inmate. It should be stressed, however, that rape is not a unified behavior pattern but rather is a complicated, often poorly understood, individualized behavior that appears to be precipitated by a variety of internal and external stimuli.

The Massachusetts Treatment Center (MTC) has identified four major categories of rapists: (1) displaced aggression, (2) compensatory, (3) sexual aggressive, and (4) impulsive rapists. **Displaced aggression rapists** (also called in other classification systems *displaced anger* or **anger-retaliation rapists**) are primarily violent and aggressive in their attack, displaying minimum or total absence of sexual feeling. These men use the act of rape to harm, humiliate, and degrade the woman. The victim is brutally assaulted and subjected to sadistic acts like biting, cutting, or tearing. In most instances, the victim is a complete stranger who happens to be the best available object or stimulus for the violence, although she may possess characteristics that attract the assailant's attention. The assault is not sexually arousing for the displaced aggression rapist, and he often demands oral manipulation or masturbation from the victim to become tumescent. Available evidence suggests that resisting this type of rapist only makes him more violent.

According to Knight and Prentky (1987), an offender must demonstrate the following characteristics during the attack in order to be assigned to the displaced aggression category:

1. The presence of a high degree of nonsexualized aggression or rage expressed either through verbal and/or physical assault that clearly exceed what is necessary to force compliance of the victim.
2. Clear evidence, in verbalization or behavior, of the intent to demean, degrade, or humiliate the victim.

3. No evidence that the aggressive behavior is eroticized or that sexual pleasure is derived from the injurious acts.
4. The injurious acts are not focused on parts of the body that have sexual significance.

Although many of these rapists are married, they are usually ambivalent toward the women in their lives (Cohen et al., 1971), and their relationships with women are often characterized by frequent irritation and periodic violence. They perceive women as being hostile, demanding, and unfaithful. In addition, they often select as their targets for sexual assault women whom they consider active, assertive, and independent. The occupational history of these assailants is stable and often shows some level of success. Usually, the work is "masculine," such as truck driving, carpentry, construction, or mechanics. The attack typically follows an incident that has upset or angered the rapist, particularly about women and their behavior. The term *displaced aggression* is derived from the fact that the victim rarely has played any direct role in generating the aggression and arousal. This offender often attributes his offense to "uncontrollable impulses."

Compared to other rapists, the childhood of the displaced aggression offender is often chaotic and unstable. Many were physically and emotionally neglected. A large number were adopted or placed in foster homes. About 80 percent were brought up in single parent homes.

Compensatory rapists rape in response to an intense sexual arousal initiated by stimuli in the environment, often quite specific stimuli. This type of rapist is sometimes referred to in the clinical and research literature as the "power-reassurance," "sexual aim," "ego dystonic," or "true" sex offender. Aggression is not a significant feature here; the basic motivation is a desire to prove sexual prowess and adequacy. In their day-to-day lives, compensatory rapists tend to be extremely passive, withdrawn, and socially inept. They live in a world of fantasy that centers on images of eagerly yielding victims who will submit to pleasurable intercourse and find the rapist's performance so outstanding that they will plead for a return engagement. The compensatory rapist's fantasies or personal versions of the world may so distort his view of the victim that he may seek further contact with her, even if she strongly resisted the sexual assault.

Although his victim is usually a stranger, the compensatory rapist has probably seen her frequently, watched her, or followed her. Specific stimuli associated with her probably excite him. For example, he may be drawn to college women but may feel the attraction would not be mutual if he approached them via a socially accepted route. He cannot face the prospect of rejection. However, if he can prove his sexual prowess, the victim will appreciate his value. If the victim vigorously resists the compensatory rapist, he is likely to flee; if she submits passively, he will rape without much force or violence. This sexually aroused passive assailant will often ejaculate spontaneously, even on mere physical contact with the victim. In general, he does not demonstrate other kinds of antisocial behavior.

The compensatory rapist is often described by others as a quiet, shy, submissive, lonely "nice man." Although he is a reliable worker, his withdrawn, introverted behavior, lack of self-esteem, and low levels of need for achievement usually preclude academic, occupational, or social success. His rapes—or attempts at rape—are an effort to compensate for his sense of inadequacy, hence the category to which he is assigned. More recent research by Knight and Prentky (1987) questions the incompetence issue. They found that, compared to the other rapist types, the compensatory rapist evidenced the best heterosexual adaptation and achieved the highest employment skill level. If this finding is replicated, the very term *compensatory rapist* would become misleading.

The **sexual aggressive** or **sadist rapist** is the one in whom sexual and aggressive features seem to coexist at equal or near equal levels. In order for him to experience sexual arousal, it must be associated with violence and pain, which excite him. He rapes, therefore, because of the combination of violence and sexual features in the act. He is convinced that women enjoy being forcefully raped and being dominated and controlled by men. This, he believes, is part of woman's nature. Anger and aggression are not always present during the early stages of the assault, which may actually begin as a seduction. In this sense, the sexual aggressive rapist considers the victim's resistance and struggle a game, a form of protesting too much; what she really wants is to be sexually assaulted and raped. This belief appears deeply ingrained and widely accepted in many Western societies (Edwards, 1983). Consider the following remarks made by a Scottish attorney general: "M.P.s would do well to remember that rape involves an activity which was normal ... it was part of the business of men and women that they hunted and were hunted and said 'yes' and 'no' and meant the opposite" (Edwards, 1983, p. 114).

Sexual aggressive offenders are often married, but because they display little commitment or loyalty, they also often have a history of multiple marriages, separations, and divorces. They also may be frequently involved in domestic violence. In fact, their backgrounds include antisocial behaviors beginning during adolescence or before and ranging from truancy to rape-murder. They have been severe management problems in school. Throughout their childhood, adolescence, and adulthood, they exhibit poor behavior controls and a low frustration tolerance. Their childhoods are characterized by physical abuse and neglect.

In the extreme, these rapists engage in sexual sadism much like the displaced aggression rapists: Their victims may be viciously violated, beaten, and even killed. The difference between the two types is that the sexual aggressive rapist derives intense sexual satisfaction from aggression, pain, and violence. In order to qualify for assignment to this category, the offender needs to demonstrate (1) a level of aggression or violence that clearly exceeds what is necessary to force compliance of the victim; and (2) the explicit, unambiguous evidence that aggression is sexually exciting to him.

A fourth type of rapist, the **impulsive** or **exploitative rapist**, demonstrates neither strong sexual nor aggressive features, but engages in spontaneous rape when the opportunity presents itself. The rape is usually carried out in the context of another crime, such as robbery or burglary. The victims simply happen to be available, and they are sexually assaulted with minimum extra-rape violence or sexual feeling. Generally, this offender has a long history of criminal offenses other than rape. In order to be assigned to this group, the offender must show (1) callous indifference to the welfare and comfort of victim; and (2) the presence of no more force than is necessary to gain the compliance of the victim.

THE MTC:R3

The Massachusetts Treatment Classification scheme offers a rough framework for conceptualizing and simplifying the behaviors and motives involved in rape. However, it needs refinement and reconstruction, a process the group has been pursuing for a number of years (e.g., Knight & Prentky, 1990). After a series of analyses and further development, the new Massachusetts Treatment Classification scheme (called the MTC:R3) finds that rape offenders can be classified into nine types. The basic four offender types are still in the equation but the researchers discovered there are subtle differences within the original four types. The researchers decided that four primary motivations for rape could improve the MTC significantly: opportunity, pervasive anger, sexual gratification, and vindictiveness (Knight, Warren, Reboussin, & Soley, 1998). Knight and his colleagues (Knight et al., 1998) concluded that these four motivations appeared to describe enduring behavioral patterns that distinguished most rapists. The opportunistic types (types 1 and 2) are similar to the fourth type of rapist described above. Their sexual assaults appear to be impulsive, predatory acts as a result of being in a situation where the opportunity for the sexual attack arises, and they are not primarily driven by sexual fantasy or explicit anger at women. However, analysis of offender data showed that the opportunistic type can be subdivided on the basis of their social competence (see Figure 10-2). Type 1 offenders are higher in social competence and first exhibited their impulsive sexual tendencies in adulthood.

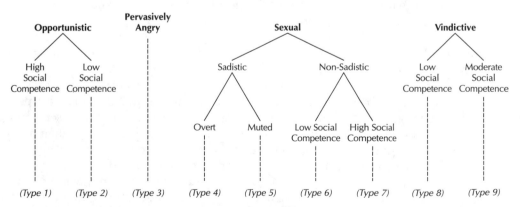

Figure 10-2   Breakdown of Four Categorizations of Rapist Type into Nine Rapist Subtypes
(Source: R. A. Knight et al., *Journal of Interpersonal Violence, 25*, p. 57, Figure 2. Copyright © 1998 by Sage Publications, Inc. Reprinted by permission of Sage Publications, Inc.)

Type 2 offenders, on the other hand, are lower in social competence and first demonstrated their impulsive sexual actions during adolescence.

The pervasive anger type (type 3) is similar to displaced aggression rapists but with the difference that his generalized anger pervades all areas of his life. Their pervasive anger is not simply directed at women but at everyone. Consequently, they often have a long history of antisocial, violent behavior of all kinds and they tend to inflict high levels of physical injury on their victims, especially their rape victims. In many ways they manifest behaviors similar to the life-course-persistent offender. Sexual motivations and preoccupation characterized four types of rapists in the newly developed MTC classification scheme (types 4, 5, 6 and 7; see Figure 10-1). The sadistic rapists (types 4 and 5) are subdivided in overt and muted types "on the basis of whether their sexual-aggressive fantasies are directly expressed in violent attacks or are only fantasized" (Knight et al., 1998, p. 58). The nonsadistic sexual rapists (types 6 and 7) are subdivided on the basis of their social competence.

The new MTC:R3 also includes vindictive offender types (types 8 and 9), characterized by anger directed exclusively at women. These types are highly similar to the displaced aggressive type described in the original MTC. "The sexual assaults of these men are distinguished by behaviors that are explicitly intended to harm the woman physically, as well as to degrade and humiliate her" (Knight et al., 1998, p. 58). Similar to the opportunistic and nonsadistic rapists, the vindictive types can be subdivided in high social competence and low social competence people.

Knight et al. (1998) postulate that these nine rape-offender classifications can help substantially in providing additional clues in crime-scene investigations. With refinement and continuing research, the MTC:R3 should ultimately enable investigators to identify "type" based on parameters gathered at the crime scene. The MTC:R3 also underscores the multiple strategies and cognitive beliefs possessed by rapists and discourage dogmatic proclamations about why rape occurs. The MTC:R3 increases the understanding of the etiology of sexual offending and helps mental health professions predict recidivism.

A frequently-asked question is: To what extent should a woman fight back or resist the attack? The MTC rape categories suggest alternative strategies to women who may wonder to what extent they should resist a rapist. In an interesting study, Sarah Ullman and Raymond Knight (1993) examined the police reports and court testimonies of 274 women who were either raped or avoided rape by violent stranger rapists. They found that forceful resistance (fighting, screaming, fleeing, or pushing the offender) was more effective for avoiding rape than nonresistance. This strategy was especially effective in dangerous situations where the offender had a weapon. However, although the victim avoided being raped or sexually assaulted, she often received more physical injury when the offender had a weapon, even if the weapon was not used. Nonresistance strategies were largely ineffective in avoiding rape or physical injury. In fact, victims who used nonresistant strategies—such as pleading, crying, or reasoning with the offender—were more likely to be sexually and physically assaulted than women who strongly resisted. Pleading, crying, or reasoning seem to encourage the offender even further. One thing to keep in mind is that the Ullman-Knight study focused on violent, stranger offenders who were committed as sexually dangerous to the Massachusetts Treatment Center. Whether the same results would occur when examining another type of offender, such as date or acquaintance rape, is unclear. Moreover, the MTC rape categories make it fairly clear that compensatory rapists and impulsive rapists—and possibly many sexual aggressive rapists—will be deterred by a victim who struggles. However, the displaced aggression rapists are apt to respond with more violence as the victim resists.

THE GROTH TYPOLOGY

Groth (1979) has developed a typology with many similarities to the MTC scheme. The Groth proposal is based on the presumed motivations and aims that underlie almost all rapes. Rape is seen as a "pseudo-sexual act" in which sex serves merely as a vehicle for the primary motivations of power and aggression. Groth—rather dogmatically—asserts, "Rape is never the result simply of sexual arousal that has no other opportunity for gratification.... Rape is always a symptom of some psychological dysfunction, either temporary and transient or chronic and repetitive" (p. 5). Later, he states, "Rape is always and foremost an aggressive act" (p. 12). Consequently, Groth divides rape behavior into three major categories: anger rape, power rape, and sadistic rape.

In **anger rape**, the offender uses more force than necessary for compliance and engages in a variety of sexual acts that are particularly degrading or humiliating to the female (such as sodomy, fellatio, or even urinating on her). He also expresses his contempt for the victim through abusive and profane language. Thus, for the anger rapist, rape is an act of conscious anger and rage toward women, and he expresses his fury physically and verbally. Sex is actually dirty, offensive, and disgusting to him and this is why he uses it to defile and degrade the victim. Very often his attacks are prompted by some previous conflict or humiliation by some significant woman (often a wife, a boss, or a mother). The assault is characterized by considerable physical brutality.

In **power rape**, the assailant seeks to establish power and control over his victim. Thus, the amount of force and threat used depends on the degree of submission shown by the victim. "I told her to undress and when she refused I struck her across the face to show her I meant business" (Groth, 1979, p. 26). His goal is sexual conquest, and he will try to overcome any resistance. Sexual intercourse is his way of asserting identity, authority, potency, mastery, and domination rather than strictly sexual gratification. Often the victim is kidnapped or held captive in some fashion, and she may be subjected to repeated assaults over an extended period of time. The sexual assault is sometimes disappointing to the power rapist because it fails to live up to his frequent fantasies of rape. "Everything was pleasurable in the fantasy, and there was acceptance, whereas in the reality of the situation, it wasn't pleasurable, and the girl was scared, not turned on to me" (Groth, 1979, p. 27).

The third pattern of rape, **sadistic rape**, includes both sexual and aggressive components. In other words, aggression is eroticized. The sadistic rapist experiences sexual arousal and excitement in the victim's maltreatment, torment, distress, helplessness, and suffering. The assault usually involves bondage and torture, and he directs considerable abuse and injury on various areas of the victim's body. Prostitutes, women he considers promiscuous, or women representing symbols of something he wants to punish or destroy often incur the wrath of the sadistic rapist. The victim may be stalked, abducted, abused, and sometimes murdered.

Groth (1979) reports that over half of the offenders evaluated or treated by his agency (Connecticut Sex Offender Program) were power rapists, 40 percent were anger rapists, and only 5 percent were sadistic rapists. The similarities between Groth's scheme and the MTC typology are multiple. The anger rapist is similar to the displaced aggressive rapist, the sadistic rapist is similar to the sexual aggressive rapist, and the power rapist shows many commonalities with the compensatory rapist.

ETIOLOGY

Generally speaking, sexual socialization plays a crucial role in the rapist's perceptions of what the rape accomplishes and what is "masculine." It is important to realize that sexual socialization (or sexual training) is rarely acquired entirely from home or school; much of it comes from peers, friends, the entertainment media, and experimentation. Most of us, even as children, were fed misconceptions, taboos, and strategies for dealing with the opposite sex. Males often learn it is "manly" to take the sexual initiative and to persist, even against resistance. Details of a sexual conquest, related to buddies, represent the badge of masculinity and self-worth. On the other hand, if attempts to conquer turn into a comedy of errors, they are seen as personal failure and sexual inadequacy. In addition, some people (both men and women) believe that a woman cannot be raped unless she wants to be. Others learn that women want to be dominated and controlled and that successful lovers demonstrate the "I'm-the-boss" syndrome. It is interesting to note in this context that some victims actually receive marriage proposals from their assailants (Russell, 1975). Other rapists ask their victims to evaluate their performance during or after the act.

Some researchers have proposed an immaturity hypothesis to account for much rape. Goldstein (1977) found that a sample of convicted sex offenders (who were mostly rapists) continued in adulthood to derive most of their sexual pleasure from fantasizing sexual stimuli they had derived from the media or from their own imagination. Average males (controls), by contrast, drew much of their sexual pleasure from real-life sexual encounters. Goldstein also discovered that many rapists have pervasive and obsessive preoccupations with sexual matters, to the point where the sexual preoccupation permeates their lives, and where normally nonerotic material becomes vividly incorporated into sexual fantasies.

Goldstein found that rapists, compared to the average male, relied substantially more on masturbation during adulthood, and that this was frequently accompanied by erotic material derived from the entertainment media. Furthermore, *all types* of sexual offenders had on the average *fewer* contacts with erotica during their formative years than did most other males. In addition, sexual curiosity was often repressed because of a punitive parental approach to matters sexual. Together, these factors provide a conducive setting for sexual misconceptions and ignorance.

Koss and Dinero (1988) conducted a well-designed survey of approximately three thousand male students at thirty-two U.S. colleges and universities. Students were asked questions about the extent of verbal coercion and physical force they had used to become sexually intimate with women without their consent. They were also questioned about attitudes and habits. The results indicated that highly sexually aggressive men expressed greater hostility toward women, frequently used alcohol, frequently viewed violent and degrading pornography (in contrast to Goldstein's finding), and were closely involved with peer groups that reinforce highly sexualized and dominating views of women. In addition, the more sexually aggressive the student, the more likely he was to believe that force and coercion are legitimate ways to gain compliance in sexual relationships. The researchers concluded: "In short, the results provided support for a developmental sequence for sexual aggression in which early experiences and psychological characteristics establish conditions for sexual violence" (p. 144).

In summary, most rapists seem to subscribe to attitudes and ideology that encourage men to be dominant, controlling, and powerful, whereas women are expected to be submissive, permissive, and compliant. Such an orientation seems to have a particularly strong disinhibitory effect on sexually aggressive men, encouraging them to interpret the ambiguous behavior of females as come-ons, to believe that women are not really offended by coercive sexual behaviors, and to perceive rape victims as desiring and deriving gratification from being sexually assaulted (Lipton, McDonel, & McFall, 1987).

Additional evidence of rapists' deviant attitudes and beliefs comes from physiological research. Abel and his associates (Abel, Barlow, Blanchard, & Guild, 1977; Abel, Becker, Blanchard, & Djenderedjian, 1978) have found that rapists show high and nearly equal sexual arousal to audiotaped portrayals of both rape and consenting sexual acts. The degree of sexual arousal was indicated by the subject's penile tumescence, which is measured by a device called a plethysmograph. Male nonrapists, on the other hand, show significantly less penile tumescence to rape depictions. In fact, convicted rapists became highly aroused by rape depictions in which the victim experiences abhorrence and pain rather than sexual pleasure. Encouraged by these findings, Abel developed a physiological measure called the "rape index." The index is arrived at by dividing the average percent of full penile erection to rape stimuli by the average percent of full penile erection to consenting sexual stimuli. Avery-Clark and Laws (1984) have developed a similar indicator for pedophiles called the "Dangerous Child Abuser Index." Today, many investigators use this measure in the diagnosis and treatment of rapists as well as child molesters. Generally, research suggests that rapists tend to have a higher rape index than nonrapists. The overall accuracy of the penile plethysmograph and its sensitivity to extraneous factors and faking remain very much in question, however.

Abel and his group also discovered that some rapists became highly sexually aroused even to scenes of *nonsexual* aggression, such as a man beating a woman with his fists. Thus, it appears that some men strongly associate aggression and violence toward women with sexual arousal, a pattern very similar to that of the sexual aggressive rapist described earlier. In fact, in rapists the intensity of this deviant arousal has been found to be positively related to the number of rapes committed and the degree of injury inflicted on victims (Abel et al., 1978). Some rapists apparently find scenes that show women being beaten exciting and pleasurable. In addition, male spouse abusers may, in part, be motivated by such arousal. On the other hand, a majority of men (70 percent) in the general population find the presence of aggression inhibiting to sexual arousal (Malamuth, Check, & Briere, 1986). Interestingly, men in the general population who are sexually aroused by force also are more accepting of an ideology that justifies male aggression against and dominance over women. These men also admit that they would probably rape if the opportunity were presented.

The role played by fantasy and imagination in the development of sexually aggressive behavior is becoming an increasingly important topic (Laws & Marshall, in press). Self-reports by sexual offenders find that frequent imagery and fantasy of sexually aggressive scenes is extremely important in motivating and guiding overt sexual aggression. Aggressive fantasies are particularly exciting to men convicted of rape (Abel et al., 1977). Interestingly, in a SR survey of 114 college men conducted by Greendlinger and Byrne (1987), over one-third indicated they fantasize about aggressively raping a woman, and 54 percent fantasize about forcing a woman to have sex.

Related to the role played by fantasy in the development of sexual deviance is the role played by masturbation. The intrinsically physiological pleasure and arousal generated by masturbation can serve as a strong bonding agent, particularly if paired repeatedly with some fantasized object or person. Also, it is important to realize that there are two powerfully reinforcing processes in masturbatory activity: sexual arousal and the reduction of that arousal at orgasm. Fantasized or actual behaviors that are sexually arousing and that result in sexual satisfaction (i.e., orgasm) are likely to increase in strength and frequency. This process is known as "masturbatory conditioning" (Marshall & Barbaree, 1988). On the basis of clinical studies (e.g., Groth, 1979; Marshall, 1988; George & Marlatt, 1989), it appears that masturbatory conditioning may play an integral part in the development of both normal and deviant sexual behavior.

In sum, the evidence to date indicates overwhelmingly that rapists learn to be rapists and that much of the teaching is done by equally naive peers, parents, significant social models, and the entertainment media. Rape springs from a culture, characterized by violence, that communicates a dominant ideology that degrades women and justifies coercive sexuality. Fortunately, most males eventually acquire a close approximation of sexual sophistication and some understanding of the needs of others. Many rapists, however, seem to remain sexually and, in some ways socially, immature.

Attitudes that promote the denigration of women may be widespread, however. There is distressing evidence that rapists may reflect the explicit and implicit beliefs held by many others. For example, in one study, 35 percent of male college students on several different campuses felt there was some likelihood that they would rape if they could be sure of getting away with it (Malamuth, 1981). In another study, 60 percent of a group of 352 male undergraduates indicated there was some likelihood they would rape or force a female to perform a sexual act against her will if given the opportunity (Briere, Malamuth, & Ceniti, 1981).

Malamuth (1989) cautions, however, that one does not conclude that subjects who indicate they would sexually force a woman are necessarily "potential rapists." The scale used in his research, Attraction to Sexual Aggression (ASA), is designed to measure the belief that actually engaging in sexual aggression would be an arousing, attractive experience. Whether they would act on that belief is dictated by a myriad of factors across a wide spectrum of influences, including the degree of motivation to commit the act, the internal and external inhibitions present, and the opportunity to commit the act.

RAPE AND PORNOGRAPHY

The relationship between rape and pornography is shrouded with confusion and surrounded by debate. Two Presidential Commissions established to study the effect of pornography on crime and human behavior reached opposite conclusions. The first and most comprehensive, established in 1967, was directed not to issue recommendations unless the effects were clearcut. Because of the complexity it uncovered, the Commission could not conclude whether explicit sexual material contributed significantly to sex crimes, prompting then President Richard M. Nixon to remark that the Commission was "morally bankrupt." Many have used this conclusion to support their contention that pornography is not harmful. The second National Commission on Obscenity and Pornography, which issued a report in 1984, recommended widespread restrictions of pornographic material. This Commission has been extensively criticized for its lack of scientific objectivity.

Research evidence has suggested that under certain conditions pornography facilitates aggressive, sexual behavior toward women. Studies by Donnerstein (1983) and Malamuth (Malamuth, Haber, & Feshbach, 1980; Malamuth, Heim, & Feshbach, 1980; Malamuth & Check, 1981) indicate, for example, that a general statement that pornography does not negatively influence people needs several qualifiers. In a series of ongoing experiments, Donnerstein finds evidence that three factors influence the relationship between erotica and human aggression: (1) the level of arousal elicited by erotic films; (2) the level of aggressive content; and (3) the reactions of the victims portrayed in these films and photographs. Donnerstein and others (e.g., Meyer, 1972; Zillman, 1971) angered male subjects in a variety of ways, then found that erotica shown to these aroused subjects significantly increased their aggressive behavior toward others. Because of their arousing properties, the erotic stimuli apparently may promote aggression under certain conditions. This finding accords with Berkowitz's theory (discussed in Chapter 7) on the relationship between arousal and aggression. Anything—sexual or not—that increases the arousal level of an already aroused subject will increase aggressive behavior in situations where aggression is the dominant behavior. The increased arousal may also draw the subject away from his own internal control or self-regulatory mechanisms, thereby allowing him to be less concerned about the consequences of his behavior. Furthermore, pornography investigations reveal that if the subject was angered by a woman, he would be even more aggressive toward other women after being exposed to the erotic film. These findings corroborate the frequent clinical observation that prior to a rape many rapists had been angered, upset, humiliated, or insulted, often by a woman (e.g., Groth, 1979).

Extremely violent stimuli, both erotic and nonerotic, can also facilitate aggression toward women even in nonangered males under certain conditions. The level of violence in the film appears significant. Portrayals of women being assaulted, even nonsexually, can increase subsequent aggressive behavior by men toward women, even when the males are not angry. Therefore, highly aggressive and violent acts depicted in the media may facilitate the rape act for some males. Since many rapists regard their act as a direct aggressive attack on women, seeing films where women are physically abused may encourage and support their own violent inclinations.

The reactions of the victims portrayed in films also seem crucial. Films or photographs that depict the female victim enjoying rape (common in pornography) encourage acceptance of the rape myth and promote violence against women (Malamuth & Check, 1981). If, on the other hand, the victim finds the rape both painful and abhorrent (negative aggressive erotica), male observers are disinclined to act aggressively. However, several qualifiers must be attached to this finding. If the male observer is already angered (aroused), seeing the victim suffer may make him more aggressive, since any arousal increase in an already aroused subject will increase subsequent aggressive behavior. The specific content of the film becomes irrelevant, as long as it meets the minimum criterion of being somehow arousing. On the other hand, males who are not upset or aroused before seeing a female victim suffer are less likely to aggress against women.

For some individuals, however, due to their conditioning history, pain cues are reinforcing if they are repeatedly associated with sexual gratification. Precisely how they react to various erotic portrayals is unclear, but it seems reasonable to suggest that they would find depictions of pain both highly arousing and supportive of their belief that pain and sexual gratification go together. They might also conclude that the pain-pleasure relationship is inherently characteristic of everyone's sexual gratification and that women really enjoy being "roughed up."

The relationship between violent pornography and sexual aggression remains complex and troubling. Although sexually arousing nonviolent pornography should be available in a free society and arguably has social value, violent pornography has no redeeming value. Its harmful effects, however, are difficult to document except as they relate to a subgroup of individuals. If all violent pornography were eradicated today, sex crimes would likely decrease. The same argument could be made to support confiscation of handguns and rifles, or random, unannounced drug testing of the citizenry. The extent to which a society should be asked to barter freedom in exchange for security remains a topic about which reasonable people consistently disagree.

PEDOPHILIA

Pedophilia, commonly known as "child molestation" or child sexual abuse, is defined in a variety of ways. The DSM-IV (1994) defines the term as a condition in which, "over a period of at least 6 months, recurrent, intense sexually arousing fantasies, sexual urges, or behaviors involving sexual activity with a prepubescent child or children (generally age 13 years or younger) occur" (p. 528). The DSM-IV further specifies that some pedophiles are sexually attracted only to children (the exclusive type); whereas others are sexually attracted to both children and adults (nonexclusive type). According to Finkelhor and Araji (1986), pedophilia is a male adult's conscious sexual interest in prepubertal children. One of two behaviors signifies that interest. Either the adult has had some sexual contact with a child (touched the child or had the child touch him with the purpose of his becoming sexually aroused), or the adult has masturbated to sexual fantasies involving children. The last definition recognizes that a male adult may have very strong sexual interest in children and be blocked only by circumstances from acting on it more directly. Occasionally, researchers extend the definition to include ages thirteen through fifteen, but most literature reserves the term **hebephilia** for sexual contact by adult males with young adolescents. Traditionally, most definitions of pedophilia were restricted to sexual contact between an adult or child who are not closely related. Sexual acts between members of a family when at least one participant is a minor were typically labeled "incest." More recent research and commentary, however, have placed all sexual contacts between an adult and a child into the pedophilia category. For purposes of clarity, we will use pedophilia and child molestation interchangeably as umbrella terms for all categories of child sexual abuse.

INCIDENCE AND PREVALENCE

As with sexual offenses in general, a caveat pertaining to the statistics is necessary. Data on pedophilia are difficult to obtain, since there are no central or national objective recording systems for tabulating sexual offenses against children. Also, as just noted, offenders may be arrested and prosecuted under a variety of statutes and for a variety of offenses, including child rape, aggravated assault, sodomy, incest, indecent exposure, or lewd and lascivious behavior. Although the UCR lists sex offenses, it does not differentiate pedophilia from the mixture of other possible sexual offenses. However, a variety of retrospective surveys of the general population indicate that from a quarter to a third of all females and a tenth or more of all males were molested during childhood (Finkelhor & Lewis, 1988; Peters, Wyatt, & Finkelhor, 1986). Moreover, only 35 percent of the children who are sexually victimized report it to anyone (Finkelhor, 1979). Russell (1984) found that in her sample only 2 percent of all incestuous abuse cases and 6 percent of all cases of extrafamilial abuse of females under eighteen had ever been reported to the police. From a national survey of about 1200 American males

(Finkelhor & Lewis, 1988), it is estimated that between 5 and 10 percent of the male population has engaged or will engage in child sexual abuse at some time in their lives. It is important to note, however, that this figure may include a one-time incident that—although still to be condemned—may not represent the offender's usual behavior and would not qualify him as a pedophile for purposes of this chapter. However, these data indicate that children are sexually victimized at levels that far exceed those reported for adults (see Finkelhor & Dziuba-Leatherman, 1994).

In the Russell (1984) survey, 930 randomly selected female residents of San Francisco were interviewed throughout the summer of 1978. The purpose of the project was to obtain an estimate of the incidence and prevalence of rape and other forms of sexual assault, including the amount of sexual abuse respondents experienced as children. Twelve percent of the women said they had been sexually abused by a relative before the age of fourteen. Twenty-nine percent reported at least one experience of sexual abuse by a nonrelative before reaching the age of fourteen. Overall, 28 percent of the 930 women reported at least one incident of sexual abuse before reaching the age of fourteen.

SITUATIONAL AND VICTIMIZATION CHARACTERISTICS

The offender, or pedophile, is almost always male, but the victim may be of either gender. Heterosexual pedophilia—male adult with female child—appears to be the more common type, with available data indicating that three-quarters of pedophiles choose female victims exclusively (Lanyon, 1986; Langevin, 1983). Homosexual pedophilia—male adult preference for male child—appears to be substantially less frequent (about 20 to 23 percent of the reported cases). A small minority of pedophiles choose their victims from both sexes. The behavior of the pedophile or child molester is usually limited to caressing the child's body, fondling the child's genitals, and/or inducing the child to manipulate his or her genitals. Heterosexual penetration is apparently involved in only a small proportion of the total number of offenses.

The offender and the victim know one another in most instances, often very well (McCaghy, 1967; Virkkunen, 1975; Schultz, 1975). Many victims were actively seeking natural affection from their offenders, as a child seeks to be hugged or cuddled. Some victims feel kindly and lovingly toward the offender, who sometimes interprets this behavior as "seductive." Clinical observations suggest that pedophiles, as a group, tend to have positive feelings toward their victims, generally perceive them as being willing participants, and frequently victimize children living in their immediate households (Miner, Day, & Nafpaktitis, 1989). It is not uncommon for the sexual behavior between the offender and victim to have gone on for a sustained period of time.

The form of the sexual contact seems to depend on three factors: the degree to which the offender had previous nonsexual interactions with children, the nature of the relationship between the child and the offender, and the age of each. Offenders who have had limited interaction with children are more likely to perform or expect genital-genital and oral-genital contact, rather than to indulge only in caressing or fondling. Furthermore, the more familiar the offender and the victim are with one another, the greater the tendency for genital-genital or oral-genital contact.

There is some disagreement about the extent to which child molesters harm the child physically or use physical force. According to most research, pedophiles do not usually use overt physical coercion. McCaghy (1967) found no evidence of any kind of coercion, verbal or physical, in three-fourths of the child molestation cases he examined. Research by Groth and his colleagues (Groth, Hobson, & Gary, 1982) supports these findings. Lanyon (1986), summarizing the research, concluded that violence is involved in about 10 to 15 percent of child sexual abuse cases. However, Hall, Proctor, and Nelson (1988) report that 28 percent of a sample of convicted pedophiles (122 nonpsychotic patients of a state mental hospital) were officially identified as having used physical force or the threat of force beyond what was necessary to gain the victim's compliance. Marshall and Christie (1981) found that in a sample of forty-one pedophiles incarcerated in Canadian federal penitentiaries, twenty-nine had used physical force. In an earlier study of 150 pedophiles, Christie, Marshall, and Lanthier (1979) had reported that 58 percent used excessive force in their attack, and 42 percent of the child victims had sustained notable injury. The researchers suggested that the offenders in their sample were highly sexually aroused by physical violence, significantly more so than other nonaggressive sex offenders. The reported differences in the use of violence and force by pedophiles appears to be explained by the sample used. Studies reporting a high incidence of violence or aggression focus on incarcerated, relatively hard-core offenders, while those reporting little or no violence sampled less-criminal or nonincarcerated pedophiles, generally those on probation.

Groth, Hobson, and Gary (1982) recommend that the few offenders using violence or force and causing physical harm to the child should be labeled "child rapists." On the other hand, those offenders only using psychological pressures should be considered child molesters or pedophiles. Although Groth's suggestion has merit, researchers in this area have used pedophile or child molester as umbrella terms to cover all child sexual abusers.

Research offers strong support for the assumption that sexual abuse in childhood (both violent and nonviolent) produces long-term psychological problems in many children (Briere, 1988). Reports of depression, guilt, feelings of inferiority, substance abuse, suicidality, anxiety, chronic tension, sleep problems, and fears and phobias are common. Depression is the symptom most commonly reported among adults who were molested as children. The extent of psychological damage to the child produced by sexual abuse is dependent on several factors. Groth (1978) contends that the greatest trauma occurs in children who have been victims for long periods of time, are victimized by a closely related person (such as a stepfather), when the victimization involves penetration, and when it is accompanied by aggression. In their careful review of the research literature on pedophilia, Browne and Finkelhor (1986) concluded that: (1) Younger children appear to be somewhat more vulnerable to trauma than older children; (2) the closer the relationship between offender and victim the greater the trauma; and (3) the greater the force used the greater the trauma. They also concluded, however, that there is no conclusive support for the contention that the longer and more frequent the abuse the greater the trauma. Nor is there any clear evidence that traumas are related to the *type* of sexual abuse (intercourse, fondling, fellatio, cunnilingus, etc.). This suggests that "mild" abuse may be as traumatizing as intercourse, especially if the victim is young and closely related to the offender. The Browne and Finkelhor review also suggests that, for some unexplained reason, victims of child sexual abuse are more likely than nonvictims to be sexually assaulted again as adults.

OFFENDER CHARACTERISTICS

Pedophilia is primarily committed by males, but it is not exclusively a male offense. The National Center on Child Abuse and Neglect (1981) reported that 46 percent of the abusive sexual experiences encountered by children included a female perpetrator. This figure is misleading, however, in that it includes any female caretaker who "permitted acts of sexual abuse to occur" (Russell & Finkelhor, 1984). In other words, leaving the child with a boyfriend as a babysitter who in turn molests the child would be considered sexual abuse by the mother. The mother who fails to report her suspicions that her husband is sexually abusing her daughter may also be included in the statistic. If only those women who actually *committed* child sexual abuse are included, the percentage of female offenders drops to 13 percent in the case of female victims and 24 percent in the case of males (Russell & Finkelhor, 1984). On the basis of their research, Russell and Finkelhor (1984) suggest that females are involved in about 5 percent of the sexual abuse of girls and about 20 percent of the cases of boys. Because sexual abuse of children by females is so little explored, we will concentrate in the remainder of this chapter on what is known about male pedophiles.

Although there is considerable age variability, the average age of convicted male child molesters ranges between thirty-six and forty. While about 75 percent of convicted rapists are under thirty, about 75 percent of convicted child molesters are over that age (Henn, Herjanic, & Vanderpearl, 1976b). Groth (1978), however, notes that all the child molesters he and colleagues have worked with had committed their first child molestation offense before age forty. Over 80 percent were first offenders by age thirty, and about 5 percent had committed their first sexual assault before they reached adolescence. However, despite the statistical finding that child molesters tend to be older than most other sexual offenders, there seems to be a pattern of victim preference as a function of age. Older pedophiles (over fifty) seek out immature children (ten or younger); younger pedophiles (under age forty) prefer girls between the ages of twelve and fifteen (Revitch & Weiss, 1962). The latter are technically classified as hebrophiles.

Perhaps because of the extremely negative attitude society displays toward child molesters, pedophiles almost always resist taking full responsibility for their offenses (McCaghy, 1967). Many claim that they went blank, were too drunk to know what they were doing, could not help themselves, or did not know what came over them. They show a strong preference to attribute the cause of their behavior to external forces or motivating factors largely beyond their personal control.

However, those charged with child molestation rarely manifest any serious or pronounced behavioral or emotional problems other than the pedophilia (Henn, Herjanic, & Vanderpearl, 1976b). When clinical diagnoses are made, they are most often organic brain syndrome (damage) or mental retardation, but still these represent only a small percentage of the total pedophile population. Since pedophilia and exhibitionism are the most common sexual offenses committed by senile and arteriosclerotic men (Coleman, 1976), the organic brain syndrome classification is not really surprising.

Many aggressive pedophiles demonstrate a large number of similarities with rapists and the prison population in general (Knight, Rosenberg, & Schneider, 1985). The most notable commonalities are the following: (1) They have problems with alcohol; (2) they have a high rate of high school failure and dropout; (3) they tend to have unstable work histories in unskilled occupations; and (4) they tend to come from the low socioeconomic class.

Alcohol abuse is frequently a problem in sex offenders. While about one-third to one-half of convicted rapists have serious problems with alcohol, about one-quarter to one-third of convicted pedophiles have such problems (Knight, Rosenberg, & Schneider, 1985). Research also indicates that a large segment of pedophiles do not progress much beyond the eighth grade in school (Christie, Marshall, & Lanthier, 1979), and many show signs of mental deficiencies on traditional IQ tests (Knight, Rosenberg, & Schneider, 1985; Swanson, 1968).

About two-thirds of those arrested and convicted for child molestation offenses come from the unskilled or semiskilled occupational groups (McCaghy, 1967; Gebhard et al., 1965). However, other occupational groups may handle the incident quite differently to prevent additional trauma for the victim and social embarrassment for their families during the legal investigation and process. In the 1980s, the media were filled with accounts of the alarming increase in child sex abuse rates. These same accounts note that it knows no economic or social barriers: Child offenders exist in all levels of society and among all occupational groups.

CLASSIFICATION OF CHILD OFFENDER PATTERNS

The Massachusetts Treatment Center (MTC) (Cohen, Seghorn, & Calmas, 1969; Knight, Rosenberg, & Schneider, 1985; Knight, 1988) has been developing a widely cited typology of pedophile behavioral patterns, similar to the rape typology presented earlier. Four major pedophiliac patterns have been identified: (1) the fixated type, (2) the regressed type, (3) the exploitative type, and (4) the aggressive or sadistic type.

The **fixated** (or **immature**) **pedophile** demonstrates a long-standing, exclusive preference for children as both sexual and social companions. He has never been able to develop a mature relationship with his adult peers, male or female, and he is considered socially immature, passive, timid, and dependent by most people who know him. He feels most comfortable relating to children, whom he seeks out as companions. Sexual contact usually occurs only after the adult and child have become well acquainted. Fixated pedophiles rarely marry, and their social background lacks much evidence of dating peers or even any sustained, long-term friendship with an adult (outside of relatives). This pedophile wishes to touch, fondle, caress, and taste the child. He rarely expects genital intercourse, and very rarely does he use physical force or aggression.

The fixated pedophile generally has average intelligence. His work history is steady, although it is often work that is below his ability. His social skills are adequate for day-to-day functioning. Probably most troubling about the fixated or immature pedophile is that he is not concerned or disturbed about his exclusive preference for children as companions, nor can he see why others are concerned. Therefore, he is difficult to treat and is most likely to recidivate.

The **regressed pedophile** had a fairly normal adolescence and good peer relationships and heterosexual experiences, but later developed feelings of masculine inadequacy and self-doubt. Problems in the individual's occupational, social, and sexual lives followed. The regressed child offender's background commonly includes alcohol abuse, divorce, and a poor employment record. Each pedophilial act is usually precipitated by a significant jolt to the offender's sexual adequacy, either by female or male peers. For example, the pedophile may perceive other males as being more successful with women. Unlike the immature child offender, the regressed child offender usually prefers victims who are strangers and who live outside his neighborhood. The victims are nearly always female. Unlike the fixated pedophile, he seeks genital sex with his victim. Because he feels remorseful and expresses disbelief after that act, clinicians usually find him a good prospect for rehabilitation. As long as stressful events are kept to a minimum and he learns to cope adequately with those he does have, he is unlikely to reoffend.

The **exploitative pedophile** seeks children primarily to satisfy his sexual needs. He exploits the child's weaknesses any way he can, and tries various kinds of strategies and tricks to get him or her to comply. He is usually unknown to the child and commonly tries to get the child isolated from others and his familiar surroundings. If necessary, he will use aggression and physical force to get the child to comply with his wishes. The exploitative offender does not care about the emotional or physical well-being of the child, but only sees the victim as a sexual object.

The exploitative offender exhibits a long history of criminal or antisocial conduct. His relationships with peers are unpredictable and stormy. He is unpleasant to be around and is often avoided by others who know him. He tends to be highly impulsive, irritable, and moody. His markedly defective interpersonal skills may be the principal reason that he chooses children as victims (Knight, Rosenberg, & Schneider, 1985). Clinicians find him difficult to treat, as his deficiencies extend to all phases of his daily life.

The **aggressive** (or **sadistic**) **pedophile** is drawn to children for both sexual and aggressive reasons. Pedophiles in this group are apt to have a long history of antisocial behavior and poor adaptation to their environments. Most prefer victims of the same sex (homosexual pedophilia). Since the primary aim is to obtain stimulation without consideration for the victim, this group often assaults the child viciously and sadistically. The more harm and pain inflicted, the more this offender becomes sexually excited. Aggressive or sadistic pedophiles are most often responsible for child abductions and murders. Clinicians find this type not only dangerous to children, but among the most difficult to treat. Fortunately, this type is rare.

An example of an aggressive child molester was Albert Fish (1870–1936), whose background is discussed by Nash (1975). Fish, called the Moon Maniac, admitted sexually molesting more than four hundred children over a span of twenty years. In addition, he confessed to six child murders and made vague reference to numerous others. He was eventually convicted of murdering a twelve-year-old girl and was electrocuted in 1936. A more contemporary example might well be John Wayne Gacy Jr., who sadistically murdered thirty-three teenage boys and young men and buried their bodies in the cellar of his suburban Chicago home.

Fish thought the conditions of his childhood led to a "perverted" life of crime. He was abandoned at an early age and placed in an orphanage, where he first witnessed and experienced brutal acts of sadism. Fish was quoted as saying, "Misery leads to crime. I saw so many boys whipped it ruined my mind." He apparently began his career of child molesting in earnest when his wife deserted him for another man. This suggests that, like regressed offenders, aggressive offenders may begin their crimes in response to precipitating events involving rejection and feelings of sexual inadequacy.

THE MTC:CM3

Similar to the Massachusetts Treatment Center classification scheme on rapists, the MTC classification system of child molesters has also undergone some refinement in recent years. In an effort to depict more accurately the complexity involved in classifying pedophiles, the MTC:CM3 (referring to Massachusetts Treatment Center: child molester, version 3) has made some tentative changes to the original scheme described above. Three significant changes are recommended: (1) Divide the regressed and fixated types into three separate factors—degree of fixation on children, the level of social competence achieved, and the amount of contact an offender has with children; (2) incorporate into the scheme a new narcissistic offender type; and (3) partition the violence of the sexual assault into physical injury and sadistic components (Knight, 1989).

The researchers discovered that, although the regressed or fixated pedophile classification is a valid one, it was also more complicated then originally supposed. Researchers found that the regression or fixated (immature) classification could be further subdivided into the molester's style of offending, his interpersonal relationships with children, the intensity of the offender's interest, and the level of social competence achieved by the offender. For example, offenders could be classified according to their level of fixation and social competence. Level of fixation refers to the strength of an offender's sexual interest in children (Knight, Carter, & Prentky, 1989). For example, to what extent are children the major focus of the offender's thought and attention? If children are the central focus of the offender's sexual and interpersonal fantasies and thoughts for more than six months, then the offender qualifies for high fixation. Social competence refers to the degree to which the offender can participate effectively in daily living. An offender would have high social competence if he has demonstrated at least two of the following behaviors: (a) has had a single job lasting three or more years; (b) has had a sexual relationship with an adult for at least a year; (c) has assumed responsibility in parenting a child for three or more years; (d) has been an active member in an adult-oriented organization (e.g., church group, business group) for one or more years; or (e) has had a social friendship with adult for at least one year. The dimensions of fixation and social competence result in four types of child molesters: high fixation, low social competence (type 0); high fixation, high social competence (type 1); low fixation, low social competence (type 2); and low fixation, high social competence (type 3). The regressed type was dropped in MTC:CM3 in favor of the term "low fixation."

Research further revealed that pedophiles can also be distinguished on the basis of how much daily contact with children they seek (see Figure 10-3). A high contact offender demonstrates regular contact with children in both sexual offense and non-sexual contexts (Knight et al., 1989). Offenders of high contact often become involved in an occupation or recreation that brings them in considerable contact with children, such as bus drivers, school teachers, Boy Scout leader, or Little

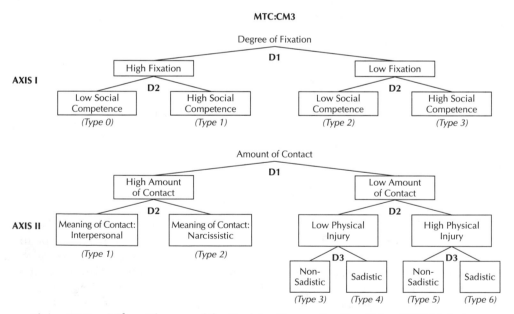

Figure 10-3   A Flow Diagram of the Decision Process for Classifying Child Molesters on Axis I and Axis II of MTC:CM3
(Note: D1 = Decision 1; D2 = Decision 2; D3 = Decision 3.)
(Source: R. A. Knight et al., *Journal of Interpersonal Violence*, 4, p. 8, Figure 1. Copyright © 1989 by Sage Publications, Inc. Reprinted by permission of Sage Publications, Inc.)

League coach. Research data revealed there are two kinds of offenders who seek more extensive involvement with children beyond their sexual offenses. The first high-contact type, the *interpersonal offender* (type 1), seeks the extensive company of children for both social and sexual needs. He sees the child as an appropriate companion in a relationship, and feels his friendship is mutually satisfying. The second type, the *narcissistic offender* (type 2), solicits the company of children only to increase his opportunities for sexual experiences. Similar to the exploitative offender, they typically molest children they do not know and their sexual acts with children are typically genitally oriented (Knight, 1989). Furthermore, there is little or no concern about the needs, comfort, or welfare of the child (Knight et al., 1989).

Another group of pedophiles are low-contact seekers. Low-contact offenders' only contacts with children are in the context of sexual assault. Low-contact offenders are evaluated according to the amount of physical injury they administer to their victims. Two types of low-contact seekers tend to administer very little physical injury to their victims: the exploitative type and the muted sadistic type. Low injury refers to the absence of physical injury to victim and the presence of such acts as pushing, shoving, slapping, holding, or verbal threats. None of the acts of low injury results in a lasting injury (e.g., cuts, bruises, contusions). The *exploitative, nonsadistic offender* (type 3) uses no more aggression or violence than is necessary to secure victim compliance. Furthermore, the assault does not reveal evidence that sadistic actions engender sexual arousal in the offender. The *muted or symbolic sadistic offender* (type 4) engages in a variety of distressing, painful, and threatening acts, none of which causes physical injury to the child.

Finally, the MTC:CM3 classifies two offenders who have often administered a high amount of physical injury to their victims: the aggressive offender and the sadistic offender. High injury is characterized by hitting, punching, choking, sodomy, or forcing the child to ingest urine or feces (Knight et al., 1989). The *aggressive, nonsadistic offender* (type 5) is similar to the aggressive pedophile described earlier except that sadism is not a primarily aim of the assault. This offender is extremely angry about all things in his life and is generally violent toward people in his life, including children. The *sadistic offender* (type 6) obtains sexual pleasure from the pain, fear, and physical harm he inflicts on the child.

The newly developed MTC:CM3 helps identify offender type based on crime scene information and perhaps presents a more refined classification system of child molester types. However, research beyond the MTC population is needed before investigators feel comfortable about adopting this promising scheme.

THE GROTH CLASSIFICATION MODEL

In a classification system similar to that of the Massachusetts Treatment Center, Groth (1978; Groth & Burgess, 1977) classifies child offenders on the basis of the longevity of the behavioral patterns and the offender's psychological aims. If the sexual preference for children has existed persistently since adolescence, he is classified an *immature* or *fixated child offender*. Like the MTC classification system, the fixated child offender has been sexually attracted primarily or exclusively to significantly younger people throughout his life, regardless of what other sexual experiences he has had. Groth believes that this fixation is due to an arresting of psychological maturation, resulting from unresolved formative issues that persist and underlie subsequent development. On the other hand, if the offender has managed to develop some normalcy to his relationships with adults, but resorts to child offending when stressed or suffers a devastating blow to his self-esteem, he is called a *regressed* child offender.

Based on his clinical research, Groth also has subdivided child offenders according to their intentions or psychological aims. He identifies two basic categories: (1) sex pressure offenders, and (2) sex force offenders. In sex pressure offenses, the offender's typical modus operandi is to entice children into sexuality through persuasion or cajolement, or to entrap them by placing them in a situation in which they feel indebted or obligated. A child may feel he owes something to the person who taught him to swim or bought him a bike. The sex force offense, on the other hand, is characterized by threat of harm and/or the use of physical force in the commission of the offense. The offender either intimidates the child by exploiting the child's relative helplessness, naiveté, and awe of adults, or attacks and physically overpowers his victim.

Groth finds he can further subdivide the sex force group into the *exploitative type*, in which the threat of force is used to overcome victim resistance, or the *sadistic type*, who derives great pleasure in hurting the child. The exploitative type typically employs verbal threats, restraint, manipulation, intimidation, and physical strength to overcome any resistance on the part of the child. His intent is not necessarily to hurt the child but to obtain compliance. The sadistic type, which fortunately is rare, eroticizes physical aggression and pain. He uses more force than is necessary to overpower the victim and may commit a so-called lust murder. Therefore, the physical and psychological abuse and/or degradation of the child is necessary for him to experience sexual excitement and gratification. Often, the child is beaten, choked, tortured, and violently sexually abused.

Certainly the Groth typology has strong commonalities with the MTC typology. The immature and the regressed child offenders display features of the sex pressure offender, and the aggressive child offender shows strong similarities to the sex force offender. It may be more appropriate for the present time to classify the child offender according to the degree of coercion or force he uses rather than according to personality features. The first method focuses on offender behavior, a criterion that is more objective and clearcut. The second focuses on "understanding" the behavior by assuming a variety of personality constructs. We have too little information about child offenders at this point to do that with total confidence.

RECIDIVISM

If pedophilia is learned, we would expect a fairly high incidence of recidivism. Like the national recidivism rates for most offenses, however, pedophile recidivism rates are difficult to confirm. Moreover, the second time around, the pedophile is undoubtedly more careful about detection. In the California study by Frisbie (1965), recidivism rates over a five-year period were reported to be 18.2 percent for heterosexual pedophiles and 34.5 percent for homosexual pedophiles.

However, as Schultz (1975) noted, most pedophile offenses go unreported. Abel and colleagues (Abel, Becker, Murphy, & Flanagan, 1981) reported that incarcerated homosexual pedophiles had, on the average, thirty-one victims, while heterosexual pedophiles had an average of sixty-two victims. A Dutch study (Bernard, 1975) reported that at least half of its respondents claimed sexual contacts with at least ten or more children. Fourteen percent of the sample—which included both arrested and unarrested pedophiles—admitted to sexual contacts with more than fifty, and 6 percent to contacts with between one hundred and three hundred children. Fifty-six percent of this sample indicated they had one or more "regular" sexual contacts with children. Fully 90 percent asserted that they did not want to stop their pedophilial activities.

Abel and colleagues (Abel, Mittelman, Becker, Rathner, & Rouleau, 1988) report that of the 192 nonincarcerated child offenders who voluntarily participated in a treatment program, the men most likely to drop out of treatment were those with a history of considerable and varied pedophilic behavior. That is, 70 percent of the frequent child offenders who demonstrated no age preference (child or adolescent) or gender preference (male or female) dropped out of treatment, usually early in the process. The treatment program consisted of thirty ninety-minute group sessions given weekly and directed at decreasing deviant arousal, developing cognitive restructuring of distorted sexual attitudes and beliefs, and increasing subjects' social competence with adults. In addition, those subjects who managed to complete the program, and who had varied child offending behavior and multiple victims were the ones who were most likely to recidivate within one year after treatment.

Further indications of recidivism rates of child offenders can be garnered from the thirteen-year outpatient treatment program described by Marshall and Barbaree (1988). This Canadian project offered psychological treatment of deviant sexual behavior on a voluntary basis to a variety of sexual offenders. Forty percent of the child offenders refused treatment. The project had access to official records (charges and convictions) throughout North America as well as to information from "unofficial" files of local police departments and Children's Aid Societies in the towns where the offenders lived. Thirty-two percent of the untreated child offenders reoffended, compared to 14 percent of the treated offenders. The average follow-up period for both groups was approximately three and one-half years. In reference to the twenty-six men who recidivated, only eleven were identified "officially" (charges and convictions), whereas the remainder were identified through the "unofficial" information. Even so, the unofficial measures of recidivism were still official in that they were collected by public agencies, which leaves us still wondering how high the "unofficial" recidivism rates for child offenders really are.

ETIOLOGY

Most explanations of pedophilia focus on a single factor as the principal cause of sexual and social preferences for children by adults. One clinical hypothesis, for example, suggests that pedophiles select children as sex objects because they are haunted by feelings of masculine and sexual inadequacy in adult relationships (e.g., Groth, Hobson, & Gary, 1982). They are terrified of being ridiculed in their sexual and social behavior by the adult world. In the world of the child, they can be safely curious, awkward, and inexperienced. This observation might help explain why pedophiles rarely engage in heterosexual intercourse. Although this inadequacy hypothesis appears to have some validity, it fails to explain the full range and diversity of pedophilic behavior.

Finkelhor and Araji (1986) find four basic explanations for pedophilia in the research and clinical literature: emotional congruence, sexual arousal, blockage, and disinhibition theories. The most common is what they call *emotional congruence theories*. These theories try to explain why a person would find relating sexually to a child to be emotionally gratifying and congruent with their needs. Finkelhor and Araji refer to these explanations as emotional congruence theories, since they convey the idea of a fit between the adult's emotional needs and the child's characteristics. Most congruence theories are psychoanalytic in origin and focus on "arrested psychological development." According to this perspective, pedophiles see themselves as children with childish emotional needs and dependency, and consequently they feel most comfortable with children. A similar version focuses on the low self-esteem and a loss of efficacy pedophiles experience in their daily lives. Relating to a child is congruent, because the inadequate adult finally feels powerful, omnipotent, and in control of a relationship. In short, relating to a child provides a sense of mastery and control in their lives.

The second group of theories tries to explain why pedophiles become sexually aroused by certain characteristics of children. Sexual arousal is typically measured by penile tumescence to the presence of children or to sexual fantasies of children. Called *sexual arousal theories*, this perspective contends that pedophiles become sexually aroused to stimuli (features of children) that, for a variety of reasons, do not generate sexual arousal in normal males. One set of theories within this group posits that it is a common childhood experience to engage in sexual play with playmates. For the pedophile, the childhood sexual play may have been particularly vivid, rewarding, stimulating, and even possibly the most sexually exciting experience he has ever had. Adult sexual play, by comparison, was less arousing, satisfying, or rewarding, perhaps even nonexistent. The pedophile's shyness, for example, may have precluded adult sexual contacts. Under these conditions, he probably took the most available sexual avenue, masturbation. As noted earlier, the powerful reinforcing role of masturbatory behavior (masturbatory conditioning) has been demonstrated in clinical studies of most sexual offenses (Marshall, 1988). During masturbation, the pedophile's fantasies may focus on the satisfying sexual experiences he had during childhood. Repetitive masturbatory activity, therefore, reinforces the immature level of sexual behavior associated with childhood. Whereas masturbation of itself may be a normal outlet for sexual tension, for the pedophile it becomes an act that reinforces his attraction to children. Continual association between the pleasurable masturbatory activities and fantasies about childhood sexual experiences results in a strong bond between sexual arousal and children.

Eventually, the children become sexual stimuli capable of arousing high levels of sexual excitation.

Another version of the sexual arousal perspective links traumatic sexual victimization to pedophilic behavior. Many researchers have found unusually high amounts of childhood sexual victimization in the background of pedophiles (Bard, Carter, Cerce, Knight, Rosenberg, & Schneider, 1987). It is unclear, however, how sexual trauma, which is aversive, becomes conditioned or associated with the sexual pleasures of pedophilia.

Blockage theories assume that pedophilia is the result of blockage of normal sexual and emotional gratification from adult relationships. Frustrated in his quest for normal channels of sexual gratification, the offender seeks the company of children. Blockage theories emphasize the unassertive, timid, inadequate, and awkward personalities of the pedophile, arguing that these social deficiencies make it nearly impossible for him to develop normal social and sexual relationships with adult women. When the marital relationship breaks down, for example, the pedophile may turn to his daughter as a substitute.

The fourth set of explanations focus on the loss of self control and personal constraints on behavior. *Disinhibition theories* outline a variety of circumstances that presumably propel the offender to his deeds. Poor impulse control, excessive use of alcohol and drugs, and an assortment of stressors could all lead him over the brink to his favorite deviant sexual practices. As mentioned earlier, many pedophiles refuse to take blame, but attribute the cause of their pedophilic behavior to forces outside themselves. "I couldn't help myself" or "I don't know what came over me" are frequent pleas.

Which theoretical perspective has the inside track for the explanation of pedophilia? By themselves none can account for the multiple causes and the full range of learning experiences, beliefs, motivations, and attitudes of pedophiles.

EXHIBITIONISM

Exhibitionism is the deliberate exposure of the genitals to another person to achieve sexual gratification. Several authors have reported that in some parts of the world exhibitionism—often called *indecent exposure*—is the most frequent sexual offense known to the police (e.g., Wincze, 1977; Coleman, 1976). In Canada and the United States, exhibitionism—usually called lewd and licentious behavior in the legal system—accounts for about one-third of all sex crimes (Evans, 1970; Rooth, 1974), and in the United Kingdom it accounts for one-fourth (Feldman, 1977). Bancroft (1976) estimates that exhibitionism is the second most common sexual deviation treated at mental health facilities in England. Rooth (1973, 1974) argues that the practice of exposing oneself is primarily a Western phenomenon, however. In India, extensive surveys have failed to uncover a single case (Rooth, 1974). In Japan, the incidence for one year was fifty-nine convicted cases, compared to 2,767 in England and Wales during the same year. Rooth (1973) also supposes that exhibitionism is rare in Latin America and Third World countries.

To what extent exhibitionism is exclusively a Western phenomenon remains open to debate. Much depends on the culture and police discretion in each country. In Latin American countries, for example, it is a common sight to see men and women openly urinating in public (Rhoads & Borjes, 1981). If a society reacts so casually to nudity or exposure of sexual organs, exhibitionism will lose its shock value. In an effort to determine comparable rates of exhibitionism, Rhoads and Borjes asked working women in both the United States and Guatemala how often men had exposed themselves to them in public. The survey indicated no difference in number of incidences, but the official records of the two countries were drastically different. This may reflect a reluctance on the part of the Guatemalan women to report exhibitionism, since officers are likely to ridicule the victims.

Exhibitionists are almost always males who delight in surprising and shocking their audiences. They differ from "strippers"—both male and female—in that the former expose themselves for economic gain rather than sexual gratification. In addition, of course, persons watching strippers do so deliberately and voluntarily. Exhibitionists sometimes masturbate during the exposure, but most prefer to do so in private, immediately following their exposure.

SITUATIONAL CHARACTERISTICS

If the offender is not particularly brazen, he may habitually hide behind the curtain of a window in his home when school lets out and, as young girls walk by, tap on the window, quickly expose himself, and make a fast retreat behind the curtain. This is risky, however, since his identity is easily traceable. Another favorite procedure is to use a car, drive slowly by a female or group of females, open the car door, show himself, and quickly drive away. The bolder exhibitionist is often the "street flasher" who opens his coat to a selected victim, makes certain the impression registers, and then runs or walks away.

Favorite locations for exposure vary, but most exhibitionists prefer public places like parks, theaters, stores, or relatively uncrowded streets. A Toronto study (Mohr, Turner, & Jerry, 1964) reported that 74 percent of a sample studied preferred open places, and most displayed themselves from a parked car. The remainder of the sample generally preferred their own homes, often exhibiting themselves through windows or doorways.

The overwhelming majority of exhibitionists prefer strangers for victims, and rarely expose more than once to the same victim. Although the preferred victim is usually female, an exhibitionist will occasionally expose himself to adult males and male children. Exhibitionists who prefer adult women will usually expose to them individually, while those who prefer female children will generally expose to small groups of two or three (Evans, 1970; Mohr, Turner, & Jerry, 1964). Most adult female victims are in their late teens or early twenties, usually unmarried. This supports the theory that most exhibitionists deliberately select their victims on the basis of specific stimuli. For example, an exhibitionist may have a definite preference for exhibiting to young girls between the ages of nine and eleven who look "naive." Another may search for a pretty face, dark hair, shapely legs, or various other physical features. Exhibitionists also tend to be consistent in the setting and time of day they choose for exposure. In fact, many are so predictable that, once the incident is reported, they are easily detected and arrested.

OFFENDER CHARACTERISTICS

Most exhibitionists begin their behavior at puberty, with a peak period occurring between ages fifteen and thirty (Evans, 1970). Contrary to popular belief, onset after age thirty is extremely rare, except in men with mental impairment due to organic brain damage or senility. Compared to the general population, exhibitionists usually have at least average intelligence, educational levels, and vocational interests (Blair & Lanyon, 1981). The majority also appear to have a reliable work record (Mohr, Turner, & Jerry, 1964).

Psychosis or other mental disorders are found no more frequently in exhibitionists than in the general population (Blair & Lanyon, 1981). However, exhibitionists show an above average incidence of previous sexual offenses other than exhibitionism, including voyeurism and even attempted rape. In the main, however, exhibitionists neither assault their audience physically nor desire sexual intercourse with them. It is highly probable that if victims expressed interest in sexual activity, most exhibitionists would be frightened and confused and would flee. In most cases, the primary motive behind the exhibitionism is the sexual excitation (reinforcement) the offender receives from shocking, surprising, or mildly frightening his victims. These reactions generate considerable sexual arousal. Later, he will probably masturbate to that image. On the other hand, if his exposure fails to engender the anticipated fright or surprise, and produces instead a disinterested, noncommittal facial expression, the offender is disappointed and suffers some loss of self-esteem.

Although many exhibitionists are married, most are considered socially and sexually inadequate both by themselves and those around them. Many are introverted, shy, socially reserved individuals who feel uncomfortable in most social situations. Generally, they are described as unassertive, self-effacing, timid, and passive. A majority of exhibitionists feel the urge to expose following a blow to their fragile self-esteem, which prompts heightened feelings of inadequacy and stress.

Therefore, like other sexual offenses, exhibitionism is a learned behavioral pattern reinforced by sexual arousal and the subsequent tension reduction achieved through masturbation. Many exhibitionists indicate that their behavior was initially acquired through some preadolescent sex play or by chance. For example, the history of most exhibitionists includes a vivid memory of a young girl expressing amazement or fear at their penis, viewed either accidentally or during sexual play. Characteristically, this attention was sexually exciting to the male, and he masturbated to the imagery of the incident. This not uncommon incident by itself is usually not sufficient to establish exhibitionism. However, a repeated pairing of the memory of the event with the sexual arousal derived from masturbation may lead to a proclivity for exhibitionism in individuals who lack sufficient self-control or self-regulatory mechanisms. That is, pleasurable, repetitive masturbatory activities in the presence of this mental imagery strongly encourage eventual exposure of the penis to victims who are perceived as similar to the initial observer. If the first, real-life exposure is sexually arousing, a strongly reinforcing chain of events is established. Each time the exhibitionist exposes and receives this sequence of rewards, the behavior pattern becomes that much more firmly entrenched.

During subsequent periods of stress and inadequacy, exposure becomes an increasingly effective way of dealing with uncomfortable emotions, especially when preferred victims are available. Therefore, because exhibitionism is a learned response, it continues to be repetitive and resistant to extinction. Furthermore, exhibitionists may expose themselves many thousands of times without complaints from victims. Irate adults do not report an incidence of exhibitionism unless the victim was their offspring. Even then they may not report in order to protect the child from having to describe the incident to police.

It is important to note that exhibitionists, in contrast to many pedophiles, often express a desire to change their behavior. Although they may expose themselves numerous times, once detected they are more likely to seek therapeutic help. Moreover, it is also not uncommon for an exhibitionist to seek professional help prior to being arrested for his behavior.

VOYEURISM AND FETISHISM

Voyeurism, also known as scoptophilia or inspectionalism, is the tendency to gain sexual excitement and gratification from observing unsuspecting others naked, undressing, or engaging in sexual activity. The term **fetishism** refers specifically to a sexual attraction to inanimate objects rather than to people. It is distinct from **partialism**, which is an exaggerated sexual interest in some part of the human anatomy not usually associated with sexual arousal, such as the knee. The individual with a fetish may become sexually aroused at the sight of boots, handbags, stockings, panties, fur, or even tailpipes on motor vehicles. The fetish object may be kissed, fondled, tasted, smelled, or just looked at.

Both voyeurism and fetishism are little more than minor sexual offenses, since they usually do not seriously harm the community. They are, of course, egregious violations of other people's privacy, because "victims" are being observed without their knowledge or their possessions are appropriated for "deviant" purposes. The voyeur or the fetishist runs afoul of the law when he harasses, trespasses, burglarizes, damages property, or steals objects.

Recall that the voyeur is sometimes an exhibitionist, and vice versa. However, the voyeur is less likely than the exhibitionist to become involved in serious forms of antisocial behavior, such as rape or other forms of violence. He does not harm his victims physically, and, like the exhibitionist, he is often described as a passive, shy, introverted, submissive, and harmless person. Clinical studies reveal that he suffers from strong heterosexual anxieties and immaturity.

One observation made in the Queen's Bench Foundation study (1978) demands attention. About 10 percent of the convicted rapists interviewed stated that they had watched their victim through a window before attacking her. The authors suggested that, in view of this finding, some "peeping Toms" should be watched for possible rape tendencies. However, some distinguishing aspects about voyeurism should be noted. All but one offender had intentions of raping before observing. The one rapist who said that he did not intend to rape when he watched his victim admitted that he did intend to "have sex" with her. In addition, all but one of these offenders had weapons in their possession at the time of their arrest (knives, guns, meat fork), even though they ordinarily did not carry them. Also, forceful entry into the victim's apartment was the common approach, and the victim was often raped with extreme violence.

These rapists, therefore, probably had little in common with the typical voyeur. Their intention from the outset was to attack the victim violently. They apparently watched the victim to determine her habits, whether anyone else was at home, and the best way to get into her residence. In other words, they were stalking their victims. The typical voyeur gets his satisfaction from watching, imagining, and eventually masturbating, with no intention of having sexual contact, forced or otherwise, with the victim.

Voyeurism, like other forms of sexual deviation, is a learned behavior. Although each individual has a unique approach to viewing, many voyeurs report the preadolescent experience of becoming sexually aroused while watching an unsuspecting woman undress. A common theme running through clinical studies is that the mental imagery of that scene is later coupled with sexual arousal, again perhaps satisfied through masturbation. Eventually, this conditioning produces a desire to observe different, realistic sexual scenes. Keep in mind that an important component of the sexual excitement experienced by the voyeur is his victim's unawareness of his presence. Erotic films or pornography, by themselves, are not likely to serve his purpose.

Fetishism is principally a male phenomenon pursued in the privacy of one's home, without interference in the lives of others. A fetish refers to the use of nonliving objects as a repeatedly and strongly preferred method of achieving sexual excitement. The fetish object is most often some women's wearing apparel, such as undergarments, shoes, boots, or stockings. The person with a fetish typically masturbates while rubbing, holding, or smelling the fetish object or may ask the sexual partner to wear the object during their sexual encounters (DSM-IV, 1994, p. 526). Through classical conditioning, virtually any object may assume sexual significance. Gosselin and Wilson (1984) describe a study of a man who was strongly attracted to safety pins. From the age of eight, he had experienced extreme sexual pleasure from gazing at these shiny objects in the privacy of his bathroom. "When he was 23 his wife observed the complete sequence, which began with him staring at the safety pin for about a minute. This was followed by a glassy-eyed appearance, vocal humming noises, sucking movements of the lips and total immobility for another minute or two" (Gosselin & Wilson, 1984, p. 104).

As mentioned previously, most fetish objects are those worn by the female, such as undergarments, shoes, boots, or hosiery. Chalkley and Powell (1983) found that underwear, stockings, and other types of lingerie were most popular for British fetish collectors. Next most common were rubber and certain rubber articles such as Mackintoshes, tubes, dolls, and paraphernalia for giving enemas.

In an excellent if controversial demonstration of fetish conditioning, Rachman (1966) showed male subjects a slide of a pair of women's black boots, followed immediately by slides of attractive, naked women (sexual arousal). After a number of such trials, the subjects became sexually excited, as measured by penile circumference, in response to the boots slide itself. There were also indications that the subjects not only became aroused by the particular boots, but also by slides of other boots and shoes as well.

Fetishism merits attention here primarily because the person with a strong attachment to an object might commit larceny or burglary to get it. One of the major avenues for obtaining fetishes is to steal, and, since clothes dryers are more in vogue in modern society than clotheslines, the fetishist's traditional method of stealing from the backyard clothesline has been replaced by more daring techniques. Chalkley and Powell (1983), in their British sample of forty-eight cases of fetishism, found that 38 percent experienced considerable excitement and sexual arousal when stealing the fetish. In this sense, it is conceivable that an indeterminant number of unexplained burglaries (when minor things are taken but more valuable items remain untouched) are a result of an impatient quest for fetishes! Some fetish burglars find sexual excitement just being in someone's house without his or her knowledge and presence. It is also not unusual for the fetish burglar to take valuable objects along with his fetish, however, either to throw off suspicion or to offer a face-saving "reasonable" explanation for the burglary if he is apprehended. In one serious fetish case described by Hazelwood and Burgess (1987), the offender admitted committing over five thousand burglaries primarily to obtain panties to satisfy his fetish. He also estimated that he stole valuables in about one-half of his burglaries.

TREATMENT OF SEXUAL OFFENDERS

Sexual offenders are often highly resistant to changing their deviant behavior patterns. Although a wide variety of treatment programs have been tried, very few have been successful in eradicating sexual offending. A 1994 survey of therapeutic services for sex offenders revealed that there were 710 adult and 684 juvenile treatment programs (Longo, Bird, Stevenson, & Fiske, 1994), compared to 297 adult and 346 juvenile treatment programs in 1985 (Knopp, Rosenberg, & Stevenson, 1986). Despite the increase in treatment programs, the success ratio remains disappointingly low. After careful review of the research and clinical literature, Furby, Weinrott, and Blackshaw (1989, p. 27) concluded: "There is as yet no evidence that clinical treatment reduces rates of sex reoffenses in general and no appropriate data for assessing whether it may be differentially effective for different types of offenders." The Furby review included all variants of therapeutic approaches.

Prentky, Knight, and Lee (1997) conclude that sex offender therapy can be categorized into four broad approaches. One approach is **evocative therapy**, a treatment that focuses on (a) helping offenders to understand the causes and motivations of their sexual behavior; and (b) increasing their empathy for the victims of the sexual assault. Evocative therapy may include individual, group, couples/marital, and family counseling. A second approach is **psychoeducational counseling**, which utilizes a group or class setting to remedy deficits in social and interpersonal skills. Psychoeducational strategies include anger management, the principles of Relapse Prevention, and other topics such as human sexuality, dating, and myths about sexuality and relationships. A third approach is **drug treatment**. This approach concentrates on "reducing sexual arousability and the frequency of deviant sexual fantasies through the use of antiandrogen and antidepressant medication" (Prentky et al., 1997, p. 13). The fourth approach is **cognitive behavior therapy**, which focuses on changing beliefs, fantasies, attitudes, and rationalizations that justify and perpetuate sexually violent behavior. Prentky et al. (1997) suggest that the most effective approach probably resides in using some combination of the four, although which specific combination remains unclear. They agree, however, that cognitive-behavioral approaches (complemented on occasion with some medication) continue to offer the most effective technique in the temporary cessation of deviant sexual behavior in motivated individuals. Cognitive-behavior therapy argues that maladaptive sexual behaviors are learned according to the same rules as normal sexual behavior, by means of classical and/or instrumental conditioning, modeling, reinforcement, generalization, and punishment. They are, therefore, modifiable. Cognitive-behavioral therapy, compared to traditional verbal, insight-oriented therapy, has demonstrated short-term effectiveness in eliminating exhibitionism and fetishism (Kilmann, Sabalis, Gearing, Bukstel, & Scovern, 1982), some forms of pedophilia (Hall, 1995; Marshall & Barbaree, 1988), and sexual aggression and arousal (Quinsey & Marshall, 1983).

The major problem, however, is not with getting the motivated offender to stop his deviant sexual pattern, but with preventing his relapse across time and situations. It is analogous to dieting. Most diet regimens do work in getting the motivated individual to lose weight. However, they offer little help in preventing people from eventually relapsing into old eating habits.

A treatment approach showing much promise in the treatment of sex offenders is called **Relapse Prevention (RP)**. "RP is a self-control program designed to teach individuals who are trying to change their behavior how to anticipate and cope with the problem of relapse" (George & Marlatt, 1989, p. 2). The program emphasizes self-management; clients are considered responsible not for the cause but for the solution of the problem. And as the name implies, the program concentrates on preventing a *relapse* of deviant sexual behavior. Therefore, RP distinguishes treatment from maintenance. As stated earlier, behavior therapy is effective in cessation of the behavior, but RP is specifically designed to be effective in helping the individual *maintain* the "cure." Distinctions are made between the terms *relapse* and *lapse*. "Relapse is a violation of a self-imposed rule or set of rules governing the rate or pattern of a selected target behavior" (George & Marlatt, 1989, p. 6). A lapse on the other hand, refers to "a single instance of violating the rule" (p. 6). "With sex offenders, the term relapse will refer to any occurrence of a sexual offense, thus connoting full-scale reestablishment of the problematic behavior. The term *lapse* will refer to any occurrence of willful and elaborate fantasizing about sexual offending or any return to sources of stimulation associated with the sexual offense pattern, but short of performance of the offense behavior" (p. 6).

RP, as a system of maintenance-oriented principles and interventions, has two central objectives: It teaches individuals (1) to cope effectively with "high-risk situations" (HRSs); and (2) to identify and respond to early warning signals of urges and "apparently irrelevant decisions" (AIDs). An HRS is any situation that poses a threat to the individual's sense of control over his behavior and consequently increases the probability of lapse or relapse. Examples of HRSs that may predispose an individual toward relapse include negative emotional states, such as anger and depression, interpersonal conflict, and various social pressures (George & Marlatt, 1989). Research by Pithers and associates (Pithers, Kashima, Cumming, Beal, & Buell, 1988; Pithers et al., 1989) has found that rapists often experience anger and use alcohol or other drugs before engaging in sexual aggression. Pedophiles, on the other hand, often experience anxiety or depression before seeking a child. A feeling of low self-esteem is experienced by both groups. These precursors reflect the beginning stages of an HRS. In other words, they psychologically predispose the individual toward a relapse.

Relapse seems to follow a sequence of events, all representing HRSs (Pithers, Marques, Gibat, & Marlatt, 1983; George & Marlatt, 1989). First, an urge, fleeting thought, or dream about committing an offense occurs. This is followed by elaborations of fantasies about committing the offense. Then, the aroused individual engages in masturbation coupled with fantasies and/or pornography related to the imagined sexual activity. The individual then plans how he is going to commit the act. Finally, the individual engages in the act. RP provides a framework within which a variety of behavioral, cognitive, educational, and skill-training techniques are used to train sex offenders to recognize and interrupt these chains of events (Marshall & Barbaree, 1988).

If the individual does not know how to cope with these HRSs, there is a high probability that he may lapse or relapse. On the other hand, if he learns how to cope, and he successfully manages to get through the HRS without violating his newly adopted rules, perceived control strengthens and the probability of relapse declines. The individual experiences a sense of mastery and self-efficacy and is better prepared for the next bout with an HRS.

The second component in RP intervention is AIDs—apparently irrelevant decisions. What at first glance seems to be an innocuous decision, unrelated to an HRS, may well be the first step toward relapse. For example, a pedophile's decision to take walks by parks and schoolyards at times when they are predictably crowded with children might be an early warning sign. It is important, therefore, that the individual learn to recognize and interrupt these apparently irrelevant decisions.

Critical to RP treatment intervention is the motivation of the offender. Without motivation, the program will not work. Remember, another key feature is that RP is for *maintaining* a cessation of the deviant behavior, not cessation itself. Therefore, a behavior therapy program or other conventional treatment intervention that stops the behavior must precede RP. The treatment phase normally takes a relatively short period of time. Another important point outlined by George and

Marlatt (1989) is that incarceration without treatment will not prevent reoffending. They offer three reasons for this. First, externally imposed, forced control does little to encourage an offender to seek help in changing his ways. Second, the offender can still maintain attachment to his offense pattern through fantasy. Third, it is conceivable that an offender could continue to actually engage in some semblance of his offense patterns even during confinement.

A volunteer outpatient treatment program for child molesters described by Marshall and Barbaree (1988) illustrates very well some of the procedures used to *stop* the behavior. The program uses a variety of behavior techniques. First, clinicians utilize aversive conditioning by linking electric shock to an offender's deviant visual and verbal images. Second, they reduce the attraction of deviant fantasies during masturbation through satiation therapy. Satiation therapy attempts to reduce the sex drive by having the patient masturbate at a frequency that will substantially reduce urges and cravings. Third, they eliminate the occurrence of deviant thoughts elicited by children or by daydreams during their day-to-day living pattern through smelling salts. That is, each patient carries smelling salts, and each time a deviant thought occurs, the patient is instructed to place the salts close to his nose and to inhale deeply. Through aversive conditioning, deviant thoughts are soon strongly associated with the experience of unpleasant smelling salts. Currently, there is no evidence that this aversive therapy has a negative impact on "normal" sexual thoughts and behavior.

The program also enhances the social competence of the child molester by training him in the skills of conversation with adult partners as well as reducing the anxiety in the presence of adult partners. The treatment also addresses training in assertiveness, and counsels the patient in financial management, use of leisure time, and alcohol or drug use. So far, Marshall and Barbaree have been able to do a three-and-a-half year follow-up on 117 patients, some of whom received the treatment described and some who did not. While 32 percent of the nontreatment group has reoffended, only 14 percent of the treated group has reoffended. In another RP project, Pithers et al. (1988) found a 10 percent relapse rate for rapists, and a 3 percent relapse rate for pedophiles during a short follow-up (less than one year).

RP is a relatively recent development and its long-term success has yet to be established. However, it does have substantial promise for the elimination of deviant behavior in offenders motivated to change. And as noted by Prentky et al. (1997, p. 14), "Continuity of treatment is considered a critical factor in managing sex offenders. Maintenance is forever, and Relapse Prevention never ends. Community-based clinical management must be supportive, vigilant, and informed by current wisdom about maximally effective maintenance."

SUMMARY AND CONCLUSIONS

Rape is committed for a variety of reasons by a variety of offenders. A major motivation appears to be to harm, derogate, or embarrass the victim. In some situations, the rapist may interpret his behavior as harmless, believing that his victims enjoy being "roughed up." Nevertheless, the effect is invariably the opposite. The psychological and social damages to the victim are incalculable. Sexual assault by husbands, dates, and intimate friends is more frequent than commonly supposed.

Most rapists are young and often show a history of rape and other violent actions. Several attempts at typologies or classification systems of sex offenders have been tried, the most notable being those developed by the Massachusetts Treatment Center and Groth.

Rape behavior appears due, in part, to the type of socialization experiences the offender has had. He has constructed, from information received from a variety of sources and models, a belief and value system that encourages and justifies the rape behavior. Further, most rapists have attitudes and an ideology that encourage men to be dominant, controlling, and powerful, while expecting women to be submissive, permissive, and compliant. This attitudinal pattern may be much more prevalent in society in both men and women than commonly realized.

We also learned that under very high levels of arousal, any consideration of the rightness of a sexual assaulter's behavior or its consequences may be obliterated. As we saw with reference to homicide and assault, high levels of arousal reduce attention to private self-awareness and personal standards of appropriate conduct. Under high levels of excitement, some normally law-abiding persons may become rapists, or at least use the high excitement as a justification for their rape behavior. Of course, some people possess a value system that justifies rape or the resolution of interpersonal conflict through violence, regardless of their arousal level.

Pedophilia, also potentially a very serious offense from the victim standpoint, appears to involve less aggression and violence, except, of course, for the pedophilia that includes rape and assault. Pedophilia appears to be motivated by both sexual desire and an expectation of sexual adequacy. Like rape, it is engaged in for a variety of reasons by a variety of offenders. There is no such thing as a common "molester profile." Each has his own construct system and beliefs about his behavior and motivations. Some offenders, for whatever reason, are vicious and violent; others are passive, relatively meek people who enjoy the companionship of children. Most pedophiles are the latter. They appear to see themselves as sexually and interpersonally inept adults who feel more comfortable interacting with children. Classical conditioning also appears to play a prominent role in the development of pedophilia, perhaps much more so than in rape.

We closed this chapter with some attention to the minor sexual offenses of exhibitionism, voyeurism, and fetishes. Classical conditioning, particularly masturbatory conditioning, also appears to play a crucial role in the development of these sexual deviations. Sexual arousal repeatedly linked with objects and persons seems especially important.

Treatment of sexual offenses can be highly successful if the offender's motivation to change is evident. Successful treatment strategies must not only focus on the cessation of the antisocial sexual conduct, but on maintenance as well.

ECONOMIC CRIME, PUBLIC ORDER CRIME, AND OTHER CRIME

conomic crimes generally involve the illegal acquisition of money and material goods, or the illegal destruction of property for financial gain. Crimes against the public order are actions against public or moral decency, or other conduct that is interpreted as a threat to the orderly operations of a given society. Examples include prostitution, pornography, gambling, vagrancy, disorderly conduct, public drunkenness, and drug use. Often, these violations are called "victimless crimes" because of the difficulty of pinpointing an identifiable victim of the offense. Later in this chapter we will concentrate on the public order crime of prostitution. In the next chapter we will turn our attention to drug use and its relationship to criminal behavior. Most of this chapter will focus on the various kinds of economic offenses.

Economic crimes are similar to the violent offenses discussed in earlier chapters in one important psychological aspect. Most of them involve a dehumanization of the victim, although in a different sense from the dehumanization that often occurs in violence. In most economic crimes (such as larceny and burglary), the offenders avoid confronting their victims directly. Therefore, they do not directly observe or experience the economic, social, and psychological discomfort of their victims. In the victim's absence, internal values and social constraints are less effective, allowing the offender to repress, deny, or justify the crime more easily. As Gresham Sykes (1956) puts it, the individual's internal sentiments are more easily neutralized by the physical absence of the victim. The offender does not have to think of the effects his or her actions have on the victim, because the offender does not know the victim as a human being, only as a target. The exception, of course, is robbery, but even in this case, victim contact is usually fleeting.

We will focus specifically on the economic crimes of robbery, burglary, shoplifting, larceny-theft, and auto theft. Figure 11-1 provides a percentage breakdown of the UCR index crimes for 1996. As you can see, larceny-theft, burglary, and motor vehicle theft account for nearly 73 percent of the total index crimes, with larceny-theft accounting for a large majority. In addition, offenses subsumed under the label "white-collar" crime will also be covered. Finally, we will touch on hostage taking (kidnapping), bombings, and arson, which could also be classi-

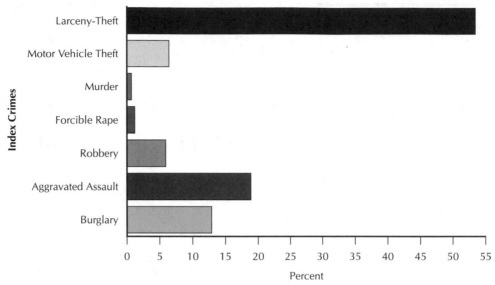

Figure 11-1   Percent Distribution of Index Crimes in the United States
(Source: U.S. Department of Justice, *Uniform Crime Reports, 1997.*)

fied as violent offenses. Because they are often motivated by the desire to acquire property, social status, or psychological rewards, they are included here as economic crimes. Robbery is also considered a violent crime, but in most cases the primary motive again is the desire for material gain.

Obviously, most people engage in economic crime for the money, or for other tangible rewards that meet biological, psychological, or social needs. Sykes notes, however, that this does not tell us why some people commit economic crime under certain social conditions, while others do not. Explanations based strictly on economic necessity and the satisfaction of basic human needs do not go far enough. Sykes proposes the concept of **relative deprivation** as one additional factor. To assess the economic want associated with economic crime, we should consider not what the person has or is making in personal income, but rather how great the discrepancy is between what he or she has and would like to have. Specifically, relative deprivation is the psychological distance between what people perceive they have now and what they feel they can realistically attain—their goal. Goals are strongly influenced by the social groups to which people belong or reference groups with which they identify.

From a psychological perspective, economic crimes cannot be simply explained by biological needs, material wants, or even in terms of relative deprivation. Powerful cognitive motivators must also be considered. These cognitive factors are in the form of outcome expectations and the capacity to predict and appreciate future consequences of one's behavior. Furthermore, the cognitive forces may be relatively independent of external reinforcements like tangible rewards or even social and status rewards. Self-reinforcements, including self-rewards and self-punishments, may represent a major motivating factor in many economic crimes.

Cognitive factors are also extremely important in another sense: They allow the offender to justify his or her behavior. A strong theme of this chapter is the tendency of economic offenders to minimize, distort, or deny misconduct or reprehensible behavior. The aforementioned psychological separation from the victim helps them to do this. We will expand on these psychological issues of motivation and justification throughout the following pages.

BURGLARY

Burglary is the unlawful entry of a structure, with or without force, with intent to commit a felony or theft. Over 2.5 million burglaries occurred in the United States during 1996 (FBI, 1997). Nationwide, the residential burglary rate is 18 per 1,000 households. Over one-third of these household burglaries do not involve forced entry. That is, the offenders entered through an unlatched window or unlocked door or used a key "hidden" in an obvious place, such as under a doormat.

Consistently, two-thirds of all reported burglaries involve residential property, while the remaining one-third involves commercial establishments. Burglaries are more likely to occur during the warmer months, especially August, apparently because people are more likely to be outdoors or away on vacation and are more likely to leave doors and windows open, making their residences vulnerable. A study by Langer and Miranksy (1983) reveals that a large segment of the population does not take responsibility for burglary prevention. Approximately half of the New York City residents questioned admitted they did not lock all their doors when away from home, even if they had been burglarized before. Interestingly, while 66 percent believed that burglary could be prevented, 61 percent of these subjects did not use all their locks. They believed that it was the responsibility of others (e.g., the police, the landlord, the building superintendent) to guard the premises, rather than their own personal responsibility. Furthermore, those who thought their neighborhoods were unsafe and burglary-prone were less likely to use locks than those who considered their neighborhoods safe and less burglary-prone. Possibly, people in burglary prone areas are convinced that if someone decides to burglarize their homes there is not much they can do about it, locks or no locks.

Like other criminal offenses, burglary seems to be primarily a crime committed by the young; nearly two-thirds of those arrested in 1996 were under twenty-five, with the average age being about twenty-two (FBI, 1997). To some extent, this arrest ratio may reflect the lack of sophistication of younger burglars who, because of their inexperience, are more likely to be detected. However, researchers have noted that, with increasing age, some burglars find they are not as nimble and athletic as they once were. Crawling through small open windows and climbing fences take their toll, and these strenuous activities become more burdensome with age. Thus, many older burglars turn to shoplifting (Cromwell, Olson, & Avary, 1991). Shoplifting is considerably easier, less risky, and more cost efficient. Shoplifted items are more easily converted to cash and are more profitable than items gained through burglary, because they are new, untraceable, and have their pricetags attached. Furthermore, the criminal penalties are significantly less for shoplifting than they are for burglary.

Burglary is largely a male enterprise, with only 9 percent of those arrested being women. Although 68 percent of those arrested are white, minorities (30 percent are African American) are overrepresented in proportion to their numbers in the general population (Eskridge, 1983; FBI, 1997).

As noted earlier, about two of every three burglaries are residential. Burglary of residences usually occurs during the daytime and on weekdays, whereas commercial establishments are usually burglarized late at night and on weekends (Cromwell et al., 1991; Pope, 1977b). This is not surprising, since burglary is a passive crime; the offender selects times and places that will minimize the possibility of an encounter with victims. Almost all experienced burglars (well over 90 percent) assert they will not even enter a residence when the occupants are believed to be at home (Cromwell et al., 1991). The home is occupied during the day most commonly by women or retired individuals. However, burglars know that occupants develop predictable patterns regarding the use of discretionary time for the purposes of shopping, errands, or visiting friends or relatives. Women who work outside the home also show similar patterns on weekends. Generally, the prime time for these errands and visits tends to be between 10:00 and 11:00 A.M., and from 1:00 to 3:00 P.M. (Cromwell et al., 1991). Parents, on the other hand, often develop predictable patterns of taking children to school and picking them up after school.

Of all crimes, burglary also offers the greatest probability of success with the least amount of risk. Not only is it a crime without victim contact and probability of identification, but it does not require weapons. Furthermore, the penalties usually are less severe than those for robbery. Juvenile offenders are more likely than their older counterparts to burglarize during the daytime hours (Pope, 1977c). In fact, a prime time for many juvenile burglaries is at the end of the school day, often between 3 P.M. and 6 P.M.

BURGLARY CUES AND SELECTED TARGETS

The identification of situational cues are especially important in successful burglary. Nee and Taylor (1988) found that there are at least four broad categories of relevant cues used by experienced residential burglars. They are as follows:

1. Occupancy cues, such as letters or newspapers visible in mailbox, motor vehicles present, windows, blinds, and curtains shut or open
2. Wealth cues, such as the appearance of the house, the neighborhood, the quality of the landscaping, the make(s) of car(s) driven, and visible furnishings
3. Layout cues, such as how easy it would be to gain access to the house or building, as well as escape
4. Security cues, such as alarm systems, window locks, and deadbolt locks

Taylor and Nee (1988) designed a study that tested the possible differences in identifying these cues between burglars and homeowners. The burglars consisted of a group of fifteen experienced burglars serving time in Cork Prison, and the homeowners consisted of fifteen Irish homeowners. Each subject was requested to explore a simulated environment made up of slides and maps of five different houses. The researchers found that burglars were better able to discern security provisions and were more concerned about escaping successfully from the scene than were homeowners. Most surprising, however, was the high amount of agreement between burglars and homeowners on which houses were most vulnerable to burglary. More research needs to be done in this area and the range of relevant cues better identified.

Bennett and Wright (1984) conducted an extensive three-year project on convicted burglars confined in various prisons throughout southern England. The researchers' primary interest was to learn the decision-making processes and perceptions of the residential burglars at the time of the crime. The principal method of data collection in the study was through semistructured interviews with the burglars themselves. Although a majority of the burglars had committed a variety of other economic crimes, almost all of them considered burglary their main criminal activity. Therefore, most of them probably qualify as professionals rather than amateurs.

Bennett and Wright discovered that almost all the burglaries were planned. Very few of the burglaries were the result of spur-of-the-moment decisions, nor were there any constant or irrepressible urges to burglarize. The two main aspects that went into the planning were the situational cues of surveillability and occupancy. Surveillability cues were related to the amount of cover or openness around the house, whether it was overlooked by neighboring houses, the availability of access to the rear, and the presence or proximity of neighbors. Occupancy cues were similar to the ones reported by Nee and Taylor, such as a car in the driveway, lights on in the house, the presence of mail, whether the walks were shoveled or the lawn was cut, and so forth. Experienced burglars said that "occupancy proxies" were the major deterrents in attempts to burglarize. Specifically, burglar alarms and dogs were extremely important in the prevention of burglary. This was also a consistent finding of Cromwell and colleagues (1991). In fact, Cromwell and colleagues found that the dog does not have to be a large one. Any dog will do, since a large one poses a physical threat and the small dog will be noisy. Cromwell and his associates also found that deadbolts caused burglars considerable difficulty in entry, even though some of the experienced burglars claimed such locks would not be any problem. However, Cromwell and colleagues not only obtained self-report data from experienced burglars, but also had them demonstrate their claims. Security locks and deadbolts caused all kinds of trouble, even for highly experienced burglars—even though they said prior to the demonstration these locks would not give them any trouble. Much of the research on burglary, on the other hand, finds that increased police patrols, and other such strategies, have very little influence on decisions to burglarize, or on its success rate. However, nosy neighbors tend to be strong deterrents for burglars. This observation is supported by both experienced burglars and crime statistics.

Research data suggest that, although burglary is a "planned" behavior, burglars identify a large number of potential targets, and then select the most vulnerable. Cromwell and his colleagues admonish, however, that although much of the research on burglary suggests that a high percentage of burglars make carefully planned, highly rational decisions based on a detailed evaluation of environmental cues, the crime seems to be more of finding the right opportunity from an array of potential targets. Burglary is not generally an impulsive crime, but it isn't usually planned to precise detail either.

The Cromwell and colleagues study found that many burglars engage in what they referred to as **rational reconstruction**. That is, "Our findings indicate that burglars interviewed in prison or those recalling crimes from the past, either consciously or unconsciously, may engage in rational reconstruction—a reinterpretation of past behavior through which the actor recasts activities in a manner consistent with 'what should have been,' rather than 'what was'" (Cromwell et al., 1991, p. 42). Thus, self-report data from burglars may indicate that there was considerable planning involved in the burglary, but actually the crime was one of opportunity. The Cromwell project not only gathered data from self-reports, but also had the experienced burglars simulate their burglaries. Moreover, the research team went on "ride-alongs" during which the burglars described their previous burglaries or described how they would burglarize a residence they perceived as vulnerable. Thus, the researchers were able to identify some of the disparities between what the professional burglars told them and what they actually did before, during, and after the real burglary. These findings suggest that research based exclusively on self-report data may be incomplete or suspect.

Cromwell and his colleagues (1991) also found in their systematic study of experienced burglars that one of the most popular entry methods was through sliding glass patio doors. Burglars said that these doors are easily popped out of their sliding tracks by hand or with aid of a crowbar or screwdriver. Entry is therefore quick and noiseless. Another common method is to remove, cut, or gently break a window pane and crawl through the open window. A skillful burglar will carefully remove the pane, crawl through, and then replace the pane in a professional manner. Other commonly preferred methods for residential burglary include: forcing the rear door open with a pry tool or kicking it down; or opening the garage door and forcing open the door between the garage and the house.

WHO BURGLARIZES?

National research data on arrested burglars in the United States indicate that a large proportion commit the offense near their own residence. This seems especially true for juvenile offenders (Pope, 1977a). The Santa Clara Criminal Justice Pilot Program (1972) found that over one-half of the apprehended offenders traveled no more than a mile from their own home to commit the offenses. It is difficult to generalize from this statistic, however, because apprehended burglars are presumably less skillful and thus more detectable than burglars who succeed. It is possible that successful burglars operate farther away from home. Eskridge (1983) found that those who burglarized commercial establishments were more willing to travel much greater distances.

Over half the apprehended burglars worked with an accomplice (Chimbos, 1973; Pope, 1977a). Eskridge (1983), who conducted a survey of crime in Lincoln, Nebraska, reports that nearly two-thirds of the identified burglars worked in groups of two or more. On a national level, groups of two or more are responsible for just under half (42 percent) of all burglary incidents. National data also suggest that very few burglars work with more than three accomplices. Younger offenders and females are more likely to use accomplices than older males (Pope, 1977a). However, this pattern also depends to some extent on the sophistication of the offender. Experienced, competent offenders who realize the formidable challenge presented by protection instruments (alarms or safes) may also be more likely to take on assistants (Shover, 1972).

As for other criminal offenses, the best predictor of burglary is an offender's record. In a California analysis, 80 percent of the offenders studied had a prior arrest record (Pope, 1977c). Of these, 58 percent had a prior burglary arrest and 47 percent had prior drug arrests, usually selling. Males were far more likely to have a previous criminal record than females.

USE OF ALCOHOL AND OTHER SUBSTANCES

Although a well-known Santa Clara 1972 project concluded that burglars are rarely under the influence of alcohol and other drugs at the time of their crime, the more recent data reported by the Cromwell and associates (1991) study indicates this is not so. Ninety-three percent of the professional burglars studied by the Cromwell group said they "fixed" or "got high" before entering a residence. These experienced, professional burglars admitted they needed to lower their anxiety levels and reduce their fear prior to the burglary. The vast majority of these burglars reported moderate amounts of alcohol or drugs simply made them better burglars, because these substances increased their alertness, vigilance, and improved their nerve to stay in the residences long enough to search for and locate a variety of items to steal. Specifically, the calming effects of drugs and alcohol enabled them to focus more on environmental cues related to risk, as well as valuable items hidden in the house that they normally would not find. Psychologically, this observation makes sense because high levels of arousal do narrow one's attention span and reduce one's focus on environmental cues under certain pressure situations (Easterbrook, 1959). Also, the Cromwell study found that heroin-using burglars tend to be more rational, more professional, and less likely to be arrested than burglars using cocaine or speed (or more generally, stimulants). Moreover, the heroin user was able to exercise considerable control over the amount of the drug used for maximum proficiency in burglarizing.

WHAT HAPPENS TO THE MERCHANDISE?

Amateur burglars usually take money or personal items that they need, whereas the professional takes items with excellent resale value, like stereos, cameras, television sets, jewelry, and furs (Vetter & Silverman, 1978). The professional usually has access to a "fence," whereas the amateur rarely has that kind of contact. A fence, an integral component in the professional burglary cycle, is a person who knowingly buys stolen merchandise for the purpose of resale. Professional burglars also have individually distinctive methods and not infrequently leave their mark (their signature) to goad the investigators they have foiled.

The Cromwell and associates (1991) research raises serious questions concerning the extent to which professional fences are used today. In their investigation of experienced burglars operating in an urban Texas metropolitan area of 250,000, they found considerable diversity in the channels through which stolen property was distributed. Some burglars sold their stolen property to pawnshops, others to friends and acquaintances, and still others traded their property for drugs. Some resold the merchandise to legitimate businesses or strangers. The researchers, therefore, suggest that today the "professional fence may have been displaced by a more diverse and readily accessed market for stolen property" (p. 73).

MOTIVES

As you might expect, the motives for burglary are varied, but the primary factor for professionals is undoubtedly monetary gain. When performed competently, burglary is a lucrative business with low risks and with monetary rewards far surpassing those the burglar might earn in the "straight" world. David (1974) learned that a husband and wife team he interviewed made, on the average, $400 to $500 a day; a solitary offender in his sample made about $500 per week. These figures will obviously be much larger in today's market. Many professionals also conceive of their behavior as a challenging skill to be continually developed and refined. Some even said they get a "rush" of excitement during the planning and commission of the crime, especially if they are good at it (Cromwell et al., 1991). In this sense, burglary is highly adaptive and represents an instrumental behavior supported by strong reinforcement. For many burglars, however, a simple conclusion that they participate in their crimes as their sole profession or lucrative business may be unwarranted. A vast majority of burglary is committed to *supplement* the offender's incomes and to improve their quality of life (Rengert & Wasilchick, 1985). The income gained from burglary enables the offender to buy drugs, alcohol, expensive goods, and, more broadly, to be able "to party." Subsistence needs are often met through other sources of income, such as a regular job.

Shover (1972) discusses some of the outstanding features of the competent professional burglar, whom he calls the "good burglar." This burglar demonstrates technical skill, maintains a good reputation for personal integrity among colleagues in the criminal subculture, gets most of his income from burglary, and has been at least relatively successful at the crime. A good reputation means that the burglar is closed-mouth, stands up to police, and is sympathetic to the criminal way of life.

The professional burglar, then, is primarily motivated by money but also by self-satisfaction and accomplishment. When self-satisfaction and self-reinforcement are conditioned on certain accomplishments, people are motivated to expend the effort needed to attain the desired goal, perhaps even independently of monetary gain. Thus, a burglar who takes great pride in developing ingenious techniques and stumping police is even more likely to continue his illegal conduct. While external reinforcements (tangible rewards) are important, internal reinforcement may be a very powerful motivating and regulating factor.

LARCENY AND MOTOR VEHICLE THEFT

McCaghy (1980) refers to the larceny-theft category as a "garbage can" because it is heterogeneous and hard to classify. Larceny-theft is defined as the "unlawful taking, carrying, leading, or riding away of property from the possession or constructive possession of another" (FBI, 1997, p. 43). It differs from burglary in that it does not involve unlawful entry. Larceny includes pickpocketing, purse snatching, shoplifting, stealing from vending machines or from motor vehicles, and theft of property left outdoors (bicycles, pedigreed dogs, lawnmowers), and so on. Over 50 percent of all economic crimes fall into the larceny category. Figure 11-2 provides a percentage distribution of the more common types of theft.

The 1996 larceny-theft rate in the United States was 2,976 per 100,000 people (FBI, 1997). Thefts of motor vehicle parts, accessories, and things left in cars made up the largest portion of reported larcenies (23 percent).

Motor vehicle theft is defined as the theft or attempted theft of a motor vehicle, including the stealing of automobiles, trucks, buses, motorcycles, motorscooters, and snowmobiles (FBI, 1997). An estimated total of 1.4 million thefts of motor vehicles occurred in the United States during 1996 (FBI, 1997). The 1996 national motor vehicle theft rate was about 526 per 100,000 people, and about one of every 135 registered motor vehicles.

Larceny and motor vehicle theft are common and widespread offenses, but research reporting specifically on these areas is rarely available. To some extent, the

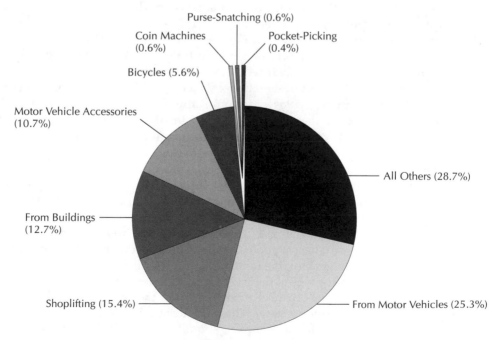

Figure 11-2   Larceny-Theft Offenses in the United States
(Source: U.S. Department of Justice, *Uniform Crime Reports, 1997*.)

motivating factors that apply to burglary apply here as well. On the other hand, larceny is more likely to be committed by the nonprofessional and the desperate.

SHOPLIFTING

Shoplifting is a very frequent and costly type of crime. Although shoplifting comprises about 15 percent of all arrests for larceny-theft in 1996 (Figure 11-2), it is obviously underreported by a large margin. The actual incidence of shoplifting, therefore, is largely unknown.

ESTIMATES OF INCIDENCE AND PREVALENCE

The data on all other economic crimes are difficult to obtain, but data acquisition for shoplifting offenses is especially difficult, since store personnel exercise wide discretion in reporting offenses. Hindelang (1974) found that whether charges were filed depended on the retail value of the stolen object, what was stolen, and the manner in which it was taken, rather than demographic and personality characteristics of the shoplifter. Specifically, the offender's race did not seem to matter, nor whether the offender was male or female, poor or middle class. What determined referral for arrest was whether the item was expensive, had resale value, or was stolen in a professional, skillful manner. However, research by Davis, Lundman, and Martinez (1991) found that shoplifters are more likely to be arrested not only when they take expensive items, but also when they resist being apprehended, have no local address, and/or live in poor neighborhoods. In England, on the other hand, store managers consider the age of the shoplifter as well as the value of the stolen item (Farrington & Burrows, 1993). The British study found that, generally, store managers did not report to the police the very young (under age seventeen) or very old (over sixty), the mentally impaired, or those shoplifters in an advanced stage of pregnancy, unless they were caught repeatedly. In a series of observational studies (also in England) by Abigail Buckle and David Farrington (1984), random samples of customers were followed by trained observers as they shopped. Approximately one in fifty were observed to steal. The amount of shoplifting, however, differed dramatically from store to store. Shoplifting characteristics in supermarkets are likely to differ significantly from those exhibited in retail department stores or hardware stores. Buckle and Farrington (1994) conducted a replication of the 1984 study. Again, trained observers randomly followed approximately five hundred customers in a small department store located in another city. The proportion of customers who shoplifted were between 1 and 2 percent and a majority were male. Most of the shoplifters also purchased goods as they checked out of the store, probably to allay suspicion. In general, the items stolen were small, low-cost items. In contrast to the original study where there was a preponderance of older shoplifters (age fifty-five or over), Buckle and Farrington found that most of the shoplifters were young (age twenty-five or less). These studies underscore the warning that estimations concerning the incidence of shoplifting must be placed within a situational, cultural, and historical context. Furthermore, apprehension statistics may tell us more about the store security personnel practices and biases than about the shoplifting population (Klemke, 1992). In fact, it is not uncommon for security personnel to claim that they have developed a "sixth sense" for picking out likely suspects. This "sixth sense" is, in some cases, a bias or stereotype against certain segments of the population more than any all-encompassing, accurate skill.

WHO SHOPLIFTS?

It has been assumed that shoplifting is committed primarily by adolescent girls and women. Among the explanations offered for women's greater involvement in shoplifting, the most common is that women have greater opportunity to steal small items from merchants than do men. Gibbens (1981) notes that women are more likely to be in stores where detectives are stationed. As men join the ranks of frequent shoppers, however, their shoplifting rates are beginning to increase, and the gap between men and women is narrowing (Moore, 1984). Baumer and Rosenbaum (1984), in an extensive review of the available research, conclude that gender ratio appears to be about fifty-fifty today. Farrington and Burrows (1993) report a similar gender ratio in England. Although women apparently shoplifted more than men in the past, more men than women were actually *convicted* (Smart, 1976).

There has also been a widespread belief that a vast majority of shoplifters are juveniles under age eighteen. Currently, most studies indicate that, although juveniles make up a large proportion of shoplifters, they are by no means the majority (Baumer & Rosenbaum, 1984). Moreover, about 70 percent of apprehended juvenile offenders were working in groups, compared to about 20 percent of apprehended adult shoplifters (Baumer & Rosenbaum, 1984). It should also be noted that shoplifting by juveniles is more likely to be evenly proportioned among males and females (Russell, 1973; Baumer & Rosenbaum, 1984). This is also apparently true for shoplifting by the elderly, a phenomenon on the increase and engaged in by both men and women in nearly equal numbers (Fyfe, 1984).

Shoplifting activity appears to change dramatically along the lifespan. Self-report data indicate that many individuals reported shoplifting when they were under age ten, but the frequency—for most individuals—declined as they got older (Klemke, 1992). The decline is particularly noticeable between ages seventeen and twenty-three. Klemke notes that this pattern supports the **invariance hypothesis**, proposed by Gottfredson and Hirschi (1990), that crime declines with age everywhere and at all times. For some reason, however, the tendency to shoplift reemerges during middle age, especially for women. A majority of apprehended shoplifters are in the middle-income bracket and generally carry enough money or credit cards to pay for the items stolen (Baumer & Rosenbaum, 1984).

Baumer and Rosenbaum outline some of the psychological characteristics and behavioral patterns of shoplifters. They note that such things as extreme nervousness, aimless walking up and down the aisles, looking around frequently, glancing up from the merchandise frequently, and leaving the store and returning a number of times are some of the indicators that suggest shoplifting.

In spite of its traditional prominence in economic crime, shoplifting has received little psychological research attention. The most heavily quoted source on the subject, Mary Owen Cameron's *The Booster and the Snitch: Department Store*

Shoplifting (1964), reported data accumulated in the 1940s and early 1950s. Cameron divided her shoplifters into two groups: Commercial shoplifters were "boosters," and amateur pilferers were "snitches." All of her data were subsequently explained with reference to this dichotomy. The boosters were professionals, accepted members of the criminal subculture: They stole for substantial financial gain by choosing items from preselected locations. Boosters used a wide range of techniques such as "booster boxes," packages designed for concealing items inserted through hidden slots or hinged openings, or "stalls," containers with hidden compartments (large handbags, coats with hidden pockets). Snitches, on the other hand, were "respectable" persons who rarely had criminal records. They did not consider themselves thieves, and the idea that they may actually be arrested and prosecuted rarely crossed their minds. Very often, once apprehended, they claimed they stole the item on impulse and did not know what came over them.

Some social science research has focused on elderly shoplifters. Feinberg (1984) found that shoplifting was neither a female-dominated offense nor undertaken for subsistence purposes. Elderly shoplifters, he notes, are neither indigent, lonely, nor victims of poor memory. He attributes their criminal offenses to changes in status that separate the elderly from mainstream society. Often, they must reevaluate their past values and try out different selves and meanings. To what extent Feinberg's research may be generalized to other age groups remains an open question.

MOTIVES

The motives behind commercial shoplifting may be clearer than those behind the amateur type. Whereas boosters take merchandise of value, snitches tend to take inexpensive items they can use. Some research has noted that male snitches prefer items of more value, such as stereo equipment, records, and jewelry. Women snitches seem to take clothing, cosmetics, and food. The boosters shoplift for the money; the snitches for more obscure reasons.

Theories concerning the intentions of snitches range from economic ones, like attempts to stretch the family budget (Cameron, 1964), to emotional ones, like attempts to satisfy needs centering around matrimonial stress, loneliness, and depression (Russell, 1973). In recent years, some "experts" have even concluded that most shoplifting is an addiction, much like gambling and alcoholism. The notion of shoplifting as a means of alleviating unmet needs or addiction is weak and poorly documented, however. The behavior gains attention, but it also becomes aversive. On the other hand, the contention that shoplifting has primarily an economic motivation seems oversimplified. Shoplifting is pursued by different people for different reasons.

METHODS OF SHOPLIFTING

Males tend to favor concealing stolen merchandise in pockets or clothing, while females generally prefer purses or shopping bags. The method of concealment, however, depends considerably on the merchandise, the gender of the offender, and the type of store. In clothing stores, shoplifters would more likely attempt to walk out wearing the clothing after leaving the fitting room, for example. Males prefer to hide items beneath their clothing in supermarkets, while pockets are preferred in drug and discount stores. Females tend to prefer purses for concealment in supermarkets or grocery stores, and packages and bags in drug and discount stores. Two things that draw the attention of store security personnel are false broken arm casts and large shopping bags obtained from a prior visit.

The item most commonly stolen in supermarkets or grocery stores is meat, while in drug stores clothing tends to be the more common, followed by health and beauty aids. A common trick for some shoplifters in a supermarket is to do a lot of "grazing" while shopping. That is, the shopper eats, drinks (commonly soda), or "tastes" while shopping, especially in the fruit section, and fails to pay for the items while checking out. Klemke (1992) notes that some shoplifters prefer to conceal the items, while others do not. Some walk out the door with the item(s) nonchalantly, as though nothing is amiss.

TYPES OF SHOPLIFTERS

Moore (1984), studying three hundred convicted shoplifters referred for presentence investigation, identified five patterns of offending. Although no shoplifters were considered professional to the degree of Cameron's booster category (the professionals may have escaped detection), 11.7 percent were semiprofessional, reporting shoplifting behavior at least once a week. Their "take" amounted to approximately $1,250 a year.

The most frequent type of shoplifter in Moore's study was the "amateur" (56.4 percent), who stole small personal items when the opportunity arose. The methods used by amateurs were less sophisticated than those of the semiprofessionals, and unlike the semiprofessionals, the amateurs admitted that their behavior was morally wrong or illegal. Both types of shoplifting were premeditated, habitual, and directed toward financial gain. Persons in the amateur category were more likely to exhibit mild personality disorders or to be plagued by psychosocial stressors associated with interpersonal problems, such as family disruption.

Approximately 17 percent of Moore's offender population were impaired by mental or emotional problems. However, very few individuals (1.7 percent) had severe mental or emotional problems that directly "compelled" them to shoplift. The persons in this latter category were called "episodic" offenders.

Fifteen percent of the sample were "impulse" shoplifters, and another 15 percent were "occasional" offenders. Impulse shoplifters typically had seen an item that they desired but were unable to afford. They had picked it up and pocketed it or carried it around the store, often in a daze, trying to decide whether to steal it. Eventually they tried to walk out but were detected. Later, they could not recall at what point they had made the decision to shoplift. Occasional offenders were less impulsive, but more likely to steal for excitement or a dare. Both impulse and occasional offenders were extremely embarrassed when detected, pleaded with officials to give them another chance, and were considered unlikely to shoplift again.

Although Moore found no significant gender differences in overall shoplifting, 68 percent of the teenage offenders were male, whereas 56.5 percent of the adult offenders were female. Moore also found interesting differences between male and female adult offenders with respect to psychological stress. More women reported being under great stress in their lives than did men (28.9 percent of the women compared to 13.5 percent of the men). However, this difference may also be due to the greater reluctance of men to report stress or other emotional problems in general. Mental disorders, found only in a small percentage of the total shoplifter population, appeared twice as often in women as in men. There were no gender differences in the incidence of milder mental disorders, however. Substance abuse, on the other hand, was more common among men than women (52 percent to 26 percent).

One thing does appear clear, however. Clinicians and researchers have been unable to substantiate evidence of **kleptomania**, the *irresistible* impulse to steal unneeded objects. Some have even questioned its very existence as a behavior pattern. According to the DSM-IV, the kleptomaniac "experiences a rising subjective sense of tension before the theft and feels pleasure, gratification, or relief when committing the theft" (p. 612). A strong argument against kleptomania is that shoplifters display exceedingly low recidivism rates. Once apprehended, the amateur rarely shoplifts again (Cameron, 1964; Russell, 1973). If kleptomania were an important ingredient, we would expect the individual to steal repeatedly as the tension increases.

Lloyd Klemke (1992) suggests that kleptomania is a psychiatric label intended to ease the guilt of affluent women caught stealing during the turn of the century. Merchants, Klemke points out, did not want to antagonize their affluent clientele. Furthermore, affluent families wanted to keep their moral reputations untarnished and keep their women at home. Nor did the courts want to convict "respectable ladies" as common criminals. Thus, kleptomania (the Greek word for "stealing madness," a term presumably coined by Esquirol in 1838) legitimized the actions of the merchants and the courts to dismiss or acquit the "afflicted" woman and excuse her from being held personally responsible for her actions.

If kleptomania does exist, it seems to be a rare phenomenon. For example, in a recent study conducted by Sarasalo, Bergman and Toth (1997), fifty (twenty-nine male, twenty-one female) shoplifters were interviewed immediately after being caught red-handed in central Stockholm, Sweden. None of the persons interviewed fulfilled the DSM-IV criteria for kleptomania. Much of the literature on the causes of kleptomania focuses on its relationship to anxiety, depression, or sexual disturbances (Goldman, 1991). Citing sexual disturbances as a cause for kleptomania is primarily based in the psychoanalytic tradition. But as Marcus Goldman (1991, p. 990) notes, "there are no modern data available to refute or confirm these earlier psychoanalytic findings." Overall, much of the recent research has found depression to be a common symptom of people who engage in "nonsensical shoplifting." Yates (1986) claims that 80 percent of those who engaged in nonsensical shoplifting were depressed. McElroy and colleagues (McElroy, Pope, Hudson, Keck, & White, 1991) found that all twenty patients they studied, who engaged in nonsensical shoplifting, met the DSM-III-R criteria for a lifetime diagnosis of a major mood (depression) disorder. In addition, many of these patients said they engaged in nonsensical shoplifting far more often when they were depressed. It seems that some depressed people may engage in nonsensical shoplifting as a stimulating, exciting activity that moves them away from feelings of helplessness. In fact, Goldman (1991) finds that depressive states are often reported throughout the literature as precursors to many kinds of theft that are not related to profit.

For some unexplained reason, women seem to engage in nonsensical shoplifting more often than men. According to Marcus Goldman (1991, p. 994), "It would appear that the average person suffering from kleptomania is a 35-year-old married woman who has been apprehended for the theft of objects she could easily afford and does not need." However, statistics on "kleptomania" are incomplete and largely unknown. Therefore, any statement concerning gender differences in nonsensical shoplifting should be made very cautiously.

ROBBERY

Robbery is taking or attempting to take anything of value from a person by force or threat of force. There were 537,050 robberies reported in 1996, reflecting a national robbery rate of 202 per 100,000 people (FBI, 1997). These figures represent about an 8 percent drop from 1995. Like many other crimes, it is primarily an offense of the young male. Over half of those arrested for robbery are under twenty-one, and three out of every four are under twenty-five. Over 90 percent are male.

Robbery accounts for only about 4 percent of all arrests for economic crimes (but 35 percent of the violent crimes). However, because of its potential physical harm to victims, it is among the crimes most feared by the American population (Garofalo, 1977). It involves a high probability of physical harm from a stranger, and it can happen to anyone. (More than half of the robberies occur on streets and highways.) One in three victims is injured in robbery (also called stickup, holdup, mugging), and one in ten so seriously that he or she requires medical attention (U.S. Department of Justice, 1988). Furthermore, robbery offenders are more likely to use weapons than other violent offenders. In fact, firearms are discharged in about one-fifth of all robberies. Yet, it is among the least studied criminal offenses.

One reason for the lack of research interest in robbery is that robbery seems so obvious and straightforward: People rob to obtain money. The process is quick, and the potential returns are lucrative. Compared to burglary, however, the risks are great and the penalties substantial. Much of this may be true, but as we have seen, human behavior should not be oversimplified. The motives of offenders may be extremely varied. People behave a certain way because they have convinced themselves that is what works best for them.

ECONOMIC CRIME OR VIOLENT CRIME?

The major distinctions between robbery and other economic crimes are the direct contact between the offender and the victim and the threat or use of force. The offender threatens bodily harm if the victim resists or impedes the offender's progress; usually this threat is backed up by a clearly visible lethal weapon, such as a firearm.

The combination of taking property and threatening physical harm to a victim creates problems for the researcher or criminologist classifying the offense. Should robbery be considered an economic crime or a violent crime? Wolfgang and Ferracuti (1967) argue that robbery—like homicide, rape, and aggravated assault—develops within a subculture of violence and should be classified as a violent crime. Norandeau (1968), on the other hand, contends that robbers are generally not violent and are associated with a subculture of theft rather than one of violence. Normandeau based his judgment on a study of Philadelphia robberies, in which he discovered that 44 percent involved no physical injury to the victim. While 56 percent of the victims did sustain some injury, only 5 percent needed to be hospitalized.

If Wolfgang and Ferracuti are correct in saying that robbery is a crime of violence springing from a violent subculture, the backgrounds of offenders should support this. We would expect to find criminal records and a social history peppered with violent incidents. In a study of Boston robberies during 1964 and again during 1968, Conklin (1972) found no "excessive amount" of prior criminal violence in the backgrounds of robbery offenders compared with the "general criminal populations of the country." In addition, fewer than one-third of the robbery victims had sustained injuries in the incidents. Similar findings are reported by Normandeau (1968) and Spencer (1966), neither of whom found that robbers had high conviction rates for violent conduct. However, research does suggest that robbers who did rely on violence in the past are more likely to use it in the future, whether in robbery or in other crimes.

One way to solve the problem of classifying robbery is to consider it both an economic crime and a violent crime. In fact, Vetter and Silverman (1978) suggest that it is more accurately catalogued as a violent economic crime. Most robbers, they point out, try to intimidate and frighten victims through threats of violence. The offender rationalizes that the more fear can be induced (without panic) the less resistance will be encountered. If the offender feels his or her control over the situation is weakening, he or she may flee, exert greater threat, or become more violent.

Strong-arm robbery (without a weapon) is more likely to result in injury to the victim than is robbery with a firearm or knife. Presumably, victims are less fearful (and thus more daring) when confronted by an unarmed individual. In the absence of a gun or other weapon, the victim's resistance to losing valuable personal property is stronger, and he or she is more apt to hamper the progress of the strong-arm offender. The tendency to resist, therefore, may partly account for the higher rates of victim injury in these no-weapon situations. Furthermore, the offender is likely to feel more confident, powerful, and in control of the incident when he or she has a weapon. Because of this increase in confidence, the offender is less likely to be anxious and disorganized in response patterns, and thus is better able to think clearly and evaluate the consequences of actions.

Assessing skilled robbery, Peter Letkemann (1973) offers pertinent remarks about the successful robber's confidence and victim "management." First, he or she analogizes between the technical skills of the burglar and the mechanic, and between the professional skills of the robber and the clinician. Burglars do not have to be concerned with people, but professional robbers must be able to maintain control and handle their victims at all times. Bank robbers, for example, assert that the keys to a successful heist are confidence and the ability to control people under highly stressful conditions. Confidence, they believe, is reflected in the robber's tone of voice and general behavior. High levels of self-confidence are crucial if robbers are to maintain control of the situation. Successful robbers also note that the posture and physical location of the victims are deliberately designed to enhance the offender's control over them.

According to Letkemann, professional robbers often express dismay over media treatment of robbery. Television and movies generally downplay the seriousness of bank robbery, for example; the offenders therefore must work harder to convince their victims that they mean business. The entertainment media also encourage some victims to be heroes; robbers consider heroes irrational and extremely dangerous.

In a revealing study, Richard Wright and Scott Decker (1997) interviewed eighty-six individuals who were actively engaged in armed robbery on a regular basis in St. Louis. One of the unique aspects about the study is that none of the robbers interviewed were incarcerated, and they were outside the clutches of the criminal justice system (not on probation, not under arrest, not on parole). Most studies of armed robbery interview prisoners who either admit engaging in the offense or have been convicted for robbery.

Wright and Decker focused on determining what factors influenced the robbers in their decisions of when, how, and whom to rob. The researchers were also interested in the offenders' thoughts and actions during the commission of the crime. In addition to interviewing, the researchers took ten of the robbers to the site of a recent holdup for which they had not been apprehended and asked them to reconstruct the crime. The sample was overwhelmingly black, poor, male, and uneducated. Although the sample represented all ages, a majority were between the ages of eighteen and twenty-nine. Most of the offenders had committed numerous robberies in their lifetimes—so many in fact that a majority found it impossible to specify the exact number. Despite the very high number of armed robberies they had committed, 60 percent of the sample had never been convicted of armed robbery. Almost all the sample (96 percent) reported committing many other offenses, particularly theft, burglary, assault, and drug selling. A majority (85 percent) typically did their robbery on the street, while 12 percent preferred to rob commercial establishments (e.g., pawn shops, jewelry stores, liquor stores).

Wright and Decker found that a vast majority of the offenders did not plan the armed robbery. "The reality for many offenders is that crime commission had become so routinized that it emerges almost naturally in the course of their daily lives, often occurring without substantial planning or deliberation" (Wright & Decker, 1997, p. 30). The researchers discovered that, with few exceptions, the decision to rob was strongly influenced by a pressing need for cash to support their hedonistic, carefree lifestyle. The robbers in this sample were deeply enmeshed in the street culture where immediate gratification reigned supreme. Many robbers spend their loot with reckless abandon without much thought to financial obligations or commitments. The offenders chose armed robbery as a lifestyle because it provides quick cash as the need arises. Armed robbery offered immediate cash compared to the delays inherent in disposing of hot merchandise acquired through burglary, shoplifting, and motor vehicle theft.

Although the need for cash was the overwhelming reason for armed robbery, a secondary gain expressed by some robbers was the control they held over their frightened victims. However, this secondary gain seemed to be restricted primarily to law-abiding citizens. Many of these offenders preferred to rob white victims because they usually complied with their demands and did not offer much resistance, particularly white women. According to many of these offenders, black victims are more likely to resist and fight back. However, many robbers in this sample reported that whites were more likely to carry credit cards and checkbooks rather than cash; the opposite was true for blacks. As one offender, who preferred to rob individuals in black neighborhoods, reported, "People in the ghetto got lots of money. The ghetto ain't poor. [The people] there got more money on them than the people downtown. All they got is plastic and checks" (Wright & Decker, 1997, p. 77). Another offender stated:

> [Whites] usually don't resist.... A black person will try to grab the gun out of your hand. They will make you shoot them if you have to.... Black people say, "I don't care if you do have a gun," and they'll put up a hassle, whereas a white person might say, "Look here, take the watch, take this here, just don't hurt me."... A black person will say, "No, you got to kill me. You ain't gonna take my money like that." (Wright & Decker, 1997, p. 84)

One of the favorite targets of the street robbers in this sample were individuals who themselves were involved in lawbreaking, especially drug sellers and wealthy drug users. Drug dealers carry considerable amounts of cash as a result of their illegal activities. Of course, the risks are higher when targeting drug users because they are more likely to be armed, more prone to resist, and are sometimes connected to a powerful drug organization. Wealthy drug users tend to be white persons who come into a neighborhood looking to buy drugs with considerable cash. They can be easily victimized, and like other lawbreakers, they are unlikely to report the robbery to the police.

The Wright and Decker study provides far more meaningful information about the perceptions and cognitive processes of armed robbers than studies that rely exclusively on information gathered from inmates who realize or are fearful that their statements will be reviewed by criminal justice authorities. One of the major findings of the Wright-Decker project is that there is little psychological mystery behind the motives of armed robbery: They need cash now to support their impulsive, hedonistic lifestyle, and robbery provides the best alternative to that cash. Some also enjoy dominating their victims and frightening them, but this motive is only secondary to cash acquisition. One caveat about the Wright-

Decker study is necessary. Generalizations to other robbers in other cities should be made cautiously until similar studies are conducted in other geographical areas.

WHITE-COLLAR AND OCCUPATIONAL CRIME

The term **white-collar crime** was coined by Edwin H. Sutherland, in his presidential address to the American Sociological Society in 1939. In his speech, Sutherland urged his fellow sociologists to pay attention to the law-violating behavior of businesses, particularly large corporations. He had uncovered these violations by reviewing government files on seventy large American corporations and had learned that breaking rules was commonplace. In 1949, Sutherland published his now classic book, *White-Collar Crime*, in which he detailed his findings without naming the corporations. A later edition of the book (Sutherland, 1983) did include the names.

Following Sutherland's lead, a considerable amount of pioneering research was done on white-collar crime between 1939 and 1963 (Geis, 1988). This was followed by a decade of inactivity. Since 1975, there has been a revival of interest in studying the area, although criminological literature gives far less attention to white-collar crime than to other forms of criminal behavior.

According to Sutherland, "white-collar crime may be defined approximately as a crime committed by a person of respectability and high social status in the course of his occupation (1949, p. 9). Although Sutherland used the word "crime," he did not intend it strictly in the legal sense. He recognized that numerous laws and regulations violated by persons of high social status carried *civil* rather than *criminal* sanctions, and he wanted these violations to be condemned. In fact, this was a critical factor to Sutherland, who saw a double standard phenomenon at work. The law-violating behavior of the poor carried criminal penalties; the law-violating behavior of the rich often did not. This was so despite the fact that "(t)he financial cost of white-collar crime is probably several times as great as the financial cost of all the crimes which are customarily regarded as 'the crime problem'" (Sutherland, 1949, p. 12).

Although Sutherland's call to study white-collar crime was heeded, his working definition produced numerous problems for subsequent criminologists. Some, most notably Paul Tappan (1947), argued that white-collar "crime" could not really be crime unless it violated the criminal law. The terms "respectability" and "high social status" were considered vague. Over the past three decades, researchers have tried to improve on Sutherland's definition. Marshall Clinard and Richard Quinney (1980) preferred to dichotomize the concept into (1) occupational crime, committed by an individual for his or her own profit, and (2) corporate crime, committed by the corporation through its agents. Horning (1970) proposed a tripartition to distinguish the various behaviors that might be at issue. He reserved white-collar crime for acts committed by salaried employees in which their place of employment is either the victim or the locale for the commission of an illegal act from which they personally benefit. Embezzlement would be a good example of this. Corporate crime refers to illegal acts by employees in the course of their employment that primarily benefit the company or corporation. Illegal dumping of hazardous wastes is an example. **Blue-collar crime** refers to the whole array of illegal acts committed by non-salaried workers against their place of employment. Theft of machinery is an example.

Gary Green (1997) has made significant contributions to clarifying the definitional dilemmas associated with the term white-collar crime by proposing the concept of *occupational crime*. Green's term encompasses all of the behaviors previously subsumed under white-collar crime, blue-collar crime, and their variants. To Green, occupational crime is "any act punishable by law that is committed through opportunity created in the course of an occupation that is legal" (Green, 1997, p. 15). Green then subdivides occupational crime into four categories: (1) organizational (which includes corporate crime); (2) professional; (3) state-authority, and (4) individual.

In *organizational occupational crime*, a legal entity such as a company, corporation, firm, or foundation profits by the law-violating behavior. An example would be the Chief Financial Officer of a company falsifying the company's tax records with the tacit approval of its Board of Directors. Other examples are anti-trust violations, violations of Occupational Safety and Health Administration (OSHA) standards, and political bribery of foreign officials. *Professional occupational crime* includes illegal behavior by persons such as lawyers, physicians, psychologists, and teachers committed through their occupation. A physician's Medicaid fraud or a lawyer's suborning the perjury of a client are illustrations.

State-authority occupational crime encompasses the wide range of law violation by persons imbued with legal authority; the individual who commits state-authority occupational crime is essentially violating the public trust. Bribe-taking by a public official and police brutality are illustrative. Finally, Green uses the category *individual occupational crime* to cover all violations not included under one of the above categories. The employee who steals equipment from his employer and the person who deliberately under-reports income to the IRS are covered in this category.

As evident from the above examples, the concept of occupational crime proposed by Green covers a wide variety of offenses, not all of which are economic in nature and not all of which are committed by persons of high social status. A therapist who sexually assaults a patient and a correctional officer who uses excessive force against an inmate are both committing violent occupational crimes. Neither the therapist's nor the correctional officer's behavior would qualify as white-collar crime in its classic sense. Some criminologists also have contended that certain corporate crimes should qualify as violent crimes, however. James Coleman (1998), for example, cites unsafe working conditions, illegal disposal of toxic waste, and the manufacture of unsafe products as examples of violent crime.

Green argues convincingly that his four-part division allows us to move away from the conceptual quagmire of "white-collar crime" and study a significant amount of workplace-facilitated illegal behavior in a logical, ordered manner. Although the term white-collar crime continues to be widely used, perhaps in deference to Sutherland's contributions to criminology, Green's approach offers an appealing alternative.

Regardless of which term is used, the extent of occupationally-linked illegal behavior is extremely difficult to measure. The standard methods of measuring crime discussed in Chapter 1 rarely apply. The typical UCR report, for example, does not tell us whether a reported crime or an arrest was related to the perpetrator's occupation. Fraud, for example, can be committed by a bank executive, a college student, a Fortune 500 Corporation, or a recipient of welfare benefits. Even when uncovered, the violations we have been discussing are often not recorded. Rather than publicize a theft by an employee, for example, a business might prefer to demand restitution, dismiss the employee, or force a resignation. It does not benefit the company's public image to file a criminal complaint.

When an organization is itself the violator, civil suits are often preferred to criminal charges. Additionally, the government regulatory process is widely acknowledged to be inefficient in preventing, uncovering, and punishing violators. When it comes to the professions, law violation is often shielded from the public, because society authorizes them to police themselves by means of standards, codes of ethics, and licensing.

Without settling the difficult definitional morass associated with "white-collar crime," we will nevertheless proceed to discuss in more detail one example of this serious crime problem, specifically crime committed by corporations and their agents. Sutherland, you will recall, focused on corporations in his original research. Following that discussion, we will consider crimes at the opposite end of the continuum, wherein individual employees victimize their employers. Although not necessarily white-collar crimes, these latter behaviors qualify as individual occupational crimes according to Green's approach.

CORPORATE CRIME

For purposes of the criminal law, a corporation is a person; that is, a corporation can be charged, tried, sentenced, and punished. Nevertheless, individuals within that organization are making decisions that render the corporate behavior a crime. Therefore, in discussing explanations for corporate crime, we will focus on the behavior of persons, despite the fact that the organizational culture as well as the economic structure of society may facilitate and reward the illegal behavior.

Corporate crime covers offenses ranging from price fixing to failure to recall a product known to have a serious defect which could potentially cause physical harm. The offenses are so varied, in fact, that most criminologists subdivide the crimes into more manageable categories. Thus, we hear of crimes against consumers, crimes against the environment, institutional corruption, and fiduciary fraud (Rosoff, Pontell, & Tillman, 1998); fraud and deception, manipulating the marketplace, violating civil liberties, and—as noted above—violent white-collar crimes (Coleman, 1998); crimes of fraud, offenses against public administration, and regulatory offenses (Albanese, 1995); and false and misleading advertising, defrauding the government, antitrust crimes, manufacture and sale of unsafe consumer products, unfair labor practices, unsafe working conditions, crimes against the environment, and political bribegiving (Green, 1997).

The estimated costs of the above—both financial and from a human-suffering standpoint—are staggering. The financial cost of corporate crime has been estimated to be between 20 and 40 billion dollars a year (Kramer, 1984), and most scholars in this area would consider even that a very conservative estimate. Kramer (1984) estimated that over 100,000 deaths a year could be attributed to occupationally related diseases, most caused by the knowing and willful violation of occupational health and safety standards by businesses and industries. Annually, 20 million serious injuries are associated with unsafe and defective consumer products—unsafe foods and drugs, and defective autos, tires, or appliances. About 110,000 of these injuries result in permanent disability, and 30,000 result in death (Schrager & Short, 1978). Obviously, not all of these accidents, injuries, and deaths are due to corporate neglect or illegal action, but the data suggest that many are (Hochstedler, 1984).

Explanations for corporate criminality often focus on the criminogenic or crime-producing nature of the business environment; that is, in order to survive, law breaking is essential. Conklin (1977), for example, argued that law breaking in American business was normative and that executives often believe that some dishonesty or deceit has to be tolerated in the best interest of the company. In response to comments such as these, corporations proclaim that they have entered an era of social responsibility and that the extent of corporate malfeasance is exaggerated. Business schools note that business ethics courses are a requirement in virtually all programs. Gilbert Geis (1997), however, a prominent scholar in the area of white-collar crime, chastises business schools for using "lulling terms, especially 'ethics,' to camouflage what essentially are considerations of criminal behavior" (Geis, p. xii).

You may recall that in the summary section of Chapter 9, we referred to strategies people use to neutralize some of their violent conduct and separate it from their personal codes. The strategies, proposed by Bandura (1978) are worth repeating here. Although they operate with reference to a wide range of reprehensible conduct, they are particularly relevant to the discussion of corporate crime. The strategies may be used individually or in combination. One set operates at the level of behavior. What is culpable is made honorable through moral justifications and euphemistic jargon. A normally reprehensible act becomes personally and socially acceptable when it is associated with beneficial or moral ends. "We did it in the best interest of the company, the employees and their families, and the country." Similarly, corporate decision makers may regard the laws they are violating as unfair, unjust, or simply not in keeping with good business practices. Cressey (1953) has called such justifications "vocabularies of adjustment." Conklin (1977) asserts that vocabularies of adjustment may even play a more crucial role in corporate crime than in juvenile delinquency, where they are frequently encountered.

A second set of neutralizing or dissociative strategies obscures or distorts the relationship between actions and their effects. In this group of strategies, people do not see themselves as personally responsible or accountable for their actions. They may disregard or deny the consequences of their actions—"It simply didn't happen the way the press reported it." Alternately, they may displace responsibility to the victim—"Consumers often don't use the appliance properly"—or diffuse the responsibility among the decision-making group—"After careful deliberation the board decided this would be the right decision."

A third set of strategies addresses the effects of the action on the recipients. Here, the dignifying qualities of the victims are removed. "Most consumers are greedy and stupid." "Third World countries are overcrowded anyway." We saw this strategy in action earlier in this text, when aggressors regarded their victims as less than human. This dehumanizing approach also seems to be a hallmark of prejudice and scapegoating.

In sum, through cognitive restructuring supported by corporate norms, decisionmakers can justify and rationalize behavior that appears reprehensible to outsiders. The restructuring process prevents the manager or executive from labeling him or herself "criminal." In fact, in some corporations, the extent to which the norms and justifying mechanisms are embraced may well determine how far up the corporate ladder one climbs.

INDIVIDUAL OCCUPATIONAL CRIME

When illegal behavior is pursued for the direct benefit of the individual, and the individual is neither a professional nor someone with state authority, Green refers to it as individual occupational crime. In this largely solitary pursuit, the offender is guided primarily by his or her own personal justifications and reasoning. An embezzler, for example, is operating outside organizational norms, although he may justify the behavior in much the same way as the corporate criminal may. In other words, an embezzler may convince himself that the activity really is not a crime, since he is merely borrowing the money temporarily and will put it to good use. Later, he will reimburse the company (secretly, of course).

One common type of illegal behavior in which the workplace is the victim is employee theft, which is an enormous drain on American business. One estimate has it costing business and industry five to ten billion dollars a year (Clark & Hollinger, 1983). In a survey of employees from forty-seven retail, manufacturing, and service organizations, one-third admitted stealing company property (Clark & Hollinger, 1983). The property included merchandise, supplies, tools, and equipment. In addition, almost two-thirds of the employees surveyed reported other types of misconduct, such as sick leave abuse, drug or alcohol use on the job, long lunch and coffee breaks, slow and sloppy workmanship, and falsifying time sheets. Collectively, these are counterproductive behaviors. They do not involve actual removal of material goods from the organization, but they do reduce production and services.

Explanations for employee theft and counterproductive behaviors are multiple, but most cluster around the themes of age, dissatisfaction, and one's normative group at the workplace. The highest levels of theft and counterproductive behaviors are reported by younger, unmarried male employees (age sixteen to mid-twenties). Apparently, these younger employees do not feel any commitment or loyalty to the organization, probably because they do not expect to spend their lives in that situation. Many are college and high school students working only until they graduate. High levels of theft and counterproductive behaviors are also found among employees expressing dissatisfaction with some aspect of their employment, especially with their immediate supervisor. Another component of job dissatisfaction is the workers' perception of the company's attitude toward them. If the workers perceive the organization as caring little about them, job dissatisfaction and the concomitant theft and counterproductive behaviors tend to follow.

While age and job dissatisfaction are highly correlated with theft and counterproductive behavior, normative support offers a viable explanation. **Normative support** refers to the standards, perceptions, and values the work group has established for itself, with or without the organization's implicit (or explicit) approval. In short, normative support refers to group norms. For example, the group may consider pilfered material a supplement to one's hourly wages, a fringe benefit. Vocabularies of adjustment are frequently employed. "It goes with the job." "The company expects you to take a little on the side." Another example is the work group verbally neutralizing the societal and organizational prohibitions against theft. "Everyone does it." "No one cares if we take a few things." "This is not really stealing." Sieh (1987) found that garment workers took "only what was owed them" and rarely stole items of substantial value.

Whether the group considers it acceptable to take something and where it decides a line should be drawn ("You can help yourself to ballpoint pens, but staplers are hands off"), depends on many variables. For example, the size of the organization is likely to be a factor. Smigel (1970) found that when workers were "forced" (in a questionnaire) to select an organization they would be most inclined to victimize, they first chose large businesses, then government, and lastly, small businesses. They considered large corporations and big government impersonal bureaucratic giants able to absorb losses more easily than smaller organizations.

Regardless of the explanation, employee theft seems to require some subjective justification on the part of the worker. He or she does not perceive his or her conduct as illegal or even unethical, either because the behavior is in line with group norms, in line with internal standards, or both. From the group's or worker's perspective, the theft or the counterproductive behavior are either expected or they adjust the imbalances inherent in working for the company. It is interesting to note that employee theft diminishes when an organization clarifies for the workforce precisely what constitutes misconduct and what is expected (Clark & Hollinger, 1983). This approach, combined with working conditions that convince employees their organization cares about them, seems to be the most effective in reducing employee theft and counterproductive behavior. Furthermore, improvement in the work environment functions both ways; the worker is also expected to demonstrate loyalty and commitment to the organization, setting up appropriate models for new workers. But loyalty to a company may go too far, as when it represents a higher obligation than commitment to law and ethics. Individual blind loyalty often leads to corporate crime.

CYBERCRIME

Cybercrime (or computer crime) refers to any illegal act that involves a computer system. The main types of cybercrime are unauthorized access to computers (hacking), mischief to data (virus generation), theft of communications, copyright violations of computer software, and transmission of pornographic material, including child pornography. Another cybercrime that is becoming popular is illegal gambling on the internet.

The extent of computer crimes is expanding rapidly and its economic impact is staggering (Carter & Katz, 1996). The British Banking Association reports that the world loss to computer fraud alone is approximately $8 billion each year (Carter & Katz, 1996). Software piracy is estimated to cost American software companies around $7.5 billion annually.

The fastest growing computer-related crime is theft, with the most common stolen commodity being information such as new product plans, new product descriptions, research, marketing plans, and prospective customer lists (Carter & Katz, 1996). Since the theft of intellectual property often has no tangible value, the offender does not as readily perceive it as being wrong.

In response to the dramatic increase in computer crimes, the U.S. Congress passed the Federal Computer Fraud and Abuse Act of 1984, which was amended and expanded in the Computer Abuse Amendments Act of 1994. Computer crime is a serious problem that will continue to draw considerable attention from law enforcement agencies across the globe. In 1997, eight of the world's industrial nations joined forces to fight computer crime, particularly security intrusions and telecommunications fraud. Research focusing on the psychological characteristics of cybercrime is just beginning.

Let's now turn our attention to three offenses that are somewhat outside the realm of economic crimes, but nonetheless have many of the same features and motives.

HOSTAGE-TAKING OFFENSES

The hostage taker holds victims against their will and uses them to obtain material gain or personal advantage. Typically, this offender threatens to take the lives of the victims if certain demands are not met within a specified time period. Included in the broad hostage-taking category are abductions and kidnappings, skyjackings, and some acts of terrorism.

Miron and Goldstein (1978) divide hostage-taking offenses into two major categories based on the offender's primary motivation: **instrumental** and **expressive hostage taking.** In instrumental hostage taking, the offender's goal is recognizable—material gain. An example is kidnapping a child and holding him or her for ransom. The goal in expressive hostage taking is psychological: The offender wants to become significant and to take control over his or her fate. Expressive offenders generally feel that they have little control over events in their lives. They want to become important, and they believe the media coverage accompanying their hostage taking will help them to achieve this goal. To the observer, the conduct of the expressive offender often seems senseless and even suicidal. A skyjacker who demands that a pilot fly an aircraft full of passengers from one continent to another, for no apparent reason, is an example. Hostage-taking offenses sometimes begin as instrumental acts but develop into expressive ones. An offender who initially kidnaps someone for material gain may find that his demands are unrealistic and not likely to be met; in this case, the person may decide to play out the scenario for the attention, significance, and control it affords. Sometimes both instrumental and expressive motives are clearly involved from the beginning. That is, the offender expects both material and psychological gain from the abduction.

Since the 1970s, the FBI has classified hostage-taking incidents into four broad categories: terrorism, the prison situation, the criminal, and the mentally disordered (Fuselier & Noesner, 1990). Research suggests that over 50 percent of all hostage-taking incidents are perpetrated by mentally disordered individuals (Borum & Strentz, 1993), thus representing the largest category. Research also indicates that the average terrorist hostage-taker is not as sophisticated as commonly believed (Fuselier & Noesner, 1990). Training for his or her terrorist activity is marginal or nonexistent. Terrorist hostage takers are usually young males with little formal education and from deprived socioeconomic backgrounds. Moreover, they are very willing to kill innocent victims, and therefore they are considered more dangerous than the more sophisticated hostage taker. However, "negotiation strategies and tactics for terrorist incidents are identical to those that would be used during any hostage or barricade incident, regardless of the political or religious backgrounds of the subjects" (Fuselier & Noesner, 1990, p. 10).

Experienced negotiators suggest strategies for dealing with hostage takers or barricaded individuals (see Table 11-1). A **barricade situation** is one in which an individual has fortified or barricaded himself or herself in a building or residence, and threatens violence, either to himself or to others. First, that person should be denied the excitement and stimulation he or she hopes to initiate; this requires that a potentially chaotic situation be handled as calmly as possible, with minimum media attention. As noted in Chapter 5, very high levels of arousal tend to promote disorganized response patterns and reduce internal thought processes. Under high excitement and chaos, the offender is more likely to revert to "mindless" behavior, which may include violence. The most dangerous phase in most hostage or barricade situations is the first fifteen to forty-five minutes (Noesner & Dolan, 1992). Therefore, the first officers on the scene should hold their positions until additional resources, including the negotiation team, arrive at the scene. If possible, the officers who are first on the scene should try to engage the hostage taker in conversation, emphasizing that they wish no harm to the individual. Experienced negotiators believe that conversation distracts the

Table 11-1   Guidelines for Negotiation

Stabilize and contain the situation

Take your time when negotiating

Allow the subject to speak: It is more important to be a good listener than a good talker

Don't offer the subject anything

Avoid directing frequent attention to the victims; do not call them hostages

Be as honest as possible; avoid tricks

Never dismiss any request as trivial

Never say "no"

Never set a deadline; try not to accept a deadline

Do not make alternate suggestions

Do not introduce outsiders (non-law enforcement) into the negotiation process

Do not allow any exchange of hostages, especially do not exchange a negotiator for a hostage

Source: Fuselier & Noesner (1990). *FBI Law Enforcement Bulletin*, p. 10.

offender from violence and generally calms the situation, especially if the negotiator maintains a calm and steady demeanor.

Second, offenders must be allowed to feel that they are in some control of the situation. Helplessness and powerlessness may have prompted the offense in the first place. If the captors do not feel they have attained any control, they may take steps to prove the opposite, such as shooting one of the hostages.

Third, in hostage or barricade situations time is a strong ally. Once the early stages of a crisis have passed and some stability and calm have been achieved, the passage of time plays a positive role. Time has several effects. After the initial high-arousal state, the body winds down and eventually the offender begins to feel tired, sluggish, and depressed. Under these conditions the event takes on aversive properties for the hostage taker, and the offender is likely to begin to wish the situation were over. Time also promotes, in the hostage taker, some thought processes and greater reliance on internal standards of conduct. If the offender has incorporated some values of society, he (or she) may begin to appreciate the ramifications of his (or her) behavior. However, the hostage taker may also begin to construct justifications. Either process, however, may enable the offender to accede more easily to police requests. Experienced negotiators strongly recommend that the negotiator act as spokesperson for the authorities and a conduit of information, emphasizing to the hostage taker that things will take time. Consequently, the negotiator should not be a decision maker or in command. Otherwise, if the hostage taker is under the impression that the negotiator (or anyone in the immediate environment) has the power and decision-making authority, he or she will believe that decisions should be made quickly and directly. Under these conditions, any delay generates frustration in the captor and further increases arousal.

Time also affects the relationship with the hostage. According to social psychological research, the more familiar one is with an object or person, the more one tends to become attracted to it (e.g., Freedman, Sears, & Carlsmith, 1978). In many hostage situations, the more the victim and captor get to know one another, the more they begin to accept one another. Furthermore, if the hostage was a stranger to the captor, the hostage takes on human qualities with the passage of time.

The attraction between victim and captor is called the **Stockholm effect**, after a hostage-taking incident in Sweden that resulted in marriage between a female hostage and one of her abductors. Police negotiations have noted that on occasion the hostage will side with the captor in working out demands. Although this may simply reflect a wish to end the terrifying ordeal as quickly as possible, it may also signify some attraction to the abductor. When hostages act this way, experts sometimes maintain that they have been brainwashed. An alternate explanation is that they have become attracted to their captors and temporarily identified with their values and goals.

How can a hostage-taking incident, which by its very nature is stressful, generate attraction? We have already noted that mere familiarity can increase attraction to an object or person. There is evidence, also, that unpleasant emotion may intensify attraction (Middlebrook, 1974). Research by Schachter (1971) suggests that when people are physiologically aroused, they may have difficulty labeling the arousal with the appropriate emotion, because several conflicting emotional labels may be available. It does not seem to matter whether the arousal derives from negative or from positive circumstances. For example, sexual deprivation may lead to physiological arousal, which may be labeled love. The same process may operate in a highly charged hostage-taking incident, where familiarity combined with very high arousal leads to mutual attraction. If the victim or kidnapper is deindividualized by a hood or a mask, the incident is much less likely to develop into attraction. Also, ideals and purpose may override any tendency to humanize and be attracted to the victims.

Thomas Strentz (1987) outlines some rules to follow should you personally ever be taken hostage, especially if you plan to travel abroad with some regularity. His suggestions are based on the psychological reactions of those hostages who survive (survivors) compared to those who do not (succumbers). Survivors, Strentz notes, are those "who returned to a meaningful existence with strong self-esteem, and who went on to live healthy and productive lives with little evidence of long-term depression, nightmares, or serious stress-induced illness" (p. 4). Although survivors do not ever forget the hostage experience, the experience does not prevent them from living relatively normal lives. Succumbers, on the other hand, are those who either did not live through the ordeal, or upon release or rescue have considerable difficulty dealing with the emotional trauma caused by the ordeal. They have great trouble getting on with their lives.

Strentz emphasizes, as we did earlier, that the most dangerous phase of any hostage situation is the moment of the abduction, and the early minutes thereafter. Arousal levels are extremely high for the abductors and the hostages. Unpredictable and unforeseen things can happen. Strentz asserts that, without exception, any form of resistance is extremely dangerous and should not be tried. He recommends playing the subordinate role immediately. Furthermore, throughout the entire abduction, maintaining a positive mental attitude that things will be all right in the end is absolutely essential. Feelings of hopelessness, abandonment, and isolation can lead to serious depression. On the other hand, a mature, controlled, and stable appearance—even if you are terrified—also helps settle the hostage taker(s). Anything that calms the situation increases survival for everyone. Furthermore, hostile feelings toward your captors must be masked as best they can, again to keep the situation calm. Do not get into arguments with captors about politics, religion, social issues, or anything else. Strentz refers to the opposite strategy as the **London syndrome**, a behavioral pattern demonstrated by the Iranian press secretary, Abbas Lavasani, during a six-day hostage situation in the Iranian Embassy in London. Lavasani refused to compromise his dedication to his cause, constantly and stubbornly proclaiming his beliefs, and seemingly intent on martyrdom. Despite the pleas of his fellow hostages for silence, he kept arguing and was eventually killed by his captors.

Your chances of survival improve greatly if you try to blend in with your fellow captives. The individual who stands out in the crowd "by crying, by being overly polite and helpful, or by doing more than the abductors require, is immediately setting himself or herself up as an easy mark to be exploited" (p. 6). If you are more comfortable in the leadership role, be prepared to take the brunt of the abuse from the captors, and you may be killed as an example to the rest of the hostages. Individuals who have experienced a hostage-taking episode say that being able to fantasize during the many empty hours is one of the critical factors in dealing with the situation. Some imagine travel to various places or dream what they plan to do after the episode. Also, trying to keep a normal routine as much as possible will relieve stress. Exercise, personal hygiene, writing letters, or keeping logs are examples. This is especially recommended for people who have a strong need to control the situation. Finally, Strentz recommends that no matter what the circumstances, you should never blame yourself or ruminate about what you should have done to avoid the abduction. Accept your status, and follow the patterns described here. Survival will be greatly enhanced if you do.

ARSON

According to the UCR, **arson** is defined as "any willful or malicious burning or attempt to burn, with or without intent to defraud, a dwelling house, public building, motor vehicle or aircraft, personal property of another, etc." (FBI, 1997, p. 395). Arson joined the list of UCR index crimes in 1978, signifying both its seriousness and its frequency. About one-fifth of all property loss in the United States is due to arson, exceeding $2 billion annually. Tragically, arson also claims an estimated seven hundred to eight hundred lives a year.

INCIDENCE AND PREVALENCE

Arson statistics in the United States are collected by the National Fire Protection Association (NFPA) and the FBI. The NFPA definition, however, focuses on structure fires only and combines both established arsons and suspicious structure fires in compiling their statistics (Douglas, Burgess, Burgess, & Ressler, 1992). On the other hand, the FBI statistics, as reported in the UCR, exclude fires of suspicious or unknown origins. Still, the statistics reported by the NFPA are similar to the UCR data. According to the NFPA, arson is responsible for about 14 percent of all structure fires. The UCR reports that while about one-half of the arson fires are directed at structures (mostly residential), another 29 percent involve mobile property, such as motor vehicles or trailers (FBI, 1997).

Arson is difficult to prove or identify because the evidence is often destroyed in the fire. Even with evidence that the fire was set, the motive is often unknown. The annual clearance rate for arson averages about 15 percent (Douglas et al., 1992; FBI, 1997). Most of the known arsonists are young. About 50 percent are under the age of eighteen. However, it is generally acknowledged that only a small proportion of fires set by juveniles are ever reported, probably fewer than 10 percent (Adler et al., 1994).

Over 1,000 civilians and about 120 firefighters die each year in deliberately set fires; an additional 30,000 civilians and 4,000 firefighters are injured (Brady, 1983; Carter, 1980).

MOTIVES

There appears to be a wide variety of motives for arson. In an effort to systematize the reasons, Boudreau and his associates (Boudreau, Kwan, Faragher, & Denault, 1977) list six primary motives for arson and estimate their relative frequencies:

Revenge, Spite, or Jealousy   Arsonists in this category include jilted lovers, feuding neighbors, disenchanted employees, and people who want to get back at someone they believe cheated or abused them. Alcohol and/or drugs are often associated with this motive.

Vandalism or Malicious Mischief   Fires set to challenge authority or to relieve boredom are by far the most common of those set by juveniles.

Crime Concealment or Diversionary Tactics   At least 7 to 9 percent of convicted arsonists are believed to be trying to obliterate evidence of burglaries, larcenies, and murders (Robbins & Robbins, 1964; Inciardi, 1970). The offender in this category expects that the fire will destroy any evidence that a crime was committed. Usually the fire is set near the object or incident the offender wishes to conceal. In some cases, the firesetter may try to cover his or her suicide for insurance purposes. Some arsonists try to destroy records that may link them to embezzlement or other occupational crime. Arson has also been used to divert attention while the offender burglarizes another building or residence.

Profit, Insurance Fraud   This is the category most likely to attract professional or semiprofessional arsonists, who generally escape detection. Consequently, there are few hard data and few statistics to support this motive. However, since the profits gained from arson of this type are so large and the probability of detection so small, actual incidence is believed to be much higher than reported statistically. The property may be residential property, businesses, or modes of transportation (vehicles, boats, planes). According to Douglas et al. (1992), this type of arson usually has two offenders: the primary offender who is the dominant personality in the offense, and the secondary offender who is the "torch for hire." The torch for hire is usually male, twenty-five to forty years of age, and unemployed. The torch is likely to have a prior arrest record for a variety of offenses, including burglary, assault, and public intoxication.

Intimidation, Extortion, Terrorism, Sabotage   This category refers to fires set for the purpose of frightening or deterring. Examples are fires set by striking workers or employees to intimidate management or by extortionists to show that they mean business. Another example is the destruction of abortion clinics, presumably set by antiabortionists wishing to intimidate. By most accounts, arson with this motive is extremely rare. Douglas et al. (1992) refer to this group as extremist-motivated arsonists who are committed to further a social, political, or religious case.

Pyromania and Other Psychological Motives   **Pyromania** is a psychiatric term for an "irresistible urge" or passion to set fires along with an intense fascination with flames. Before setting the fire, the individual is said to experience a build-up of tension; once the fire is underway, he or she experiences intense pleasure or release (DSM-IV, 1994). Although the fire-setting urge is believed to be uncontrollable, the individual often provides many clues about his or her intention before setting the fire. Pyromania is believed to be a motive in only a small percentage of all arsons, but we will discuss it in more detail to illustrate how some crimes lend themselves well to psychoanalytical interpretation.

Douglas et al. (1992) suggests an additional category that is close to the pyromaniac classification: **excitement-motivated (E-M) arson**. Excitement-motivated arsonists set fires because they crave stimulation that is satisfied by firesetting and by watching all the excitement that accompanies the fighting of the fire. The offender often selects a location that offers a good vantage point from which to safely observe the firefighting and investigation. Sometimes he mingles with the crowd watching the fire, primarily to hear comments and see the excitement of the crowd. This E-M arsonist is usually a juvenile or young adult, usually unemployed and living with his (or her) parents. Generally, the E-M arsonist is socially inadequate and has poor interpersonal skills.

In a comprehensive study of 1,016 juveniles and adults arrested for arson and fire-related crimes, Icove and Estepp (1987) report that vandalism is the most frequently identified motive, accounting for 49 percent of the arsons in the sample. The second most frequent motive was excitement (25 percent), followed by revenge (14 percent), crime concealment (2 percent), profit (1 percent), and other or unspecified motive (8 percent). Research (e.g., Robbins & Robbins, 1964) has consistently shown that most fires set by juveniles appear to be motivated by wishes to get back at authority or gain status, or prompted by a dare or a need for excitement. Therefore, it is not surprising that the Icove-Estepp investigation revealed that a vast majority (96 percent) of vandalism fires were set by juveniles, who often set the fire within one mile from their homes and were accompanied by one or more individuals. About half of these juvenile offenders remained at the scene. Excitement-motive fires (69 percent) also tended to be set by juveniles, who also tended to live within one mile of the crime scene, but who preferred to set the blaze alone.

On the other hand, revenge fires tended to be set by adults (81 percent), who tended to be single males and who used alcohol, drugs, or both, prior to or during the offense. Earlier research (Robbins & Robbins, 1964; Inciardi, 1970) also concluded that revenge was almost exclusively an adult crime. According to Icove and Estepp, approximately two-thirds of revenge firesetters have a prior arrest record. Crime concealment fires were also most likely set by adults (72 percent), who were predominately single, male, low income, and who also used alcohol and/or drugs prior to or during the offense. Virtually all the concealment firesetters had prior arrest records. Both the revenge and crime-concealment firesetters usually left the scene of the crime, usually to begin establishing an alibi.

Harmon, Rosner, and Wiederlight (1985) studied the psychological and demographic characteristics of twenty-seven women arsonists who were evaluated in the Forensic Psychiatric Clinics for the Criminal and Supreme Courts of New York between 1980 and 1983. Although the sample is small and restricted to a specific geographical area, the researchers found these female arsonists were somewhat older (mid-thirties), African American, and with a history of alcohol and drug abuse. Generally, the group was uneducated, unmarried, and relying on public assistance for support. Most often, their motivation was revenge, a consistent finding also reported by Icove and Estepp for female arsonists. In their revenge, the women tended to act impulsively, responding to a perceived wrong committed against them or a perceived threat to their persons. In their haste, they used whatever flammable material was handy to set the fire. Generally, they set fires to places they lived in—apartments or common, public spaces of their buildings.

PYROMANIA

According to the DSM-IV, pyromania is "the presence of multiple episodes of deliberate and purposeful fire setting" (p. 614). Moreover, it is characterized by high levels of tension or emotional arousal before the act, and there is relief or reduction of this tension when setting fires, or when observing or participating in their aftermath. Pyromaniacs are believed to be regular spectators at fires in their neighborhoods and communities. They are also believed to set off false alarms and to show unusual interest in firefighting paraphernalia.

Pyromania was coined in the early nineteenth century to refer to a form of "insanity" identified by the impulse to set fires without apparent motive (Schmideberg, 1953). In the mid-1800s, clinicians suggested that there was a relationship between firesetting and sexual disturbances, and psychoanalytic and psychiatric literature in particular continued to promote that link. For instance,

Gold (1962, p. 416) contends that the roots of arson are "deep within the personality and have some relationship to sexual disturbance and urinary malfunction." Abrahamsen (1960, p. 129) writes: "Firesetting is a substitute for a sexual thrill, and the devastating and destructive powers of fire reflect the intensity of the pyromaniac's sexual desires, as well as his sadism."

Orthodox psychoanalytic thinking draws a connection between pleasurable urination (urethral eroticism) and firesetting. Fenichel (1945, p. 371) concluded: "Regularly deep-seated relationship to urethral eroticism is to be found.... In the same way that there are coprophilic perversions based on urethral eroticism, perversions may also be developed based on the derivative of urethral eroticism, pleasure in fire." This theory is based in part on the presumption that many firesetters are or have been enuretic (bedwetters) (Halleck, 1967). The theory does not suggest that enuretic people are likely to be firesetters, only that firesetters have more than their share of bedwetting behavior. Whether this relationship actually exists is still very unclear from the available research.

The relationship between sexual arousal and firesetting is plausible, since, through the process of classical conditioning, virtually any object or event can become associated with sexual arousal and gratification. The fact that some arsonists have fetishes or records of previous arrests for sexual offenses (MacDonald, 1977) lends some support to this possibility. Individuals who are sexually aroused by fire may, in general, be highly conditionable introverts. We may also expect them to be sexually, socially, and vocationally inadequate (as noted by Levin, 1976). Firesetting could be a way of feeling significant and resolving conflicts.

While some firesetters may obtain sexual arousal and gratification from fire, there is very little evidence that many do. In an extensive analysis of sixty-eight convicted arsonists imprisoned in Florida, South Carolina, and North Carolina, sexual "abnormality" was no more in evidence than it was in a comparable group of controls (nonarsonist offenders) (Wolford, 1972). Nor is there much evidence for the diagnostic label "pyromaniac." Koson and Dvoskin (1982) were unable to find any arsonists in their sample that met the DSM-III criteria of pyromania. More specifically, even though 38 percent of the sample were repetitive arsonists, none qualified as exhibiting a recurrent failure to resist impulses to set fires compounded by an intense fascination with firesetting and seeing the fires burn.

In their investigation of 1,016 offenders of arson and fire-related crimes in the Prince George's County area of Maryland, Icove and Estepp (1987) reported only two offenders who may have qualified as pyromaniacs. In Canada, Bradford (1982) found only one individual out of thirty-four repetitive arsonists who could even remotely qualify as a pyromaniac, and Hill and colleagues (Hill, Langevin, Paitich, Handy, Russon, & Wilkinson, 1982), in another Canadian sample of thirty-eight arsonists, found none. Yesavage and associates (Yesavage, Benezech, Ceccaldi, Bourgeois, & Addad, 1983) also found no indications that fifty French arsonists were attracted to fire for sexual reasons. Similar findings have been reported for child firesetters (Kuhnley, Hendren, & Quinlan, 1982; Stewart & Culver, 1982).

REPETITIVE AND PERSISTENT ARSONISTS

Research on repetitive or serial arsonists is beginning to identify some common features. A repetitive or serial arsonist is one who sets three or more separate fires. The time between the firesetting episodes may be days, weeks, or even years. Douglas and colleagues (1992) suggest that a distinction also be made between spree arsonists and mass arsonists. A **spree arsonist** sets fires at three or more separate locations with no emotional "cooling-off" period between them. The **mass arsonist**, on the other hand, sets three or more fires at the same location within a limited period of time. For example, a mass arsonist may set fires to several floors of the same apartment building, simultaneously or within minutes of each other. The most frightening of these repetitive arsonists is the one who randomly selects structures for revenge, excitement, or political (or religious) ideology. An entire community may sleep in fear until the offender either stops or is detected.

The most consistent research finding on the psychology of adult repetitive arsonists is that they, as a group, experience and perceive little control over their environment or personal lives. They are usually from a socially disadvantaged segment of the population (Jackson, Glass, & Hope, 1987). Their plight is usually compounded by an assortment of physical, mental, and psychological handicaps (Koson & Dvoskin, 1982). Compared to other criminal groups, their intellectual level (IQ scores) and educational attainment are low (Wolford, 1972; Lewis & Yarnell, 1951). They also lack social or interpersonal skills for dealing with their social environment, and consequently often lack self-esteem (Hurley & Monahan, 1969; Vreeland & Levin, 1980).

Nearly all children who set fires beyond the normal fascination stage tend to have poor relationships with their parents and were also victims of physical and emotional abuse (Jackson, Glass, & Hope, 1987). Depression is commonly reported in other studies, and sometimes the offenders display serious suicide inclinations (Jackson, Glass, & Hope, 1987).

Therefore, the overall picture of the adult serial arsonist is one of inadequacy, frequent failure, social passivity, and social isolation. Adult arsonists who began setting fires as children tend to be unassertive, have limited interpersonal skills, be underemployed or unemployed, and be prone toward depression and feelings of helplessness (Murphy & Clare, 1996). Theoretically, repetitive fire setting may be motivated by an attempt to gain some control over his or her life and some social recognition. For example, the firesetting seems to be precipitated by events that exacerbate the arsonist's feelings of low self-esteem, sadness, and depression (Bumpass, Fagelman, & Birx, 1983). In addition, following a firesetting, many arsonists stay at the scene of the fire, often sound the alarm, and even help fight the fire. In some cases they take heroic action to save lives. The recognition they receive for these actions probably enhances their self-esteem and instills a sense of control in their lives.

Jackson, Glass, and Hope (1987) note that most acts of firesetting by repetitive arsonists progress from small fires to large fires, and the arsonists also become increasingly involved in fighting the fire. Furthermore, repetitive arsonists set fires alone and in secret, with virtually no one aware of their actions until caught. If caught, their history of firesetting presents an additional opportunity for them to gain attention and recognition from others.

What are the etiological factors in repetitive firesetting? Fascination and experimentation with fire appear to be a common feature of normal child development. Kafrey (1980) discovered that interest and fascination with fire appear to be nearly universal in children between five and seven years old. Furthermore, this fascination with fire begins early, with about one in five children setting fires before the age of three. Firesetting behavior appears to decline after age seven, probably due to frequent admonishments of its dangers from parents and other adults. Those children who continue to set fires tend to be more mischievous, energetic, adventurous, and impulsive than their peers. Persistent firesetters are more likely to demonstrate symptoms of ADHD during childhood (Forehand et al., 1991), and many were regarded as "conduct problems" by their teachers. Not surprisingly, most persistent firesetters are males (about 80 percent). Kafrey (1980) refers to these behavioral patterns as the "rascality pattern." The rascality pattern has also been noted by Kuhnley, Hendren, and Quinlan (1982), Stewart and Culver (1982), and Kolko, Kazdin, and Meyer (1985).

The frequent observation that youthful firesetters are conduct problems, impulsive, more hyperactive, and even more aggressive than their peers appears to be in sharp contrast to the behavior of repetitive adult firesetters, described previously. As noted in Chapter 2, aggressive, acting-out, and hyperactive children are often unpopular with peers (Hartup, 1983; Maccoby, 1986), and demonstrate poor interpersonal and social skills for dealing with others. Patterson (1982) writes that impulsive, hyperactive children with a low frustration tolerance and inadequate social skills tend to be social isolates. Moreover, other research (e.g., Caspi, Elder, & Bem, 1987) indicates that ill-tempered children have considerable personal, marital, social and financial failure throughout their lifetimes, a pattern very similar to repetitive arsonists. In addition, both the frequent childhood firesetter and repetitive adult arsonist exhibit a continual battle against the social environment as demonstrated by frequent contacts with criminal justice agencies. In their conclusion on child and adult firesetting, Vreeland and Levin (1980, p. 44) write:

> The picture turns out to be one of an individual with several maladaptive behaviour patterns, of which firesetting is one. We have identified social ineffectiveness as a common factor in the general tendency of firesetters to have drinking problems, marital, occupational and sexual problems, and to exhibit a variety of other criminal and antisocial behaviours.

Thus, firesetting may be just one component in the constellation of maladaptive behaviors displayed by these individuals. Firesetting may be among these behaviors because of previous experiences with fire. Ritvo, Shanok, & Lewis (1983) found that a surprisingly large number of firesetters had been burned and maltreated with fire as children. They describe how one frequent firesetter during his early childhood had his feet severely burned by his father as a punishment for lighting fires. Another boy had been beaten on his buttocks with a hot spatula by his father. Still another had his hands held over a lighted stove burner by his mother until burned for lighting fires. Ritvo, Shanok, and Lewis (1983, p. 266) speculate that these punishments may have "conveyed the message that the use of fire was an acceptable mode of retaliation."

In this section we have concentrated on the repetitive or serial arsonists who set fires primarily for psychological and social gain. This focus is not to imply that a majority of arson fires are set by these individuals. Obviously, arson is committed for a variety of reasons by a variety of offenders, although much of it is probably committed for monetary gain, such as insurance.

BOMBINGS

In 1995, bombing incidents in the United States decreased 18.5 percent to 2,577 from the 3,163 reported in 1994 (FBI, 1996). Bombs killed 193 people in 1995 and injured 744, a dramatic increase from the 31 fatalities and 308 injured in 1994. This increase is largely due to the tragic bombing incident that killed 168 people and injured 518 in Oklahoma City. In addition, each year there are a substantial number of hoaxes, involving threats of bombing and bogus bomb devices, usually involving businesses. About one-third of these incidences are preceded by a threatening note, letter, or telephone call.

MOTIVES

In over half of all bombings, the motives were unknown. In bombings where the motives were identified, the most frequent was mischief or vandalism (nearly 50 percent). In about 25 percent of all incidents, revenge or intimidation was the primary motive. Personal animosity accounted for 15 percent, and sabotage or subversion another 7 percent.

Many of the motives for bombing are believed to resemble those for arson. However, it would appear that some bombers are more intent on destruction and injury than arsonists are, and they do not wish to cover up the cause of the destruction. Moreover, the bombing generally requires more technical knowledge than arson and it is also more dangerous. The planning, construction, safe transportation, placing, and activating of an explosive device require more skill than dropping a match onto gasoline-soaked rags under a stairwell.

The apparent motives for bombings change with the times. Between the years 1968 and 1971, nearly half of the bombings in the United States were a result of "social protest" (Moll, 1974), while in 1975 over a third of the bombings were due to "personal animosity," and another third to "malicious destruction" (U.S. Department of Justice, 1976). In 1975 only 10 percent of the bombings were related to social protest. From 1980 to 1983, there was a steady decline of bombings in this country, the incidence leveled for a couple of years, then there has been a dramatic increase since 1987.

While there is certainly no single bomber-type personality, MacDonald (1977) contends that there is a personality pattern drawn to bombing that demonstrates most of the characteristics of the "compulsive firesetter"; he calls it the "compulsive bomber." *Compulsive* implies that the individual is drawn to the activity again and again, the behavior seemingly out of the individual's control.

MacDonald reports that the compulsive bombers he has known exhibited a fascination with bombs from childhood. In addition, he found them keenly interested in discussing explosive devices and various techniques of detonating. Large segments of their life appear devoted to the study, development, and experience of bombing. More important, they derive excitement from their actions and are aroused by only one aspect of the explosion: the power, the fire, or the noise. One bomber confessed, "I want to become more than what I am" (MacDonald, 1977, p. 40).

In line with the psychoanalytic tradition, however, MacDonald links sexual gratification with bombing, claiming that one in six compulsive bombers obtains sexual pleasure from his or her explosions. This is apparently based on his observation that sexual deviation is prominent in many bombers.

Two of the more dramatic and best known bombers were George Metesky, a fifty-six-year-old, known as the Mad Bomber of New York, and Theodore Kaczynski, a fifty-five-year-old mathematical genius known as the Unabomber. Metesky planted thirty-two different pipe bombs between 1940 and 1956, all supposedly designed to draw attention to the alleged unfair labor practices of a major utility. Metesky was working for United Electric (now known as Consolidated Edison, or Con Ed) in 1931 when a gush of hot gas from a boiler knocked him down. At the time, he got up and walked away without apparent injury, but he later claimed illness and inability to work as a result of the accident, and he expected compensation. When the company repeatedly denied his requests, Metesky undertook an intense campaign designed to bring attention to Con Ed's "dastardly deeds." He planted bombs in locations that would receive heavy press coverage (Macy's Department Store, the New York Public Library, Grand Central Station), but he maintained he did not intend to harm anyone. Fortunately, no one was killed during his bombing missions, but some twenty-two people were injured. Although his first bombing attempt failed, he subsequently became more sophisticated, technically competent, and successful.

Metesky at one point wrote a letter to the editor of a New York newspaper:

> Have you noticed the bombs in your city, if you are worried, I am sorry, and also if anyone is injured. But it cannot be helped, for justice will be served, I am not well and for this I will make the Con Edison sorry. Yes, they will regret their dastardly deeds. I will bring them before the bar of justice, public opinion will condemn them, for beware, I will place more units under theater seats in the near future. F. P. (MacDonald, 1977, p. 47)

The phrase "dastardly deeds" eventually spelled Metesky's downfall. Investigators searching the files of Con Ed for evidence of disgruntled employees uncovered it in the file folder of Metesky, who had used it in a letter to the company many years before.

Brussel (1978), the consulting psychiatrist in the Mad Bomber case, wrote a detailed account of the events surrounding the search for the bomber and the arrest, when over a half-dozen law enforcement agents closed in on Metesky's home. He greeted them cordially and immediately guessed their purpose. He smiled frequently and appeared to be in a state of high self-satisfaction at capture. Throughout the trial, Metesky beamed and seemed to be enjoying the excitement he had created and the attention he was gaining. In 1957, the court found him "insane" (Brussel contends he was suffering from "paranoia"), and he was committed to Matteawan State Hospital. Metesky was released in 1973.

Although he was considered insane, he displayed a lifelong design to draw attention to his plight and the perceived injustice done to him. Metesky's behavior probably was his way of coping with his feelings about helplessness. Possibly another principal reason for his bombings was to add excitement to his life or to become famous as the Mad Bomber. Overall, it appears that Metesky was successful in creating some significance for himself.

The search for the Unabomber—Theodore Kaczynski—was one of the longest, most difficult, and most frustrating cases in the history of the FBI. The search took over seventeen years until he was apprehended in 1996. In 1993, a UNABOM Task Force (UTF) was established in the search for Kaczynski, with fifty FBI agents assigned full time to the unit. The UTF investigated more than 2,400 suspects, and accumulated 3,600 volumes of information, 175 computer bases, 82 million records, 12,000 event records, 8,182 items of evidence, 22,000 pages of evidentiary documents, and 9,000 evidence photographs.

The Unabomber was responsible for the deaths of three innocent victims and for twenty-three serious injuries by mailing sixteen explosive devices to carefully selected target persons. The first few bombings were directed at individuals at universities and airlines—thus the "un" and the "a" in the FBI's code name. His victims included the chief lobbyist for the California Forestry Association; an Engineering professor at University of California, Berkeley; a geneticist at University of California-San Francisco; a computer science professor at Yale; the assistant to psychology professor James McConnell; and the president of United Airlines.

The Unabomber continually changed and improved both his bombs and his tactics, indicating a strong intelligence, and he maintained his cover for a long time. Investigators were continually impressed by the combination of intellect, malice, and showmanship during the seventeen years. The primary motive of Kaczynski was his desire to have society return to the era before electric power and aircraft. He also believed that mail bombs, mostly sent to universities and airlines, could lead to a massive uprising against technology.

Kaczynski grew up in the Chicago suburb of Evergreen Park, graduated from Harvard University at the age of twenty, majoring in mathematics and physics. He went on to earn a Ph.D. in mathematics from the University of Michigan, and appeared headed for a brilliant career in academics. Instead, he became a recluse who shunned family and friends and lived in a remote, isolated cabin in Montana.

The Unabomber downfall resulted when his brother, David Kaczynski, recognized his brother's work—a 35,000 word personal and political manifesto—published in the *New York Times* and the *Washington Post*. The piece was published in the *Times* and *Post* after the Unabomber promised he would stop mailing bombs if his statement was published in full. Although his lawyers wanted to use the insanity defense on his behalf before his trial, Kaczynski strongly rejected the defense. On January 22, 1998, Kaczynski pleaded guilty and agreed to a life sentence in prison without possibility of parole. He is currently serving his sentence.

PROSTITUTION

Prostitution is illegal in all states except Nevada. Nevada does, however, prohibit prostitution in counties in the state that exceed two hundred thousand in population (Miller, 1991). In the popular literature, it is blamed for decreases in neighborhood property values, increases in drug abuse and violent crime, and deterioration of the American family. On the other hand, cogent arguments have been advanced in favor of its legalization. Some commentators note that prostitutes (especially female prostitutes) are more often victims than offenders, and more than one author suggests that the criminal justice system shares the role of victimizer with pimps and persons who patronize prostitutes (James, 1978). On the other hand, some social scientists and social commentators suggest that adult prostitution is a lucrative career, and that the time may be ripe for society to recruit prostitutes as social workers specializing in treating some sexual problems (Adler, 1975).

Because prostitution is presently a crime, and one that holds a dominant place in female criminality, it merits our consideration. Obviously, males as well as females become prostitutes. In the past, female prostitutes accounted for approximately one-third of the female jail and prison population (James, 1978), whereas male prostitutes were rarely incarcerated. Conservative estimates suggest that prostitution is the primary source of personal income for at least one million women and girls in the United States (Miller, 1991). In 1988, there were 24,293 arrests of males for prostitution, compared to 52,871 female arrests (U.S. Department of Justice, 1989a). Prostitution is also relevant to this text because it is a "deviant behavior" that lends itself well to psychological examination. Our purpose in discussing prostitution is not to consider its moral and policy implications, but to focus on the sociological and psychological myths and misconceptions that surround it. We will not, however, address the exploitation of juveniles of both sexes for prostitution purposes, a phenomenon quickly gaining the attention of social science researchers. Miller (1991) argues that prostitution is a form of sexual exploitation and a form of sexual coercion for all women, because they are compelled or forced (usually by men), physically and psychologically, to engage in a sexual act.

Prostitution is defined as the offering, agreement to offer, or provision of sexual relations in return for tangible rewards or special favors. It may involve either a heterosexual or homosexual pairing, or it may involve group behavior. Although it most commonly refers to the procurement of sexual intercourse with a woman by a man, a variety of sexual activities may be involved.

It is impossible to estimate the number of commercial prostitutes in the United States, since police agencies interpret the criminality of the behavior very subjectively and arbitrarily. Arrests are often dependent on social and political pressures. It is also generally recognized that prostitutes are often harassed and detained, with or without formal arrest, and for purposes other than the idealized goal of eliminating the practice. Primary clientele are believed to be white, middle-class men between the ages of thirty and sixty (Haft, 1976).

Theorists and researchers have traditionally offered biased, subjective generalizations about the female prostitute. They have alternately called her feeble-minded, emotionally disturbed, a latent or manifest homosexual, oversexed, sexually deprived, a primitive creature, or an individual rigidly fixated at her Oedipal (or Electra) stage of psychosexual development. From all indications, none of these labels adequately describes the prostitute. Women who become prostitutes appear to come from many different walks of life, possess varied educational and family backgrounds, demonstrate a wide range of personality types, and express a great variety of motives for involvement in prostitution.

Several researchers have brought attention to a system of class structure among prostitutes. At the lower end of the continuum are the streetwalkers who work the streets; at the uppermost level are call girls, who cater to a select clientele and who are rarely arrested. The call girl is usually more sophisticated and educated than the streetwalker, and is more often protected from the physical brutality and humiliation women at the lower levels of prostitution hierarchy encounter (D'Emilio & Freedman, 1988). In between are a variety of categories, which may (but do not inevitably) include stag party workers, escorts, masseuses, conventioneers, and circuit travelers. Coleman (1976) found that, as we go up the social class structure, the women are increasingly physically attractive, intelligent, well-educated, and sophisticated. Adler (1975) points out that the contemporary prostitute is, in many instances, socially and culturally indistinguishable from women in general.

The flashy and distinctive styles of dress have either disappeared altogether or have faded into the commonplace as they have been adopted as fashion by the rest of society. It is often no longer possible to distinguish the prostitute from the matrons, college girls, or debutantes who might congregate at any public gathering (Adler, 1975).

It was generally believed that many prostitutes, especially at the lower status levels, came from lower- or lower-middle-class homes, but even this is now in question. James (1978) noted that a full 64 percent of her sample of streetwalkers reported their childhood family's income as middle or upper class. There seems little doubt, however, that most prostitutes come from conflictual families, where patterns of alienation from a single parent or from both parents are discernible. Many prostitutes also report negative sexual experiences in the home during preadolescence or adolescence. In an oft-cited study, 41 percent of 136 prostitutes reported incestuous experiences, usually with their fathers (James, 1976). Forty-seven percent reported they had been raped, and 17 percent had been raped more than once, most before reaching the age of sixteen. Studies of juvenile prostitutes lend support to these findings. Silberman (cited in Bracey, 1982) interviewed over two hundred juvenile prostitutes and reported that 61 percent had been sexually molested by a member of their household. Bracey (1982) found that 50 percent of juvenile prostitutes in her sample reported forcible sexual advances by older men before they reached puberty.

Contrary to popular assumption, a majority of prostitutes do not appear to be lured into the activity by organized crime, brutal pimps, under false pretenses, or to support drug habits. Recruitment by pimps, madames, or organized crime appears to have been a factor for only about 20 percent of the prostitute population. The assumption of heavy drug use among prostitutes also appears questionable. James (1978) suggests that the prostitutes apprehended by police (and who thus end up in the criminal statistics) tend to be the "hypes"—the addicts working as prostitutes to support a drug habit. They "form a special, lower class in the hierarchy of the 'fast life'"(James, 1978, p. 306). Inciardi (1980) surveyed 149 female heroin users and found a high incidence of prostitution (about one-third) among them. However, he did not find evidence for a strong causal link. The women who committed crimes to support their drug habits were much more likely to choose economic offenses, like larceny or fraud, rather than prostitution.

MOTIVES

What motivates women to engage in prostitution? An obvious, although oversimplistic answer, is money. It is important to distinguish between financial necessity and financial comfort, however. James (1976) found that only 8.4 percent of her sample started prostitution out of economic necessity, but 56.5 percent did out of a desire for money and material goods. They saw prostitution as a lucrative business that offered material rewards they otherwise might not have attained. Social rewards like parties, dancing, and expensive dining were also a factor.

The James study and others like it have dispelled several alleged motives for entering into prostitution—narcissism, frigidity, hatred of men, fears of lesbianism, or an unresolved sexual attachment to one's father (Electra complex). Some studies have reported that prostitutes may be more sexually responsive in their own personal lives than women in general (Pomeroy, 1965; James, 1976). James' finding that only 1 percent of her sample demonstrated hostility toward men damages Gibbens' (1957) "Circe complex" theory, which suggests that prostitutes have burning desires to turn men into swine. Greenwald's (1958) suggestion that prostitution is a way of combating a fear of homosexuality and a way of proving "normality" also seems to be on shaky ground. James found that, although 35 percent of her sample had experienced a lesbian relationship, only 7 percent had frequent homosexual activity. An additional 7 percent considered themselves exclusively lesbian. Although these figures appear high compared to the general female population, it should be emphasized that the prostitution sample was drawn from women who were blasé about so-called deviant behavior. They had ample opportunity for lesbian contact, yet did not apparently pursue it.

Finally, the Freudian theory that prostitution is a result of early sexual love for the opposite-sex parent, and that subsequent sexual partners represent insufficient surrogates, seems weak. According to this theory, the bulk of sexual energy and attraction is directed to the initial love object; later partners are unsatisfactory. Therefore, the sexually promiscuous female endlessly but subconsciously searches for the treasured first love object, the father (or in the case of male prostitutes, the mother). The Freudian perspective sees prostitution as individual psychopathology rather than a social phenomenon. Since a consistent finding in the research literature is that more than half of all prostitutes did not have an available father figure in the home, it is questionable whether they would develop unconscious, imagined incestuous relationships.

To conclude that women go into prostitution and remain there for financial gain is premature, however, and it oversimplifies human behavior. Why do not more women opt for that life style? Furthermore, although material gains may provide an initial incentive, it is widely recognized that most prostitutes—with the possible exception of independent, high-class call girls—do not directly profit much from their work, given the obligatory payoffs to pimps, police, hotel clerks, and taxi drivers.

Human behavior represents an infinite array of learned response patterns, and prostitution as a complex behavior should be no exception. It is frequently observed that most prostitutes find out about prostitution through friends and get started through their efforts and encouragement (James, 1978). These personal contacts provide significant models and opportunities for imitative learning. In addition, the sex-for-sale behaviors offer greater reward possibilities (money, excitement, adventure) than a previous life predicament. For some, prostitution offers a more positive and potentially exciting alternative than the home situation. Furthermore, the relationship with a pimp who often serves as husband, boyfriend, father, lover, agent, and protector (James, 1976) may be considerably more rewarding than the relationship with family.

Once these expectations and potentially rewarding behaviors are acquired, continued involvement depends partly on the actual rewards obtained. Do the positives of prostitution outweigh the negatives? Even given "good money" and an ideal situation in which the prostitute is relatively independent, few personalities would seem suited for long-term prostitution. To be habitually used solely as a sexual object would appear to require, among other things, a learned method of detachment and the availability of other sources of self-esteem.

Prostitution appears to be an emotionally stressful and psychologically draining occupation. James found that at least 50 percent of her sample listed emotional stress, worry about physical harm at the hands of a customer, or low self-esteem as major disadvantages. Another 20 percent listed the stress of worrying about venereal disease, reactions of family and society, personal vulnerability, and feelings of helplessness as primary disadvantages.

Legalization may alleviate some of the stress, but it is unlikely that it would change the situation substantially. As one prostitute interviewed by Millett (1974) remarked: "The worst part about prostitution is that you're obliged not to sell sex only, but your humanity. That's the worst part of it: that what you're selling is your human dignity. Not really so much in bed, but in accepting the agreement—in becoming a bought person" (p. 140).

SUMMARY AND CONCLUSIONS

The main theme of this chapter centers on the ways economic offenders minimize, neutralize, deny, and justify their actions to themselves and others. We have reviewed the economic crimes of burglary, larceny, motor vehicle theft, shoplifting, robbery, white-collar crime, and the tangential economic crimes of arson, bombing, and hostage taking. Perceived control of one's environment is a secondary theme. We also covered briefly an example of a crime against the public order, namely prostitution. We found that this "victimless" crime is replete with myths and misunderstandings, and is characterized by limited systematic study, especially recent, up-to-date research.

While monetary gain is certainly a powerful motive in economic crimes, the cognitive standards against which the offender's behavior is judged and regulated are crucial. These points of reference are strongly influenced by the social context and by one's immediate reference groups, such as fellow workers or peers. Reference groups and the social context are especially powerful influences in white-collar crimes, specifically corporate crime and the occupational offenses. By restructuring their cognitions to align them with the social climate, white-collar offenders are able to engage in behavior that they would otherwise perceive as reprehensible. Conventional economic offenders are less likely to restructure their cognitions drastically, although they too may do so. White-collar, occupational, corporate, and computer offenders often deny they are doing anything wrong; traditional economic offenders are more likely to admit wrongdoing, although like most criminals, they also justify it.

In discussing white-collar crime, we focused on Bandura's strategies for justifying or denying unlawful behavior. Each type of strategy involves either restructuring cognitions or denying consequences of one's conduct. All strategies promote a neutralization of any guilt feelings or self-punishment. The price we pay for the human brain is its powerful ability to justify even heinous and reprehensible actions. It may be that, in the long run, we have more to fear from corporate and organizational behavior than from any collection of conventional crimes.

12

DRUGS AND CRIME

In a poll by Strasser (1989a) of one thousand individuals randomly selected across the continental United States, two-thirds of the respondents felt that the sale and usage of drugs was the key cause of crime. In this chapter we will review the evidence in support of or against this public perception.

The relationship between drugs and crime may be viewed from two perspectives: (1) the use, sale, and possession of an illegal drug as a crime; and (2) the effect of drugs on antisocial behavior. In 1995, 1.5 million people were arrested for either the sale and/or manufacture or possession of illegal drugs (FBI, 1997). The majority of arrests for the offense of drug abuse violations are for possession, mostly involving marijuana. However, concentrating on drug possession and consumption in this chapter would require sifting through varied regulations and statistics, many of which are ambiguous and most of which differ from state to state. There is considerable evidence that violence accompanies drug distribution in the course of territorial disputes between rival organizations, or in conflicts between the buyer and the seller (Roth, 1996). Places where drug deals occur bring together valuable drugs, big money, weapons, and people accustomed to violence. This volatile mix creates a high potential for violence. For our purposes in this chapter, however, we are most concerned with the effect various drugs have on the criminal behaviors discussed throughout this text. Is a person more likely to be violent while under the influence of drugs? And if so, which drugs? Are people more sexually aroused and aggressive under the influence of certain drugs and thus more likely to rape or otherwise sexually assault? A considerable body of research is available to help answer these questions.

Four major categories of **psychoactive drugs** will be covered. To keep the chapter within manageable limits, however, we will focus on only one or two representative drugs within each group, usually the one most often associated with crime. The **hallucinogens** or **psychedelics**, which include LSD (lysergic acid diethylamide), mescaline, psilocybin, phencyclidine, ketamine, marijuana, and hashish, will be our first category. So called because they sometimes generate hallucinations, the hallucinogens are chemicals that lead to a change in consciousness involving an alteration of reality. In some respects they replace the present world with an alternative one, although persons using them can generally attend to their altered state and to reality simultaneously. Marijuana, classified as a hallucinogen, is certainly a mild one for a majority who use it. Because of its widespread use and the public's tendency to mistakenly associate it with crime and bizarre behavior, it will be the main drug covered under the hallucinogens category. We will also include phencyclidine (PCP), a powerful drug that has been linked to crime during the 1980s.

Next, we will discuss the **stimulants**, so called because they appear to stimulate central nervous system functions. They include amphetamines, clinical antidepressants, cocaine, caffeine, and nicotine. Again because of an alleged relationship with crime, the amphetamines and cocaine will be highlighted.

The third group includes the **opiate narcotics**, which generally have sedative (sleep-inducing) and analgesic (pain-relieving) effects. Heroin will be featured in this section. The heroin addict appears frequently in crime statistics, since it is believed that he or she often turns to crime—particularly property crime—to finance this expensive habit.

Finally, alcohol will represent the **sedative-hypnotic** chemicals that depress central nervous system functions. In most instances, the sedative-hypnotics are all capable of sedating the nervous system and reducing anxiety and tension.

The relationship between drugs and crimes is complicated by a threefold interaction: (1) the pharmacological effects of the drug, which refer to the chemical impact of the drug on the body; (2) the psychological characteristics of the individual using the drug; and (3) the psychosocial conditions under which the drug is taken. Discussion of pharmacological effects includes features of the nervous system, such as the amount of neurotransmitter substances within neurons, and body weight, blood composition, and other neurophysiological features that significantly influence the chemical effects of the drug. Psychological variables include the mood of the person at the time the drug is consumed, previous experience with the drug, and the person's expectancies about the drug's effects. Psychosocial variables include the social atmosphere under which the drug is taken. The people who are present and their expectations, moods, and behavior all may influence an individual's reactions to a drug.

In order to understand the effects of any drug, therefore, the pharmacological, psychological, and psychosocial variables all must be taken into account. Considering the fact that crime is complex to begin with, deciphering the crime-drug connection becomes very difficult, and the conclusions are necessarily that much more elusive and tentative.

The relationship between drugs and crime is further complicated by the cultural, subcultural, and ethnographic aspects of drug consumption. Age groups and cultures have different attitudes and perceptions about specific drugs that are often in a state of flux. Cultural preferences shift and change depending on drug availability, law enforcement priorities, and changes in cultural attitudes. In addition, demographic studies have shown drug popularity and epidemics go through four distinct stages: incubation, expansion, plateau, and decline (Golub

& Johnson, 1997). During the incubation stage, users experiment with the new and emerging drug, learn how to use it, and develop techniques for its use. During the expansion stage, prices drop, it becomes easy to use, its availability increases, and word gets around about the drug, all of which contribute to its popularity. During the plateau stage, there is a relatively high and constant use of the drug. But during the decline stage, the drug is shunned—usually by a new generation of youth—and a new drug emerges in popularity.

Furthermore, certain professional criminal groups often prefer one drug over another. Professional pickpockets, shoplifters, and burglars, for example—when they use drugs—have a distinct preference for those that steady their nerves and provide relief from the pressures of their occupation (Inciardi, 1981). Professional pickpockets often consider opiates instrumental in furthering their careers. To some extent, this has a cyclical effect, since their material gain from their crimes is used to obtain the drugs.

Before proceeding, we must distinguish two terms that are consistently used in the drug literature: **tolerance** and **dependence**. Drug tolerance is the "state of progressively decreased responsiveness to a drug" (Julien, 1975, p. 29). Tolerance is indicated if the individual requires a larger dose of the drug to reach the same effects he or she has previously experienced. In other words, the person has become psychologically and physiologically used to, or habituated to, the drug.

Dependence may be physical or psychological, or both. In simple terms, physical dependence refers to the physiological distress and physical pain a person suffers if he or she goes without the drug for any length of time. Psychological dependence is difficult to distinguish from physical dependence, but it is characterized by an overwhelming desire to use the drug for a favorable effect. The person is convinced that he or she needs the drug to maintain an optimal sense of well-being. The degree of psychological dependence varies widely from person to person and drug to drug. In its extreme form, the person's life is permeated with thoughts of procuring and using the drug, and he or she may resort to crime to obtain it. In common parlance, the person who is extremely psychologically and/or physically dependent is the addict.

Secondary psychological dependence may also develop. While primary dependence is associated with the reward of the drug experience (positive reinforcement), secondary dependence refers to expectancies about aversive withdrawal or the painful effects that will accompany absence of the drug. Thus, to avoid the anticipated pain and discomfort associated with withdrawal, the individual continues to take the drug (negative reinforcement).

The data reported in this chapter concerning illicit drug use were primarily gathered from the *National Household Survey on Drug Abuse* (*NHSDA*), currently sponsored by the Substance Abuse and Mental Health Services Administration. This survey was described in more detail in Chapter 1. In 1996, the NHSDA estimated that 13 million Americans were current drug users, meaning they had used an illicit drug in the month prior to the interview. The 1996 figure is essentially the same as the 1995 data, suggesting that illicit drug use has hit a plateau.

According to the NDSDA, the number of illicit drug users was at its highest level in 1979 when there were 25 million users.

THE HALLUCINOGENS: CANNABIS

Marijuana, which apparently originated in Asia, is among the oldest and most frequently used intoxicants. It remains the most commonly used illicit drug in the United States. The 1996 NHSDA reported that about 68.5 million Americans (32 percent) had tried marijuana at least once in their lifetimes, and 18 million (8.6 million) had used it during the past year. In addition, the survey reported that marijuana use among youth ages twelve to seventeen had nearly doubled in two years.

The earliest reference to marijuana was found in a book on pharmacy written by the Chinese emperor Shen Nung in 2737 B.C. (Ray, 1972). It was called the "Liberator of Sin" and recommended for such ailments as "female weakness," constipation, and absentmindedness. The word marijuana is commonly believed to have derived from "mary jane," Mexican slang for cheap tobacco, or from the Portuguese word mariguano, meaning intoxicant. Street names for the drug include pot, grass, reefer, weed, Mary Jane, and Acapulco gold.

The drug is prepared from the plant **cannabis**, an annual that is cultivated or grows freely as a weed in both tropical and temperate climates. There are at least three species of cannabis—sativa, indica, and ruderalis—each differing in psychoactive potency. The psychoactive (intoxicating) properties of the plant reside principally in the chemical Delta-9 tetrahydrocannabinol (THC), found mainly in its resin. Thus, the concentration and quality of THC within parts of the plant determine the potency or psychoactive power of the drug.

THC content varies from one preparation to another, partly due to the quality of the plant itself, but also due to its environment. The strain of the plant, the climate, and the soil conditions all affect THC content. For example, the resin is believed to retard the dehydration of the flowering elements and thus is produced in greater quantities in hot, tropical climates than in temperate zones (Hofmann, 1975). Consequently, cannabis grown in the tropics (Mexico, Columbia, Jamaica, and North Africa) presumably has greater psychoactive potential than American grown hemp, a product not highly prized by experienced cannabis users. More recent information suggests, however, that THC potency is more a feature of the species of the cannabis plant than of geographic area or climatic conditions (Ray, 1983).

The cannabis extracts used most commonly in the United States are marijuana and hashish. Marijuana is usually prepared by cutting the stem beneath the lowest branches, air drying, and stripping seeds, bracts, flowers, leaves, and small stems from the plant. There is no evidence that the female cannabis plant contains more THC than the male. Hashish, the Arabic word for "dry grass," is produced by scraping or in some other way extracting the resin secreted by the flowers. Therefore, hashish, which is usually sold in this country in small cubes, cakes, or even cookie-like shapes, has more THC content than marijuana. Hofmann (1975) reports that the THC content in hashish ranges from 5 to 12 percent, while the more potent forms of marijuana (e.g., ganja from Jamaica) contain about 4 to 8 percent THC. Currently, the most select product, sinsemilla (Spanish for "without seed"), is believed to contain as much as 8 percent THC (Abadinsky, 1993). Mexican varieties often contain less than 1 percent of THC, and American varieties often less than 0.2 percent. Hashish oil is produced by repeated extractions of cannabis plant materials, a process that results in a dark, viscous liquid with a THC content as high as 20 percent (Abadinsky, 1993). A drop or two on a regular cigarette usually has the effect of one marijuana cigarette. When exposed to air over a period of time, marijuana appears to lose its psychoactive potency, since THC is converted to cannabinol and other inactive compounds (Mechoulam, 1970). Cannabis extracts with higher levels of resin deteriorate more rapidly than those with lower levels.

In the United States, marijuana and hashish are usually smoked, most often in hand-rolled cigarettes. It is becoming increasingly popular to lace the cigarette with other drugs, such as PCP. A common practice in other countries is to consume cannabis as "tea," or mixed with other beverages or food.

The psychological effects of cannabis are so subjective and depend on such a wide range of variables that any generalizations must be accompanied by the warning that there are numerous exceptions. Reactions to cannabis, like all psychoactive drugs, depend on the complex interactions of both pharmacological and extrapharmacological factors. As we noted, these include the mood of the user, the user's expectations about the drug, the social context in which it is used, and the user's past experiences with the drug. The strong influence of these extrapharmacological factors together with the widespread variation in THC content in any sample of cannabis make it exceedingly difficult to obtain comparable research data. Essentially, the effects of cannabis are unique to each individual. Except for increases in heart rate, increases in peripheral blood flow, and reddening of the membranes around the eyes, there are few consistent physiological changes reported for all persons (Hofmann, 1975; National Commission, 1972; Canadian Government's Commission of Inquiry, 1971).

Addiction to THC does occur, but only at doses and continued use far above what is now used recreationally (Ray, 1983). Furthermore, the person who uses marijuana must learn to use the drug to reach a euphoric "stoned" or "high" state. Ray (1983) reports that a three-stage learning process is involved. First, users must inhale the smoke deeply and hold it in their lungs for twenty to forty seconds. Then, they must learn to identify and control the effects. Finally, they must learn to label the effects as pleasant.

CANNABIS AND CRIME

Public concern about the connection between cannabis and crime was stimulated by a number of articles printed in a New Orleans newspaper as long ago as 1926 (Ray, 1972). In 1931, a popular article concluded that one out of every four persons arrested in New Orleans was addicted to cannabis. With public interest activated, a drive to get the "dangerous" drug outlawed was soon underway. It was spearheaded by the then Commissioner of Narcotics, Harry Anslinger, who convinced Congress and many states that marijuana often led to serious crime and was a threat to the moral fabric of American society. During this time (the 1930s), marijuana use was often linked with both violent and "perverted" crime.

In 1937, Congress passed the *Marijuana Tax Act*, a bill intended to add muscle to antimarijuana laws that by then existed in forty-six states. The Tax Act did not actually outlaw cannabis, but it taxed the grower, distributor, seller, and buyer prohibitively and established so many requirements that it was nearly impossible to have anything to do with any form of cannabis (Ray, 1972). Interestingly, none of the attitudes or regulations were supported by comprehensive scientific investigations or evidence that marijuana was harmful. The information communicated was anecdotal; the "documentation" consisted of testimony of the "I know a case where" variety. The U.S. Supreme Court eventually declared the Marijuana Tax Act unconstitutional.

In 1939, Bromberg published results of a study conducted in New York between the years 1932 and 1937. Out of a total of 16,854 prisoners, only sixty-seven said they were cannabis users, and only six of those were indicted for a violent crime. Bromberg concluded that the relationship between marijuana use and crime was not substantiated, but staunch advocates of the marijuana-crime connection were not swayed.

Numerous research projects directed at the effects of cannabis were launched during the 1950s, 1960s, and early 1970s. Many of these studies had methodological shortcomings and did not control for parity of dosage levels, means of administering the drug, and THC content in the drug itself. Psychological factors associated with the subjects were not considered carefully enough, and experimental settings and instructions were haphazard. At first, some of the research suggested a relationship between cannabis use and criminal behavior. However, with more sophisticated statistical analyses that controlled demographic and criminal background variables, the earlier results were found to be spurious (National Commission, 1972). To date, no investigation has established a causal link between the use of cannabis and criminal activity. Of course, this assertion excludes the illegal acts of selling, possessing, or using the drug.

Recent independent research as well as investigations conducted by government-sponsored commissions strongly indicate that marijuana does not directly contribute to criminal behavior. After an extensive review of available literature, the National Commission on Marijuana and Drug Abuse (1972, p. 470) came to this conclusion: "There is no systematic empirical evidence, at least that is drawn from the American experience, to support the thesis that the use of marijuana either inevitably or generally causes, leads to or precipitates criminal, violent, aggressive or delinquent behavior of sexual or nonsexual nature." The Commission Report (p. 470) adds: "If anything, the effects observed suggest that marijuana may be more likely to neutralize criminal behavior and to militate against the commission of aggressive acts."

One of the predominant effects of THC is relaxation and a marked decrease in physical activity (Tinklenberg & Stillman, 1970). THC induces muscular weakness and inability to sustain physical effort, so that the user wishes nothing more strenuous than to stay relatively motionless. As Tinklenberg and Stillman (1970, p. 341) note, "'being stoned' summarizes these sensations of demobilizing lethargy." It is difficult to imagine "stoned" users engaging in assaultive or violent activity. If anything, THC should reduce the likelihood of criminal activity, particularly aggressive conduct, as the Commission suggested. There is some evidence to support this conclusion.

Tinklenberg and Woodrow (1974) found that drug users who use mainly marijuana seem less inclined toward violence and aggression than their counterparts who prefer other drugs, such as alcohol or amphetamines. After examining drug usage among lower-class minority youth, Blumer and his associates (Blumer, Sutter, Ahmed, & Smith, 1967) made the same observation. In fact, they found that marijuana users deliberately shunned aggression and violence; in order to maintain one's status in the group, it was important to remain "cool" and nonaggressive, regardless of provocation.

Although the empirical evidence so far indicates that cannabis does not, as a rule, stimulate aggressive behavior or other criminal actions, whenever we deal with human behavior there will be exceptions. Individuals familiar with the effects of cannabis have heard of occasional negative experiences produced by THC. Although the phenomenon is rare, some people do report feelings of panic, hypersensitivity, feelings of being out of contact with their surroundings, and bizarre behavior. Some individuals have experienced rapid, disorganized intrusions of irrelevant thoughts, which prompted them to feel they were losing control of their mind. Under these conditions, it is plausible that one would interpret the actions of others as threatening. It is also possible that these panicked individuals might attack those surrounding them.

However, those who investigate cannabis effects usually agree that people who act violently under the influence of the drug were probably predisposed to act that way, with or without the drug (National Commission, 1972). The evidence indicates that violent marijuana users were violent prior to using cannabis. In other words, they learned the behavioral pattern independently of cannabis. In addition, they have come to expect that the drug will "bring out" aggression or violence in them.

In summary, there is no solid evidence to indicate that cannabis contributes to or encourages violent or property crime, in spite of continuing beliefs that this relationship exists. In fact, there is evidence to suggest that cannabis users are less criminally or violently prone under the influence of the drug than users of other drugs, such as alcohol and amphetamines. There are also no supportive data that cannabis is habit-forming to the point where the user must get a "fix" and will burglarize or rob to obtain funds to purchase the drug.

PHENCYCLIDINE (PCP)

PCP may be classified as a central nervous system depressant, anesthetic, tranquilizer, or hallucinogen. It has many effects, but most pronounced is its barbiturate-like downer effect, perceptual distortions and hallucinations, and its amphetamine-like upper effects, such as excitation and hyperactivity. An overdosed person, for example, may show signs of both moving from upper to downer effects, while having hallucinations.

PCP was first synthesized in 1957, but due to its psychotic and hallucinogenic reactions, it was taken off the market for human consumption in 1965 and limited to veterinary medicine as an animal immobilizing agent. Because of its serious and numerous side effects, it is no longer used even in veterinary medicine. Between 1973 and 1979 its popularity increased, but then declined briefly between 1979 and 1981. Since 1982, however, it has showed a resurgence in popularity (Crider, 1986). Most users are male, African American, and between the ages of twenty and twenty-nine (Crider, 1986). The behavior of some individuals under the influence of PCP is highly unpredictable and may lead to life-threatening situations. Under the spell of PCP psychosis, delusions of superhuman strength, persecution, and grandiosity are not uncommon. On occasion, individuals under the influence of PCP may use weapons to defend themselves and to commit other acts of violence. However, the incidence of violence caused by PCP influence is unknown.

There is wide variation in degree of purity and dosage forms of PCP manufactured in clandestine laboratories. It comes in capsules, tablets, liquids, or powders. It may be administered orally, by inhalation (snorted or smoked), and at times by intravenous injection. If it is smoked, PCP is often applied to leafy material such as mint, parsley, oregano, or marijuana. Users usually combine PCP with other drugs, particularly marijuana and alcohol. It can cause death, although the majority of fatal doses were combined with alcohol (Brunet, Reiffenstein, Williams, & Wong, 1985–1986). Because of its adverse and negative effects, the reasons for its popularity remain obscure.

The available evidence clearly indicates that PCP users tend to be multiple illicit drug users (polydrug users). In addition, it continues to be one of the more common drugs found in arrestee populations. Wish (1986) reports that in an urinalysis study of nearly five thousand male arrestees in Manhattan in 1984, 12 percent showed evidence of PCP. Furthermore, 49 percent of those using PCP were also using other drugs at the time of the arrest, usually cocaine. In a similar project conducted in Washington, DC, 30 percent of the male arrestees were using PCP. In both studies, the vast majority of the subjects were arrested for goal-oriented, income-generating crimes rather than violent offenses. To what extent PCP propels a person toward a life of crime is largely unknown, but it does not seem likely that the PCP user regularly engages in crime to support his or her habit. PCP users are generally polydrug users who have demonstrated a variety of types of antisocial conduct prior to PCP usage. Polydrug usage is more likely to be one symptom within a complicated matrix of other symptoms found in certain individuals habitually "going against" their environment.

AMPHETAMINES AND COCAINE

Amphetamines and cocaine are classified as central nervous system stimulants and have highly similar effects. Amphetamines are part of a group of synthetic drugs known collectively as **amines**. Cocaine (coke, snow, candy) is a chemical extracted from the coca plant (Erythroxylon coca), an extremely hardy plant native to Peru. The amines in particular produce effects in the sympathetic nervous system, a subdivision of the autonomic nervous system, which arouse the person to action that might include fighting or fleeing from a frightening situation. Amphetamines are traditionally classified into three major categories: (1) amphetamine (Benzedrine); (2) dextroamphetamine (Dexedrine); and (3) methamphetamine (Methedrine or Desoxyn). Of the three, Benzedrine is the least potent. All may be taken orally, inhaled, or injected, and all act directly on the central nervous system, particularly the reticular activating system (Bloomquist, 1970). Methamphetamine has traditionally been the drug of preference when the user injects the amphetamines directly into the bloodstream. Its use has increased significantly in the United States in recent years, particularly in the West and Southwest, and is a matter of growing concern (Feucht & Kyle, 1996). Once the drug is taken, it is rapidly assimilated into the bloodstream, but it is metabolized and eliminated from the body relatively slowly. Both psychological and physiological reactions to these drugs vary dramatically with the dose; in addition, the effects of massive quantities intravenously injected differ substantially from low doses administered orally. Reactions to the drugs also vary widely among individuals.

The common street names for amphetamines include bennies, dexies, copilots, meth, speed, white cross, uppers, crank, cryptol, crystal, quill, pep pills, yellow bam, tweek, eye openers, wakeups, hearts, footballs, bombitas, coast-to-coasts, splash, and purple hearts. The street names are derived from the various effects, the purposes to which the drug is put, the shape and color of the drug, or the trade name of the manufacturers.

The amphetamines are synthetic compounds, and, unlike cannabis or cocaine, can be easily produced by self-appointed chemists for large-scale illegal distribution. The manufacture of methamphetamine, for example, requires precursor drugs (drugs that are necessary in the manufacture of another) such as ephedrine or pseudoephedrine, which are widely available in Mexico and are believe to be smuggled into the United States in large quantities (Feucht & Kyle, 1996). Therefore, it is exceedingly difficult to estimate the quantity of amphetamines consumed each year in the Unites States. Available research does indicate, however, that methamphetamines may be used more frequently by females than males (Feucht & Klye, 1996).

Methamphetamine is currently the amphetamine most popular with drug abusers in the United States. Methamphetamine hydrochloride, clear chunky crystals resembling ice (therefore, often referred to as "ice," "crystal," and "glass"), is usually smoked; whereas regular methamphetamine is usually either taken orally, injected or inhaled (snorting the powder). Currently, the popular method of administration is through smoking. The 1996 data reported by the *Monitoring the Future Study* indicates that crystal methamphetamine is becoming increasingly popular among high school seniors.

Cocaine has traditionally been much more expensive than amphetamines, partly because it is a natural organic substance and cannot be produced synthetically. The coca plant from which it is extracted thrives at elevations of two thousand to eight thousand feet with heavy rainfall (one hundred inches per year). It is an evergreen shrub, growing to about three feet tall, and generally found on the eastern slopes of the Andes. It has long been used by Peruvians living in or near the Andes. Mountain natives chew coca leaves almost continuously and commonly keep them tucked in their cheek (Ray, 1972). Coca leaves are also used for tea. There are at least two hundred strains of coca plants, but the vast majority contain little if any cocaine. However, with the increasing appetite of North Americans for cocaine, South American growers and entrepreneurs have not only developed vast new areas for the cultivation of coca but also new, more vigorous strains of the plant (Inciardi, 1986).

In the United States and Canada, cocaine is usually administered nasally (sniffing), inhaling (smoking), or intravenously. Cocaine taken orally is poorly absorbed because it is hydrolyzed by gastrointestinal secretions. Light users normally sniff the drug to obtain their "high," but chronic sniffing can result in nasal irritation and inflammation. The common unit in the black market is the "spoon," which approximates one gram of the diluted drug. In most cases, cocaine is diluted twenty to thirty times its weight. It is estimated that there are 6 million (3 percent of the population) regular cocaine users in the United States (White & Azel, 1989, p. 25).

Coca Cola contained cocaine as an active ingredient until 1903, when caffeine was substituted (Kleber, 1988). In fact, around the turn of the century, cocaine was used not only in soft drinks (such as Kos-Kola, Wiseola, and Care-Cola), but even in cigarettes and cigars, various tonics, foods, sprays, and ointments (including hemorrhoid salves) (Smart, 1986). The famous drink "Vin Mariani," so popular among the wealthy at the time, was a combination of vintage French wine and cocaine. However, cocaine began to fall into disfavor when people became concerned about its dangerous and undesirable effects. By 1910, cocaine had become the most hated and feared drug in North America (Kleber, 1988). The Harrison Narcotics Act of 1914 in the United States, and the Propriety and Patents Medicines Act of 1908 in Canada, sharply curtailed or terminated its usage, and the popularity of cocaine correspondingly declined until the 1960s.

In national surveys conducted in the early 1980s in Canada, about 4 percent of the college students and 3 percent of the adults said they used cocaine at least once during the year (Smart, 1986). More recent research suggests that the high level of cocaine use in Canada during the 1980s seems to be declining during the early 1990s (Smart & Adlaf, 1992). In the United States, the incidence was high during the 1980s, with about 16 to 20 percent of the college students using cocaine at least once during the year (Johnson, Bachman, & O'Malley, 1983), and about 28 percent of the adults saying they used the drug at least once in their lifetimes (Miller, Cisin, Gardner-Keaton, Harrell, Wirtz, Abelson, & Fishburne, 1983). The 1996 NHSDA found that 22 million Americans (or 10 percent) age twelve and older had tried cocaine at least once in their lifetimes; about 4 million (or 1.8 percent) had used cocaine during the past year; and about 1.7 (less than 1 percent) million had used cocaine in the past month. These figures also suggest that there has been a discernible drop or leveling off of cocaine use in recent years.

PSYCHOLOGICAL EFFECTS

In small doses, both amphetamines and cocaine increase wakefulness, alertness, and vigilance, improve concentration, and produce a feeling of clear thinking. There is generally an elevation of mood, mild euphoria, increased sociability, and a belief that one can do just about anything. The duration of the stimulant's euphoric effects depends on the route of administration. The faster the absorption, the more intense the high. In large doses, the effects may be irritability, hypersensitivity, delirium, panic aggression, hallucinations, and psychosis. Injected at chronically high doses, these drugs may precipitate "toxic psychosis," a syndrome with many of the psychotic features of paranoid schizophrenia. With the metabolization and elimination of the drug, the psychotic episode usually dissipates.

STIMULANTS, COCAINE, AND CRIME

As pointed out, heavy users of amphetamines typically prefer to inject methamphetamine directly into the bloodstream, cranking up with several hundred milligrams at one time. During these speed "runs" the user may engage in aggressive or violent behavior (Tinklenberg & Stillman, 1970; Hofmann, 1975; National Commission on Marijuana and Drug Abuse, 1973).

At this point in our knowledge, however, there is little evidence to support a relationship between stimulants and crime. Both amphetamines and cocaine, in small doses, increase alertness and concentration. In large doses, they generally produce negative psychological effects. But, to date, virtually no study has shown that stimulants or cocaine facilitate either property crime or violent crime. In an exhaustive review of the literature, the *Panel on the Understanding and Control of Violent Behavior* concluded that "there is no evidence to support the claim that snorting or injecting cocaine stimulates violent behavior. However, research is urgently needed on the behavioral effects of smoking cocaine in crack form, which affects the brain more directly" (Roth, 1996, p. 6).

CRACK

The most common form of cocaine smoking in the United States is freebasing. Freebase is prepared by dissolving cocaine hydrochloride in water, and then adding a strong base such as ammonia or baking soda to the solution (Weiss & Mirin, 1987). This cocaine freebase is generally dissolved in ether to extract the cocaine, and then the ether is removed by drying. Other methods may be used that bypass the ether method. The result is a product ranging from 37 to 96 percent purity (Weiss & Mirin, 1987).

During the 1980s, a purified, high-potency form of freebase cocaine known as "crack" exploded in popularity. It was, according to Howard Abadinsky (1993), the drug abuser's answer to fast food. The drug is called "crack" because it makes a crackling sound when smoked (Abadinsky, 1993; Gold, 1984). Several times more pure than ordinary street cocaine, crack smoking generates a very rapid, intense state of euphoria, which peaks in about five minutes. The psychological and physical effects of crack are as powerful as any intravenously injected cocaine. However, the euphoria is short-lived, ending in about ten to twenty minutes after inhalation, and is followed by depression, irritability, and often an intense craving for more. Although most users limit themselves to one or two "hits," some users seek multiple hits. Crack smokers, in order to stay high, often find a place where crack can be safely smoked, such as a "crack house," because the smoke and smell are difficult to hide.

During the 1980s crack cocaine generated much concern to local officials across the United States because of its popularity, illegal drug trafficking, and health hazards to adolescents and young adults. At one point, some experts regarded crack as the most addictive drug currently available on the street (Weiss & Mirin, 1987). Furthermore, it was thought that the craving for the drug might become so severe for some individuals that the user would lie, steal, or commit acts of violence in order to obtain more of the drug (Rosecan, Spitz, & Gross, 1987). Its popularity probably resided in the instantaneous psychological effects it provides, its inexpensiveness, and its wide availability throughout most major U.S. cities. The drug also provided tremendous profitability for the sellers. For awhile, about one-third of all arrests made by the New York City Narcotics Division involved cocaine, and over half of them involved crack (Cohn, 1986). Because it was so inexpensive and available, it became a very popular drug for the young—including preteenagers. It is also extremely dangerous to the user and may result in a rapid, irregular heartbeat, respiratory failure, seizures, or a cerebral hemorrhage.

Beginning in the early 1990s, the use of crack cocaine has begun to decline (Golub & Johnson, 1997). The reasons for the decline are multiple, but the most prominent appear to be its health risks and the changes in attitude among the new generation concerning its use. The youth today consider crack users "dumb" and "crackhead" a dirty word (Golub & Johnson, 1997). In some cities, many youths abuse crackheads or avoid them altogether. Overall, it appears that the primary users of crack cocaine who began using the drug during the 1980s continue to be the heavy users of the drug today. However, the more recent generation of youth called Generation X tend to avoid using the drug.

The relationship between crack and crime remains obscure. One thing that does emerge from the research literature is that crack users, especially persistent users, are often polydrug users. Surveys indicate that virtually all crack users have been frequent users of other drugs, and most also had an extensive history of prior drug use, drug selling, and nondrug criminality (Golub & Johnson, 1997). While it is difficult at this point in our knowledge to determine which comes first, drug use or involvement in crime, the evidence does suggest that persistent offenders have engaged in a variety of illegal activities and troublesome conduct throughout their lifetimes, probably before extensive drug abuse. One thing appears clear: Crack use by itself does not appear to be associated with the initiation of violent behavior (Golub & Johnson, 1997).

NARCOTIC DRUGS

The word **narcotics** usually provokes intense negative reactions and very often is quickly associated with crime. Like the word dope, it is widely misused to denote all illegal drugs. In this chapter, narcotic drugs refer only to the derivatives of or products pharmacologically similar to products of the opium or poppy plant, Papaver sominferum.

The opium plant, an annual, grows to about three to five feet in height. Today, most opium is grown in two regions: (1) the Golden Triangle: Laos, which produces 70 metric tons of opium per year; Burma, which produces 532 metric tons; and Thailand, which produces 36 metric tons; and (2) the Golden Crescent: Iran, Afghanistan, and Pakistan, which together produce about 865 metric tons annually (Inciardi, 1986). Interestingly, it is estimated that about 150 metric tons of opium per year are sufficient to meet the needs of all the world's narcotic addicts (Ray, 1983).

Narcotic drugs can be divided into three major categories on the basis of the kind of preparation they require: (1) natural narcotics, which include the grown opium; (2) semisynthetic narcotics, which include the chemically prepared heroin; and (3) synthetic narcotics, which are wholly prepared chemically and include methadone, meperidine, and phenazocine. All are narcotics because they produce similar effects: relief of pain, relaxation, peacefulness, and sleep (narco, of Greek origin, means "to sleep"). The narcotics are highly addictive for some individuals; they develop a relentless and strong craving for the drug. Many heavy narcotic users, however, lead successful, productive lives, without significant interference in their daily routine. There is no single type of opium user.

HEROIN

The most heavily used illegal narcotic in this country is heroin. During the 1970s, it was estimated that there were 400,000 to 600,000 heroin addicts in any given year. During the 1990s, it is estimated that there are 229,000 "casual users and 500,000 "heavy" users per year (Epstein & Gfroerer, 1997). Data from the 1996 NHSDA indicated that there were approximately 2.4 million Americans who tried heroin at least once in their lifetime and approximately 455,000 Americans who used heroin at least once during the past year.

Although the street scene continually changes with respect to the use of illegal drugs, heroin use has hit a plateau over the past three decades. Current heroin users tend to be a "leftover" group of older, experienced, long-term addicts. About two-thirds are over age thirty, and males outnumber females by a margin of two to one. Unlike other drugs, heroin sellers usually do not use the drug themselves. Street sales are becoming increasingly managed by young nonusers who sell both heroin and cocaine, a practice known as "double breasting."

The availability of heroin continues to be high in almost all areas of the country, although the purity varies considerably from region to region. In early 1998, heroin was selling for $10 to $25 per bag for one-eighth ounce of the drug. The "bag" may be a glassine bag, capsules or "pills," or balloons. When heroin is sold by the "bag," its price does not always vary according to its purity. For example, the time of day it is sold or the geographic area may strongly influence the price due to the risks of detection perceived by the seller. Usually, heroin looks like a white, crystalline material and is characterized by the bitter taste of alkaloid. Its appearance is largely dictated by its diluents, which in most cases make up 95 to

98 percent of its total weight. In some instances, heroin will have a dark brown appearance due to the impurities left from the manufacturing process or the presence of additives.

Mexican "black tar" heroin has hit the streets in recent years. It is a dark brown substance that has the appearance of black tar and is sticky like roofing tar or, in some instances, hard like coal. The color and consistency of black tar heroin is due to the crude processing methods used to manufacture the drug. High quality Mexican black tar heroin sells for $600 to $800 per gram, and ranges in purity from 20 to 80 percent. In many areas, heroin users combine heroin with cocaine powder (HCl) or with crack, and then inject the mixture. This practice is known as "speedballing." In some regions, particularly in the West, users often mix heroin and methamphetamine and then inject. In New York, cocaine and heroin are often alternately inhaled, a practice called "criss-crossing." Heroin is rarely taken orally, because the absorption rate is slow and incomplete. It may be administered intramuscularly, subcutaneously ("skin popping"), or intra-venously ("mainlining"), or it may be inhaled ("snorted"). Heroin inhalers usu-ally choose to use heroin and crack simultaneously. In the past, experienced heroin users strongly preferred mainlining because of the sensational thrill, splash, rush, or kick it provided. Injection is probably the most practical and effi-cient way to administer low-purity heroin. However, in recent years, the dra-matic increase in heroin purity has changed the preferred method of administra-tion. Users now can snort or smoke the drug. And with the fear of HIV/AIDS and hepatitis from contaminated needles in recent years, a majority of young users prefer to snort or smoke heroin rather than injecting it.

The effects of heroin depend on the quantity taken, the method of administra-tion, the interval between administrations, the tolerance and dependence of the user, the setting, and the user's expectations. Effects usually wear off in from five to eight hours, depending on the user's tolerance.

Like all the narcotics, heroin is a central nervous system depressant. For many users, it promotes mental clouding, dreamlike states, light sleep punctuated by vivid dreams, and a general feeling of "sublime contentment." The body may become permeated with a feeling of warmth, and the extremities may feel heavy. There is little inclination toward physical activity; the user prefers to sit motion-less and in a fog.

HEROIN AND CRIME

No other drug group is as closely associated with crime as the narcotics, particu-larly heroin. The image of the desperate "junkie" looking for a fix is widespread. Furthermore, because of the adverse effects of the drug, it is assumed that the heroin user is bizarre, unpredictable, and therefore dangerous. However, high doses of narcotics produce sleep rather than the psychotic or paranoid panic states sometimes produced by high doses of amphetamines. Therefore, narcotics users rarely become violent or dangerous. Research strongly indicates that addicts do not, as a general rule, participate in violent crimes such as assault, rape, or homi-cide (National Institute on Drug Abuse, 1978; Canadian Government's

Commission of Inquiry, 1971; National Commission on Marijuana and Drug Abuse, 1973; Tinklenberg & Stillman, 1970).

Research evidence does suggest a relationship between heroin addiction and money-producing crime. A study in Miami of 573 narcotics users found that they were responsible for almost 6,000 robberies, 6,700 burglaries, 900 stolen vehicles, 25,000 instances of shoplifting, and 46,000 other events of larceny and fraud (Inciardi, 1986). Self-report surveys find that heroin users report financing their habits largely through "acquisitive crime" (Jarvis & Parker, 1989; Mott, 1986). Parker and Newcombe (1987) studied crime patterns and heroin use in the English community of Wirral, located in northwest England. They found that many heroin users were from the poor sections of the community and were young. The researchers were also able to divide their sample into three groups: (1) the largest group, consisting of young offenders who were not known to be using heroin but were highly criminally active; (2) heroin users who engaged in considerable acquisitive crime, but were involved in this type of crime prior to their heroin addiction; and (3) heroin users who started engaging in acquisitive crime after their habit in order to support the habit. The Parker-Newcombe investigation suggests that some heroin addicts do support their habit through crime.

Ball, Shaffer, and Nurco (1983) found that heroin addicts committed more money-producing crime when they were addicted compared to times when they were not. Still, it may be misleading to examine the heroin-crime relationship in isolation without considering the possible interactions between polydrug use and crime, or to conclude that heroin addiction causes crime. All we can say with some confidence at this point is that those who use heroin also seem to be deeply involved in money-producing crime. Heroin users, however, may not be driven to crime by the needs of their addiction. Heroin users, particularly polydrug users, may represent a segment of society that runs counter to society's rules and expectations in multiple ways, drug use and larceny among them. It may well be that most heroin-addicted criminals were involved in crime before they became addicted. Research by Faupel (1991) does support this hypothesis. However, studies also suggest that, although many heroin users have criminal records prior to their addiction, their criminal activity increases substantially during periods of heavy drug consumption (Faupel, 1991). Furthermore, polydrug users tend to switch from drug to drug, depending on what is available and inexpensive at the time, and do not seem physiologically desperate for any one particular drug. They simply substitute one drug for the other. Overall, the relationship between heroin use and criminal behavior is a complex one and varies throughout the addict's career.

THE DEPRESSANTS: ALCOHOL

Despite the public concern over heroin, opium, marijuana, cocaine, and the amphetamines, the number one drug of abuse has been and continues to be alcohol (ethanol, ethyl alcohol, grain alcohol). According to the 1996 NHSDA, 109 million Americans age twelve and older had used alcohol in the past month (51 percent of the population). About 32 million engaged in binge drinking (five or more drinks on at least one occasion in the past month) and about 11 million were heavy drinkers (drinking five or more drinks per occasion on five or more days in the past thirty days). Approximately 4.4 million of the binge drinkers were between the age of twelve and twenty, and 1.9 million of this age group were heavy drinkers. Men are more likely to be binge drinkers than women (22.8 and 8.7 percent, respectively), and they are also more likely to be heavy drinkers (9.3 and 1.9 percent, respectively).

Alcohol is responsible for more deaths and violence (it is the third major cause of death) than all other drugs combined. Approximately 25,000 individuals are killed each year, for example, in traffic accidents in which a driver was under the influence of alcohol.

PSYCHOLOGICAL EFFECTS

The social, psychological, and physical effects of excessive use of alcohol can be just as destructive to the individual, his or her family, and society in general, as heroin abuse. And similar to heroin, the alcoholic can develop a strong psychological and physical dependence on the drug. Society's attitudes toward alcohol are dramatically different from its attitudes toward other drugs of abuse, however. In virtually every part of the United States, it is legal and socially acceptable to consume the drug. In public, drinking behavior is generally unregulated unless it involves heavy intoxication and correspondingly unacceptable conduct, like disturbing the peace or operating a motor vehicle. In private, one can get as drunk as one wishes, a privilege not granted with respect to other drugs.

The effects of alcohol are complex, and we can provide only a cursory treatment here. At low doses (two or four ounces of whiskey, for example) alcohol seems to act as a stimulant on the central nervous system. Initially, it appears to affect the inhibitory chemical process of nervous system transmission, producing in the individual feelings of euphoria, good cheer, and social and physical warmth. In moderate and high quantities, however, alcohol begins to depress the excitatory processes of the central nervous system, as well as its inhibitory processes. Consequently, the individual's neuromuscular coordination and visual acuity are reduced, and he or she perceives pain and fatigue. The ability to concentrate is also impaired. Very often, self-confidence increases and the person becomes more daring, sometimes foolishly so. It is believed that alcohol at moderate levels begins to "numb" the higher brain centers that process cognitive information, especially judgment and abstract thought. It should be emphasized at this point that the levels of intoxication are not necessarily dependent on the amount of alcohol ingested; as for other psychoactive drugs, the effects depend on a myriad of interacting variables.

ALCOHOL AND CRIME

The belief that alcohol is a major cause of crime appears to be deeply embedded in American society. Surveys, for example, suggest that over 50 percent of the population is convinced that alcohol is a major factor in crimes of violence (Critchlow,

1986). This pervasive belief appears to be based on the premise that alcohol instigates aggressive conduct in some individuals, or somehow diminishes the checks and balances of nonaggressive, nonviolent behavior.

Coleman (1976) calls alcohol a "catalyst for violence," noting that about one out of every three arrests in the United States results from alcohol abuse. A survey of state prisons in 1974 found that 43 percent of all inmates had been drinking when they committed the crime for which they were serving time (Law Enforcement Assistance Administration, 1976). In a Missouri study, 55 percent of all males charged with capital or first-degree murder over a three-year period were taking alcohol, drugs, or a combination of both at the time of the homicide (Holcomb & Anderson, 1983). Cole, Fisher, and Cole (1968) reported that 51 percent of a sample of California women arrested for homicide had been drinking at the time of their offenses. Fifty-five percent of those convicted for murder in Britain (Gillies, 1965), and 51 percent of those convicted in France (Derville, L'Epee, Lazarin, & Derville, 1961) were drinking at the time of the violence. Nichol and colleagues (Nichol, Gunn, Gristwood, Foggett, & Watson, 1973) found that the more severe the drinking problem, the more serious the violent offense. Mayfield (1976) reports that 57 percent of a sample of convicted American murderers were drinking when they killed. Rada (1975) cites evidence that 50 percent of a sample of rapists were drinking at the time of their offenses. Tinklenberg (1973) found that 53 percent of a sample of California youth under age nineteen convicted of murder, manslaughter, or assault were under the influence of alcohol at the time of their offenses. A national survey of twelve thousand inmates indicated that 38 percent of the inmates were daily or almost daily drinkers in the year prior to their incarceration, and approximately 50 percent had been drinking just prior to the offense that resulted in their incarceration (Kalish, 1983). Glaser (1978, p. 275) estimates that "about half of the people arrested on any charge in the United States either are under the influence of alcohol when taken into custody, or are held for acts committed when drunk, or both." Roizen (1997), in summarizing the research on alcohol and violence, found that up to 86 percent of homicide offenders had been drinking at the time of the offense. Roizen further discovered that 60 percent of sexual offenders, 37 percent of assault offenders, 57 percent of males in marital violence, and 13 percent of child abusers had also been drinking at the time of the crime.

In summary, the evidence is quite clear that approximately half of all offenders who commit violent crime were drinking at the time of offense, and many were highly intoxicated. In an up-to-date, extensive literature review, Reiss and Roth (1993, p. 185) conclude: "In studies of prison inmates, those classified as 'heavy' or 'problem' drinkers had accumulated more previous arrests for violent crime, and reported higher average frequencies of assaults than did other inmates." And the *National Institute on Alcohol Abuse and Alcoholism* (1990, p. 92) asserts: "In both animals and human studies, alcohol more than any other drug, has been linked with a high incidence of violence and aggression."

While the relationship between alcohol and violence has long been suspected, the landmark study by Wolfgang (1958) on 588 Philadelphia homicides brought the alcohol-violence relationship into clear focus and stamped it with some scientific confirmation. The Wolfgang survey reported that in 9 percent of the homicides, the victims had been drinking alcohol at the time of the offense; 11 percent of the offenders had been drinking. More important, however, in an additional 44 percent of the cases, alcohol was present in both the offender and the victim. The Wolfgang findings suggest that people become volatile under the influence of alcohol, and that the danger increases greatly when both parties have been drinking. Research continues to support this finding.

High blood alcohol content (BAC) has been consistently reported in about 50 percent of homicide victims (e.g., Cleveland, 1955; Fisher, 1951; Bowden, Wilson, & Turner, 1958; Verkko, 1951; Wilentz, 1953; Bensing & Schroeder, 1960; Spain, Bradess, & Eggson, 1951). In a recent study (Welte & Abel, 1989), 46 percent of the homicide victims had significant amounts of alcohol, and many had substantial amounts. Specifically, 70 percent had BAC amounts higher than 0.10. This was especially the case for victims involved in fight-related homicides. The high BAC-victim connection, however, should not be read as simply supporting the conclusion that most victims precipitate their own demise. Although this may be the case in a proportion of violent events, the relationship should also be viewed as underscoring the importance of the social context within which violence occurs. Violence frequently occurs in social situations where drinking is heavy, physiological arousal is high (such as anger), interpersonal conflict is evident, and cognitive processes—especially judgment and abstract reasoning—are impaired.

Research in the psychology laboratory also finds strong evidence that drinking alcohol facilitates physical aggression. In the typical laboratory experiment, subjects are placed in a variety of conditions (independent variables) and can administer "electric shock" (simulated) to another person (the amount and frequency of the shock is the dependent variable). The independent variable may be the drug conditions to which subjects are randomly assigned (e.g., drug, placebo—in which subjects believe they are receiving a drug but do not, and non-drug conditions in which the subjects believe they are not receiving a drug and do not). To create another common independent variable, researchers may place subjects into aroused (usually anger) and nonaroused conditions.

Research using these paradigms has consistently found that drinking alcohol facilitates aggression, measured by shocking behavior (Taylor & Leonard, 1983; Taylor & Sears, 1988). Furthermore, as the quantity of alcohol consumed increases, so does the tendency to be aggressive, at least up to the point when the subject "passes out." We will return to these two findings shortly.

It should be mentioned that the alcohol-violence connection appears to be strongest in the United States, even though the amount of alcohol consumption in this country is by no means the highest in the world. Many countries, including France, Italy, Spain, West Germany, Portugal, and Russia, consume substantially more alcohol per capita than the United States. In addition to obvious cultural differences between the countries, drinking patterns are also different. In some countries, alcohol consumption is spread out across the day, including meal times, whereas in the United States drinking is generally reserved for the end of the day, particularly during weekends and holidays. It appears to be this episodic heavy drinking pattern that is most strongly related to aggression, violence and antisocial behavior.

The relationship between episodic heavy drinking of alcohol and aggression or violence is well supported, but how is it explained? Many models and theories have been proposed during the past twenty years, but a majority can be subsumed into two major categories: *Disinhibitory models* and *social-cognitive models*. Disinhibitory models contend that alcohol, directly or indirectly, influences neurological or psychological mechanisms that normally control aggressive and antisocial behavior. One disinhibitory perspective hypothesizes that alcohol chemically influences the portion of the brain that controls the expression of aggression. The more intoxicated the person, the less control he or she has of his or her behavior. Another disinhibitory perspective, and by far the most popular in American society, supposes that certain people have a particular sensitivity or susceptibility to alcohol. This perspective views problem drinking as a biological abnormality or disease. This approach, known as the "American disease model" (Miller & Hester, 1989), is deeply entrenched in American society and forms the fundamental assumption of Alcoholics Anonymous (AA). Polls show, for example, that 79 percent of Americans believe that alcoholism is a disease that requires medical treatment (Peele, 1984). The disease conception is not confined to the United States, however. Seventy percent of the general public in Scotland are also convinced that alcoholism is a disease (Crawford & Heather, 1987). The basic AA version is that chronic problem drinking is a disease reflected in an individual's inability to control alcoholic drinking, a disease that exists within the individual even before the first drink is taken. Furthermore, "The condition is irreversible and progressive and requires complete and utter abstinence" (Peele, 1984, p. 1339).

All disinhibitory models assume that alcohol has the power to disinhibit impulses that are normally held in check, and consequently this disinhibition may result in drink-induced criminal behavior (Critchlow, 1986). Furthermore, alcohol also provides a powerful excuse for undesirable behaviors that are often accompanied by such pleas as "I couldn't help myself" or "Alcohol always does this to me." Peele (1984, p. 1348) writes, "Disease conceptions may be alluring to our contemporary society because they are congruent with general ideas about the self and personal responsibility. Alcoholism viewed as an uncontrollable urge is after all part of a larger trend in which premenstrual tension, drug use and drug withdrawal, eating junk foods, and lovesickness are presented as defenses for murder."

While disinhibitory viewpoints focus on internal influences or predispositions, social-cognitive models emphasize the interactions between subjective belief systems or expectancies and the social environment. They reject the disease or loss of control assumptions of disinhibitory models. Social-cognitive models argue that problem drinking and much of the psychoactive influences of alcohol are learned and situationally determined. The contention that one cannot help oneself or that alcohol directly instigates a loss of control is a subjective, cognitive expectancy that feeds on itself, rather than a disease. A person's expectations or cognitions influence how he or she responds to alcohol. Alcohol serves as a cue for acting intoxicated and doing things one normally would not do, or acting the way one believes alcohol makes one act.

There is considerable empirical support for social-cognitive models of drinking behavior, and actually very little empirical support for disinhibitory models. For example, disinhibitory models advocate total abstinence if alcoholic-prone people are to control themselves, otherwise "one drink leads to one drunk." However, a large body of research shows that the most effective treatment for heavy drinkers is to train them to be responsible light to moderate drinkers rather than have them abstain completely over their lifespans (see Peele, 1984). Research continually shows that total abstinence has a poor track record over the long haul, especially for younger single men, since the abstinence requirement does not dovetail with their lifestyles and the opportunities and pressures they face to drink (Peele, 1984).

Among the proponents of social-cognitive theory are Marlatt and Rohsenow (1980) and Lang and his colleagues (Lang, Goeckner, Adesso, & Marlatt, 1975), who found that the amount of alcohol consumed may not be as important as what the person expects from the drug. Independent of the pharmacological effects, some people expect to become giddy, or loud, or boisterous after one or more drinks. Some anticipate acting more aggressively under the influence, because alcohol is "supposed" to have that effect. According to Lang, if a person expects alcohol to influence behavior in a preconceived way, it probably will. Moreover, as mentioned earlier, the person avoids blame for some of his or her actions, because society tends to accept the "I was drunk" explanation. In fact, Sobell and Sobell (1973) suggested that one of the rewarding aspects of heavy drinking is that it provides a socially acceptable excuse for engaging in inappropriate behavior.

In the Lang and colleagues (1975) experiment, half of the subjects were told they would be drinking alcohol, which actually was either vodka or tonic water. The other half were told they would be drinking tonic water, not alcohol. However, half the members of this second group were actually given vodka, and the other half received the tonic water they expected. Results indicated that "the only significant determinant of aggression was the expectation factor; subjects who believed they had consumed alcohol were more aggressive than subjects who believed they had consumed a nonalcoholic beverage, regardless of the actual alcohol content of the drinks administered" (p. 508).

According to social-cognitive theory, therefore, the consumer's expectancy becomes the crucial factor. As long as consumers believe they drank alcohol, they expect to feel intoxicated. Furthermore, being "intoxicated," they tend to feel less responsible for their behavior, including violent or criminal behavior. Interestingly, convicted murderers who were intoxicated during the crime often claim they cannot remember the incident at all (Schacter, 1986a). Whether these claims of amnesia are genuine remain very much in doubt.

Critchlow (1986) asserts that the pharmacological action of alcohol cannot account for the many transformations in social behavior that occur when people drink, as those transformations vary widely from culture to culture and in the same culture across time periods. She argues that the effects of alcohol on social behavior are found largely at the cultural level. Expectations about what alcohol can do behaviorally can be learned through a particular culture by anyone, even before taking the first drink. Critchlow writes:

> On a cultural level, it seems to be the negative consequences of alcohol that hold the most powerful sway over our thinking.... Thus, by believing that alcohol makes people act badly, we give it a great deal of power. Drinking becomes a tool that legitimates irrationality and excuses violence without permanently destroying an individual's moral standing or society's systems of rules and ethics. (pp. 761–762)

While cognitive expectancies play an extremely important role, we should not downplay the pharmacological effects of alcohol. Alcohol does affect the neurochemistry of the central nervous system by depressing many functions. Anyone who has tried to act sober with marginal success, no matter how they tried, can attest to this effect. Research confirms that alcohol has a strong pharmacological effect on behavior, somewhat independent of subjective expectancies. For example, Shuntich and Taylor (1972) found that actually intoxicated subjects were more aggressive than both subjects who consumed a placebo beverage (thinking they had consumed alcohol) and subjects who did not consume any beverage. Zeichner and Pihl (1979, 1980) also found that subjects in a nonalcohol condition were as aggressive as placebo subjects who thought they had consumed alcohol.

Social cognitive theory also predicts that the amount of alcohol consumed should make little difference in overall behavior. If subjects believe they are consuming large amounts, they will, correspondingly, act more intoxicated (and hence more aggressive). If, on the other hand, they do not believe they have consumed much alcohol, even though they actually have, they will be less aggressive and less likely to act intoxicated. In other words, the misled subjects will behave at the level of aggressiveness that corresponds with their expectations, regardless of the amount of alcohol they consume.

In evaluating this implication, a series of studies by Stuart Taylor and his associates (Taylor & Gammon, 1975; Taylor, Gammon, & Capasso, 1976; Taylor, Vardaris, Ravitch, Gammon, Cranston, & Lubetkin, 1976; Taylor, Schmutte, Leonard, & Cranston, 1979) are instructive. The Taylor projects found that small doses of alcohol (e.g., 0.5 ounces of vodka or bourbon per forty pounds of body weight) tend to inhibit aggression, while larger doses (1.5 ounces per forty pounds) tend to facilitate aggression. Therefore, depending on the amount, alcohol may either inhibit or facilitate expressions of aggression and violence.

The Taylor experiments are in agreement with the known pharmacological effects of alcohol. At small amounts, alcohol appears to stimulate the central nervous system, generating mild euphoria and a sense of well-being. This good cheer becomes readily apparent at a party, when, after the first round of drinks, people tend to take on a happy frame of mind. As alcoholic intake increases, however, the integrating functions of the cortex are depressed, causing some disorganization and impairment of complex cognitive functions. At extreme levels of intoxication, even simple cognitive processes like attention and sustained concentration break down, eventually ending in stupor and sleep. Therefore, violent behavior, if it is to occur, will most likely occur at moderate levels of intoxication.

In the Taylor investigation, when subjects were informed that they would be consuming alcohol, aggression was positively related only to the amount of alcohol actually consumed, not to the amount they thought they had consumed (Taylor & Gammon, 1975). In a later study (Taylor et al., 1976), subjects were informed that they would be consuming one of three drugs: alcohol, marijuana, or a tranquilizer. Therefore, all subjects within each group had the same drug expectancy. They then received either a high or low dose of THC or alcohol. The results demonstrated that the high dose of alcohol facilitated aggression, while the high dose of THC suppressed it.

Overall, Taylor's data strongly suggest that the aggression demonstrated by intoxicated subjects is a joint function of the pharmacological state produced by alcohol and cognitive and situational factors. The researchers maintain that alcohol consumption by itself does not produce aggressive behavior (Taylor & Leonard, 1983). Physiological effects of alcohol do influence behavior, but they also interact with expectancies and with what is happening in the person's environment at any given time.

Emotions may be important also. Jaffe, Babor, and Fishbein (1988) observe that alcoholics exhibit more aggressive, violent behavior than do nonalcoholics, especially when drinking. Beyond this, however, the researchers also noted that alcoholics frequently report highly negative emotions when drinking, such as anger and depression. They concluded, "Thus it is possible that when these states are experienced by alcoholics with a prior history of aggressive behavior, the likelihood of alcohol-related aggression increases and such behavior can be predicted with some degree of reliability" (p. 217). Similarly, unhappy or depressive thoughts presumably activate other negative memories and feelings and therefore are likely to promote aggressive, violent inclinations (Berkowitz & Heimer, 1989).

Situational factors are crucial. In all of Taylor's studies, aggression was not automatically produced by alcohol, even alcohol in large amounts. Rather, subjects were provoked, threatened, or at least were in the presence of aggressive cues before they displayed aggressive behavior. Therefore, in order for aggression to occur, there must be provocative, incitive, or instigative cues along with intoxication. Something or someone must anger, threaten, or in some other way arouse the intoxicated subject. But external cues are certainly not the whole story. Internal cues, such as thoughts, beliefs, or even imagined slights or provocations can serve as instigating cues for aggressive or violent behavior.

SUMMARY AND CONCLUSIONS

This chapter reviewed the relationship between crime and a number of drugs commonly associated with criminal behavior. Four major drug categories were identified: (1) the hallucinogens; (2) the stimulants; (3) the opiate narcotics; and (4) the sedative-hypnotics. Rather than discuss most of the drugs in each category, we considered only those commonly believed to be connected with criminal conduct. Moreover, we did not examine the crimes of drug distribution or possession. We are mainly concerned with whether the substance itself facilitates or instigates illegal action, especially violence. In other words, are persons under the influence of marijuana more violent than they are normally? Or, to what extent does alcohol directly contribute to loss of control or reduce self-regulatory mechanisms?

Cannabis, which includes marijuana and hashish, is a relatively mild hallucinogen with few psychological or physiological side effects. No significant relationship between cannabis use and crime has been consistently reported in the research literature. If anything, marijuana seems to reduce the likelihood of violence, since its psychoactive ingredient, THC, induces muscle weakness and promotes feelings of lethargy.

Amphetamines and cocaine (especially crack) represented the stimulant group. Most illegal users do not participate in crime other than the possession or sale of these drugs. Similar to marijuana, amphetamines are plentiful and inexpensive. However, there are some documented cases in which heavy users of amphetamines entered psychological states that presumably predisposed them to violence and paranoia. In addition, several studies have found correlations between violent offenders and a history of amphetamine abuse. As in all correlations, however, it is difficult to determine what contributes to what. Cocaine, a natural drug that grows only in certain parts of the world, has traditionally been quite expensive. In recent years, the drug has become widely available and its cost less prohibitive. There is no hard evidence, however, that cocaine generally renders one more violent, more out of control, or more likely to engage in property crimes.

We discussed heroin as the representative of the opiate narcotics. Like most other narcotics, heroin appears to be highly addictive, particularly in the sense that it creates a strong psychological dependency. Narcotics in general are so addictive and so expensive that substantial funds are needed to support a user's habit. Thus, some researchers have found a moderate correlation between narcotics and various income-generating crimes. On the other hand, others have noted that most addicts turned to drugs after they had developed criminal patterns.

Of all the drugs reviewed, alcohol—representing the sedative-hypnotic group—shows the strongest relationship with violent offenses, such as rape, homicide, and assault. At intermediate and high levels, alcohol appears to impair or disrupt the brain operations responsible for self-control. Alcohol may also impair information processing, thereby leading a person to misjudge social cues and encouraging overreactions to a perceived threat. However, it is likely that violent behavior associated with alcohol use is a joint function of pharmacological effects, cognitive expectancies, and situational influences. If the individual expects that alcohol will make him or her act aggressively, and if the social environment provides appropriate cues, aggression or violent behavior will be facilitated. The National Institute on Alcohol Abuse and Alcoholism (1997, p. 4) concluded in its extensive review of the relevant research literature that "alcohol apparently may increase the risk of violent behavior only for certain individuals or subpopulations and only under some situations and social/cultural influences." Furthermore, the National Institute noted, "intoxication alone does not cause violence" (p. 2). However, the relationship between alcohol consumption and violence is a strong one in Western civilization. The Panel on the Understanding and Control of Violent Behavior concludes "For at least the last several decades, alcohol drinking—by the perpetrator of a crime, the victim, or both—has immediately preceded at least half of all violent events, including murders, in the sample studied by researchers" (Roth, 1996, p. 3). While the relationship between alcohol and violence clearly exists, the nature of that relationship is largely unknown.

In conclusion, the relationships between crime and all the drugs discussed in this chapter are complex, involving interactions among numerous pharmacological, social, and psychological variables. Research is beginning to ease some data out of the complexity, but additional studies employing well-designed methodology are greatly needed to understand the many possible influences of psychoactive drugs on human behavior, particularly criminal behavior. It appears at this point in our knowledge that substance abuse appears to be more of a health problem to those who use them rather than a "crime problem." Individuals who are chronic, persistent criminals often are polydrug users, but it is unlikely that the drugs they ingest directly cause them to engage in criminal activity. It is more likely they were criminally prone prior to and independent of polydrug use.

13

CORRECTIONAL PSYCHOLOGY

In this text we have concentrated on the genetic, neuropsychological, psychological, and social characteristics of the serious offender. We have seen that persistent offenders engage in various crimes in a variety of ways for a variety of reasons. However, there are some generalizations that can be made. We have learned that the antisocial behavior of persistent offenders often begins early in life. Some demonstrate a discernible pattern of going against the environment as early as the first grade, ranging from lying, stealing, and truancy to bullying and frequent fighting with peers. Most of the time they are male. They are often disliked and socially rejected by a majority of their peers, who are not interested in opposing the social environment themselves. In many instances, antisocial children grow up with below-average interpersonal skills for dealing with others in a socially appropriate manner. Their friends tend to be delinquent, antisocial peers.

Antisocial children also often do poorly in school work, a pattern that accumulates in disinterest and dropping out—mentally as well as behaviorally. Their work history tends to be spotty, with extended periods of unemployment followed by unskilled labor. For some unknown reasons, persistent offenders often score below the norm on "intelligence" tests, although in other ways some demonstrate an uncanny "intelligence" or street sense of how to survive.

Persistent offenders, particularly those who are aggressive and violent, often come from multiassaultive families where physical and other kinds of abuse are commonplace. In addition, they often have family members, especially parents and/or siblings, who are also frequent offenders and antisocial themselves (Blumstein, Farrington, & Moitra, 1985).

As we discussed in the previous chapter, many persistent offenders tend to be polydrug users, using whatever combinations are on the market at an affordable price. They do not specialize in any one type of offending, but tend to demonstrate a wide variety of antisocial behavior, ranging from theft to rape. In fact, the frequency, seriousness, and variety of offending are highly correlated (Farrington, 1987). Moreover, the frequency of offending seems to decline with age, especially around age forty. However, the reasons for this decline are unknown.

Although there are some solid indications that persistent offenders have nervous systems that require high amounts of stimulation, there is little reason to believe that these neurological propensities cannot be overcome by learning and cognitive factors, as well as by the influences of the social environment. Human beings are not simply driven by animal instincts, genetic programming, chromosomal anomalies, or primitive biological urges or proclivities from their evolutionary past. They are also thinking, active agents with dreams, goals, and unique versions of the world. These versions and goals influence their ongoing behavior, including behavior that violates criminal law. Cognitive processes and constructs can override biology in human action and conduct. Nor is there convincing evidence that any sizable portion of criminal behavior is propelled by some mental disease, biological abnormality, or addiction. Sexual addiction, alcohol addiction, shoplifting addiction, and all the other variants of addiction portrayed by the media are not strongly supported by empirical research. Human beings are highly adaptable and changeable, a topic we will review later in this chapter.

The focus of this chapter will be on the work of correctional psychologists in predicting and changing criminal behavior patterns. The three main services provided by correctional psychologists are (1) diagnosis and classification, (2) treatment or intervention; and (3) research, planning, and evaluation. A majority of correctional psychologists are located in assessment or reception centers that operate centrally or regionally to screen and classify newly received offenders (Clements, 1987). Some psychologists also provide treatment services at these centers. Other correctional psychologists treat inmates diagnosed as having mental disorders or adjustment problems within the correctional facility itself. In fact, psychologists make up about half of the professionally trained mental health staff in prisons and outnumber psychiatrists by at least five to one (Clements, 1987).

In a nationwide survey of 120 American correctional psychologists, we (Bartol, Griffin, & Clark, 1993) discovered that the *direct* services most commonly provided by psychologists working full-time in the correctional setting are counseling (14.1 percent) and psychological assessment (12.9 percent). A great percentage of their time is also spent in various administrative duties (14.3 percent) or consulting with correctional staff (9.1 percent) (see Figure 13-1). Most of the correctional psychologists worked in state institutions (64.2 percent) or federal facilities (6.2 percent). The remainder worked in private, county, municipal correctional institutions. The survey revealed that psychologists who work in the federal correctional system are paid a median salary of $60,500, compared to a $50,000 median salary for correctional psychologists working in state systems. A majority of the correctional psychologists (around 80 percent) thought that employment opportunities for psychologists in corrections will be excellent or very good in the future.

Since diagnosis, classification, and treatment are increasingly guided by research evaluation, the need for psychologists in research areas is expanding rapidly. We will review each of these functions in the remainder of this chapter. Before we do, however, it is important that we have some familiarity with the correctional system as a whole.

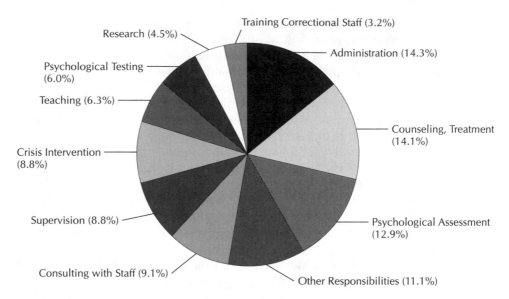

Figure 13-1   Percent Distribution of What Correctional Psychologists Do

THE CORRECTIONAL SYSTEM

In the United States, detained, accused, and convicted persons—when incarcerated—are housed in three types of facilities: jails, community-based facilities, and prisons. **Jails** are operated by local (or sometimes state) governments to hold persons temporarily detained, awaiting trial, or sentenced to confinement for a misdemeanor, usually for less than one year. However, in some states, misdemeanors may carry a maximum sentence of up to two years. Therefore, jails house a mixture of persons at various stages of criminal justice processing. About 50 to 60 percent of the jail population have not been convicted.

Community-based corrections facilities are operated by public or private organizations (under governmental contract). They hold persons for less than twenty-four hours of each day to allow them limited opportunity to work, attend school, or make other community contacts. This plan is an option in lieu of continuing prison or jail confinement. Overall, community-based facilities house about 4 percent of all those confined in the correctional system.

Prisons are operated by state and federal governments to hold persons sentenced under state and federal laws to terms of more than one year. Prisons are often classified according to three levels of security: maximum, medium, and minimum security. They may also hold special categories of offenders, such as those found to be mentally disordered, or chronically violent inmates. Maximum or close security prisons are typically surrounded by a double fence or wall (usually eighteen to twenty-five feet high) guarded by armed correctional officers in observation towers. Medium security prisons typically are enclosed within double fences topped with barbed wire. About 90 percent of medium security prisons were built after 1925. Minimum security prisons usually do not have armed guards and may or may not have fences surrounding the buildings. More than 60 percent of these prisons were built after 1950. In the United States (as of 1995), states operated 1,375 correctional facilities and the Federal Bureau of Prisons operated 125 facilities.

Approximately 1,158,763 inmates were housed in state and federal prisons in this country in 1997 (Gilliard & Beck, 1998). About ninety-four percent of all inmates are men and 6 percent women. In both 1990 and 1995, about 20 percent of inmates in U.S. correctional facilities were classified as maximum security risk, 40 percent as medium security, and 33 percent as minimum security (Stephan et al., 1997). On June 30, 1997, an estimated 567,079 persons were held in local jails. At any given time, the total is affected by changes in judicial and legislative philosophies about deterrence and incapacitation, the amount of space available, law enforcement practices, and economic conditions. In recent years, there has been a substantial increase in prison and jail populations (see Figure 13-2). Moreover, the inmate population for women appears to be increasing at a rate higher than for men (Decostanza & Scholes, 1988). In the time period between 1990 and 1995, for example, the male inmate population in state and federal correctional facilities increased by 42 percent, while the female inmate population increased by 56 percent (Stephan et al., 1997). These increases probably reflect a judicial and societal change in attitude about what should be done about offenders, rather than any dramatic increase in crime rates. For example, the dramatic increase in women inmates during the 1980s appears to be primarily due to substance abuse (Decostanza & Scholes, 1988).

Nearly 64 percent of all adult inmates have experienced prior incarceration—

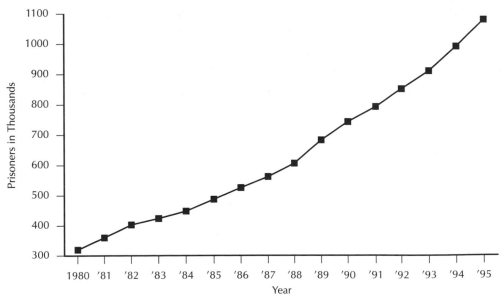

Figure 13-2   Prison Population in the United States
(Source: U.S. Bureau of Justice Statistics, 1996.)

either in juvenile facilities, adult institutions, or both. After release from prison, about 12 percent are likely to be back in prison within one year. After three years, about 24 percent of the parolees return to prison. Decostanza and Scholes (1988) estimate that one out of every three women inmates returns to prison at some point. More than half of all prison returns are for technical violations of parole. The remainder are for new, major convictions. When former inmates reach age thirty, there is a high probability that they will not return to prison. The reasons are multiple, but one viable explanation is that the justice system, in effect, physically "wears down" offenders (U.S. Department of Justice, 1993). The process of repeatedly being arrested, appearing in court, and adjusting to prison life is eventually perceived by offenders as an exhausting ordeal.

Table 13-1 lists the types of offenses of which inmates in U.S. federal prisons have been convicted. Notice that 60 percent of the inmates serving time in U.S. federal prisons have been incarcerated for drug offenses.

SOCIETAL RATIONALE FOR IMPRISONMENT OF OFFENDERS

Four fundamental considerations are usually in operation when offenders are sentenced: (1) protection of other members of society, frequently called **incapacitation**; (2) **rehabilitation**; (3) **punishment** (or **retribution**); and (4) **deterrence**. The first is the most straightforward justification for confining convicted individuals against their will. If the criminal is believed dangerous to society, on the basis of past conduct, it is obvious that society must be protected from future injury. However, if we rely heavily on incapacitation to remove the offender from the streets, we are in danger of increasing the inmate population dramatically and far beyond the present capacity of correctional facilities. On the other hand, we have seen that only a small percentage—around 8 to 10 percent—of the criminal popu-

Table 13-1 Offense Conviction Categories of Federal Prison Inmates

Type of Offense	Number of Inmates	Percentage
Drug Offenses	51,848	60.18
Robbery	8,063	9.36
Firearms, Explosives, Arson	7,826	9.08
Extortion, Fraud, Bribery	5,020	5.83
Property Offenses	4,843	5.62
Violent Offenses	2,396	2.78
Immigration	2,877	3.34
Continuing Criminal Enterprise	663	0.77
White Collar	626	0.73
Courts or Corrections	542	0.63
National Security	76	0.09
Miscellaneous	1,378	1.60

Source: Federal Bureau of Prisons (1997).

lation commit, by far, an inordinate amount of the crime—perhaps more than 50 percent of the total. For example, Peterson, Braiker, and Polich (1981) reported that the average prisoner committed about three serious crimes per year of street time, while the most frequent offender (about 8 percent of the inmate population) committed over sixty serious crimes per year of street time. Incapacitation directed at this 8 percent might be a more effective means of reducing crime, a strategy called **selective incapacitation**.

In recent years, the effectiveness of incapacitation has been questioned seriously (Blumstein, Cohen, Roth, & Visher, 1986; Cohen, 1983; Visher, 1987). And rehabilitation "is being revived, reaffirmed, and resold" (Visher, 1987, p. 514). Rehabilitation as a justification for confinement often creates heated debate. Rehabilitation is essentially restoring the person to a useful life, either through education, training, treatment (e.g., psychotherapy, behavior modification, plastic surgery) or a combination of these. During the 1970s, rehabilitation lost favor with much of society, including courts and criminal justice practitioners. Contributing to this disenchantment was a provocative article by R. M. Martinson (1974), arguing that the concept of rehabilitation, especially in the form of treatment methods then in operation, did not work. Correctional administrators were put on notice that rehabilitation programs were not efficacious (Adams, 1977). The concept of rehabilitation has yet to regain a comfortable foothold within the correctional system. In the scholarly community, however, rehabilitation remains a viable alternative (Cullen & Gilbert, 1982; Gendreau & Ross, 1983; Greenwood & Zimring, 1985).

Punishment and deterrence are closely linked. Society has for a very long time assumed that some form of punishment—defined as aversive consequences for one's behavior—is an effective method of behavior control. With reference to criminal behavior, punishment supposedly works in two ways.

First, it is believed that punishment and its public disclosure reveal to the members of a society what the consequence of criminal behavior will be (the informative role). "If you choose to violate this rule, this is what will happen." Thus, the threat and fear of punishment should act as a potent deterrent. Second, punishment applied directly to the offender should deter him or her personally from future violations (the inhibitory role). It is usually assumed that direct application of aversive stimuli is more effective than the observation or knowledge of punishing consequences. In other words, many shoplifters are not deterred from a first offense by signs that warn them of possible prosecution, or by reading or hearing about other offenders. However, the embarrassment of having one's name published in the local newspaper and the pain of paying a fine or spending time in confinement is much more likely to prevent future violations. This theory does not hold as easily for more serious offenses, however.

Theoretical discussions on the effectiveness of punishment as a deterrent often revolve around the aforementioned dichotomy. The term **general deterrence** is used for the threat of punishment on the public at large; **special deterrence** refers to the actual experience of punishment by the offender (Andenaes, 1968). The long-debated question surrounding the relationship between deterrence and criminal conduct has never been satisfactorily answered. It is reasonable to assume, however, that general deterrence or the threat of punishment does prevent a significant number of people from violating the law.

The general deterrence associated with the legal system may not be as powerful as the threat of punishment established through socialization and moral development, however. It is reasonable to assume that a very large segment of the population will not engage in serious criminal activity, even if there is no police officer at the elbow. For most people, fear of social, parental, or self-disapproval operate as sufficient deterrents. In keeping with our theme of the complexity of human behavior, it is probable that some combination of the aforementioned internal and external checks are operating for most people.

CLASSIFICATION AND PREDICTION

Classification systems do three important things: (1) They simplify and summarize; (2) they enhance prediction; and (3) they remind us that crime and delinquency are behaviorally and psychologically heterogeneous with multiple causation. The pressures of overcrowding, scarce fiscal resources, and legal challenges have contributed to a renewed interest in classification within the jails and prisons of this country (Brennan, 1987). Inmate classification systems serve a number of important, if not critical, functions within the correctional system. First, they help corrections officials make decisions about inmate placement in order to provide a safe environment for all inmates and staff. Second, they provide information for treatment, intervention, and rehabilitation. If we do not intend to treat all offenders alike and do not intend to behave haphazardly toward them, then some form of classification for treatment is necessary (Sechrest, 1987). Third, classification systems help in making predictions about recidivism and other risks to society.

Although a good many schemes or systems of classification have been proposed and used over the years, their impact has been limited (Sechrest, 1987). The situation is much the same for juveniles and adults, but more emphasis has been placed on classification of juvenile offenders for treatment (Sechrest, 1987). Eleven of the better known and researched classification schemes are the Megargee system, Toch's Prison Preference Inventory, Risk Assessment, Quay's AIMS, Quay's juvenile typology, the Jesness Inventory Classification System, the Interpersonal Maturity Level Classification System, the Federal Bureau of Prison Classification System, the National Institute of Corrections Model, the Illinois Adult Classification System, and the California Prison Classification System. We will briefly review only Megargee's system and Quay's systems in this section.

The Megargee system was developed and validated on large samples of youthful offenders, ages eighteen to twenty-seven (Megargee & Bohn, 1979). Classification is based on response patterns to questions from the Minnesota Multiphasic Personality Inventory (MMPI), one of the oldest and most widely used personality measurements in the world today. The MMPI is also the most commonly used classification and diagnostic instrument in state and federal correctional facilities (Carlson, 1990). Through years of research, the following ten types of offenders have been identified on the basis of MMPI profiles (descriptions adapted from Zager, 1988; Sechrest, 1987; and Megargee & Bohn, 1977):

1. Well-adjusted individuals who lack conflicts with authorities
2. Well-adjusted underachievers with good interpersonal skills
3. Inadequate individuals who are anxious, constricted, dogmatic, and with a tendency to abuse alcohol
4. Charming individuals who tend to be impulsive, manipulative, and achievement oriented
5. Submissive and anxious individuals who are hardworking and reliable
6. Hedonistic, manipulative individuals who have poor interpersonal relations with peers and staff
7. Individuals from deprived backgrounds who do better in prison as well as on release than expected
8. Individuals with extensive criminal records who are tough, streetwise, cynical, and generally antisocial
9. Individuals with extensive criminal records, polydrug abuse, who are described as hostile, misanthropic, alienated, and antisocial
10. Individuals characterized as being unstable and emotionally disturbed

Quay (1984) developed a system called the Adult Internal Management System (AIMS). AIMS classifies male inmates into five categories. Much of the following descriptions of the five groups was taken from a recent study by Levinson (1988). Group I consists of inmates who presently exhibit or have histories of aggressive and sometimes violent behavior. Members of this group are most likely to cause major disturbances within the institution. Group II inmates do not demonstrate the same degree of aggressive behavior as Group I inmates, but they tend to be master manipulators in obtaining things they want as well as causing trouble within the institution. Group III members do not have an extensive criminal history and generally are those the staff can rely on. Group IV represents prisoners who are withdrawn, unhappy, whiny, socially isolated, complaining, and unreliable. They are easily victimized within the institution. Group V inmates are anxious, maladjusted, depressed, chronically worried, and easily upset. They, too, are easily victimized.

Often the AIMS groups are further classified according to potential for aggressive behavior. Groups I and II are considered the "heavies" in that they are violence-prone and manipulative predators. Group III members are evaluated as "moderates," and Groups IV and V are considered "lights." It is often recommended that "heavies" be housed in the facility's most secure living quarters, while the "lights" should be housed in quarters as distant from the "heavies" as possible. "Moderates" can be placed in either living area without anticipated problems. As the reader can discern, AIMS appears to be more designed for management than treatment purposes. Currently, AIMS has been implemented in Pennsylvania, South Carolina, and some institutions of the federal prison system (Posey, 1988).

Quay (1987) has also developed a classification system for juvenile offenders that delineates four categories: (1) the undersocialized or unsocialized delinquent; (2) the socialized delinquent; (3) the attention deficit disorder (ADD) delinquent; and (4) the anxiety-withdrawal-dysphoria delinquent. Undersocialized delinquents display aggression, negativism, resistance, and lack of concern for others. Basically, they follow the characteristics of the adult psychopath. Undersocialized youths, as the label implies, have not become adequately socialized to mainstream social values and standards. Youths institutionalized for repetitive, serious offenses tend to be undersocialized, and they also tend to be the group who are constant disciplinary problems and unresponsive to institutional treatment and rehabilitation programs. Socialized delinquents, on the other hand, have become socialized not so much to mainstream societal standards but to the norms and values of a delinquent subculture or group. Compared to the undersocialized group, they tend to be less overtly aggressive, less interpersonally alienated, and more responsive to treatment. The third type is plagued by an attentional deficit (previously labeled hyperactivity). Youths in this category have problems in focusing and sustaining attention and in coming to grips with task demands. The cognitive and social-behavioral correlates of this pattern and the accompanying frustrations leave the child especially susceptible to environmental influences, including those that foster delinquency. The fourth pattern carries the intimidating clinical label anxiety-withdrawal-dysphoria and is characterized by neurotic, overinhibited, anxious, and socially withdrawn behavior. Those following this pattern do not deal competently with the social environment and generally prefer to avoid it by withdrawing from social interactions. Delinquent or deviant acts in this category are motivated by a need to escape or avoid stressful situations. Examples include truancy from school, running away from home, or theft of a motor vehicle.

Classification systems have become useful tools for decision making and placement within the correctional system in recent years. Some have drawn considerable research and evaluation, especially the Megargee MMPI-based system. All current classification systems, however, have their problems and need much more research before they fulfill their missions. Sechrest (1987) asserts that they lack theoretical sophistication and the methodologies used to develop them have been generally inadequate. Furthermore, the lack of dependable means of treatment or intervention for offenders, both juvenile and adults, makes classification difficult (Sechrest, 1987). Finally, the rapid proliferation of classification systems demands some empirical attempts to integrate and organize them in line with the various philosophies of correctional facilities and administrations.

PSYCHOLOGICAL EFFECTS OF IMPRISONMENT

Clinical case studies on the effects of prison life have often concluded that, for many individuals, imprisonment can be brutal, demeaning, and generally devastating. These studies often describe a variety of psychological symptoms believed to be caused directly by imprisonment, including psychosis, severe depression, inhibiting anxiety, and social withdrawal. However, more recent research (e.g., Adams, 1992; Toch & Adams, with Grant, 1989; Toch & Adams, 1989; Zamble &

Porporino, 1988) raises serious questions about the extent of serious psychological deterioration that is caused by imprisonment. Before we continue, it must be emphasized that there are wide individual differences in reactions to imprisonment. Some people do react to imprisonment with severe emotional or mental disorders, but the number appears smaller than originally supposed.

Zamble and Porporino (1988) examined the coping strategies and adjustment characteristics of inmates in Canadian penitentiaries. They found that emotional disruption and adjustment were clearly problems for most inmates during the beginning of their sentences, particularly signs of serious to moderate depression. This deleterious reaction came as no surprise, as prison produces a dramatic disruption in customary behavior, compounded by restrictions, deprivations, and constraints. However, these initial reactions soon dissipated for most inmates, and no lasting emotional disturbance was discernible as the inmate became adjusted to his surroundings and prison routine. Toch and Adams (with Grant, 1989) report a similar pattern in their study on American prisoners. The Toch-Adams data suggest that inmates with emotional problems also tend to be disruptive in prison. Furthermore, their data support the frequent observation that age is a consistent correlate of prison violations, with young inmates being much more prone to engage in prison misbehavior than older inmates.

Inmate reactions to prison life appear to follow a curvilinear pattern, with stress indicators increasing at the beginning of the term, then dropping, and then rising again as the end of their term approaches (Bukstel & Kilmann, 1980). Sometimes referred to as the "short-timer's syndrome," many inmates exhibit signs of distress, sleeplessness, restlessness, and anxiety, probably in anticipation of the new coping strategies required for the outside.

Zamble and Porporino write, "We conclude that prisons do not produce permanent harm to the psychological well-being of inmates" (p. 149). On the other hand, they did not find positive effects either. "Our data show very little positive behavioral change in prison, just as earlier we could see little evidence for generalized negative effects" (p. 151). Interestingly, Toch and Adams suggest that prison experiences actually temper or even improve inmate misbehavior, most particularly in the young inmate under age twenty-five. "Young inmates, who are presumably more rambunctious and less mature than older inmates, appear to derive some benefit from this forced environment ... it is encouraging to find that prison inmates who are initially most resistant to restrictions on their personal liberty demonstrate increasing levels of conformity over time" (pp. 19–20). Why this happens remains largely a mystery, but Toch and Adams (with Grant, 1989) suggest that the maturation process facilitated by humane prison environments plays a crucial role. The researchers contend that inmate behavior is likely to improve when inmates learn the association between behavior and its positive or negative consequences within the institution, and when they have psychological support, the opportunity to participate in conventional activities, form attachment bonds, and build relationships.

In summary, a vast majority of inmates do not demonstrate long-lasting psychological impairment or problems as a result of imprisonment. However, there are certain conditions where this conclusion may not hold, namely crowding and isolation.

PSYCHOLOGICAL EFFECTS OF CROWDING

Prison crowding has become an increasingly important topic as the prison population reaches critical numbers. Prison crowding has probably always been a concern, but the sheer number of offenders being currently processed through the system is without precedent. Prison officials estimate that the United States is currently at least 11 percent short in bed space in state prisons and jails, a situation likely to get much worse (Patrick, 1988). While the United States has the highest proportion of its population incarcerated, the crowding problem is worldwide (Patrick, 1988). Prison populations everywhere appear to be increasing.

Prison and jail overcrowding does seem related to a higher incidence of physical illness, socially disruptive behavior, and emotional distress (Bukstel & Kilmann, 1980). Some researchers have suggested that disruptive behavior in correctional facilities increases directly as the available space decreases (Megargee, 1976; Nacci, Teitelbaum, & Prather, 1977). This relationship seems to be particularly pronounced for juvenile institutions (Megargee, 1976), and for women's prisons (Ruback & Carr, 1984). In most cases, inmates are housed in units with fifty or more inmates with less than twenty square feet of space per person.

In a fifteen-year project on prison crowding, Paulus (1988) concluded that increasing the number of residents in correctional housing units significantly increased the negative psychological (e.g., tension, anxiety, depression) and physical reactions (e.g., headaches, high blood pressure, cardiovascular problems) in inmates. The critical factor appears to be the number of residents sharing a space and not simply the amount of space available. For example, providing some privacy and limiting the visual and physical access of other inmates, such as providing cubicles in open dormitories, reduces the negative impact of living there.

Paulus also found that socioeconomic level, education level, and prior prison or jail confinements were related to inmate reactions to crowded conditions. Specifically, the higher the socioeconomic and education level, the more difficult the adjustment to, and the lower the tolerance for, crowded conditions. Presumably, many members of the lower socioeconomic class are used to living under crowded conditions and therefore are more tolerant of invasions of privacy and other factors involved in crowded environments. Surprisingly, prior confinement interfered with adjustment to crowded conditions. Prisoners who had some history of prior imprisonment exhibited more problems in adjustments than those without prior time. A reason suggested by Paulus is that individuals with extensive prison histories are likely to have spent part of their time in single cells or under less crowded conditions. This may have made them particularly sensitive to crowded conditions, such as living in a dormitory setting. Paulus also found that men and women, and blacks and whites, react similarly to variations in social density.

Paulus hypothesizes that crowding has its primary impact through its influence on social interaction. For one thing, crowding reduces one's sense of control over the social environment, and with that many people, things become unpredictable and uncertain. Secondly, crowded situations interfere with one's goals, such as carrying out desired activities, restrict freedom and privacy, and expose one to a variety of undesired intrusions. And thirdly, crowded situations produce much more activity, noise, interactions, smells, violations of personal space, and generally excessive stimulation.

In summary, the available research does indicate that crowding is related to negative psychological and physical problems in confinement. However, individuals react differently to crowded conditions, some demonstrating much better adjustment than others. There are many other variables that have to be considered also, such as the type of institution, the institution's orientation, the type of social milieu, the degree of crowding, and the phase an individual is in his or her sentence.

PSYCHOLOGICAL EFFECTS OF ISOLATION

Prison inmates may be physically isolated from each other for a variety of reasons and under a wide range of conditions. There are two main categories: (1) isolation as a form of punishment; and (2) isolation for inmate protection. Isolation, solitary confinement, and restrictive housing are some of the terms used to designate various kinds of isolation for punishment. For example, "disciplinary segregation"—also called punitive isolation—is imposed as punishment for violations of prison rules and procedures. While prison authorities are investigating an incident, an inmate may be placed in "administrative isolation."

Protective custody or protective seclusion, on the other hand, is reserved for isolation that is for the protection of the inmate, either from himself or herself, or from the other inmates. In 1990, seventy-six prison homicides were reported in state and federal facilities, and there were close to ten thousand inmate-on-inmate assaults that required medical attention (Camp & Camp, 1991; McCorkle, 1992). Correctional staff may also be fearful of possible suicide, especially correctional staff working in jails. Jails have a higher suicide rate than prisons (Lester & Danto, 1993). Suicide in custody is usually committed by young, unmarried white males during the early stages of confinement. The most common method is by hanging. Under protective-suicide conditions, the level of social and perceptual-sensory isolation may be even more extreme than solitary, because many materials and items must be removed from the cell so that the inmate cannot use the objects to accomplish the suicide.

Systematic knowledge of the psychological effects of isolation comes primarily from the psychological laboratory, using volunteers who allow themselves to be socially isolated, sometimes with sensory restrictions such as a blindfold or earphones, for varying periods of time. The research so far demonstrates that individuals respond differently to solitude; some show great tolerance and often welcome the quiet solitude from the hustle and bustle of daily living. Others experience stress and anxiety, even after relatively short periods of isolation. In general, however, the research shows that most individuals are able to tolerate and even adjust to isolation, if the isolation is short in duration, such as a few days.

In the past, the conditions of solitary or protective custody in institutions have often been deplorable. Offenders have been held in cells without adequate ventilation, heat, clothing, light, sanitary and bathroom facilities for long periods of time. Since no published research has examined the effects of such adverse conditions, it is difficult to determine what the psychological effects might be. Fortunately, the courts are beginning to set up minimum conditions that must be met during isolation as well as due process requirements. At this time, there is not enough evidence to conclude, one way or the other, whether isolation under deplorable conditions or over extended periods of time causes gross psychological disruption or impairment.

TREATMENT AND REHABILITATION

One of the fundamental goals of corrections is to inhibit unlawful, antisocial behavior, at the very least by keeping perpetrators confined and away from society. During the 1970s and 1980s, because of a variety of factors, including budgetary considerations, widespread disenchantment with the concept of rehabilitation, and a hard-line approach to offenders, the correctional system made punishment and confinement its primary goal. In so doing, however, the system risks promoting more unlawful behavior, since prison confinement per se reinforces learned deviant responses. Unless we opt for a drastic change in our methods of punishment, such as corporal punishment (Newman, 1982) or irreversible banishment, we must somehow reconcile prison confinement with the realities of postconfinement and effective living on the outside.

This brings us to the subject of rehabilitation, whose fundamental goal is to develop lawful alternative behavior that will generalize beyond the institution. If rehabilitation is thought of in terms of training, this goal is difficult—some would say impossible—to achieve. First, the positive, alternative behavior to be developed must be capable of bringing to the individual significant social, psychological, and material rewards. Second, different approaches would be needed for different types of offenders. Training may be inappropriate for the violent or sexual offender; for the property offender, it would involve developing skills that would translate to the outside world and provide better rewards than obtained from criminal behavior. Third, rehabilitation of this sort necessitates educating the general public, legislators, and professionals about its long-term benefits and the probabilities of success, and there are always many failures.

Alternative behavioral development as a viable rehabilitative goal would likely require large financial investments in facilities, well-trained and motivated staff, offender job placement, elimination of prejudice toward former felons, and long-term, carefully executed research on the effectiveness of the programs. The correctional system as it now operates is a poor setting in which to implement this approach. Furthermore, during the 1970s and 1980s, public expressions of sympathy toward prisoners have been very rare.

Yet most would agree that there is a strong relationship between personally meaningful employment and recidivism, particularly for economically motivated crimes (Halleck & Witte, 1977; Kennedy, 1976; Jenkins & Barton, 1973). Individuals engaged in rewarding employment are less apt to be involved in unlawful activity. This requires not only the availability of a job, but also the appropriate social and occupational skills to maintain it. Moreover, the rewards must be greater than the rewards offered by the criminal activity. Too frequently, ex-offenders cannot meet even the first criteria, obtaining a job. Glaser (1964) writes, "Unemployment may be among the principal causal factors involved in the recidivism of adult male offenders" (p. 329). Moreover, it is estimated that the unemployment rate for ex-offenders is three times the rate for the general population, and that most who received "vocational training" are not able to use it (Dale, 1976).

Additionally, the recidivism rate for the unemployed is four times that of the fully employed ex-offender. This relationship does not necessarily prove that unemployment is a causal factor. It might be that offenders who are prone toward continuing unlawful behavior are also less likely to find and maintain suitable employment because of personal inadequacy. However, it is difficult to ignore statements like the following, which, although dated, still rings true:

> An opportunity to live a normal, non-criminal productive life is denied the ex-offender immediately upon his release from the penal institution. We effectively preclude his rehabilitation by failing to train and educate him, by refusing to hire him, by allowing the private bonding industry to intimidate employers, and by enacting restrictive occupational licensing requirements at the behest of self-serving economic groups. (Dale, 1976, p. 336)

If we shift the focus from rehabilitative training to psychological rehabilitation (treatment), we may find some reason for guarded optimism. The dilemma still remains that any type of rehabilitation proposal may sound like an idealized package delivered many times before. Correctional officers exposed to wide varieties of hardcore offenders on a daily basis and under adverse conditions are apt to view the prison population as totally incorrigible and to suspect and resist any notion that offenders can be changed. Many correctional personnel come to view criminals as less-than-human creatures who have few dignifying qualities. The reasons that criminals have become this way are irrelevant; what matters is that little can be done about them now. On the other hand, there is ample evidence that the prison system as it exists dehumanizes many correctional officers as well as prisoners.

Some offenders, especially habitually violent ones, are unlikely to benefit from psychological rehabilitation and should remain in prison for society's protection. Moreover, if you believe that aggression and selfishness are integral features of human nature (the difference-in-degrees perspective), then warehousing prisoners makes good sense. Those who believe in inherent selfishness and violence tend to be strongly pessimistic about what can be done about the crime problem. More prisons, stricter law enforcement, and a more efficient judicial process offer the only solution. Those less inclined to believe that humans are locked in the natural fate of inherent violence, selfishness, and deceit may be more optimistic about whether anything can be done about the crime problem. If humans learn to be criminal, and are guided by changeable construct systems and self-regulatory mechanisms rather than by genetic programming, then creative rehabilitation using learning principles may be extremely effective.

The overwhelming bulk of the psychological and social research indicates that humans learn behavior, including deviant and unlawful behavior, from significant members of their society. Furthermore, they are constantly perceiving and interpreting their actions and the actions of others in accordance with internal standards and cognitive constructs. To understand their behavior, it seems most fruitful to examine these mediated processes and the justifying mechanisms that accompany them. To change their actions over an extended period of time, it will be necessary to change the cognitive templates or schema they use to perceive, interpret, and expect.

REHABILITATION AND PSYCHOLOGICAL TREATMENT

Several years ago, Carlson wrote that rehabilitation by means of psychological treatment "is out of fashion today. It is not dead yet, but the literature is littered with death warrants" (1976, p. 32). He implies that behavioral science professionals (e.g., psychologists, psychiatrists, and social workers) are responsible for overselling their goods to the correctional system.

Numerous other practitioners, administrators, and academicians have come to the same or similar conclusions. Martinson (1974), one of the chief critics of rehabilitation, reviewed 231 studies of prison rehabilitative programs and concluded: "With few and isolated exceptions, the rehabilitative efforts that have been reported so far have had no appreciable effect on recidivism" (p. 25). His conclusion that "nothing works," together with growing disenchantment about rehabilitation within the criminal justice system, had a powerful effect on criminal justice administration. There was an immediate shift away from rehabilitation and toward other models of corrections, such as strict punishment with minimal efforts to rehabilitate. Later, the dust settled somewhat and administrators became more reluctant to discard rehabilitative programs in their entirety. Even Martinson eventually reduced his onslaught to "almost nothing works" (Lipton, Martinson, & Wilks, 1975).

One of the first to criticize Martinson's "nothing works" doctrine was Palmer (1975), who noted that Martinson tended to reject any type of rehabilitative treatment that was not highly successful. According to Palmer, Martinson was seeking a cure-all approach that would work for everyone, all or almost all of the time. He was not interested in partial success, and he appeared indifferent to the fact that about one-half (48 percent) of his 231 sample studies showed success with at least some subjects.

Adams (1977) pointed out that correctional treatments appear to be as effective as the partial success rate achieved thus far by traditional psychotherapy offered to the general population. Many of the projects that Martinson considered failures demonstrated behavioral improvement during the treatment, but there was regression to original behavior upon return to the original environment

(Adams, 1977). In some cases, the return to criminal behavior occurred years after the improved behavior during treatment. Martinson's tendency to accept only the long-term signs of "cure" masks the short-term effect of correctional treatment. If individuals have no sufficient alternatives and skills for coping in the outside world, it is not surprising that they will return to their original deviant ways once back in the social environment from which these ways were acquired and which supports them.

Halleck and Witte (1977) note that Martinson's critique spanned the years 1945 to 1967, when evaluation and research methodology relating to corrections was in its infancy. "Evaluations since 1967 have, in general, been more thorough and more reliable statistically than those before that date" (Halleck & Witte, 1977, p. 376). Halleck and Witte believe that the later evaluations are more promising and cite, as examples, two work-release programs in California that significantly reduced the recidivism rate.

Quay (1977), in a cogent argument against the view that nothing works, noted that evaluations of correctional treatment concentrated too much on the adequacy of the research designs and measurement of outcomes and too little on the integrity of the program being assessed. To evaluate a program, a researcher must consider the rationale and goals of the treatment as well as how that treatment is delivered. Labeling a program "treatment" or "counseling" tells us nothing about what happened in the program. For example, were counseling sessions actually held? How well were they attended? Were inmates coerced into participating in the program, or were they able to volunteer freely without implicit threat?

Quay also advocates scrutinizing the delivery of treatment. Were the "counselors" untrained prison guards or community volunteers? Quay suggests that some evidence of competence to deliver treatment might be measured by the counselors' past educational experience, academic degrees, or similar qualifications. In evaluating rehabilitation programs, we should also examine the nature of the training and orientation given to the counselors, particularly if they were non-professionals. Was the training provided in two one-hour lectures by disinterested instructors, or was it provided intensively over a period of weeks by interested personnel? What kind of supervision did the treatment personnel receive?

Finally, Quay asks, how generalizable is a particular treatment approach to all inmates? To be maximally effective, any treatment-rehabilitative program should be formulated in relation to the needs and capabilities of each person, a concept referred to as **differential treatment**.

In his review of the literature, Quay finds that studies evaluating correctional treatment provide little information concerning the foregoing considerations. In one of the two studies that did describe goals, personnel, and treatment procedures in some detail (Kassebaum, Ward, & Wilner, 1971), it was quite evident that the planning, goal definition, and implementation of the program were poorly done.

Before proclaiming correctional psychological treatment per se ineffective and worthless, critics should give it a chance to perform under sophisticated planning, careful and dedicated execution, and well-designed methods of evaluation. It would be a mistake to discard a potentially useful concept because of misunder-standing and poorly conceived evaluation methods, and to wait for the rehabilita-tive treatment pendulum to swing back several decades later.

PSYCHOTHERAPY

The main problem with rehabilitative treatment programs, however, might not be so much their evaluation as their validity. In other words, are any forms of psy-chological treatment effective in changing criminal behavior? Before answering this difficult question, we must describe briefly what is meant by psychological treatment, or psychotherapy.

The terms psychotherapy, therapy, counseling, and treatment are used inter-changeably by clinicians. Broadly, they refer to a set of procedures or techniques used to help individuals or groups alter their maladaptive behavior, develop adaptive behavior, or both. The behavior must be considered maladaptive by the individual, however. In other words, the person must want to change.

Psychotherapy can be divided into six very broad and overlapping areas: psy-choanalytic, behavioral, humanistic-existential, interpersonal, group, and cogni-tive therapy. Each approach is designed to change a person's way of thinking about the world to some extent. Most psychotherapies try to change cognitive constructs about ourselves, others, or both. Skinnerian behaviorism is probably least inclined to worry about cognitive constructs, since it focuses heavily on overt behavior to the exclusion of the mediational processes. Lately, most behaviorists have shifted to a more cognitive-behavioral approach.

Each variant of the psychotherapies has been tried to some extent within the correctional system under wide variations in method and purpose and different degrees of commitment. Overall, they have been marginally successful or unsuc-cessful in reducing criminal behavior, depending on one's point of view. To assess the many therapies used is not the purpose of this chapter. We will focus briefly on behavioral therapy, however, since it has drawn considerable attention and controversy over the past two decades. Following that, we will give some atten-tion to cognitive therapy, which appears to offer the most realistic approach to rehabilitative treatment.

MULTISYSTEMIC THERAPY

Scott Henggeler and his colleagues have developed a treatment approach for seri-ous juvenile offenders that is responsive to the many social systems influencing the child's delinquent behavior (Henggeler & Borduin, 1990; Henggeler, Melton, & Smith, 1992; Scherer et al., 1994). *Multisystemic therapy* (*MST*) focuses on the family system, and a major ingredient of the treatment is that the family must be actively involved in the program. Together, counselors and family collaborate to develop pertinent treatment goals as well as appropriate plans to meet these goals (Henggeler, 1996). Impediments to the plan, such as uncooperative family mem-bers, teachers, and school administrators, are directly and actively worked with. MST is an action-based treatment program that tries to get the involved family members to take "action" (behaviorally do something) rather than simply talk.

MST is an intensive, time-limited intervention wherein trained therapists have daily contact with the adolescent and his or her family for approximately sixty hours over a four-month period. The caseload of each therapist is small, averaging four to six families per counselor. MST therapists identify both strengths and problem areas within the individual, the family, peers, school officials, social service agencies, and the parents' workplace. The therapy emphasizes family strengths and focuses on providing the parent(s) with the resources needed for effective parenting and attempts to develop a better-functioning and more cohesive family unit. For instance, the therapists might work with the parents on improving communication and problem-solving skills, teaching them to be less susceptible to manipulation by the child, enhancing their consistency in administering discipline and rewards, helping them find ways to reduce stress, and reducing parental drug and alcohol abuse.

MST therapists also work with the delinquent youth to remediate deficits in interpersonal skills that hinder acceptance by prosocial peers. Youth and therapist may work on modifying thought processes and coping mechanisms that may interfere with the family, peer, school, and neighborhood systems. Other MST methods include decreasing the teenager's antisocial peer contacts and increasing affiliation with prosocial peers and activities. Another strategy is developing ways to monitor and promote the youth's school performance. For example, the MST therapist might work toward opening and maintaining effective lines of communication among parents, teachers, and administrators.

In one study, Henggeler et al. (1992) found that, in comparison with the typical intensive probation services, teenagers from families participating in MST treatment had significantly lower rearrest rates during a follow-up period of 2.4 years. The follow-up period in the study was a relatively long one compared to other studies, and demonstrates that the program has considerable promise in the treatment of serious juvenile offenders. In another study (Borduin et al., 1995), MST was found very effective in reducing long-term rates of violent offending, and drug-related offending, compared to other forms of treatment and intervention.

BEHAVIOR THERAPY

Behavior therapy was developed from learning-conditioning principles derived from well-controlled, precise laboratory environments or small-scale, well-designed demonstration projects. The social and physical environments are crucial considerations in the planning of any behavior therapy program. Before the treatment program can be effectively implemented, the target behaviors and the environmental events that accompany them must be accurately described and carefully evaluated as to how, when, and where they occur for a particular individual. This information is normally gathered through direct observation of the individual within situations where he or she typically exhibits the target behavior, and through interviews with the individual and acquaintances. In the planning stage, these initial data concerning the target behavior (such as frequency) provide baseline or pretreatment information that is useful for later determinations of how effective the treatment plan has been. Once the target behaviors and the conditions under which they occur are determined, the next step usually involves establishing a twofold plan: (1) The associative or reinforcement bond between the target behavior and the environmental event must be weakened; (2) more desirable behavior must be instituted through reinforcement. When the plan has been implemented, comparing treatment data with baseline data helps to determine whether or not it is working. If the original treatment plan does not work, the conditions will be reassessed and a modified plan will be introduced.

Behavior therapy (also called behavior modification) seems to have a number of advantages. It has been shown to be highly effective in changing and developing specific behaviors under controlled, experimental conditions. Its apparent simplicity and the ease with which it can be applied by paraprofessionals with minimal training are also appealing. Furthermore, it is economical, because it does not require a legion of high-level, expensive professionals, and it can be immediately beneficial for controlling unmanageable behavior within the institution. Finally, because it quantifies observable behaviors, it lends itself very well to evaluation and research.

However, behavior therapy has a number of problems. While it seems to offer a simple, straightforward method of alleviating pressing behavior problems, it actually requires sophistication on the part of the therapist, stringent environmental control, and a high degree of cooperation and commitment from those even remotely involved in the program. Transferring behavior techniques from the controlled psychological laboratory to the correctional institution, where there are bound to be numerous constraints, is an extremely difficult task. Another flaw is behavior therapy's lack of demonstrated generalizability to the natural environment outside the prison, where powerful, significant models and reference groups often dilute the short-term effectiveness of many behavior therapy approaches. Finally, and perhaps most important, behavior therapy in the correctional setting raises many questions about the rights of inmates, especially if there is any indication that they are being coerced to participate.

Behavior therapy, well applied and with the inmate's willing participation, may be useful for controlling institutional behavior and can promote the acquisition of specific social and academic skills. Furthermore, when combined with social cognitive therapy, it is beginning to demonstrate its effectiveness in inhibiting or even reducing criminal behavior in the natural environment, such as with sex offenders discussed in Chapter 9.

In all fairness, treatment programs within institutions are often handicapped by inadequate facilities, staff, programs, and financial support. Added to these restraints are legal, political, and social pressures. If some restrictions were reduced, the scientific community might be able to design and formulate effective, generalizable programs that would involve more personal commitment and freedom of choice on the part of the inmate.

Another feature of the prison system that makes treatment and rehabilitation difficult is that two systems are at work—the formal system dictated by authorities and the informal system run by inmates. In the latter, two processes may be identified: **criminalization** and **prisonization**. In criminalization, inmates exchange, share, and support one another's construct systems, beliefs, attitudes, and feelings. The system creates a "deviant" culture where inmates form subgroups and develop friendships, loyalty, and commitment. Prisonization is the process whereby inmates learn the specific rules, general culture, and expectation of the prison community. With these two learning processes at work, which are often in conflict with society, it seems that the longer the time inmates spend in prison, the more likely they will crystallize their thinking about their deviant lifestyles and become "better criminals." Research continually reveals that, in general, the more time one spends in prison, the more likely one is to reoffend.

The processes of criminalization and prisonization underscore the traditionally recognized influence of normative or reference groups on human behavior. Criminal behavior, however, is not simply the result of imitating others in the social environment, or even the result of external reinforcement. Recent research in cognitive psychology goes one step further. "If actions were determined solely by external rewards and punishments, people would behave like weathervanes, constantly shifting in different directions to conform to the momentary influence impinging on them. They would act corruptly with unprincipled individuals and honorably with righteous ones, and liberally with libertarians and dogmatically with authoritarians" (Bandura, 1977, p. 128). Instead, most human behavior is motivated and regulated in large part by personally adopted beliefs, values, and expectations.

COGNITIVE THERAPY

During the past two decades, cognitive theories have come to dominate the research on learning, memory, personality, motivation, and social psychology (Mahoney & Lyddon, 1988). The growth of **cognition** has also been very strong in the areas of counseling and psychotherapy.

One of the forerunners of the cognitive approaches was **reality therapy**, a form of self-control therapy developed by the psychiatrist William Glasser (1965) and still commonly used in corrections today. The basic principles for the approach were developed at the Ventura (California) School for Girls, whose residents were seriously delinquent adolescent girls. The popularity of reality therapy stems partly from its straightforward approach and easy-to-understand procedures. Because of its apparent simplicity, paraprofessionals and front line correctional staff can be easily trained to offer personal and group therapy to inmates. Reality therapy is based on the perspective that offenders must face reality—no matter what happened to them in the past—and take full responsibility for their behavior now. In essence, the focus is to teach offenders responsible behavior. A major contribution of reality therapy has been to focus attention on the irresponsible nature of crime and delinquency, rather than viewing them as the result of some psychological sickness or disorder.

Other important forerunners of commonly used cognitive treatment approaches are George Kelly's (1955) *personal construct therapy*, Albert Ellis' (1962) *rational-emotive therapy*, and Aron T. Beck's (1970) *cognitive therapy*. All of these early approaches have undergone extensive revision since their initial formulation, and have splintered into many different therapeutic perspectives.

In recent years, **constructivist therapy** has emerged as a viable, rapidly growing approach across a wide area of cognitive therapies. "The basic assertion of constructivism is that each individual creates his or her own representational model of the world. This experiential scaffolding ... in turn becomes a framework from which the individual orders and assigns meaning to new experience" (Mahoney & Lyddon, 1988, p. 200). The basic idea of the constructivist approach is that individuals do not formulate static templates through which ongoing experience is filtered, but rather develop more *dynamic* constructs that are always subject to change as a result of new experiences. Thus, "the constructivist does not view cognitive structures as static, storage entities but rather as systems of transformation" (Mahoney & Lyddon, 1988, p. 203).

From a constructivist perspective, developing human beings are active information processors, who explore and adapt to the environment, and who continually organize information about the world and oneself into increasingly complex views (Greenberg, 1988). On the other hand, repetitively violent and antisocial individuals may be those who are essentially trapped in an isolated, socially closed-off, and self-constructive cognitive system that relies on simple, straightforward aggressive solutions to survival. Moreover, they continually fall out of mainstream society, which results in their already isolated cognitive systems becoming more narrow, restrictive, and deviant. Instead of becoming more complex and integrative, the world versions of the repetitive offender may stagnate or deteriorate. Many repetitive offenders may become so caught up in their personal versions of the world that they refuse to allow alternative views to pierce their cognitive armor. Yochelson and Samenow (1976), for example, contend that there are fifty-two basic errors in thinking practiced by the hard-core criminals that must be corrected before there is any hope of change. It would seem that cognitive therapies offer the best hope for changing the thinking and belief systems of the repetitive offender.

We also need to have a better understanding of the relationships among the vast array of swirling systems that affect delinquent and criminal behavior before we can have highly effective treatment or prevention programs. "Human action is ... regulated by multilevel systems of control" (Bandura, 1989, p. 1181). One such approach is a social systems theory. A social systems approach facilitates a synthesis of what we know across the various disciplines and perspectives, whether we are discussing social class, neighborhood, community, culture, family, siblings, or the individual (Bartol, 1988). Social systems theory assumes that while it is helpful to study personality variables, family, the neighborhood, and the culture in isolation, it is far more effective to study these variables in relationship to one another. In order to change criminal behavior over long periods of time, we need to study not only the offenders themselves but also their families, peers, schools, neighborhoods, communities, and cultures, all in relationship to one another. The offender affects the other systems and the systems affect the offender in complex, poorly understood ways. Treatment and preventive approaches that are fully able to appreciate this dynamic interplay are far more likely to be successful than those that only concentrate on one aspect of an individual's life.

Of course, it is easier to describe the factors that might contribute to criminal behavior than to offer a comprehensive, realistic proposal for dealing with it. The primary mission of this text was to propose some explanations for criminal behavior from a psychological perspective. Whether these explanations will be accepted and applied to solving the crime problem remains to be seen. We can only reiterate that the defeatist attitude toward rehabilitation espoused by much of society, together with the emphasis on punishment for its own sake, cannot improve the situation. Undoubtedly, the ideal way of dealing with crime is by attacking its origins; from a psychological point of view this means examining the values we communicate to our young. Nevertheless, it is not too optimistic to hope that the psychological principles we have discussed may be applied to at least some offenders presently housed in correctional institutions.

Cases Cited

Addington v. Texas, 99 S.Ct. 1804 (1979)
Baxstrom v. Herold, 383 U.S. 107 (1966)
Carter v. U.S., 252 F.2d 608 (D.C. Cir. 1957)
Dixon v. Attorney General of the Commonwealth of Pennsylvania, 325 F.Supp. 966 (M.D. Pa. 1971)
Durham v. U.S., 214 F.2d 862 (D.C. Cir. 1954)
Dusky v. U.S., 363 U.S. 402 (1960)
Foucha v. Louisiana, 51 Cr.L. 2084 (1992)
Jackson v. Indiana, 406 U.S. 715 (1972)
Jones v. U.S., 463 U.S. 354 (1983)
M'Naghten, 10 Clark & Fin. 200, 210, 8 Eng.Rep 718, 722 (1843)
Miller v. State, 318 N.W.2d 673 (S.D. 1983)
Riggins v. Nevada, 504 U.S. (1992)
State v. Bianchi, No. 79-10116 (Wash. Super. Ct., October 19, 1979)
State v. Campanaro, Nos. 632–79, 1309–79, 1317–79, 514–80, & 707–80 (Superior Court of New Jersey Crim. Div., Union County, 1980)
State v. Felde, 422 So.2d 370 (La. 1982)
State v. Lafferty, 192 Conn. 571, 472 A.2d 1275 (1984)
State v. Milligan, No. 77-CR-11-2908 (Franklin Co., Ohio, Dec. 4, 1978)
State v. Rodrigues, 679 P.2d 615 (Hawaii 1984)
Tan Van Khiem v. U.S., 51 Cr.L. 1061 (D.C. Cir. 1992)
Tarasoff v. Regents of the University of California, 529 F.2d 553 (Cal. 1974). vac., reheard en banc, & aff'd 131 Cal.Rptr. 1, 551 P.2d 334 (1976)
U.S. v. Brawner, 471 F.2d 969 (D.C. Cir. 1972)
U.S. v. Charters, 863 F.2d 302 (4th Cir. 1988)
U.S. v. Crosby, 713 F.2d 1066 (1983)
U.S. v. Davis, 772 F.2d 1339 (7th Cir. 1985), cert. denied, 106 S.Ct. 603 (1985)
U.S. v. Gillis, 773 F.2d 549 (4th Cir. 1985)
U.S. v. Gould, 741 F.2d 45 (4th Cir. 1984)
U.S. v. Krutschewski, 509 F.Supp. 1186 (D. Mass. 1981)
U.S. v. Lewellyn, 723 F.2d 615 (8th Cir. 1983)
Vitek v. Jones, 445 U.S. 480 (1980)

GLOSSARY

adolescent-limited (AL) offender   An individual who usually demonstrates delinquent or antisocial behavior only during his or her teen years and then stops offending during his or her young adult years.

aggression, hostile (expressive)   Aggressive behavior characterized by the intent to cause the target discomfort or pain.

aggression, instrumental   Aggressive behavior characterized by the intent to gain material or financial rewards from the target.

aggressive (sadistic) pedophile   An adult drawn to children for both sexual and aggressive (violent) purposes.

amines   A group of synthetically produced stimulants.

amnesia   Complete or partial memory loss of an incident, series of incidents, or some aspects of life's experiences.

anger rape   A rape situation, identified by Goth, where an offender uses more force than necessary for compliance and engages in a variety of sexual acts that are particularly degrading or humiliating to the victim (such as sodomy, fellatio, or even urinating on her).

anger retaliation rapist   A classification of rapists proposed by the Massachusetts Research Center to identify those individuals who are more motivated to humiliate the victim than to gain sexual gratification. See also *displaced anger rapist*.

antisocial personality disorder (ASP)   A disorder characterized by a history of continuous behavior where the rights of others are violated.

anxiety disorder   Mental disorder caused by high levels of physiological arousal that interfere with daily functioning.

arson   Any willful or malicious burning or attempt to burn, with or without intent to defraud, a dwelling house, public building, motor vehicle, aircraft, or personal property of another.

assault   The intentional inflicting of bodily injury on another person, or the attempt to inflict such injury.

assault, aggravated   Inflicting, or attempting to inflict, bodily injury on another person, with the intent to inflict serious injury.

assault, simple   The unlawful, intentional inflicting of less than serious bodily injury without a deadly or dangerous weapon, or the attempt to inflict such bodily injury, again without a deadly or dangerous weapon.

atavism   A biological throwback to prehistoric times.

attention deficit hyperactivity disorder (ADHD)   Traditionally considered a chronic neurobiological condition characterized by developmentally poor attention, impulsivity, and hyperactivity. More contemporary perspectives see the behavioral pattern as a deficiency in interpersonal skills.

autoeroticism   A term coined by Havelock Ellis that refers to self-arousal and self-gratification of sexual desire.

availability heuristic   The cognitive shortcuts that people use to make quick inferences about their world. It is the information that is most readily available to us mentally, and is usually based extensively on the most recent material we gain from the news or entertainment media.

avoidance learning   A process whereby, if a person responds in time to a warning signal, he or she avoids painful or aversive stimuli.

barricade situation   A hostage situation in which an individual has fortified himself or herself in a building or residence, threatening violence to himself or herself, or to others.

battered child syndrome   A cluster of behavioral and psychological characteristics believed common to children who have been abused, physically or emotionally.

battered woman syndrome   A cluster of behavioral and psychological characteristics believed common to women who have been abused in relationships.

behaviorism   A perspective that focuses on observable, measurable behavior and argues that the social environment and learning are the key determinants of human behavior.

blue-collar crime   A term that encompasses the whole array of illegal acts committed by nonsalaried workers and where the place of employment is the victim. Examples include the theft of company property, the destruction of company property, or the falsification of production records for pay increase or overtime.

Brawner Rule   A standard for evaluating the insanity defense that recognizes that the defendant suffers from a condition that substantially (1) affects mental or emotional processes or (2) impairs behavior controls. This rule expands on the ALI Rule.

burglary   The unlawful entry of a structure, with or without force, with intent to commit a felony or theft.

cannabis   The plant that contains marijuana.

caveat paragraph   A section of the ALI/Brawner Rule that excludes abnormality manifested only by repeated criminal or antisocial conduct. It was specifically designed to disallow the insanity defense for psychopaths.

classic mass murder   A situation in which an individual barricades himself or herself inside a public building, such as a fast food restaurant, randomly killing the patrons and other individuals he or she has contact with.

classical (Pavlovian) conditioning   The process of learning to respond to a formerly neutral stimulus that has been paired with another stimulus that already elicits a response. Also called *Pavlovian conditioning*.

classical school perspective   The theoretical position that in order to deter criminal behavior the punishment should fit the crime. It is also a perspective that believes humans presumably act according to their free will and therefore should be held completely responsible for their actions.

clearance rate   The proportion of reported crimes that have been "solved."

cognition   The internal processes that enable humans to imagine, to gain knowledge, to reason, and to evaluate.

cognitive behavior therapy   An approach to sex offender therapy that focuses on changing beliefs, fantasies, attitudes, and rationalizations that justify and perpetuate sexually violent behavior.

cognitive-neoassociation model   A revised theory of the frustration-aggression hypothesis proposed by Leonard Berkowitz.

cognitive scripts   Mental images of how one feels he or she should act in a variety of situations.

cognitive scripts model   Rowell Huesmann's theory that social behavior in general and aggressive behavior in particular are controlled largely by cognitive scripts learned and memorized through daily experiences.

community-based corrections   Supervisory facilities that hold individuals for less than twenty-four hours of each day to give them the opportunity to work, attend school, receive treatment, or participate in other community activities.

compensatory rapist   An offender who rapes in response to an intense sexual arousal initiated by stimuli in the environment, often quite specific stimuli (e.g., rich college girls). His main motive is to prove his sexual prowess.

compulsion   An action a person feels compelled (driven) by internal thoughts to take, even though it may be irrational.

compulsive gambling   A psychiatric syndrome characterized by anxiety and an insatiable, unconscious desire to lose what was gained in previous gambling.

concordance   A term used in genetics to represent the degree to which related pairs of subjects both show a particular behavior or condition. It is usually expressed in percentages.

conduct disorder   A diagnostic label used to identify children who demonstrate habitual misbehavior.

conformity perspective   The theoretical position that humans are born basically good and generally try to do the right and just thing.

constructivist therapy   Psychotherapy based on the view that the therapist must begin and work with each person's unique version of the world.

contagion effect   A tendency for some people to model or copy a behavior or activity portrayed by the news or entertainment media.

copycat effect   See *contagion effect*.

corporate crime   Illegal acts by employees in the course of their employment that benefit the company or corporation.

correlation   A mathematical index that reflects the nature of the relationship between two variables.

criminal investigative analysis (CIA)   An attempt to derive hypotheses about an offender based on the analysis of a crime scene, victim information, and current knowledge of offenders from previous research. Also called crime scene analysis.

criminal homicide   A term that encompasses both murder and nonnegligent homicide.

criminal profiling   See *profiling*.

criminal psychopath   A primary psychopath who engages in repetitive antisocial or criminal behavior.

criminalization   The process whereby inmates exchange, share, and support one another's beliefs, attitudes, and feelings, which in the long run promotes criminal activity.

criminology   The multidisciplinary study of crime.

criminology, psychiatric   The branch of criminology that focuses on individual aspects of behavior, particularly internal forces and unconscious drives. Also called *forensic psychiatry*.

criminology, psychological   The branch of criminology that examines the individual behavior and especially the mental processes involved in criminal behavior.

criminology, sociological   The branch of criminology that examines the demographic and group variables related to crime.

cybercrime   Any illegal act that involves a computer system. Also called computer crime.

cyberstalking   The use of the internet for stalking.

dark figure   The number of crimes that go unreported in official crime data reports.

Darwinism   In psychology, a belief that humans should be placed on a single continuum along with all creatures in the animal kingdom.

dehumanize   To engage in actions that obscure the identity of the victim, such as excessive facial battery.

deindividuation   A process by which individuals feel they cannot be identified.

delusional (paranoid) disorder   Mental disorder characterized by a system of false beliefs.

dependence   A condition that may be physical, psychological, or both, whereby a person develops an intense craving for (and feels he or she cannot live without) a drug.

dependent variable   The variable that is measured to see how it is changed by manipulations on the independent variable.

determinism   The study of the nature and location of causes of human behavior.

determinism, biological   See *determinism, neurobiological*.

determinism, external   The belief that the causes of human behavior are largely determined by forces and events outside ourselves, such as the social environment. Also called *situationism*.

determinism, hard   The belief that all behavior is caused by forces or events that follow the natural laws of the universe, and that, ultimately, all behaviors are predictable.

determinism, internal   The belief that the causes of human behavior are largely determined by powerful instinctual drives or biological needs.

determinism, neurobiological   The belief that the causes of human behavior are determined largely by heredity, bodily constitution, physique, neurophysiological factors, or other characteristics of the nervous system.

determinism, psychological   The belief that the causes of behavior are determined by psychological factors (personality, cognitions, learning) rather than neurobiological ones.

determinism, soft   The belief that although some behavior is caused by outside forces and events, self-control or self-determinism plays an equally important role in determining behavior.

deterrence   One of the four goals or purposes of punishment; refers to the use of punishment to dissuade individuals from committing crime in the future. General deterrence refers to the overall symbolic impact punishment has on the population as a whole. Specific deterrence is based on the actual experience of punishment, which presumably will deter the punished individual from engaging in future transgressions.

Diagnostic and Statistical Manual of Mental Disorders (DSM)   The official guidebook or manual, published by the American Psychiatric Association, used to define and diagnose specific mental disorders.

difference in degree   The perspective of human nature that argues that humans are intimately tied to their animal ancestry in important and significant ways. For example, this perspective might argue that human violence is a result of innate, biological needs to obtain sufficient food supplies, territory, or mates.

difference in kind   The perspective of human nature that argues that humans are distinctly different from animals, spiritually, psychologically, and/or mentally.

differential association theory   Formulated by Edwin Sutherland, a theory of crime that states that criminal behavior is primarily due to socializing with criminal people. The critical factors include with whom a person associates, for how long, how frequently, how personally meaningful the associations are, and how they occur in a person's development.

differential association-reinforcement (DAR) theory   A theory of deviance developed by Ronald Akers that combines Skinner's behaviorism and Sutherland's differential association theory. The theory states that people learn deviant behavior through the reinforcements they receive from the social environment.

differential treatment   Any treatment program formulated to meet the needs and capabilities of each person in a correctional setting.

disorganized crime scene   Demonstrates that the offender committed the crime without premeditation or planning. In other words, the crime scene indicators suggest the individual acted on impulse or in rage, or under extreme excitement.

displaced aggression rapist   The rapist whose attack is violent and aggressive, displaying minimum or total absence of sexual feeling.

disposition   A term that signifies internal or personality determinants of human behavior. Dispositional theorists look to inner conflicts, beliefs, drives, personal needs, traits, or attitudes to explain behavior.

dissociative disorders   Mental disorders characterized by memory loss or loss of identity.

dissociative identity disorder   A psychiatric syndrome characterized by a number of personalities or personality states. Also called *multiple personality disorder (MPD)*.

drug treatment   An approach to sex offender therapy that concentrates on reducing the targeted behavior through the use of antiandrogen and antidepressant medication.

DSM   See *Diagnostic and Statistical Manual*.

Durham Rule   A legal standard of insanity that holds that an accused is not criminally responsible if his or her unlawful act was the product of mental disease or defect. Also known as the Product Rule.

dyssocial psychopath   Individual who is antisocial because of social learning.

ecological fallacy   Making incorrect conclusions about an individual based on group data or stereotypes. For example, "since he is Irish, he will act like all Irish."

ectomorph   A body type characterized by thinness and fragility in structure.

endomorph   A body type characterized by roundness and fatty tissue.

equivocal death analysis   See *reconstructive psychological evaluation (RPE)*.

escalation   A process whereby each party in a conflict increases the magnitude or intensity of a response in reaction to the increased response received from the other party.

evocative therapy   An approach to sex offender therapy that focuses on (1) helping offenders to understand the causes and motivations of their sexual behavior and (2) increasing their empathy for the victims of the sexual assault.

excitation transfer theory   Theory explaining how physiological arousal can generalize from one situation to another; based on the assumption that physiological arousal, however produced, dissipates slowly over time.

excitement-motivated (E-M) arson   A category suggested by the FBI to classify those people who set fires simply for excitement.

exhibitionism   The deliberate exposure of the genitals to another person to achieve sexual gratification. Also called indecent exposure.

exploitative pedophile   An adult who seeks children almost exclusively for sexual gratification.

exploitative rapist   See *impulsive rapist*.

expressive hostage taking   Hostage-taking situation where the primary goal of the offender is to gain some control over his or her life.

expressive sexual aggression   A rape situation in which the offender's primary aim is to harm the victim physically as well as psychologically.

extended suicide   A situation in which the person committing suicide kills others in the environment as well. Sometimes referred to as a murder-suicide.

extinction   The decline and eventual disappearance of a conditioned or learned response when it is no longer reinforced.

extraversion   In Eysenck's theory, a personality dimension that represents needs for stimulation.

false memory syndrome   A mental state wherein an individual believes that an incident has happened, although the incident has not actually happened.

family mass murder   A situation in which at least three family members are killed (usually by another family member).

fetishism   Sexual attraction to inanimate objects.

filicide   The killing of a child who is more than twenty-four-hours old.

fixated pedophile   A male who demonstrates a long-standing, exclusive preference for children as both sexual and social companions.

forcible rape   The carnal knowledge of a female, forcibly and against her will. It includes rape by force, assault to rape, and attempted rape.

forensic psychiatry   See *criminology, psychiatric*.

forensic psychology   The production and application of psychological knowledge to the civil and criminal justice systems.

frustration-aggression hypothesis   The theory that frustration leads to aggressive behavior. The theory has been revised several times, with most substantial changes coming from the work of Leonard Berkowitz.

fundamental attribution error   A tendency to underestimate the importance of situational determinates and to overestimate the importance of personality or dispositional factors in identifying the causes of human behavior.

general deterrence   See *deterrence*.

Guilty but Mentally Ill (GBMI)   A new verdict alternative intended as an alternative to, not a substitute for, the NGRI verdict.

habituation   Getting used to or adapting to a stimulus.

hallucinogens   Those psychoactive drugs that sometimes generate hallucinations and lead to changes in perceptions of reality. Also called *psychedelics*.

Hate Crime Statistics Act   A statute that mandates the FBI to collect data on all crimes motivated by racial, ethnic, religious, or sexual orientation hate or bias.

hebephilia   The use of young adolescent girls or boys for sexual gratification by adult males.

homicide   Causing the death of another person without legal justification or excuse.

hostile attribution model   A cognitive model of aggression developed by Kenneth Dodge and colleagues. See also *hostile attributional bias*.

hostile attributional bias   The tendency to perceive hostile intent in others even when it is totally lacking.

hyperactivity   A behavioral pattern demonstrated by both children and adults wherein there is considerable motor activity in an attempt to gain adequate amounts of cortical stimulation.

I-theory   Developed by Sullivan, Grant, and Grant, the interpersonal maturity theory was originally formulated to account for the disturbed interpersonal relationships of juvenile delinquents.

iatrogenic   A process whereby mental or physical disorders are unintentionally induced or developed in patients by physicians, clinicians, or psychotherapists.

imitational learning   See *observational learning*.

immature pedophile   See *fixated pedophile*.

impulsive rapist A rapist who demonstrates neither strong sexual nor aggressive features, but engages in spontaneous rape when the opportunity presents itself. The rape is usually carried out in the context of another crime, such as robbery or burglary.

incapacitation One of the four goals or purposes of punishment. Isolation of the individual from society so that he or she cannot commit more crime.

incidence The total number of reported cases (frequency) per year.

Incompetent to Stand Trial (IST) A judicial determination that a defendant lacks sufficient ability to understand the legal process against him or her and/or to assist a lawyer in the preparation of a defense.

independent variable The measure whose effect is being studied, and, in most scientific investigations, that is manipulated by the experimenter in a controlled fashion.

index crimes (Part I crimes) The crimes that are of most concern, as defined by the FBI's Uniform Crime Reports, and are used to indicate the seriousness of the crime problem. The eight index crimes are murder and nonnegligent manslaughter, aggravated assault, robbery, rape, burglary, larceny, theft, arson, and motor-vehicle theft.

individual offender A person who consistently violates the law because of a series of frustrations and disappointments.

infanticide Although this term literally means the killing of an infant, it has become synonymous with the killing of a child by a parent.

insanity In the legal context, judicial determination that an individual's degree or quantity of mental disorder relieves him or her of criminal responsibility for illegal actions.

Insanity Defense Reform Act of 1984 A law designed to make it more difficult for defendants using the insanity defense in the federal courts to be acquitted.

instrumental conditioning See *instrumental learning*.

instrumental hostage taking A hostage situation in which the primary goal of the offender is material or monetary gain.

instrumental learning A form of learning in which a voluntary response is strengthened or diminished by its consequences. Also called *operant conditioning*.

instrumental sexual aggression When the sexual offender uses just enough coercion to gain compliance from his victim.

interactionism The perspective that argues that human behavior is determined or influenced by both internal (biological, psychological, cognitive) and external (social environmental) factors.

Interpersonal-Maturity Theory See *I-theory*.

invariance hypothesis Proposed by Gottfredson and Hirschi, this hypothesis refers to the observation that crime seems to decline with age, no matter where in history or no matter what culture is being considered.

irrationality   A basic ingredient of the insanity standard. Refers to the legal assumption that a person cannot be held criminally responsible for his or her actions if it is determined he or she could not control his or her behavior.

irresistible (uncontrollable) impulse test   A legal standard whereby a defendant argues that he or she could not control his or her actions, even though he or she knew it was wrong.

jail   A facility operated by a local government to hold persons temporarily detained, awaiting trial, or sentenced to confinement, after having been convicted of a misdemeanor.

just world hypothesis   A belief that one gets what one deserves in this world.

Juvenile Court Act   A statute passed by the Illinois legislature in 1899 that marks the official beginning of juvenile justice in the United States.

kleptomania   The irresistible urge to steal unneeded objects. Whether there is such an urge is highly debatable.

learned helplessness   A learned passive and withdrawing response in the face of perceived hopelessness, as theorized by Martin Seligman (1975).

learning approach   The theoretical position that humans are born basically neutral and behaviorally a blank slate. What they become as individuals depends on their learning experiences rather than innate predispositions.

life-course-persistent (LCP) offenders   A term by Terrie Moffitt to represent offenders who demonstrate a life-long pattern of antisocial behavior and who are not responsive to treatment or rehabilitation.

limited amnesia   A pathological inability to remember a specific episode, or small number of episodes, from the recent past.

London syndrome   A behavioral pattern observed during a hostage situation at the Iranian Embassy in London. Refers to the explicit and consistent resistance and refusals by hostages to do what is expected by captors. This behavior often results in death or serious injury to the blatant resistors.

M'Naghten Rule   An insanity standard based on the conclusion that if a defendant has a defect of reason, or a disease of the mind, so as not to know the nature and quality of his or her actions, then he or she cannot be held criminally responsible. Also called the *right and wrong test*.

mass arsonist   A person who sets three or more fires in quick succession at the same location without a cooling-off period.

mass murder   Murdering three or more persons at a single location with no cooling-off period between murders.

maturation retardation hypothesis   Robert Hare's theory that suggests that the neurological development of psychopaths may be slower than normal.

mental illness A disorder of the mind judged by experts to interfere significantly with a person's ability to cope with life on a daily basis. Preferred term today is mental disorder.

Mentally Disordered Sex Offender (MDSO) A classification established by some state legislatures to identify those mentally disordered individuals prone toward repetitive sexual attacks on children, women, or both.

mesomorph A muscular and well-developed body type. Some research has indicated that this body type is more likely to be involved in violent crime.

mixed crime scene Indicates that the nature of the crime demonstrates both organized and disorganized behavioral patterns.

modeling A process whereby an individual learns new behavior by watching others.

modus operandi (MO) The actions and procedures an offender uses to commit a crime successfully.

multiple personality disorder (MPD) A mental disorder characterized by the existence within an individual of two or more distinct personalities, each of which may be dominant at any given moment.

multisystemic therapy A treatment approach for serious juvenile offenders that focuses on the family while being responsive to the many other contexts surrounding the family, such as the welfare system, the neighborhood, and the school.

murder The felonious killing of one human being by another with malice aforethought. See also *criminal homicide*.

narcotics Psychoactive drugs that produce sleep and are derivatives of the poppy plant.

National Crime Victimization Survey (NCVS) A survey conducted by the Bureau of Census for the Department of Justice that involves contacts with a large national sample of households to learn the extent of criminal victimization. Originally called the National Crime Survey (NCS).

neoclassical school of criminology A theoretical perspective that is similar to the classical perspective, except that it challenges the absolute belief in free will and total criminal responsibility advocated by the classical school.

neonaticide The killing of a newborn within the first twenty-four hours after birth.

neurosis A mild form of mental disorder characterized by anxiety. The term is used infrequently by clinicians today.

neurotic disorders Anxiety disorders, somatoform disorders, and dissociative disorders.

neuroticism A dimension of personality according to Hans J. Eysenck that theoretically reflects arousal levels of the autonomic nervous system.

nonconformist perspective   The theoretical perspective that humans will naturally try to get away with anything they can, including illegal conduct, unless social controls are imposed.

nonindex crimes (Part II crimes)   Crimes not considered serious by the FBI.

normative support   Refers to the standards, perceptions, and values a work group has established for itself, with or without the company's or organization's approval. More specifically, normative support standards identify what "illegal" behavior is permitted in the workplace.

Not Guilty by Reason of Insanity (NGRI)   See *insanity*.

observational learning (modeling)   The hypothesis that individuals may learn patterns of behavior simply by observing another person performing the action.

operant conditioning   See *instrumental conditioning*.

opiate narcotics   Psychoactive drugs that have sedative (sleep-inducing) and analgesic (pain-relieving) effects.

organized crime scene   Indicates planning and premeditation on the part of the offender. In other words, the crime scene shows signs that the offender maintained control of himself or herself and the victim.

overcontrolled personality   A person who has well-established inhibitions against aggressive behavior and rigidly adheres to them, even in the face of provocation.

partialism   An exaggerated sexual interest in some part of the human anatomy not usually associated with sexual arousal, such as an ankle or elbow.

Pavlovian conditioning   See *classical conditioning*.

pedophilia   The use of children by adults for sexual gratification and companionship.

personation   See *signature*.

positive school of criminology   A perspective developed through the early efforts of Enrico Ferri and Raffaele Garofalo, sometimes referred to as the Italian School. This perspective was largely biological in its explanations of criminal behavior, but its major contribution was its heavy reliance on positivism for studying crime, an approach that forms the basis of modern criminological research methods.

positivism   The firm belief that the best way to acquire knowledge about our world is strictly through observable facts and other information gained through the senses. This orientation follows the classical methods (the experimental method) used by the natural sciences to gain knowledge.

post-traumatic stress disorder (PTSD)   A cluster of behavioral patterns that result from a psychologically distressing event outside the usual range of human experience.

power rape   A rape situation, identified by Groth, where the assailant seeks to establish power and control over his victim. Thus, the amount of force and threats used depends on the degree of submission shown by the victim.

premenstrual syndrome (PMS)   The cluster of behavioral patterns and psychological changes that are believed to accompany the cyclic physiological changes that occur prior to the onset of menstruation in some women. The prevalence and existence of PMS is widely disputed.

prevalence   The proportion or ratio of the population involved (e.g., the number of children experiencing abuse per 1,000 children in the general population).

primary prevention   An intervention program designed to prevent behavior or disorders before any signs of the behavioral pattern develops.

primary psychopath   Robert Hare's classification of the "true" psychopath. That is, the individual who demonstrates those behavioral features that represent psychopathy—in contrast to secondary psychopaths, who commit antisocial acts because of severe emotional problems or inner conflicts, and dyssocial psychopaths, who are antisocial because of social learning.

prisonization   The process by which inmates adopt and internalize the prisoner subculture within a particular correctional facility.

prisons   Correctional facilities operated by state and federal governments to hold persons convicted of felonies and sentenced generally to terms of more than one year.

profiling   The process of identifying personality traits, behavioral tendencies, and demographic variables of an offender based on characteristics of the crime.

psychedelics   A broad psychoactive drug classification characterized by elevated mood, hallucinations, and altered states of consciousness.

psychoactive drugs   Drugs that exert their primary effect on the brain, thus altering mood or behavior.

psychodynamic (hydraulic) model   The theoretical perspective that argues that human behavior can be best explained through the use of psychological forces and pressures.

psychoeducational counseling   An approach to sex offender therapy that utilizes a group or class setting to remedy deficits in social and interpersonal skills.

psychogenic amnesia   Amnesia caused by psychological or mental factors, in contrast to biological or organic causes.

psychological autopsy   Postmortem analysis often reserved for suicide cases. The psychological autopsy is frequently done to determine the reasons and precipitating factors for the suicide.

psychometric approach   The perspective that human characteristics, attributes, and traits can be measured and quantified.

psychometric intelligence (PI)   A more contemporary designation of intelligence as measured by intelligence or IQ tests.

psychopath   An individual who demonstrates a distinct behavioral pattern that differs from the general population in its level of sensitivity, empathy, compassion, and guilt.

Psychopathy Checklist (PCL)   Developed by Robert Hare, currently the best measuring instrument of criminal psychopathy.

psychosis   A severe form of mental disorder characterized by hallucinations, delusions, and other indications of loss of contact with reality.

psychotechnology   Methods of permanently altering brain tissue through surgical, electrical (direct current), or chemical means.

psychoticism   A personality dimension, proposed by Eysenck, characterized by cold cruelty, social insensitivity, unemotionality, high risk taking, troublesome behavior, and a dislike of others.

punishment (retribution)   An event by which a person receives a noxious, painful, or aversive stimulus, usually as a consequence of behavior.

pyromania   A psychiatric term for an irresistible urge to set fires along with an intense fascination (usually sexual) with fire. The existence of this behavioral phenomenon has been seriously questioned by the available research.

rape by fraud   The act of having sexual relations with a supposedly consenting adult female under fraudulent conditions, such as when a physician or psychotherapist has sexual intercourse with a patient under the guise of "effective treatment."

rational reconstruction   A mental process whereby an individual engages in a reinterpretation of past behavior through which he or she recasts activities in a manner consistent with "what should have been" rather than "what was." The term in this book was used specifically for explaining research on burglary.

reality therapy   Treatment based on the view that the patient must face reality and take full responsibility for his or her behavior.

reciprocal influence   The observation that family influences do not flow in one direction, but tend to be multidirectional in their effects.

Reconstructive Psychological Evaluation (RPE)   Reconstruction of the personality profile and cognitive features (especially intentions) of deceased individuals.

recovered memory syndrome   Based on the assumption that emotionally painful or traumatic events can be unconsciously pushed into the deep recesses of the mind and reside there until brought out by skillful, systematic digging by a therapist or hypnotist. However, there is considerable debate over whether the mind actually works this way.

reductionism   A research approach that argues that in order to understand highly complex events or phenomenon, one must start examining the simplest parts first.

regressed pedophile   A male who had a fairly normal relationship with adults but later reverted to children for sexual and social companionship because of feelings of inadequacy.

rehabilitation   Any attempt intended to bring about change in behavior patterns or attitudes.

reinforcement   Anything that increases the probability of responding.

reinforcement, negative   The reward received for avoiding a painful or aversive condition, or stimuli.

reinforcement, positive   The acquisition of something desired as a result of one's behavior.

relapse prevention (RP)   A method of treatment primarily designed to prevent a relapse of an undesired behavioral pattern.

relative deprivation   A concept developed by Gresham Sykes for explaining economic crime. It refers to the perceived discrepancy between what an individual has and what he or she would like to have. It is a condition that is especially prominent when people of wealth and people of poverty live in close proximity.

right and wrong test   See *M'Naghten Rule.*

ritual abuse   Child abuse as a result of satanic cult practices.

sadist rapist   See *sexual aggressive rapist.*

sadistic rape   The rape situation, identified by Groth, where the offender experiences sexual arousal and excitement in the victim's maltreatment, torment, distress, helplessness, and suffering. The assault usually involves bondage and torture, and the rapist directs considerable abuse and injury on various areas of the victim's body.

satanic cult   A group of people who worship the devil and aspire to possess some of his powers.

satanic ritual abuse   See *ritual abuse.*

schizophrenic disorders   Mental disorders characterized by severe breakdowns in thought patterns, emotions, and perceptions. It is the disorder most commonly associated with the term "crazy behavior."

secondary prevention   An intervention program designed for individuals who demonstrate early signs or indicators of behavioral problems or antisocial behavior.

secondary psychopath   Individual who commits antisocial acts because of severe emotional problems or inner conflicts.

sedative-hypnotic   Psychoactive drugs that depress central nervous system functioning, generally reducing anxiety and tension.

selective incapacitation   The imprisonment for longer terms of offenders who are believed to pose the greatest threat to society.

self-fulfilling prophecy   A tendency to act on one's expectations in such a way as to make the expectations come true.

self-regulatory mechanisms   Personal standards that people develop by which they compare and evaluate their own conduct.

self-serving bias   A tendency to attribute positive things that happen to us to our abilities and personalities, and to attribute negative events to some cause outside ourselves or beyond our control.

semantic aphasia   A characteristic found in psychopaths whereby the words they speak are devoid of emotional sincerity.

serial murder   Incidents in which an individual (or individuals) kill a number of individuals (usually a minimum of three) over time.

sexual aggressive rapist   A rapist who demonstrates both sexual and aggressive features in his attack. In order for him to experience sexual arousal, it must be associated with violence and pain, which excite him. Also called *sadist rapist*.

sexual bondage   The restriction of movement of a victim in a way that enhances the sexual arousal of the offender.

sexual sadism   A deviation characterized by torture and/or killing and mutilation of other persons in order to achieve sexual gratification.

signature   Any behavior that goes beyond what is necessary to commit the crime. Also called *personation*.

simulation   Research conducted in a laboratory setting that is designed to mimic as closely as possible the "real world."

situationism   A theoretical perspective that argues that environmental stimuli control behavior.

social class   Socioeconomic status based on one's family income.

social status   Refers to a person's own socioeconomic status, rather than one's family socioeconomic status.

social control theory   A theory proposed by Travis Hirschi that contends that crime and delinquency occur when an individual's ties to the conventional order or normative standards are weak or largely nonexistent.

social learning theory   A theory of human behavior based on learning from watching others in the social environment.

socialized offender   A person who violates the law consistently because of learning the behavioral patterns from his or her social environment.

sociopath   A person who is repetitively in conflict with the law, apparently with very limited capacity to learn from past experience.

somatoform disorders   Mental disorders characterized by vague bodily ailments and dysfunctions caused by psychological factors.

somatotyping   William H. Sheldon's theory relating physique to delinquency;

based on delineating three basic body builds: endomorphic, ectomorphic, and mesomorphic.

special deterrence   See *deterrence*.

spree arsonist   A person who sets fires at three or more locations with no emotional cooling-off period between them.

spree murder   The killing of three or more individuals without any cooling-off period, usually at two or more locations.

staging   The intentional alteration of a crime scene prior to the arrival of the police.

strain theory   A prominent sociological explanation for crime based on Robert Merton's theory that crime and delinquency occur when there is a perceived discrepancy between the materialistic values and goals cherished and held in high esteem by a society and the availability of the legitimate means for reaching these goals.

status offenses   A class of illegal behavior that only persons with certain characteristics or status can commit, such as persons below a certain age. Examples include running away from home, violating curfew, buying alcohol, or skipping school.

statutory rape   Rape for which the age of the victim is the crucial distinction, on the premise that a victim below a certain age (usually sixteen) cannot validly consent to sexual intercourse with an adult.

stimulants   A broad drug classification that refers to those psychoactive drugs that "stimulate" the central nervous system and elevate mood.

Stockholm effect   A term coined after a hostage situation in Sweden, it refers to the phenomenon of hostages becoming attracted to their captors.

territoriality   The tendency to attack space violators.

tolerance   A condition in which only increasing dosages of the drug produce the desired effect.

tertiary prevention   Intervention strategy designed to reduce or eliminate behavioral problems or antisocial behavior that is fully developed in individuals. Generally called treatment or counseling.

uncontrollable (irresistible) impulse attribution   A psychological state in which the normal restraints of self-control are substantially reduced or virtually eliminated by an overwhelming sex drive.

undercontrolled personality   A person who has few inhibitions against aggressive behavior and frequently engages in violence when frustrated or provoked.

undoing   A behavioral pattern found at the crime scene whereby the offender tries to psychologically "undo" the murder.

unique defenses   Legal defenses that have not been attempted in previous court cases.

victimological perspective   A proposal that suggests we can gain substantial amounts of knowledge on offender characteristics by also studying the nature of the victims selected by offenders such as serial murderers or rapists.

volitional prong   The part of the insanity defense that requires acceptance of the possibility that a defendant could not control his or her behavior to conform to the requirements of the law.

voyeurism   The tendency to gain sexual excitement and gratification from observing unsuspecting others naked, undressing, or engaging in sexual activity.

white-collar crime   A term coined in 1939 by Edwin Sutherland, it refers to illegal acts committed by salaried employees, in which the company or organization of their employment is either the victim of or the location for the commission of the crime. It is restricted to the workplace crimes where the salaried employee personally benefits.

woozle effect   A term, first used in a Winnie-the-Pooh story and later adopted by Houghton (1979), that refers to the tendency of one study to cite another study's data or conclusions without mentioning the methodological limitations and problems inherent in the first study.

REFERENCES

Abadinsky, H. (1993). *Drug Abuse* (2nd edition). Chicago, IL: Nelson-Hall.

Abel, G. G., Barlow, D. H., Blanchard, E. B., & Guild, D. (1977). The components of rapists' sexual arousal. *Archives of General Psychiatry, 34,* 895–903.

Abel, G. G., Becker, J. V., Blanchard, E. B., & Djenderedjian, A. (1978). Differentiating sexual aggressives with penile measures. *Criminal Justice and Behavior, 5,* 315–332.

Abel, G. G., Becker, J. V., Murphy, W. D., & Flanagan, B. (1981). Identifying dangerous child molesters. In R. B. Stuart (Ed.), *Violent behavior: Social learning approaches to prediction, management and treatment.* New York: Brunner/Mazel.

Abel, G. G., Mittelman, M. S., & Becker, J. V. (1985). Sexual offenders: Results of assessment and recommendations for treatment. In H. H. Ben-Aron, S. I. Hucker, C. D. Webster (Eds.), *Clinical criminology.* Toronto: MM Graphics.

Abel, G. G., Mittelman, M., Becker, J. V., Rathner, J., & Rouleau, J. (1988). Predicting child molesters' response to treatment. R. A. Prentky & V. L. Quinsey (Eds.), *Human sexual aggression: Current perspectives.* New York: New York Academy of Sciences.

Abrahamsen, D. (1952). *Who are the guilty?* Westport, CT: Greenwood Press.

Abrahamsen, D. (1960). *The psychology of crime.* New York: Columbia University Press.

Adams, D. (1992). Biology does not make men more aggressive than women. In K. Bjorkquist & P. Niemela (Eds.), *Of mice and women: Aspects of female aggression.* San Diego, CA: Academic Press.

Adams, S. S. (1977). Evaluating correctional treatments. *Criminal Justice and Behavior, 4,* 323–340.

Adler, F. (1975). Sisters in crime. New York: McGraw-Hill.

Adler, R., Nunn, R., Northam, E., Lebnan, V., & Ross, R. (1994). Secondary prevention of childhood firesetting. *Journal of the American Academy of Child and Adolescent Psychiatry, 33,* 1194–1202.

Akers, R. L. (1977). *Deviant behavior: A social learning approach* (2nd edition). Belmont, CA: Wadsworth.

Akers, R. L. (1985). *Deviant behavior: A social learning approach* (3rd edition). Belmont, CA: Wadsworth.

Albanese, J. S. (1995). *White-collar crime in America*. Englewood Cliffs, NJ: Prentice Hall.

Allsopp, J. F. (1976). Criminality and delinquency. In H. J. Eysenck & G. D. Wilson (Eds.), *A textbook of human psychology*. Baltimore, MD: University Park Press.

Allsopp, J. F., & Feldman, M. P. (1976). Personality and antisocial behaviour in schoolboys: Item analysis of questionnaire measures. *British Journal of Criminology, 16*, 337–351.

American Bar Association. (1979). *Juvenile justice standards project*. Chicago, IL: Author.

American Humane Association. (1987). *Highlights of official child neglect and abuse reporting—1985*. Denver, CO: Author.

American Psychiatric Association. (1993). *Draft version of DSM-IV*. Washington, DC: Author.

Amir, M. (1971). *Patterns in forcible rape*. Chicago, IL: University of Chicago Press.

Amsel, A. (1958). The role of frustrative nonreward in noncontinuous reward situations. *Psychological Bulletin, 55*, 102–119.

Andenaes, J. (1968). Does punishment deter crime? *The Criminal Law Quarterly, 11*, 76–93.

Anderson, C. A. (1987). Temperature and aggression: Effects on quarterly, yearly, and city rates of violent and nonviolent crime. *Journal of Personality and Social Psychology, 52*, 1161–1173.

Anderson, C. A. (1989). Temperature and aggression: Ubiquitous effects of heat on occurrence of human violence. *Psychological Bulletin, 106*, 74–96.

Anderson, C. A., & Anderson, D. C. (1984). Ambient temperature and violent crime: Tests of the linear and curvilinear hypothesis. *Journal of Personality and Social Psychology, 46*, 91–97.

Andreasen, N. C., & Carpenter, W. T. (1993). Diagnosis and classification of schizophrenia. *Schizophrenia Bulletin, 19*, 199–214.

Andrew, J. M. (1978). Laterality on the tapping test among legal offenders. *Journal of Clinical Psychology, 7*, 149–150.

Andrew, J. M. (1980). Are left-handers less violent? *Journal of Youth and Adolescence, 9*, 1–9.

Andrews, D. A., & Bonta, J. (1994). *The psychology of criminal conduct*. Cincinnati, OH: Anderson.

Appelbaum, P. S., Jick, R. Z., Grisso, T., Givelbar, D., Silver, E., & Steadman, H. J. (1993). Use of posttraumatic stress. *Psychiatry, 150*, 229–234.

Ardrey, R. (1966). *The territorial imperative*. New York: Atheneum.

Arthur, R. G., & Cahoon, E. B. (1964). A clinical and electroencephalographic survey of psychopathic personality. *American Journal of Psychiatry, 120*, 875–882.

Ault, R., & Reese, J. T. (1980). A psychological assessment of criminal profiling. *FBI Law Enforcement Bulletin, 49*, 22–25.

Avery-Clark, C. A., & Laws, D. R. (1984). Differential erection response patterns of sexual child abusers to stimuli describing activities with children. *Behavior Therapy, 15*, 71–83.

Babcock, J. C., Waltz, J., Jacobson, N. S., & Gottman, J. M. (1993). Power and violence: The relation between communication patterns, power discrepancies, and domestic violence. *Journal of Consulting and Clinical Psychology, 61*, 40–50.

Bachman, R. (1992). *Death and violence on the reservation.* New York: Auburn House.

Bailey, W. C. (1984). Poverty, inequality and city homicide rates. *Criminology, 22,* 531–550.

Ball, J. C., Shaffer, J. W., & Nurco, D. N. (1983). The day-to-day criminality of heroin addicts in Baltimore—a study in the continuity of offense rates. *Drug and Alcohol Dependence, 12,* 119–142.

Bancroft, H. (1976). Behavioral treatments of sexual deviations. In N. H. Leitenberg (Ed.), *Handbook of behavioral modifications and behavioral therapy.* Englewood Cliffs, NJ: Prentice Hall.

Bandura, A. (1965). Influence of models' reinforcement contingencies on the acquisition of imitative responses. *Journal of Personality and Social Psychology, 1,* 589–595.

Bandura, A. (1973a). *Aggression: A social learning analysis.* Englewood Cliffs, NJ: Prentice Hall.

Bandura, A. (1973b). Social learning theory of aggression. In J. F. Knutson (Ed.), *The control of aggression.* Chicago, IL: Aldine.

Bandura, A. (1977). *Social learning theory.* Englewood Cliffs, NJ: Prentice Hall.

Bandura, A. (1978). The self-system in reciprocal determinism. *American Psychologist, 33,* 344–358.

Bandura, A. (1983). Psychological mechanisms of aggression. In R. G. Geen & E. I. Donnerstein (Eds.), *Aggression: Theoretical and empirical reviews* (Vol. 1). New York: Academic Press.

Bandura, A. (1986). *Social foundations in thought and action: A social cognitive theory.* Englewood Cliffs, NJ: Prentice Hall.

Bandura, A. (1989). Human agency in social cognitive theory. *American Psychologist, 44,* 1175–1184.

Bandura, A., & Huston, A. (1961). Identification as a process of incidental learning. *Journal of Abnormal and Social Psychology, 63,* 311–318.

Bandura, A., Ross, D., & Ross, S. (1963). Vicarious reinforcement and imitative learning. *Journal of Abnormal and Social Psychology, 67,* 601–607.

Bandura, A., Underwood, B., & Fromson, M. E. (1975). Disinhibition of aggression through diffusion of responsibility and dehumanization of victims. *Journal of Research in Personality, 9,* 253–269.

Bandura, A., & Walters, R. H. (1959). *Adolescent aggression.* New York: Ronald Press.

Bard, L. A., Carter, D. L., Cerce, D. D., Knight, R. A., Rosenberg, R., & Schneider, B. (1987). *Behavioral Sciences & the Law, 5,* 203–220.

Bardone, A. M., Moffitt, T. E., & Caspi, A. (in press). Adult mental health and social outcomes of adolescent girls with depression and conduct disorder. *Development and Psychopathology.*

Baron, L. (1993). Gender inequality and child homicide: A state-level analysis. In A. V. Wilson (Ed.), *Homicide: The victim/offender connection.* Cincinnati, OH: Anderson.

Baron, R. A. (1977). *Human aggression.* New York: Plenum.

Baron, R. A. (1983). The control of human aggression: An optimistic perspective. *Journal of Social and Clinical Psychology, 1,* 97–119.

Baron, R. A., & Bell, P. A. (1975). Aggression and heat: Mediating effects of prior provocation and exposure to an aggressive model. *Journal of Personality and Social Psychology, 31,* 825–832.

Baron, R. A., & Byrne, D. (1977). *Social psychology* (2nd edition). Boston, MA: Allyn and Bacon.

Baron, R. A., & Lawton, S. F. (1972). Environmental influences on aggression: The facilitation of modeling effects by high ambient temperatures. *Psychonomic Science, 26,* 80–83.

Baron, R. A., & Ransberger, V. M. (1978). Ambient temperature and the occurrence of collective violence: The "long, hot summer" revisited. *Journal of Personality and Social Psychology, 36,* 361–366.

Bartol, C. R. (1975). The effects of chlorpromazine and detroamphetamine sulfate on the visual stimulation preferences of extraverts and introverts. *Psychophysiology, 12,* 22–31.

Bartol, C. R. (1988). Understanding delinquency: Causal loops and social systems. *Criminal Justice and Behavior, 15,* 394–401.

Bartol, C. R., & Bartol, A. M. (1994). *Psychology and law: Research and application* (2nd edition). Pacific Grove, CA: Brooks/Cole.

Bartol, C. R., & Bartol, A. M. (1998). *Delinquency and justice: A psychosocial approach* (2nd edition). Upper Saddle River, NJ: Prentice Hall.

Bartol, C. R., Griffin, R., & Clark, M. (1993, July). Nationwide survey of American correctional psychologists. Unpublished manuscript.

Bartol, C. R., & Holanchock, H. A. (1979). A test of Eysenck's theory of criminality on an American prisoner population. *Criminal Justice and Behavior, 6,* 245–249.

Battelle Law and Justice Center Report. (1977). *Forcible rape: An analysis of the legal issue.* Washington, DC: National Institute of Law Enforcement and Criminal Justice.

Baumer, T. L., & Rosenbaum, D. P. (1984). *Combating retail theft: Programs and strategies.* Boston, MA: Butterworth.

Beck, A. T. (1970). Cognitive therapy: Nature and relation to behavior therapy. *Behavior Therapy, 1,* 184–200.

Bell, P. A., & Baron, R. A. (1977). Aggression and ambient temperature: The inhibiting and facilitating effects of hot and cold environments. *Bulletin of the Psychonomic Society, 6,* 240–242.

Belsky, J., Lerner, R. M., & Spanier, G. B. (1984). *The child in the family.* New York: Random House.

Bennett, T., & Wright, R. (1984). *Burglars on burglary: Prevention and the offender.* Brookfield, VT: Gower.

Bensing, R. C., & Schroeder, O. (1960). *Homicide in an urban community.* Springfield, IL: Charles C. Thomas.

Berger, H. (1929). Uber das Electrenkephalogram des Menschen. *Archiv fur Psychiatrie und Nervenkrankheiten, 87,* 527–570.

Berkowitz, L. (1962). *Aggression: A social-psychological analysis.* New York: McGraw-Hill.

Berkowitz, L. (1969). The frustration-aggression hypothesis revisited. In L. Berkowitz (Ed.), *Roots of aggression.* New York: Atherton Press.

Berkowitz, L. (1970). The contagion of violence: An S-R mediational analysis of some effects of observed aggression. In W. J. Arnold & M. M. Page (Eds.), *Nebraska symposium on motivation*. Lincoln, NE: University of Nebraska Press.

Berkowitz, L. (1973). Words and symbols as stimuli to aggressive responses. In J. F. Knutson (Ed.), *The control of aggression*. Chicago, IL: Aldine.

Berkowitz, L. (1983). The experience of anger as a parallel process in the display of impulsive, "angry" aggression. In R. G. Geen & E. I. Donnerstein (Eds.), *Aggression: Theoretical and empirical reviews* (Vol. 1). New York: Academic Press.

Berkowitz, L. (1989). Frustration-aggression hypothesis: Examination and reformulation. *Psychological Bulletin, 106*, 59–73.

Berkowitz, L. (1994). Guns and youth. In L. E. Eron, J. H. Gentry, & P. Schlegel (Eds.), *Reason to hope: A psychosocial perspective on violence and youth*. Washington, DC: American Psychological Association.

Berkowitz, L., & Heimer, K. (1989). On the construction of the anger experience: Aversive events and negative priming in the formation of feelings. In L. Berkowitz (Ed.), *Advances in experimental social psychology* (Vol. 22). New York: Academic Press.

Berkowitz, L., & LePage, A. (1967). Weapons as aggression-eliciting stimuli. *Journal of Personality and Social Psychology, 7*, 202–207.

Berlyne, D. E. (1960). *Conflict, arousal, and curiosity*. New York: McGraw-Hill.

Berman, T., & Paisey, T. (1984). Personality in assaultive and non-assaultive juvenile male offenders. *Psychological Reports, 54*, 527–530.

Bernard, F. (1975). An inquiry among a group of pedophiles. *Journal of Sex Research, 11*, 242–255.

Berndt, T. (1979). Developmental changes in conformity to peers and parents. *Developmental Psychology, 15*, 608–616.

Berrueta-Clement, J. R., Schweinhart, L. J., Barnett, W. S., & Weikart. D. P. (1987). The effects of early educational intervention in adolescence and early adulthood. In J. D. Burhcard & S. N. Burchard (Eds.), *Prevention of delinquent behavior*. Newbury Park, CA: Sage.

Best, J. (1991). Endangered children in antisatanist rhetoric. In J. T. Richardson, J. Best, & D. G. Bromley (Eds.), *The satanism scare*. New York: Aldine De Gruyter.

Binder, A. (1988). Juvenile delinquency. *Annual Review of Psychology, 39*, 253–282.

Biskupic, J. (1994). Court: Insanity defense not a right. *Washington Post*, March 29, A2.

Björkqvist, K., Lagerspetz, M. J., & Kaukianinen, A. (1992). Do girls manipulate and boys fight? Developmental trends in regard to direct and indirect aggression. *Aggressive Behavior, 18*, 117–127.

Black, S. L., & Bevan, S. (1992). At the movies with Buss and Durkee: A natural experiment on film violence. *Aggressive Behavior, 18*, 37–45.

Blackburn, N., Weiss, J., & Lamberti, J. (1960). The sudden murderer. *Archives of General Psychiatry, 2*, 670–678.

Blackburn, R. (1968). Personality in relation to extreme aggression in psychiatric offenders. *British Journal of Psychiatry, 114*, 821–828.

Blackburn, R. (1988). On moral judgments and personality disorders. *British Journal of Psychiatry, 153,* 505–512.

Blackburn, R. (1993). *The psychology of criminal conduct: Theory, research and practice.* Chichester, Eng.: Wiley.

Blackburn, R. (1998). Criminality and the interpersonal circle in mentally disordered offenders. *Criminal Justice and Behavior, 25,* 155–176.

Blair, C. D., & Lanyon, R. I. (1981). Exhibitionism: An etiology and treatment. *Psychological Bulletin, 89,* 439–463.

Blau, J. R., & Blau, P. M. (1982). Metropolitan structure and violent crime. *American Sociological Review, 47,* 114–128.

Block, R. (1977). *Violent crime.* Lexington: MA: Lexington Books.

Bloomquist, E. R. (1970). The use and abuse of stimulants. In W. G. Clark & J. DelGiudice (Eds.), *Principles of psychopharmacology.* New York: Academic Press.

Blumer, D. (1976). Epilepsy and violence. In D. J. Madden & J. R. Lion (Eds.), *Rage, hate, assault, and other forms of violence.* New York: Spectrum Publishing.

Blumer, D., & Migeon, C. (1973). Treatment of impulsive behavior disorders in males with medroxy-progesterone acetate. Paper presented at the Annual Meeting of the American Psychiatric Association.

Blumer, H., Sutter, A., Ahmed, S., & Smith, R. (1967). *ADD center final report: The world of youthful drug use.* Berkeley, CA: University of California Press.

Blumstein, A., Cohen, J., Roth, J., & Visher, C. (Eds.) (1986). *Criminal careers and career criminals.* Washington, DC: National Academy Press.

Blumstein, A., Farrington, D. P., & Moitra, S. (1985). Delinquency careers: Innocents, desisters and persisters. In M. Tonry and N. Morris (Eds.), *Crime and justice: An annual review of research* (Vol. 6). Chicago, IL: University of Chicago Press.

Boehnert, C. E. (1989). Characteristics of successful and unsuccessful insanity pleas. *Law and Human Behavior, 13,* 31–39.

Bonta, J., Law, M., & Hanson, K. (1998). The prediction of criminal and violent recidivism among mentally disordered offenders: A meta-analysis. *Psychological Bulletin, 123,* 123–142.

Borduin, C. M., Mann, B. J., Cone, L. T., Henggeler, S. W., Fucci, B. R., Blaske, D. M., & Williams, R. (1995). Multisystemic treatment of serious juvenile offenders: Long-term prevention of criminality and violence. *Journal of Consulting and Clinical Psychology, 63,* 569–578.

Borgida, E. (1980). Evidentiary reform of rape laws: A psychological approach. In P. D. Lipsitt & B. D. Sales (Eds.), *New directions in psycholegal research.* New York: Van Nostrand Reinhold.

Borum, R. (1996). Improving the clinical practice of violence risk assessment. *American Psychologist, 51,* 945–956.

Borum, R., & Strentz, T. (1993, April). The borderline personality: Negotiation strategies. *FBI Law Enforcement Bulletin,* pp. 6–10.

Boudreau, J., Kwan, Q., Faragher, W., & Denault, G. (1977). *Arson and arson investigation.* Washington, DC: USGPO.

Bowden, K. M., Wilson, D. W., & Turner, L. K. (1958). A survey of blood alcohol testing in Victoria (1951–56). *Medical Journal of Australia, 45,* 13–15.

Bowker, L. H. (1983). *Beating wife-battering*. Lexington, MA: Lexington Books.

Boykin, A. W. (1986). The triple quandary and the schooling of Afro-American children. In U. Neisser (Ed.), *The school achievement of minority children*. Hillsdale, NJ: Erlbaum.

Boykin, A. W. (1994). Harvesting talent and culture: African-American children and educational reform. In R. Rossi (Ed.), *Schools and students at risk*. New York: Teachers College Press.

Bracey, D. H. (1982). Concurrent and consecutive abuse: The juvenile prostitute. In B. R. Price and N. Sokoloff (Eds.), *The criminal justice system and women*. New York: Clark Boardman.

Bradford, J. M. W. (1982). Arson: A clinical study. *Canadian Journal of Psychiatry, 27*, 188–193.

Brady, J. (1983). Arson, urban economy, and organized crime: The case of Boston. *Social Problems, 31*, 1–27.

Braithwaite, J. (1981). The myth of class and criminality reconsidered. *American Sociological Review, 46*, 36–57.

Brennan, T. (1987). Classification: An overview of selected methodological issues. In J. M. Gottfredson & M. Tonry (Eds.), *Prediction and classification: Criminal justice decision making* (Vol. 9). Chicago, IL: University of Chicago Press.

Brennan, P., Mednick, S. A., & Kandel, E. (1993). Congenital determinants of violent and property offending. In D. J. Pepler & K. H. Rubin (Eds.), *The development and treatment of childhood aggression*. Hillsdale, NJ: Erlbaum.

Brent, D. A. (1989). The psychological autopsy: Methodological issues for the study of adolescent suicide. *Suicide and Life Threatening Behavior, 19*, 43–57.

Brier, N. (1989). The relationship between learning disability and delinquency: A review and reappraisal. *Journal of Learning Disabilities, 22*, 546–553.

Briere, J. (1988). The long term clinical correlates of childhood sexual victimization. In R. A. Prentky & V. L. Quinsey (Eds.), *Human sexual aggression: Current perspectives*. New York: New York Academy of Sciences.

Briere, J., Malamuth, N., & Ceniti, J. (1981). Self-assessed rape proclivity: Attitudinal and sexual correlates. Paper presented at APA Meeting, Los Angeles, CA.

Brittain, R. P. (1970). The sadistic murderer. *Medicine, Science and the Law, 10*, 198–207.

Brodsky, S. L. (1973). *Psychologists in the criminal justice system*. Urbana, IL: University of Illinois Press.

Brodsky, S. L. (1977). Criminal and dangerous behavior. In D. Rimm & J. Somervill (Eds.), *Abnormal psychology*. New York: Academic Press.

Bromley, D. G. (1991). Satanism: The new cult scare. In J. T. Richardson, J. Best, & D. G. Bromley (Eds.), *The satanism scare*. New York: Aldine De Gruyter.

Brown, J. S., & Farber, I. E. (1951). Emotions conceptualized as intervening variables—with suggestions toward a theory of frustration. *Psychological Bulletin, 48*, 465–495.

Browne, A. (1987). *When battered women kill*. New York: Free Press.

Browne, A., & Finkelhor, D. (1986). Impact of child sexual abuse: A review of the research. *Psychological Bulletin, 99*, 66–77.

Brunet, B. L., Reiffenstein, R. J., Williams, T., & Wong, L. (1985–1986). Toxicity of phencyclidine and ethanol in combination. *Alcohol and Drug Research, 6,* 341–349.

Brussel, J. A. (1978). Casebook of a crime psychiatrist. New York: Bernard Geis Associates.

Buckle, A., & Farrington, D. P. (1984). An observational study of shoplifting. *British Journal of Criminology, 24,* 63–73.

Buckle, A., & Farrington, D. P. (1994). Measuring shoplifting by systematic observation: A replication study. *Psychology, Crime & Law, 1,* 133–141.

Buikhuisen, W., & Hemmel, J. J. (1972). Crime and conditioning. *British Journal of Criminology, 17,* 147–157.

Bukstel, L. H., & Kilmann, P. R. (1980). Psychological effects of imprisonment on confined individuals. *Psychological Bulletin, 88,* 469–493.

Bullock, H. A. (1955). Urban homicide in theory and fact. *Journal of Criminal Law, Criminology and Police Science, 45,* 565–575.

Bumpass, E. R., Fagelman, F. D., & Birx, R. J. (1983). Intervention with children who set fires. *American Journal of Psychotherapy, 37,* 328–345.

Burgess, P. K. (1972). Eysenck's theory of criminality: A test of some objectives of disconfirmatory evidence. *British Journal of Social and Clinical Psychology, 11,* 248–256.

Burgess, R. L., & Akers, R. L. (1966). A differential association-reinforcement theory of criminal behavior. *Social Problems, 14,* 128–147.

Burnam, M. A., Stein, J. A., Golding, J. M., Siegel, J. M., Sorenson, S. B., Forsythe, A. B., & Telles, C. A. (1988). Sexual assault and mental disorders in a community population. *Journal of Consulting and Clinical Psychology, 56,* 843–850.

Burton, N., & Steadman, H. J. (1978). Legal professionals' perceptions of the insanity defense. *Journal of Psychiatry and Law, 6,* 173–187.

Buss, A. H. (1966). *Psychopathology.* New York: Wiley.

Butler, R. A. (1954). Curiosity in monkeys. *Scientific American* (reprint #426). San Francisco, CA: W. H. Freeman.

Cairns, R. B., & Cairns, B. D. (1991). Social cognition and social networks: A developmental perspective. In D. J. Pepler & K. H. Rubin (Eds.), *The development and treatment of childhood aggression.* Hillsdale, NJ: Erlbaum.

Cairns, R. B., Cairns, B. D., Neckerman, H. J., Ferguson, L. L., & Gariépy, J. L. (1989). Growth and aggression: I. Childhood to early adolescence. *Developmental Psychology, 25,* 320–330.

Cairns, R. B., Cairns, B. D., Neckerman, H. J., Gest, S. D., & Gariépy, J. L. (1988). Social networks and aggressive behavior: Peer support or peer rejection. *Developmental Psychology, 24,* 815–826.

Calhoun, J. B. (1961). Phenomena associated with population density. *Proceedings of the National Academy of Sciences, 47,* 428–429.

Calhoun, J. B. (1962). Population density and social pathology. *Scientific American, 206,* 139–148.

Callahan, L. A., McGreevy, M. A., Cirincione, C., & Steadman, H. J. (1992). Measuring the effects of the guilty but mentally ill (GBMI) verdict. *Law and Human Behavior, 16,* 447–462.

Callahan, L. A., Steadman, H. J., McGreevy, M. A., Robbins, P. C. (1991). The volume and characteristics of insanity defense pleas: An eight-state study. *Bulletin of Psychiatry and the Law, 19,* 331–338.

Cameron, M. O. (1964). *The booster and the snitch.* New York: Free Press.

Camp, G. M., & Camp, C. G. (1991). *Corrections yearbook.* South Salem, NY: Criminal Justice Institute.

Campbell, A. (1993). *Men, women, and aggression.* New York: Basic Books.

Campbell, A., Muncer, S., & Coyle, E. (1992). Social representation of aggression as an explanation of gender differences: A preliminary study. *Aggressive Behavior, 18,* 95–108.

Canadian Government's Commission of Inquiry. (1971). *The non-medical use of drugs: Interim report.* London: Penguin Books.

Canter, S. (1973). Personality traits in twins. In G. Claridge, S. Canter, & W. I. Hume (Eds.), *Personality differences and biological variations: A study of twins.* Oxford, Eng.: Pergamon Press.

Cantwell, D. P. (1975). A medical model for research and clinical use with hyperactive children. In D. P. Cantwell (Ed.), *The hyperactive child.* New York: Spectrum.

Capute, A. J., Niedermeyer, E. F. L., & Richardson, I. (1968). The electroencephalogram in children with minimal cerebral dysfunction. *Pediatrics, 41,* 1104.

Carlson, K. A. (1990). 1989 survey of psychological testing practices in prisons. *Correctional Psychologist, 22,* 9–11.

Carlson, M., Marcus-Newhall, A., & Miller, N. (1990). Effects of situational aggression cues: A quantitative review. *Journal of Personality and Social Psychology, 58,* 622–633.

Carlson, R. J. (1976). *The dilemmas of corrections.* Lexington, MA: Lexington Books.

Carnes, P. (1983). Out of the shadows: Understanding sexual addiction. Minneapolis, MN: Compcare Publications.

Carney, R. M., & Williams, B. D. (1983). Premenstrual syndrome: A criminal defense. *Notre Dame Law Review, 59,* 253–269.

Carraher, T. N., Carraher, D., & Schliemann, A. D. (1985). Mathematics in the streets and schools. *British Journal of Developmental Psychology, 3,* 21–29.

Carter, D. L., & Katz, A. J. (1996). *Computer crime: An emerging challenge for law enforcement.* Washington, DC: U.S. Department of Justice. Available: www.fbi.gov/leb/dec961.txt.

Carter, R. (1980). Arson and arson investigation in the United States. *Fire Journal, 74,* 40–47.

Caspi, A., Elder, G. H., & Bem, D. J. (1987). Moving against the world: Life course patterns of explosive children. *Developmental Psychology, 23,* 308–313.

Cavior, N., & Howard, L. R. (1973). Facial attractiveness and juvenile delinquency among black offenders and white offenders. *Journal of Abnormal Child Psychology, 1,* 202–213.

Ceci, S. J., & Bruck, M. (1993). Suggestibility of the child witness: A historical review and synthesis. *Psychological Bulletin, 113,* 403–439.

Chaffee, S. H., & McLeod, J. M. (1971). Adolescents, parents, and television violence. Paper presented at the meeting of the American Psychological Association, Washington, DC.

Chalkley, A. J., & Powell, G. E. (1983). The clinical description of forty-eight cases of clinical fetishism. *British Journal of Psychiatry, 142,* 292–295.

Chamberlain, P. (1996). Treatment foster care for adolescents with conduct disorders and delinquency. In P. S. Jensen & D. Hibbs (Eds.), *Psychological treatment with research with children and adolescents.* Rockville, MD: National Institute of Mental Health.

Chappell, D. (1977a). *Forcible rape: A national survey of the response by police (LEAA).* Washington, DC: USPGO.

Chappell, D. (1977b). *Forcible rape: A national survey of the response by prosecutors* (LEAA). Washington, DC: USPGO.

Charney, J. (1980). The new diagnostic and statistical manual of mental disorders: Or, what's in a name? *Philosophical Psychology, 1,* 59–71.

Cheatwood, D. (1988). Is there a season for homicide? *Criminology, 26,* 287–306.

Chesney-Lind, M. (1986). Women and crime. *Signs, 12,* 78–96.

Chesno, F. A., & Kilmann, P. R. (1975). Effects of stimulation intensity on sociopathic avoidance learning. *Journal of Abnormal Psychology, 84,* 144–150.

Chimbos, P. D. (1973). A study of breaking and entering offenses in "Northern City," Ontario. *Canadian Journal of Criminology and Corrections, 15,* 316–325.

Chorover, S. L. (1980). Violence: A localizable problem? In E. S. Valenstein (Ed.), *The psychosurgery debate.* San Francisco, CA: W. H. Freeman.

Christiansen, K. O. (1977). A review of studies of criminality among twins. In S. Mednick & K. O. Christiansen (Eds.), *Biosocial bases of criminal behavior.* New York: Gardiner Press.

Christie, M. M., Marshall, W. L., & Lanthier. R. D. (1979). *A descriptive study of incarcerated rapists and pedophiles.* Ottawa: Report to the Solicitor General of Canada.

Christoffel, K. K., & Liu, K. (1983). Homicide death rates in childhood in 23 developed countries: U.S. rates atypically high. *Child Abuse and Neglect, 7,* 339–345.

Churgin, M. M. (1983). The transfer of inmates of mental health facilities: Developments in the law. In J. Monahan & H. J. Steadman (Eds.), *Mentally disordered offenders.* New York: Plenum.

Chute, C. L. (1949). Fifty years of the juvenile court. In M. Bell (Ed.), *Current approaches to delinquency.* New York: National Probation and Parole Association.

Claridge, G. (1973). Final remarks. In G. Claridge, S. Canter, & W. I. Hume (Eds.), *Personality differences and biological variations.* Oxford, Eng.: Pergamon Press.

Clark, J. P., & Hollinger, R. C. (1983). *Theft by employees in work organizations.* Washington, DC: USGPO.

Clark, K. B. (1971). The pathos of power: A psychological perspective. *American Psychologist, 26,* 1047–1057.

Cleckley, H. (1976). *The mask of sanity* (5th edition). St. Louis, MO: Mosby.

Clements, C. B. (1987). Psychologists in adult correctional institutions: Getting off the treadmill. In E. K. Morris & C. J. Braukmann (Eds.), *Behavioral approaches to crime and delinquency.* New York: Plenum.

Cleveland, F. P. (1955). Problems in homicide investigation IV: The relationship of alcohol to homicide. *Cincinnati Journal of Medicine, 36,* 28–30.

Cline, V. B., Croft, R. G., & Courrier, S. (1973). Desensitization of children to television violence. *Journal of Personality and Social Psychology, 27,* 360–365.

Cochrane, R. (1974). Crime and personality: Theory and evidence. *Bulletin of the British Psychological Society, 27,* 19–22.

Cocozza, J. J., & Steadman, H. J. (1976). The failure of psychiatric prediction of dangerousness: Clear and convincing evidence. *Rutgers Law Review, 29,* 1084–1101.

Cohen, F. (1980). *The law of deprivation of liberty: A study in social control.* St. Paul, MN: West.

Cohen, J. (1983). Incapacitation as a strategy for crime control. In M. Tonry & N. Morris (Eds.), *Crime and justice: An annual review of research* (Vol. 5). Chicago, IL: University of Chicago Press.

Cohen, M. L., Garafalo, R., Boucher, R., & Seghorn, T. (1971). The psychology of rapists. *Seminars in Psychiatry, 3,* 307–327.

Cohen, M., Seghorn, T., & Calmas, W. (1969). Sociometric study of the sex offender. *Journal of Abnormal Psychology, 74,* 249–255.

Cohen, P., Cohen, J., & Brook, J. (1993). An epidemiological study of disorders in late childhood and adolescence—II. Persistent disorders. *Journal of Child Psychology and Psychiatry, 34,* 869–877.

Cohn, V. (1986). Crack use. *NIDA Notes, 1,* 6.

Coie, J. D., Belding, M., & Underwood, M. (1988). Aggression and peer rejection in childhood. In B. Lahey & A. Kazdin (Eds.), *Advances in clinical child psychology.* Vol. 2. New York: Plenum.

Coie, J. D., Dodge, K., & Kupersmith, J. (1990). Peer group behavior and social status. In S. R. Asher & J. D. Coie (Eds.), *Peer rejection in childhood.* Cambridge, Eng.: Cambridge University Press.

Coie, J. D., Underwood, M., & Lochman, J. E. (1991). Programmatic intervention with aggressive children in the school setting. In D. J. Pepler & K. H. Rubin (Eds.), *The development and treatment of childhood aggression.* Hillsdale, NJ: Erlbaum.

Cole, K. E., Fisher, G., & Cole, S. S. (1968). Women who kill. *Archives of General Psychiatry, 19,* 1–8.

Coleman, J. C. (1976). *Abnormal psychology and modern life* (5th edition). Glenview, IL: Scott, Foresman.

Coleman, J. W. (1998). *The criminal elite* (4th edition). New York: St. Martin's Press.

Collins, J. J. (1981). Alcohol use and criminal behavior. In J. J. Collins (Ed.), *Drinking and crime.* New York: Guilford.

Comer, R. J. (1992). *Abnormal psychology.* New York: W. H. Freeman.

Conklin, J. E. (1972). *Robbery and the criminal justice system.* Philadelphia, PA: Lippincott.

Conklin, J. E. (1977). *"Illegal but not criminal."* Englewood Cliffs, NJ: Prentice Hall.

Conly, C., & McEwan, J. T. (1990, January/February). Computer crime. *NIJ Reports.* Washington, DC: USGPO.

Cook, P. J., & Ludwig, J. (1997). Guns in America: National survey on private ownership and use of firearms. *NIJ Research in Brief.* Washington, DC: National Institute of Justice.

Correctional Service of Canada. (1990). *Forum on corrections research, 2*, No. 1. Ottawa: Author.

Cortes, J. B., & Gatti, F. M. (1972). *Delinquency and crime: A biopsychosocial approach.* New York: Seminar Press.

Coscina, D. V. (1997). The biopsychology of impulsivity: Focus on brain serotonin. In C. D. Webster & M. A. Jackson (Eds.), *Impulsivity: Theory, assessment, and treatment.* New York: Guilford Press.

Cowley, G. (1993, July 26). The not-young and the restless. *Newsweek,* pp. 48–49.

Craft, M. (1966). The meanings of the term "psychopath." In M. Craft (Ed.), *Psychopathic disorders and their assessment.* Oxford, Eng.: Pergamon Press.

Craft, M., Stephenson, G., & Granger, C. (1964). A controlled trial of authoritarian and self-governing regimes with adolescent psychopaths. *American Journal of Orthopsychiatry, 34,* 543–554.

Crawford, J., & Heather, N. (1987). Public attitudes to the disease concept of alcoholism. *The International Journal of Addiction, 22,* 1129–1138.

Cressey, D. R. (1953). *A study in the social psychology of embezzlement: Other people's money.* Glencoe, IL: Free Press.

Crick, N. R. (1995). Relational aggression: The role of intent attributions, feelings of distress, and provocation type. *Development and Psychopathology, 7,* 313–322.

Crick, N. R., & Grotpeter, J. K. (1995). Relational aggression, gender, and social-psychological adjustment. *Child Development, 66,* 710–722.

Crider, R. (1986). Phencyclidine: Changing abuse patterns. In D. H. Clovet (Ed.), *Phencyclidine: An update.* Rockville, MD: National Institute of Drug Abuse.

Critchley, M. (1951). *The trial of Neville George Clevely Heath.* London: William Hodge.

Critchlow, B. (1986). The powers of John Barleycorn: Beliefs about the effects of alcohol on social behavior. *American Psychologist, 41,* 751–764.

Critchton, R. (1959). *The great imposter.* New York: Random House.

Crocker, A. G., & Hodgins, S. (1997). The criminality of noninstitutionalized mentally retarded person: Evidence from a birth cohort followed to age 30. *Criminal Justice and Behavior, 24,* 432–454.

Cromwell, P. F., Olson, J. F., & Avary, D. W. (1991). *Breaking and entering: An ethnographic analysis of burglary.* Newbury Park, CA: Sage.

Crowe, R. R. (1974). An adoptive study of antisocial personality. *Archives of General Psychiatry, 31,* 785–791.

Cruise, K. R., & Rogers, R. (1998). An analysis of competency to stand trial: An integration of case law and clinical knowledge. *Behavioral Sciences and the Law, 16,* 35–50.

Culberton, F. M., Feral, C. H., & Gabby, S. (1989). Pattern analysis of Wechlser Intelligence Scale for Children-Revised profiles of delinquent boys. *Journal of Clinical Psychology, 45,* 651–660.

Cullen, F., & Gilbert, K. E. (1982). *Reaffirming rehabilitation.* Cincinnati, OH: Anderson.

Cunnien, A. J. (1985). Pathological gambling as an insanity defense. *Behavioral Sciences and the Law, 3,* 85–101.

Dale, M. W. (1976). Barriers to the rehabilitation of ex-offenders. *Crime and Delinquency, 22,* 322–337.

Dalgaard, O. S., & Kringlen, E. (1976). A Norwegian twin study of criminality. *British Journal of Criminology, 16,* 213–233.

Dalton, K. (1961). Menstruation and crime. *British Medical Journal, 2,* 1752–1753.

Dalton, K. (1964). *The premenstrual syndrome.* Springfield, IL: Charles C. Thomas.

Daniels, D. N., & Gilula, M. F. (1970). Violence and the struggle for existence. In D. Daniels, M. Gilula, & F. Ochberg (Eds.), *Violence and the struggle for existence.* Boston, MA: Little, Brown.

David, P. R. (1974). *The world of the burglar.* Albuquerque, NM: University of New Mexico Press.

Davis, G. E., & Leitenberg, H. (1987). Adolescent sex offenders. *Psychological Bulletin, 101,* 417–427.

Davis, M. G., Lundman, R. J., & Martinez, R. (1991). Private corporate justice: Store police, shoplifters, and civil recovery. *Social Problems, 38,* 395–411.

Decostanza, E., & Scholes, H. (1988). Women behind bars: Their numbers increase. *Corrections Today, 50,* 104–108.

Delgado-Escueta, A., Mattson, R., & King, L. (1981). The nature of aggression during epileptic seizures. *New England Journal of Medicine, 305,* 711–716.

D'Emilio, J., & Freedman, E. B. (1988). *Intimate matters: A history of sexuality in America.* New York: Harper & Row.

Derville, P., L'Epee, P., Lazarin, H. J., & Derville, E. (1961). Statistical indications of a possible relationship between alcoholism and criminality: An inquiry into the Bordeaux region. *Revue Alcoholisme, 7,* 20–21.

Diener, E. (1980). Deindividuation: The absence of self-awareness and self-regulation in group members. In P. Paulus (Ed.), *The psychology of group influence.* Hillsdale, NJ: Erlbaum.

Dietz, P. E., Hazelwood, R. R., & Warren, J. (1990). The sexually sadistic criminal and his offenses. *Bulletin of the American Academy of Psychiatry and Law, 18,* 163–178.

Dion, K. (1972). Physical attractiveness and evaluations of children's transgressions. *Journal of Personality and Social Psychology, 24,* 207–213.

Dion, K., Berscheid, E., & Walster, E. (1972). What is beautiful is good. *Journal of Personality and Social Psychology, 24,* 285–290.

Diserens, C. M. (1925). Psychological objectivism. *Psychological Review, 32,* 121–152.

Dishion, T. J., & Andrews, D. W. (1995). Preventing escalation in problem behaviors with high-risk young adolescents: Immediate and 1-year outcomes. *Journal of Consulting and Clinical Psychology, 63,* 538–548.

Dix, G. E. (1976). Differential processing of abnormal sex offenders. *Journal of Criminal Law and Criminology, 67,* 233–243.

Dix, G. E. (1980). Clinical evaluation of the "dangerous" if "normal" criminal defendants. *Virginia Law Review, 66,* 523–581.

Dix, G. E. (1983). Special dispositional alternatives for abnormal offenders: Developments in the law. In J. Monahan & H. J. Steadman (Eds.), *Mentally disordered offenders.* New York: Plenum.

Dodge, K. A. (1986). A social information processing model of social competence in children. In M. Perlmutter (Ed.), *The Minnesota symposium on child psychology*. Hillsdale, NJ: Erlbaum.

Dodge, K. A. (1993a). The future of research on the treatment of conduct disorder. *Development and Psychopathology, 5*, 311–319.

Dodge, K. A. (1993b). Social-cognitive mechanisms in the development of conduct disorder and depression. *Annual Review of Psychology, 44*, 559–584.

Dodge, K. A., & Coie, J. D. (1987). Social information processing factors in reactive and proactive aggression in children's peer groups. *Journal of Personality and Social Psychology, 53*, 1146–1158.

Doerner, W. G. (1988). The impact of medical resources on criminally induced lethality: A further examination. *Criminology, 26*, 171–179.

Doerner, W. G., & Speir, J. C. (1986). Stitch and sew: The impact of medical resources upon criminally induced lethality. *Criminology, 24*, 319–330.

Dollard, J., Doob, L. W., Miller, N. E., Mowrer, O. H., & Sears, R. R. (1939). *Frustration and aggression*. New Haven, CT: Yale University Press.

Donnerstein, E. (1983). Erotica and human aggression. In R. G. Geen & E. I. Donnerstein (Eds.), *Aggression: Theoretical and empirical reviews* (Vol. 2). New York: Academic Press.

d'Orban, P. T., & O'Connor, A. (1989). Women who kill their parents. *British Journal of Psychiatry, 154*, 27–33.

Douglas, J. E., Burgess, A. W., Burgess, A. G., & Ressler, R. K. (1992). *Crime classification manual*. New York: Lexington Books.

Douglas, J. E., & Munn, C. (1992a). The detection of staging and personation at the crime scene. In J. E. Douglas, A. W. Burgess, A. G. Burgess, & R. K. Ressler (Eds.), *Crime classification manual*. New York: Lexington Books.

Douglas, J. E., & Munn, C. (1992b). Modus operandi and the signature aspects of violent crime. In J. E. Douglas, A. W. Burgess, A. G. Burgess, & R. K. Ressler (Eds.), *Crime classification manual*. New York: Lexington Books.

Douglas, J. E., & Munn, C. (1992c, February). Violent crime scene analysis. *FBI Law Enforcement Bulletin*, pp. 1–10.

Douglas, J. E., Ressler, R. K., Burgess, A. W., & Hartman. C. R. (1986). Criminal profiling from crime scene analysis. *Behavioral Sciences and the Law, 4*, 401–421.

Driver, E. D. (1961). Interaction and criminal homicide in India. *Social Forces, 40*, 153–158.

DSM-II. (1968). *Diagnostic and statistical manual of mental disorders* (2nd edition). Washington, DC: American Psychiatric Association.

DSM-III. (1980). *Diagnostic and statistical manual of mental disorders* (3rd edition). Washington, DC: American Psychiatric Association.

DSM-III-R. (1987). *Diagnostic and statistical manual of mental disorders* (Revised edition). Washington, DC: American Psychiatric Association.

DSM-IV. (1994). *Diagnostic and statistical manual of mental disorders* (4th edition). Washington, DC: American Psychiatric Association.

Dull, R. T., & Giacopassi, D. J. (1987). Demographic correlates of sexual and dating attitudes: A study of date rape. *Criminal Justice and Behavior, 14*, 175–193.

Dunn, C. S. (1976). *The patterns and distribution of assault incident characteristics among social areas.* Albany, NY: Criminal Justice Research Center, Analytic Report 14.

Easterbrook, J. A. (1959). The effect of emotion on cue utilization and the organization of behavior. *Psychological Review, 66*, 183–201.

Eaton, J., & Polk, K. (1961). *Measuring delinquency.* Pittsburgh, PA: University of Pittsburgh Press.

Ebert, B. W. (1987). Guide to conducting a psychological autopsy. *Professional Psychology: Research and Practice, 18*, 52–56.

Edwards, S. (1983). Sexuality, sexual offenses, and conception of victims in the criminal justice process. *Victimology: An International Journal, 8*, 113–128.

Efran, M. G., & Cheyne, J. A. (1974). Affective concomitants of the invasion of shared space: Behavioral, physiological, and verbal indicators. *Journal of Personality and Social Psychology, 29*, 219–226.

Ehrlich, S. K., & Keogh, R. P. (1956). The psychopath in a mental institution. *Archives of Neurology and Psychiatry, 76*, 286–295.

Eisenhower, M. S. (Chairman). (1969). *Commission statement on violence in television entertainment programs.* Washington, DC: USGPO.

Elliott, D. S. (1989). Criminal justice procedures in family violence crimes. In L. Ohlin & M. Tonry (Eds.), *Family violence* (Vol. 11). Chicago, IL: University of Chicago Press.

Elliott, D. S., Ageton, S. S., & Huizinga, D. (1980). *The national youth survey.* Boulder, CO: Behavioral Research Institute.

Elliott, D. S., Dunford, T. W., & Huizinga, D. (1987). The identification and prediction of career offenders utilizing self-reported and official data. In J. D. Burchard & S. N. Burchard (Eds.), *Prevention of delinquent behavior.* Newbury Park, CA: Sage.

Elliott, D. S., Huizinga, D., & Ageton, S. S. (1985). *Explaining delinquency and drug use.* Beverly Hills, CA: Sage.

Ellis, A. (1962). *Reason and emotion in psychotherapy.* New York: Lyle Stuart.

Ellis, L. (1982). Genetics and criminal behavior: Evidence through the end of the 1970's. *Criminology, 20*, 43–66.

Emery, R. E., & Laumann-Billings, L. (1998). An overview of the nature, causes, and consequences of abusive family relationships. *American Psychologist, 53*, 121–135.

Epstein, J. F., & Gfroerer, J. C. (1997, August). *Heroin abuse in the United States.* Rockville, MD: Substance Abuse and Mental Health Services Administration.

Epstein, S., & Taylor, S. P. (1967). Instigation to aggression as a function of degree of defeat and perceived aggressive intent of the opponent. *Journal of Personality, 35*, 265–289.

Eron, L. D. (1963). Relationship of TV violence habits and aggressive behavior in children. *Journal of Abnormal and Social Psychology, 67*, 193–196.

Eron, L. D., & Huesmann, L. P. (1984). The relation of prosocial behavior to the development of aggression and psychopathology. *Aggressive Behavior, 10*, 201–211.

Eron, L. D., & Huesmann, L. R. (1986). The role of television in the development of prosocial and antisocial behavior. In D. Olweus, J. Block, and M. Radke-

Yarrow (Eds.), *Development of antisocial and prosocial behavior: Research, theories and issues*. Orlando, FL: Academic Press.

Eron, L. D., Huesmann, L. P., & Zelli, A. (1991). The role of parental variables in the learning of aggression. In D. J. Pepler & K. H. Rubin (Eds.), *The development and treatment of childhood aggression*. Hillsdale, NJ: Erlbaum.

Eron, L. D., & Slaby, R. G. (1994). Introduction. In L. D. Eron, J. H. Gentry, & P. Schlegel (Eds.), *Reason to hope: A psychosocial perspective on violence and youth*. Washington, DC: American Psychological Association.

Eskridge, C. W. (1983). Prediction of burglary: A research note. *Journal of Criminal Justice, 11*, 67–75.

Esquirol, E. (1838). *Des maladies mentales*. Paris: Bailliére.

Evans, D. (1970). Exhibitionism. In C. G. Costello (Ed.), *Symptoms of psychopathology: A handbook*. New York: Wiley.

Ewing, C. P. (1990). Psychological self-defense: A proposed justification for battered women who kill. *Law and Human Behavior, 14*, 579–594.

Eysenck, H. J. (1964). *Crime and personality*. London: Routledge & Kegan Paul.

Eysenck, H. J. (1967). *The biological basis of personality*. Springfield, IL: Charles C. Thomas.

Eysenck, H. J. (1971). *Readings in extraversion-introversion*. Volume 2. *Fields of application*. New York: Wiley-Interscience.

Eysenck, H. J. (1973). *The inequality of man*. San Diego, CA: EDITS Publishers.

Eysenck, H. J. (1977). *Crime and personality* (2nd edition). London: Routledge & Kegan Paul.

Eysenck, H. J. (1981). *A model for personality*. New York: Springer.

Eysenck, H. J. (1983). Personality, conditioning, and antisocial behavior. In W. S. Laufer & J. M. Day (Eds.), *Personality theory, moral development, and criminal behavior*. Lexington, MA: Lexington Books.

Eysenck, H. J. (1996). Personality and crime: Where do we stand? *Psychology, Crime & Law, 2*, 143–152.

Eysenck, H. J., & Eysenck, S. B. G. (1971). A comparative study of criminals and matched controls on three dimensions of personality. *British Journal of Social and Clinical Psychology, 10*, 362–366.

Eysenck, H. J., & Gudjonsson, G. H. (1989). *The causes and cures of criminality*. New York: Plenum.

Eysenck, H. J., & Rachman, S. (1965). *The causes and cures of neurosis*. San Diego, CA: Robert R. Knapp.

Eysenck, S. B. G., & Eysenck, H. J. (1970). Crime and personality: An empirical study of the three-factor theory. *British Journal of Criminology, 10*, 225–239.

Fagan, J. (1989). Cessation of family violence. In L. Ohlin & M. Tonry (Eds.), *Family violence* (Vol. 11). Chicago, IL: University of Chicago Press.

Farrington, D. P. (1979). Environmental stress, delinquent behavior, and conviction. In I. G. Sarason & C. D. Spielberger (Eds.), *Stress and anxiety* (Vol. 6). Washington, DC: Hemisphere.

Farrington, D. P. (1987). Predicting individual crime rates. In D. M. Gottfredson & M. Tonry (Eds.), *Prediction and classification* (Vol. 10). Chicago, IL: University of Chicago Press.

Farrington, D. P. (1991). Childhood aggression and adult violence: Early precursors and later life outcomes. In D. J. Pepler & K. H. Rubin (Eds.), *The development and treatment of childhood aggression*. Hillsdale, NJ: Erlbaum.

Farrington, D. P., Biron, L., & LeBlanc, M. (1982). Personality and delinquency in London and Montreal. In J. Gunn & D. P. Farrington (Eds.), *Abnormal offenders, delinquency, and the criminal justice system*. Chichester, Eng.: Wiley.

Farrington, D. P., & Burrows, J. N. (1993). Did shoplifting really decrease? *British Journal of Criminology, 33*, 57–59.

Farrington, D. P., & Hawkins, J. D. (1991). Predicting participation, early onset, and later persistence in officially recorded offending. *Criminal Behavior and Mental Health, 1*, 1–33.

Faupel, C. E. (1991). *Shooting dope: Career patterns of hard-core heroin users*. Gainsville, FL: University of Florida Press.

Federal Bureau of Investigation. (1992). *Killed in the line of duty: A study of selected felonious killings of law enforcement officers*. Washington, DC: U.S. Department of Justice.

Federal Bureau of Investigation. (1996). *Terrorism in the United States, 1995*. Washington, DC: USGPO.

Federal Bureau of Investigation. (1997). *Uniform Crime Reports 1996*. Washington, DC: USGPO.

Fehrenbach, P. A., Smith, W., Monastersky, C., & Deisher, R. W. (1986). Adolescent sexual offenders: Offender and offense characteristics. *American Journal of Orthopsychiatry, 56*, 225–233.

Feinberg, G. (1984). Profile for the elderly shoplifter. In E. S. Newman, D. J. Newman, & M. L. Gewirtz (Eds.), *Elderly criminals*. Cambridge, MA: Oelgeschlager, Gunn & Hain.

Feldman, M. P. (1977). *Criminal behavior: A psychological analysis*. London: Wiley.

Fenichel, O. (1945). *The psychoanalytic theory of neurosis*. New York: W. W. Norton.

Feshbach, S. (1964). The function of aggression and the regulation of aggressive drive. *Psychological Review, 71*, 257–272.

Feucht, T. W., & Kyle, G. M. (1996, November). Methamphetamine use among adult arrestees: Findings of the DUF program. *NIJ Research in Brief*. Washington, DC: U.S. Department of Justice.

Field, S. (1992). The effect of temperature on crime. *British Journal of Criminology, 32*, 340–351.

Finkelhor, D. (1979). *Sexually victimized children*. New York: Free Press.

Finkelhor, D., & Araji, S. (1986). Explanations of pedophilia: A four factor model. *The Journal of Sex Research, 22*, 145–161.

Finkelhor, D., & Dziuba-Leatherman, J. (1994). Children as victims of violence: A national survey. *Pediatrics, 94*, 413–420.

Finkelhor, D., & Lewis, I. A. (1988). An epidemiologic approach to the study of child molestation. In R. A. Prentky & V. L. Quinsey (Eds.), *Human sexual aggression: Current perspectives*. New York: New York Academy of Sciences.

Fisher, R. S. (1951). Symposium on the compulsory use of chemical tests for alcoholic intoxication. *Maryland Medical Journal, 3*, 291–292.

Fiske, D. E., & Maddi, S. R. (1961). *Functions of varied experience*. Homewood, IL: Dorsey.

Fitzhugh, K. B. (1973). Some neuropsychological features of delinquent subjects. *Perceptual and Motor Skills, 36*, 494.

Flor-Henry, P. (1973). Psychiatric syndromes considered as manifestations of lateralized temporal-limbic dysfunction. In L. V. Latiner & K. E. Livingston (Eds.), *Surgical approaches in psychiatry*. Lancaster, Eng.: Medical and Technical Publishing.

Flor-Henry, P., & Yeudall, L. T. (1973). Lateralized cerebral dysfunction in depression and in aggressive criminal psychopathy. *International Research Communications, 7*, 31.

Flynn, E. E. (1983). Crime as a major social issue. *American Behavioral Scientist, 27*, 7–42.

Fois, A. (1961). *The electroencephalogram of the normal child*. Springfield, IL: Charles C. Thomas.

Forehand, R., Wierson, M., Frame, C. L., Kemptom, T., & Armistead, L. (1991). Juvenile firesetting: A unique syndrome or an advanced level of antisocial behavior? *Behavioral Research and Therapy, 29*, 125–128.

Fox, R. G. (1971). The XYY offender: A modern myth? *Journal of Criminal Law, Criminology, and Police Science, 62*, 59–73.

Franke, D. (1975). *The torture doctor*. New York: Avon.

Freedman, J. L. (1975). *Crowding and behavior*. San Francisco, CA: W. H. Freeman.

Freedman, J. L. (1988). Television violence and aggression: What the evidence shows. In S. Oskamp (Ed.), *Applied social psychology annual: Television as a social issue* (Vol. 8). Newbury Park, CA: Sage.

Freedman, J. L., Levy, A., Buchanan, R. W., & Price, J. (1972). Crowding and human aggressiveness. *Journal of Experimental Social Psychology, 8*, 528–548.

Freedman, J. L., Sears, D. O., & Carlsmith, J. J. (1978). *Social psychology* (3rd edition). Englewood Cliffs, NJ: Prentice Hall.

French, J. D. (1957). The reticular formation. *Scientific American, 196*, 54–60.

Frieze, I. H., & Browne, A. (1989). Violence in marriage. In L. Ohlin & M. Tonry (Eds.), *Family violence* (Vol. 11). Chicago, IL: University of Chicago Press.

Frisbie, L. V. (1965). Treated sex offenders who reverted to sexually deviant behavior. *Federal Probation, 29*, 52–57.

Funk, J. B., & Buchman, D. D. (1996). Playing violent video and computer games and the adolescent self-concept. *Journal of Communication, Spring*, 84–89.

Fuselier, G. D., & Noesner, G. W. (1990, July). Confronting the terrorist hostage taker. *FBI Law Enforcement Bulletin*, pp. 6–11.

Furby, L., Weinrott, M. R., & Blackshaw, L. (1989). Sex offender recidivism: A review. *Psychological Bulletin, 105*, 3–30.

Fyfe, J. F. (1984). Police dilemmas in processing elderly offenders. In E. S. Newman, D. J. Newman, & M. L. Gewirtz (Eds.), *Elderly criminals*. Cambridge, MA: Oelgeschalger, Gunn & Hain.

Gabrielli, W. F., & Mednick, S. A. (1983). Genetic correlates of criminal behavior. *American Behavioral Scientist, 27*, 59–74.

Galanter, M. (1974). Why the "haves" come out ahead: Speculations on the limits of social change. *Law & Society Review, 9*, 95–160.

Gallup, G. E., & Castelli, J. (1987). *The American Catholic people*. Garden City, NY: Doubleday.

Galvin, J., & Polk, K. (1983). Juvenile justice: Time for new direction? *Delinquency and Crime, 29,* 325–332.

Garbarino, J. (1989). The incidence and prevalence of child maltreatment. In L. Ohlin & M. Tonry (Eds.), *Family violence* (Vol. 11). Chicago, IL: University of Chicago Press.

Garbarino, J., & Asp, C. E. (1981). *Successful schools and competent students.* Lexington, MA: Lexington Books.

Gardner, M. (1993). The false memory syndrome. *Skeptical Inquirer, 17,* 370–375.

Garofalo, J. (1977). *Public opinion about crime: The attitudes of victims and nonvictims in selected cities.* Washington, DC: USGPO.

Gebhard, P. H., Gagnon, J. H., Pomeroy, W. B., & Christenson, C. V. (1965). *Sex offenders.* New York: Harper & Row.

Geis, G. (1988). From Deuteronomy to deniability: A historical perlustration on white-collar crime. *Justice Quarterly, 5,* 7–32.

Geis, G. (1997). Preface. In G. Green, *Occupational crime* (2nd edition). Chicago, IL: Nelson-Hall.

Geis, G., & Monahan, J. (1976). The social ecology of violence. In T. Lickona (Ed.), *Moral development and behavior.* New York: Holt, Rinehart & Winston.

Gelles, R. J. (1982). Domestic criminal violence. In M. E. Wolfgang & N. A. Weiner (Eds.), *Criminal violence.* Beverly Hills, CA: Sage.

Gendreau, P., Little, T., & Goggin, C. (1996). A meta-analysis of the predictors of adult offender recidivism: What works! *Criminology, 34,* 575–607.

Gendreau, P., & Ross, P. (1983). Correctional treatment. *Juvenile and Family Court Journal, Winter,* 31–39.

George, W. H., & Marlatt, G. A. (1989). Introduction. In D. R. Laws (Ed.), *Relapse prevention with sex offenders.* New York: Guilford Press.

Gerbner, G., & Gross, L. (1976). Living with television: The violence profile. *Journal of Communications, 26,* 173–199.

Gerbner, G., Gross, L., Morgan, M., & Signorielli, N. (1981). Health and medicine on television. *The New England Journal of Medicine, 305,* 901–904.

Gibbens, T. C. (1957). Female offenders. *British Journal of Delinquency, 8,* 23–25.

Gibbens, T. C. (1981). Female crime in England and Wales. In F. Adler (Ed.), *The incidence of female criminality in the contemporary world.* New York: New York University Press.

Gibbens, T. C., Pond, D. A., & Stafford-Clark, D. (1955). A follow-up study of criminal psychopaths. *British Journal of Delinquency, 5,* 126–136.

Gibbons, D. C. (1977). *Society, crime and criminal careers* (3rd edition). Englewood Cliffs, NJ: Prentice Hall.

Gibbons, D. C. (1988). Some critical observation on criminal types and criminal careers. *Criminal Justice and Behavior, 15,* 8–23.

Gibson, E., & Klein, S. (1961). *Murder.* London: H.M.S.O.

Gibson, H. B. (1967). Self-reported delinquency among schoolboys, and their attitudes to the police. *British Journal of Social and Clinical Psychology, 6,* 168–173.

Gil, D. (1970). *Violence against children: Physical child abuse in the United States.* Cambridge, MA: Harvard University Press.

Gilliard, D. K., & Beck, A. J. (1998). Prison and jail inmates at midyear 1997. *Bureau of Justice Statistics Bulletin.* Washington, DC: USGPO.

Gillies, H. (1965). Murder in West Scotland. *British Journal of Psychiatry, 111*, 1087–1094.

Gillin, J. C., & Ochberg, F. M. (1970). Firearms control and violence. In D. N. Daniels, M. F. Gilula, & F. M. Ochberg (Eds.), *Violence and the struggle for existence*. Boston, MA: Little, Brown.

Glaser, D. (1964). *The effectiveness of a prison and parole system*. Indianapolis, IN: Bobbs-Merrill.

Glaser, D. (1978). *Crime in our changing society*. New York: Holt, Rinehart & Winston.

Glasser, W. D. (1965). *Reality therapy*. New York: Harper & Row.

Glueck, S., & Glueck, E. (1950). *Unraveling juvenile delinquency*. New York: Harper & Row.

Glueck, S., & Glueck, E. (1956). *Physique and delinquency*. New York: Harper & Row.

Gold, L. H. (1962). Psychiatric profile of the firesetter. *Journal of Forensic Sciences, 7*, 404–417.

Gold, M. S. (1984). *800-cocaine*. New York: Bantam.

Golding, S. L., & Roesch, R. (1987). The assessment of criminal responsibility: A historical approach to a current controversy. In I. B. Weiner & A. K. Hess (Eds.), *Handbook of forensic psychology*. New York: Wiley.

Goldman, H. (1977). The limits of clockwork: The neurobiology of violent behavior. In J. P. Conrad & S. Dinitz (Eds.), *In fear of each other*. Lexington, MA: Lexington Books.

Goldman, M. J. (1991). Kleptomania: Making sense of the nonsensical. *American Journal of Psychiatry, 148*, 986–995.

Goldstein, J. H. (1975). *Aggression and crimes of violence*. New York: Oxford University Press.

Goldstein, M. (1974). Brain research and violent behavior. *Archives of Neurology, 30*, 1–34.

Goldstein, M. J. (1977). A behavioral scientist looks at obscenity. In B. D. Sales (Ed.), *The criminal justice system* (Vol. 1). New York: Plenum.

Golub, A. L., & Johnson, B. D. (1997, July). *Crack's decline: Some surprises across U.S. cities*. NIJ Research in Brief. Washington, DC: U.S. Department of Justice.

Gorenstein, E. E. (1982). Frontal lobe functions in psychopaths. *Journal of Abnormal Psychology, 91*, 368–379.

Goring, C. (1913/1972). The English convict: A statistical study. Montclair, NJ: Patterson Smith.

Gorman-Smith, D., Tolan, P. H., Huesmann, L. R., & Zelli, A. (1996). The relation of family functioning to violence among inner-city minority youths. *Journal of Family Psychology, 10*, 115–129.

Gosselin, C., & Wilson, G. (1984). Fetishism, sadomasochism and related behaviours. In K. Howells (Ed.), *The psychology of sexual diversity*. London: Basil Blackwell.

Gossop, M. R., & Kristjansson, I. (1977). Crime and personality. *British Journal of Criminology, 17*, 264–273.

Gottfredson, M. R., & Hirschi, T. (1990). *A general theory of crime*. Stanford, CA: Stanford University Press.

Gove, W. R., & Crutchfield, R. D. (1982). The family and delinquency. *The Sociological Quarterly, 23*, 301–319.

Gove, W. R., Hughes, M., & Galle, O. R. (1977). Overcrowding in the home: An empirical investigation of its possible pathological consequences. *American Sociological Review, 44*, 59–80.

Grant, V. (1977). *The menacing stranger.* New York: Dover.

Gray, K. G., & Hutchison, H. C. (1964). The psychopathic personality: A survey of Canadian psychiatrists' opinions. *Canadian Psychiatric Association Journal, 9*, 452–461.

Green, G. S. (1997). *Occupational crime* (2nd edition). Chicago, IL: Nelson-Hall.

Greenberg, L. S. (1988). Constructive cognition: Cognitive therapy coming of age. *The Counseling Psychologist, 16*, 235–238.

Greendlinger, V., & Byrne, D. (1987). Coercive sexual fantasies of college men as predictors of self-reported likelihood to rape and overt sexual aggression. *The Journal of Sex Research, 23*, 1–11.

Greenwald, H. (1958). *The call girl.* New York: Ballantine Books.

Greenwood, P. J., & Zimring, F. (1985). One more chance: The role of rehabilitation in reducing the criminality of chronic serious juvenile offenders. *Rand Report R-3214-OJJDP.* Santa Monica, CA: Rand Corporation.

Greer, S. (1964). Study of parental loss in neurotics and sociopaths. *Archives of General Psychiatry, 11*, 177–180.

Griffith, W., & Veitch, R. (1971). Hot and crowded: Influences of population density and temperature on interpersonal affective behavior. *Journal of Personality and Social Psychology, 17*, 92–98.

Grisso, T. (1986). *Evaluating competencies: Forensic assessments and instruments.* New York: Plenum.

Groth, A. N. (1978). Patterns of sexual assault against children and adolescents. In A. W. Burgess, A. N. Groth, L. L. Holmstrom, & S. M. Sgroi (Eds.), *Sexual assault of children and adolescents.* Lexington, MA: Lexington Books.

Groth, A. N. (1979). *Men who rape: The psychology of the offender.* New York: Plenum.

Groth, A. N., & Burgess, A. W. (1977). Motivational intent in the sexual assault of children. *Criminal Justice and Behavior, 4*, 253–271.

Groth, A. N., Hobson, W. F., & Gary, T. S. (1982). The child molester: Clinical observation. *Journal of Social Work and Human Sexuality, 1*, 129–144.

Guerra, N. G., Huesmann, L. R., Tolan, P. H., Van Acker, R., & Eron, L. D. (1995). Stressful events and individual beliefs as correlates of economic disadvantage and aggression among urban children. *Journal of Consulting and Clinical Psychology, 63*, 518–528.

Guze, S. B. (1976). *Criminality and psychiatric disorders.* New York: Oxford University Press.

Häfner, H., & Böker, W. (1973). Mentally disordered violent offenders. *Social Psychiatry, 8*, 220–229.

Haft, M. G. (1976). Hustling for rights. In L. Crites (Ed.), *The female offender.* Lexington, MA: Lexington Books.

Hall, D. M. (1998). The victims of stalking. In J. R. Meloy (Ed.), *The psychology of stalking: Clinical and forensic perspectives.* San Diego, CA: Academic Press.

Hall, C. S., & Lindzey, G. (1970). *Theories of personality* (2nd edition). New York: Wiley.

Hall, G. C. N. (1995). Sexual offender recidivism revisited: A meta-analysis of recent treatment studies. *Journal of Consulting and Clinical Psychology, 63,* 802–809

Hall, G. C. N., Proctor, W. C., & Nelson, G. M. (1988). Validity of physiological measures of pedophilic sexual arousal in a sexual offender population. *Journal of Consulting and Clinical Psychology, 56,* 118–122.

Halleck, S. L. (1967). *Psychiatry and the dilemmas of crime.* New York: Harper & Row.

Halleck, S. L., & Witte, A. D. (1977). Is rehabilitation dead? *Crime and Delinquency, 23,* 372–382.

Halloran, J. D., Brown, R. L., & Chaney, D. (1969). *Mass media and crime.* Leicester, Eng.: Leicester University Press.

Halverson, C. F., & Victor, J. B. (1976). Minor physical anomalies and problem behavior in elementary school children. *Child Development, 47,* 281–285.

Hämäläinen, T., & Haapasalo, J. (1996). Retrospective reports of childhood abuse and neglect among violent and property offenders. *Psychology, Crime & Law, 3,* 1–13.

Hammond, W. R., & Yung, B. (1993). Psychology's role in the public health response to assaultive violence among young African-American men. *American Psychologist, 48,* 142–154.

Hammond, W. R., & Yung, B. (1994). African Americans. In L. D. Eron, J. H. Gentry, & P. Schlegel (Eds.), *Reason to hope: A psychosocial perspective on violence and youth.* Washington, DC: American Psychological Association.

Haney, C. W. (1983). The good, the bad, and the lawful: An essay on psychological injustice. In W. S. Laufer & J. M. Day (Eds.), *Personality theory, moral development, and criminal behavior.* Lexington, MA: Lexington Books.

Hare, R. D. (1965a). A conflict and learning theory analysis of psychopathic behavior. *Journal of Research in Crime and Delinquency, 2,* 12–19.

Hare, R. D. (1965b). Acquisition and generalization of a conditioned-fear response in psychopathic and nonpsychopathic criminals. *Journal of Psychology, 59,* 367–370.

Hare, R. D. (1968). Psychopathy, autonomic functioning, and the orienting response. *Journal of Abnormal Psychology, 73,* 1–24.

Hare, R. D. (1970). *Psychopathy: Theory and research.* New York: Wiley.

Hare, R. D. (1976). Anxiety, stress and psychopathy. In G. Shean (Ed.), *Dimensions in abnormal psychology.* Chicago, IL: Rand McNally.

Hare, R. D. (1980). A research scale for the assessment of psychopathy in criminal populations. *Personality and Individual Differences, 1,* 111–119.

Hare, R. D. (1986). Criminal psychopaths. In J. C. Yuille (Ed.), *Selection and training: The role of psychology.* Boston, MA: Martinus Nijhoff.

Hare, R. D. (1991). *The Hare psychopathy checklist-revised.* Toronto: Multi-Health Systems.

Hare, R. D. (1996). Psychopathy: A clinical construct whose time has come. *Criminal Justice and Behavior, 23,* 25–54.

Hare, R. D., & Connolly, J. F. (1987). Perceptual asymmetries and information processing in psychopaths. In S. A. Mednick, T. E. Moffitt, & S. A. Stack (Eds.), *The causes of crime: New biological approaches.* Cambridge, Eng.: Cambridge University Press.

Hare, R. D., & Craigen, D. (1974). Psychopathy and physiological activity in a mixed-motive game. *Psychophysiology, 11,* 197–206.

Hare, R. D., Forth, A. E., & Stachan, K. E. (1992). Psychopathy and crime across the life span. In R. D. Peters, R. J. McMahon, & V. L. Quinsey (Eds.), *Aggression and violence throughout the life span.* Newbury Park, CA: Sage.

Hare, R. D., Hart, S. D., & Harpur, T. J. (1991). Psychopathy and the DSM-IV criteria for antisocial personality disorder. *Journal of Abnormal Psychology, 100,* 391–398.

Hare, R. D., & Jutai, J. W. (1983). Criminal history of the male psychopath: Some preliminary data. In K. T. Van Dusen & S. A. Mednick (Eds.), *Prospective studies of crime and delinquency.* Boston, MA: Kluwer-Nijhoff.

Hare, R. D., & McPherson, L. M. (1984). Violent and aggressive behavior by criminal psychopaths. *International Journal of Law and Psychiatry, 7,* 35–50.

Hare, R. D., & McPherson, L. M., & Forth, A. E. (1988). Male psychopaths and their criminal careers. *Journal of Consulting and Clinical Psychology, 56,* 710–714.

Hare, R. D., & Quinn, M. (1971). Psychopathy and autonomic conditioning. *Journal of Abnormal Psychology, 77,* 223–239.

Harmon, R. B., Rosner, R., & Wiederlight, M. (1985). Women and arson: A demographic study. *Journal of Forensic Sciences, 10,* 467–477.

Harpur, J. T., & Hare, R. D. (1994). The assessment of psychopathy as a function of age. *Journal of Abnormal Psychology, 103,* 604–609.

Harries, K. D. (1980). *Crime and the environment.* Springfield, IL: Charles C. Thomas.

Harris, G. T., Rice, M. E., & Quinsey, V. L. (1993). Violent recidivism of mentally disordered offenders: The development of a statistical prediction instrument. *Criminal Justice and Behavior, 20,* 315–335.

Harry, B., & Balcer, C. M. (1987). Menstruation and crime: A critical review from a clinical criminology perspective. *Behavioral Sciences and the Law, 5,* 307–321.

Hart, H. M., Jr., & Sacks, A. M. (1958). *The legal process: Basic problems in the making and application of law.* Unpublished manuscript.

Hart, S. D., Cox, D. N., & Hare, R. D. (1995). *The Hare Psychopathy Checklist: Screening Version.* Toronto: Multihealth Systems.

Hart, S. D., & Dempster, R. J. (1997). Impulsivity and psychopathy. In C. D. Webster & M. A. Jackson (Eds.), *Impulsivity: Theory, assessment and treatment.* New York: Guilford.

Hart, S. D., Hare, R. D., & Forth, A. E. (1993). Psychopathy as a risk marker for violence: Development and validation of a screening version of the Revised Psychopathy Checklist. In J. Monahan & H. Steadman (Eds.), *Violence and mental disorder: Developmental in risk assessment.* Chicago, IL: University of Chicago Press.

Hartl, E. M., Monnelly, E. P., & Elderkin, R. D. (1982). *Physique and delinquent behavior.* New York: Academic Press.

Hartnagel, T. F. (1987). Correlates of criminal behaviour. In R. Linden (Ed.), *Criminology: A Canadian perspective*. Toronto: Holt, Rinehart & Winston.

Hartshorne, H., & May, M. A. (1928–1930). *Studies in deceit*. New York: Macmillan.

Hartup, W. W. (1983). Peer relations. In P. H. Mussen (Ed.), *Manual of child psychology*. New York: Wiley.

Hawke, C. C. (1950). Castration and sex crimes. *American Journal of Mental Deficiency, 55*, 220–226.

Hawkins, D. F. (1985). Black homicide: The adequacy of existing research for devising prevention strategies. *Crime and Delinquency, 31*, 83–103.

Hazelwood, R. R., & Burgess, A. W. (1987, September). An introduction to the serial rapist. *FBI Law Enforcement Bulletin*, pp. 16–24.

Hebb, D. O. (1955). Drives and the C.N.S. (Conceptual Nervous System). *Psychological Review, 62*, 243–254.

Henderson, M. (1983). An empirical classification of non-violent offenders using the MMPI. *Personality and Individual Differences, 4*, 671–677.

Hendrick, C., & Taylor, S. P. (1971). The effects of belief similarity and aggression on attraction and counter aggression. *Journal of Personality and Social Psychology, 17*, 342–349.

Henggeler, S. W. (1996). Treatment of violent juvenile offenders—we have the knowledge. *Journal of Family Psychology, 10*, 137–141.

Henggeler, S. W., & Borduin, C. M. (1990). *Family therapy and beyond: A multisystemic approach to treating the behavior problems of children and adolescents*. Pacific Grove, CA: Brooks/Cole.

Henggeler, S. W., Melton, G. B., & Smith, L. A. (1992). Family preservation using multisystemic therapy—an effective alternative to incarcerating serious juvenile offenders. *Journal of Consulting and Clinical Psychology, 60*, 953–961.

Henker, B., & Whalen, C. K. (1989). Hyperactivity and attention deficits. *American Psychologist, 44*, 216–244.

Henn, F. A., Herjanic, M., & Vanderpearl, R. H. (1976a). Forensic psychiatry: Profiles of two types of sex offenders. *American Journal of Psychiatry, 133*, 694–696.

Henn, F. A., Herjanic, M., & Vanderpearl, R. H. (1976b). Forensic psychiatry: Diagnosis of criminal responsibility. *The Journal of Nervous and Mental Disease, 162*, 423–429.

Hepburn, J., & Voss, H. L. (1970). Patterns of criminal homicide: A comparison of Chicago and Philadelphia. *Criminology, 8*, 19–45.

Herzberg, J. L., & Fenwick, P. B. C. (1988). The aetiology of aggression in temporal lobe epilepsy. *British Journal of Psychiatry, 153*, 50–55.

Hetherington, E. M., & Parke, R. D. (1975). *Child psychology: A contemporary viewpoint*. New York: McGraw-Hill.

Hewitt, J. D. (1988). The victim-offender relationship in convicted homicide cases: 1960–1984. *Journal of Criminal Justice, 16*, 25–33.

Hickey, E. (1991). *Serial killers and their victims*. Pacific Grove, CA: Brooks/Cole.

Hill, D., & Watterson, D. (1942). Electroencephalographic studies of the psychopathic personality. *Journal of Neurology and Psychiatry, 5*, 47–64.

Hill, H. M., Soriano, F. I., Chen, S. A., & LaFromboise, T. D. (1994). Sociocultural factors in the etiology and prevention of violence among ethnic minority youth. In L. D. Eron, J. H. Gentry, & P. Schlegel (Eds.), *Reason to hope: A psychosocial perspective on violence and youth*. Washington, DC: American Psychological Association.

Hill, P. (1960). *Portrait of a sadist*. New York: Avon.

Hill, R. W., Langevin, R., Paitich, D., Handy, L., Russon, A., & Wilkinson, L. (1982). Is arson an aggressive act or a property offense? *Canadian Journal of Psychiatry, 27*, 648–654.

Hindelang, M. J. (1974). Decisions of shoplifting victims to invoke the criminal justice process. *Social Process, 21*, 580–593.

Hindelang, M. J., Dunn, C. S., Sutton, L. P., & Aumick, A. (1976). *Sourcebook of criminal justice statistics, 1975*. Washington, DC: USGPO.

Hindelang, M. J., Hirschi, T., & Weis, J. G. (1981). *Measuring delinquency*. Beverly Hills, CA: Sage.

Hirschi, T., & Hindelang, M. J. (1977). Intelligence and delinquency. *American Sociological Review, 42*, 571–587.

Hochstedler, E. (Ed.). (1984). *Corporations as criminals*. Beverly Hills, CA: Sage.

Hoffman, J. J., Hall, R. W., & Bartsch, T. W. (1987). On the relative importance of "psychopathic" personality and alcoholism measures of frontal lobe dysfunction. *Journal of Abnormal Psychology, 96*, 158–160.

Hofmann, F. G. (1975). *A handbook on drug and alcohol abuse: The biomedical aspects*. New York: Oxford University Press.

Hoghughi, M. S., & Forrest, A. R. (1970). Eysenck's theory of criminality: An examination with approved school boys. *British Journal of Criminology, 10*, 240–254.

Holcomb, W. R., & Anderson, W. P. (1983). Alcohol and multiple drug abuse in accused murderers. *Psychological Reports, 52*, 159–164.

Holmes, R. M., & DeBurger, J. (1988). *Serial murder*. Newbury Park, CA: Sage.

Holmes, S. T., Hickey, E., & Holmes, R. M. (1991). Female serial murderesses: Constructing differentiating typologies. *Journal of Contemporary Criminal Justice, 7*, 245–256.

Holtzworth-Monroe, A., & Stuart, G. L. (1994). Typologies of male batterers: Three subtypes and the differences among them. *Psychological Bulletin, 116*, 476–497.

Homant, R. J., & Kennedy, D. B. (1998). Psychological aspects of crime scene profiling: Validity research. *Criminal Justice and Behavior, 25*, 319–343.

Home Office. (1986). *Criminal statistics: England and Wales 1985*. London: HMSO.

Horney, J. (1978). Menstrual cycles and criminal responsibility. *Law and Human Behavior, 2*, 25–36.

Horning, D. N. M. (1970). Blue-collar theft: Conceptions of property, attitudes toward pilfering, and work group norms in a modern industrial plant. In E. O. Smigel & H. L. Ross (Eds.), *Crimes against bureaucracy*. New York: Van Nostrand Reinhold.

Hornung, C. A., McCullough, B. C., & Sugimoto, T. (1981). Status relationships in marriage: Risk factors in spouse abuse. *Journal of Marriage and the Family, 43*, 675–692.

Hotaling, G. T., & Straus, M. A. (1989). Intrafamily violence, and crime and violence outside the family. In L. Ohlin & M. Tonry (Eds.), *Family violence* (Vol. 11). Chicago, IL: University of Chicago Press.

Houghton, B. (1979). Review of research on women abuse. Paper presented at the annual meeting of American Society of Criminology, Philadelphia, PA.

Howard, R. C. (1990). Psychopathy checklist scores in mentally abnormal offenders: A re-examination. *Personality and Individual Differences, 11,* 1087–1091.

Hudson, M. I. (1986). Elder maltreatment: Current research. In K. A. Pillemer & R. S. Wolf (Eds.), *Elder abuse: Conflict in the family.* Dover, MA: Auburn House.

Huesmann, L. R. (1988). An information processing model for the development of aggression. *Aggressive Behavior, 14,* 13–24.

Huesmann, L. R. (1997). Observational learning of violent behavior: Social and biosocial processes. In A. Raine, P. A. Brennan, D. P. Farrington, & S. A. Mednick (Eds.), *Biosocial bases of violence.* New York: Plenum.

Huesmann, L. R., & Eron, L. D. (1986). *Television and the aggressive child: A cross national comparison.* Hillsdale, NJ: Erlbaum.

Hughes, R., Crawford, G., Barker N., Schumann, S., & Jaffe, J. (1971). The social structure of a heroin copping community. *American Journal of Psychiatry, 128,* 554.

Humphrey, J. A., & Palmer, S. (1987). Race, sex, and criminal homicide offender-victim relationships. *Journal of Black Studies, 18,* 45–57.

Hurley, W., & Monahan, T. M. (1969). Arson: The criminal and the crime. *British Journal of Criminology, 9,* 4–21.

Hutchings, B., & Mednick, S. A. (1975). Registered criminality in the adoptive and biological parents of registered male criminal adoptees. In R. R. Fieve, D. Rosenthal, & H. Brill (Eds.), *Genetic research in psychiatry.* Baltimore, MD: John Hopkins University Press.

Icove, D. J., & Estepp, M. H. (1987, April). Motive-based offender profiles of arson and fire-related crime. *FBI Law Enforcement Bulletin,* pp. 17–23.

Inciardi, J. A. (1970). The adult firesetter, a typology. *Criminology, 3,* 145–155.

Inciardi, J. A. (1980). Women, heroin, and property crime. In S. K. Datesman & F. R. Scarpitti (Eds.), *Women, crime and justice.* New York: Oxford University Press.

Inciardi, J. A. (1981). Crime and alternative patterns of substance abuse. In S. E. Gardner (Ed.), *Drug and alcohol abuse.* Rockville, MD: National Institute on Drug Abuse.

Inciardi, J. A. (1986). *The war on drugs: Heroin, cocaine, crime and public policy.* Palo Alto, CA: Mayfield Publishing.

Insight Canada Research. (1998). *Prevalence of problem and pathological gambling in Ontario using the South Oaks Gambling Screen.* Ottawa: Canadian Foundation on Compulsive Gambling. Available: www.cfcg.on.ca.

Jackson, H. F., Glass, C., & Hope, S. (1987). A functional analysis of recidivistic arson. *British Journal of Clinical Psychology, 26,* 175–185.

Jaffe, J. H., Babor, T. F., & Fishbein, D. H. (1988). Alcoholics, aggression and antisocial behavior. *Journal of Studies on Alcohol, 49,* 211–218.

James, J. (1976). Motivations for entrance into prostitution. In L. Crites (Ed.), *The female offender.* Lexington, MA: Lexington Books.

James, J. (1978). The prostitute as victim. In J. R. Chapman & M. Gates (Eds.), *The victimization of women.* Beverly Hills, CA: Sage.

Jamison, R. N. (1980). Psychoticism, deviancy, and perception of risk in normal children. *Personality and Individual Differences, 1,* 87–91.

Jarvik, L. F., Klodin, V., & Matsuyama, S. S. (1973). Human aggression and the extra Y chromosome. *American Psychologist, 28,* 674–682.

Jarvis, G., & Parker, H. (1989). Young heroin users and crime. *British Journal of Criminology, 29,* 175–185.

Jeffrey, C. R. (1965). Criminal behavior and learning theory. *The Journal of Criminal Law, Criminology, and Police Science, 56,* 294–300.

Jenkins, P. (1988). Serial murder in England 1940–1985. *Journal of Criminal Justice, 16,* 1–15.

Jenkins, P. (1993). Chance or choice: The selection of serial murder victims. In A. V. Wilson (Ed.), *Homicide: The victim/offender connection.* Cincinnati, OH: Anderson.

Jenkins, P., & Maier-Katkin, D. (1991). Occult survivors: The making of a myth. In J. T. Richardson, J. Best, & D. G. Bromley (Eds.), *The satanism scare.* New York: Aldine De Gruyter.

Jenkins, W. O., & Barton, M. C. (1973). *Longitudinal follow-up investigation of the post release behavior of paroled and released offenders.* Elmore, AL: Rehabilitation Research Foundation.

Jenson, B. (1996 May). *Cyberstalking: Crime, enforcement and personal responsibility in the on-line world.* Available: www. law.ucla.edu/Classes/Archive.S96/340/cyberlaw.htm.

Johns, J. H., & Quay, H. C. (1962). The effect of social reward on verbal conditioning in psychopathic military offenders. *Journal of Consulting Psychology, 26,* 217–220.

Johnson, L. G., Bachman, J. G., & O'Malley, P. M. (1983). *Student drug use, attitudes and beliefs: National trends 1975–1983.* Rockville, MD: National Institute on Drug Abuse.

Johnson, R. E., Marcos, A. C., & Bahr, J. (1987). The role of peers in the complex etiology of adolescent drug use. *Criminology, 25,* 323–340.

Johnson, R. N. (1972). *Aggression in man and animals.* Philadelphia, PA: W. B. Saunders.

Jones, C., & Aronson, E. (1973). Attribution of fault to a rape victim as a function of respectability of the victim. *Journal of Personality and Social Psychology, 26,* 415–419.

Jones, J. W., & Bogat, G. A. (1978). Air pollution and human aggression. *Psychological Reports, 43,* 721–722.

Julien, R. M. (1975). *A primer of drug action.* San Francisco, CA: W. H. Freeman.

Julien, R. M. (1992). *A primer of drug action* (6th edition). New York: W. H. Freeman.

Kafrey, D. (1980). Playing with matches: Children and fire. In D. Canter (Ed.), *Fires and human behaviour.* Chichester, Eng.: Wiley.

Kahaner, L. (1988). *Cults that kill.* New York: Warner.

Kahn, E. (1931). *Psychopathic personalities.* New Haven, CT: Yale University Press.

Kalish, C. B. (1983). *Prisoners and alcohol.* Washington, DC: U.S. Department of Justice.

Kandel, E., Mednick, S. A., Kirkegaard-Sorenson, L., Hutchings, B., Knop, J.,

Rosenberg, R., & Schulsinger, F. (1988). IQ as a protective factor for subjects at high risk for antisocial behavior. *Journal of Consulting and Clinical Psychology, 56,* 224–226.

Kanin, E. J. (1984). Date rape: Unofficial criminals and victims. *Victimology, 9,* 95–108.

Kassebaum, G., Ward, D., & Wilner, D. (1971). *Prison treatment and parole survival: An empirical assessment.* New York: Wiley.

Kato, P. S., & Ruble, D. N. (1992). Toward an understanding of women's experience of menstrual cycle symptoms. In V. Adesso, D. Reddy, & R. Fleming (Eds.), *Psychological perspectives in women's health.* Washington, DC: Hemisphere.

Kelleher, M. D. (1997). *Profiling the lethal employee: Case studies of violence in the workplace.* Westport, CT: Praeger.

Kelly, D. H. (1980). The educational experience and evolving delinquent careers: A neglected institutional link. In D. Schichor & D. H. Kelly (Eds.), *Critical issues in juvenile delinquency.* Lexington, MA: Lexington Books.

Kelly, G. A. (1955). *The psychology of personal constructs.* New York: Norton.

Kelman, H. C., & Hamilton, V. L. (1989). *Crimes of obedience: Toward a social psychology of authority and responsibility.* New Haven, CT: Yale University Press.

Kempe, C. H., Silverman, F. N., Steele, B. B., Droegemueller, W., & Silver, H. K. (1962). The battered-child syndrome. *Journal of the American Medical Association, 181,* 17–24.

Kennedy, R. E. (1976). Behavior modification in prisons. In W. Craighead, A. Kasdin, & M. Mahoney (Eds.), *Behavior modification: Principles, issues and applications.* Boston, MA: Houghton Mifflin.

Kenrick, D. T., & MacFarland, S. W. (1986). Ambient temperature and horn honking. *Environment and Behavior, 18,* 179–191.

Kilmann, P. R., Sabalis, R. F., Gearing, M. L., Bukstel, L. H., & Scovern, A. W. (1982). The treatment of sexual paraphilias: A review of the outcome research. *The Journal of Sex Research, 18,* 193–252.

Kilpatrick, D. G., Best, C. L., Saunders, B. E., & Veronen, L. J. (1988). Rape in marriage and in dating relationships: How bad is it for mental health? In R. A. Prentky & V. L. Quinsey (Eds.), *Human sexual aggression: Current perspectives.* New York: New York Academy of Sciences.

Kirmeyer, S. L. (1978). Urban density and pathology—a review of research. *Environment and Behavior, 10,* 247–269.

Klassen, D., & O'Connor, W. (1988). Crime, inpatient admissions, and violence among male mental patients. *International Journal of Law and Psychiatry, 11,* 305–312.

Klassen, D., & O'Connor, W. (1990). Assessing the risk of violence in released mental patients: A cross-validation study. *Psychological Assessment: A Journal of Consulting and Clinical Psychology, 1,* 75–81.

Kleber, H. D. (1988). Epidemic cocaine abuse: America's present, Britain's future. *British Journal of Addiction, 83,* 1359–1371.

Klemke, L. W. (1992). *The sociology of shoplifting: Boosters and snitches today.* Westport, CT: Praeger.

Klinteberg, B., Magnusson, D., & Schalling, D. (1989). Hyperactive behavior in childhood and adult impulsivity: A longitudinal study of male subjects. *Personality and Individual Differences, 10*, 43–50.

Knight, R. A. (1988). A taxonomic analysis of child molesters. In R. A. Prentky & V. L. Quinsey (Eds.), *Human sexual aggression: Current perspectives.* New York: New York Academy of Science.

Knight, R. A. (1989). An assessment of the concurrent validity of a child molester typology. *Journal of Interpersonal Violence, 4*, 131–150.

Knight, R. A., Carter, D. L., & Prentky, R. A. (1989). A system for the classification of child molesters: Reliability and application. *Journal of Interpersonal Violence, 4*, 3–23.

Knight, R. A., & Prentky, R. A. (1987). The developmental antecedents and adult adaptations of rapist subtypes. *Criminal Justice and Behavior, 14*, 403–426.

Knight, R. A., & Prentky, R. A. (1990). Classifying sexual offenders: The development and corroboration of taxonomic models. In W. L. Marshall, D. R. Laws, & H. E. Barbaree (Eds.), *The handbook of sexual assault: Issues, theories, and treatment of the offender.* New York: Plenum.

Knight, R. A., Rosenberg, R., & Schneider, B. A. (1985). Classification of sexual offenders: Perspectives, methods, and validation. In A. W. Burgess (Ed.), *Rape and sexual assault.* New York: Garland.

Knight, R. A., Warren, J. I., Reboussin, R., & Soley, B. J. (1998). Predicting rapist type from crime-scene variables. *Criminal Justice and Behavior, 25*, 46–80.

Knopp, F. H., Rosenberg, J., & Stevenson, W. (1986). *Report on nationwide survey of juvenile and adult sex-offender treatment programs and providers.* Syracuse, NY: Safer Society Press.

Knott, J. R., Platt, E. B., Ashby, M. C., & Gottlieb, J. S. (1953). A familial evaluation of the electroencephalogram of patients with primary behavior disorder and psychopathic personality. *EEG and Clinical Neurophysiology, 5*, 363–370.

Kohlmeier, L. M. (1976, September 26). The bribe busters. *The New York Times Magazine*, pp. 44–58, 91–99.

Kolko, D. J., Kazdin, A. E., & Meyer, E. C. (1985). Aggression and psychopathology in childhood firesetters: Parent and child reports. *Journal of Consulting and Clinical Psychology, 53*, 377–385.

Konečni, V. J. (1975). The mediation of aggressive behavior: Arousal levels vs. anger and cognitive labeling. *Journal of Personality and Social Psychology, 32*, 706–712.

Konečni, V. J., Mulcahy, E. M., & Ebbesen, E. B. (1980). Prison or mental hospital: Factors affecting the processing of persons suspected of being "mentally disordered sex offenders." In P. D. Lipsett & B. D. Sales (Eds.), *New directions in psycholegal research.* New York: Van Nostrand Reinhold.

Kornhauser, R. R. (1978). *Social sources of delinquency.* Chicago, IL: University of Chicago Press.

Korman, A. (1974). *The psychology of motivation.* Englewood Cliffs, NJ: Prentice Hall.

Koson, D. F., & Dvoskin, J. (1982). Arson: A diagnostic study. *Bulletin of the American Academy of Psychiatry and the Law, 10*, 39–49.

Koss, M. P., & Dinero, T. E. (1988). Predictors of sexual aggression among a national sample of male college students. In R. A. Prentky and V. L. Quinsey (Eds.), *Human sexual aggression: Current perspectives.* New York: New York Academy of Sciences.

Koss, M. P., Gidycz, C. A., & Wisniewski, N. (1987). The scope of rape: Incidence and prevalence of sexual aggression and victimization in a national sample of higher education students. *Journal of Consulting and Clinical Psychology, 55,* 162–170.

Kosson, D. S., Smith, S. S., & Newman, J. P. (1990). Evaluating the construct validity of psychopathy in black and white male inmates: Three preliminary studies. *Journal of Abnormal Psychology, 99,* 250–259.

Kozol, H. L., Boucher, R. L., & Garofalo, P. F. (1972). The diagnosis and treatment of dangerousness. *Crime and Delinquency, 8,* 371–392.

Kramer, R. C. (1984). Corporate criminality: The development of an idea. In E. Hochstedler (Ed.), *Corporations as criminals.* Beverly Hills, CA: Sage.

Krapelin, E. (1913). *Clinical psychiatry: A textbook for physicians.* New York: Macmillan.

Kretschmer, E. (1925). *Physique and character.* New York: Harcourt Brace Jovanovich.

Krisberg, B. (1992). Youth crime and its prevention: A research agenda. In I. M. Schwartz (Ed.), *Juvenile justice and public policy.* New York: Lexington Books.

Krisberg, B. (1995). The legacy of juvenile corrections. *Corrections Today, 57,* 122–126.

Krisberg, B., & Schwartz, I. (1983). Rethinking juvenile justice. *Crime and Delinquency, 29,* 333–364.

Kuhnley, E. J., Hendren, R. L., & Quinlan, D. M. (1982). *Journal of the American Academy of Child Psychiatry, 21,* 560–563.

Kulka, R. A., Schlenger, W. E., Fairbank, J. A., Jordan, B. K., Hough, R. L., Marmar, C. R., & Weiss, D. S. (1991). Assessment of post-traumatic stress disorder in the community: Prospects and pitfalls from recent studies of Vietnam veterans. *Psychological Assessment: A Journal of Consulting and Clinical Psychology, 4,* 547–560.

Kurland, H. D., Yeager, C. T., & Arthur, R. J. (1963). Psychophysiologic aspects of severe behavior disorders. *Archives of General Psychiatry, 8,* 599–604.

Kurtzberg, R. L., Mandell, W., Lewin, M., Lipton, D. S., & Shuster, M. (1978). Plastic surgery on offenders. In N. Johnson & L. Savitz (Eds.), *Justice and corrections.* New York: Wiley.

Lance, D. (1988, April). Product tampering. *FBI Law Enforcement Bulletin,* pp. 20–23.

Landau, S. F., Drapkin, E., & Arad, S. (1974). Homicide victims and offenders: An Israeli study. *The Journal of Criminal Law and Criminology, 65,* 390–396.

Landy, D., & Aronson, E. (1969). The influence of the character of the criminal and his victim on the decisions of simulated jurors. *Journal of Experimental Social Psychology, 5,* 141–152.

Lane, D. A. (1987). Personality and antisocial behaviour: A long term study. *Personality and Individual Differences, 8,* 799–806.

Lang, A. R., Goeckner, D. J., Adesso, V. G., & Marlatt, G. A. (1975). Effects of alcohol on aggression in male social drinkers. *Journal of Abnormal Psychology, 84,* 508–518.

Lange, J. (1929). *Vebrechen als Schicksal*. Leipzig: Georg Thieme Verlag.

Langer, E. J., & Miransky, J. (1983). Burglary (non) prevention. In E. J. Langer (Ed.), *The psychology of control*. Beverly Hills, CA: Sage.

Langevin, R. (1983). *Sexual strands*. Hillsdale, NJ: Erlbaum.

Lanning, K. V. (1989, October). Satanic, occult, ritualistic crime: A law enforcement perspective. *The Police Chief*, 62–83.

Lanyon, R. I. (1986). Theory and treatment in child molestation. *Journal of Consulting and Clinical Psychology, 54*, 176–182.

Larson, B. (1989). *Satanism: The seduction of America's youth*. Nashville, TN: Thomas Nelson.

Laub, J. H. (1983). Trends in serious juvenile crime. *Criminal Justice and Behavior, 10*, 485–506.

Laws, D. R., & Marshall, W. L. (in press). A conditioning theory of the etiology and maintenance of deviant sexual preference and behavior. In W. L. Marshall, D. R. Laws, and H. E. Barabaree (Eds.), *Handbook of sexual assault*. New York: Plenum.

Leach, E. (1973). Don't say "boo" to a goose. In A. Montagu (Ed.), *Man and aggression* (2nd edition). London: Oxford University Press.

Lee, M., Zimbardo, P. G., & Bertholf, M. (1977, November). Shy murderers. *Psychology Today*, pp. 68–70, 148.

Lefkowitz, M., Eron, L., Walder, L., & Huesmann, L. (1977). *Growing up to be violent: A longitudinal study of the development of aggression*. New York: Pergamon Press.

Legras, A. M. (1932). *Psychese en Criminaliteit bij Twellingen*. Utrecht: Keminken ZOON N. V.

Le Maire, L. (1956). Danish experiences regarding the castration of sexual offenders. *Journal of Criminal Law and Criminology, 47*, 294–310.

Lerner, M. J. (1970). The desire for justice and reactions to victims. In J. Macaulay & L. Berkowitz (Eds.), *Altruism and helping behavior*. New York: Academic Press.

Lerner, M. J. (1980). *The belief in a just world: A fundamental delusion*. New York: Plenum.

Lester, D., & Danto, B. L. (1993). *Suicide behind bars: Prediction and prevention*. Philadelphia, PA: The Charles Press.

Letkemann, P. (1973). *Crime as work*. Englewood Cliffs, NJ: Prentice Hall.

Levin, B. (1976). Psychological characteristics of firesetters. *Fire Journal, 70*, 36–41.

Levinson, R. (1988). Developments in the classification process: Quay's AIMS approach. *Criminal Justice and Behavior, 15*, 24–38.

Lewis, N. D. C., & Yarnell, H. (1951). Pathological firesetting (pyromania). *Nervous and Mental Disease Monographs*, No. 82.

Light, R. J. (1973). Abused and neglected children in America: A study of alternative policies. *Harvard Educational Review, 43*, 556–598.

Lipton, D., Martinson, R. M., & Wilks, J. (1975). *The effectiveness of correctional treatment*. New York: Praeger.

Lipton, D. N., McDonel, E. C., & McFall, R. M. (1987). Heterosocial perception in rapists. *Journal of Consulting and Clinical Psychology, 55*, 17–21.

Little, A. (1963). Professor Eysenck's theory of crime: An empirical test on adolescent offenders. *British Journal of Criminology, 4*, 152–163.

Loeber, R. (1990). Development and risk factors of juvenile antisocial behavior and delinquency. *Clinical Psychology Review, 10*, 1–41.

Loeber, R., & Dishion, T. (1983). Early predictors of male delinquency: A review. *Psychological Bulletin, 94*, 68–99.

Loeber, R., Lahey, B. B., & Thomas, C. (1991). The diagnostic conundrum of oppositional defiant disorder and conduct disorder. *Journal of Abnormal Psychology, 100*, 379–390.

Loeber, R., & Stouthamer-Loeber, M. (1986). Family factors as correlates and predictors of juvenile conduct problems and delinquency. In N. Morris & M. Tonry (Eds.), *Crime and justice: An annual review of research* (Vol. 7). Chicago, IL: University of Chicago Press.

Loeber, R., & Stouthamer-Loeber, M. (1998). Development of juvenile aggression and violence: Some common misconceptions and controversies. *American Psychologist, 53*, 242–259.

Lombardo, V. S., & Lombardo, E. F. (1991). The link between learning disabilities and juvenile delinquency: Fact or fiction? *International Journal of Biosocial and Medical Research, 13*, 112–117.

Lombroso, C. (1876). *L'uomo delinquente*. Milan, Italy: Torin.

Lombroso, C. (1911/1968). *Crime: Its causes and remedies*. Montclair, NJ: Patterson Smith.

Lombroso-Ferrero, G. (1972). *Criminal man*. Montclair, NJ: Patterson Smith.

Longo, R. F., Bird, S., Stevenson, W. F., & Fiske, J. A. (1995). *1994 nationwide survey of treatment programs and models*. Brandon, VT: The Safer Society Program and Press.

Lore, R. K., & Schultz, L. A. (1993). Control of human aggression: A comparative perspective. *American Psychologist, 48*, 16–25.

Lorenz, K. (1966). *On aggression*. New York: Harcourt Brace Jovanovich.

Lottes, I. L. (1988). Sexual socialization and attitudes toward rape. In A. W. Burgess (Ed.), *Rape and sexual assault II*. New York: Garland Publishing.

Lubenow, G. C. (1983, June 27). When kids kill their parents. *Newsweek*, pp. 35–36.

Lunde, D. T. (1976). *Murder and madness*. San Francisco, CA: San Francisco Book Co.

Lung, C. T., & Daro, D. (1996). *Current trends in child abuse reporting and fatalities: The results of the 1995 annual fifty state survey*. Chicago, IL: National Committee to Prevent Child Abuse.

Lykken, D. T. (1955). *A study of anxiety in the sociopathic personality* (Doctoral dissertation, University of Minnesota). Ann Arbor, MI: University Microfilms, No. 55–944.

Lykken, D. T. (1957). A study of anxiety in the sociopathic personality. *Journal of Abnormal and Social Psychology, 55*, 6–10.

Lykken, D. T. (1978). The psychopath and the lie detector. *Psychophysiology, 15*, 137–142.

Lykken, D. T., & Venables, P. H. (1971). Direct measurement of skin conductance: A proposal for standardization. *Psychophysiology, 8*, 856–872.

Lynam, D., Moffitt, T., & Stouthamer-Loeber, M. (1993). Explaining the relation between IQ and delinquency: Class, race, test motivation, school failure, or self control? *Journal of Abnormal Psychology, 102,* 187–196.

Maccoby, E. E. (1986). Social groupings in childhood. In D. Olweus, J. Block, & M. Radke-Yarrow (Eds.), *Development of antisocial and prosocial behavior: Research, theories, and issues.* New York: Academic Press.

MacDonald, J. M. (1977). *Bombers and firesetters.* Springfield, IL: C. C. Thomas.

MacHovec, F. (1992). Cults: Forensic and therapeutic aspects. *Behavioral Sciences and the Law, 10,* 31–37.

Mahoney, M. J., & Lyddon, W. J. (1988). Recent developments in cognitive approaches to counseling and psychotherapy. *The Counseling Psychologist, 16,* 190–234.

Malamuth, N. M. (1981). Rape proclivity among males. *Journal of Social Issues, 37,* 138–157.

Malamuth, N. M. (1989). The attraction to sexual aggression scale: Part one. *The Journal of Sex Research, 26,* 26–49.

Malamuth, N. M., & Check, J. V. P. (1981). The effects of violent-sexual movies: A field experiment. *Journal of Research in Personality, 15,* 436–446.

Malamuth, N. M., Check, J. V. P., & Briere, J. (1986). Sexual arousal in response to aggression: Ideological, aggressive, and sexual correlates. *Journal of Personality and Social Psychology, 50,* 330–340.

Malamuth, N. M., Haber, S., & Feshbach, S. (1980). Testing hypothesis regarding rape: Exposure to sexual violence, sex differences, and the "normality" of rape. *Journal of Research in Personality, 14,* 121–137.

Malamuth, N. M., Heim, M., & Feshbach, S. (1980). The sexual responsiveness of college students to rape depictions: Inhibitory and disinhibitory effects. *Journal of Personality and Social Psychology, 38,* 399–408.

Mann, C. R. (1993). Maternal filicide of preschoolers. In A. V. Wilson (Ed.), *Homicide: The victim/offender connection.* Cincinnati, OH: Anderson.

Mark, V. H., & Ervin, F. R. (1970). *Violence and the brain.* Hagerstown, MD: Harper & Row.

Marlatt, G. A., & Rohsenow, D. J. (1980). Cognitive processes in alcohol use: Expectancy and the balanced placebo design. In N. K. Mello (Ed.), *Advances in substance abuse: Behavioral and biological research.* Greenwich, CT: JAI Press.

Marques, J. K., & Nelson, C. (1989). Elements of high-risk situations for sex offenders. In D. R. Laws (Ed.), *Relapse prevention with sex offenders.* New York: Guilford.

Marshall, W. L. (1988). The use of sexually explicit stimuli by rapists, child molesters, and nonoffenders. *The Journal of Sex Research, 25,* 267–288.

Marshall, W. L., & Barbaree, H. E. (1988). An outpatient treatment program for child molesters. In R. A. Prentky and V. L. Quinsey (Eds.), *Human sexual aggression: Current perspectives.* New York: New York Academy of Sciences.

Marshall, W. L., & Christie, M. M. (1981). Pedophilia and aggression. *Criminal Justice and Behavior, 8,* 145–158.

Martinson, R. M. (1974). What works—questions and answers about prison reform. *Public Interest, 35,* 22–54.

Maslow, A. H. (1954). *Motivation and personality.* New York: Harper.

Mayfield, D. (1976). Alcoholism, alcohol, intoxication, and assaultive behavior. *Diseases of the Nervous System, 37,* 288–291.

McCaghy, C. H. (1967). Child molesters: A study of their careers as deviants. In M. Clinard & R. Quinney (Eds.), *Criminal behavior systems: A typology.* New York: Holt, Rinehart & Winston.

McCaghy, C. H. (1980). *Crime in American society.* New York: Macmillan.

McCandless, B. R., Persons, W. S., & Roberts, A. (1972). Perceived opportunity, delinquency, race and body build among delinquent youth. *Journal of Consulting and Clinical Psychology, 38,* 281–287.

McClearn, G. E., & DeFries, J. C. (1973). *Introduction to behavioral genetics.* San Francisco, CA: W. H. Freeman.

McCord, D. (1987). Syndromes, profiles and other mental exotica: A new approach to the admissibility of nontraditional psychological evidence in criminal cases. *Oregon Law Review, 66,* 19–108.

McCord, J. (1979). Some child rearing antecedents of criminal behavior in adult men. *Journal of Personality and Social Psychology, 37,* 1477–1486.

McCord, W., & McCord, J. (1964). *The psychopath: An essay on the criminal mind.* Princeton, NJ: Van Nostrand.

McCord, W., McCord, J., & Zola, I. K. (1959). *Origins of crime: A new evaluation of the Cambridge-Somerville Youth Study.* New York: Columbia University Press.

McCorkle, R. C. (1992). Personal precaution to violence in prison. *Criminal Justice and Behavior, 19,* 160–173.

McDermott, M. J., & Hindelang, M. J. (1981). *Juvenile criminal behavior in the United States: Its trends and patterns.* Washington, DC: USGPO.

McElroy, S. L., Pope, H. G., Hudson, J. I., Keck, P. E., & White, K. L. (1991). Kleptomania: A report of 20 cases. *American Journal of Psychiatry, 148,* 652–657.

McFarland, C., Ross, M., & DeCourville, N. (1989). Women's theories of menstruation and biases in recall of menstrual symptoms. *Journal of Personality and Social Psychology, 57,* 522–531.

McGinley, H., & Paswark, R. A. (1989). National survey of the frequency and success of the insanity plea and alternate pleas. *Journal of Psychiatry and Law, 17,* 205–221.

McShane, D. A., & Plas, J. M. (1984a). Response to a critique of the McShane & Plas review of American Indian performance on the Wecshler Intelligence Scales. *School Psychology Review, 13,* 83–88.

McShane, D. A., & Plas, J. M. (1984b). The cognitive functioning of American Indian children: Moving from the WISC to the WISC-R. *School Psychology Review, 13,* 61–73.

Mechoulam, R. (1970). Marihuana chemistry. *Science, 168,* 1159–1166.

Mednick, S. A., Gabrielli, W. F., & Hutchings, B. (1984). Genetic influences in criminal convictions: Evidence from an adoption cohort. *Science, 234,* 891–894.

Mednick, S. A., Gabrielli, W. F., & Hutchings, B. (1987). Genetic factors in the etiology of criminal behavior. In S. A. Mednick, T. F. Moffitt, & S. A. Stack (Eds.), *The causes of crime: New biological approaches.* Cambridge, Eng.: Cambridge University Press.

Mednick, S. A., & Kandel, E. (1988). Genetic and perinatal factors in violence. In S.

A. Mednick & T. Moffitt (Eds.), *Biological contributions to crime causation.* Dordrecht, North Holland: Martinus Nijhoff.

Megargee, E. I. (1966). Undercontrolled and overcontrolled personality types in extreme antisocial aggression. *Psychological Monographs, 80*, No. 3.

Megargee, E. I. (1976). Population density and disruptive behavior in prison settings. In A. K. Cohen, F. G. Cole, & R. G. Bailey (Eds.), *Prison violence.* Lexington, MA: Lexington Books.

Megargee, E. I. (1982). Psychological determinants and correlates of criminal violence. In M. E. Wolfgang & N. A. Weinder (Eds.), *Criminal violence.* Beverly Hills, CA: Sage.

Megargee, E. I., & Bohn, M. J. (1977). Empirically determined characteristics of the ten types. *Criminal Justice and Behavior, 4*, 149–210.

Megargee, E. I., & Bohn, M. J. (1979). *Classifying criminal offenders.* Newbury Park, CA: Sage.

Meloy, J. R. (1998). The psychology of stalking. In J. R. Meloy (Ed.), *The psychology of stalking: Clinical and forensic perspectives.* San Diego, CA: Academic Press.

Mendelson, W., Johnson, N., & Steward, M. A. (1971). Hyperactive children as teenagers: A follow-up study. *Journal of Nervous and Mental Disease, 153*, 273–279.

Mercy, J., & Salzman, L. (1989). Fatal violence among spouses in the United States, 1986–1987. *American Journal of Public Health, 79*, 595–599.

Meyer, T. P. (1972). The effects of sexually arousing and violent films on aggressive behavior. *Journal of Sex Research, 8*, 324–333.

Middlebrook, P. M. (1974). *Social psychology and modern life.* New York: Knopf.

Milgram, S. (1963). Behavioral study of obedience. *Journal of Abnormal and Social Psychology, 67*, 371–378.

Milgram, S. (1977). *The individual in a social world.* Reading, MA: Addison-Wesley.

Miller, J. D., Cisin, I. H., Gardner-Keaton, H., Harrell, A. V., Wirtz, P. W., Abelson, H. I., & Fishburne, P. M. (1983). *National survey on drug abuse: Main findings.* Rockville, MD: National Institute on Drug Abuse.

Miller, J. L. (1991). Prostitution in contemporary American society. In E. Graverholtz & M. A. Koralewski (Eds.), *Sexual coercion: A sourcebook on its nature, causes, and prevention.* Lexington, MA: Lexington Books.

Miller, W. R., & Hester, R. K. (1989). Treating alcohol problems: Toward an informed eclecticism. In R. K. Hester & W. R. Miller (Eds.), *Handbook of alcoholism treatment approaches: Effective alternatives.* New York: Pergamon Press.

Millett, K. (1974). "J," the life. In E. Goode & R. Troiden (Eds.), *Sexual deviance and sexual deviants.* New York: William Morrow.

Milstein, V. (1988). EEG topology in patients with aggressive violent behavior. In T. E. Moffitt & S. A. Mednick (Eds.), *Biological contributions to crime causation.* Dordrecht, North Holland: Martinus Nijhoff.

Miner, M. H., Day, D. M., & Nafpaktitis, M. K. (1989). Assessment of coping skills: Development of situational competency test. In D. R. Laws (Ed.), *Relapse prevention with sex offenders.* New York: Guilford.

Miron, M. S., & Goldstein, A. P. (1978). *Hostage.* Kalamazoo, MI: Behaviordelia.

Mischel, W. (1973). Toward a cognitive social learning reconceptualization of personality. *Psychological Review, 80*, 252–283.

Mischel, W. (1976). *Introduction to personality* (2nd edition). New York: Holt, Rinehart & Winston.

Moffitt, T. E. (1990a). The neuropsychology of juvenile delinquency: A critical review. In M. Tonry & N. Morris (Eds.), *Crime and justice: A review of research*. Chicago, IL: University of Chicago Press.

Moffitt, T. E. (1990b). Juvenile delinquency and attention deficit disorder: Boys' developmental trajectories from age 13 to age 15. *Child Development, 61,* 893–910.

Moffitt, T. E. (1993a). Adolescence-limited and life-course-persistent antisocial behavior: A developmental taxonomy. *Psychological Review, 100,* 674–701.

Moffitt, T. E. (1993b). The neuropsychology of conduct disorder. *Development and Psychopathology, 5,* 135–151.

Moffitt, T. E., Caspi, A., Dickson, N., Silva, P., & Stanton, W. (1996). Childhood-onset versus adolescent-onset antisocial conduct problems in males: Natural history from ages 3 to 18. *Development and Psychopathology, 8,* 399–424.

Moffitt, T. E., & Silva, P. A. (1988). Self-reported delinquency, neuropsychological deficit, and history of attention deficit disorder. *Journal of Abnormal Child Psychology, 16,* 553–569.

Mohr, J. W., Turner, R. E., & Jerry, N. B. (1964). *Pedophilia and exhibitionism*. Toronto: University of Toronto Press.

Moll, K. D. (1974). *Arson, vandalism and violence: Law enforcement problems affecting fire departments (LEAA)*. Washington, DC: USGPO.

Monahan, J. (1976). The prevention of crime. In J. Monahan (Ed.), *Community mental health and the criminal justice system*. New York: Pergamon Press.

Monahan, J. (1981). *Predicting violent behavior*. Beverly Hills, CA: Sage.

Monahan, J. (1984). The prediction of violent behavior: Toward a second generation of theory and policy. *American Journal of Psychiatry, 141,* 10–15.

Monahan, J. (1988). Risk assessment of violence among the mentally disordered: Generating useful knowledge. *International Journal of Law and Psychiatry, 11,* 249–257.

Monahan, J. (1992). Mental disorder and violent behavior: Perceptions and evidence. *American Psychologist, 47,* 511–521.

Monahan, J. (1996). Mental illness and violent crime. *NIJ Research Preview*. Washington, DC: National Institute of Justice.

Monahan, J., & Geis, G. (1976). Controlling "dangerous" people. *Annals of the American Academy of Political and Social Science, 423,* 142–151.

Monahan, J., & Shah, S. A. (1989). Dangerousness and commitment of the mentally disordered in the United States. *Schizophrenia Bulletin, 15,* 541–553.

Monahan, J., & Walker, L. (1990). *Social science and law: Cases and materials* (2nd edition). Westbury, NY: Foundation Press.

Monahan, J., & Walker, L. (1994). *Social science and law: Cases and materials* (3rd edition). Waterbury, NY: Foundation Press.

Monahan, T. P. (1957). Family status and the delinquent child: A reappraisal and some new findings. *Social Forces, 35,* 250–258.

Montagu, A. (1973). *Man and aggression* (2nd edition). London: Oxford University Press.

Montagu, A. (1976). *The nature of human aggression*. New York: Oxford University Press.

Moore, R. H. (1984). Shoplifting in middle America: Patterns and motivational correlates. *International Journal of Offender Therapy and Comparative Criminology, 28*, 53–64.

Morash, M. (1983). An explanation of juvenile delinquency: The integration of moral reasoning theory and sociological knowledge. In W. S. Laufer & J. M. Day (Eds.), *Personality theory, moral development, and criminal behavior*. Lexington, MA: Lexington Books.

Morris, D. (1967). *The naked ape*. New York: McGraw-Hill.

Morris, N. (1982). *Madness and the criminal law*. Chicago, IL: University of Chicago Press.

Morris, N., & Miller, M. (1985). Prediction of dangerousness. In M. Tonry & N. Morris (Eds.), *Crime and justice: An annual review of research*. Chicago, IL: University of Chicago Press.

Morse, S. J. (1978). Behavior, morals, and science: An analysis of mental health law. *Southern California Law Review, 51*, 527–654.

Morse, S. J. (1985). Excusing the crazy: The insanity defense reconsidered. *Southern California Law Review, 58*, 777–836.

Morse, S. J. (1986). Why amnesia and the law is not a useful topic. *Behavioral Science and the Law, 4*, 99–102.

Morton, J., Addison, H., Addison, R., Hunt, L., & Sullivan, J. (1953). A clinical study of premenstrual tension. *American Journal of Obstetrics and Gynecology, 65*, 1182–1191.

Mott, J. (1986). Opoid use and burglary. *British Journal of Addiction, 81*, 671–677.

Moyer, K. E. (1971). The physiology of aggression and the implication for aggression control. In J. L. Singer (Ed.), *The control of aggression and violence*. New York: Academic Press.

Moyer, K. E. (1976). *The psychobiology of aggression*. New York: Harper & Row.

Mueller, C. W. (1983). Environmental stressors and aggressive behavior. In R. G. Geen & E. I. Donnerstein (Eds.), *Aggression: Theoretical and empirical reviews* (Vol. 2). New York: Academic Press.

Mulder, R. T., Wells, J. E., Joyce, P. R., & Bushnell, J. A. (1994). Antisocial women. *Journal of Personality Disorders, 8*, 279–287.

Mulhern, S. (1991). Satanism and psychotherapy: A rumor in search of an inquisition. In J. T. Richardson, J. Best, & D. G. Bromley (Eds.), *The satanism scare*. New York: Aldine De Gruyter.

Mulvey, E. P., Arthur, M. W., & Reppucci, N. D. (1993). The prevention and treatment of juvenile delinquency: A review of the research. *Clinical Psychology Review, 13*, 133–167.

Munford, R. S., Kazer, R., Feldman, R., & Stivers, R. (1976). Homicide trends in Atlanta. *Criminology, 142*, 213–231.

Murphy, G. H., & Clare, C. H. (1996). Analysis of motivation in people with mild learning disabilities (mental handicap) who set fires. *Psychology, Crime, & Law, 2*, 153–164.

Murphy, J. M., & Gilligan, C. (1980). Moral development in late adolescence and adulthood: A critique and reconstruction of Kohlberg's theory. *Human Development, 23,* 77–104.

Myers, D. G. (1996). *Social psychology* (5th edition). New York: McGraw-Hill.

Nacci, P. L., Teitelbaum, H. E., & Prather, J. (1977). Population density and inmate misconduct rates in the federal prison system. *Federal Probation, 41,* 26–31.

Nachshon, I. (1983). Hemisphere dysfunction in psychopathy and behavior disorders. In M. Myslobodsky (Ed.), *Hemisyndromes: Psychobiology, neurology, psychiatry.* New York: Academic Press.

Nachshon, I., & Denno, D. (1987). Violent behavior and cerebral hemisphere function. In S. A. Mednick, T. E. Moffitt, & S. A. Stack (Eds.), *The causes of crime: New biological approaches.* Cambridge, Eng.: Cambridge University Press.

Nagi, S. G. (1975). Child abuse and neglect programs: A national overview. *Children Today, 4,* 13–17.

Nagin, D. S., Farrington, D. P., & Moffitt, T. (1995). Life-course trajectories of different types of offenders. *Criminology, 33,* 111–139.

Nagin, D. S., & Land, K. C. (1993). Age, criminal careers, and population heterogeneity: Specification and estimation of a nonparametric mixed Poisson model. *Criminology, 31,* 163–189.

Nash, J. R. (1975). *Bloodletters and badmen: Book 3.* New York: Warner Books.

Nathan, D. (1991). Satanism and child molestation: Constructing the ritual abuse scare. In J. T. Richardson, J. Best, & D. G. Bromley (Eds.), *The satanism scare.* New York: Aldine De Gruyter.

National Cable Television Association. (1998). *National Television Violence Study* (Vol. 3). Thousand Oaks, CA: Sage.

National Commission on Marihuana and Drug Abuse. (1972). *Marihuana: A signal of misunderstanding. Appendix, Vol. 1.* Washington, DC: USGPO.

National Commission on Marihuana and Drug Abuse. (1973). *Drug use in America: Problem in perspective* (2nd report). Washington, DC: USGPO.

National Institute on Alcohol Abuse and Alcoholism. (1990). *Alcohol and health: Neuroscience.* Rockville, MD: USGPO.

National Institute on Alcohol Abuse and Alcoholism. (1997, October). *Alcohol, violence, and aggression.* Alcohol Alert. Rockville, MD: USGPO.

National Institute on Drug Abuse. (1978). Drug abuse and crime. In L. D. Savitz & N. Johnson (Eds.), *Crime in society.* New York: Wiley.

National Media Archive. (1990 September). Stories emphasized violence against women and children. *On Balance, 3,* No. 8.

Nebylitsyn, V. D., & Gray, J. A. (1972). *Biological bases of individual behavior.* New York: Academic Press.

Nee, C., & Taylor, M. (1988). Residential burglary in the Republic of Ireland: A situational perspective. *Howard Journal, 27,* 105–116.

Neisser, U., et al. (1996). Intelligence: Knowns and unknowns. *American Psychologist, 51,* 77–101.

Nelson, S., & Amir, M. (1975). The hitchhike victim of rape: A research report. In I. Drapkin & E. Viano (Eds.), *Victimology: A new focus* (Vol. 5). Lexington, MA: Lexington Books.

Nettler, G. (1982). *Killing one another.* Cincinnati, OH: Anderson.

Nettler, G. (1984). *Explaining crime* (3rd edition). New York: McGraw-Hill.

Newman, E. S., Newman, D. J., & Gewirtz, M. L. (Eds.). (1984). *Elderly criminals.* Cambridge, MA: Oelgeschlager, Gunn & Hain.

Newman, G. (1982). *Just and painful: A case for the corporal punishment of criminals.* New York: Macmillan.

Newman, J. P. (1987). Reaction to punishment in extroverts and psychopaths: Implications for the impulsive behavior of disinhibited individuals. *Journal of Research in Personality, 21,* 464–480.

Newman, J. P., & Kosson, D. S. (1986). Passive avoidance learning in psychopathic and nonpsychopathic offenders. *Journal of Abnormal Psychology, 95,* 252–256.

Newman, J. P., Patterson, C. M., Howland, E. W., & Nichols, S. L. (1990). Passive avoidance in psychopaths: The effects of reward. *Personality and Individual Differences, 11,* 1101–1114.

Newman, J. P., Patterson, C. M., & Kosson, D. S. (1987). Response preservation in psychopaths. *Journal of Abnormal Psychology, 96,* 145–148.

Nichol, A. R., Gunn, J. C., Gristwood, J., Foggett, R. H., & Watson, J. P. (1973). The relationship of alcoholism to violent behaviors resulting in long-term imprisonment. *British Journal of Psychiatry, 123,* 47–51.

Nicholson, R. A., & Kugler, K. E. (1991). Competent and incompetent criminal defendants: A quantitative review of comparative research. *Psychological Bulletin, 109,* 355–370.

Niedermeyer, A. A. (1963). *Der Nervenarzt, 34,* 168.

Nietzel, M. T. (1979). *Crime and its modification: A social learning perspective.* New York: Pergamon.

NIOSH. (1993). *Fatal injuries to workers in the United States, 1980–1989: A decade of surveillance.* Cincinnati, OH: U.S. Department of Health and Human Services.

Noesner, G. W., & Dolan, J. T. (1992, August). First responder negotiation training. *FBI Law Enforcement Bulletin,* pp. 1–4.

Normandeau, A. (1968). Patterns in robbery. *Criminologica, 1,* 2–13.

Nunn, C. Z. (1974). The rising credibility of the devil in America. *Listening, 9,* 84–99.

Offord, D. R., Boyle, M. C., & Racine, Y. A. (1991). The epidemiology of antisocial behavior in childhood and adolescence. In D. J. Pepler & K. H. Rubin (Eds.), *The development and treatment of childhood aggression.* Hillsdale, NJ: Erlbaum.

Ogloff, J. R., & Pfeifer, J. E. (1992). Cults and the law: A discussion of the legality of alleged cult activities. *Behavioral Sciences and the Law, 10,* 117–140.

Ogloff, J. R., & Wong, S. (1990) Electrodermal and cardiovascular evidence of a coping response in psychopaths. *Criminal Justice and Behavior, 17,* 231–245.

Ohlin, L. E. (1983). The future of juvenile justice policy and research. *Crime and Delinquency, 29,* 463–472.

Ohlin, L. E., & Tonry, M. (1989). Family violence in perspective. In L. Ohlin & M. Tonry (Eds.), *Family violence* (Vol. 11). Chicago, IL: University of Chicago Press.

O'Leary, K. D. (1988). Physical aggression between spouses: A social learning perspective. In V. B. Van Hasselt, R. L. Morrison, A. S. Bellack, & M. Hersen (Eds.), *Handbook of family violence.* New York: Plenum.

O'Leary, K. D., Barling, J., Arias, I., Rosenbaum, A., Malone, J., & Tyree, A. (1989).

Prevalence and stability of physical aggression between spouses: A longitudinal analysis. *Journal of Consulting and Clinical Psychology, 57,* 263–268.

O'Leary, K. D., & Curley, A. D. (1986). Assertion and family violence: Correlates of spouse abuse. *Journal of Marital and Family Therapy, 12,* 281–289.

O'Leary, M. R., & Dengerink, H. A. (1973). Aggression as a function of the intensity and pattern of attack. *Journal of Experimental Research in Personality, 7,* 61–70.

Oltman, J., & Friedman, S. (1967). Parental deprivation in psychiatric conditions. *Diseases of the Nervous System, 28,* 298–303.

Olweus, D. (1978). *Aggression in the schools.* New York: Wiley.

Ondrovik, J., & Hamilton, D. (1991). Credibility of victims diagnosed as multiple personality: A case study. *American Journal of Forensic Psychology, 9,* 13–17.

Orne, M. T., Dinges, D. F., & Orne, E. C. (1984). On the differential diagnosis of multiple personality in the forensic context. *The International Journal of Clinical and Experimental Hypnosis, 32,* 118–169.

Orris, J. B. (1969). Visual monitoring performance in three subgroups of male delinquents. *Journal of Abnormal Psychology, 74,* 227–229.

Pacht, A., & Cowden, J. (1974). An exploratory study of five hundred sex offenders. *Criminal Justice and Behavior, 1,* 13–20.

Pagelow, M. D. (1989). The incidence and prevalence of criminal abuse of other family members. In L. Ohlin & M. Tonry (Eds.), *Family violence* (Vol. 11). Chicago, IL: University of Chicago Press.

Palmer, T. (1975). Martinson revisited. *Journal of Research in Crime and Delinquency, 12,* 3–14.

Parker, H., & Newcombe, R. (1987). Heroin use and acquisitive crime in an English community. *British Journal of Sociology, 38,* 331–350.

Passantino, G., & Passantino, B. (1989). Satan's sideshow, *Cornerstone, 18,* 23–28.

Passingham, R. E. (1972). Crime and personality: A review of Eysenck's theory. In V. D. Nebylitsyn & J. A. Gray (Eds.), *Biological bases of individual behavior.* New York: Academic Press.

Patrick, A. (1988). The crowding crisis: A global view. *Corrections Today, 50,* 110–111, 114–115.

Patrick, C. J., Bradley, M. M., & Lang, P. J. (1993). Emotion in the criminal psychopath: Start reflex modulation. *Journal of Abnormal Psychology, 102,* 82–92.

Patterson, G. R. (1982). *Coercive family processes.* Eugene, OR: Castalia Press.

Patterson, G. R. (1986). Performance models for antisocial boys. *American Psychologist, 41,* 432–444.

Paulhus, D. L., & Martin, C. L. (1986). Predicting adult temperament from minor physical anomalies. *Journal of Personality and Social Psychology, 50,* 1235–1239.

Paull, D. (1993). *Fitness to stand trial.* Springfield, IL: C. C. Thomas.

Paulus, P. B. (1988). *Prison crowding: A psychological perspective.* New York: Springer-Verlag.

Pazder, L., & Smith, M. (1980). *Michelle remembers.* New York: Congdon and Lattes.

Peele, S. (1984). The cultural context of psychological approaches to alcoholism. *American Psychologist, 39,* 1337–1351.

Pennington, L. A. (1966). Psychopathic and criminal behavior. In L. A. Pennington & I. A. Berg (Eds.), *An introduction to clinical psychology*. New York: Ronald Press.

Penrod, S. (1983). *Social psychology*. Englewood Cliffs, NJ: Prentice Hall.

Pepler, D. J., & Slaby, R. G. (1994). Theoretical and development perspectives on youth and violence. In L. D. Eron, J. H. Gentry, & P. Schlegel (Eds.), *Reason to hope: A psychosocial perspective on violence and youth*. Washington, DC: American Psychological Association.

Peters, S. D., Wyatt, G. E., & Finkelhor, D. (1986). Prevalence. In D. Finkelhor (Ed.), *Sourcebook on child sexual abuse*. Beverly Hills, CA: Sage.

Petersen, E. (1977). *A reassessment of the concept of criminality*. New York: Halstead Press.

Peterson, M. A., Braiker, H. B., & Polich, S. M. (1981). *Who commits crimes?* Cambridge, MA: Oelgeschlager, Gunn & Hain.

Phares, E. J. (1972). A social learning theory approach to psychopathology. In J. Rotter, J. Chana, & E. J. Phares (Eds.), *Applications of a social learning theory of personality*. New York: Holt, Rinehart & Winston.

Piaget, J. (1948). *The moral judgment of the child*. New York: Free Press.

Pillemer, K., & Finkelhor, D. (1988). The prevalence of elder abuse: A random sample survey. *The Gerontologist, 28*, 51–57.

Pillemer, K., & Suitor, J. J. (1988). Elder abuse. In V. B. van Hasselt, R. L. Morrison, A. S. Morrison, A. S. Bellak, & M. Hersen (Eds.), *Handbook of family violence*. New York: Plenum.

Pincus, J. H. (1980). Can violence be a manifestation of epilepsy? *Neurology, 30*, 304–306.

Pinizzotto, A. J. (1984). Forensic psychology: Criminal personality profiling. *Journal of Police Science and Administration, 12*, 32–40.

Pinizzotto, A. J., & Finkel, N. J. (1990). Criminal personality profiling: An outcome and process study. *Law and Human Behavior, 14*, 215–234.

Pithers, W. D., Beal, L. S., Armstrong, J., & Petty, J. (1989). Identification of risk factors through clinical interviews and analysis of records. In D. R. Laws (Ed.), *Relapse prevention with sex offenders*. New York: Guilford.

Pithers, W. D., Kashima, K. M., Cumming, G. F., Beal, L. S., & Buell, M. M. (1988). Relapse prevention of sexual aggression. In R. A. Prentky & V. L. Quinsey (Eds.), *Human sexual aggression: Current perspectives*. New York: New York Academy of Sciences.

Pithers, W. D., Marques, J. K., Gibat, C. C., & Marlatt, G. A. (1983). Relapse prevention with sexual aggressives. In J. G. Greer & I. R. Stuart (Eds.), *The sexual aggressor: Current perspectives on treatment*. New York: Van Nostrand Reinhold.

Plass, P. S. (1993). African-American family homicide: Patterns in partner, parent, and child victimization, 1985–1987. *Journal of Black Studies, 23*, 515–538.

Pleck, E. (1989). Criminal approaches to family violence, 1640–1980. In L. Ohlin & M. Tonry (Eds.), *Family violence* (Vol. 11). Chicago, IL: University of Chicago Press.

Pokorny, A. D. (1965). A comparison of homicide in two cities. *Journal of Criminal Law, Criminology and Police Science, 56*, 479–484.

Pomeroy, W. (1965). Some aspects of prostitution. *Journal of Sex Research, 5,* 177–187.

Pope, C. E. (1977a). *Crime-specific analysis: An empirical examination of burglary offender characteristics (LEAA).* Washington, DC: USGPO.

Pope, C. E. (1977b). *Crime-specific analysis: The characteristics of burglary incidents (LEAA).* Washington, DC: USGPO.

Pope, C. E. (1977c). *Crime-specific analysis: An empirical examination of burglary offense and offense characteristics (LEAA).* Washington, DC: USGPO.

Powell, G. E., & Stewart, R. A. (1983). The relationship of personality to antisocial and neurotic behaviours as observed by teachers. *Personality and Individual Differences, 4,* 97–100.

Poythress, N. G., Otto, R. K., Darkes, J., & Starr, L. (1993). APA's expert panel in the Congressional review of the USS Iowa incident. *American Psychologist, 48,* 8–15.

Prentice-Dunn, S., & Rogers, R. (1982). Effects of public and private self-awareness on deindividuation and aggression. *Journal of Personality and Social Psychology, 43,* 503–513.

Prentice-Dunn, S., & Rogers, R. (1983). Deindividuation in aggression. In R. G. Geen & E. I. Donnerstein (Eds.), *Aggression: Theoretical and empirical reviews* (Vol. 2). New York: Academic Press.

Prentky, R. A., & Knight, R. A. (1986). Impulsivity in the life style and criminal behavior of sexual offenders. *Criminal Justice and Behavior, 13,* 141–164.

Prentky, R. A., Knight, R. A., & Lee, A. F. S. (1997). Child sexual molestation: Research issues. *NIJ Research Report.* Rockville, MD: National Criminal Justice Reference Service. Available: www.ncjrs.org/txtfiles/163390.txt.

President's Commission on Law Enforcement and Administration of Justice. (1967). *The challenge of crime in free society.* Washington, DC: USGPO.

Price, J. B. (1968). Some results on the Maudsley Personality Inventory from a sample of girls in Borstal. *British Journal of Criminology, 8,* 383–401.

Price, W. H., & Whatmore, P. B. (1967). Behaviour disorders and patterns of crime among XYY males identified at a maximum security hospital. *British Medical Journal, 1,* 533–536.

Quay, H. C. (1964). Dimensions of personality in delinquent boys as inferred from the factor analysis of case history data. *Child Development, 35,* 479–484.

Quay, H. C. (1965). Psychopathic personality: Pathological stimulation-seeking. *American Journal of Psychiatry, 122,* 180–183.

Quay, H. C. (1972). Patterns of aggression, withdrawal, and immaturity. In H. Quay & J. Werry (Eds.), *Psychopathological disorders of childhood.* New York: Wiley.

Quay, H. C. (1977). The three faces of evaluation: What can be expected to work. *Criminal Justice and Behavior, 4,* 341–354.

Quay, H. C. (1987b). Intelligence. In H. C. Quay (Ed.), *Handbook of juvenile delinquency.* New York: Wiley.

Queen's Bench Foundation. (1978). The rapist and his crime. In L. D. Savitz & N. Johnson (Eds.), *Crime in society.* New York: Wiley.

Quinsey, V. L., & Marshall, W. L. (1983). Procedures for reducing inappropriate sexual arousal: An evaluation review. In J. G. Greer & I. R. Stuart (Eds.), *The sexual aggressor*. New York: Van Nostrand Reinhold.

Quinsey, V. L., Rice, M. E., & Harris, G. T. (1995). Actuarial prediction of sexual recidivism. *Journal of Interpersonal Violence, 10*, 85–105.

Rabkin, J. G. (1979). Criminal behavior of discharged mental patients: A critical appraisal of the research. *Psychological Bulletin, 86*, 1–27.

Rachman, S. J. (1966). Sexual fetishism: An experimental analogue. *Psychological Record, 16*, 293–296.

Rada, R. T. (1975). Alcoholism and forcible rape. *American Journal of Psychiatry, 121*, 776–783.

Raine, A. (1993). *The psychopathology of crime: Criminal behavior as a clinical disorder*. San Diego, CA: Academic Press.

Raskin, D. C., & Hare, R. D. (1978). Psychopathy and detection of deception in a prison population. *Psychophysiology, 15*, 126–136.

Ray, O. (1972). *Drugs, society and human behavior*. St. Louis, MO: C. V. Mosby.

Ray, O. (1983). *Drugs, society and human behavior* (3rd edition). St. Louis, MO: C. V. Mosby.

Reid, J. B. (1993). Prevention of conduct disorder before and after school entry: Relating interventions to developmental findings. *Development and Psychopathology, 5*, 243–262.

Reiss, A. J., & Roth, J. A. (Eds.) (1993). *Understanding and preventing violence*. Washington, DC: National Academy Press.

Reiss, J. (1977). "Voluntary" castration of mentally disordered sex offenders. *Criminal Law Bulletin, 13*, 30–48.

Rengert, G., & Wasilchick, J. (1985). *Suburban burglary: A time and place for everything*. Springfield, IL: C. C. Thomas

Resnick, P. J. (1969). Child murder by parents. *American Journal of Psychiatry, 126*, 325–334.

Resnick, P. J. (1970). Murder of the newborn: A psychiatric review of neonaticide. *American Journal of Psychiatry, 126*, 1414–1420.

Revitch, E., & Schlesinger, L. B. (1988). Clinical reflections on sexual aggression. In R. A. Prentky & V. L. Quinsey (Eds.), *Human sexual aggression: Current perspectives*. New York: New York Academy of Sciences.

Revitch, E., & Weiss, R. G. (1962). The pedophiliac offender. *Diseases of the Nervous System, 23*, 73–78.

Rhoads, J. M., & Borjes, E. D. (1981). The incidence of exhibitionism in Guatemala and U.S. *British Journal of Psychiatry, 139*, 242–244.

Rice, M. E. (1997). Violent offender research and implications for the criminal justice system. *American Psychologist, 52*, 414–423.

Rice, M. E., Harris, G. T., & Cormier, C. A. (1992). An evaluation of a maximum security therapeutic community for psychopaths and other mentally disordered offenders. *Law and Human Behavior, 16*, 399–412.

Riedel, M., Zahn, M., & Mock, L. F. (1985). *The nature and patterns of American homicide*. Washington, DC: USGPO.

Ritvo, E., Shanok, S. S., & Lewis, D. O. (1983). Firesetting and nonfiresetting delinquents. *Child Psychiatry and Human Development, 13*, 259–267.

Rivera, G. (1988, Oct 25). *Devil worship: Exposing Satan's underground*. NBC Television Documentary.

Robbins, E., & Robbins, L. (1964). Arson with special reference to pyromania. *New York State Journal of Medicine, 2*, 795–798.

Robins, L. N. (1966). *Deviant children grow up*. Baltimore, MD: Williams & Wilkins.

Roche, P. Q. (1958). *The criminal mind: A study of communication between criminal law and psychiatry*. New York: Grove Press.

Rodman, H., & Grams, P. (1967). Juvenile delinquency and the family: A review and discussion. In *Task Force Report: Juvenile delinquency and youth crime*. Washington, DC: USGPO.

Rogers, R. W., & Ketcher, C. M. (1979). Effects of anonymity and arousal on aggression. *Journal of Psychology, 102*, 13–19.

Roizen, J. (1997). Epidemiological issues in alcohol-related violence. In M. Galanter (Ed.), *Recent developments in alcoholism* (Vol. 13). New York: Plenum.

Roncek, D. W. (1975). Density and crime: A methodological critique. *American Behavioral Scientist, 18*, 843–860.

Rooth, G. (1973). Exhibitionism outside Europe and America. *Archives of Sexual Behavior, 2*, 351–363.

Rooth, G. (1974). Exhibitionists around the world. *Human Behavior, 3*, 61.

Rosecan, J. S., Spitz, H. I., & Gross, B. (1987). Contemporary issues in the treatment of cocaine abuse. In H. I. Spitz & J. S. Rosecan (Eds.), *Cocaine abuse: New directions in treatment and research*. New York: Brunner/Mazel.

Rosenthal, D. (1970). *Genetic theory and abnormal behavior*. New York: McGraw-Hill.

Rosenthal, D. (1971). *Genetics of psychopathology*. New York: McGraw-Hill.

Rosenthal, D. (1975). Heredity in criminality. *Criminal Justice and Behavior, 2*, 3–21.

Rosoff, S. M., Pontell, H. N., & Tillman, R. (1998). *Profit without honor: White-collar crime and the looting of America*. Upper Saddle River, NJ: Prentice Hall.

Rotenberg, M., & Diamond, B. (1971). The biblical conception of psychopathy: The law of the stubborn and rebellious son. *Journal of the History of the Behavioral Sciences, 12*, 29–38.

Roth, J. A. (1996). *Psychoactive substances and violence*. Washington, DC: U.S. Department of Justice. Available: www.ncjrs.org/txtfile/psycho.txt.

Rotton, J. (1983). Affective and cognitive consequences of malodorous pollution. *Basic and Applied Psychology, 4*, 171–191.

Rotton, J., & Frey, J. (1985). Air pollution, weather, and violent crimes: Concomitant time-series analysis of archival data. *Journal of Personality and Social Psychology, 49*, 1207–1220.

Ruback, R. B., & Carr, T. S. (1984). Crowding in a women's prison: Attitudinal and behavioral effects. *Journal of Applied Social Psychology, 14*, 57–68.

Rubin, B. (1972). Predictions of dangerousness in mentally ill criminals. *Archives of General Psychiatry, 27*, 397–407.

Rubinsky, E. W., & Brandt, J. (1986). Amnesia and criminal law: A clinical overview. *Behavioral Sciences and the Law, 4*, 27–46.

Rushton, J. P., & Chrisjohn, R. D. (1981). Extraversion, neuroticism, psychoticism, and self-reported delinquency: Evidence from eight separate samples. *Personality and Individual Differences, 2*, 11–20.

Russell, D. (1973). Emotional aspects of shoplifting. *Psychiatric Annals, 3*, 77–86.

Russell, D. E. H. (1975). *The politics of rape: The victim's perspective.* New York: Stein & Day.

Russell, D. E. H. (1983). The prevalence and incidence of forcible rape and attempted rape of females. *Victimology: An International Journal, 7,* 81–93.

Russell, D. E. H. (1984). *Sexual exploitation.* Beverly Hills, CA: Sage.

Russell, D. E. H., & Finkelhor, D. (1984). The gender gap among perpetrators of child sexual abuse. In D. E. H. Russell (Ed.), *Sexual exploitation.* Beverly Hills, CA: Sage.

Russell, D. E. H., & Howell, N. (1983). The prevalence of rape in the United States revisited. *Signs: Journal of Women in Culture and Society, 8,* 688–695.

Rutter, M., & Giller, H. (1984). *Juvenile delinquency: Trends and perspectives.* New York: Guilford Press.

Salekin, R. T., Rogers, R., & Sewell, K. W. (1997). Construct validity of psychopathy in a female offender sample: A multitrait-multimethod evaluation. *Journal of Abnormal Psychology, 106,* 576–585.

Salekin, R. T., Rogers, R., Ustad, K. L., & Sewell, K. W. (1998). Psychopathy and recidivism among female inmates. *Law and Human Behavior, 22,* 109–128.

Sampson, R. J., & Laub, J. H. (1997). Unraveling the social context of physique and delinquency: A new, long-term look at the Gluecks' classic study. In A. Raine, P. A. Brennan, D. P. Farrington, & S. A. Mednick (Eds.), *Biosocial bases of violence.* New York: Plenum.

Sampson, R. J., & Lauritsen, J. L. (1994). Violent victimization and offending: Individual, situational and community-level risk factors. In A. T. Reiss Jr. & J. Roth (Eds.), *Understanding and preventing violence: Social Influences* (Vol. 3). Washington, DC: National Academy Press.

Sampson, R. J., & Wilson, W. J. (1993). Toward a theory of race, crime, and urban inequality. In J. Hagan & R. Peterson (Eds.), *Crime and inequality.* Stanford, CA: Stanford University Press.

Santa Clara Criminal Justice Pilot Program. (1972). *Burglary in San Jose.* Springfield, VA: U.S. Department of Commerce.

Sarasalo, E., Bergman, B., & Toth, J. (1997). Kleptomania-like behaviour and psychosocial characteristics among shoplifters. *Legal and Criminological Psychology, 2,* 1–10.

Sarbin, T. R. (1979). The myth of the criminal type. In T. R. Sarbin (Ed.), *Challenges to the criminal justice system: The perspective of community psychology.* New York: Human Services Press.

Satterfield, J. H. (1973). EEG issues in children with minimal brain dysfunction. *Seminars in Psychiatry, 5,* 35–46.

Satterfield, J. H. (1978). The hyperactive child syndrome: A precursor of adult psychopathy? In R. D. Hare & D. Schalling (Eds.), *Psychopathic behaviour: Approaches to research.* Chichester, Eng.: Wiley.

Satterfield, J. H. (1987). Childhood diagnostic and neurophysiological predictors of teenage arrest rates: An eight year prospective study. In S. A. Mednick, T. A. Moffitt, & S. A. Stack (Eds.), *The causes of crime: New biological approaches.* Cambridge, Eng.: Cambridge University Press.

Satterfield, J. H., Atoian, G., Brashears, G. C., Burleigh, A. C., & Dawson, M. E. (1974). Electrodermal studies of minimal brain dysfunction in children. In *Clinical use of stimulant drugs in children.* The Hague: Excerpta Medica.

Satterfield, J. H., & Dawson, M. E. (1971). Electrodermal correlates of hyperactivity in children. *Psychophysiology, 8,* 191–197.

Satterfield, J. H., Swanson, J., Schell, A., & Lee, F. (1994). Prediction of antisocial behavior in attention-deficit hyperactivity disorder boys from aggression/defiance scores. *Journal of the American Academy of Child and Adolescent Psychiatry, 33,* 185–191.

Saulnier, K., & Perlman, D. (1981). The actor-observer bias is alive and well in prison: A sequel to Wells. *Personality and Social Psychology, 7,* 559–564.

Saunders, D. G., & Azar, S. T. (1989). Treatment programs for family violence. In L. Ohlin & M. Tonry (Eds.), *Family violence* (Vol. 11). Chicago, IL: University of Chicago Press.

Savitz, L. D. (1972). Introduction. In G. Lombroso-Ferrero, *Criminal man.* Montclair, NJ: Patterson Smith.

Scaret, D., & Wilgosh, L. (1989). Learning disabilities and juvenile delinquency: A causal relationship? *International Journal for the Advancement of Counselling, 12,* 113–123.

Schacht, T. E. (1985). DSM-III and the politics of truth. *American Psychologist, 40,* 513–521.

Schachter, S. (1971). *Emotion, obesity and crime.* New York: Academic Press.

Schachter, S., & Latane, B. (1964). Crime, cognition, and the autonomic nervous system. In M. R. Jones (Ed.), *Nebraska symposium on motivation.* Lincoln, NE: University of Nebraska Press.

Schacter, D. L. (1986a). Amnesia and crime: How much do we really know? *American Psychologist, 41,* 286–295.

Schacter, D. L. (1986b). On the relation between genuine and simulated amnesia. *Behavioral Sciences and the Law, 4,* 47–64.

Schafer, W. E., & Polk, K. (1967). Delinquency and the schools. *Task force report: Juvenile delinquency and youth crime.* Washington, DC: USGPO.

Scherer, D. G., Brondino, M. J., Henggeler, S. W., Melton, G. B., & Hanley, J. H. (1994). Multisystemic family preservation therapy: Preliminary findings from a study of rural and minority serious adolescent offenders. *Journal of Emotional and Behavioral Disorders, 2,* 198–206.

Schlossman, S., & Sedlak, M. (1983). The Chicago area project revisited. *Crime and Delinquency, 29,* 398–462.

Schmideberg, M. (1953). Pathological firesetters. *Journal of Criminal Law, Criminology and Police Science, 44,* 30–39.

Schrager, L., & Short, J. (1978). Toward a sociology of organizational crime. *Social Problems, 25,* 407–419.

Schuller, R. A., & Vidmar, V. (1992). Battered woman syndrome evidence in the courtroom: A review of the literature. *Law and Human Behavior, 16,* 272–292.

Schulsinger, F. (1972). Psychopathy: Heredity and environment. *International Journal of Mental Health, 1,* 190–206.

Schultz, J. L., & Cohen, F. (1976). Isolationism in juvenile court jurisprudence. In M. Rosenhan (Ed.), *Pursuing justice for the child.* Chicago, IL: University of Chicago Press.

Schultz, L. G. (1975). *Rape victimology.* Springfield, IL: C. C. Thomas.

Scully, D., & Marolla, J. (1984). Convicted rapists' vocabulary of motive: Excuses and justifications. *Social Problems, 31*, 530–544.

Scully, D., & Marolla, J. (1985). Rape and vocabularies of motive: Alternative perspectives. In A. W. Burgess (Ed.), *Rape and sexual assault*. New York: Garland Publishing.

Sears, R., Maccoby, E., & Levin, H. (1957). *Patterns of child rearing*. Evanston, IL: Row, Peterson.

Sebald, H. (1986). Adolescents' shifting orientations toward parents and peers: A curvilinear trend over recent decades. *Journal of Marriage and the Family, 48*, 5–13.

Sechrest, L. (1987). Classification for treatment. In D. M. Gottfredson & M. Tonry (Eds.), *Prediction and classification: Criminal justice decision making* (Vol. 9). Chicago, IL: University of Chicago Press.

Sedlak, A. J., & Broadhurst, D. D. (1996). *Executive summary of the third national incidence study of child abuse and neglect*. Washington, DC: U.S. Department of Health and Human Services.

Seligman, M. E. (1975). *Helplessness: On depression, development, and death*. San Francisco, CA: W. H. Freeman.

Selkin, J. (1987). *Psychological autopsy in the courtroom*. Denver, CO: Author.

Sellin, T. (1970). A sociological approach. In M. E. Wolfgang, L. Savitz, & N. Johnson (Eds.), *The sociology of crime and delinquency* (2nd edition). New York: Wiley.

Serin, R. C., & Amos, N. L. (1995). The role of psychopathy in the assessment of dangerousness. *International Journal of Law & Psychiatry, 18*, 231–238.

Serin, R. C., Peters, R. D., & Barbaree, H. E. (1990). Predictors of psychopathy and release outcome in a criminal population. *Psychological Assessment, 2*, 419–422.

Shafer, S. (1976). *Introduction to criminology*. Reston, VA: Reston Publishing.

Shain, R., & Phillips, J. (1991). The stigma of mental illness: Labeling and stereotyping in the news. In L. Wilkins & P. Patterson (Eds.), *Risky business: Communicating issues of science, risk, and public policy*. Westport, CT: Greenwood Press.

Sheldon, W. H., Hartl, E. M., & McDermott, E. (1949). *Varieties of delinquent youth: An introduction to constitutional psychiatry*. New York: Harper.

Sheldon, W. H., & Stevens, S. S. (1942). *The varieties of temperament*. New York: Harper.

Sherman, L. W., & Berk, R. A. (1984). The specific deterrent effects of arrest for domestic assault. *American Sociological Review, 49*, 261–272.

Shields, J. (1962). *Monozygotic twins brought up apart and together*. Oxford, Eng.: Oxford University Press.

Short, J. F. (1968). *Gang delinquency and delinquency subcultures*. New York: Harper & Row.

Short, J. F., & Nye, I. (1957). Reported behavior as a criterion of deviant behavior. *Social Problems, 5*, 207–213.

Shover, N. (1972). Structures and careers in burglary. *Journal of Criminal Law, Criminology and Police Science, 63*, 540–548.

Shuntich, R. J., & Taylor, S. P. (1972). The effects of alcohol on human physical aggressions. *Journal of Experimental Research in Personality, 6*, 34–38.

Sickmund, M., Snyder, H. N., & Poe-Yamagata, E. (1997). *Juvenile offenders and victims: 1997 update on violence*. Washington, DC: Office of Juvenile Justice and Delinquency Prevention.

Siegel, A., & Kohn, L. (1959). Permissiveness, permission, and aggression: The effect of adult presence or absence on aggression in children's play. *Child Development, 30,* 131–141.

Siegel, J. M., Sorenson, S. B., Golding, J. M., Burnam, M. A., & Stein, J. A. (1987). The prevalence of childhood sexual assault: The Los Angeles Epidemiological Catchment Area Project. *American Journal of Epidemiology, 126,* 1141–1153.

Sieh, E. W. (1987). Garment workers: Perceptions of inequity and employee theft. *British Journal of Criminology, 27,* 174–190.

Sigall, H., & Ostrove, N. (1978). Physical attractiveness and jury decisions. In N. Johnson & L. Savitz (Eds.), *Justice and corrections*. New York: Wiley.

Silva, F., Martorell, C., & Clemente, A. (1986). Socialization and personality: Study through questionnaires in a preadult Spanish population. *Personality and Individual Differences, 7,* 355–372.

Silverman, R. A., & Mukherjee, S. K. (1987). Intimate homicide: An analysis of violent social relationships. *Behavioral Sciences and the Law, 5,* 37–47.

Simon, R. J., & Aaronson, D. E. (1988). *The insanity defense*. New York: Praeger.

Simon, R. J., & Cockerham, W. (1977). Civil commitment, burden of proof, and dangerous acts: A comparison of the perspectives of judges and psychiatrists. *Journal of Psychiatry and Law, 5,* 571–594.

Skinner, B. F. (1964). Behaviorism at fifty. In T. W. Wann (Ed.), *Behaviorism and phenomenology*. Chicago, IL: University of Chicago Press.

Skogan, W. G. (1977). Dimensions of the dark figure of unreported crime. *Crime and Delinquency, 23,* 41–50.

Skrzpek, G. J. (1969). The effects of perceptual isolation and arousal on anxiety, complexity preference, and novelty preference in psychopathic and neurotic delinquents. *Journal of Abnormal Psychology, 74,* 321–329.

Slobogin, C. (1985). The guilty but mentally ill verdict: An idea whose time should not have come. *George Washington Law Review, 53,* 494–580.

Slovenko, R. (1989). The multiple personality: A challenge to legal concepts. *The Journal of Psychiatry and Law, 17,* 681–719.

Smart, C. (1976). *Women, crime, and criminology: A feminist critique*. London: Routledge & Kegan Paul.

Smart, R. G. (1986). Cocaine use and problems in North America. *British Journal of Criminology, 28,* 109–128.

Smart, R. G., & Adlaf, E. M. (1992). Recent studies of cocaine use and abuse in Canada. *Canadian Journal of Criminology, 34,* 1–13.

Smigel, E. O. (1970). Public attitudes toward stealing as related to the size of the victim organization. In E. O. Smigel & H. L. Ross (Eds.), *Crimes against bureaucracy*. New York: Van Nostrand Reinhold.

Smith, M. D., & Bennett, N. (1985). Poverty, inequality, and theories of forcible rape. *Crime and Delinquency, 31,* 295–305.

Smith, S. S., & Newman, J. P. (1990). Alcohol and drug abuse-dependence disorder in psychopathic and nonpsychopathic criminal offenders. *Journal of Abnormal Psychology, 99,* 430–439.

Sobell, M. B., & Sobell, L. C. (1973). Individualized behavior for alcoholics. *Behavior Therapy, 4,* 49–72.

Solomon, J., & King, P. (1993, July 19). Waging war in the workplace. *Newsweek,* pp. 30–34.

Sommer, D. A. (1983). How does menstruation affect cognitive competence and psychophysiological response? *Women and Health, 8,* 53–90.

Sorenson, S. B., Stein, J. A., Siegel, J. M., Golding, J. M., & Burnam, M. A. (1987). The prevalence of adult sexual assault: The Los Angeles Epidemiological Catchment Area Project. *American Journal of Epidemiology, 126,* 1154–1164.

Southerland, M. D., Collins, P. A., & Scarborough, K. E. (1997). *Workplace violence.* Cincinnati, OH: Anderson.

Spain, D. M., Bradess, F. A., & Eggson, A. A. (1951). Alcohol and violent death. *Journal of the American Medical Association, 146,* 334–335.

Spencer, C. (1966). *A typology of violent offenders.* Administrative Abstract No. 23, California Department of Corrections, September.

Spencer, J. (1989). *Suffer the child.* New York: Pocket.

Staffieri, J. R. (1967). A study of social stereotypes of body image in children. *Journal of Personality and Social Psychology, 1,* 101–104.

Stanger, C., Achenbach, T. M., & Verhulst, F. C. (1997). Accelerated longitudinal comparisons of aggressive versus delinquent syndromes. *Development and Psychopathology, 9,* 43–58.

Steadman, H. J. (1976). Predicting dangerousness. In D. J. Madden & J. R. Lion (Eds.), *Rage, hate, assault, and other forms of violence.* New York: Spectrum Publishers.

Steadman, H. J. (1979). *Beating a rap? Defendants found incompetent to stand trial.* Chicago, IL: University of Chicago Press.

Steadman, H. J., & Braff, J. (1983). Defendants not guilty by reason of insanity. In J. Mohanan & H. J. Steadman (Eds.), *Mentally disordered offenders.* New York: Plenum.

Steadman, H. J., & Cocozza, J. J. (1974). *Careers of the criminally insane.* Lexington, MA: Lexington Books.

Steadman, H. J., Fabisiak, S., Dvoskin, J., & Holobean, E. (1987). A survey of mental disability among state prison inmates. *Hospital and Community Psychiatry, 38,* 1086–1090.

Steadman, H. J., & Hartstone, E. (1983). Defendants incompetent to stand trial. In J. Monahan & H. J. Steadman (Eds.), *Mentally disordered offenders.* New York: Plenum.

Steadman, H. J., McGreevy, M. A., Morrissey, J. P., Callahan, L. A., Robbins, P. C., & Cirincione, C. (1993). *Before and after Hinckley: Evaluating insanity defense reform.* New York: Guilford Press.

Steadman, H. J., Monahan, J., Applebaum, P. S., Grisso, T., Mulvery, E. P., Roth, L. H., Robbins, P. C., & Klassen, D. (1994). Designing a new generation of risk assessment research. In J. Monahan & H. Steadman (Eds.), *Violence and mental disorder: Developments in risk assessment.* Chicago, IL: University of Chicago Press.

Steadman, H. J., Monahan, J., Hartstone, E., Davis, S. K., & Robbins, D. C. (1982). Mentally disordered offenders: A national survey of patients and facilities. *Law and Human Behavior, 6,* 31–38.

Steinmetz, S. K. (1977). *The cycle of violence: Assaultive, aggressive, and abusive family interaction*. New York: Praeger.

Steinmetz, S. K. (1981). A cross-cultural comparison of sibling violence. *International Journal of Family Psychiatry, 2*, 337–351.

Stephan, J. J., et al. (1997). *Census of state and federal correctional facilities, 1995*. Washington, DC: U.S. Bureau of Justice Statistics. Available: www.ojp.usdoj.gov/bjs/.

Stevens, P. (1991). The demonology of satanism: An anthropological view. In J. T. Richardson, J. Best, & D. G. Bromley (Eds.), *The satanism scare*. New York: Aldine De Gruyter.

Stewart, M. A., & Culver, K. W. (1982). Children who set fires: The clinical picture and a follow-up. *British Journal of Psychiatry, 140*, 357–363.

Stone, A. (1975). *Mental health law: A system in transition*. Washington, DC: USGPO.

Stratford, Lauren (1988). *Satan's underground: The extraordinary story of one woman's escape*. Eugene, OR: Harvest House.

Straus, M. (1991). Discipline and deviance: Physical punishment of children and violence and other crime in adulthood. *Social Problems, 38*, 133–154.

Straus, M. A., & Gelles, R. J. (1986). Societal change and change in family violence from 1975 to 1985 as revealed by two national surveys. *Journal of Marriage and the Family, 48*, 465–479.

Straus, M. A., Gelles, R. J., & Steinmetz, S. K. (1980). *Behind closed doors: Violence in the American family*. New York: Doubleday.

Strentz, T. (1987, November). A hostage psychological survival guide. *FBI Law Enforcement Bulletin*, pp. 1–7.

Sturgeon, V., & Taylor, J. (1980). Report of a five year follow-up study of mentally disordered sex offenders released from Atascadero State Hospital in 1973. *Criminal Justice Journal of Western State University, San Diego, 4*, 31–64.

Sutherland, E. H. (1983). *White-collar crime: The uncut version*. New Haven, CT: Yale University Press.

Sutherland, E. H., & Cressey, D. R. (1974). *Criminology* (9th edition). Philadelphia, PA: J. B. Lippincott.

Sutker, P. B., & Allain, A. N. (1983). Behavior and personality assessment in men labeled adaptive sociopaths. *Journal of Behavioral Assessment, 5*, 65–79.

Sutker, P. B., Uddo-Crane, M., & Allain, A. N. (1991). Clinical and research assessment of posttraumatic stress disorder: A conceptual overview. *Psychological Assessment: A Journal of Consulting and Clinical Psychology, 3*, 520–530.

Svalastoga, K. (1956). Homicide and social contact in Denmark. *American Journal of Sociology, 62*, 37–41.

Swanson, D. W. (1968). Adult sexual abuse of children: The man and circumstances. *Diseases of the Nervous System, 29*, 677–683.

Swanson, J., & Holzer, C. (1991). Violence and the ECA data. *Hospital and Community Psychiatry, 42*, 79–80.

Swanson, J., Holzer, C., Ganju, V., & Jono, R. (1990). Violence and psychiatric disorder in the community: Evidence from the Epidemiologic Catchment Area surveys. *Hospital and Community Psychiatry, 41*, 761–770.

Sykes, G. M. (1956). *Crime and society*. New York: Random House.

Symons, D. (1979). *The evolution of human sexuality.* New York: Oxford University Press.

Tappan, P. W. (1947). Who is the criminal? *American Sociological Review, 12,* 100–110.

Tappan, P. W. (1949). *Juvenile delinquency.* New York: McGraw-Hill.

Tasto, D., & Insel, P. (1977). The premenstrual and menstrual syndromes. In S. Rachman (Ed.), *Contributions to medical psychology* (Vol. 1). Oxford, Eng.: Pergamon Press.

Taylor, M., & Nee, C. (1988). The role of cues in simulated residential burglary. *British Journal of Criminology, 28,* 396–401.

Taylor, S. P. (1967). Aggressive behavior and physiological arousal as a function of provocation and the tendency to inhibit aggression. *Journal of Personality, 35,* 297–310.

Taylor, S. P., & Gammon, C. B. (1975). Effects of type and dose of alcohol on human physical aggression. *Journal of Personality and Social Psychology, 32,* 169–175.

Taylor, S. P., Gammon, C. B., & Capasso, D. R. (1976). Aggression as a function of the interaction of alcohol and threat. *Journal of Personality and Social Psychology, 34,* 938–941.

Taylor, S. P., & Leonard, K. E. (1983). Alcohol and human physical aggression. In R. G. Geen & E. I. Donnerstein (Eds.), *Aggression: Theoretical and empirical reviews* (Vol. 2). New York: Academic Press.

Taylor, S. P., Schmutte, G. T., Leonard, K. E., & Cranston, J. W. (1979). The effects of alcohol and extreme provocation on the use of highly noxious shock. *Motivation and Emotion, 3,* 73–81.

Taylor, S. P., & Sears, J. D. (1988). The effects of alcohol and persuasive social pressure on human physical aggression. *Aggressive Behavior, 14,* 237–244.

Taylor, S. P., Vardaris, R. M., Ravitch, A. B., Gammon, C. B., Cranston, J. W., & Lubetkin, A. E. (1976). The effects of alcohol and delta-9-tetrahydrocannabinol on human physical aggression. *Aggressive Behavior, 2,* 153–161.

Teplin, J. (1990). The prevalence of severe mental disorder among male urban jail detainees: Comparisons with the Epidemiologic Catchment Area program. *American Journal of Public Health, 80,* 663–669.

Teplin, L. (1984). Criminalizing mental disorder. *American Psychologist, 39,* 794–803.

Thomas, M. H. (1982). Physiological arousal, exposure to a relatively lengthy aggressive film, and aggressive behavior. *Journal of Research in Personality, 16,* 72–81.

Thompson, K. M. (1990). Refacing inmates: A critical appraisal of plastic surgery programs in prison. *Criminal Justice and Behavior, 17,* 448–466.

Thorley, G. (1984). Review of follow-up and follow-back studies of childhood hyperactivity. *Psychological Bulletin, 96,* 116–132.

Thornberry, T. P., & Farnworth, M. (1982). Social correlates of criminal involvement: Further evidence on the relationships between social status and criminal behavior. *American Sociological Review, 47,* 505–518.

Thornberry, T. P., & Jacoby, J. E. (1979). *The criminally insane: A community follow-up of mentally ill offenders.* Chicago, IL: University of Chicago Press.

Tinklenberg, J. R. (1973). Alcohol and violence. In P. G. Bourne (Ed.), *Alcoholism: Progress in research and treatment*. New York: Academic Press.

Tinklenberg, J. R., & Stillman, R. C. (1970). Drug use and violence. In D. Daniels, M. Gilula, & F. Ochberg (Eds.), *Violence and the struggle for existence*. Boston, MA: Little, Brown.

Tinklenberg, J. R., & Woodrow, K. M. (1974). Drug use among youthful assaultive and sexual offenders. In S. H. Frazier (Ed.), *Aggression*. Baltimore, MD: Williams & Wilkins.

Titchener, E. B. (1914). On "psychology as the behaviorist views it." *Proceedings of the American Philosophical Society, 53*, 213.

Tittle, C. R. (1983). Social class and criminal behavior: A critique of the theoretical foundation. *Social Forces, 62*, 334–358.

Tittle, C. R., & Villemez, W. J. (1977). Social class and criminality. *Social Forces, 56*, 474–502.

Tjaden, P. (1997, November). The crime of stalking: How big is the problem? *NIJ Research Preview*. Washington, DC: U.S. Department of Justice.

Tjaden, P., & Thoennes, N. (1997). *Stalking in America: Findings from the national violence against women survey*. Denver, CO: Center for Policy Research.

Tjaden, P., & Thoennes, N. (1998). *Stalking in America: Findings from the national violence against women survey*. Washington, DC: U.S. Department of Justice.

Toch, H. (1969). *Violent men: An inquiry into the psychology of violence*. Chicago, IL: Aldine.

Toch, H. (1977). *Police, prisons, and the problems of violence*. National Institute of Mental Health. Washington, DC: USGPO.

Toch, H., & Adams, K. (1989). *The disturbed violent offender*. New Haven, CT: Yale University Press.

Toch, H., & Adams, K., with Grant, J. D. (1989). *Coping: Maladaptation in prisons*. New Brunswick, NJ: Transaction Publishers.

Tolan, P. H., & Guerra, N. G. (1994). Prevention of delinquency: Current status and issues. *Applied and Preventive Psychology, 3*, 251–273.

Tolan, P. H., & Thomas, P. (1995). The implications of age of onset for delinquency II: Longitudinal data. *Journal of Abnormal Child Psychology, 23*, 157–169.

Trasler, G. (1987). Some cautions for the biological approach to crime causation. In S. A. Mednick, E. Moffitt, & S. A. Stack (Eds.), *The causes of crime: New biological approach*. Cambridge, Eng.: Cambridge University Press.

Tucker, D. M. (1981). Lateral brain function, emotion and conceptualization. *Psychological Bulletin, 89*, 19–46.

Tupin, J. P., Mahar, D., & Smith, D. (1973). Two types of violent offenders with psychosocial descriptors. *Diseases of the Nervous System, 34*, 356–363.

Ullman, S. E., & Knight, R. A. (1993). The efficacy of women's resistance strategies in rape situations. *Psychology of Women Quarterly, 17*, 23–38.

U.S. Department of Health and Human Services. (1988). *Study findings: Study of national incidence of child abuse and neglect*. Washington, DC: USGPO.

U.S. Department of Justice. (1976). *Bomb summary—1975*. Washington, DC: USGPO.

U.S. Department of Justice. (1988). *Report to the nation on crime and justice: The data* (2nd edition). Washington, DC: USGPO.

U.S. Department of Justice. (1989a). *Uniform crime reports.* Washington, DC: USGPO.

U.S. Department of Justice. (1989b). *Criminal victimization in the United States, 1987.* Washington, DC: USGPO.

U.S. Department of Justice. (1993). *Uniform crime reports.* Washington, DC: USGPO.

Valenstein, E. S. (1973). *Brain control.* New York: Wiley.

Verkko, V. (1951). *Homicides and suicides in Finland and their dependence on national character.* Copenhagen: C. E. R. Gad.

Vetter, H. J., & Silverman, I. J. (1978). *The nature of crime.* Philadelphia, PA: W. B. Saunders.

Victor, J. S. (1993). *Satanic panic: The creation of a contemporary legend.* Chicago, IL: Open Court.

Vincent, K. R. (1991). Black/white IQ difference? *Journal of Clinical Psychology, 47,* 266–270.

Virkkunen, M. (1975). Victim-precipitated pedophilia offenses. *British Journal of Criminology, 15,* 175–180.

Visher, C. A. (1987). Incapacitation and crime control. *Justice Quarterly, 4,* 513–543.

Volavka, J. (1987). Electroencephalogram among criminals. In S. A. Mednick, T. E. Moffitt, & S. Stack (Eds.), *The causes of crime: New biological approaches.* Cambridge, Eng.: Cambridge University Press.

Vold, G. B. (1958). *Theoretical criminology.* New York: Oxford University Press.

Voss, H. L., & Hepburn, J. (1968). Patterns in criminal homicide in Chicago. *Journal of Criminal Law, Criminology, and Police Science, 59,* 499–506.

Vreeland, R. G., & Levin, B. M. (1980). Psychological aspects of firesetting. In D. Canter (Ed.), *Fires and human behaviour.* Chichester, Eng.: Wiley.

Wadsworth, M. E. J. (1979). *Roots of delinquency: Infancy, adolescence and crime.* Oxford, Eng.: Martin Robinson.

Wakefield, J. C. (1992). Disorder as harmful dysfunction: A conceptual critique of DSM-III-R's definition of mental disorder. *Psychological Review, 99,* 232–247.

Walker, L. E. (1979). *The battered woman.* New York: Harper Colophon Books.

Walker, N. (1978). Dangerous people. *International Journal of Law and Psychiatry, 1,* 37–49.

Wallerstein, J. S., & Wyle, J. (1947). Our law-abiding law breakers. *Probation, 25,* 107–112.

Walster, E. (1966). Assignment of responsibility for an accident. *Journal of Personality and Social Psychology, 3,* 73–79.

Walters, G. C., & Grusec, J. E. (1977). *Punishment.* San Francisco, CA: W. H. Freeman.

Walters, H. F., & Malamud, P. (1975, March 10). Drop that gun, Captain Video. *Newsweek,* pp. 81–82.

Watson, R. I. (1973). Investigation into deindividuation using a cross-cultural survey technique. *Journal of Personality and Social Psychology, 25,* 342–345.

Webster, C. D., Douglas, K. S., Eaves, D., & Hart, S. D. (1997). Assessing risk to violence to others. In C. D. Webster & M. A. Jackson (eds.), *Impulsivity: Theory, assessment and treatment.* New York: Guilford.

Webster, C. D., & Menzies, R. J. (1993). Supervision in the deinstitutionalized community. In S. Hodgins (Ed.), *Mental disorder and crime*. Newbury Park, CA: Sage.

Weis, J. G. (1989). Family violence methodology and design. In L. Ohlin & M. Tonry (Eds.), *Family violence* (Vol. 11). Chicago, IL: University of Chicago Press.

Weis, J. G., & Sederstrom, J. (1981). *The prevention of serious delinquency. What to do?* Washington, DC: U.S. Department of Justice.

Weiss, G., Minde, K., Werry, J., Douglas, V., & Nemeth, E. (1971). Studies on the hyperactive child: Five-year follow-up. *Archives of General Psychiatry, 24,* 409–414.

Weiss, J., Lamberti, J., & Blackburn, N. (1960). The sudden murderers. *Archives of General Psychiatry, 2,* 670–678.

Weiss, R. D., & Mirin, S. M. (1987). *Cocaine*. Washington, DC: American Psychiatric Press.

Welte, J. W., & Abel, E. L. (1989). Homicide: Drinking by the victim. *Journal of Studies on Alcohol, 50,* 197–201.

Wenk, E. A., Robison, J. O., & Smith, G. W. (1972). Can violence be predicted? *Crime and Delinquency, 18,* 393–402.

West, D. J., & Farrington, D. P. (1973). *Who becomes delinquent?* London: Heinemann Educational.

Wettstein, R. M. (1984). The prediction of violent behavior and the duty to protect third parties. *Behavioral Science and the Law, 2,* 291–316.

Wetzel, R. D., McClure, J. N., & Reich, T. (1971). Premenstrual symptoms in self-referrals to a suicide prevention service. *British Journal of Psychiatry, 119,* 525–526.

Wexler, D. B. (1977). Criminal commitment contingency structures. In R. D. Sales (Ed.), *The criminal justice system* (Vol. 1). New York: Plenum.

Wexler, D. B. (1981). *Mental health law*. New York: Plenum.

White, J. L., Moffitt, T. E., & Silva, P. A. (1989). A prospective replication of the protective effects of IQ in subjects at high risk for juvenile delinquency. *Journal of Consulting and Clinical Psychology, 57,* 719–724.

White, P. T., & Azel, J. (1989, January). Coca—an ancient herb turns deadly. *National Geographic*, pp. 3–47.

Whitehill, M., DeMyer-Gapin, S., & Scott, T. G. (1976). Stimulation seeking in antisocial preadolescent children. *Journal of Abnormal Psychology, 85,* 101–104.

Widiger, T. A., Frances, A. J., Pincus, H. A., Davis, W. W., & First, M. B. (1991). Toward an empirical classification of the DSM IV. *Journal of Abnormal Psychology, 100,* 280–288.

Wiesen, A. E. (1965). Differential reinforcing effects of onset and offset of stimulation on the operant behavior of normals, neurotics, and psychopaths. (Doctoral dissertation, University of Florida). Ann Arbor, MI: University Microfilms, No. 65–9625.

Wilczynski, A. (1991). Images of women who kill their infants: The mad and the bad. *Women & Criminal Justice, 2,* 71–88.

Wilczynski, A. (1997). Mad or bad? Child-killers, gender, and the courts. *British Journal of Criminology, 37,* 419–436.

Wilentz, W. C. (1953). The alcohol factor in violent deaths. *American Practitioner: Digest of Treatment, 4*, 21–24.

Williams, J. E., & Holmes, K. A. (1981). *The second assault: Rape and public attitudes.* Westport, CT: Greenwood Press.

Williams, K. (1984). Economic sources of homicides: Re-estimating the effects of poverty and inequality. *American Sociological Review, 49*, 283–289.

Williams, W., & Miller, K. S. (1981). The processing and disposition of incompetent mentally ill offenders. *Law and Human Behavior, 5*, 245–261.

Williamson, S., Hare, R. D., & Wong, S. (1987). Violence: Criminal psychopaths and their victims. *Canadian Journal of Behavioral Science, 19*, 454–462.

Wilson, J. Q., & Herrnstein, R. J. (1985). *Crime and human nature.* New York: Simon & Schuster.

Wincze, J. P. (1977). Sexual deviance and dysfunction. In D. Rimm & J. Somervill (Eds.), *Abnormal psychology.* New York: Academic Press.

Wish, E. D. (1986). PCP and crime: Just another illicit drug? In D. H. Clouet (Ed.), *Phencyclidine: An update.* Rockville, MD: National Institute on Drug Abuse.

Wolfe, D. A. (1985). Child-abusive parents: An empirical review and analysis. *Psychological Bulletin, 97*, 462–582.

Wolfgang, M. E. (1958). *Patterns in criminal homicide.* Philadelphia, PA: University of Pennsylvania Press.

Wolfgang, M. E. (1961). A sociological analysis of criminal homicide. *Federal Probation, 25*, 48–55.

Wolfgang, M. E. (1972). Cesare Lombroso (1835–1909). In H. Mannheim (Ed.), *Pioneers in criminality.* Montclair, NJ: Patterson Smith.

Wolfgang, M. E., & Ferracuti, F. (1967). *The subculture of violence.* London: Tavistock.

Wolford, M. R. (1972). Some attitudinal, psychological and sociological characteristics of incarcerated arsonists. *Fire and Arson Investigator, 16*, 8–13.

Wong, M., & Singer, K. (1973). Abnormal homicide in Hong Kong. *British Journal of Psychiatry, 123*, 37–46.

Wood, W., Wong, F. Y., & Chachere, J. G. (1991). The effects of media violence on viewers' aggression in unconstrained social interaction. *Psychological Bulletin, 109*, 371–383.

Woodbury, R. (1989, April 24). Cult of the red-haired devil. *Time*, p. 30.

Wright, L. (1993a, May 17). Remembering Satan—Part I. *The New Yorker*, pp. 60–81.

Wright, L. (1993b, May 24). Remembering Satan—Part II. *The New Yorker*, pp. 54–76.

Wright, R. (1980). Rape and physical violence. In D. J. West (Ed.), *Sex offenders in the criminal justice system.* Cambridge, Eng.: Cambridge University Institute of Criminology.

Wright, R. T., & Decker, S. (1997). *Armed robbers in action: Stickup and street culture.* Boston, MA: Northeastern University Press.

Yates, E. (1986). The influence of psychosocial factors on nonsensical shoplifting. *International Journal of Offender Therapy and Comparative Criminology, 30*, 203–211.

Yegidis, B. L. (1986). Date rape and other forced sexual encounters among college students. *Journal of Sex Education and Therapy, 12*, 51–54.

Yesavage, J. A., Benezech, M., Ceccaldi, P., Bourgeois, M., & Addad, M. (1983). Arson in mentally ill and criminal populations. *Journal of Clinical Psychiatry, 44*, 128–130.

Yochelson, S., & Samenow, S. E. (1976). *The criminal personality* (Vol. 1). New York: Jason Aronson.

Zager, L. D. (1988). The MMPI-based criminal classification system. *Criminal Justice and Behavior, 15*, 39–57.

Zahn, M. A., & Rickle, W. C. (1986). Murder and minorities: The Hispanic case. Paper presented at the Academy of Criminal Justice Sciences annual meeting, Orlando, FL.

Zamble, E., & Porporino, F. G. (1988). *Coping, behavior, and adaptation in prison inmates.* New York: Springer-Verlag.

Zeichner, A., & Pihl, R. O. (1979). Effects of alcohol and behavior contingencies on human aggression. *Journal of Abnormal Psychology, 88*, 152–160.

Zeichner, A., & Pihl, R. O. (1980). Effects of alcohol and instigator intent on human aggression. *Journal of Studies on Alcohol, 41*, 265–276.

Zigler, E. (1994). Reshaping early childhood interventions to be a more effective weapon against poverty. *American Journal of Community Psychology, 22*, 37–47.

Zillman, D. (1971). Excitation transfer in communication-mediated aggressive behavior. *Journal of Experimental Social Psychology, 7*, 419–434.

Zillman, D. (1979). *Hostility and aggression.* Hillsdale, NJ: Erlbaum.

Zillman, D. (1983). Arousal and aggression. In R. G. Geen & E. I. Donnerstein (Eds.), *Aggression: Theoretical and empirical reviews* (Vol. 1). New York: Academic Press.

Zillman, D. (1988). Cognitive-excitation interdependencies in aggressive behavior. *Aggressive Behavior, 14*, 51–64.

Zillman, D., Baron, R., & Tamborini, R. (1981). Social costs of smoking: Effects of tobacco smoke on hostile behavior. *Journal of Applied Social Psychology, 11*, 548–561.

Zimbardo, P. G. (1970). The human choice. Individuation, reason, and order versus deindividuation, impulse, and chaos. In W. J. Arnold & D. Levine (Eds.), *Nebraska symposium on motivation 1969.* Lincoln, NE: University of Nebraska Press.

Zimbardo, P. G. (1973). The psychological power and pathology of imprisonment. In E. Aronson and R. Helmreich (Eds.), *Social psychology.* New York: Van Nostrand.

Zimring, F. G., Mukhergee, S. K., & Van Winkle, B. (1983). Intimate violence: A study of intersexual homicide in Chicago. *University of Chicago Law Review, 50*, 910–930.

Zoccoulillo, M. (1993). Gender and the development of conduct disorder. *Development and Psychopathology, 5*, 65–78.

Author Index

SUBJECT INDEX